# DOING QUALITATIVE RESEARCH: DESIGNS, METHODS, AND TECHNIQUES

**Greg Scott and Roberta Garner**

*DePaul University*

Boston   Columbus   Indianapolis   New York   San Francisco   Upper Saddle River   Amsterdam
Cape Town   Dubai   London   Madrid   Milan   Munich   Paris   Montreal   Toronto   Delhi
Mexico City   Sao Paulo   Sydney   Hong Kong   Seoul   Singapore   Taipei   Tokyo

**Editorial Director:** Craig Campanella
**Editor in Chief:** Dickson Musslewhite
**Publisher:** Karen Hanson
**Editorial Assistant:** Joseph Jantas
**Director of Marketing:** Brandy Dawson
**Executive Marketing Manager:** Kelly May
**Marketing Assistant:** Diane Griffin
**Production Project Manager:** Elizabeth Gale Napolitano

**Production Editor:** Maria Piper
**Manager, Cover Design:** Jayne Conte
**Editorial Production and Composition**
  **Service:** Integra
**Cover Designer:** Karen Noferi
**Cover Image:** Courtesy of Scott M. Garner
**Printer/Binder/Cover Printer:** COURIER/Westford
**Text Font:** Minion 10/12

**Photos:** Courtesy of Scott M. Garner. **Text:** p. 57: "Guiding Principles of Human Subjects Protection": Glesne, Corrine, *Becoming Qualitative Researchers: An Introduction*, 3rd Edition, © 2006. Reprinted by permission of Pearson Educuation, Inc., Upper Saddle River NJ; p. 115: Michael Agar excerpt used by permission of Forum Qualitative Sozialforschung/Forum: Qualitative Social Research, 2006; p. 135: Reprinted from Klinenberg, Eric (2002), *Heat Wave: A Social Autopsy of Disaster in Chicago*. Copyright © 2002. Reprinted by permission of the University of Chicago Press.; p. 179: excerpt from Rury, John L. and Frank A. Cassell, *Seeds of Crisis: Public Schooling in Milwaukee Since 1920*. © 1993 by the Board of Regents of the University of Wisconsin System. Reprinted by permission of The University of Wisconsin Press; p. 209: Michael Agar excerpt used by permission of Forum Qualitative Sozialforschung/Forum: Qualitative Social Research, 2006; p. 266: excerpt from Widick, Richard, "Money Traders," *Theory and Society*, 32 (2003); p. 680: Reprinted with kind permission from Springer Science+Business Media B.V.; p. 287: excerpt from Schatzman and Strauss, *Field Research Strategies for a Natural Society*, 1st Edition, © 1973. Reprinted by permission of Pearson Education, Inc., Upper Saddle River, NJ; p. 336: excerpt used by permission of Dr. Anne Bamford; p. 359: Fig. 22.1: Reprinted by permission of QSR International Pty Ltd.; p. 361, 363: figures reprinted by permission of ATLAS.ti; pp. 396–397: Michael Buraway, *Ethnography Unbound: Power and Resistance in the Modern Metropolis*. © 1991 by the Regents of the University of California. Reprinted by permission of University of California Press.

**Library of Congress Cataloging-in-Publication Data**
Scott, Greg.
   Doing qualitative research : designs, methods, and techniques / Greg Scott, Roberta Garner.
      p. cm.
   Includes bibliographical references.
   ISBN-13: 978-0-205-69593-5 (alk. paper)
   ISBN-10: 0-205-69593-0 (alk. paper)
   1. Qualitative research.   I. Title.
   H62.G256 2013
   001.4'2—dc23

                                                                        2011040749


10 9 8 7 6 5 4 3 2 1

ISBN-10:    0-205-69593-0
ISBN-13: 978-0-205-69593-5

# CONTENTS

# PREFACE

We are excited about sharing with you the pleasure of qualitative research. *Doing Qualitative Research* is a text designed not only for sociologists but also for anyone exploring cultural studies, anthropology, political science, ethnic studies, women and gender studies, the media, journalism and communications, organizational behavior, and many other fields that prize the telling of evidence-based stories of social life. By the time you finish reading this book and doing your own research in reference to it, we hope that you, too, will share our passion for the pleasures *and the perils* of qualitative research.

We believe you'll find that *Doing Qualitative Research* isn't your standard run-of-the-mill textbook on methods. It's different from most others in several ways. Most notably, perhaps, is the fact that we start with the assumption that the world is a *messy* place; therefore, conducting research on it will invariably be complicated, maze-like at times, and often quite "messy" itself. There's no absolutely right or definitely wrong approach to qualitative research, but there are more and less effective and appropriate ways of doing it. We'll help you understand how to develop and assess these ways of research. The world's a dynamic, electrically charged place to be. We believe that the qualitative research enterprise can be just as dynamic and exciting, even when it's making you absolutely miserable! We advocate anything but a lockstep, formulaic, and mandatorily linear approach to methodology. Both of us are committed to having fun doing what we do, and we want you to have fun too. In writing this book, we've tried to give you lots of opportunities for *enjoying the work*.

In addition to acknowledging and embracing messiness and committing ourselves to enjoyment, six other main ideas have guided tour writing.

- We continue to feel confidence in the scientific method, broadly defined and adapted to understanding human beings. We believe that human beings and their actions can be studied in a rigorous and systematic way. Research does not have to be numeric to be accurate and scientific. We realize that the scientific method used in the natural sciences needs to be modified to be effective in studying social reality. Our goal, as in all science, is to enhance our understanding of the world in which we live; ultimately we may want to change it as well, but we need to have a picture of "how it works" before we can effectively. Our research yields stories, gathered and told systematically, about the world we live in; it is not primarily a story about ourselves (and our feelings, relationships, and experiences), although these matters are important, and in doing research, we may learn about ourselves as well.
- We are committed to a critical and reflexive style of research. We give thoughtful and consistent attention to the goal of producing objective information. We do not believe that this goal can be accomplished by mechanically following technical procedures, but neither do we reject it altogether. Reflexive sociology means thinking about our own social location, experiences, beliefs, education, and interests—not in order to dismiss our conclusions as "just opinions" but in order to see how our characteristics shape our research choices. In every research study, the researcher and the project appear as "variables" with a life of their own, operating in relation to those being studied. In other words, every research study involves collecting data from and/or about humans, but the research study itself is always a potential source of rich data.
- We encourage linking theory and research. Research questions should draw on theory; theories can guide research, and research contributes to theories. Theory does not mean pointless, abstruse abstraction, but attention to concepts, in-depth understanding of social phenomena, and discussion of the larger implications of our research.
- We emphasize macro–micro linkages that are created by connecting our research experiences and empirical observations (which are usually obtained locally and at a micro- or mesolevel) to macrolevel and historical concepts such as inequalities, stratification, and political and economic systems. The link from the micro-, the local, and the experiential to the macro-level contexts helps build theory. Empirical research is usually at the micro- and meso-levels. We can only observe interactions,

individual actions, and cultural objects and discourses produced by individuals and interacting groups; we cannot directly observe "the economy," "the political field," and "a stratification system" (as Blumer insisted), but we want to connect our empirical observations to macro-level analysis.

- Research is about choices. The data are not "lying around out there"—like fruit fallen from a tree. We produce them, and by our choices we can make the data and our representation of them an accurate and truthful representation of the world in which we live. The choices are not bound by mechanical rules; we need to be aware of these choices. Technical decisions must be guided by research questions, goals, and theories. We need to think about the choices as we make them, document them carefully, and explain them in our writing.
- We emphasize learning from examples of research; beginning researchers can be inspired by seeing how others have framed research questions and made choices from the methods toolbox. Many of our examples are drawn from the work of students and newly minted researchers; although the designs are relatively simple, the research questions can be complex. These examples provide models for student research projects.

Three additional principles have influenced our writing.

1. We maintain a completely open mind about the choice of quantitative and qualitative strategies. One is not better than the other; what matters is how well the research strategy matches the research question.
2. In the spirit of the preceding comment, we want to introduce the reader to a broad range of research strategies and designs, not just fieldwork. Many methods—the items in our "tool-kit"—can be used in many different kinds of design and can be combined with each other successfully. The organization of our book encourages thoughtful choices of method-mixes.
3. We continue to emphasize the value of triangulation as did the great qualitative researchers of the Chicago School and the postwar period (Denzin 1978; Janevich in Denzin: 46–47). Multiple sources of data, multiple methods, competing theoretical perspectives, several researchers, and perhaps even multiple disciplines—all can contribute to a more complete understanding of social reality.

**Instructor's Manual and Test Bank (ISBN 0205695949):** The Instructor's Manual and Test Bank has been prepared to assist teachers in their efforts to prepare lectures and evaluate student learning. For each chapter of the text, the Instructor's Manual offers different types of resources, including detailed chapter summaries and outlines, learning objectives, discussion questions, classroom activities and much more.

Also included in this manual is a test bank offering multiple-choice, true/false, fill-in-the-blank, and/or essay questions for each chapter. The Instructor's Manual and Test Bank is available to adopters at HYPERLINK "http://www.pearsonhighered.com" www.pearsonhighered.com.

**MyTest (ISBN 0205225292):** The Test Bank is also available online through Pearson's computerized testing system, MyTest. MyTest allows instructors to create their own personalized exams, to edit any of the existing test questions, and to add new questions. Other special features of this program include random generation of test questions, creation of alternative versions of the same test, scrambling question sequence, and test preview before printing. Search and sort features allow you to locate questions quickly and to arrange them in whatever order you prefer. The test bank can be accessed from anywhere with a free MyTest user account. There is no need to download a program or file to your computer.

**PowerPoint Presentations (0205226752):** Lecture PowerPoints are available for this text. The Lecture PowerPoint slides outline each chapter to help you convey sociological principles in a visual and exciting way. They are available to adopters at HYPERLINK "http://www.pearsonhighered.com" www.pearsonhighered.com.

**MySearchLab** MySearchLab contains writing, grammar, and research tools and access to a variety of academic journals, census data, Associated Press news feeds, and discipline-specific readings to help you hone your writing and research skills. In addition, a complete eText is included. MySearchLab can be purchased with the text (ISBN 0205231667) or separately (ISBN 0205239927)

# ABOUT THE AUTHORS

*Greg Scott*, Associate Professor of Sociology and Director of the Social Science Research Center (SSRC) at DePaul University in Chicago, Illinois, received his doctorate in sociology in 1998 from the University of California at Santa Barbara. From 1995 to 2000, he served as Director of Research and Associate Director of the Illinois Attorney General's Gang Crime Prevention Center where he conducted and supervised primary and evaluation research on community prevention and intervention programs.

Since arriving at DePaul University in 2000, he has conducted quantitative, qualitative, and ethnographic research on injection drug use (hepatitis B vaccination clinical trials, syringe-facilitated HIV/AIDS transmission, opiate overdose, the network impact of sterile syringe exchange efforts, and injection practices and interventions) and on the relationship between street gangs and the reintegration of ex-offenders. Between 1990 and 2001, Greg conducted extensive ethnographic fieldwork on drug-dealing street gangs, immersing himself in the world of illegal drug trade. In 2001, he began to examine the "demand and use" side of the drug market. At this point, he took up living with homeless and precariously housed injection drug users, habitual crack smokers, sex workers, burglars, thieves, and drug dealers. Greg has become an independent documentary filmmaker, concentrating his efforts on the social, economic, cultural, political, and health issues facing illicit drug users; he produces training films for health professionals and laypersons in order to contribute to safe injection practices and overdose prevention, as well as social documentaries to educate the public and policy makers on the lives of drug users. He is making a documentary called *The Brickyard*, a feature-length film on a West Side Chicago encampment of homeless people among whom Greg has lived and worked for the past seven years.

In 2005, Greg established a nonprofit organization ("Sawbuck Productions") whose mission revolves around creating and producing multimedia educational and political materials concerning the well-being of illicit drug users. Recently, Greg began using his films as a catalyst for organizing a social movement in Chicago, Chicago Area Network of Drug Users (CANDU), whose goal is to create the city's first-ever "drug users' union" to improve the well-being and life chances of illicit drug users.

In addition to conducting ethnographic research and producing doc films and radio documentaries (and trying to keep up with his teenage son Ben), Greg teaches upper-division courses on ethnographic filmmaking, substance use and abuse, public health and high-risk behavior, and urban cultural research. Greg also runs the Social Science Research Center (SSRC) at DePaul University. To find out more about the SSRC's work and Greg's involvement in the enterprise, visit the website www.depaul.edu/~ssrc.

*Roberta Garner*, Professor of Sociology at DePaul University, earned a PhD at the University of Chicago in the late 1960s, coming of age in the sixties between the Beatniks and the hippy/baby-boom generation. Her PhD dissertation was based on 250 life narratives of first-generation college students, and since then she has conducted qualitative research in the Italian school system and written (with a colleague and grad students) a mixed qualitative–quantitative study of Midwestern high school students' aspirations, school engagement, and perceptions of their schools.

She has traveled extensively in Europe and Latin America and was field director of four DePaul Study Abroad trips and programs. She lived in Italy in 1979 during a period of intense political activism there, in Budapest, Hungary, in 1984 in the waning years of the socialist era, in Merida, Mexico, in 1986, in Florence, Italy, in 1987–1988 (where she used a "parent-as-researcher" method to write about schooling in Italy), and most recently in Paris.

Her interests include political sociology, urban sociology, sociology of youth and education, and sociological theory; and she enjoys teaching stats and methods courses. She was one of the six editors of *The New Chicago*, a collection of essays that explored changes in Chicago in recent decades, including the making of a postindustrial economy, the impact of immigration, and the process of gentrification and displacement in the inner city. Recently she co-authored (with Black Hawk Hancock) a book on contemporary sociological theories (*Changing Theories: New Directions in Sociology*) and translated (from French) an interview with Loïc Wacquant about his experiences as an ethnographer, a critical-reflexive theorist in France and the United States, and an apprentice boxer engaged in carnal sociology (published in the journal *Qualitative Sociology* in 2009). As you will see when you read the book, she is open to both qualitative and statistical methods and is enthusiastic about integrating research and theory.

The authors would like to thank the crew at Pearson-Allyn and Bacon, especially Jeff Lasser for his encouragement during the crucial early launch phase, Lauren Macey, and Seanna Breen. Anandakrishnan Natarajan at Integra was essential to the production process, and his patience under pressure and grace under fire are exemplary.

We would like to thank all the following reviewers: Matthew Brown, University of Colorado; Gerardo Marti, Davidson College; and Carol Ward, Brigham and Young University. We'd also like to thank all of our chapter co-authors, and Roberta is especially grateful to Krista Harper for inspiration and support. Greg is particularly grateful to Gerry Suttles, whose extensive and impeccable fieldwork-based scholarship continues to fuel Greg's passion for social research methodologies.

Here at DePaul, it wouldn't have been possible without Valerie Paulson, Jessica Chiarella, Kathleen Tallmadge, Josh Covell, Brandy Peak, Linda Levendusky, and of course, Glenance Green. Our colleagues in the Sociology Department and the Social Science Research Center provided a supportive, collegial environment.

Roberta would like to thank her family for patience, love, and laughter. Greg wishes to thank his wife Erin and his son Ben for their unflagging love and devotion, and he wishes to dedicate his efforts on this book to his grandparents: Thomas Briggs, a methodical railroad man who went to his grave still mystified as to what Greg actually does for a living, but loving him all the same, and Ruth Briggs, whose inimitable embodiment of insatiable curiosity and delightful capacity for surprise will always be one of Greg's main sources of sociological inspiration.

# Getting Started— Thinking about Research Choices

You've got a research topic. You're really excited about it and have a lot of ideas for exploring it. But how do you start ... The Project?

Doing research is kind of like farming, or more specifically, cultivating a plot of land for the harvest of vegetables. Imagine planting a crop of organic vegetables, tending your field, bringing in the harvest, and getting your vegetables to the folks who want to eat them. First, you learn about the properties of the soil and the characteristics of plants you want to grow. Next, you assemble your tools and seeds and prepare the field. You become familiar with the goals, procedures, and regulations that govern organic farming so that your claim of "organic produce" will be valid, legal, and ethical. You confirm your title to the land and think about the people you will need to help you—the people with whom you will interact, whether they are hired hands or family. Starting your crop requires a vision of the possibilities, an overall plan for the project from the beginning to the harvest, the marketing, and the eating. Learning about other organic farmers' experiences may help you make the right choices for your terrain, resources, and goals.

It's the same process for a research project. In research projects, we *grow* our data in very much the way we grow vegetables. We don't collect stuff that just happens to be lying on the ground, but neither do we have nearly complete control over creating the product (as we do when we build a house or make a painting). Our crop—our harvest of data—is produced in interaction with the "world out there" in which these results grow. You will need to have a vision of what you want to accomplish, a design for doing it, knowledge of available tools and resources, and a sense of the social context—the personal, ethical, and political context in which you work, within which you make your choices of research questions, designs, methods, and the telling of the story. In the doing of research, your plans will depend especially *on your imagination*, but also on your knowledge of concepts and theory, your skills in using the methods tool-kit correctly, your ability to interact with others, and usually an intense physical effort out in the field. And like a newcomer to farming, you can look at others' accomplishments to find designs that inspire you.

Chapter 1 provides an overview of the book as a whole and explains the logic of its organization.

We will briefly review the many research traditions that contribute to contemporary qualitative research in Chapter 2. We will discuss the overall design, vision and purpose—in Chapter 3 and look at the ethics and politics of writing about the lives of others in Chapters 4 and 5. Chapter 6 highlights the importance of theory in research.

In Part II, we will look more closely at how to choose a design. Part III examines one type of design: ethnography. Part IV presents a flexible, multipurpose "methods tool kit" that can be used to implement the designs. And Part V is about "telling the story"—to ourselves and others—in other words, about ways of bringing our crop to the table.

# 1

# Introduction: Logic of Inquiry, Research Designs and Strategies, and the Methods Tool-Kit

## OVERVIEW

In this chapter we welcome you to the book, explain its organization, define basic terms, and explain where qualitative research fits in the research tradition.

## GUIDING PRINCIPLES

Three concepts guided our writing. First, in every study the researcher makes countless conscious *choices*. For example, the researcher must decide what question(s) to answer and how to design a research project to answer the question(s). Our choices of methods should be guided by good practices for producing and analyzing data, but the research is never a matter of just mechanically following specific technical steps; at all stages of a project, we should be asking ourselves why we are doing what we are doing and whether we could or should do it differently. Our intellectual goals and values guide us; we don't operate robotically or in a lock-step manner, obeying technique alone.

The importance of choice is directly related to our second guiding principle: The **research question** determines, to a great extent, the research choices available to us, and it affects how we actually make the choices. The research question (or the set of related research questions) articulates what we want to learn about social reality. We have to be clear on what knowledge we want to create and therefore what data and information we need to produce—not simply collect in a wily-nily manner. Information and data are not just "out there" lying around like apples fallen from a tree, waiting to be "collected" by the eager researcher; rather, the researcher brings the data into existence through her research choices and activities, which unfold in reference to the research questions. In a word, the qualitative researcher *produces* data; she does not *discover* it as an archaeologist finds artifacts. Throughout the book, we will emphasize this process of matching research designs and methods to research questions.

Our third guiding principle is that research should always be linked logically to **theory**. Research without theory is just a pile of information with a relatively short shelf life. Theory is the "soul" of a research project, giving it a larger meaning and a longer future. Theories influence the statement of the research question, and the knowledge gained in the research project informs and enriches theory. For instance, when Emile Durkheim wrote about the distribution of suicide rates in Europe in the 1890s, he was not just amassing statistics about a particular moment in time—he was trying to understand variation in two fundamental characteristics of society: social integration and normative regulation. He wanted to learn how these characteristics shape people's lives and the choice to go on living. These basic theoretical concepts are just as vital to our understanding of society today as they were in 1898.

## THE BOOK'S ORGANIZATION

The book is divided into five parts: (1) an introductory section that covers the goals and history of qualitative methods, including ethical and political challenges; (2) a discussion of **research designs** or basic strategies for organizing research; (3) a focus on **ethnography**, the qualitative research design *par excellence* and one that poses many complex challenges; (4) a part that introduces the methods "toolbox" and describes **methods** that can be used to implement the designs; and (5) a section that discusses preparing the research report and disengaging from the field—a reflection on how to tell the story of the research to the public, colleagues, participants, and oneself.

### Part I: Getting Started—Thinking about Research Choices

In the first part, we discuss the basics of qualitative research, define key terms, explain why and how to formulate research questions, review the history of qualitative research, challenge the reader to think about ethical and political issues in research, and conclude this part by highlighting the importance of the link between research and theory. Part I gets the reader started on thinking about research.

### Part II: Choosing a Research Design

In the second part, we identify several basic designs or strategies used in qualitative inquiry. These strategies, designs, or logics of research are the overall plans for conducting research. The basic designs differ in the purpose of the research, the types of research questions that are answered, and the way that specific methods are selected from the "methods toolbox" and brought together to implement the design. We will introduce five basic designs or strategies: **ethnography**, **historical-comparative research**, the **social autopsy**, **community-based participatory research** or participatory action research, and **discourse/cultural artifact analysis**. A sixth type of design is the **mixed or multimethod design** that combines major approaches. Each type of design requires certain tools, which we call "methods," but these tools can be used for more than one design, and each design can use several of these tools. Each design will be illustrated with examples of research. Part II encourages the reader to think about choosing designs and matching them to the larger purposes and questions that guide research.

Here is a brief summary of the designs we will discuss; later chapters will explain them in more detail.

The word **ethnography** comes from the Greek words for "people" (*ethnos*) and "writing" (*grapho*) and means "writing about a people." It is an effort to present as complete an account of the way of life and culture of a group as possible. It could be any group with a shared culture.

The second design is **historical-comparative research**. This type of research tries to reach conclusions about large-scale social processes that take place in whole societies. It tries to explain differences in institutions among societies (e.g., Why do countries have different types of health care systems?) and the differences in how societies are "put together," how their institutions emerged, and how these institutions are connected to each other. Historical-comparative designs require methods that can "bring up" information from the past. The methods of historians—such as archival research, analysis of documents and artifacts, oral histories, and eyewitness accounts—form the basis of the conclusions that historical-comparative researchers try to formulate. Researchers do not always put together and analyze primary sources themselves, but they have to be able to judge the reliability of the findings that historians develop on the basis of these types of methods and materials.

The third design we will discuss is the **social autopsy**. A social autopsy is research that begins with an adverse event—a disaster such as Hurricane Katrina, an accident, or an intentional act of harm—and then tries to explain how and why this event happened the way it did. The analysis of the causes, consequences, and impact of the event is used to dissect social relationships and practices; it is used to gain an understanding of the society and culture within which this problematic event was possible.

Our fourth design is **community-based participatory research**, also called participatory action research, or PAR. This approach involves the researcher and the "subjects" working together to drastically reduce the distance that separates them in more typical research studies. Instead of the researcher standing "outside" of the research, he or she interacts with the community participants to develop a research project that will answer their questions and address their practical concerns, not just to find answers to the researchers' questions. The research questions, the choice of specific methods, and the strategy of collecting information emerge from interaction and agreement between researcher and participants—it is their study, not a study "owned" by the researcher. This commitment creates a very different set of conditions for making research decisions than the more traditional designs.

Our fifth design is the **analysis of cultural artifacts and discourses**. The object of analysis is a product of human activities—writing texts, creating artwork, making music, or making ordinary utensils and tools, for example. The emphasis in this type of cultural analysis is not the way people live their culture (the focus of ethnographies), but the culture as a total and highly revealing product in its own right, apart from the actions and interactions of the people who construct and live it.

Our sixth design is the **mixed quantitative/qualitative design** that blends any one of the preceding five qualitative designs (or strategies) with the production and analysis of quantitative data. The mixed design uses qualitative methods in combination with quantitative ones, drawing on methods such as surveys and analysis of statistical records from the "quantitative toolbox."

Each of the above designs has a distinct logic. How research questions can be asked, the types of hypotheses that are set forth, the choices of specific methods, the integration of the results in the analysis, and the strategy for reaching conclusions differ depending on which design the researcher has chosen.

### Part III: Focus on Ethnography

This part focuses exclusively on ethnography. We discuss preparing to enter the field, entering the field, producing data, recording observations, and organizing a range of methods into a coherent project to study a culture.

### Part IV: Choices from the Methods Tool-Kit

In Part IV, we review key tools in the methods toolbox. These methods involve **research activities** needed to implement the design or strategy. Many of these methods—such as **observing**, **interviewing, focus groups**, and **visual methods**—can be used in several or even all of the designs; they are widely used and versatile. In each chapter in this part, we will give a broad overview of the method, suggest ways in which it needs to be modified to fit different types of designs, provide tips for "how to do it," and discuss examples of research.

### Part V: Telling the Story

Part V is about life after the research experience and covers how to write about research and the personal, ethical, and legal complications that we may encounter afterwards. We discuss the challenges of telling the story of the research—not only to colleagues in the research community but also to the participants in the study, the public, and to ourselves. Every research project generates many different stories. In the end, however, the researcher must choose which story (or stories) to tell, and which not to tell. Decisions concerning which stories to tell and how to tell them can be very complicated, involving personal, political, professional, economic, and moral considerations.

## KEY CONCEPTS

In this book, you'll come across dozens of new concepts and terms. Here are the definitions of some of the most important terms that will be useful as you read the book:

Our most fundamental term is **research question**. A research question (RQ) is a question relating to an overarching concern that a researcher wants to address through gathering and analyzing data on a specific phenomenon involving people, groups, organizations, institutions, cultures, situations, societies, and so on. A research question is *not* the same as a question on a survey or questionnaire. Survey questions exist to help you gather the data you need to analyze in order to form an answer to your overarching research question. In short, the RQ is a question about people and anything they do, say, or think. Most important, it must be possible to answer the question with *evidence*, or data that you can create, produce, shape, and assemble through your deliberate (though often serendipitous) interactions with the world.

We need to distinguish **empirical inquiry** from *theory*. The word "empirical" means information or knowledge that we can obtain through our five senses. It is knowledge about the world around us. The empirical world is the "realm of the senses." Theories refer to clusters of ideas and concepts that we form in our minds. They may be influenced by our sense experience but they are not quite the same thing as that experience. When I pet a dog, I may form the word "pit bull" in my mind, but that is not identical to the feeling of touching the dog. The concept "dog" or "pit bull" is in my brain, whereas the feeling of the dog's hair is empirical, an observation that involves direct contact with the outside world in which the dog exists. Of course, "pit bull" is not much of a theory, but it is one step toward a theory—for instance, one about the causes of ferocious, unpredictable behavior in animals (maybe such behavior is the result of both genetic factors and a dog's brutal experiences in the environment). Or perhaps it's a step toward a theory about how dogs are classified officially and legally as compared with how humans classify dogs in their everyday experience.

In the social sciences, a lot of empirical inquiry is already heavily laced with theory. We are rarely in the situation of petting a dog just to learn the feel of its hair and body. We usually are observing empirically with a rather conceptual research question in mind that guides the empirical observation. But we also remain open to empirical experience that may change our concepts and theories.

**Research design or strategy** (or logic of inquiry) is an overall plan for answering our research questions. It specifies *research methods, activities,* and *techniques* that we will need in order to answer our question in a satisfactory way. For example, because Durkheim wanted to understand differences in suicide rates between groups of people, he had to find data that enabled him to see the differences in rates, for instance, government statistics collected in different countries. Looking at a couple of suicide notes would have been heart-rending, but they would not have helped him understand the differences in rates among many groups of people.

Research design is in large part dictated by the question and must bring evidence to bear on the question. For example, if our research question is, "Does Drug Rehab Program X work?" it would not be very smart to confine our research design to interviewing the founders and employees of Program X. Interviewing them might be a good method to include in a design that attempts to answer other questions, such as "What was the history of the program?" or "Do employees feel satisfied with their work?" or "What are the demographic characteristics of the owners and employees of the program?" But if we want to know whether the program works, we have to assemble systematic and uniformly collected information that compares its rate of success (however we define that) to other programs' outcomes or to the situation of being in no program at all.

**Research methods** are recognized ways of collecting empirical information. They are usually clusters of related research activities. For example, we often talk about "survey methods" in the social sciences, and that means a lot of related activities such as writing a questionnaire, identifying a sample of people to fill it out, and analyzing the resulting data. All of these activities are part of "survey methods." In qualitative research, our methods toolbox includes interviewing, observing as an outside viewer, participating at the same time that we are observing, looking at historical records, and analyzing documents or cultural artifacts such as buildings or works of art. We use one or more of these methods to implement a research design. Some of these methods can be used for several different designs. For example, interviewing and observing are versatile methods that can be used to implement many types of designs.

**Research activities** are things we do to carry out the research design and to collect the empirical information that we will need to answer our research questions. The activities have to be linked to the research questions so that they help us to answer them. These activities are actions to make the research happen—some may be part of specific methods/techniques but the activities also include things we do that are preliminary or supplementary to applying the methods. They include actions that set the stage, lay the ground work, or support the actual research methods. For example, we may be working on an ethnography—a broad, multifaceted study of a community. To implement that basic design, we may choose the methods of interviewing. In order to make the interviewing happen, we may have to engage in activities that are not strictly part of the interview—for example, driving a homeless person to a doctor's appointment or meeting with a media relations staff person of a large corporation in order to arrange an interview with the CEO.

Social scientists distinguish between research *methods* and *methodologies*, although in everyday usage these terms are often confused with each other. The research method is a recognized way of collecting or producing empirical information, such as a survey, an interview, and **content analysis** of documents. **Methodology** refers to a broader and more conceptual way of thinking about research than any one method or even any given research design. It means systematic reflection on the theoretical and philosophical reasons for using specific designs and methods.

**Research techniques** are specific procedures for implementing research methods. For example, if we decide to use a survey method, we need to become familiar with techniques for writing survey questions, sampling a population, and statistical analysis of the results. If we decide to use qualitative methods such as semi-structured interviews, we need to learn the techniques for preparing an interview guide (the set of questions that we ask our respondent), for taking notes during the interview, and for transcribing and editing the audiotape that we recorded during the interview. A technique is a practical and specific way of doing things. Techniques often involve step-by-step procedures. Researchers can be trained in techniques, while research design, the logic of inquiry, and the choice of methods require a broader, more reflective way of learning.

## An Example: Studying the Unhoused

In our example, our research question is, "What are the conditions in which precariously housed people live—what is the world of the homeless?"

We could decide that this question as worded must be answered with a research design based on ethnography, on a complete description of the world of the homeless and the precariously housed, one that requires the researcher to be in prolonged contact with a community of homeless people, perhaps to live with them. It would not be enough to simply interview them or have some other type of fleeting and limited contact with them.

Once we have decided that the research design must involve ethnography, we would probably include a variety of methods, such as **participant-observation,** collection of **life narratives,** unstructured interviews, and documentary film.

These methods in turn have their own techniques, such as writing and organizing good field notes, selecting the right kind of camera for making a documentary film, using the camera effectively in the field, and careful coding of themes in the life stories told by homeless people and video recordings of their everyday behavior.

And the research methods (as well as the larger ethnographic research design) would engender a large number of research activities: Some might be directly related to the methods, such as filming, conducting unstructured interviews, and keeping field notes, but other activities would turn out to be necessary as well, although they are not guided by any specific technique that can be learned from a textbook. These activities might include helping individuals build huts along the railroad tracks, driving them to a food store, obtaining medical care for them, or just hanging out with them. These activities are part of the fieldwork method and ethnographic research design, but because they are not research techniques, textbooks do not usually explain how to do them. Many formal research reports—especially article-length ones—are rather vague about the types of activities in which the researcher actually engaged.

## QUANTITATIVE VERSUS QUALITATIVE RESEARCH

Research design is often classified into two types: **quantitative and qualitative.** In quantitative research, we are interested in reaching conclusions based on counting or measuring characteristics of the world around us. We formulate research questions that can be answered with numerical and statistically analyzed data, questions that might begin with "How many...?" "How often...?" "Are the rates different among ...?" We strive to collect information that can be analyzed statistically. We follow strict guidelines to ensure that our results can be generalized. And the variables—characteristics of the world in which we are interested—are defined precisely enough to allow counting and measurement.

Examples of quantitative research methods and designs include surveys and secondary data analysis. Secondary data analysis is a design based on the statistical analysis of existing surveys or of statistics collected by governments or large survey organizations. An example of a survey is the General Social Survey (GSS), a regular survey of American adults that asks respondents questions about their demographic characteristics and their feelings on a wide range of topics including their own happiness, frequency of sexual relations, and views of controversial issues such as abortion and gun control. An example of secondary data analysis is provided by Monique Payne's use of a large, nationally representative data set to explore the effect of residential mobility on adolescents' educational achievement—more mobility turned out to be related to diminished achievement, with many other variables controlled. She did not collect the data herself, but rather posed a new research question that could be answered using the information in an existing and publicly available data set (2008).

Finally, one simple way to characterize quantitative research is this: It deals with a large number of **cases** but a small number of **variables**. For instance, in this line of research it's not uncommon for the researcher to be asking a research question regarding the social life of 10,000 or even 10 million people. But when you're working with many cases, you can't be asking a question whose answering will require you to examine a large number of each person's attributes. Instead, the researcher focuses on a relatively small number of attributes/characteristics when answering the question.

Qualitative research is based on observations that can be written, spoken about, filmed, and interpreted, but not so easily measured, counted, "put into numbers," or generalized about on the basis of statistical reasoning. The basic research designs used in qualitative research tend to produce information that is not readily and immediately in quantitative form, although in many cases it can be transformed into numbers later in the research process.

Qualitative research is best suited for answering research questions that lend themselves to the analysis of a relatively small number of **cases** but a large number of attributes/variables. So, in contrast with quantitative research, you're going to be working with a relatively small population, but you're going to learn a great deal about each case in the population. In other words, you're going to be digging deep, as opposed to the very wide but not so deep digging you'll do in a quantitative research project.

Examples of qualitative research include ethnographies in which the researcher lives in a community and describes its way of life. This design might include some counting and measurement, but these activities would not be the primary research activities. An example of qualitative research is Horowitz's *Honor and the American Dream*, in which the author lived in a Mexican American neighborhood in Chicago and tried to understand the appeal of gangs and the reasons young people do or do not join them.

Collection of life narratives is a specific method that is a major component of many ethnographic studies and could also be used as a method for conducting historical-comparative research. For example, in *Nan: The Life of an Irish Traveling Woman*, Sharon Gmelch presents and discusses the life story of Nan, an Irish "Traveller" (a low-status caste of traditionally nomadic people). The story of one person illuminates the lives of Travellers, their customs, relationships with other Irish and with British, the loss of their traditional nomadic way of life, their economic situation, and—as seen in Nan's perspective—the problem of domestic violence in the community.

Neither Horowitz nor Gmelch reports a lot of statistics. They do not claim to have a statistical basis for their conclusions, and they are careful not to make claims that what they heard and saw is true of all urban Mexican American communities or every Irish Traveller (let alone of every Irish citizen, woman on the planet, or human being). Their interpretation of the observations gives us a different kind of understanding than quantitative data; we feel that we have gained an understanding of the ideas and experiences of the people in the study. We feel that we have "gotten into their heads." We have also learned about a specific place and time and have gained a strongly contextualized understanding.

In later chapters, we will look at how the quantitative/qualitative distinction—which used to be a major and rancorous division in sociology—is now being bridged by many studies. Researchers collect quantitative data in their field research; for example, Greg Scott has filmed over 400 instances of drug injection and converted the video recordings into numeric data, with each case (i.e., "injection episode") comprising dozens of numeric variables relating to the type of activity (cleaning the skin, inserting the needle, etc.) and the level of disease transmission risk associated with the activity. Thus he has taken audio-visual representations and out of them created a statistically analyzable database that allows for (1) the development of a systematic understanding of exactly how heroin and crack injectors perform their injections and (2) the identifying of patterns in risky behavior across injectors. Ultimately, this evidence-based understanding of injection risk will be helpful to those who attempt to help drug injectors improve the hygiene of their injections and thereby reduce their risk of contracting or spreading a viral infection. This is just one of thousands of instances in which a researcher has derived quantitative data from data that were originally qualitative in nature.

Many researchers carry out quantitative analysis of qualitative data such as texts and discourses, which are coded using special software. And many researchers create combined research designs in which both types of methods are used to in order to provide two different perspectives on the research question.

### Unobtrusive and "Obtrusive" (or Interactive) Research

In addition to the distinction between quantitative and qualitative research, many social scientists make a distinction between obtrusive and unobtrusive designs, methods, and research activities. Unobtrusive methods do not require interaction with research subjects or respondents. We can carry out many of them in the privacy of our own home wearing pajamas—and we don't have to talk to anyone!

Table 1.1 shows both of these dimensions, placing research designs and specific methods on two axes.

## FIELDWORK

The terms **fieldwork** and "in the field" refer to a basic way of thinking and feeling that is unique to qualitative research and ethnography. A major difference exists between work that is done in labs, libraries, and offices and work that is done in the open, free, exciting, and unpredictable terrain of "the field." The field can be as distant and remote as a village in the mountains of Tibet or as close as a walk from campus, but it is always territory that the researcher does not control, always "someone else's turf."

| | **TABLE 1.1** A Comparison of Different Types of Methods and Designs | |
|---|---|---|
| | **Qualitative** | **Quantitative** |
| **Obtrusive** | **Designs**: ethnography and most of its methods; community-based participatory research<br><br>**Methods**: ethnographic documentary film; participant-observation and carnal sociology; interviewing | **Designs**: survey research; quantitative data in fieldwork; experimental design |
| | **Method**: Focus groups | |
| **Unobtrusive** | **Designs**: historical-comparative analysis; analysis of art and cultural artifacts; content/discourse analysis of documents. | **Designs**: secondary data analysis; some archival research |

When the researcher is engaged in fieldwork, she is seeing and listening to people engaged in *their* world and not answering to *her* demands and questions. It is true that quantitative researchers can conduct surveys and even experiments "in the field," but when they do so, they make every effort to interact with people in the field in limited, predictable ways. They administer a survey to them or ask them to engage in a scripted series of interactions. The researcher's interaction with the respondents and subjects remains fleeting, impersonal, and carefully structured. But when qualitative and ethnographic researchers enter the field, it is an experience of uncontrolled immersion in a natural setting. "Natural" is a tricky word with a long history, and nothing that humans do is entirely natural; suffice it to say that in the context of qualitative methods, it means that the researcher has not brought about the situation she is studying. She has not assembled individuals for a focus group or a controlled lab experiment. Uncontrolled immersion means that the researcher does not decide who participates in this situation, where it takes place, and when it starts and ends. The interaction moves at its own pace.

The "obtrusiveness" of fieldwork is a two-way street. The researcher is "obtrusive" into the lives and actions of the research subjects (as is also the case when a survey is administered), but the research subjects can also "obtrude" into the researcher's life and actions (which almost never happens in survey or focus group research).

Therefore, whether "the field" is a remote village in a distant country or a neighborhood near campus, it always is unpredictable. Because many qualitative and ethnographic designs and methods call for going into the field, they contrast with the controlled and predictable research activities associated with quantitative and experimental designs in which unpredictable events are much less likely to occur and far more limited in scope.

## UNDERSTANDING THE EXPERIENCES OF OTHERS

A basic principle of qualitative and ethnographic research is the goal of understanding the experiences of others and not merely recording their opinions and behavior. Qualitative researchers want to "get into the heads" of the research subjects. This kind of research often begins with questions such as "What is it like to be, to do, to experience....?" Researchers try to immerse themselves in the world experienced through the senses of other human beings by interviewing, observing, listening, reading documents, looking at artifacts, and sometimes by having the same bodily experiences as their research subjects ( "carnal sociology," discussed in a later chapter).

During and after this immersion in the world of others, qualitative researchers return to their own world and engage in an "analysis of the data," the application of their own concepts and perspectives to the world of the others. This back-and-forth between immersion and extraction often leads to a kind of "split identity" or "dual consciousness" in the researcher. Out of this dialogue of evidence and ideas and from within the crack between the world of the subjects and the world of the researcher comes the analysis, the sociological story. The point of immersion is not mere description, but rather the development of a new, theory-informed perspective on the social phenomena of interest, often framed as the research question.

We may smile at the clichéd question, "How did you feel...?" as the reporter thrusts the microphone in front of the face of the winning pitcher, the losing quarterback, the crime victim, the convicted murderer . . . but this question is not so distant from the impulses that move qualitative researchers. We do want to know what others feel and experience. Some researchers refer to this goal as the phenomenological perspective. Radical psychologist R.D. Laing wrote, "I cannot experience your experience. You cannot experience my experience. We are both invisible men. All men are invisible to one another. Experience is man's invisibility to man." Qualitative researchers are often impelled to try to break through this veil that separates us from one another; and this desire is as strong as the desire to carry out scientific research and expand knowledge about human beings in society. Exciting research emerges from the tensions between immersion in experience and scientific analysis, between objective knowledge and subjective understanding, and between phenomenological awareness and statistical reason.

As qualitative researchers trying to understand the meaning of others' experience, we need to first understand how our own views, interests, and prejudgments were formed and to recognize the influence of our own background and experiences—to gain reflexive understanding of ourselves.

## Exercises

1. Identify five topics that interest you and that you think could be studied using qualitative methods. Explain why you find these topics of interest and what you would like to learn from your research. Are they only suitable for qualitative designs or could they also be studied using quantitative methods such as a survey or analysis of existing statistics (secondary data analysis)? Discuss how the data might be different depending on which type of methods you use.

2. The chapter identifies five designs: ethnography, social autopsy, community-based participatory research, historical-comparative research, and analysis of cultural artifacts. Identify a topic for each one of these designs. Explain why the research design is the best choice for the topic that you've chosen.

3. The next time you go out in public (or maybe you're in public as you're reading this), shift your focus from the things you ordinarily notice to the things that you ordinarily ignore. Make a list of the people, places, things, and occurrences that you ordinarily ignore when out in public doing whatever you're doing. Now, ask yourself why you tend to ignore them. Do these things you ignore have anything in common? Are they similar? Is there a common denominator? This exercise will help you to better understand the kinds of things that make their way into your "social viewfinder" and the kinds of things that you block out. We all are guilty of selective perception . . . it's a necessary skill for getting through the day. But a big part of qualitative research is reflexivity, which in part entails knowing how your perceptual, moral, ethical, and social biases affect the kinds of research questions you ask and also how you go about answering them.

4. From everyday life, identify a phenomenon that seems bizarre, strange, alien, or even totally incomprehensible to you. Maybe it's a group of people, or it could be an activity or event. Whatever the case, you should believe it to be pointless, or even irrational. Now, spend some time figuring out how this activity or group is utterly logical, reasonable, and rational given the circumstances in which it occurs. Step outside of yourself, your own identity, and try to assume the position of those who engage in the phenomenon. What have you learned?

## Key Terms

cases *9*

designs: analysis of cultural artifacts and discourses; community-based participatory research; ethnography; historical-comparative research; mixed quantitative/qualitative; social autopsy *5*

empirical inquiry *6*

fieldwork *10*

methodology *8*

methods: content analysis; focus groups; interviewing; life narratives; participant-observation; visual methods *8*

quantitative and qualitative research *9*

research: activities; design or strategy; methods; question; techniques *6*

theory *4*

unobtrusive research and obtrusive (interactive) research *10*

variables *9*

# 2

# A Brief History of Qualitative Research

## OVERVIEW

As a research tradition in sociology and other social sciences, qualitative methodology springs from diverse origins and does not have a single linear history. In this chapter, we examine these origins and tell our story of how qualitative research has unfolded and matured over time. We emphasize the central ideas, purposes, theories, and designs of pioneering studies, as opposed to overwhelming you with details concerning the development of specific data gathering and data analysis techniques.

## CLASSICAL IDEAS

The notion of employing systematic methods in conducting social science research dates back to the late nineteenth century, the same time as the emergence of classical theories such as those of Weber, Marx and Engels, Simmel, and Durkheim. Up to this point, explorers and natural historians wrote accounts of life in non-Western societies, travelers recorded their impressions, social reformers, partisan pamphleteers, and "muck-raking" professional journalists revealed the experiences and troubles of poor people living in cities. At the same time, scholars affiliated with universities and social movements were planning more systematic surveys of social life (such as Marx's draft of an extremely long questionnaire for working people), and so scientific and popular interest in statistics began to grow rapidly.

Two great classical theorists—Emile Durkheim in France and Max Weber in Germany—not only made major conceptual/theoretical contributions but also were pioneers of research methods. Their methodological choices grew organically from their theoretical views: Emile Durkheim, for instance, was convinced that social behavior was structured into regular patterns that reflected normative regulation in society. It therefore made sense for him to develop an affinity with statistical analysis, which he used as a way to look for evidence of behavioral patterns and their underlying unspoken norms. In his masterpiece *Suicide*, he used quantitative data and statistical analysis to reveal the social conditions that determine suicide rates. His approach and his findings went against the grain of popular belief that suicide was solely an individualistic, pathological event without any sort of connection to society's "normal" ways of operating.

## MAX WEBER

In contrast to Durkheim, Max Weber gave little attention to quantitative data and was one of the founders of qualitative research. He developed three concepts that are still central to qualitative research.

### *Verstehen*—Understanding

Social researchers must *understand* the ideas, thoughts, and meanings of the people they study. In today's terms, this fundamental tenet might translate into interviewing individuals to learn about their opinions and experiences. Ultimately, though, Weber was interested in the cultures of the past and more specifically how literate elites had formed and expressed these cultures. It therefore made sense for him to study the texts that elites had produced—the words of the Hebrew prophets, sacred Sanskrit texts of Indian sages, the teachings of Confucius, the Protestant ethic revealed in the writings of Calvin and Luther, and the "spirit of capitalism" that animated the writing of Benjamin Franklin. A careful reading of these texts was required for "getting into the heads" of the writers and to begin the task of interpreting their ideas in order to connect their ideas and values to other characteristics of their epoch, such as economic activity and the organization of states.

### The Historical-Comparative Method

In this method, the **units of analysis** (UOA) are not individuals but rather the collective units that individuals comprise—their cultures, societies, and civilizations. The **historical-comparative method** enables the researchers to understand why and how civilizations varied, diverged, and took on specific forms. Why, for instance, did capitalism as a system emerge in the Protestant regions of Northern Europe while Italy and China—places with vibrant cultures and intense commercial activity—did not develop the institutions and ideologies of modern capitalism? Another example of the historical-comparative method was Weber's effort to explain the conditions under which bureaucracies appear as the dominant form of organization in a society, displacing patrimonial organizations in which rulers rely on close personal ties to "friends and family."

### The Construction of "Ideal-Types"

The **ideal type** is not an ideal in the sense of something good, desirable, or valued; one could construct the ideal type of a criminal gang, a concentration camp, or a system of racial dominance. The ideal type is an abstract construct—an idea—that identifies key or essential features of an institution or situation if it were to exist in "pure form." For example, in *Asylums*, Erving Goffman (1961) constructed the ideal type of the "total institution," characterized by confinement, batch processing, staff–inmate hierarchy, and degradation and mortification of inmates in order to break down their resistance and transform their character and actions. Prisons, mental hospitals, boot camps, and cults are real-life instances that share these key defining features of the total institution. Establishing the ideal type of an institution or mode of action allows us to answer questions such as these: In what circumstances do they emerge, what are their effects, when did they first appear historically, and how are they related to other institutions (if indeed they are)?

## THE CHICAGO SCHOOL AND ITS LEGACY

The contributions of Max Weber influenced the **Chicago School of sociology**, noted for its contributions to urban sociology from the 1920s into the 1950s, but his ideas were absorbed and changed almost beyond recognition by the empirical priorities of the Chicago School. Over time, the Chicago School has become an institution in its own right. As Americans, early Chicago School sociologists were less interested than their European colleagues in reading the "great texts" of the "great civilizations," and they gave less attention to the big historical issues such as the rise of capitalism or the influence of the Hebrew prophets on Western values and social organization. Chicago School sociologists focused on what was happening in the neighborhoods of Chicago in the first half of the twentieth century—ethnic turnover, movement out of the inner city to the suburbs, immigration and assimilation, gangs and organized crime, racial tensions, and everyday life in all its myriad forms and experiences.

Chicago School sociologists developed several qualitative methods that are still in use.

### Spatial Mapping and Spatial Analysis

They observed the distribution of activities and people in space and time. Most famously, Ernest Burgess suggested a "concentric zone" hypothesis of urban growth, in which market forces led to deterioration of older areas around the center of the city while more attractive new areas cropped up further away from the center, as seen, for example, in the proliferation of suburbs. Observations were supplemented by quantitative data such as census records and real-estate listings, which were as yet unwieldy and unsophisticated compared to contemporary data. Students of Burgess extended this theoretical device to various issues, most notably juvenile delinquency. Clifford Shaw and Henry McKay, for example, found much higher criminal offending rates in the "inner ring" (i.e., "inner city") over time *regardless* of which ethnic group happened to occupy the area, and lower rates of offending in the outer rings of the concentric model (i.e., the suburbs). Out of this they developed a theory of "social disorganization," which traces delinquency/crime to the deterioration of social institutions that ordinarily keep young people "in check," such as schools, churches, and legitimate economic activity.

### The Life History Method

Chicago School sociologists collected the **life histories** of Polish immigrants, jack rollers (a type of mugger), taxi dancers (women working in multiple establishments as paid dance partners), and other denizens of the urban landscape. These narratives enabled them to understand processes of immigration, assimilation, recruitment to crime, and many other "down to earth" experiences of city life. They were able to see how larger social forces affected individuals, a central focus of the **sociological imagination**.

In the 1980s, a contemporary student of the Chicago School, Douglas Harper, took a teaching job at a college in a small upstate New York town. When it came time to get his old Saab repaired, a colleague referred him to "Willie," the local mechanic and jack-of-all-trades. Over the next few years, Harper and Willie became close friends. Throughout the course of their friendship, Harper documented (field notes, maps, photos, drawings) how Willie did his job, what it meant to him and to the folks who employed him, and how his way of work reflected larger issues in the American economy. The net result, *Working Knowledge* (1992)—part ethnography, part biography, and part photo-essay— documents the work life of Willie; it's a remarkable illustration of how sociological imagination can infuse deep meaning into even the most mundane aspects of the world.

## Analysis of Documents

Beginning with W.I. Thomas's accidental discovery of a packet of discarded letters in a Polish neighborhood in Chicago (1918–1920, five volumes), Chicago School sociologists read and interpreted texts produced by ordinary people—letters and local newspapers of the ethnic and immigrant presses such as the African American–oriented *Chicago Defender*. These **documents** showed how ordinary people experienced their world and "defined their situation."

## Observations and Descriptions of Neighborhood Life

Zorbaugh (1929) observed "the gold coast and the slum"—the area of Chicago where the fabulous homes of the wealthy along the lakefront were in close proximity to communities of poor Italian immigrants and African Americans. In their magisterial study of urban African American life in the 1930s and 1940s, *Black Metropolis*, St. Clair Drake and Horace Cayton (1945/1993) described the lives, hopes, dreams, successes, transgressions, and political struggles of the residents of Bronzeville, the core area of the Black Belt and the heart of Chicago's growing ghetto.

One of the more famous of the Chicago School sociologists Robert Park was a "newsman" before getting his PhD in Sociology and joining the University of Chicago faculty. He roundly criticized "armchair theories" of social life—theories disconnected from the nitty-gritty of daily life. Instead, he advocated strenuously for sociologists to get out of their offices, hit the streets, and literally get themselves dirty with research. He once wrote the following passage:

> Go and sit in the lounges of luxury hotels and on the doorsteps of the flophouses; sit on the Gold Coast settees and on the slum shakedowns; sit in the Orchestra Hall and in the Star and Garter Burlesque. In short go and get the seat of your pants dirty in real research. (Blumer 1984: 97)

## Occupational Studies

Chicago School researchers, most notably Everett Hughes, studied the complexities and dilemmas of work, charting the ethical issues people encountered in many jobs (i.e., "when good people do dirty work") and their collective and interactive efforts to solve problems encountered in work-related situations. This approach still influences many qualitative researchers who explore the lives of people in jobs such as the madame of the brothel (Albert 2001), the professional dominatrix (Lindemann, forthcoming), the nightclub bouncer (Rivera 2010), the phone-sex worker (Mattley 2002), the options trader (Widick 2003), and the street vendor (Duneier 1999).

## ETHNOGRAPHIC RESEARCH IN ANTHROPOLOGY

A very large, powerful stream of qualitative research ran alongside the sociological current: the research tradition of anthropology. Beginning with the work of natural historians such as Alexander Von Humboldt, who explored the Amazon region and wrote about its peoples as well as its flora and fauna, European and North American explorers compiled accounts of the "lives of savages." Initially, many of these studies espoused evolutionary ideas with a racial subtext that the "subjects" represented earlier and more primitive stages in the history of humankind's triumphal march to European civilization. Nevertheless, these early field studies yielded valuable information about the lifeways and material cultures of societies that were being exposed to the destructive effects of colonialism, disease, displacement, and adoption of

Christianity and "modern life." Examples of these studies included the inhabitants of Tierra del Fuego at the southern tip of South America, Polynesians, peoples of the Amazon, the Inuit, and the many ethnic groups of Africa.

Meticulous drawings and photographs—and, beginning in the 1920s, motion pictures (film)—supplemented the written accounts of marriage customs, initiation rites, beliefs and rituals honoring gods and spirits, body ornamentation, economic activities, artifacts, and food habits. Many of these early anthropological accounts circulated in mainstream society, in silent movie theaters and museums, in world exposition exhibits and libraries, and so forth.

By the early twentieth century, these accounts were organized more systematically and scientifically (Stocking 1992). The researcher was trained in the theories of the social sciences, systematic observations were made during a long period of fieldwork, and in most cases the voyeuristic and racist subtext was buried more deeply, if not eliminated altogether. The purpose was no longer to use observations to construct an evolutionary model of human progress, but to understand variation and difference in human cultures. At the same time, the general public became keenly interested in anthropological films and, even more so, fictional films based on anthropological-like characterizations of the "noble savage," such as Edward Curtis's *In the Land of the Headhunters* (1914) and Robert Flaherty's *Nanook of the North* (1922).

## Anthropologists of the Early 1900s

In the early twentieth century, key contributions were made by Bronislaw Malinowski's study of the Trobriand Islanders in the Pacific (1922, 1935), Margaret Mead's observations in Samoa, New Guinea (1935/2001), and later (with Gregory Bateson 1942) in Bali, and the **"British School" of anthropology**, especially Evans-Prichard's research among the Nuer of the Upper Nile (1950). The findings were often organized into comprehensive categories such as kinship, economic activities, religion and beliefs, warfare, marriage and the family, and reflected the theoretical position that these various institutions and activities "hang together" in a comprehensible and coherent way. In some instances, the studies addressed research questions that probed variation in human social and cultural arrangements: Mead wondered whether adolescence was as stressful in Samoa as in the United States and whether gender roles in New Guinea were just like those in the United States. Malinowski explored the implications of a matrilineal kinship system and probed the relationship among trading, economic activity, kinship, and spiritual beliefs.

Fieldwork in a remote and physically uncomfortable setting became the rite of passage for the aspiring cultural anthropologist. Ethnography—"writing about a people or ethnic group"—became a holistic and systematic methodology for understanding variation in the human condition (Stocking 1992). A variety of research strategies and techniques were developed that remain important components of ethnography today: learning the language or dialect of the community; spatial mapping of a village and its environs; tracing kinship relations and genealogies; documenting life narratives to understand life cycles, historical change, and individual variation in experiences, dispositions, and character; recording rituals and economic activities; and above all, keeping and organizing field notes.

## Sociology and Anthropology: An Often Uneasy Union

Sociology and anthropology were often placed together in a single department in North American universities, and the boundaries between them were not sharply defined beyond the fact that up until the last decades of the twentieth century, anthropologists eschewed quantitative methods and sociologists studied modern or industrialized societies while anthropologists studied "the others." In this situation, anthropological research influenced sociologists. For example, Lloyd Warner, an anthropologist by training, studied "Yankee City," a New England town, as if he were conducting an ethnographic study of a tribal community (1963). He compiled a rich record of the life, beliefs, and subjective views of the townspeople. Although we identified Emile Durkheim as the father of quantitative research, his theories influenced the Yankee City study, because Warner was a Durkheimian who sought to identify the symbolic order that underpinned life in Yankee City—the values, norms, tastes, and worldviews that organized behaviors and sustained the stratification system of the community.

Most of the "pioneering" qualitative researchers we've discussed so far were keenly interested in fairly small, often tight-knit "communities"—villages, tribes, towns, neighborhoods, families, or even units as small as the friendship network or the individual person's biography. But there's a whole other tradition of studying culture qualitatively and critically. This tradition's origins can be traced back to the early works of researchers at the "Frankfurt Institute."

## THE FRANKFURT INSTITUTE

The Frankfurt Institute was comprised of a group of social scientists working in Germany between World War I and World War II (Jay 1996). Two momentous societal changes were underway: On one hand, the researchers observed the emergence of *new media* such as radio, film, the recording industry, the circulation of magazines and pulp fiction, and spectator sports; and on the other hand, they saw the nefarious rise of Fascism and Nazism. To the Frankfurt researchers, these two phenomena were related: that is, the media functioned to distract the masses and to make them passive and uncritical.

The media were channels for carrying seductive, irrational, and emotional messages that inspired support for right-wing extremists. The Frankfurt scholars examined the products of the culture industry, the media and entertainment firms that generated subtle and not-so-subtle messages of passivity, escapism, stupefaction, and emotions such as fear, anger, racism, and the worship of strong leaders. These messages were easily used and manipulated by right-wing politicians such as Hitler and Mussolini. The Frankfurt researchers were influenced not only by Marxism but also by **psychoanalysis** in their analysis of the political impact of the media.

Walter Benjamin also examined the spaces of consumption, specifically the Paris Arcades or passageways, shopping areas of the nineteenth century that were forerunners of the shopping mall. In these lavishly ornamented spaces with their shops and restaurants, the rich bought luxury goods and the poor gaped at them longingly, carried away by fantasies of consumption (Buck-Morss 1989; McRobbie 1999; Benjamin 2002). By examining the unthinking consumption of mass media products and the mindless sojourning into fantasy-inspiring spaces ruled by the "look but don't touch" rule, the scholars associated with the Frankfurt Institute used qualitative methods to examine the interrelationship of culture, social stratification, and injustice.

In short, the Frankfurt Institute pioneered the analysis of media and cultural artifacts, organizing their research around politically and theoretically charged critical research questions that linked material objects and products (shop windows, magazines, movies, pulp fiction, radio broadcasts), inner lives of fantasies and fears, and political movements and outcomes.

Passage Jouffroy (1845).   Paris, May 2006.

When the Nazis came to power in Germany, the Frankfurt scholars had to flee and many came to the United States where they made crucial contributions in the development of both quantitative and qualitative research. They contributed to the U.S. love affair with Dr. Freud's psychoanalysis, though his gloomy and radical insights were greatly toned down for U.S. popular culture. Psychoanalytic perspectives influenced sociology, anthropology, and political science (more than mainstream psychology) and led to imaginative qualitative methods such as the use of life histories, data collection about child-raising practices and gender roles, interest in sexual

Passage Vivienne (1823).   Paris, May 2006.

behavior, the use and interpretation of **projective tests** (such as the Thematic Apperception Test and the Rorschach inkblot test), the interpretation of religious and magical beliefs as projections of sexual and aggressive drives and fears, and psychoanalytic interpretations of art and myths (Adorno et al. 1993). Chicago School sociologists had already been using life history methods, but without reference to psychoanalytic concepts and with little attention to the effects of childrearing on personality.

Passage du Panorama (1800).    Paris, May 2006.

The arcades or passages were splendid glass and iron structures of nineteenth-century Paris where new consumer goods were beautifully displayed in shop windows that opened into a public space. They were forerunners of great shopping boulevards such as Fifth Avenue in New York and contemporary shopping malls. They ran through the middle of city blocks and seemed both "inside" and "outside." Many of them were decorated with paintings and dioramas, as well as "Orientalist" ornamentation inspired by French conquests in Egypt and the Middle East.

## STREET CORNER SOCIETY: PARAGON OF EARLY QUALITATIVE RESEARCH

We feel compelled to make special mention of William F. Whyte's *Street Corner Society* (1943/1993). In many respects, this study of a predominantly Italian American community in Boston in the late 1930s was similar to Chicago School studies. It focused on a specific area ("Cornerville"), described the life of the neighborhood primarily through the experiences and actions of its young men, and provided accounts of racketeering and politics. But *Street Corner Society* differed from Chicago School studies in its careful attention to the fieldwork experience and the lessons the researcher had to learn—such as living in an apartment without a bathroom, not dating local women, and carefully and respectfully listening to conversations instead of asking direct questions about murders and police payoffs.

Whyte wrote a long appendix to the 1954 edition, in which he described his entry into the community in great detail—and his frank reliance on a guide, a man named Doc who enabled Whyte to meet many neighborhood people, including the "corner guys" and racketeers. Doc interpreted these experiences for the researcher. Whyte met Doc through a mutual acquaintance who worked in a settlement house in the neighborhood, and without Doc the study would have been vastly different, much less revealing, and perhaps altogether impossible to conduct. Whyte's book broached the issues of entry, reliance on a guide, and the ethics of the guide–researcher relationship, all of which have continued to be key problems in qualitative and ethnographic fieldwork. Methodologically speaking, Whyte's approach was innovative. His trailblazing use of systematic social observation (SSO), geospatial network mapping, and group hierarchy charting laid the foundation upon which thousands of future scholars pursued their own field studies.

Whyte tapped into and inspired the further development of several new "subfields" of social science, including "participatory action research" and **critical community studies**. We now turn to a brief explanation of the latter.

## CRITICAL COMMUNITY STUDIES

Throughout the period from the 1930s to the last decades of the twentieth century, critical community studies were a major area of qualitative research. They provided an unflinching look at the harshness of American community life. Although superficially similar in research techniques to ethnographies and Chicago School research, the critical community studies were driven by theoretical concerns based on conflict theories. They had a much sharper political edge than the ethnographies and Chicago School observations, and their research questions focused on inequalities in the communities, power structures, and the myths and ideologies that legitimated the status quo. The researchers showed how townspeople clung to the myth of their community as a friendly, self-reliant place when it was really deeply class-divided and at the mercy of larger economic and political forces.

Among the first of these studies were the two volumes written by the Lynds about Middletown, a community in Indiana that passed from 1920s prosperity to an unsettled economic condition during the depression of the 1930s (Lynd and Lynd 1959). The Lynds focused on stratification and economic inequalities in the community, the dominance of the business class and its allies, and the conservative ideology espoused not only by the elite but by many folks further down the economic ladder.

After World War II, Vidich and Bensman (1969) offered a devastating and sarcastically toned picture of small town life in upstate New York—*Small Town in Mass Society*. Not only did they analyze the town's class structure, emphasizing its deep divisions and contending interests; they also highlighted the townspeople's *misrecognition* of their condition. Despite self-congratulatory boosterism about small town independence, self-reliance, and traditional values, the town was economically and politically dependent on larger forces—the regional and national economy and political decisions made beyond the local level.

In a similar but more topically focused study, Hollingshead (1975) examined the interplay between class inequality and high school experiences in a small town in Northern Illinois. He showed how both the formal education system and the informal student culture favored and nurtured the children of local business owners and managers, while children of the poor were marginalized and induced to drop out of school.

These studies were driven by theoretical projects of showing the mismatch between the realities of stratification, class and power inequalities, and economic dependency on the one hand and on the other hand, the subjective (mis-)understandings (whether intentional and therefore known, or unknown) held by the townspeople as they celebrated their independence, friendliness, and virtues of small town life.

Up to this point in the development of qualitative research, scholars were mostly interested in "the collective"—they conceived "the community" or "the neighborhood," the village or the tribe, as the main unit of analysis. Certainly they interviewed and observed individuals, but their ultimate goal was to account for phenomena that occurred at a level higher than the individual . . . they were attuned to the superordinate dynamics of human life. Around midcentury, though, things began to change a bit.

## THE RISE OF MICROSOCIOLOGIES AND THE GREAT SURGE IN QUALITATIVE RESEARCH

The later 1950s and the 1960s marked a key turning point in qualitative research which now became the strategy *par excellence* of a host of new microtheories, including **symbolic interactionism** and Goffman's **dramaturgical model**. These sociologists' actual, day-to-day research activities were not very different from those of the Chicago School—in fact, this wave is sometimes referred to as the "second Chicago School." But the rationale for participant-observation and fieldwork became much more elaborated and self-conscious. All the microtheorists agreed that "society" was a meaningless abstraction, a **reification** (a nonmaterial phenomenon treated as though it's a tangible "thing"); "society" does not exist, and all that exists are human beings in interaction and in **situated actions**, actions in specific contexts.

### Foundational Concepts of Early Qualitative Research

"Society" is constituted by innumerable actions and interactions, which are not always rational and which may have unintended and unanticipated consequences. "Structure" does not exist as a "thing." So researchers can really only study the constant flux of interaction between and among individuals. The "flagship" research method is observation, and actions and interactions (as opposed to individual persons or organizations, much less "society," whatever that word means) must be the units of study in sociological research (Lindesmith and Strauss 1958; Goffman 1959, 1961, 1963; Becker 1963, 1998; Glaser and Strauss 1967; Blumer 1968).

This position had various theoretical ancestors: For the *symbolic interactionists*, the roots took hold in Weber's concept of *verstehen* and his interest in action, Simmel's observations of interaction and social forms, and the influence of social behaviorism based on Cooley's looking-glass self, the writing of George Herbert Mead, and pragmatic philosophy with its celebration of a competent, coping self. Goffman on the other hand was a "micro-Durkheimian"; like Durkheim he was interested in the normative order and normative regulation, and unlike other readers of Durkheim, he looked for evidence of this order in the high degree of patterning of interactions and the presentation of self.

Regulation takes place not only in the "big" institutions such as religion, law, and criminal justice but also at the microlevel where it is exercised through the unspoken rules of interaction, impression management, presentation of self, management of stigma, and behavior in public places. These rules regulate performance; the norms are transmuted into aesthetic criteria—Is the performance of sanity, sincerity, love, respect, integrity, respectability, competence, and so on convincing or not? The moral and normative order is embedded in aesthetic judgments of role performance. Norms are monitored and enforced by deciding whether or not people's performances are credible and convincing. When we find others' role performances to be acceptable (i.e., credible, convincing, and appropriate), we reward them through how we treat them. When we find them inappropriate, we "punish" them. Think about ordinary places you frequent in daily life. How do you reward and punish your friends, your classmates, and members of your family? Everyone "polices" everyone else; this is what keeps society running. To understand this microregulation, it is essential to observe interaction (Goffman 1959, 1961, 1963).

## The Common Denominator: Get Out of the Office and into the Mix of Real Life!

Whatever the theoretical ancestors of the new microtheorists were, they agreed that sociological method had to involve observation in social contexts. Researchers have to watch, listen, and record. They have to enter the messiness of real life and get their proverbial hands (and seat of the pants) dirty. The microsociologists had little interest in surveys and experiments, which they saw as decontextualized ways of collecting information that missed process, natural settings, duration in time, and the play of interaction.

This explicit new orientation was developed in a host of exciting field-based studies in mental hospitals, nursing homes, gynecologists' offices, jazz clubs, and medical schools. Observations focused on the use of space and time, the manipulation of power and inequality in interaction, judgment of performances, management of stigma (both visible stigma such as a scarred face or the "wrong" skin-tone and hidden ones such as a criminal record or history of mental illness). **Labeling processes** were observed not only in interactions but also in documents that expressed power, categorized people, and revealed unequal resources, such as school disciplinary files, case reports on patients and social work clients, and police records. As you might imagine, students delighted in these opportunities for fieldwork and "hands-on" research experiences in real-life contexts. In contrast to the enormous resources, large teams, and tedious data analysis (in the age of punched cards) required by survey research, students and young scholars found it was easy to start the adventure of sociological inquiry using participant-observation. All they had to do was grab a notebook and pencil and venture out into the world, eyes wide open and ears calibrated to the nuances of life.

## Principles of the New Qualitative Methodology

By the early 1970s, qualitative research had reached maturity. Researchers understandably grew increasingly concerned about *refining* the systematic use of techniques for collecting data. They were more conscious of theoretical frameworks. And they were committed to elucidating the conceptual and technical features of their data collection while also reflecting critically on the data production enterprise. In a word, they had become methodologists, for **methodology** is *the reflexive and recursive application of concept/theory-informed techniques for producing and analyzing information to tell a sociological story* about a given phenomenon. A core set of principles comprised the foundation on which many researchers conceived and conducted qualitative research.

**SITUATED ACTION**   "Situated" means that observers must look at what people are doing and saying *in situ*, or in their normal settings, in contrast to bringing them into the stale environment of a university office and asking them questions in a survey (which means the respondents are never seen in action) or subjecting them to an experiment (which is an "unnatural" condition set up by the researcher and detached from real contexts).

**ACTION AND INTERACTION**   Symbolic interactionists avoided the term "behavior" because it implies that all the researcher needs to accomplish is to observe what people do and then analyze these data "objectively" regardless of the words, ideas, meanings, and intentions of the subjects. In contrast, symbolic interactionists held to Weber's emphasis on "social action," which refers to behavior that is infused with and shaped by meaning, understanding, and interpretation; in this approach, they honored his insistence that human beings generally act with a purpose and attempt to express their will. Human beings are not rats or pigeons, but symbol-using animals.

**NATURAL SETTINGS**   As noted above, microsociologists believed that social context was crucial to the understanding and interpretation of actions and interactions, so that most of their research was carried out in the settings of everyday life—nursing homes, street corners, medical school classrooms, jazz clubs, and every other "real place" to be found.

**GROUNDED THEORY**   While Goffman's dramaturgical model was rooted in Durkheim's theories of normative regulation and social order, the symbolic interactionists claimed to be developing theories inductively. The term **grounded theory** implied that the researcher should not go into fieldwork with a definite set of theories in mind, but should let concepts and explanations emerge from careful observation. This position was a bit disingenuous—the symbolic interactionists did have theoretical perspectives of their own, and in fact these very theories often motivated their choice of research topics; in addition, it was extremely unlikely that their fieldwork methods would ever lead to theoretical formulations that were far removed from the premises of symbolic interactionism.

The practice of grounded theory tended to reinforce the idea that social institutions are not structures nor the product of individual characteristics but processes embedded in clusters of oft-repeated interactions and symbolic usage. For example, residential segregation in the United States was not "a structure" nor simply the result of individual prejudice, but rather the outcome of myriad constantly repeated situated actions, interactions, and use of words and symbols among real-estate agents, home buyers, mortgage lenders, elected officials, and so on.

## Ethnomethodologists and "Breaching" Experiments

A daring extension of the microtheorists' position was developed by **ethnomethodologists** and examined through **breaching experiments**. Ethnomethodologists shared Goffman's view that interaction is highly regulated by shared, unspoken norms and they went even further, emphasizing the way shared meanings are embedded in our use of language. Every conversation operates on the basis of these unspoken shared understandings that underlie our interpretation of others' words and gestures. Garfinkel (1967) believed that a way of "finding" these shared hidden rules of interaction was to breach the rules and see what happens. For example, he had his students "act like boarders" (i.e., tenants) in their parents' homes, speaking formally and politely asking whether they could help themselves to food in the fridge. The students recorded the way their parents became confused, disoriented, and angry by this violation of the unspoken norms of family interaction. Garfinkel was also interested in an unintentional breaching of gender norms, resulting from a botched circumcision and the consequent effort of the child's parent to reorient their former little boy to a feminine gender identity.

## The Birth of a Contentious Divide

This era of sociology—from the 1960s to the last decade of the twentieth century—was marked by divergence between the ever-more-sophisticated qualitative, observational, and interpretive methods of the microsociologists and the increasingly rarefied quantitative analysis that was often identified as the mainstream approach to research. The two camps tended to be hostile to each other. Quantitative researchers relied heavily on identifying and operationalizing variables prior to entering the field and they conceived of the field as a vast aggregate of cases best selected by probability sampling. **Microsociology**, the interpretive paradigm, and grounded theory were based on the observation of situated actions, quite a different object of analysis than the decontextualized and predefined variables of quantitative research.

Microresearchers believed that only qualitative methods of observations in contexts, analysis of the flow and process of interaction, and attention to situated action were adequate for understanding the human condition. Neither large historical change (studied by historical-comparative methods and often linked to Weberian or Marxian conflict theories) nor the search for statistically discernible patterns (linked to Durkheimian quantitative analysis) can fully capture human life.

To this day, the qualitative–quantitative rift persists, though the passage of time has ushered in multimethodological approaches to research and new perspectives on the many conceptual and logical similarities between the two "camps" of research. We intend for this book to present this type of perspective.

## FEMINIST AND POSTMODERNIST APPROACHES: NEW DIRECTIONS AT THE END OF THE TWENTIETH CENTURY

### Feminist Research Strategies

Many **feminist theorists** writing in the last decades of the twentieth century supported and expanded the perspectives of the microsociologists; they agreed that interpretations of people's words and actions were crucial to understanding their experiences. Dorothy Smith (1990, 1992) and other feminists linked these perspectives to a criticism of what they considered a masculinist way of doing sociology. In their view, "masculinist sociology" meant the stance of being objective, keeping a distance from the research subjects (who are treated as objects of research, not real participants in it), and being indifferent to the experiences, ideas, and knowledge of the people who were being researched.

Masculinist researchers had little interest in the labor and knowledge of women and other people in subaltern positions in society, such as poor people and ethnic minorities. In the view of the feminists, the masculinist researcher claimed to have a practically omniscient position and imposed his (*sic*) own categories and variables on the data. Behavior was recorded, findings stated, and conclusions formulated and published as if the researchers were studying insects or lab animals, not human beings. Feminists believed that this detached and objectifying approach was a typically masculine way of understanding the world and relating to people. In contrast, feminist scholars claimed that they invite people they studied to become research participants (rather than research subjects or objects of scientific scrutiny), actively involve them in defining the goals of the study and interpreting their own life situations to the researcher (Reinharz and Davidman 1992). The local knowledge of the researched community is valued, and the dominant–subordinate relationship of researcher to researched is made markedly more equal.

The portrayal of "masculinist research" was often a caricature, and not all male researchers were indifferent objectifiers nor were all women researchers sensitive egalitarian research partners. Nevertheless, the feminist critique and the effort to develop specifically feminist research orientations reflected researchers' discomfort with aspects of qualitative research and ethnographic writing, such as objectification and the feeling that communities and individuals— often the most disadvantaged ones—are vulnerable to exploitation by researchers who obtain a PhD, a tenured professorship, or a book from the relationship and give little in return.

## Postmodernism in Qualitative Research

Another way in which Lingering doubts about qualitative research also found expression in the subjectivist and **postmodern** turn in ethnography. This current was strongly influenced by the intellectual trend of "deconstruction"—the position that texts and categories of thought are socially constructed and that the process of construction needs to be revealed and made transparent. A somewhat simplified version of the complex philosophical work of Jacques Derrida had a profound effect on sociological theory and cultural studies. The impact on qualitative methods was twofold.

A first step in the process was the critical reading of famous ethnographies, especially anthropological studies. For example, Bronislaw Malinowski's observations of the Trobriand Islanders in the South Pacific were revisited in light of his links to the colonial administration and unseemly and racist comments he made in his diaries (Malinowski 1967; Stocking 1992). So postmodernists observed the observers and drew attention to their political and personal positions. The formation of the researchers' own points of view became the focus of a new wave of analyzing ethnographies and other types of fieldwork.

The second critical step was to emphasize the textual nature of all ethnographic writing. It is never a faithful and perfect mirror of a community's reality but always a product created by the choices of the individual observer/writer. The reader can see the community's world only "through a glass darkly"—through the ethnographer's writing. It is usually filtered through the preconceptions of Western culture (most ethnographers, until very recently, were Westerners and generally of European heritage), organized according to the norms of academic writing, and above all, composed according to the code that generates an illusion of objectivity and truth. For example, the ethnographer (like all social science researchers) rarely uses the pronoun "I" in the writing and keeps up the illusion that "facts" and "findings" are being presented, that we are reading the truth, rather than a story.

These reflections made postmodern ethnographers decide to dispel this illusion by focusing on themselves—the ethnographers—showing how the researchers experience the life of the community, revealing prejudices and ethnocentrism, and making transparent their observation and writing choices (Adler and Adler 2008). Of course, some of this reflexive writing had appeared in earlier and more traditional ethnographies, as we noted in our discussion of William F. Whyte's *Street Corner Society*; the unusual aspect of the postmodern ethnography was its extreme degree of self-contemplation. One critic says that postmodern ethnographies "threw themselves into the well of subjectivity" (Wacquant 2009). Postmodern ethnographies were no longer about a community but about the act and experience of doing ethnography and about the inner life of the ethnographer.

It is worth noting that a similar trend appeared in journalism after a long twentieth-century romance with objectivity, which was defined by careful attention to "balance" and "getting both sides of the story." In the era of the war in Vietnam, many journalists and writers such as Norman Mailer and Hunter Thompson were dismayed that the consequence of the cult of objectivity was to lose the truth of the story; and they decided that the only course of action was to focus the story on their own presence in the unfolding events and to write about their writing (Schudson 1978). Their basic premise was that objectivity is chimerical—it's a ruse, "necessary illusion" (Chomsky 1989) that we, the media-consuming public, uphold in order to achieve a stability vis-à-vis information flows in society. But true objectivity cannot be achieved; hence, it must be abandoned and replaced by "reports" that explain events and also expose the inner workings of the writer's various perceptual filters, which affords readers the opportunity to assess the truthfulness and/or accuracy of the report.

## Toward More Comprehensive Orientations

Not all qualitative researchers believe that feminist, deconstructionist, and postmodern ethnography are the best antidotes to the ethical and intellectual problems of classical ethnography and participant-observation. They agree that these ethical and intellectual problems need to be resolved but believe that can be accomplished without taking a position as extreme as the postmodernists' renunciation of all claims to objectivity, accuracy, and truthful representation.

In the next chapters, we will explore contemporary approaches to resolving these problems, such as:

- Combining quantitative and qualitative methods
- Community-based participatory research which addresses the concerns expressed in the feminist critique
- Reflexive sociology and theory construction, especially as influenced by the work of Pierre Bourdieu and Loïc Wacquant.

## CONCLUSION

This chapter has introduced the reader to the diverse traditions of qualitative research that influence contemporary qualitative research, and it has broached several issues which we will explore in this book:

1. What is the purpose of the research? Is it to obtain a broad understanding of the way of life of a community or is it more theoretically focused and driven by specific research questions?
2. What is the relationship between theories and research? Are theories believed to emerge from the research (inductively and as "grounded theory") or does a theory inform the research project from the very start, shaping the research questions and influencing the choice of research strategies ("foundational theory")?
3. What is the researcher's relationship to the research subjects/participants? Are the research subjects treated distantly, with their lives and views held up to objective scrutiny, or are they partners in the research with their subjective understandings incorporated not only into data but also into the research process itself? Are researchers intent on enabling their subjects to send a message to a larger audience or intent on exposing the subjects' "misrecognitions"?

4. Do researchers rely on the people they are studying to be their guides, and if so, what are the intellectual, political, and ethical implications of this relationship? And if not, how can researchers ever hope to enter the field and interact with the community?

5. What are the appropriate research techniques—the research tools and strategies—in view of research questions, purposes, and ethical and political commitments?

6. How are researchers to write about research experience? Will they write a broad, multi-method ethnography, a discussion of theoretical constructs focused on theoretically oriented research questions, a brief on behalf of the community as its advocates, or a "postmodern" personal account about their own experiences and feelings (Adler and Adler 2008)?

## Exercises

1. Read one of the studies discussed in this chapter and write a response paper. Is the topic still of interest? Did the author explain the choice of methods? Were the conclusions convincing? Do you think this study could be replicated today—what might be different?

2. Think about the origins of qualitative research and how the tradition has changed over time. Which of the early studies interests you most? Why do you find it so interesting?

3. Spend some time talking with someone whose life is "interesting" to you in some way. Write up your notes. Then write a brief analysis of what this person's life, as you have come to understand it, says about the larger society in which we all live. In other words, through your interactions with the other person produce data on which you can apply your sociological imagination.

4. Conduct your own "norm breaching" experiment and document what the experiment reveals about

the regulatory norms of the situation whose unwritten rules (protocol) you have broken. For instance, enter an elevator occupied by several other people, and when the doors close, turn around and face the direction opposite that which all others are facing. What is their response? Alternatively, visit a space in which people work to accomplish non-interaction (e.g., a doctor's office waiting room, a public bus, or even bus stop). Rather than abide by the tacit "don't talk" rule, just start blabbing to the nearest person about personal issues (nothing too revealing, though!). Then start to include others in the conversation. Talk to as many people as possible. In your analysis, try to discern the various norms that people ordinarily enact in order to regulate their own and others' behaviors in the situation. Also reflect on the various "punishments" ( scolding glances, the "shush" sound, averted eyes, etc.) you received as you broke protocol.

## Key Terms

breaching experiments *26*
"British School" of anthropology *18*
Chicago School of sociology *16*
critical community studies *23*
documents *17*
dramaturgical model *24*
ethnographic research in anthropology *17*
ethnomethodology *26*
feminist theorists *27*

Frankfurt Institute 19
grounded theory *26*
historical-comparative method *15*
ideal type *15*
labeling processes *25*
life histories *16*
methodology *26*
microsociology *24*
occupational studies *17*
postmodernism *28*

projective tests *21*
psychoanalysis *19*
reification *24*
situated action *24*
sociological imagination *16*
symbolic interactionsim *24*
spatial mapping and spatial analysis *16*
units of analysis *15*
*verstehen 24*

# 3

# Asking Research Questions

## OVERVIEW

The **research question** guides the empirical research study. It sets in motion research activities that yield information and lead to a special type of story, a research report. These activities aim at producing data that meet the criteria of "the scientific method," a particular way of knowing. The "findings," or the answers you create by analyzing the data you gathered in response to the research question, must be **objective, generalizable, falsifiable**, and **reproducible**. The research question and the story that answers it (i.e., the findings) must be conveyed in a **science vernacular**. Qualitative research differs from quantitative research in being more flexible in organizing evidence and framing of the stories. In this chapter, we discuss the research question, offer you guidance on developing your own RQ, and present two examples to help you think through some of the key issues pertaining to the asking and answering of RQs. We also offer tips on where to get ideas for research questions and how to word them.

## INTRODUCTION: WHAT IS A RESEARCH QUESTION?

Research questions guide research projects. Nowadays, few research projects simply describe, blow-by-blow, a slice of social "reality" in the manner of a well-written blog, a vivid piece of journalism, or detailed nonfiction writing. Almost all empirical studies, qualitative or quantitative, attempt to answer a particular question or cluster of questions, usually about variation and diversity in social arrangements or behaviours. Some studies are concerned with how similar **cases** or situations produce different outcomes, while others examine how very different cases or situations yield similar outcomes. Why do some cities have higher crime rates than other cities? Does identifying as a man or a woman affect individuals' voting choices and political views? Which religious groups have the highest suicide rates and what accounts for the differences? Why and how do some youth end up dropping out of high school? Why does the United States have a high rate of incarceration? Sometimes the research question focuses on uniformities or a lack of variability in arrangements and behaviours. For example, why do all Western societies shun mutilation as a method of punishment? What similarities can we find in the organization of drug gangs in large U.S. cities, and what social forces account for these similarities?

Without a guiding research question (or cluster of related questions), empirical studies would be mere reports of observations, at best entertaining to read but more likely amounting to a disorganized set of field notes or a hot mess of aimless numbers. The research question motivates and structures data and their collection, the process of analyzing data, the creation of theories to make sense of the data, and the composing of a story that brings it all together. In short, the research question is a necessary catalyst in a sociological study, and it plays an integral role in every phase of the research process. When in doubt about any phase or aspect of your study, pay a visit to your research question—it almost always will bring some clarity to the matter.

We hasten to mention that your research question is likely to change *substantially* throughout your study, as you move from formulating the question to strategizing data production, and then possibly continue to change as you conduct your analyses. Many textbooks treat the research question as though it's a static "thing," an unyielding foundation on which you build a study. As we'll see, this couldn't be further from the truth, especially in qualitative research, where the research question sways and bobs on the dynamic current of the "dialogue of evidence and ideas" (Ragin 1994) of the research process. At some point, however, you will have to solidify your research question, but this point could be much later in the game than most other textbooks (or instructor-scholars) might admit!

## WHAT DOES A RESEARCH QUESTION PRODUCE?

The research question gets you going on a number of research activities that produce a special type of information called "data," and a final report that organizes the data and your manipulation and interpretation of it into a compelling "story." Research and the stories we tell about what we find—called **research reports**—generally follow a set of rules derived from natural science methods. Every scientist's activities, including her choices, occur within a very large framework, a **way of knowing** that is called the **scientific method**. Not all social scientists adhere strictly to the scientific method but all are influenced by it—even if they decide to reject it explicitly. The scientific method lurks in the back of the sociologist's mind as she asks her research questions, and she typically avoids asking questions that cannot be answered within this framework (e.g., Is there a higher power running everything?)

### The Sociologist's Way

Sociology is the study of people doing things—and/or not doing things—together. As a qualitative researcher, your job is to craft a **representation of social life** (Becker 2007). This means that you will be using the scientific method, as it applies to qualitative research, to "tell a story" about a social phenomenon that interests you and to answer questions that you have formulated about it. These questions are formulated well in advance of carrying out research activities, but in qualitative research, they often change dramatically during the initial research experiences.

You might be telling a sociological story of how customers and artists interact in tattoo parlors, how upper-class families in France raise their children, how street gangs participate in the illicit drug economy or how they contribute value to their communities, how binge drinking happens among college students. Or, you might be trying to explain "accomplished noninteraction," the ways people go about *not* interacting with each other in public spaces, such as doctor's office waiting rooms, public transportation vehicles (trains and buses), or lines at the grocery store cash register.

## The Scientific Method

Every single day we "represent" social life: We tell our friends and families stories about what happened during the day, we go to parties where we exchange comic or tragic stories of events we have witnessed or heard about, and we review our day's activities—complete with characters, events, and theories of why things happened the way they did—as we fall asleep at night. But sociological representations differ from these more casual storytelling forays. And they differ from the structured representations that journalists compose for newspapers and television news programs. Sociological representations have their own structure and often must adhere to a different set of rules. These **rules of sociological representation** enable *and* constrain the sociologist's way of making representations of social life and telling stories about it. Our shorthand name for these rules is the *scientific method*. It is a way of knowing, of arriving at knowledge of the world around us.

There is considerable controversy about the extent to which the social sciences—and especially qualitative research—can and should use the scientific method, but a majority of researchers would say that in very broad terms the scientific method does apply to the study of social phenomena, although it needs to be suitably adjusted to the fact that human action takes place in a **historical context** and that humans are **self-reflexive and symbol-using beings**, not inanimate or wordless objects. Moreover, the scientist in this case is a human; the same goes for the "subjects" of the study. This can make everything much more complicated—in terms of rules—than it is when the scientist is a chemist and the subject is polyisoprene vulcanization (burning rubber latex).

## The Scientific Method: A Set of Rules Guiding Procedures, Presentation of Evidence, and Storytelling

The criteria that comprise the scientific method resemble the **rules of evidence** applicable to legal proceedings in Anglo-American law, where the evidentiary standard is "proof beyond a reasonable doubt that the accused party is guilty," a cornerstone of the American criminal justice system known as the "presumption of innocence." From this premise flows a further set of rules governing the stringent procedures that the prosecution must use to convince a judge or jury that no "reasonable person" could conclude that the defendant is innocent of the crime. These rules play out in an "adversarial system," where the defense and prosecution go up against each other in constructing two different, competing stories of what happened. In presenting evidence to the judge or jury, each side attempts to "falsify"—in the sense of "cast doubt on"—the story told by the adversary. In the United States, it is believed that truth is most likely to emerge from this battle of representations, in contrast to the continental systems in which a lone investigating magistrate sets out to discover the truth. In both systems, however, the "facts" in the story (or contending stories) must meet criteria such as relevance, materiality, and competence, and there are very strict rules about presenting evidence.

The scientific method is a similar kind of framework that governs the quality of evidence and the search for "truth." Sociologists continuously strive to demonstrate the **plausibility** of their social representations. They wish to convince the reader/audience that their "proof" meets specific criteria and is therefore "rigorous" or "robust." And they assemble their various forms of "evidence" (called "data" in sociology) to construct a representation that others—usually peer scholars—will find convincing. Essentially, the sociologist follows the scientific method in her quest to demonstrate beyond a reasonable doubt that her particular story is potentially truthful, that it holds up well against challenges, and that it is supported by the evidence. In addition, every sociologist brings his "reasonable doubt" into the scrutiny of others' research findings by applying the tenets of the scientific method to determine how compelling and persuasive the other scholar's findings are.

## Principles of the Scientific Method

In the discipline of sociology, roiling debates encircle the scientific method—some scholars summarily reject it, others embrace it wholesale, and some feel either ambivalent toward it or adopt a utilitarian, practical position that entails selectively applying and adapting one or more of its basic principles. But it's a good starting point for our discussion, because even those who reject it completely still operate in reference to it.

What are these principles (or tenets)? Just as juridical systems employ rules of evidence, the field of sociology rests on a foundation of central principles that come alive in the doing of research, whether quantitative (numeric) or qualitative. These fundamental tenets include **objectivity**, **generalizability**, **falsifiability**, and **replicability** (**or reproducibility**). The researcher uses these tenets to achieve *plausibility* for the conclusions. That's a lot of big words ending in "ity" . . . let's break them down a bit.

**OBJECTIVITY**    *Objectivity means that the information is not influenced by personal feelings or opinions of anyone. Objective statements "match what is out there" regardless of how individuals feel about this match or even whether they can perceive it.* When a tree falls in the forest, the impact on the ground sets up sound waves, regardless of whether anyone is there to hear them. The principle of objectivity tacitly presupposes the existence of "facts" that do not depend upon the mind for their existence.

Scholars and laypersons argue endlessly about the problems in this definition. Statements of fact come from the human mind and almost always are constructed through interaction with other humans. Hence, every fact emerges not directly from the "world out there" but through a mix of social construction and neurologically determined workings of minds. In the social sciences and the study of human actions, statements of fact are embedded in even thicker layers of social construction than in the natural sciences. So some scholars object to the use of terms such as "objective" and "fact" at all.

Yet we would argue that it is still reasonable to say that statements formulated in research have different degrees of objectivity. For example, "El Salvador has a higher level of income inequality than Denmark" is a relatively objective statement. Once we have decided that income inequality is worth talking about (a notion that might just be a subjective value or might be related to other research questions) and decided how to measure it (thereby socially constructing income inequality as a fact), we would all agree that there is more of "it" in El Salvador than Denmark. Notice how we often assign higher degrees of objectivity to statements that are based on a prior agreement about how we define something, especially by measuring or counting.

Qualitative researchers concern themselves with objectivity as much as quantitative researchers, but they often call it something else: **believability**. Scientists realize but often do not publicly admit that facts are only facts when there is a socially agreed-upon paradigm for identifying and labeling a phenomenon as a fact or a nonfact. Every scientist, when pursuing the scientific method, works toward constructing a story about the world—natural or social—that readers will find *believable*—or **plausible**—or at the very least *not unbelievable*. Believability, as sort of substitute for complete objectivity, must entail a full, complete, and transparent description of procedures of research to convince the reader that the researcher looked at "something out there" and did not invent a story based only on her opinions and feelings, although these opinions are legitimate reasons to have *undertaken* the research to begin with. We must be convinced that if we went to the same place and situation and used the same methods, we would obtain very similar results (a conviction called *replicability*) because the results are basically a product of something "out there" in the real world even if it is filtered through human minds and interactions.

**GENERALIZABILITY**   *Generalizability means that the information applies to someone other than those people or situations for which it was directly observed or produced. We ask ourselves "Does this study's findings tell us anything convincing/believable about anyone other than the people who were studied?"*

After studying experiences of violence among gang members, for instance, the author may first decide that any gang member is more likely to be assaulted by a fellow gang member than by the member of a rival gang and then offers the conclusion that *intra*-gang victimization is more likely than *inter*-gang victimization. Let's assume that his observations of the gang were correct—believable findings supported by evidence. But what about his conclusion? Does it apply to any gang other than the one he studied? How far can he stretch this finding? Who is it really about? Does it apply to other gangs in the researcher's city, to gangs throughout the country, to all contemporary gangs across the globe, to all gangs for all times and places…? As skeptical readers who go into the reading with "reasonable doubt" about the story's "truth," we must ask ourselves and each other whether or not the researcher's methods and data were rigorously enough developed to make the story applicable to gang members *whom the researcher did not observe, interview, or otherwise study* (i.e., the "unobserved cases").

It may be useful to replace the word "generalizability" with **relevance**. A study (or scientific story) of a specific set of gang members might not be generalizable to all gang members in all cities across the planet, but it might have relevance to the way many or most or a significant number of other gangs operate. This is an important point. Very few studies, even the most scientifically rigorous, can be considered fully generalizable. Many of them, however, address "generic social processes," which Becker (2007: 395) defines as "abstracted formulations of social behaviour." A detailed study of a single urban tattoo parlor, for instance, may not be generalizable to all tattoo parlors in the world, but it may well generate broadly relevant insights concerning how the parlor operates. The study might find that social, economic, and cultural processes within this single shop have parallels in free health clinics. A study of a classroom might yield findings that illuminate the similarities between schools and prisons.

Those who are interested in generic social processes are less concerned with how all members of a particular socially constructed category are alike; they are more concerned with documenting processes that operate across social sites. This emphasis on documenting *processes* in *contexts* is particularly strong in qualitative research; we highlight both the word "processes" and the word "context." It is important to emphasize that focusing on **generic processes** as a form of generalizability is not an effort to render invisible the social-historical specificity that often gives qualitative research its depth. As Schwalbe (2004: 421) note, "To call these processes 'generic' does not imply that they are unaffected by context. It means, rather, that they occur in multiple contexts wherein social actors face similar or analogous problems."

**FALSIFIABILITY**   *Falsifiability means that conclusions from a study can be refuted or to use a common phrase, "proven wrong." The conclusion is stated in a form that allows it to be challenged, and the evidence for the conclusion is presented in a way that can be scrutinized and possibly reinterpreted to refute the conclusion.*

A simple example from personal injury suits will clarify the issue here. When a plaintiff says that an accident caused back pain, a feeling of disbelief often sets in among the jury. Unless very clear damage to the spinal cord or vertebrae can be shown, the claim of back pain (unlike that of many other injuries—mangled limbs, scarred faces, disturbed gait, etc.) is hard to observe and hence hard to challenge. How can it be refuted? If it can't be refuted, it can't be proven. It is actually its *nonfalsifiability* that makes the claim suspect.

The strongest research studies tend to exhibit a high degree of falsifiability. In other words, the more falsifiable your research study is, the stronger (i.e., more influential, more scientifically sound) it will be. This may sound backwards, weird, counterintuitive, or just plain wrong. Don't we want our theories and our findings to assume the resilience of "iron-clad truth"? The answer is a resounding "no!" The strongest hypotheses tend to make predictions about what cannot be observed—they take a risk by stating that certain things cannot happen, or more commonly, that they are unlikely to happen.

For example, we might venture the hypothesis that college students who paid their own way through college are more concerned about their grades than those whose college costs are paid by their families, with suitable definitions for terms such as "student" and "care about grades." If we wanted a ridiculously high level of falsifiability, we would specify that all self-paying students care more about their grades than all family-supported ones, in which case one counterexample would knock out our conjecture. More likely, we would be looking for statistical patterns, not complete determination, and our statement would sound something like this: Self-paying students check their grades more often, or more of them check their grades frequently, than family-supported ones. We would collect our information and be able to decide if our conjecture was supported and if so, strongly or significantly enough that we feel comfortable generalizing it beyond our sample of students and institutions.

A word of caution about falsifiability: understanding when a single counterexample challenges a hypothesis (or a theory) requires thinking about probabilistic models of behaviour. As long as the proportions of self-paying students who care about grades are significantly higher than the proportions of family-supported students, we can conclude that grades are more important to former, while recognizing that there is variability among the students—a few don't care at all and some care only slightly. Most findings in the social sciences are not fully generalizable, as we discussed above, and a finding may be of value even if there are a few cases in which it does not hold up. It is very rare in the social sciences to find a situation where a single, individual case is sufficient to dismiss a hypothesis that holds for a large number of cases. Usually instead of immediately throwing out the hypothesis because of a single counterexample, we would try to understand the reasons why it did not work in that instance. In qualitative research, we would use descriptions of behaviour and situations, rather than probability sampling and tests of statistical significance, to convince our readers of the plausibility and generalizability of our findings.

A weak theory exhibits nonfalsifiability. Nonfalsifiability is inherent in hypotheses that include beings whose existence is a matter of faith, not empirical evidence: "Space aliens cause crime" or "in accidents, guardian angels save our lives." Weakness often stems from poorly developed definitions, too much subjectivity which makes the "theory" just a restatement of opinions, and **tautologies** in which definitions and procedures for collecting information are confounded. A simple example will illustrate the point. My hypothesis is that people sing along to songs that exhibit energy. I then measure "energy" according to a scale of how likely people are to sing along to a song. Lo and behold, when I define a song as "high energy" I see and hear people singing along to it. This is *tautological*. My definition and measure of my target term, the cause, and the effect are one and the same! The theory's cause refers back to its effect, and vice versa, so it's very weak. Counterfactual historical statements are nonfalsifiable because we cannot produce data concerning their premise: "If the French had won the French and Indian War, the American Revolution would not have taken place." We can, however, muster empirical evidence for the falsifiable hypothesis that the French defeat in the war was one of the causes of the American Revolution.

**REPRODUCIBILITY**    *Reproducibility means that the research project could be repeated by another person and would produce very similar results. A research project should not be so particular and idiosyncratic that no other person could ever come along and replicate it.* This is a critical criterion in the use of the scientific method to assess a study's rigor. Every researcher concerned with generating accurate representations of actuality should do her work in such a way that others can read it, understand it, and then try to replicate the study. In other words, as a researcher you must work very hard to leave behind a methodological "footprint." If the project depends entirely on your unique personality or your personal interpretations of what you saw, then it may be the basis for an interesting story, but it is not research.

Throughout the research process, you will want to keep detailed notes and memoranda to yourself regarding decisions you make, new insights that occur to you, adjustments you make to the research program, and all of the preconceived notions you hold concerning the subject matter and/or hypotheses. Keeping detailed notes, memoranda, and a research log will go a long way toward maximizing the replicability—and therefore the scientific rigour—of your project. Just imagine that you're a criminal, and you're not only plotting a complex crime (such as a bank heist), but you're also leaving a detailed plan so that the detectives and the world at large can understand exactly why and how you pulled off the job.

One of the most important aspects of this process is **reflexivity**—thinking about what you are doing. From the get-go, you need to get on paper all of the reasons why you have chosen this particular topic. In addition, you should work very hard to specify the presuppositions, prejudices, and biases you have. Some of these might be positive/favourable, while others will be negative and might even be rooted in racism, sexism, or some other systematized pejorative belief system directed to a group, culture, or population. Being clear about the emotional responses you have during the research process will also help others to understand the choices you made. Finally, getting all of this internal matter onto paper will allow you to improve your project through becoming more clearheaded, more analytical, more precise, and more careful.

Reflexivity means always asking yourself the question, "How could someone else come along and do this research project?" Qualitative projects often revolve around the idiosyncratic dimensions of the researcher himself. You use these dimensions of personality, of self, to gain access and to create data through interaction with subjects. Try to recognize and record how you go about "trading on" these features of your identity to carry out your research project. Many identity features just are … they can't be changed. The "fact" of being white/Caucasian among African American gang members, for instance, cannot be changed. But whiteness can be used, tapped, exploited in such a way as to enhance the researcher's ability to gather valid and reliable data. To use this very simple example, being different (white, female, non-drug using, whatever) can be advantageous if the researcher learns how to assist research subjects in defining this difference as a good thing and/or as a reason for, *not against*, getting involved in the researcher's project. Your roles, identities, and unique personality traits do not make the research worthless, but they require you to be alert and aware about how you are deploying them in the research.

The bottom line is that you need to record in detail all the ways that you, as a living and breathing human researcher, affect the scene you're researching. And you need to be just as diligent in recording how the scene affects you because there's little doubt that the project's effects on you will change your behaviour down the line, which will change further the scene you're researching, and so on.

## FRAMING RESEARCH QUESTIONS

Now that we've discussed the principles of the scientific method, it's time to take up the issue of how to ask a question that will produce a research project that meets these criteria. Asking the question requires that you know the language—the vocabulary—that gives shape and meaning to the **logic of scientific inquiry**. Research in the social sciences, and specifically qualitative research, has its own **vernacular**, or specialized language belonging to a specific group of people—in this case, qualitative researchers. Let's explore how they use language to assign meaning to their ideas and activities.

### Learning the Language: Qualitative Research Vernacular

**LOST IN TRANSLATION—UNDERLYING AGREEMENT BETWEEN QUALITATIVE AND QUANTITATIVE RESEARCHERS**    Before going to spend a long period in a foreign country, you likely would try to learn the language in order to survive and thrive. In the land of social science research, you'll encounter two "nations"—the qualitative and the quantitative—whose long-storied antagonism has gradually eroded as residents of each nation begin to realize that they have a lot more in common than they thought and that they are talking the same language, albeit different dialects.

The vernaculars of qualitative and quantitative researchers arguably share more similarities than differences. As stated earlier in this book, quantitative researchers most typically work with a large number of **cases** and a relatively small number of **variables**. The qualitative approach, on the other hand, generally entails the analysis of a small number of cases and a very large number of variables. This is the main distinction between these two main "camps" of social science inquiry.

In a study of poverty, for instance, quantitative researchers might consider the level of poverty among 100,000 urban dwellers across the United States and attempt to discern the factors associated with variance in household income. These factors may include level of education, age, household size, and race/ethnicity. A qualitative researcher, on the other hand, would be more likely to choose a smaller group (or a few smaller groups) of city dwellers, and to spend a significant amount of time observing and interviewing them about their individual and collective experiences of poverty. Variation in the subjective experience and/or the objective poverty-related behaviors would still be the "thing" to explain, but the researcher would take a different approach to building an explanation.

Quantitative researchers focus primarily on the question of "what variables" are related to each other, while qualitative researchers ask questions such as, "How did these factors come to be associated?" and/or "How did these factors become factors in the first place" and/or "What kinds of meaning do people attach to these factors?" As we stated above, qualitative researchers often look for patterns in *processes* within *contexts*, rather than at variables that predict patterns in individual behavior. For example, researchers might study one school to answer the question "How do young people decide to drop out of high school?" rather than the question, "What are demographic and household characteristics that predict which individuals are likely to leave school?"—a question more typical of quantitative research. A gross simplification might sum up the main difference between these perspectives: Quantitative researchers ask questions that begin with "what?" Qualitative researchers ask questions that begin with "how?" Nevertheless, one could argue that regardless of which camp a researcher calls home, the process of formulating the question and seeking answers to it is nearly identical across camps.

So let's look more closely at **qualitative research vernacular**. We will be defining key terms in the language of qualitative researchers and, where relevant or necessary, we contrast the meaning of a term with the meaning assigned to it in the quantitative camp.

**FORMULATING A RESEARCH QUESTION AND ITS ASSOCIATED HYPOTHESES—DOS AND DON'TS**    Every research project begins with an interest, a hunch, an idea, a tickle of a question. Oftentimes these preliminary, suggestive questions seem to come out of nowhere—driving to work, exercising, walking down the street … Eventually, however, the tickle of an idea becomes a formally stated *research question* (RQ). The RQ isn't just any old question; rather, it's a question that stimulates and requires an answer that comes about through structured scientific inquiry. It leads into hypotheses, though in qualitative research these are not always stated explicitly.

**RQs must be specific and falsifiable.**    A good RQ is one that suggests hypotheses that can either be supported or refuted through the collection of information—that is, **empirical data**. We have already discussed several types of nonfalsifiable hypotheses to avoid. The hypotheses that flow from the research question should lend themselves to looking at empirical evidence, or "facts" in a broad and loose sense.

**RQs focus on behavioral outcomes**    —actions that can be observed directly or, in some cases, indirectly. Activities and ideas are both behavioral in the sense that actions can be viewed and ideas can be expressed through speech, which is a behavior ("speech act"). Some theorists prefer words such as "action," "practices," and "discourses" rather than the language of *behaviors*.

**RQs stay away from the values, beliefs, and tastes of the researchers themselves.**    You would not, for instance, ask the question, "Is it better to live in poverty and be happy than to be wealthy and miserable?" Aside from being nonspecific, the question smacks of personal taste and your own individual judgment. The next researcher down the line would have a very difficult time trying to support or refute the research you conduct around this question. Instead, you might ask the question, "How do people living under the poverty line define 'happiness'?" This is a more specific RQ, lends itself to inquiry, and could be replicated by future researchers.

**DEFINING YOUR UNIT OF ANALYSIS**    The next element of research, or vocabulary word, to explore is the **unit of analysis** (UOA), the type of case that you are studying. When you set out to conduct research, you must get your data, or information, from somewhere, and in qualitative research it often—but not always—comes from people you observe and/or interview. The **individual** is a very common level of UOA.

**Groups** of people are also common UAOs, however. These groupings could include gangs, formal organizations, informal friendship groups, and even communities. One might be interested in how so-called "street gangs" operate in relation to the supply/sale of illicit substances, for instance. Here, the RQ takes you in the direction of examining group-level phenomena, such as social network composition, level of cohesion, nature of inter-member communication, and the group's position in the "marketplace" of heroin, cocaine, and/or marijuana. You are really interested in gangs—that's your UOA—but a lot of your information will be based on observing and interviewing individuals. In qualitative analysis, these two levels are often not as distinct as they are in quantitative studies.

A special type of grouping that is a very popular UOA is the **organization**, an entity that operates at the *meso*level of society. Many sociologists (and researchers in fields such as management and public administration) would like to know more about the culture and functioning of organizations, characteristics of the whole group, not just a sum total of individual characteristics. Many scholars define the organization as a set of planned, coordinated, and purposeful actions in which people engage as they attempt to produce something (whether tangible, such as tennis shoes, or intangible, such as advice on marketing tennis shoes to the public). Social scientists often add to the definition the notions of "permanence," formality/legality, clear boundaries, and rules. The many actions required to make tennis shoes, for example, share a common frame—workers share formal membership (they're on the payroll and organizational chart) and they must subject themselves to a common set of formal rules or else risk losing their jobs.

Finally, **places** can be UOAs too. In quantitative research, we often are studying cities, states, or countries. For example, we might be comparing crime rates in different cities and try to explain the variation. In qualitative research, a whole community might be the UOA, for example, a small town, a suburb, or a city neighborhood. Ethnographers sometimes try to study all the people in a defined space or territory.

When places are our UOAs we have to be careful not to commit the **ecological fallacy**, a false generalization from rates based on one category of individuals in a place to other individuals who share the space. For example, states with a high proportion of residents who are newcomers have higher suicide rates than other states, but we cannot conclude (without further data) that the individuals who are committing suicide are the newcomers.

One of the most important things you can do as a researcher striving to craft a solid, convincing representation of the social life you're studying is to clearly define your UOA. This entails recognizing **limits** of your UOA and knowing how far your UOA can take you in terms of understanding the realm of social life you're investigating. You need to be careful in switching back and forth from observations based on individuals to conclusions about groups and places.

**AVOIDING REDUCTIONISM**     Reductionism means posing a research question in a way that points to a single cause, especially one that is less complex and interactive than causes usually are in human societies. This cause often, but not always, corresponds to psychological traits of group members. For example, a researcher might "reduce" complex phenomena, such as street gang life, to a single, psychologically inflected cause by hypothesizing that street gangs help individuals solve the problem associated with low self-esteem. This researcher then sets out to conduct psychological surveys (aka scales or measures) that assess level of self-esteem within individuals. Finding that the majority of street gang members possess low self-esteem, the researcher erroneously concludes that low self-esteem among individuals causes street gangs to form. Here the researcher has committed an act of *reductionism*, reducing complex phenomena (street gang formation and perpetuation) to a single cause (low self-esteem) and, moreover, has done so on the basis of individual-level data. This is *psychological reductionism*.

*Economic reductionism* occurs when the researcher concludes that a complex social phenomenon can be explained solely in economic terms. For instance, think about your own closest friends and the resources each has available—access to a car, private space for parties, tickets to concerts, a swimming pool, alcohol or drugs, and so on. If we were to conclude that the only reason the group formed and stuck together was access to each other's resources, without regard for people's feelings and shared interests, we would be engaged in "economic reductionism." We have "reduced" the complexity of group cohesion to a very simple material formula that doesn't capture all of reality.

**VARIABLES**    Research questions are often formulated as efforts to relate two or more variables to each other, explaining the distribution of one variable by examining the distribution of other variables. For example, in the gang research literature, we read that gangs form in neighborhoods that are disorganized; that is, the hypothesis is that the variable of gang presence is related to the variable of community disorganization.

Many students of the social sciences argue that quantitative and qualitative research differ mainly because the former deals with variables, while the latter deals with something other than variables, such as "situations," "context," or some other vague notion. This isn't accurate. Both methodological schools deal with variables. Quantitative researchers, however, make their **variable-oriented** (Ragin 1994) approach more explicit, while qualitative researchers often discuss or specify their variables in more subtle ways, by embedding them in the "thick description" (Geertz 1973) of a particular scene. In qualitative research, the variables are complex and contextualized.

Let's look at few examples of "embedded variables" from qualitative research in the sociology of education and socialization. In a number of studies, the "outcome variable" is the way young-sters are prepared for occupations and locations in the structure of social classes. Le Wita (1994) relates the continuing power of the French bourgeoisie to their methods of raising their children in the institutional settings of families and schools that encourage self-discipline and a sense of entitlement. Cookson and Persell (1985) document how prep schools teach youngsters to exercise power (the outcome variable) through their demanding curriculum, the high expectations of teachers, separation from the family, bonding with peers headed for the same elite status, and an experience of loneliness and individuation in boarding school. Anyon (1980) uses a descriptive comparison of four types of schools to show that the class origins of students are related to their teachers' behaviors and classroom interaction, and that this cluster of "independent variables" in turn produces habits of mind (the "dependent variable") appropriate for the children's probable occupations and class destinies. In all these cases, the central variable relationship is conveyed by a large amount of description that serves as evidence for the linkages. When you strip down any given piece of qualitative research, you will find many variables, many of which will be hidden in detailed accounts of events, relationships, and places.

A **variable** is a characteristic or trait of a UOA. By definition the trait must vary, either over time or between units. For example, in the study of an organizational UOA, the tattoo shop, one variable or trait that varies in a study of 30 such shops is *age* or "how long the shop has been in operation." Notice that the variable applies to the UOA, the shop, and not to individual artists or customers. And the variable of *age* is quantitative or numeric—it corresponds to a number. Don't make the all-too-common mistake of assuming that numbers aren't important in qualitative research because they are, or can be, very important.

Keeping the tattoo shop as our UOA, we might specify that they also differ in the *kind* or *aesthetic* in which their artists specialize. This is a qualitative, or non-numeric, variable, one best captured by text, perhaps accompanied by pictures. A given shop might specialize in "traditional" tattoos, the kind most popular among members of the armed services in the 1940s. Another shop might specialize in "tribal" art—artists in these shops tend to work with designs rooted in, say, indigenous Polynesian figures. Our research question might be, "What accounts for the type/kind of specialization among and between tattoo parlors?" In this case, we would specify various hypotheses, or educated guesses, regarding the **variables** or traits that we think will likely influence our **outcome variable**, the formation of a specialty within a shop.

The variable that we're trying to explain, the main outcome that interests us, in this study of specialization among tattoo parlors is their type of specialization. Qualitative in nature, "type of specialization" is our primary "outcome" of interest. It's known as a **dependent variable** because type of specialization "depends on" the particular configuration and/or confluence of other variables. For example, "type of apprenticeships the artists completed" might be one of the variables that explain the specialization a given parlor develops over time. In addition, we might hypothesize that the geographic location of a shop makes a difference because we believe that parlors in more affluent areas are more likely to deal in tribal art, whereas shops in more economically distressed locales specialize in "traditional" ink. In any event, the type of specialization is our dependent variable, and the independent variables are those traits or characteristics whose variation, or difference from each other, helps explain the differences among types of specialization.

So we know that variables vary across cases, or units, and that the trait can be expressed either with a number or with a description. And we know that our research project should have a single variable that interests us the most—the outcome, or dependent, variable. Our hypotheses, or educated guesses, lead us to specify the different variables that we think explain why the outcome variable varies, or differs, from one unit/case to another. When we look at variables, we can see quite easily how we could conclude that some variables "cause" other variables to happen. This is where things get tricky. In the social sciences, most scholars shy away from making claims about "causation." When we observe patterns in our data, across UOAs, that lead us to believe that certain variables have a relationship with our dependent variable, we must be careful to recognize the distinction between "correlation" and "causation." However careful we know we should be, we still end up making or implying causal relationships.

**HYPOTHESIS**    Hypotheses are statements linking variables. They offer tentative or provisional answers to the research questions—answers that are going to be subjected to *falsifiability* and the test of evidence. In the preceding paragraph, we loosely defined a **hypothesis** as "an educated guess." This is pretty much correct, but it's time to flesh it out a bit. At the beginning of this chapter, we emphasized the centrality redundant of the research question. The RQ is the driving force behind everything else that happens, every choice that's made, in the research process. The hypotheses are indeed educated guesses—they offer potential answers to the research question. And our research project is geared around testing the effectiveness and the viability of these answers. Hypotheses derive from our belief that certain kinds of relationships between certain variables will explain the outcome that interests us, will give us the answer (or part of an answer) to the RQ itself.

The hypothesis is therefore a formal statement that indicates a **relationship among variables**, and this relationship (we believe) explains some part of the variance in our dependent variable.

## DOUBTS AND CONCERNS: ARE WE BEING TOO SCIENTIFIC?

At this point, we can hear two cries of alarm from colleagues. The first objection is that the process that we have described for formulating research questions is too close to the scientific method; some individuals engaged in social inquiry do not use these rules and in fact explicitly reject them. These scholars use the word "positivist" as a pejorative term to label inquiry that follows the canons of the natural sciences, which they believe are inappropriate to use in inquiry into the human condition. These scholars see themselves as much closer to the humanities—literature and philosophy, for example—than to the natural sciences. Other researchers accept the rules of the scientific method but believe they have to be substantially modified to work in the study of the social world.

We will return to this issue when we discuss writing a qualitative research narrative, and we will see that some scholars engaged in social inquiry refuse to write research reports guided by the scientific method; they do indeed see themselves as engaged in social inquiry but reject what appear to them to be the trappings of natural science research. The second and closely related objection is that we have blurred the lines between quantitative and qualitative research. Later in this book, we devote a chapter to the use of multiple methods in a single study. So if you were somewhat troubled by our discussion of the scientific method we are asking you to be patient—we will return to the issue.

## CHOOSING RESEARCH ACTIVITIES

Now that we have covered the basic terms of qualitative research, the question becomes, "What do qualitative researchers actually do?" Well, in the process of examining the vernacular of qualitative research, we have ventured into some of the most important activities in which any researcher of any stripe must engage: defining the research question, specifying hypotheses, and establishing the independent and dependent variables. Ideally, every move a researcher makes in some way relates to the research question. Some research questions are best answered through the gathering and analysis of numeric data, while others would be best served with qualitative data. Remember the distinction between questions of "what?" and questions of "how?" In the qualitative realm, most questions relate to *how*? Our tattoo parlor example illustrates this quite well: How do tattoo artists distinguish themselves from their walking, talking canvases—their customers?

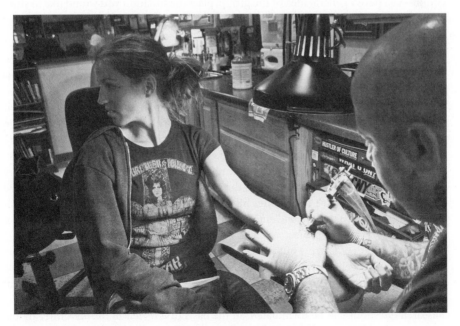

A tattoo artist working on his "canvas"   (Photo by Greg Scott)

Once you have determined that qualitative (i.e., mostly non-numeric) data would provide you with the means for best answering your research question, you must figure out how you will create the data. Yes, create. By "create" we do not mean "make it up" or "falsify" or "invent." All data, quantitative and qualitative, emerge out of a relationship between a researcher who asks questions or makes observations and a human subject who knowingly or unwittingly provides the data through speech and/or behavior. Even dead people provide data. Their act of dying places them in a pool of potential research subjects for studies that examine causes of death (e.g., heroin overdose or heat wave). Even after they discontinued life on earth, they can live on as subjects in very important studies that have the potential to prevent premature death in the future. Dead people who produced texts that shed light on social history also can be research subjects; their texts are the principle means by which we can understand the past. Okay, so back to the question of how you get the data, you need to test the hypotheses whose viability or nonviability will allow you in turn to offer an answer to your research question.

Qualitative researchers get their data from their UOAs in a wide variety of ways. Some choose to conduct in-depth interviews with a manageable number of people; others opt to spend a great deal of time observing people and speaking to them more informally (while going to great lengths to record in writing what they say); and still others decide that they will "move in" to a particular setting, group, or culture, and stay there long enough to develop an "insider's view" on life there. In Part II, we will look at all of these activities for collecting data and, ultimately, crafting a representation of social life.

## WHERE DO RESEARCH QUESTIONS COME FROM?

Research questions are the guiding device for all research projects—but where do they come from? At this point, you may be wondering how you can produce one for a project you would like to carry out—you have a general idea of the group, place, or situation you would like to study but you are not sure you can formulate a research question. There are four general sources of research questions:

- Research questions can come from you. They can arise from the *life experiences, values, and basic human curiosity* of the researcher. You should be at least somewhat passionate about your research study, as it's this passion that carries the researcher through all the tedious and frustrating moments of research. It may also provide the energy to design research that addresses social problems or seeks to change the world, rather than merely interpret it. Many older textbooks, particularly in the quantitative tradition, argue that researchers should adopt a "dispassionate" and/or "value-free" approach to their subjects. This is folly. Not only is it impossible to rid oneself entirely of his or her personal values and interest in the world but doing so would also spell the demise of one's research endeavors. Indeed, the quality of qualitative research studies hinges in part on the degree to which the researcher invests her work with passion and enthusiasm. It's the statement of the hypotheses that needs to be value-free, not the project as a whole.
- Research questions can grow out of *theory,* and we will argue later in the book that theoretically driven research questions add depth and longevity to a research project.
- Research questions can emerge from *previous research and systematic observation* carried out by the researcher.
- Research questions can be formulated on the basis of *a review of the literature*, an analytic overview of other social scientists' findings and conclusions on this topic.

All four of these sources are important in research, and they're not mutually exclusive. In most cases, a project's research question comes from a combination of these "ideal type" sources. But they are treated differently in formal social scientific writing. Scholars frequently "cover up" their debt to their own life experiences. The canons of scientific writing typically discourage any personal reflection or at most allow it limited and fleeting mention. The other three sources are viewed as "more acceptable" by the stewards of the scientific method.

In a later chapter we discuss the use of theory, as studies differ widely in the extent to which they address theoretical issues. The researchers present prior findings (both their own and those of others) in a section of the research report called the **literature review**. The review of the literature is considered to be an excellent way of reconstructing how the researchers arrived at their research question. The review of the literature is usually placed at the beginning of a final research report, and the entire research report is framed as if the research questions emerged from the review of the literature (Pan 2008). In Chapter 23, we provide suggestions for how to organize the "lit review."

Right now you are probably thinking two thoughts—that's a lot of abstract vocabulary to learn! And that's a lot of rules to follow! To address both of these objections, we will walk you through two research projects (Boxes 3.1 and 3.2) to show you how qualitative researchers actually use the scientific method, and we will provide a few down-to-earth tips for going through the process of formulating research questions.

## BOX 3.1
### Studying a Tattoo Parlor: Using the Scientific Method

To explore some examples of research questions, variables, and hypotheses in qualitative research, let's look at a project based in a tattoo parlor. Two graduate students at DePaul University in Chicago, Illinois (USA), began working on a research project centered on a single tattoo parlor in the city. They chose the site out of convenience (close to campus) and because it's arguably one of the most famous and popular parlors in the city. Choosing research locations is a question we take up in a different chapter, but suffice it to say that some of the best, most often cited research endeavors began with a scholar selecting a research site out of convenience (close to home, campus, a vacation getaway, etc.). Based on their interest in tattoo parlors (and tattooing in general) and the convenient location and strong reputation of a particular shop, Sarah Schar and Maize Jacobs-Brichford set out to conduct an ethnographic study of "getting inked."

Ethnography is one kind of qualitative research. Later in this book, we will explore this methodological branch in more detail and examine other research designs (or strategies, or logics of inquiry) such as historical-comparative analysis and social autopsies. For now, let's just say that ethnography involves deeply immersing oneself in a particular culture or setting, the goal being to understand the organization of culture from the inside out. In this case, Sarah and Maize spent a lot of time "hanging out with a purpose" in the tattoo parlor. Over time, they developed an interest in how tattoo artists differentiate themselves and their fellow artists from the clientele they serve. Using the terms we've covered so far, the outcome/dependent variable of interest here is the ways or methods that artists use to create "social distance" between themselves and their customers. The central hypothesis, or educated guess that explains the different ways artists accomplish this task, is that artists engage in "speech acts" that maintain a hierarchy of status wherein the artists are elevated above the customers, who serve as living, breathing canvases for their work.

*(continued)*

*(continued)*

In qualitative research, the central hypothesis is likely to be accompanied by at least one (and usually more than one) **buffer hypothesis**. This hypothesis essentially qualifies the central hypothesis, places conditions on it, and establishes the limits of the central hypothesis. In the tattoo parlor study, several buffer hypotheses emerged. The meaning of the term "buffer hypothesis" should become clearer as we explore them. First, tattoo artists tend to employ a nonartist "gatekeeper," someone who works at the shop's counter and is responsible for dealing directly with paying customers. This person's conversations with customers typically entail information exchange—pricing, artist availability, and other logistical matters. This is the "grunt work" that tattoo artists define as a "necessary evil" of doing art on live human beings. Only after a given customer has made her way through the gatekeeper (i.e., she has passed the seriousness-screening process) does she get to interact with an actual artist. Employing a gatekeeper to deal with the mundane aspects of this artistic enterprise reduces the overall number of speech acts that occur between artist and customer. So this is one hypothesized method that enables the creation and maintenance of social distance between artist and customer—the live canvas.

The second hypothesis is about the nature/content of the speech acts themselves. Once customers make their way past the gatekeeper and enter the realm of artists, who conventionally work in a shared space separated by a wall, gate, or counter from the customer waiting area, they become part of a series of speech acts. In this artist-centered realm, however, the speech acts tend to be exclusionary. That is, they exclude or at least render improbable and/or unwelcome, the customer's participation. In short, artists talk to each other in a way that discourages customers from joining the conversation. Artists use "inside jokes" and humorous stories as they orient their speech to other artists, not to customers. They also talk about professional development and the more rarefied aesthetics of "doing ink." This hypothesis posits that the nature of speech acts in tattoo parlors relegates the customer to little more than a

Tattoo parlor—Customers, artists, and the gate between them

"paying canvas" and the artist to an elevated position of authority.

A third buffer hypothesis is about the ways that artists increase cohesion among each other—how they solidify their "in-group" status often at the expense of customers. Here we predict (and Sarah and Maize find) that when artists find themselves alone together in the shop, without customers around, their speech acts revolve around lampooning customers who've come and gone. The speech itself may be playful, and the artists may not intend any malice, but it nevertheless serves to elevate artists above customers. In this sense, the artists are "doing difference" even when their contrapuntal foils are not present.

In this research study, Sarah and Maize conceptualized their UOAs not as individuals or networks or groups or even the shop as an organization. Rather, their UOA is the "speech act." Their dependent variable is how artists differentiate themselves from customers, and vice versa, through the social organization of speech acts in the tattoo parlor. Their independent variables include control of total volume of speech acts (gatekeeper), exclusionary language employed by artists, and in-group cohesion building (use of ridicule behind customers' backs). Hopefully, this example makes clear some of the vocabulary terms covered so far, and sheds new light on how one might go about conducting a qualitative study focused on "interaction events" as UOAs.

Remember that hypotheses should be "value free" even if your own values motivate your choice of a topic. They should *not* be statements concerning what you, as the researcher, think or believe the state of affairs "ought to" or "should" be. For instance, going back to Sarah's and Maize's project on the tattoo parlor, it would be unproductive to state the following hypothesis: "It is only right (i.e., morally correct) that tattoo artists define and see themselves as being equal in all ways to their customers." It's ok to believe this and feel that it is morally right, but it has no place in a list of hypotheses. It's a value statement that reflects how you would like the world to operate, ideally. And remember that each hypothesis needs to be specific. "Tattoo artists and customers behave in different ways" is a very vague and therefore very weak hypothesis.

## BOX 3.2
### Qualitative Research Principles in Action: Paul Willis, *Learning to Labor: How Working Class Kids Get Working Class Jobs*

Paul Willis selected the topic of how young English working-class men fail in school. The "how" question was in many respects also a "why" question—why do they fail? Willis studied "the lads"—male, working-class youth in one particular school in England. This topic was related to larger social issues of concern about the drop-out rate, preparation for an increasingly complex global economy, and the limited economic opportunities that working-class kids have when they do poorly in school or fail to complete secondary school. But beyond the concrete social problems that the study addressed, there loomed a larger question about how people in positions of class disadvantage in modern societies understand their own situation.

His research questions were the following: How is the outcome of low academic achievement produced through interaction within the context of the school? Why do some youth but not others engage in rebellious behavior? How do the lads perceive and understand their own rebellion and disengagement from school?

His answers to these three questions were that the "lads'" rebellion and their boisterous, disrespectful behavior led them into rejection of schooling and to school failure. The lads who were most involved in rebellious behaviors were the ones most strongly socialized to a working class "us versus them" view that their fathers had brought home from their experiences in factories—"the

*(continued)*

*(continued)*

shop floor." Although the lads saw class inequality clearly and indeed rebelled against it, their rebellion led to their own relegation to working-class jobs and—even more poignantly—to a rejection of "mental labor," of habits of mind and body associated with formal education and ultimately with intellectual activity of all kinds.

Willis chose qualitative methods, interviews and the observation of behaviors and interactions among young people and between them and teachers in one school in England with predominantly working-class students. He focused his observations of behaviors and his interviews on white working–class males because they seemed to be the most overtly rebellious and hostile to the school environment. This research design was his choice and he could have pursued an alternative strategy, such as looking at data based on all secondary schools in England and identifying variables correlated with noncompletion of a diploma or with low grades. The quantitative strategy would have answered a related but differently worded set of research questions than the strategy of observing and interviewing in a single school. His qualitative strategy enabled him to understand the "how" of school failure, to track interactions, behaviors, and processes that led to low achievement, disciplinary problems, and dropping out. It also gave him a close-up understanding of how the young men viewed school, their futures, and their own behaviors, and especially how they talked and gave meaning to their own actions.

The results are strongly generalizable. Willis implies that his observations in one school can be generalized to the condition of low-achieving working-class kids throughout Britain, and perhaps to any modern, economically developed capitalist country.

Willis anchored his work in Marxist theory. He analyzed the actions and choices of working-class white males ("the lads") in terms of their perceptions of class relationships and power and showed how they were able to arrive at "partial penetrations" of the capitalist system—they understood it in terms of exploitive and unequal class relationships—but they were not able to see that their rejection of mental labor limited their individual opportunities for social mobility and also kept them *as a class* from developing a larger and more analytical understanding of capitalist society. A dogmatic Marxist might insist on the nonfalsifiable premise that the working class is always ready for revolutionary action, but Willis had to come to the conclusion that the lads' rejection of mental labor left them ill-prepared for political leadership. He recognized that the young men in his study were not class-conscious revolutionaries, but rebellious lads who had a limited comprehension of their situation and held attitudes that narrowed their educational, occupational, and above all, political horizons.

This example shows us how research questions involve making choices—Willis could have asked his question in a way that would have led to different kinds of research strategies and activities, different types of data, and different ways of conceptualizing the process of school rebellion and failure. He chose to use Marxism as the foundational theory of his research. His report convinces us that the process he observed in one school could be generalized to many other schools and probably most economically developed capitalist countries.

Was his underlying hypothesis falsifiable? Yes, because his research questions, hypotheses, and methods of observing and interviewing left open the possibility of finding evidence against his main hypothesis of self-relegation to school failure. For example, he could have discovered that the young men were pushed out of school by administrators who did not like the presence of low-achieving youngsters or that they had to drop out of school to support their families.

## TIPS FOR FORMULATING A RESEARCH QUESTION

- Select a topic that interests you.
- Read what others have written about this topic. Look at how they formulated their questions, how they carried out their study, and what they found.
- Ask yourself a number of related smaller or more manageable questions that revolve around a central theme or topic. Eventually you can pull them together into a single

broader question or develop them as buffer hypotheses. Often these questions are about variation in social arrangements or behaviors and ask us to think about possible reasons, explanations, or even causes for this variation.

- Frame the questions in a way that can be answered by empirical research and the available research methods. If your research is primarily qualitative, lean toward "how" questions and away from "what predicts—" or "how many?" Qualitative research often focuses on processes within contexts, interactions, and the meanings that people assign to their situation.
- Be clear about your choice of units of analysis. Do you want to reach conclusions about individuals or about groups, organizations, or places—or both levels at the same time?
- Think in terms of variables and explanations, even if these variables are complex and contextualized.
- Experiment with stating your ideas both as questions and as hypotheses.
- Avoid reductionism and thinking only about simplistic, one-cause explanations.
- Don't let a concern with falsifiability overwhelm you, but do keep in mind that your conclusions must be evidence-based and face up to skepticism and challenge and that your evidence will need to match and support your conclusions.
- Consider the bodies of theory to which the questions can be linked to give your research deeper and more lasting value. A base in theory will tie your findings to the work of other sociologists and contribute to a bigger picture that develops our "sociological imagination."

## CONCLUSION

In this chapter, we have discussed the basic principles of qualitative research in relation to a modified scientific method paradigm. We also have examined the language, or vernacular, of the qualitative research tradition. Finally, this chapter has brought us to the point where we can draw upon a common language to formulate a strong research question. In the next couple of chapters, we explore the actual doing of research. Get ready to go out and get your hands dirty in the messy world we call "reality."

## Exercises

1. Return to the five topics that you listed for the exercise in Chapter 1. For each one, state at least one research question that you would like to answer. What would you like to explain? Can you reformulate the research question in terms of specific, testable hypotheses? Why or why not? Do your questions lead to research that meets the criteria of objectivity, generalizability, validity, replicability, and falsifiability? Can you identify a main hypothesis and buffer hypotheses for each of your topics? What are the units of analysis for each topic? What research activities would you carry out to answer your research question/test your hypotheses?

2. Begin to sketch the research question (or principle hypothesis) for a topic corresponding to each one of the designs described in Chapter 1. We will return to this exercise later in more detail in the chapters in Part II.

3. Observe a trial (or watch a criminal justice or law enforcement television show such as *Law and Order: SVU*, keeping in mind it is not reality). Based on what you've learned so far in this book, compare and contrast the legal procedures you see in the courtroom (or illustrated in the program) and the "truth-finding" process of qualitative research. Use as many of the key terms from this chapter as you possibly can.

## Key Terms

avoiding ecological fallacies  *40*
avoiding reductionism  *40*
avoiding tautologies *36*
believability *34*
buffer hypothesis *46*
cases *31*
dependent variable *42*
empirical data *39*
falsifiability *34*
falsifiable *31*
generalizability *34*
generalizable *31*
generic processes *35*
groups *39*
historical context *33*
hypothesis *42*

individual *39*
limits *40*
literature review *45*
logic of scientific inquiry *38*
objective *31*
objectivity *34*
organization *40*
outcome variable *42*
places *40*
plausibility *33*
plausible *35*
reflexivity *37*
relationship among variables *42*
relevance *35*
replicability (or reproducibility) *34*
representation of social life *32*

reproducible *31*
research question *31*
research reports *32*
rules of evidence *33*
rules of sociological representation *33*
scientific method *32*
science vernacular *31*
self-reflexive and symbol-using
    beings *33*
unit of analysis *39*
variable-oriented *41*
variables *38*
vernacular *38*
"vernacular" of qualitative
    research *39*
way of knowing *32*

# 4

# The Ethics of Qualitative Research

## OVERVIEW

Once you have gotten familiar with the vernacular of research, formulated your research question, and begun to think about going into the world to conduct your study, you need to spend time reflecting on **research ethics**, which we define loosely as the rules of proper conduct in doing social research. We start with a scenario designed to give you an idea of what it feels like to be the "subject" of a researcher's study. Then, we present a brief account of how codes of ethical conduct have evolved over time. Finally, we offer some practical insight into how you can (and will be required to) build into your research study various mechanisms for "protecting human subjects" who participate in your project.

## A MENTAL EXERCISE IN ROLE-TAKING

Picture yourself as a **research subject**—a person being studied by a sociologist—and imagine two scenarios.

### Scenario 1: You're a Survey "Respondent"

In the first situation, an interviewer asks you to participate in a survey about urban change and gentrification. The interviewer identifies herself as an employee of a large university-based research organization. She briefly describes the purpose of the survey, tells you that survey is being administered nationwide to 1200 people, and explains the procedures for assuring the **confidentiality** and anonymity of the data and the measures to ensure data security (such as putting completed forms in a safety deposit box that only the principal researcher can open and immediately replacing names by code numbers as identifiers on the forms). Then she reads you a series of questions with pre-coded multiple-choice answers. You can choose to skip an item if you feel uncomfortable about the purpose or wording of the question or the list of answers; you are assured that you can refuse to complete the interview.

A few months later when you read the results of the survey, you feel comfortable that your answers contributed to a very small part of the overall findings, that they were correctly processed in the data analysis, and that no reader of the survey can "spot" your responses in the statistically analyzed aggregated data that appears in the publication.

### Scenario 2: You're an "Informant" Neighbor

In the second scenario, a researcher moves into your neighborhood. She tells people that she is studying gentrification and urban change in the neighborhood. She conducts formal audio-recorded interviews with neighbors. The interview is preceded by your signing of an **informed consent form**, a quasi-legal document that spells out the research study's goals, procedures, risks, and benefits. Her presence in the neighborhood means that she also has informal conversations, not formally identified as interviews; presumably, she will not use any direct quotes from these conversations (because no one signed consent forms or documents of any kind). Even if they are not formally recognized as interviews, the conversations' tone and tenor may influence her conclusions. She takes pictures of buildings and spaces in the neighborhood, and—with photo release forms signed by individuals—of residents. She attends meetings of block clubs, hearings held by city agencies and the public housing authority, and meetings of community-based organizations, some of which oppose municipal and state plans for the area. These meetings are public events, but her presence at all of them gives her insights that might make some residents uncomfortable. Finding her to be a lively and interesting person, you develop a friendly relationship with her—not a close friendship but a cordial and informal one in which you sometimes forget that she is studying the neighborhood. She joins your church and sings in the choir.

After you read the book based on her research, you can "spot" yourself easily in the interview quotes and in some of the other observations. Even though the researcher used pseudonyms for individuals, you feel that you can identify many of the people about whom she writes. You are taken aback when you find that she does not see the situation in the way that you explained it to her. In fact, she's got a view of the neighborhood that's completely different from—even the opposite of—your own view. You feel that you are committed to neighborhood diversity, yet she interprets your words as those of an aggressive advocate of gentrification who would like poor people to move away (or conversely, she portrays you as an opponent of gentrification).

Confronting her directly is out of the question. At the end of her data collection period, she moved out of the neighborhood and back to her home, job, and family. In fact, *you* and your neighbors worked together to organize her "going away" party last year. Although neither she nor you made good on the promises to "stay in touch" by email, up to this point you felt "connected" to her and were looking forward to the publication of a book celebrating the wonders of life in your neighborhood. How do you feel? Angry? Betrayed? Embarrassed that you could be so naïve?

## ETHICAL CONDUCT IN QUALITATIVE RESEARCH

These two vignettes suggest that the ethical issues of human subject research are very different in quantitative and qualitative research. (To be precise, in ethnography and qualitative research involving **human subjects**; content analysis of documents and artifacts presents fewer ethical problems.) In quantitative research, the researcher–subject relationship is "functionally specific"; it is limited to a narrow range of activity and interaction—usually the reading and completion of a survey instrument. Its goals are clearly defined. It is "affectively neutral"—relatively unemotional and politely impersonal. It is very limited in time, lasting an hour or two at the most. It is very clear what is being asked and what the choices of answers are. It is easy to refuse to answer questions or to refuse to participate altogether. Procedures to safeguard confidentiality and data security are precise and easy to explain. Each participant is only one of many, and it will be essentially impossible to identify any person's responses from the statistical analysis of the data. Voices and faces are not recorded.

## Qualitative Research as a "Complicated Relationship"

The qualitative community study or ethnography has exactly the opposite characteristics. The relationship of the researcher and the subject is **diffuse** and permeates many areas of life—residence, participation in organizations and religious institutions, conversations, even friendship. It is "affective"—the relationship is a friendly one and it is difficult to discern exactly where the friendship ends and the research begins. The contact is not fleeting, but rather extends over months or even years. The researcher records the voices, faces, identities, and homes of the research "subjects" (or "informants"). Even if the researcher eventually uses pseudonyms in place of the real names of people, neighborhoods, and cities, the readers (especially those who were close to the researcher) likely will recognize a good many subjects and situations.

The research subjects have taken the researcher into their lives and shared their experiences, their worries and fears, maybe some of their deepest secrets and knowledge with her—and what have they gotten in return? In every interaction, the researcher seemed trustworthy, sensitive, caring, and most of all *circumspect*—that she would take every secret to her grave. Another common remark from subjects is this: "It seemed like the researcher agreed with me, supported my view of things…like we were in synch." So it appeared. Well, appearances can be deceiving. In fact, some would argue (as Scott has argued many times) that **deception** is integral—that is to say indispensable—to every ethnographic endeavor. Without it, the study will suffer.

## The Question of Meaning

One of the most disconcerting aspects of "the study," from the subject's point of view, is that it was not clear to her how the researcher was going to interpret her words and observed actions. At the time of the study, the researcher often withholds interpretation and instead tries to ferret out subjects' interpretations. In doing so, the researcher often seems to agree with each and every subject's interpretation. Later, when the research is published and the research subjects see that in fact the researcher had a different interpretation altogether, it's startling. Subjects often first feel surprised and then mortified when they see themselves in the "looking glass" of the research report, and they may not like their image nor find it accurate. They may feel that a person who appeared to be their friend instrumentalized the relationship, distorted their views, and by the very act of writing about them, created a sardonic distance and exposed them to a scornful gaze. In a word, the subjects often feel "used" or "exploited," or perhaps "suckered."

## Rules on the Books versus Rules in Action

All of this apparent deception and betrayal and hurting of feelings may well occur—and often does occur—in *full compliance* with the rules governing the **protection of human subjects** in research. This is to say that even the most ethically compliant study can inflict injury on the subjects who participated in it. Why? Because when it comes to protecting human subjects, there's a big difference between the "rules on the books" and the "rules in action." A researcher who follows the "letter of law" may still end up hurting a lot of people. By the same token, a researcher who violates the formal human subjects protection rules could well be considered a wonderful, caring, sensitive, and thoughtful social critic, even, or especially, by the subjects of the study. To understand how these things could be true, we need to examine the formal rules and the informal rules of conduct. And to be good, as ethical researchers, we need to know how to negotiate and navigate these formal and informal rules in reference to the relationships we have with the people we're studying.

In this chapter, we will first discuss formal safeguards for human subjects and then explore the more diffuse ethical issues in qualitative research that were raised by these vignettes.

## FORMAL SAFEGUARDS: HUMAN SUBJECTS RESEARCH, THE IRB, AND PROFESSIONAL CODES OF ETHICS

Until the last decades of the twentieth century, there were very few "controls" on the relationship between scientists and their subjects in most countries. Although most people agreed that the "experiments" performed by Nazis on concentration camp inmates and prisoners of war were not science at all, but just sadistic tortures, more respected and serious individuals in democratic societies were also responsible for abuses of power and terrible physical harm.

The most horrific of these incidents in the United States was the **Tuskegee syphilis study**, in which researchers withheld penicillin from African American men who had contracted syphilis in the course of their lives; the researchers did this in order to observe the course of the disease if left untreated. When the study began in the 1930s, there was indeed no cure for syphilis, only palliative and temporary measures, but by the later years of the study, after World War II, penicillin had become available yet the men were not provided with the treatment or even informed of its existence (Jones 1993). In other incidents of abusive research, soldiers were involuntarily exposed to radiation in nuclear tests, and prison inmates were induced to "volunteer" for experimental studies of the effects of radiation in which some were seriously burned.

The social and behavioral sciences were less susceptible to these abuses as compared with the biomedical fields. Generally speaking, subjects in psychology and the social sciences were not exposed to bodily harm, but they *were* at risk for humiliation and psychological distress. Two very revealing social psychological studies could probably not be carried out today, although the information and insights they produced continue to be very valuable and relevant to today's social issues.

### To Obey or Not to Obey: "The Milgram Study"

The first social science study we want to share with you is Stanley Milgram's (1963) famous set of experiments on "obedience." In this study, the researchers deceived research subjects into thinking that they (the subjects) were administering escalating levels of electric shocks to fellow subjects (actually the researchers' helpers, or "confederates") in a learning experiment. The researcher would ask the confederate-subject a question; if the response was incorrect, the researcher commanded the true subject to administer an electric shock to the pretend, or confederate, subject. Unbeknownst to the true subjects, the person they were "shocking" not only was a confederate and therefore "in on" the research but also was answering incorrectly on purpose; in addition, the electric shock wasn't real at all. But the confederate's screams would lead the subject to believe otherwise. Though some subjects simply refused to administer any shock at all, most of them were willing to deliver pretty intense jolts to the other subject. A high percentage of them were even willing to administer a "lethal" surge of electricity to the other subject.

Dr. Milgram captured on film the level of this obedient and brutal acquiescence to authority. Most university libraries stock at least one of the films that came out of the study. It is still disturbing to see men administer potentially lethal shocks to fellow human beings who can be heard crying out in pain and fear, with the lab coat-wearing researcher standing over the subject commanding him to administer yet a higher dose of electrical shock. Ultimately, the study raised a great many questions about the everyday life circumstances that foster this type of obedience, this willingness to succumb to the demands of authoritative figures such as police officers and prison guards, military commanders and school teachers, parents and professors. However, the degree to which Milgram and his research team *deceived* the research subjects and the extent to which they precipitated a deep and abiding sense of remorse in their subjects remain ethically questionable issues.

## "Prisoner 819 Did a Bad Thing": The Stanford Prison Experiment

Another famous study that might not be approved nowadays is Dr. Phillip Zimbardo's prison simulation, in which he randomly assigned psychologically "healthy" male college students to the roles of guards and inmates in an improvised lockup in the basement of a university building in 1971. The experiment was slated to last for two full weeks. But within a few days, distinct situational responses became visible (and were recorded on film), with the "guards" becoming capricious and sadistic while the "prisoners" became disoriented, apathetic, and despondent. One of the "prisoners" had to be released from the experiment as he became increasingly disturbed.

The experiment supported Zimbardo's contention that the behaviors and dispositions of guards and prisoners are not the result of personal/character traits but instead are fostered by and stem from the conditions of prison life itself. Therefore, anyone—no matter how "good" or "bad" a person he is—could begin acting like a "guard" or a "prisoner." Who we are, how we behave, even what we believe, are all issues determined in large measure by the situations in which we participate, and more specifically by the roles we occupy in those situations, and even more specifically by how we respond to others' expectations of us as players of a given role. Today this experiment might be considered too psychologically risky to obtain approval.

## The Spy Who Didn't Love Me: Laud Humphreys' *Tea Room Trade*

A third example of a study that generated controversy and a great deal of regulatory change in the area of research ethics is Laud Humphreys' (1970) examination of the "tearoom trade," a 1950s–1960s term that refers to largely anonymous sexual encounters between men in public washrooms (e.g., the use of "glory holes"). Humphreys gained entrée to public washrooms that served as "tea rooms" by agreeing to serve as a lookout ("watch queen") who would warn the men if he saw police coming. In serving as "lookout" for the police, he also enjoyed a good vantage from which to observe the men "servicing" each other in the washroom. Humphreys spent hundreds of hours observing sex acts between men, many of whom had no previous or subsequent connection to each other.

But Humphreys didn't stop there. Not only did he observe the "men in action," but he also made a point of writing down the license plate number of each man's car along with other identifying information. He would then call up his police officer buddy and ask him to "run the plate" and give Humphreys the man's address. Armed with this information, Humphreys traced the men to their homes and communities where the majority (about 55%) of them maintained a *heterosexual* identity. Once there, Humphreys would walk right up to the door, knock or ring the bell, and then ask if he could interview the "head of household" (in those days always the man) as part of a vaguely named and described "health study." Never did he tell the men that he had observed them engaged in homosexual/homoerotic interactions in a "tea room." By combining observational data of heterosexually identified men engaged in homosexual liaisons and interview data concerning these men's personal life histories, Humphreys' book teemed with intriguing observations and lessons learned about masculinity, such as the various ways that outwardly heterosexual men "cover" their homoerotic inclinations when circulating in the public sphere.

Humphreys never revealed the names of specific individuals he observed or interviewed, but the study was based on deception and serious breaches of the principles of **privacy** and **informed consent**. Humphrey's purpose was not to "out" or embarrass the men as individuals or to get them in trouble with police,[1] families, and employers, but to document that homosexual behavior is not confined to the small percentage of the population that identifies as gay and that it occurs more frequently than is commonly believed. Despite its thought-provoking findings, the study was seen by many as involving serious breaches of research ethics. Even today, it's not unheard of for two sociologists to argue heatedly over the ethical implications of *Tea Room Trade*. Those who argue on Humphreys behalf typically invoke a "cost-benefit" analysis; that is, they argue that the study's deception and violation of privacy were necessary elements in the production of knowledge whose value to social science knowledge is greater than the costs that accrued to the subjects of the study.

The weighing of a given study's costs and benefits, in terms of potential harm to subjects versus knowledge gained, is the basic foundation upon which the modern institutional review board is premised. In the next section, we discuss the IRB—how it developed, how it functions, and how you can effectively interact with its members.

## Institutional Review Boards

The 1970s ushered in unprecedented price inflation, gasoline rationing, a new musical form known as "disco," and a flurry of reports concerning abusive biomedical research. In response to the latter, the U.S. federal government began taking steps to regulate research involving human subjects. A document called **The Belmont Report** specified that human subjects had to be treated as autonomous (**autonomy** in effect means that they must give informed consent and be able to understand their actions in participating in the research) and that studies had to be guided by beneficence and justice. **Beneficence** means that the study must provide benefits to the subject or to society as a whole, and that whatever risks may be incurred cannot outweigh the benefits. **Justice** means in practice that the research has to be designed to include many different categories of people, so that the opportunity to participate in and benefit from the findings is not confined to narrow segments of the population. Special attention was given to **vulnerable categories** of people who might become subjects: pregnant women, fetuses, and neonates; children; and prisoners.

As early as 1974, the federal government began mandating institutional review of human subject research at universities that accepted federal funding. In 1998, the National Commission Report on Institutional Review Boards reiterated the policy of regulatory committees at universities, research labs, hospitals, and other facilities that conducted research and received federal funding. These committees are called "institutional review boards" (IRBs). Because the federal

---

[1] To the contrary, in fact, Humphreys set out to convince police departments that "tearoom" activities were largely harmless, or "victimless," and that restricted law enforcement resources should be redirected to truly serious crimes. In this he was reasonably successful.

government funds so much research in the United States, it had the power to initiate the process, but the review now also applies to unfunded or internally funded research. No research results can be published if the research was not approved by an IRB; and graduate student projects are generally also submitted to IRBs. The institution as a whole is responsible for the actions of investigators; misconduct or negligence in one research project or department may lead to a suspension of funds to the institution as a whole. Researchers submit detailed protocols of their research plans to **local review boards** (at the department level, for example) and after receiving approval at the lower level, present their plans to the **institutional review board**. The IRB is also responsible for educating and mentoring the research community at its institution.

IRBs are comprised of faculty members representing a broad spectrum of disciplines. In addition, every IRB must include at least one "community member," a nonscientist who can represent the interests and concerns of "the community at large." It's also mandatory that every IRB include a member who can represent the interests of prisoners, broadly defined as any person who is or has been under the custody of the state's criminal justice system (typically this means prisoners, jail inmates, parolees and probationers, etc.). In Canada, a similar institutional structure is implemented through the **National Council on Ethics in Human Research** and **Research Ethics Boards**.

**GUIDING PRINCIPLES OF HUMAN SUBJECTS PROTECTION:**   Five very broad principles guide the decisions of IRBs (Glesne 2006: 130):

1. The principle of informed consent: research subjects must be able to understand the purpose, procedures, risks, and benefits of the research, have sufficient information about the research to be able to decide whether to participate, and must actively agree to participate in it.
2. The principle that research subjects can withdraw from a study at any time, without penalties.
3. The elimination of unnecessary risks to subjects, including the risk of embarrassment or sanctions such as job loss or social stigma.
4. The principle that benefits to society and if at all possible to subjects as well need to outweigh the possible harm to subjects.
5. The researchers must be qualified.

We can spot tension between the first two principles and the characteristics of field research as we described it in our second vignette. In a field research setting, where the relationships that connect the researcher with her subjects are "complicated" and "open ended" at best, we can see how murky the terms "informed consent," "active agreement," and "withdrawing from a study" can get. When exactly is a subject sufficiently informed of the goals, procedures, risks, and benefits of a study? And what exactly constitutes "consent" to participate in the study? Even at the point of signing an informed consent document, most subjects don't really know *exactly what they're consenting to*. This is glaringly obvious and painful when they get their hands on the final product—be it a book or article or monograph—and see that they have been fooled, hoodwinked, bamboozled, and betrayed! Indeed, it's quite common for a subject to believe wholeheartedly that this kind, open-minded, patient, and very compassionate researcher is going to listen to me, and really hear what I have to say, and that she will "take my side" when it comes time to tell whatever story the researcher has set out to tell. After all, *it's the researcher's job* to make every subject feel this way, to convince every subject that she is the "most special" of all the special people who live in the chosen area of concern.

In the social sciences, the risk of serious physical harm is generally low, but the researcher needs to address other types of risk, such as inconvenience, and various discomforts such as frustration, embarrassment, and possible harm resulting from the invasion of privacy or recall of traumatic events. Ostracism and stigma may also result—a social harming that many researchers don't even think to consider when preparing their plan for protecting subjects. But in many settings, subjects can experience all sorts of social loss as a result of having trusted the researcher enough to reveal to her the "dirty little secrets" of community life. So risk and harm can take many forms, and it's essential that you consider as many possibilities as come to mind. Then you need to account for these possible risks—and your plan for minimizing their probability of occurrence and their impact should they occur anyway—in writing. This document is not optional; the IRB will demand it of you.

Depending on the sensitivity of the data you intend to gather, the vulnerability of the population being studied, and the level of direct contact with subjects, the IRB will review your written protocol for subject protection, and then they will classify it as **exempt** (for instance, use of publicly available records or relatively uncomplicated surveys), **expedited**, or **full board review**. A full board review may be required when the research subjects are in vulnerable categories such as minors or incarcerated individuals or when illegal behaviors are the topic of the study.

**THE RESEARCHER'S PROTOCOL:**   Before going into the world and interacting with humans for the purpose of producing data about them, the researcher (i.e., you) must write up and submit to the IRB a **protocol**, or specific plan for protecting the well-being of the human subjects who participate in the project. Every institution has a different format to which the protocol must adhere, but generally you should be prepared for the LRB/IRB to raise the following kinds of issues and concerns:

- Is the privacy and confidentiality of research subjects protected?
- Are the collected data as "secure" as they need to be given the level of risk/harm if the data's security were compromised (stored in password-protected file on non-networked computer hard drive, hard copy data stored in locked file cabinet, etc.)?
- Are subjects informed about the research and do they give informed consent to their participation? Do they really know—and describe in their own words—your study's goals, procedures, and potential risks, harms, and benefits?
- Is the research design and purpose of sufficiently high quality to warrant the use of subjects' time? (One principle that many IRBs follow is this: If the proposed research study's design is so poor as to be unlikely to produce valuable knowledge, then *no level of risk* is acceptable.)
- Is the proposed sample diverse, does it represent the community or "population," and if not, is there a valid reason for excluding some categories of people (such as women or ethnic minorities)? If subjects are not fluent in English, are the materials (including consent forms) available to them in their native language and correctly translated? What procedures will ensure the proper training in human subject protection of those who will serve as translators?
- What measures are being taken to protect **vulnerable populations** for whom "informed consent" may be problematic—such as prison inmates, minors, or mentally handicapped adults?

It is noteworthy that IRB often treats as "exempt" the use of not only archival data that are public or "de-identified" but also survey/interview research with adults, in cases where the data are recorded in an anonymous fashion and there is little risk inherent in the collection of the information. This policy underlines one of the ideas in our chapter-head vignettes—namely that quantitative survey research usually poses fewer ethical problems and less opportunity for abusive or irresponsible behavior by researchers than qualitative and ethnographic field research.

## IRB RULES AND QUALITATIVE RESEARCH PRINCIPLES—SQUARE PEG, ROUND HOLE?

Increasingly, IRBs have very strict guidelines. No aspect of the research study can begin until the IRB has approved the study in writing and provided the researcher with stamped informed consent documents. You can't even begin recruiting potential subjects by handing out flyers describing your study. Plus, once you've begun the study, you cannot make major changes in the purpose or methods of the research once it is underway.

These regulations are often more troublesome for qualitative field research than for quantitative research. Usually quantitative researchers would not "go into the field" until they have a completed survey instrument ready, and they would not be inclined to make changes in the instrument in the middle of their study. On the other hand, qualitative researchers often find that they have to change the basic aims of their research after they enter the field. The very concept of "grounded theory" implies that researchers learn about a community or a situation as they deepen their experiences in it, so that all field research has to be a "work in progress" that is constantly changing and developing.

The IRB approval process frequently *seems* designed to turn a diffuse, affective relationship into a functionally specific, impersonal one, and to make qualitative research, especially fieldwork and ethnography, more like quantitative and biomedical research.

The regulatory framework of the IRBs is valuable in ensuring responsible behavior in the community of scientists, but it leaves a number of issues in qualitative research unaddressed. It must, however, be said that IRBs have become more flexible and sensitive to issues in behavioral and social research (which are quite different from biomedical research) and even to qualitative research. The protection of human subjects is an evolving area and the body of knowledge and regulation are changing rapidly. Fortunately, most IRBs consider it their job to help researchers—faculty and students alike—figure out how to conduct their studies in the way that best protects human subjects. Certainly the IRB's central function is to protect subjects (though many cynics argue that they really exist to cover the university's rear end in case something goes wrong). But most IRBs want to see the researcher succeed and get the study off the ground and implemented effectively.

The **ethical codes of professional associations**, such as the American Sociological Association,[2] are closer to actual research in the discipline and have field-specific guidelines for ethical behavior. Still, every code is by definition a formal attempt to govern behavior through the reduction of norms, rules, and customs to writing. Hence, every regulatory or professional code is going to be static in relation to the dynamic warp and woof of real-life happenings. Does this mean that we should aspire to adhere only to "the law" when it comes to protecting the subjects of our research? No, definitely not. We need to go further. Why? Because some of the most complicated and thorny ethical issues lie outside the purview of written code. So let's turn to a discussion of "diffuse" ethical issues.

## BEYOND FORMAL CODES OF ETHICS

The formal codes of ethics of institutional review boards, federal agencies, and professional associations create a relatively uniform set of norms for researchers. But social reality—out in the field—is often more complicated, messy, and less formalized than the code of ethics. Several thorny, largely irresolvable issues often come up in research that are not fully clarified by the IRB process and the formal codes.

---

[2] You can find the ASA's code of ethics online at http://www2.asanet.org/members/ecoderev.html

## Informed Consent

The researcher's presence in the field may seem a bit obscure, vague, and unbounded (or at best bounded by the blurriest of lines—quasi-friend, confidante, lay counselor, person who does favors, etc.). It's impossible for a single formal agreement—an informed consent form—to address and govern every single contact or conversation between a researcher and a subject. Imagine an analogous phenomenon: The next time you hang out with your friends in a public place, speak with them ahead of time about how you're going to be analyzing every word they say and that you're going to be studying everyone who happens to join the group over the course of the day/evening. Then, when you're out, be sure that you sit and have a formal conversation with every person who approaches your group: Inform him or her that you're conducting a study, that you'll be watching and listening and ultimately analyzing him or her, and so on. You can see how infeasible this would be and, ultimately, results in people acting very differently than they ordinarily would act. Formal informed consent agreements not only pose practical problems with even the most basic of interactions; they also directly contribute to the production of nonvalid and nonreliable data.

## The (Hollow) Right to Withdraw

And that's just the formal informed consent requirement. What about the rule stating that every subject must have the right to withdraw from a study at any time and suffer absolutely no negative consequences as a result of the withdrawal. Well, research subjects (or **participants**) who live in a community in which a researcher is conducting fieldwork may find it essentially impossible to withdraw from a study, even if they don't like the researcher or disapprove of the project. If they do dislike the researcher and/or the study, then the researcher's continued presence in the neighborhood and the subject's continued participation in the neighborhood may mean that (1) there's no real way for the subject to withdraw from the study (unless she moves away entirely and ceases all contact with former neighbors, though even in this extreme case her involvement up to the point of departure may end up in the researcher's analyses and/or final product) and (2) the inability to truly withdraw from the study could cause the disaffected subject even more emotional or mental distress.

## Informed Consent Is a Process, *Not* a Document

In the "real life" of research, informed consent is ideally a process of mutual discovery. At the outset the researcher often has some idea, however vague, of the study's purpose, what the subjects will be doing, and what the potential **risks and benefits** are. If nothing else, the researcher knows what product will come out at the end—a paper, an article, maybe a book or even an ethnographic film. The subject, on the other hand, often knows next to nothing about any of these things. Moreover, the subject often has very different ideas and interpretations of the researcher's desired product. If, for example, the researcher says that he is writing a book on the subject's community, the subject often believes that the book will be entirely favorable, a celebration of the community in which she lives.

No matter what informed consent documents might exist and be exchanged between researcher and subject at the study's outset, they soon will become irrelevant, or at the very least incomplete and therefore inaccurate. What's actually going on changes over the course of the research, which is usually construed as a weakness from the perspective of the IRB, but from a "logic of inquiry" vantage point, this flexibility of design is one of qualitative research's central strengths.

So what it means to be "informed" and to give "consent" changes over the course of the research study. Being sensitive to this is essential for the researcher's success, and figuring out how to negotiate changes in the study's purpose, procedures, risks, and benefits with the IRB's often intransigent rules is bound to be a difficult process, one that you should talk openly about with a trusted experienced advisor.

## Some Suggestions for Resolving the Tension between Law on the Books and Law in Action

In talking with your advisor, try to explore some alternatives to the "one-time signing" of a formal informed consent document. We suggest that you raise such IRB-endorsed possibilities as the **waiver of informed consent** (which allows you to conduct a study without going through a formal consent process), an **alteration of documentation of informed consent** (which means that you must engage in an informed consent discussion with every subject but you will not be required to obtain their signature on a document), or a **step-wise consent process**. In a step-wise process, you describe roughly how you're going to enter the community or group, how and when you're going to first describe what you're doing and what their involvement will consist of as subjects, and so forth. At each step, you may or may not need documentation of consent.

In addition, you might want to explore the possibility of informing the IRB of how you're going to enter the study area/group, how the entry/observation/interviewing will pose inconsequential risk of harm to subjects, and how at some point you will ask subjects whom you've decided ultimately to include in the study to give their consent for you to do so. With this approach, you would be asking subjects to "authorize" your use of "information not collected for research purposes" as data to be analyzed in your study. These are just a few of many possible ways to deal with the flux of real-life research and still be compliant with IRB regulations. Again, we strongly advise you to seek counsel and guidance from a trusted mentor as you develop your study and its IRB protocol.

## Deception

While the code of ethics followed by IRB clearly attempts to reduce and even eliminate deception, many different qualitative research situations generate deceptive practice, and *all* of them carry the potential for it. Not all researchers agree, however, on the basic principles or on the line between outright deception and mere vagueness about one's identity and precise purpose. For example, Denzin (1989: 261–264) asserts that it is sometimes legitimate for researchers to mask their identity and he provocatively challenges each of the conventional arguments against it.

**DECEPTION IN EXAMPLE—A STUDY OF THE GARMENT INDUSTRY IN LOS ANGELES:** In Greg Scott's (1998) study of undocumented women garment workers in Los Angeles, for example, he argues that it was necessary for him to "differentially manufacture a situationally specific presentation of self" in order to gain access to the more powerful members of the clothing trade. In his interviews and observations with workers themselves, he felt that he could more freely discuss his political beliefs concerning stratification and inequality in the industry. But in order to get "sweatshop" owners to talk openly about the many labor violations they knowingly committed, Greg had to present himself as a researcher "interested in how garment contractors deal with the many challenges of the industry, how they suffer and fight to stay ahead, how they try to succeed in the face of stiff odds against them, how they go to battle against the much more powerful 'wholesalers' like Bugle Boy, Ocean Pacific, and Guess." When venturing into the wholesalers' corporate offices, however, Greg donned a suit and tie, and began his pitch with a different description of his research, saying to CEOs that he was interested in how they managed to get—and stay—at the top of the heap, how they deal with unjust regulatory practices, how they "survive the onslaught of organized labor worldwide," and so forth. You get the idea.

Each of Greg's descriptions of his study contained a core of truth. Indeed he was telling the truth when describing his interests. But what got him in the door—and what got people telling him things whose telling was against their interests—was *how* he presented his study. Those whom he theorized to be the exploiters—the contractors and wholesalers—turned over and exposed their "tender underbellies" because they believed that Greg's study would cast them in a sympathetic light (a much sought-after resource in an industry known for its human rights abuses and legal violations). Had Greg told them that his principal concern was the adverse impact of the "sweat system" on the most marginal of the industry's members, they never would have given him the time of day.

Researchers such as Greg often justify their deception by referencing some larger social good that can be achieved if the researcher were to reveal behaviors that are harmful, such as dumping of toxic materials, racist hiring, brutality to incarcerated individuals or other vulnerable populations, or unfair treatment of workers. In these cases, the research can only be carried out if the researcher deliberately misleads the subjects about the purpose of the researcher and his or her identity. Do the ends of social justice or obtaining critical information ever justify deceptive means? Finally, some researchers argue that all field research and participant-observation is inherently deceptive in the sense that human subjects rarely fully understand the purpose and underlying orientation of the research project. Unlike clinical studies in which the objective of testing drugs or vaccines is relatively easy to understand, the complex social issues that social scientists study are hard to explain in full detail; and if they were fully explained, the explanation itself might influence behaviors and affect the outcome of the study.

## "Instrumentalization" of Relationships

Every qualitative researcher uses, and arguably **exploits**, her subjects. Although many scholars view the relationship as unilaterally exploitative, with the researcher enjoying all the riches and the poor, defenseless subject/informant representing little more than a resource to be used and discarded, the reality is that in many instances the subject uses and exploits the researcher. In our experience, the relationship is bilaterally exploitative. Both parties seek to gain something—tangible or intangible—from the "research relationship" (a redundancy of terms, for as we've said, qualitative research *is* a relationship). But the question is how will each party go about getting what she wants? What form will the exploitation take?

The **instrumentalization of a personal relationship** between the researcher and a research subject is a complex issue in fieldwork and interactive qualitative research. Researchers may convince themselves and their subjects that what they have is a friendship formed in the course of fieldwork. But with few exceptions, such as blogging and social networking sites, friends don't write critically about other friends, so the relationship between the researcher and the subject wasn't really a friendship after all. What might have appeared to the subject to be a friendship in fact was more of an ongoing utilitarian "data harvest," with the researcher deploying various friendship formation and sustenance tactics, such as the doing of favors, in order to make the subject feel comfortable being vulnerable around the researcher. This vulnerability is the key to a good data harvest—for the more a subject trusts and likes you, the more "real" he will allow himself to be in the researcher's presence. The more real a subject is, the better the data will be. If the researcher does her job right and effectively convinces the subject to trust her, then the researcher will enjoy over time a diminishing of the **actuality differential**, or the difference between how the subject acts in the presence of the researcher and how the subject acts when the researcher isn't around.

## Give in Order to Take ... and Take More

Minimizing the actuality differential by forging a pseudo-friendship with subjects necessitates a fair amount of basic deception—not just simple lies about who the researcher is or what is being studied—but the fundamental lie that the relationship is a friendly and reciprocal one, when in the end the researcher writes about the subject, reduces the subject to an object of analysis, and builds a research career on the backs of all the subjects in the study. In the end, no matter what justification the researcher uses (contributing to scientific knowledge, changing policy, etc.), the final product(s) of a research study ultimately further the goals of the researcher. To the extent that the study is well-received, the researcher will enjoy potentially substantial gains in status/prestige, income, and social influence. The subjects he "befriended," studied, and left behind, on the other hand, typically continue going on about their business and in all but a very small number of cases enjoy none of the gains (e.g., royalties from book sales, advancement of career) had by the researcher. Their net yield, at best, is the feeling of loss (if they truly believed it was a friendship) and at worst, an unshakeable feeling of betrayal.

## Caveat: The Subject Is Not a Dishrag

While our characterization of the researcher–subject relationship may appear to be bleak or even cynical, we offer it confidently as a corrective to the monument of fieldwork texts that paint a rosy picture of the situation. Moreover, by no means do we wish to cast the subject as an unsuspecting, hapless, half-wit devoid of any agency. Indeed, most subjects of research studies do find ways to exploit their relationship with the researcher. It's quite common for subjects to use the researcher as a "lay therapist" whom they seek out for help in resolving a variety of emotional and psychological issues. After all, who among us doesn't like to be heard, really heard, by a patient, nonjudgmental, compassionate, even sympathetic person? Subjects also achieve all manner of material and nonmaterial gains—honoraria/stipend payments (if it's a funded study) for participating in interviews, free rides to and from places they need to frequent, personal loans, access to information (especially when subjects themselves face limitations on information access, as when they don't have an Internet connection), job references, information and insight into employment and/or educational and/or social welfare opportunities, and so on. Finally, subjects often view the researcher as a symbolic resource, a person who can finally "tell the story right," who can issue a counterassault against the forces that have depicted the community in negative terms (e.g., "gang-ridden," "crime-infested," "disorganized," or "chaotic"). Subjects often consider the act of telling the researcher "our side" of the story, and having the researcher really listen to and record it, as a gain in itself. However, insofar as the researcher represents a "resource" or a bundle of resources, his presence in the community may itself become a source of conflict, antagonism, or outright physical altercations. We address this particular issue more fully in Part III (Chapters 13–16).

## The "Gaze"

The research subject is exposed to a scientific "gaze," an objective examination that is at best cold and impersonal, and at worst ironic and demeaning. The French philosopher and social critic Michel Foucault used the term **gaze** to characterize this objective, impersonal, and unequal examination of a subject by those who hold power and expertise. Research often rests on this type of unequal scrutiny of relatively powerless subjects by scholars with expertise and social standing. Even if the IRB and ethical codes keep the researcher from doing harm and discourage disrespectful writing about the research subjects, the entire relationship is fraught with inequality and differences in power and knowledge.

Despite (or because of) the "friendship foundation" upon which the researcher built his fund of data, the ultimate objective is to produce a highly synthesized, readable account that tells some kind of meaningful sociological story. Well, as we discuss later, such storytelling requires that the researcher reduce people (i.e., the subjects) to objects on paper, analyzable "characters" or "figures" whose behaviors and words the scientist scrutinizes critically. Reductionism is one of science's fundamental tenets and arguably its emblematic mechanical function—it's what makes science work. But reductionism in human relations can be, and often is, very damaging. Just because qualitative research involves interacting in a friendly way with real people *in situ* doesn't mean that the methodology is immune to "the gaze" and its dehumanizing effect on those who wield it and those whom it targets.

## Revealing Subjects' Ignorance

Ethical issues arise particularly in those instances when the research reveals that their subjects hold **misrecognitions** about the social world, their environment, and even their own actions and choices. The researchers do not just repeat what the respondents/subjects tell them, but analyze these views and may identify them as mistaken or confused. The interpretations may be hurtful or uncomfortable for the participants. The research narrative holds up an unpleasant "looking glass" that not only reveals illegal or immoral actions on the part of the subjects but puts into question their entire understanding of the world.

## Caveat: "Studying Up" versus "Studying Down"—The Patterning of Ethical Issues

We feel compelled to note that our overwhelmingly negative characterization of the researcher–subject relationship stems in large part from the realization that most sociological field studies constitute an act of "studying down." This means that the researcher occupies a higher rung on the socioeconomic ladder than do her research subjects. Since its inception, qualitative field researchers have been much more likely to focus on communities they view as being "oppressed," "impoverished," "marginalized," "disenfranchised," or otherwise less privileged than the middle and/or upper-middle-class communities, institutions, groups, and organizations with which the researcher is familiar. The tendency to "study down" results not only, or even principally, from sociologists' lurid fascination with suffering but rather from the differential capacity of communities and groups to shield themselves from the probing eyes and ears of enquirers. Quite simply, privileged groups possess the capacity—and the desire—to keep outsiders from prying into their business. As a corollary, one manifestation of a community's "oppressed" or "marginalized" status is its inability to keep "professional strangers" (sociologists) from entering their realm, nosing around, and then reporting on what they see. Part and parcel of this patterning of community power and sociologists' interests is the fact that privileged communities are much more likely than their disprivileged counterparts to read the researcher's final product (the book or article) and to hold the researcher accountable (sometimes legally) for its contents. A full analysis of the "studying down" versus "studying up" phenomenon is outside the scope of this book, but we encourage you to seek out qualitative studies of affluent, powerful groups and compare them, in terms of ethics, with those published studies of less powerful groups and communities.

## LOOKING AHEAD AT ETHICS

We will look at the ethical issues in more detail in later chapters. They are too pervasive and complex to be resolved in a single chapter on the ethics of research. Issues of deception and compensation will be addressed in our chapters on ethnography and fieldwork. These chapters will also suggest that informed consent is a process, not a single moment or act like signing a document. Our chapter on community-based participatory research will suggest different ways that the researcher can contribute to the community, but it also probes deeper into the ethics and politics of interventions, which must not be undertaken lightly or in situations where the researchers know little about community structure, divisions, and processes. Our last chapter on "wrapping it up" will return to the issue of the "gaze" and the power dynamics of friendships in which one friend writes a book about the others. Our chapters on the politics of qualitative research and theory will look in more depth at the issue of the gap between researcher knowledge and research subjects' understandings of a situation—a gap that leads the researcher to claim that the subjects misrecognize their own situation, an assertion on the part of the researcher that may be accurate but that poses ethical challenges.

## Exercises

1. Go to Collaborative Institutional Training Initiative (CITI) https://www.citiprogram.org/ website if your institution subscribes to it (or other certification site) and obtain student certification.

2. Read the code of ethics for ASA online at the address provided in footnote 2 (or other professional association). What do you think are the most important principles in the code?

3. While the Tuskegee syphilis study is indefensible on ethical grounds, the social and behavioral science studies mentioned in this chapter (Milgram, Zimbardo, and Humphreys) are more ambiguous. Could they be redesigned to meet today's ethical standards?

4. Documentaries you may want to watch: The Deadly Deception (1993) (Nova and the *WGBH* Educational Foundation) about the Tuskegee syphilis study; Obedience, Stanley Milgram's original filming of the experiment (Pennsylvania State University, University Park, PA, 1969); Philip Zimbardo's original film on the experiment, reissued as Quiet Rage, 1992.

5. If unethical studies yielded valuable findings, do you think that this information should be used or not? For example, if the Nazi studies of the effects of cold used prisoners of war and concentration camp inmates as human subjects (many of whom died in the experiments), does that mean that no findings can ever be used?

6. How will you know if your study is "too unethical?" What are the conditions under which a study is too unethical to be conducted?

7. Conduct your own "instrumentalization" experiment with your friends or family. Identify an upcoming event or gathering (informal) or situation that you want to know more about. This need not be a research issue at all. Perhaps you just want to know where the best party's going to be Friday night. Or you want tickets to a ball game. Or you need some advice on where to get your hair done. It could be anything. Then start calling up your friends to solicit information. But in doing so, do *not* employ any of the "social niceties" we typically use to veil, enshroud, and soften the blow of instrumental requests. Instead of having five minutes of meandering "just catching up" conversation at the beginning of the call, just cut to the chase and make your intentions glaringly known: "I'm only calling you to get information on XYZ. I don't want to pretend otherwise. Let's get down to business." Once you've done this with five or six friends or family members, sit and reflect on the experience. Write up your observations. Think not only about how "instrumentalization" is dressed up in social norms but also about how it lies at the core of many of our interactions and even many of our relationships.

## Key Terms

actuality differential *62*

alteration of documentation of informed consent *61*

Belmont Report: autonomy; beneficence; and justice *56*

Canadian Association of Research Ethics Boards *57*

confidentiality *51*

critical issues in qualitative research: compensation *65*

deception *53*

"diffuse" researcher–subject relationship *53*

exploitation *62*

informed consent *56*

instrumentalization of a personal relationship *62*

the "gaze" *63*

revealing misrecognition *64*

ethical codes of professional associations *59*

exempt *58*

expedited *58*

full board reviews *58*

human subjects *52*

Humphreys' tearoom trade study *55*

informed consent *56*

informed consent form *52*

institutional review board *57*

justice in the distribution of risks and benefits *56*

local review boards *57*

Milgram obedience study *54*

National Council on Ethics in Human Research *57*

participants *60*

privacy *56*

protection of human subjects *53*

protocol *58*

research ethics *51*

risks and benefits *60*

Stanford prison experiment *55*

step-wise consent *61*

Tuskegee syphilis study *54*

vulnerable populations (or categories) *58*

waiver of informed consent *61*

# The Politics of
# Qualitative Research

## OVERVIEW

The ethics of qualitative research cannot be separated neatly from the politics of research. By "politics," we refer to the many ways that qualitative researchers think about and address larger public issues (e.g., racism, poverty, and oppression). More broadly (but still more simply), we define politics as the struggle over the distribution of material and symbolic resources. At every level the qualitative research study is a political endeavor. In this chapter, we discuss the dynamic and reciprocal relation between the researcher's personal values, ethics, and worldview (*Weltanschauung*) and the research choices and activities in which the researcher engages.

## RESEARCH AND POLITICS: TOGETHER BUT MOSTLY APART

Max Weber believed that there is tension between political goals and scientific research. The scientist's endeavors cannot and should not directly further political aims. What scientists can do is to clarify whether or not a particular set of political values and goals can be realized and what difficulties and costs might be encountered in their realization. Weber (Weber/Gerth and Mills 1965: 147, 151) admonished educators not to attempt to inculcate students with their own political views and wrote,

> The primary task of a useful teacher is to teach his students to recognize "inconvenient" facts—I mean facts that are inconvenient for their party opinions. And for every party opinion there are facts that are extremely inconvenient, for my own opinion no less than others. I believe the teacher accomplishes more than a mere intellectual task if he compels his audience to accustom itself to the existence of such facts. ...if you take such and such a stand, then according to scientific experience, you have to use such and such a *means* in order to carry out your conviction practically. Now, these means are perhaps such that you believe you

must reject them. Then you simply must choose between the end and the inevitable means....The teacher can confront you with the necessity of this choice. He cannot do more as long as he wishes to remain a teacher and not become a demagogue....

Despite Weber's warning, sociological researchers often fail to keep a clear line between their research studies and their own personal-political values. In fact, as we discussed in a previous chapter, one of the primary sources for the research question itself is the researcher's own life experiences, beliefs, values, and interests. This mix poses less of a problem for quantitative than qualitative research. Quantitative researchers must follow strict rules of research design that discourage (but by no means eliminate entirely) inappropriate mixes of politics and science. The quantitative researcher may have strong political opinions and values, which guided him or her to the research topic and the research questions, but once the project is under way, opinions and values must stay on a back burner. If the study turns up **inconvenient facts**, the quantitative researcher cannot evade them or dismiss them (though some figure out how to do just that). For the social scientist, then, personal-political values represent a double-edged sword, for there can be no better source of inspiration for a research topic nor a worse enemy to the integrity of the scientific enterprise.

## Limiting Personal Bias by Exposing It: Embracing Transparency and Falsifiability

Research canons of validity, reliability, measurement, falsifiability, and operationalizing variables *limit* the introduction of **bias** in quantitative research. For example, in designing a survey instrument, a researcher cannot ask **leading questions** (or **push/pull questions** that force the respondent into choices that support the researcher's political purposes). If leading questions are used on the questionnaire in order to elicit the response desired by the researcher, peers in the discipline will "catch" this problem and criticize the survey as biased, unprofessional, and invalid. The same holds for quantitative content analysis of documents: It's easy to spot the bias behind the coding. But qualitative fieldwork affords lots of "wiggle room" for introducing politically slanted interpretations of the observations. We are not talking about *fraudulent* science—about deliberate *mis*reporting of observations, because such behavior is completely morally and professionally unacceptable—but rather about "spin" introduced in the framing and wording of field notes and in their interpretation. Quite simply, every phase of the qualitative research enterprise opens up multiple opportunities for the researcher to inject and further his personal/political agenda.

This opportunity for "bias" in the recording and interpretation of qualitative data is not always or intrinsically a bad thing. As we will see in this chapter, many outstanding studies were deeply "biased" and organized to further a distinct point of view or to weigh in on a public issue. Bias does not need to be driven out of all research. Indeed, there is no way to eliminate entirely the bias in research, if only because there's no such thing as a completely "unbiased" study. The very complaint or criticism that "the study is biased" is predicated on the idea that out there somewhere is a completely "unbiased," or pure, way of doing the study. And this just isn't true. There is no such true way to conduct any given study. The question isn't whether or not a study *is* biased but rather, to *what degree* is it biased? How effectively does the researcher make the bias clear to those who read the study? What effect do the biases exert on the data and the researcher's interpretation of them? And so on.

**TRANSPARENCY**    Recognizing the ubiquity of bias, researchers at every step of the study should clarify their point of view, take steps to insure that they record information accurately, and be prepared to encounter results that may diverge from their initial hypotheses (i.e., "inconvenient facts"), no matter how cherished or deeply felt these conjectures might be. In essence, the researcher should work very hard to render visible the inner workings of her project—its core assumptions about the world, the moral-ethical values out of which it sprouted, and so forth.

This is what qualitative researchers mean by **transparency**: the more transparent you make your motives, interests, values, and politics—and the more carefully you delineate how you believe they may have affected your research—the *stronger* your study will be. Also, the strongest studies are those where the transparency factor is high and the researcher has gone to great lengths to seek out "inconvenient facts" and "negative cases," or phenomena that undermine or in some way contradict the researcher's working theory and/or interpretation of findings.

**PURSUING FALSIFIABILITY**    The goal of "falsifiability" in research means explicitly opening the research design to the possibility that the data will not support the hypothesized outcome; it helps to address the issue that Weber raised. Findings should not be foregone conclusions, and the researcher must be prepared to encounter "inconvenient facts." Furthermore, the qualitative researcher must be able to convince readers of the research report that the observations are accurate, regardless of how they are interpreted. The researcher must be able to explain choices that were made in recording and interpreting the observations. Accounting for "plausible alternative explanations" can be a really useful strategy in this respect. Every time you think you've had an "a-ha!" moment in which you've developed a "finding," you should think about how that same finding might be explained by someone whose beliefs/values concerning the subject are diametrically opposed. This mental exercise will help keep you "in check" and also will contribute to a more lively and interesting approach to data analysis.

## Research as a Means for Championing Rights: Social Justice and Social Science

As you might expect, not all researchers agree with Weber's cautious, skeptical, and fundamentally *apolitical* view. Marxists would consider research that is not politically engaged to be utterly pointless. In the 1960s and 1970s, many microsociologists and symbolic interactionists also saw themselves as committed to social justice. In 1967, Howard Becker's presidential address to the ASA was entitled "**Whose Side Are We On?**" In his lecture and the corresponding journal article by the same title, Becker called for a vigorous defense of the rights of the marginalized, the poor, and all those labeled as "deviants" (Becker 1967).

Many qualitative researchers have political aims in their research, but there's a lot of variation in the type of claims they have and in the degree to which their political views influence the research they do. Some qualitative researchers see themselves as champions of social justice, but that goal can mean a lot of different things in practice. Social science—and sociology in particular—enjoys a history with intricate and intimate connections with the history of social justice movements across the world. Though some sociologists fall prey to the corrosive effects of politics on science, most scholars (as exemplified by the work of Becker, for instance) have been quite successful in weaving together their social justice aims and their research objectives. But the relationship between the two always has been and always will be an uneasy one, fraught with complications and tension. Like anything worthwhile, however, it's worth the effort.

## POLITICIZING RESEARCH WITHOUT COMPROMISING SCIENCE

In the remainder of this chapter, we look at how points of view and personal values structure research, and we provide examples of how to make research both political and scientifically rigorous. We emphasize that these points of view should be made clear and transparent. The researcher must explain how his political orientation/views influenced research choices, such as selection of methods, protocol for sampling, coding categories, and even the wording and/or tone of field notes.

### Clusters of Values: Truth, Sociological Imagination, and Social Justice

Three clusters of values are especially important to many contemporary researchers. The first of these is **truth**—the belief that researchers must and can report and interpret the world accurately, both in its immediate details and in terms of larger, more long-term, and more conceptual understanding. It is the *sine qua non* of research—if the researcher does not feel this commitment, there is little point in being a social scientist. Commitment to "the truth" obviously means carefully recording observations, avoiding errors in basic facts, and being prepared to record and report different opinions that are encountered in the field. It means **documenting research choices.** It certainly means the willingness to accept "inconvenient facts." It can also mean being prepared to contradict the opinions of research subjects or to reinterpret them in a wider context. We return to this notion many times later in this book, particularly in the chapters where we discuss how one goes about "making" or "producing" qualitative data.

How the social scientist's commitment to truth-telling manifests in the documentation he produces in the course of his study resembles the manner in which certain documentary filmmakers do their work. Albert Maysles, one of the "founders" of the "direct cinema" or "observational cinema" genre of documentary film, writes,

> As a photographer and documentarian, I happily place my fate and faith in reality. Reality is my caretaker, the provider of subjects, themes, experiences—all endowed with the power of truth and the romance of discovery. The closer I adhere to reality the more honest and authentic my tales. After all, knowledge of the real world is exactly what we need to better understand and, possibly, to love one another. It's my way of making the world a better place. (2007: 15)

A belief in "reality" is a necessary condition for the social scientist, no matter the specific discipline she works in. Although we may engage in various academic debates about the *nature* of reality—how it's defined, measured, and so on—the point is that collecting data in order to answer a question about reality, as perceived by any given group, necessitates not just a belief in the existence of reality but also a commitment to recording reality as carefully and accurately as possible. Ultimately, the knowledge you gain and share from your study may or may not make the world a better place. But if you've adhered to the truth as best you can, and if you've given yourself over to the "romance of discovery," then most likely you will have made the world of social science a better place through realizing a commitment to truth-telling.

**ENLIGHTENED SKEPTICISM:**    Committing yourself to telling the truth, even when it's not the truth you prefer the world to possess, is a vital part of doing good social science. At every phase of your study, one of the best things you can do for the cause of truth-telling is to *question everything*. One mantra to keep at the fore is this: "At all times be skeptical of your interpretations." Of course, you could take this too far and find yourself plagued and paralyzed by self-doubt. That's not what we're talking about. We are saying that the qualitative researcher should, at all times, view her own scholarly work with the same degree of "enlightened skepticism" that characterizes her view of others' work and her view of whatever "injustices" propel her interest in the subject at hand. Examine your own work, your own data, and your own interpretations, as rigorously as you examine the subject of your study. This will help you adhere to whichever reality you've chosen to adopt as the principal vantage point in your study. It may seem counterintuitive, but the act of casting doubt on the "truths" you hold is the best way to make the tales you tell as truthful as they can be.

The second cluster of values that often shape research emerges from the **sociological imagination** as C. Wright Mills defined it:

> The sociological imagination enables its possessor to understand the larger historical scene in terms of its meaning for the inner life and external career of a variety of individuals. ... By such means the personal uneasiness of individuals is focused upon explicit troubles and the indifference of publics is transformed into involvement with public issues.
>
> (Mills 1959: 5)

This commitment has implications for the way in which researchers interpret their results and how they present and use their data. Mills is saying that sociologists need to identify public issues so that people can find collective, public solutions to these issues. This cluster of values is related to the formulation of research questions, to interpretation of findings, to identifying broader contexts for conclusions (a whole country rather than an individual or a household, the macrolevel as well as the micro- and mesolevels). Mills' concept of the sociological imagination suggests that the audience for research needs to be the public and not a small number of academic experts; and it suggests that the tone for writing about research needs to be politically engaged, not neutral and "value-free."

The third cluster of values and goals that many researchers share is the most overtly political—the widely shared commitment to **social justice**, and more specifically to values such as equality in access to resources and opportunities, a better quality of life for all, democratic participation, a say in the "decisions that affect our lives," a more equal distribution of power, and respect for civil rights and liberties. More controversial but nevertheless widely held is the conviction that the state can have a positive role in people's lives by regulating markets and providing social services, especially for segments of the population that historically were marginalized, excluded, or exploited. This cluster of values may be related to action and efforts to change the world rather than merely interpret it, as Marx said. Not all social scientists would agree with the idea that research should further these values.

## Politically Engaged Science: Different Strokes for Different Folks

Qualitative researchers have found a wide range of ways of making their research politically relevant. Some aim to conduct research and construct theory in ways that address political and public issues even if their audiences remain largely scholarly and academic; the underlying idea is that no political practice—no matter how impassioned—can succeed unless it is built on sound research and well-designed theory. Others choose to be public intellectuals and hope to participate directly in public debates in the media and to influence the formation of **public policy,** a difficult project in the United States and more feasible in other countries (Wacquant 2009). Finally, some choose to involve themselves not just in scholarly or public debates but also in advocacy and action at ground level, where "the rubber meets the road." One of your many challenges as a qualitative researcher involves identifying your own personal views and convictions and determining how they shape, influence, and otherwise affect the decisions you make and actions you take. This is no easy task, but we promise that if you see it through, eventually you'll be glad you did.

## POLITICAL ENGAGEMENT IN THEORY AND INTERPRETATION

In this section, we discuss various ways that researchers pursue political values in their work and precipitate political controversies. Our discussion begins with the most abstract and theoretical political perspectives and then moves toward more down-to-earth and action-oriented ones. We end the chapter by looking at how critiques of research itself can become highly politicized: When research focuses on the scientific quality or ethical soundness of commonly accepted and highly regarded research methods in a given field, political controversy within the field is almost sure to ignite.

### Mounting a Critique of Existing Concepts and Constructing Alternative Concepts That More Accurately Capture Social Realities

Superficially this goal looks theoretical and cerebral, not political and action-oriented, but French theorists Bourdieu and Wacquant argue that the construction of accurate and objective theoretical constructs is a major political project. Contrary to popular views, highly theoretical and intellectual analysis is not "up in the clouds" or "pie in the sky" but the foundation of effective action to change society. Feminist scholars, Marxists, critical race theorists, and other types of critical theorists have focused on a **critique of prevailing concepts** as a political project, to eliminate terms that perpetuate a way of thinking that sustains and encourages inequalities.

For example, Wacquant's (2004) study of life in Woodlawn, in Chicago's predominantly African American South Side, is a work of "carnal sociology" that emerged from his long-term immersion in a gym where he trained to become a boxer. This study demonstrates how the use of the label "underclass" by scholars and the media has distorted our understanding of the lives of the urban poor. The label misses the larger context of racism and a deteriorating economy in the wake of de-industrialization; and it also misses the microsituations in which people give meaning to their lives.

Similarly, Wacquant shows how use of the term "ghetto" to describe the urban periphery of French cities is an inappropriate carryover of the historical situation of segregation in the United States. In France, the urban periphery includes many public housing projects and is the home of many immigrants from northern and western Africa, but the communities are far more diverse than the U.S. "ghetto." Similarities exist in the residents' feelings of marginalization and frustration about the lack of economic opportunities, but the composition and historical process of establishing these "zones of relegation" as well as the cultural and historical contexts are too different to allow a simple transfer of the term "ghetto" from the United States to contemporary Europe.

In these studies, the central project is the construction of theoretical concepts and terms that respect the *complexity* of social conditions. Wacquant is delving beneath the surface and criticizing terms that were used in a superficial way. The political project here is to clarify theoretical and conceptual foundations so that ultimately political effort can be meaningful and effective. After all, politics is the struggle over the distribution of material and symbolic resources . . . and language is arguably the single greatest symbolic resource of all.

## Dissecting Misrecognition

Research may focus primarily on the **misrecognitions** of the research subjects themselves. This aim is closely related to the goal of theory construction.

**PARTIAL PENETRATION AND ITS CONSEQUENCES**    For example, Paul Willis in his milestone *Learning to Labor* (1981) offered a complex theoretical analysis of why and how white-working-class youths in an English high school—"the lads"—rejected the opportunities offered by the school system, their only possible route of escape from factory jobs and low-wage labor. In his study of how the "lads" were engaged in showing disrespect to school authorities, disruptive antics, disengagement from school work, and constant joking and horseplay, he reveals the causes and consequences of their rejection of schooling.

Willis traces their rejection of formal education to the beliefs and behaviors handed down over generations of social solidarity and resistance to authority in the factory. The lads' inherited worldview celebrates white, masculine solidarity in opposition to individualistic striving for academic achievement. Willis also argues that the lads' rejection of schooling is evidence that the "lads" have "partially penetrated" the capitalist ideology of "success" and individualism. Their fractious stance and actions yield what they perceive as "victories," short-term gains (positive reinforcement from peers, elders, etc.). But the penetration of capitalist ideology is only partial and therefore *deeply flawed*, for the long-term detriments far outweigh the short-term gains to be had from their kind of resistance.

The negative long-term consequences of their actions include low levels of academic achievement and therefore limited job opportunities for individuals; sexism and racism among the lads and therefore the tendency to divide and weaken the working class; and most important of all, the perpetuation of the mental/manual division of labor and with it the rejection of intellectual activity. This disregard for mental activity ultimately thwarts the working class's development of a "hegemonic" (i.e., integrated, all-encompassing, and dominant) vision of an *alternative* to capitalism; instead, members of the working class remain locked in a pattern of self-defeating oppositional behaviors. Willis is sympathetic to the lads and their working-class traditions of resistance, but his central concern is to show the limitations and political ineffectiveness that result from their "partial penetration" of capitalist ideology.

**NIKE TOWN**    Mary Pattillo (1999) offers a similarly critical account of orientations she observed in her ethnographic research in a middle-class African American community in Chicago. She dissects the "ghetto trance" and "reign of Nike" that captivated many of the community's young people, holding them in thrall to self-defeating behaviors such as drug use and consumerist values such as the purchase of expensive athletic gear. A veneer of authentic resistance to "the Man" and defiance of white-middle-class conventions accompanied these attitudes, but Pattillo tears away this veneer and argues that these orientations and behaviors not only block academic achievement and economic success but also turn into hollow substitutes for realistic political struggles.

**THE NECESSARY ILLUSION OF FAMILY:**   In Greg Scott's ethnographic documentary film *The Family at 1312*, we see a female crack dealing "pimp" by the name of "Cat" expound the belief that she and the prostitutes who work for her form a family—a few minutes later we see Cat slap and abuse one of the women for not coming up with enough money to pay a debt she owes to Cat's boyfriend. The word "family" and the narrative of the family are revealed as lies, or at best, self-deluding but "necessary myths" formed and perpetuated among some of the most marginalized and socially overlooked populations in the United States—homeless drug addicts. The viewer is tacitly encouraged to consider the abusiveness and exploitation that characterizes even the most "normal" family relationships ... and to consider how various bastardizations of the meaning of "family" result from our prejudicial treatment of stigmatized populations.

In these studies, the aim of the researchers is to identify the "misrecognitions" that limit the insights and ultimately the political efficacy of the people they observed. This critical account is "out there" for any one to read and indirectly addressed to people like the research subjects. The observer identifies with the subjects, and for that very reason, exposes their misrecognitions.

## Controversy over Context

Researchers' political commitments and points of view are often revealed in the disagreements over the **context** in which observations are interpreted. These controversies are illustrated by the intense disagreement between Loic Wacquant and several other qualitative researchers (Mitch Duneier, Elijah Anderson, and Katherine Newman). In "Scrutinizing the Street," a 2002 article in the *American Journal of Sociology*, Wacquant argued that the three researchers had made serious errors in interpreting the lives of their research subjects, respectively street vendors of books and magazines (Duneier), residents of the black ghetto of Philadelphia (Anderson), and the working poor of Harlem (Newman). Wacquant believes that these errors of interpretation have political implications, leading to a sugar-coating and romanticizing of the experience of poverty and racism and an uncritical stance toward the economic system and racial hierarchy of the United States.

Let's look more closely at Wacquant's critique of Newman's (1999) book, *No Shame in My Game: The Working Poor in the Inner City*. Newman and her research team observed and interviewed fast-food workers in New York City. The point of the study was to show that people are eager to work, and even though their jobs are low-wage, insecure, dead-end, part-time, and dull, the workers find dignity and self-esteem in their work. In many cases, the jobs provide structure and meaning in their lives. Even the rather simple skills that are needed for the jobs—punctuality, handling money and machinery, multitasking and time management, pleasant interaction with customers—are useful. Newman was combating the stereotype that poor inner-city African Americans are lazy and don't want to work.

**MAKING SENSE OF DEAD-END WORK**   Wacquant does not deny that respondents might want to have a job and express positive views about working—work is after all a source of income that is desperately needed by their families. His attack on the book ultimately centers on his contention that Newman's *interpretation* was placed in too narrow a context. Newman's positive interpretation that dead-end jobs are meaningful makes sense in the narrow context of the respondents' immediate situation; in *this context*, poor people's adherence to the work ethic and their employers' claims to be supporting their employees appear to be coherent. But Wacquant believes that theoretically and politically the *appropriate* context for thinking about the observations is not the immediate and local situation, but the economy and society as a whole with its increasingly two-tiered job structure, the growing number of precarious and poorly paid jobs at the lower end of the scale, its insecure and exploitive work conditions, the lack of benefits that workers in Europe enjoy, the weakness of unions, and the inadequate educational system that makes many native-born workers ill-prepared for better jobs.

**FALSE CONSCIOUSNESS**    Wacquant argues that once we *expand the interpretive context* from the immediate observations of the here and now to the larger system of inequality, we would have to reinterpret the work ethic espoused by the workers as a "misrecognition." Instead of feeling grateful to have a job or believing they're deriving some dignity from it, they should be angry about their limited opportunities, the racism and class prejudice they encounter on a daily basis, their weak educational preparation, and the insecure exploitive jobs in which they end up. As a corollary to this, we should also question the respondents' employers' claims that they are supportive of their workers and helping to "lift them up"; from the perspective that Wacquant advocates, we might consider these claims to be at best paternalistic, probably self-deluding, certainly self-serving, and quite possibly fraudulent and exploitative.

**TELL IT LIKE IT IS**    In short, Wacquant argues the readers of the study should not accept the positive spin Newman puts on her the observations because she does not analyze the work experience in the larger stratified, exploitive context. In Wacquant's view, researchers bear the responsibility of speaking out against an economy that fails to provide living wage jobs with job security, opportunities for promotion, and genuine skill development.

Is Wacquant right? What is the best context for interpreting findings—the immediate and local context of the world in which the respondents live or the larger sphere of the U.S. economy, which requires a critical understanding? The example shows us how the politics of qualitative research is often built into the choice of interpretive context so that the same observations might lead to opposite conclusions when they are placed in different contexts.

## ENGAGING IN PUBLIC DISCUSSION

Many scholars inflect their research with politics by challenging taken-for-granted views on how the world operates. They draw from their research insights on which they build critical theory—explanations of social phenomena that illuminate and underscore injustice. Another way of politicizing one's research is to "go public" with it. To work in the public sphere as a sociologist means to combat stereotypes and to inspire the general public to think more critically about the world we share.

### Combating Stereotypes

Qualitative researchers often hold the aim of debunking widely held stereotypes and **taken-for-granted assumptions** (TFGs), especially the ones that circulate in the media and in "conventional wisdom" about ethnic minorities and people with low incomes. **Combating stereotypes** calls for entering broader public debates in forums such as the conventional mass media (e.g., television and radio), "new social media" (e.g., blogs, social networking sites, and other computer-mediated communication), and books addressed to a wide reading public. Also, documentary film is an increasingly popular vehicle by which public intellectuals attempt to transport laypersons into new and different, sociologically shaped representations of various parts of the world, typically those most maligned, overlooked, and/or mistreated.

A pioneering study of this type was Carol Stack's (1974) *All Our Kin*, based on observations of an African American inner-city family. Stack showed how the behavior of family members was by no means "pathological," but rather expressed rational and humane adaptations to the difficult conditions of their lives. The extended "matrifocal" (i.e., mother-centered) family, intricate exchanges of resources and mutual aid (such as taking care of each other's children), and establishment of fictive kinship ("going for cousins") that enlarged their support networks were all effective practices in their circumstances. This analysis complemented Eliot Liebow's observations of "street corner men" in which he showed that apparently "lazy" and "shiftless" actions, such as intermittent work, made sense in the economic, social, and political conditions in which the men lived.

More recently, Mitch Duneier has published two books that document the dignity and self-respect of people who live on the lower rungs of the economic ladder and the racial stratification system. In *Slim's Table* (1994), he portrays the lives of elderly working-class African American men and in *Sidewalk* (2001) the world of street vendors of books and magazines. Both books show people of limited means engaged in helping relationships, establishing social networks, and generally developing humane and adaptive practices that enable them to survive in a harsh urban environment.

Greg Scott's ethnographic documentary *Matrimony* shows the tenderness and affection of a couple whose heroin addiction, homelessness, and life in shelters make it very difficult for them to fulfill the expectations that are associated with state-sanctioned marriage—even the most basic one of privacy and intimacy in their sleeping arrangement. They were punished by expulsion from a shelter for reaching under the curtain between men's and women's quarters simply so they could hold each other's hand while falling asleep.

These studies are examples of stereotype-busting endeavors that are addressed to a larger public, readers and viewers who may hold distorted and demeaning images of poor urban people. Generally, the accounts respect and reiterate the self-definitions of the subjects, diverging in this regard from the studies that analyze subjects' misrecognitions of their situations.

## Exposing Misrecognition and Debunking Stereotypes

Two studies of street gangs combine these approaches as they debunk stereotypes of the gang as a lucrative enterprise for all its members and also expose the gang members' misrecognition of their gang as a "family." Both Felix Padilla (1992) and Greg Scott in "It's a Sucker's Outfit" (2004) found that gang activity is profitable for only a small fraction of gang members. Most gang members work in dangerous conditions for very limited income. The studies not only criticized media and popular stereotypes of gangs as lucrative but also challenged gang members' own mythologizing misrecognitions, their self-images as heroic, successful, and valued in a large, cohesive family-like enterprise. Instead the researchers demonstrate by observation and the use of interview data that the young men are economically exploited, misled, self-deluding, and caught in dead-end tracks.

## The Dangers of Trying a Little Politically Motivated Tenderness

But there are pitfalls in combating stereotypes, most notably the possibility that we will lose our critical view of the larger context in which people find themselves. When we see people who are poor or who experience racial discrimination, act with dignity, self-respect, tenderness, and concern for others, we may focus so much on these positive observations that we lose sight of the unjust and unequal world in which people nevertheless struggle to act with humanity. We find ourselves seduced by our own anti-stereotyping, because if people can be so decent, the world is really an OK place after all—and so we lose some of our will to change its injustices.

The worst-case scenario for research associated with the "combating stereotypes" goal is that the researcher unconsciously censors the observation and reporting of negative behaviors that might reawaken the stereotypes and thus create a "backfire effect" whereby the reader's preexisting stereotypes are reinforced. To consciously and deliberately omit negative behavior from one's data and/or interpretations would be a serious breach of professional ethics, but the diffuse quality of qualitative observation and writing makes it relatively easy to avoid such "inconvenient facts" encountered in the field situation. For example, Wacquant argued that Duneier's very sympathetic account of street vendors of books and magazines avoids discussing their addictions and violent behavior. Wacquant charges that Duneier discretely avoided situations in which he ran the risk of seeing negative behaviors (Wacquant 2002).

## Critical Examination of the State of Social Services and Government Policies

Qualitative researchers engage not only in dissecting ideologies and images, but also in **critical analysis of institutions and practices**, and some of these studies are focused on social services and government policies. A major purpose of many qualitative studies is examining who is served by social services, the quality of service delivery and the human impact of problems in delivery, and problems associated with government policies. This approach is a good example of Mills' sociological imagination at work in qualitative research; the personal troubles of individuals turn out to be results of public issues in social services.

A recent widely discussed study of this type is Eric Klinenberg's *Heat Wave* (2002). Klinenberg organized his study as a social autopsy (see Chapter 9, "Social Autopsies," for further discussion of this design). He dissected the causes and consequences of the hundreds of deaths that occurred during the 1995 Chicago heat wave in excess of the normal July death rate. As temperatures soared over 100 degrees Fahrenheit, death rates were higher than usual and autopsies showed that the causes of death were heat-related. Most of the dead were elderly people who lived alone and were isolated from networks of friends and family. They were disproportionately likely to be white or African American rather than Latino or Asian.

But to read *Heat Wave* as a discussion of ethno-racial differences in the care of elderly relatives (as readers are inclined to do if they don't read beyond Chapter 2 of the book) is to miss Klinenberg's most important conclusions: Vibrant communities with a dense and lively social fabric are a protective factor; and the heat-related deaths are the tragic results of the reorganization of social services in the neoliberal era. By "neoliberal," Klinenberg means the withdrawal of the state from the regulation of markets and provision of social services that started during the Reagan presidency and continues to the present. Social services were not completely eliminated at the federal, state, and local level, but they were sharply cut back and reorganized along the lines of a "smart consumer" model that required an active, informed population ready to seek out information, make informed choices, and develop strategies for obtaining services from downsized, unresponsive public and privatized service providers.

This model was completely inappropriate for getting help to elderly, ill, isolated people, many of whom lived in neighborhoods they found frightening and dangerous. Klinenberg analyzes these scaled-down services, the ineffective last-minute effort to use police to rescue at-risk people—a task for which police were not adequately trained—and the cover-up of the heat wave crisis by City Hall and its compliant allies in the media. In short, this study packs a powerful punch against the institutions that should have been looking out for the ill and elderly.

## Identifying Inequalities in Service Delivery

Closely related to the preceding goal is the aim of **identifying inequalities or disparities** in the delivery of services such as health care or schooling. Qualitative research enables the researcher to "get inside" institutions and observe processes within them that result in disparities.

In quantitative data, these systematic differences in outcomes may be hard to discern or if they are discernible, they remain "opaque" and hard to explain. For example, in national quantitative data, it is difficult to assess the quality—as opposed to the quantity—of education respondents have received. The data report the number of years of schooling or the highest degree completed; they may tell us little about what has been learned. The General Social Survey (a large national survey conducted on a regular basis) only records years-completed and highest degree, and this uncritically quantitative method for measuring "educational attainment" is common in many surveys as well as government statistics. But schools are very unequal in the quality of education they provide, especially in the United States where they are administered locally and financed by a combination of state and local taxes.

The results of this policy are major differences among districts and schools in per pupil school expenditures, teacher pay, resources, and so on. For example, in the Chicago area, one of the wealthy North Shore suburban districts spends about nearly twice as much per student per year as does the Chicago Public School system. There may also be large disparities within school districts, as well as differences in how individual children are treated within schools depending on their class, race, gender, and the impressions teachers have of their families and homes. Qualitative research can reveal these disparities, and we will use examples from the sociology of education to illustrate this type of research.

Valerie Polakow (1993) observed how teachers expected less from children whose mothers received AFDC ("welfare") and provided less support and attention to these children in the classroom. Johnson and Johnson (2006), themselves experienced teachers as well as professors of education at University of Louisiana-Monroe, spent a year teaching in a poor community in Louisiana whose major asset and employer was a state prison. The children were subjected to high-stakes testing and taught to pass tests rather than enjoy learning. Teachers were poorly paid and not treated as professionals by administrators and the state education agencies. The Johnsons' observation and analysis takes us inside the school and traces practices and interactions that resulted in the children being poorly prepared for complex skills and higher education. Their qualitative methodology enables the readers to understand the whole process that produces low educational outcomes in a community and by extension, throughout the nation. Jonathan Kozol (1992) drew attention to these disparities among schools, strongly associated with school financing as well as race and class, in an influential book called *Savage Inequalities*; his work made an important contribution to public debate about school funding, but it was more journalistic and less in-depth than the Johnsons' observations in one school for an entire year.

While Polakow, the Johnsons, and Kozol all looked at unsatisfactory, inadequate, and demeaning school experiences, Jean Anyon (1980) used qualitative research focused on classroom interaction to develop a comparative analysis of four types of schools, each associated with a different social class. The school in a predominantly working-class community featured authoritarian behavior from teachers, boring drills, and student misconduct because the children were so bored and hostile.

Teachers in the lower-middle-class school emphasized "following the rules"; they appeared intent on preparing the children for a lifetime of routine clerical work that required attention to detail and compliance with regulations. The school in which children came from professional homes encouraged creative projects and freedom to make their own learning choices in a "hippy-dippy" individualistic atmosphere. The most remarkable insights came from the research team's observations in a school attended by children of business and managerial elites. In this school the teachers fostered analytic skills and in-depth knowledge. Each child was taken very seriously by the teachers, and attention was given to reasoning skills and the process of organizing knowledge. For example, children talked about different ways of solving math problems rather than having the teacher say "do it my way" and "there is only one to get the answer." While children were encouraged to develop high-level intellectual skills and knowledge in an atmosphere of discussion and the exchange of ideas, fewer opportunities for individualistic and creative projects were offered than in the school of the children of professionals.

In short, in each school teachers acted in a way that anticipated the work situations the children would face in the future and prepared them for their "class destinies." Although essentially all of the children would eventually complete elementary school, they had learned vastly different lessons. Large disparities were created in how they used knowledge, developed reasoning skills, and gained confidence in their creative and analytic capabilities. Only observation of classroom interaction—not a precoded survey item about elementary school completion—could fully reveal these disparities.

## Critique of Organizational Practices

The critique of organizational practices and behaviors is closely related to the preceding aim of examining disparities, but instead of assessing practices "from the outside" by observing harmful consequences, the researcher gets inside the organization and sees how these harmful or risky practices are conceived and implemented. This research strategy requires entry into an organization (such as a corporation or a government agency), contacts with people inside it who are prepared to talk to the interviewer, interviews with people who have left the organization, and/or scrutiny of publicly available documents that reveal information about organizational decision making. This type of research is similar to investigative journalism, but the researcher is constrained by the norms of confidentiality and anonymity; whereas the ethics of journalism call for the identification of sources, the ethics of sociological research call for confidentiality of sources.

Diana Vaughan's 1996 study of the *Challenger* launch decision is an excellent example of qualitative analysis of problems in an organization, in this case the decision to go ahead with the 1986 *Challenger* launch in very cold temperatures which resulted in the deaths of all the individuals on board. Vaughan did not work at NASA or its contractors, so her data are based on interviews and documents. She was able to reconstruct the process of decision making within these organizations that led to minimizing the risks of a launch in cold weather, eventually culminating in the fatal choice of a launch at near-freezing temperatures. She refers to this process of minimizing risks, the outcome of interaction among engineers and managers, as "routinization of deviance" and argues that it became part of the organizational culture.

Although Vaughan does not write in a polemical tone, it is clear that her position is that processes within an organization can lead to unnecessary risks and potentially harmful consequences for the public or for specific populations or individuals.

## Studying the Rich and Powerful

Anyon's analysis of the learning provided to the children of the business elite points to another political direction in qualitative research—studying people and communities of wealth and power. Many years ago when one of the authors (Roberta) was a graduate student at the University of Chicago, Professor Morris Janowitz threw out a challenge to his Social Organization class:

> It's easy to study the disadvantaged—the poor and powerless—and many socio-logists do it; but we need to study the rich and powerful—that is much harder to do because they are hard to contact, live in homes that are protected by doormen and security guards, and find it easy to keep their distance from sociological researchers . . .

The barriers to studying the rich and powerful are even more formidable 40 years later as entire communities are now gated and corporations are more inclined to be secretive and indifferent to their public image. This is one of the principal reasons that social scientists are much more likely to "study down" than they are to "study up."

This state of affairs means that much sociological research "upwards" has to rely on archival data or on the occasional sociologist of wealthy social origins who is prepared to be a "class traitor" and writes about the life of his/her community of origin. For example, in the 1950s, Digby Baltzell was able to write about the "Philadelphia gentleman" because he was one of them. Le Wita (1994) wrote about French bourgeois culture as an individual who had grown up in it. An important study of prep schools, *Preparing for Power* by Cookson and Persell (1985) used interviews, observations, and school records to present a portrait of these schools, and its insights were enhanced by the fact that Cookson had attended a prep school himself. Much like Anyon's study, it showed the sophistication, rigor, and preparation for decision making offered by the academic curriculum as well as revealing stresses in the lives of young people who lived away from parents and understood that they were destined to wield economic and political power.

As conflict theories became popular in the 1960s and 1970s, researchers devised methods for understanding the behavior of elites. One was to use public records to trace "interlocking directorates" that linked corporations to each other and created social networks among clusters of companies as well as nonprofits, lobbying firms, and public agencies. Domhoff (1975) attempted to understand the world of the power elite by observations of elites at play in a place he called "Bohemian Grove," an exclusive resort catering to the top corporate and political echelons. More recently, Sennett (in the *Corrosion of Character*, 1998) provides a brief report on his presence at the world economic forum in Davos, Switzerland, and contrasts the excitement and pleasure in market risk expressed by elites to the fears and insecurities that flexible capitalism and deregulated financial markets provoke among the less fortunate. Karen Ho's ethnography of Wall Street (2009) provides a more detailed account of a culture governed entirely by risk, impermanence, and the pursuit of money. George Marcus (1992) wrote ethnographic studies about dynastic families, entities that maintain their wealth through the construction of trusts and other legal instruments.

R. Khurana carried out a brilliant study of the CEO selection process using a mix of quantitative and qualitative methods, especially interviews, for a book entitled *Searching for a Corporate Savior* (2002). Khurana's study provides insight into several aspects of the CEO selec-tion process: Why and how do boards of directors and CEOs reproduce themselves socially and demographically, constantly replicating themselves as a group of white men of middle- to upper-class backgrounds? And why and how has the CEO selection process led to soaring CEO compen-sation in the United States, which is now  over 500 times the amount that average employees of a firm receive? Khurana explodes the myth that these astronomical amounts are necessary to "attract the most talented people" to top positions, and he shows how the increases are produced by the social dynamics of the selection process. Qualitative methods are not needed to tell us that CEOs are still predominantly white men or that they get a lot of money! But what Khurana accomplishes is documenting the process and revealing how apparently open and rational selection procedures result in social reproduction of elites and irrationally huge compensation.

Despite impressive breakthroughs such as Khurana's study, qualitative research on elites remains a difficult enterprise.

## ACTIVISM: FROM SPOKESPERSON TO CBPR

Over the years, qualitative researchers have often said that their aim is to "give voice" to the aspirations and views of communities that are marginalized or silenced. Like "empowerment" (a related aim), this political purpose is fraught with ambiguities and challenges.

One way of accomplishing this goal is combating stereotypes and presenting a fair, in-depth, and sympathetic description of communities that are frequently misrepresented or portrayed in demeaning ways. We have already discussed this purpose in the section on combating stereotypes.

Closely related to this purpose is the goal of documenting the struggles of ordinary people to improve their lives and change their circumstances. These struggles are rarely covered in the media, and when they are, they are often described in a distorted or dismissive way. Lillian Rubin's (1976) accounts of the hopes and daily lives of working-class families and the work of Michael Burawoy and his students (1991) in documenting small-scale political struggles—in a bakery, in a school, in the Cambodian-American community, and so on—are examples of this type of research. These studies still fall within the category of "struggles in representation"—the point of the research is an intellectual and representational one, to make readers more familiar and sympathetic with people whose lives they might otherwise know little about.

To go beyond these largely academic accounts and actually "give voice" in a more politically charged way is a challenging undertaking for several reasons.

**LIMITED ACCESS TO POWER**   First of all, researchers themselves usually have only limited access to public forums, public agenda-setting, and the "policy process." Most scholars in the United States have very little access to or influence on politicians, business elites, policy makers, and the media. The media are reluctant to involve scholars in their programming and think readers and viewers will not want to hear about research or follow complicated arguments based on data. One of the authors (Roberta) attended a session with the op-ed page editor of a major metropolitan daily at which would-be op-ed writers were told never to use the phrase "my research shows…" or "one of the findings of my research is…"; what is expected at the beginning of an op-ed piece is a human interest story. In recent years and even throughout U.S. history, professors were only occasionally included among top policy advisors. Sociologists who would like to become public intellectuals, following in the footsteps of W.E.B. DuBois, rarely find encouragement from peers, university administrators, or the media. The situation is more open to researchers in other countries, such as France (Wacquant 2009).

**POLITICS OF VOCALIZING FOR OTHERS**   Another issue is that "giving voice" is a highly ambiguous goal. The researcher can end up assuming a paternalistic role with the community. After all why should a researcher represent the community—shouldn't community members do this for themselves? Aren't their own voices good enough? (Just as the expression "to empower" is ambiguous—either people claim and exercise power for themselves, or they don't—why should a community be the object of empowerment and who is doing it to them?)

It is probably better to think of the researcher as a facilitator and resource person for a community, not as its spokesperson. The researcher can use connections to universities, media, the legal profession, and other institutions to help community members pursue their goals. Ideas and products (such as photo exhibits) of the community can circulate to larger audiences and viewers with the help of the researcher. The researcher can involve legal and scientific experts (such as environmental scientists) and introduce them to community organizations that can benefit from their knowledge. Another aspect of the researcher's role can be to help the community members come together to discuss and define their own goals. Research designs and methods such as photo-voice and documentary film can spark these kinds of discussions.

## Realistic Ways for Sociologists to Assist Struggling Communities

Researchers are developing ways in which their research can benefit the communities in which they work:

1. Sharing data with the community that community activists can use; providing information, data, or techniques of collection and analysis to **advocacy groups.**
2. Testifying in court or legislative hearings as **expert witnesses**, as Kai Erikson (1976) did on behalf of plaintiffs in the Buffalo Creek flood disaster and developing a **social autopsy** which reveals practices that caused or exacerbated disasters (which we will discuss in Chapter 9).
3. **Community-based participatory research** in which community members work with the researcher to define research goals and design the study so that it yields information that is meaningful to community members and not just to scholarly researchers or policy makers (see Chapter 10).

We will look at these ways of connecting research to political goals in more detail in Chapters 9 and 10.

## THE CRITICAL ANALYSIS OF RESEARCH METHODS

We already discussed how a critical purpose of qualitative research is to examine widely used concepts such as "underclass" and to challenge stereotypes in the media. Qualitative research can be used to critique not only concepts and notions but also research practices themselves. Research can reveal that research methods and techniques may be scientifically flawed or ethically questionable. The critical analysis of research methods can reveal that the methods in question do not "do what they were designed to do"—that the data they produce is not of sufficient quality to support conclusions and answer research questions.

A critical analysis of this type is almost certain to lead to controversies among researchers and disputes between the critics and defenders of the method in question. These disputes in turn are linked to power differences among individuals within professional institutions (such as funding agencies and journals) and ultimately to distribution of resources such as grants. We provide an example of this type of critical analysis of a research method and the ensuing firestorm from Greg's qualitative and ethnographic evaluation of a sampling technique called "respondent-driven sampling" that has been used in the study of "hidden populations."

## The Politics of Researching Research: A Critique of Respondent-Driven Sampling

In 2004, the Chicago Department of Public Health (CDPH) retained one of the authors (Greg) as a consultant on their public health study of HIV/AIDS risk among injection drug users (IDUs). They put him in charge of conducting a front-end "ethnographic assessment" of the city's IDUs. Greg's objective was simple enough—furnish guidance and support, grounded in empirical street-level qualitative and ethnographic research, to CDPH as they prepared to conduct a citywide survey of IDUs. Given CDPH's disengagement with the IDU population, they needed Greg to help them figure out the basics: Who are IDUs? Where do they live? How do they go about using their drugs? Where do they use their drugs? What drugs do they inject? How do they inject? The central question, however, was, "What can we do to maximize our chances of finding and then surveying people who have every reason to remain 'hidden,' unfound, and unsurveyed?"

Here's a firsthand account of how this study of a study became the centerpiece of a highly contentious, at times quite nasty, debate over the methodology. From this point forward, Greg will be writing in the first person ....

## Case Study

The U.S. Centers for Disease Control and Prevention (CDC) held the purse strings for this study, and they were funding not only CDPH but approximately 24 other cities' health departments as well. Ultimately CDC wanted to develop a kind of "snapshot" of HIV risk and protective factors among IDUs nationwide. The CDC had selected a strategy for penetrating this "hidden population" whose members are notoriously difficult to locate much less to interview. To recruit and enroll IDUs in their study, the CDC decided they would employ "respondent-driven sampling" (RDS), the then "hot commodity" on the survey sampling market.

RDS is similar to snowball sampling (i.e., "word of mouth" recruitment), except that it supposedly produces a representative, though nonrandomly obtained, subject sample. The method operates in roughly the same way a pyramid scheme runs. First, it's based on "dual incentive"—you interview a subject and pay her an "incentive" ($20 on average for this study). And you give her three nonduplicable "coupons," which she then presumably hands

out to her fellow injection drug users—the peers who comprise her closest personal network. Each one of the peers who comes in and gets interviewed receives the same $20 payment and receives three coupons himself, which he then hands out to *his* friends. For each peer who redeems a coupon and completes an interview, the person who recruited him receives a "finder's fee" (usually $10). So, if you're in the study, you get paid $20 when they interview you, and then you get $10 for each of the three coupons that your "friends" redeem. In total, you stand to make $50 from this study. For a street-level drug addict, that's really good money ... and it's easy money.

On the streets, easy money often breeds hard times, at least for some. In the first few weeks of the actual study, I observed several predictable instances in which IDUs were attempting to "hustle" the RDS system. Some of the hustles were relatively benign (e.g., teaching one's noninjector friends how to "fake" their way into the study), while others were more troubling (e.g., physically abusing a romantic

(*continued*)

*(continued)*

partner who was taking too long to redeem her coupon). Then I began to notice more systematic, or patterned, hustles, such as IDUs running "training programs" designed to teach groups of crack smokers how to pass the study's screening interview and get into the study even though they had never injected drugs before. The most distressing pattern involved "owners" of "shooting galleries" (densely populated spaces in which IDUs congregate to inject their drugs, socialize, etc.) collecting gallery occupants' coupons, strategically distributing them to carefully selected IDUs, and then reaping the rewards of finder's fees collected en masse. Several other methodological problems came to light; full details of the study can be found online at http://www.ijdp.org/article/S0955-3959(07)00250-2/abstract.

As the study's consultant, I shared my observations with the study's principal investigator at CDPH and the CDC's Chicago liaison. I sought and obtained permission to implement an ethnographic study of the RDS process. The objective was to employ qualitative methodology to investigate the use of mixed-methods—I was using methods to study methods.

Upon conclusion of the study, I decided to publish my results. Notwithstanding the findings my study generated, I still had reason to believe that RDS was (and still is) the best available mechanism for sampling IDUs and other hidden populations. In fact, I wrote this very statement in the article that was eventually (2008) published in a widely read special edition of the *International Journal of Drug Policy*. Even before the article's publication, I found myself in the middle of a political firestorm, with public health scholars attacking my article, the study, and even me as a person. Amidst rapidly elevating heat and controversy, the journal editors decided to allow a select few detractors to read my article in advance of its publication and to publish letters of response.

The select few detractors weren't chosen randomly. IJDP's editors handpicked the most vocal opponents and solicited response letters from them. The opponents were the "inventors" of RDS, the high-priced consultants whom the CDC had retained for the purpose of monitoring its implementation of RDS, the CDPH executive manager and principal investigator, the director of CDC's national surveillance project, and the Chicago-based IDU researcher whom I had "beaten out" for the position of project consultant (who later replaced me when my contract was terminated).

These highly regarded public health scholars published scathing letters of response attacking not only me and my research but ethnographic research in general. To their credit, the journal's editors allowed me to read their letters in advance and prepare my own letter of response to their responses. The letters can be found online at http://www.ijdp.org/issues/contents?issue_key=S0955-3959(08)X0005-2. The letters contained little science, but many personal attacks. In my responses I tried to refocus the discussion on the scientific issues.

A close reading of the article, the responses, and my rejoinder will lead you to form the conclusion, as stated explicitly in the article, that I was not attacking RDS or the people who use it, much less the people who "invented" it. Already in the abstract I clearly state my belief that RDS remains the best available means for sampling hidden populations. It does not follow, however, that RDS should be sheltered from critical scrutiny. My goal was to examine RDS's inner workings with an eye toward improving the method's capacity for accruing representative samples while simultaneously doing the best possible job of protecting the human subjects from whom we collect data. In the long run, my article may improve the method, but in the short run it produced trouble for me.

Since the publication of the article and the letters, I was replaced by CDPH with a scholar whom I had beaten out for the consultant position and who published one of the angry letters. I no longer received appointments as a consultant for CDC studies of IDUs, and one of my colleagues does not want to be associated with me because he worries that the association might lead to a negative decision on his application for CDC funding.

My conclusions are, however, supported by the swiftly swelling stream of published articles presenting critiques of RDS in terms of human-subjects violations and other methodological quirks. On the horizon I see (and am involved with) publication of articles that expose RDS's substantive weaknesses as well and these may produce a repeat of the angry responses.

The moral of this story is that scholarship involves funding and symbolic power in the form of status—and therefore politics. I published an article based on rigorous qualitative research, and it represented a serious critique of the core methodology of a very well-funded research study. But the powerful stakeholders prevailed, the article had little immediate effect on research practices, and I ended up without funding and in relative isolation. I would think twice before doing it again . . . anywhere.

## CONCLUSION

In this chapter, we have seen that qualitative research often flows from political engagement and is embroiled in and/or instigates political controversies. The researcher must never falsify data in order to pursue political ends and must always make clear the political commitments and goals of the study, but beyond these two safeguards, a political orientation is not necessarily a barrier to good research. Researchers must also keep in mind Weber's warning that scientific research cannot in and of itself lead to the attainment of political goals; rather, it can serve to clarify limitations and barriers to their attainment.

Political goals can be actualized in many different ways, ranging from improving theory construction and critiquing methods at the scholarly end of the spectrum to expert witness and advocacy at the applied and overtly engaged end. In the middle of the spectrum, we can find many ways of bringing research findings into **public discussion** and pursuing the commitment to the "sociological imagination" and the role of **public intellectual**.

## Exercises

1. Instead of starting with a topic for research (as you did in Chapters 1 and 3), begin with a situation that you think needs to be changed or reformed. Discuss why. Would qualitative research aimed at explaining the situation also contribute to changing it? Why or why not? (Example: Homelessness in the United States: Is this a problem? Can we study it using qualitative methods? Give an example of qualitative research on this topic. How could the information you find in your study help to solve or remedy this problem?)

2. Many people use the word "bias" to refer to the orientation or values of a researcher or journalist that have clearly influenced a study or report. What does the word mean to you? Where would you draw the line between the perspective of the researcher as a citizen and human being (which every person has) and a "biased" view that makes

the study less accurate and valuable? If you believe that "bias" is always a bad thing, how do you think researchers can guard against it? If not, when is it OK? Can you give an example of a study you read that seemed too biased to you—and discuss in what way it was biased? Can you give an example of a research project that has absolutely no bias whatsoever (i.e., it's "bias-free"), from start to finish?

3. The chapter starts with a quote from Max Weber about discovering inconvenient facts or truths. Thomas Jefferson wrote we should not be afraid to follow truth wherever it may lead. Can you give an example of a study you have read in which the researcher uncovered an inconvenient truth—what was the truth he or she found and in what way was it inconvenient? To whom was it inconvenient?

4. Many social scientists have a basically liberal political position. What does that mean? Can you identify any studies or research reports that were conservative? Radical? Some perspectives are both theoretical and political—for example, Marxism and feminism. Can you identify studies that were written by social scientists who held these viewpoints? Did their perspectives affect the way they stated research questions or framed their conclusions?

5. As you think about studies you have read, which ones seemed the most emotionally and politically neutral or "value-free"? Which seemed the most clearly committed to values? Discuss the reasons for your answers.

6. Think about a subject that you believe you know very, very well—the one thing you know better than anything else. Now, write out a sociological analysis of that subject, or thing, or whatever. Put it away for at least a day or two. Return to it as though you are a stranger to the issue. Review the analysis critically, and write up your analysis. Be sure to focus on all the ways that your analysis is biased, skewed, based on faulty taken-for-granted assumptions, value-driven theories, and so on. In other words, investigate yourself ... turn a skeptical eye on your own work. What did you learn from this?

## Key Terms

activism *81*

advocacy groups *82*

bias *68*

combating stereotypes *75*

context of interpretation *74*

critical analysis of institutions and practices *77*

critical analysis of research methods *82*

critique of: concept construction *72*

organizational practices *79*

prevailing concepts *72*

documenting research choice *70*

expert witness *82*

identifying inequalities or disparities *78*

inconvenient facts *68*

leading (or "push/pull") questions *68*

misrecognition *73*

political engagement *72*

public discussion *85*

public intellectuals *85*

public policy *72*

Community-based participatory research social justice 82

sociological imagination *71*

studying the rich and powerful *79*

taken-for-granted assumptions *75*

transparency *69*

truth *70*

"Whose Side Are We On?" *69*

# 6

# Integrating Theory Into Qualitative Research: Foundational, Grounded, and Critical-Reflexive Theories

## OVERVIEW

In this chapter, we discuss the meaning of "theory" and its significance and role in the actual doing of qualitative research. We begin with a basic introduction to theory—what it is and isn't—and then we present different ways of integrating theories into qualitative research and using our findings to build a theoretical understanding of our research topic.

## THE MEANING OF "THEORY": WHAT IT IS, WHAT IT ISN'T

Theory is a statement about how the world works; not the whole world (usually), but rather some part of the world that the researcher finds particularly interesting. It is not an explanation of one incident, a specific prediction, or an educated guess about what is likely to happen, but a general idea about what satisfactory explanations should look like. A theory is a general strategy for explaining human actions, not an explanation of any specific action or instance.

Theory and research (data collection) are dynamically intertwined, mutually influential, and constantly evolving. A study can't be good unless its theoretical and empirical foundations are connected organically. Becker's description of the relationship is insightful: "The connection between theory and research, put simply and abstractly, is that theories raise questions, suggest things to look at, point to what we don't yet know, and research answers questions but also makes us aware of things we hadn't thought of, which in turn suggest theoretical possibilities" (2008: xi). This is a lot of back and forth, and back and forth again!

How can we go from the data that we are producing to the theories that will help us organize the material and make sense of our empirical findings? Theory comes in many different forms, and they vary in their substantive focus, so let's look at different ways of bringing theory into our research.

## Foundational Theory

**Foundational theories** are selected at a very early point in the research project. They guide the way we ask research questions and directly shape why we ask the questions, how we frame them, and why we pick a particular research design. Foundational theories are commonly used by sociologists to understand the social world. Examples of these include Weberian **conflict theories, Marxist theories, structural functionalism, symbolic interaction**, and **feminist theories**. These theories provide a framework, or lens, through which we can view the world in its entirety. A foundational theory is a way of thinking about the world and explaining what we observe in daily life at the microlevel and the macrolevel.

In recent decades, new theories have become excellent candidates for foundational theories, such as the work of Pierre Bourdieu on fields and different types of capital; Michel Foucault's analysis of discourses, practices, and social control; and social constructionist theories that "take apart" or deconstruct the way gender, race, and class inequalities and structures of dominance are formed by discourses, practices, and interactions (Hancock and Garner 2009).

## Grounded Theory

**Grounded theory** is a systematic strategy for moving from specific observations to general conclusions about discourses, actions, interactions, and practices. An important step of grounded theory is comparing two situations or contexts, and this step allows us to make generalizations based on our observations. Unlike foundational theory, grounded theory avoids an explicit initial a *priori* choice of one of the "big" theories of the social sciences.

## Critical-Reflexive Theory

**Critical-reflexive theory** is built by consciously focusing on and overcoming the gaps and tensions that beset social research: the tension between the scientific method and our own individual perspectives that are based on our experiences; the tension between being an objective observer and recognizing the presence of a multiplicity of subjective points of view, including our own; and the gap between the microlevel at which we observe and the macrolevel about which we would like to reach conclusions. This approach to theory is critical and reflexive because we are always looking at our own assumptions and the prevailing "conventional wisdom" as we carry out our research; we do not take anything for granted, especially not "common sense." We scrutinize everything—the opinions of our research subjects, the conventional wisdom of the media, the prevailing notions of our field of scholarship, and our own assumptions.

These three ways of integrating theory into a research project are not mutually exclusive, and both foundational and grounded theories can be developed critically and reflexively.

# FOUNDATIONAL THEORY IN ACTION: RESEARCH ILLUSTRATIONS

In this section, we take each of the three theoretical perspectives, or levels, described earlier and demonstrate how you might go about formulating a research question and project around particular issues. We take each theory in turn, beginning with foundational theory.

## Foundational Theory in Action

To reiterate, by foundational theory we mean theories and explanations that we explicitly choose to use in our research at an early point in the process. These theories guide our research questions and subsequent research choices. They provide a vocabulary for thinking about our topic or the situation we hope to understand. Foundational theories are present from the start of a project.

Let's begin this section with an exercise in choosing theories. Currently the United States has an extremely high level of indebtedness for businesses, government, and individuals. How do we measure the level of debt of a nation? One way of measuring debt of households and individuals is to compute the ratio of personal debt for the country as a whole to the household income of the country as a whole. In the United States, this ratio has climbed steadily during recent decades from values less than 1 (meaning there is more household income than debt) to values that exceed 1 (meaning there is more debt than household income), and it currently stands at over 1.30. Why did this increase take place? Take a few minutes before you continue reading and think about how you would explain this fact. You might think about the experiences of yourself, friends, and family or about things you have read, seen, and heard in the media or in books. Terms like "shopaholic," "subprime mortgages," "foreclosures," and "student loans" might flash through your mind as you start to think about this question. Can you suggest an explanation or cause for the debt phenomenon?

OK, now that you've taken a few minutes to think about your explanation, let's look at four foundational theories that might help us understand this situation. Selecting one of these theories leads us to frame the issue in distinct ways, ask distinct questions, and make specific decisions about our research strategy.

**THEORY 1, IRRATIONAL CHOICES**    This theory focuses on irrational unconscious choices. Increasing indebtedness was the result of irrational individual thought processes. People were unable to delay gratification and they responded unthinkingly to advertising and media pressures. Infantile needs and impulses, poor impulse control, and unconscious drives that emerge from primitive parts of the brain—perhaps even "the reptilian brain"—led individuals to act without reason and self-control. People seeking to satisfy wants (not needs) and exercising little or no control over their impulses got deeply into debt.

**THEORY 2, A CULTURE OF OVERCONSUMPTION**    This theory also points to individual choices, but it does not use labels such as "infantile," "irrational," "unconscious drives," and "poor impulse control." This theory is about social pressures and culture; the explanation focuses on changes in culture, symbols, media, frames and discourses, and the reference groups to which individuals compare themselves. Individuals and families no longer compare themselves to local role models ("keeping up with the Joneses"—who lived next door) but aspire to enjoy the lifestyles of celebrities and to enter the fabulous fantasy world of advertisements (Schor 1998). As a big gap opened up between the incomes of the middle class and the incomes of the upper fifth of the population, middle-class individuals compared themselves increasingly to a segment of the population that had much more money to spend than they did; and this comparison fueled growing debt to keep up with the "moving target" of an affluent lifestyle.

Theories 1 and 2 share a social psychological approach in that both emphasize individual behaviors and orientations. But Theory 1 is more intraindividual and uses psychoanalytic concepts such as the unconscious, infantile wishes, and impulse control. It is influenced by Freudian theory, while Theory 2 points to the way people's thinking and feeling are shaped by media and peers and changed by historical shifts in symbols and culture. However, both theories posit that individuals made mistakes in assessing their needs and resources. Lacking an understanding of financial markets and the meaning of interest payment, they assumed mortgages they could not pay. Eager home-buyers assumed NINA mortgages—"no income, no assets"—with huge interest payments. As a student of ours (Jasmine Davis) put it well, they engaged in "overzealous consumption."

**THEORY 3, RATIONAL ACTION THEORY—COPING WITH THE ECONOMY**    From the perspective of rational action theory (RAT; or rational choice theory), a growing level of debt was the result of basically rational decisions by households coping with the problem of how to maintain an acceptable standard of living while facing new and increasing needs. These needs were experienced as pressures to own a home because condo conversions reduced rental stock, to own several cars because multi-earner families faced multiple long commutes on divergent routes, to pay for college tuition because educational credentials inflated, and to buy medical insurance when employer contributions declined. These pressures led U.S. residents to accumulate debt after having calculated the costs and benefits of going "into the red." In the economy of the past three decades, with declining public services and largely stagnating incomes, households were forced to assume a high level of debt to just maintain their standard of living. The huge debt of student loans is a prime example of how individuals and families went into debt to remain competitive in the job market. Rational action theory, or rational choice theory, explains debt as a rational choice—a reflection of calculation of the costs and benefits of perceived alternative solutions—of individuals and households in contemporary economic circumstances. Most people were not behaving wildly or irrationally when they went into debt; debt became a way of coping with real problems in household finances and everyday life.

**THEORY 4, THE CAPITALIST SYSTEM IN THE ERA OF GLOBALIZATION**    A Marxist theorist might say that debt was a product of social structure, an individual "solution" to the stagnation of wages after 1980. In an increasingly free-market and deregulated capitalist economy, potential discontent among working people was managed by a high level of debt. Workers were paid less than they needed or wanted, and the gap was filled by rising levels of indebtedness. This theory is substantially different from the more individual-level explanations of the first three theories. It emphasizes historical changes at the macrolevel—the whole society and the global capitalist economy. It shifts the focus from individuals and households to social classes and economic institutions.

## Evaluating Foundational Theories in Action

Which of these theoretical approaches do you like best? Which explanation of the high level of consumer debt in the United States do you think is most convincing? Why? Are they compatible with each other or do you have to pick one of them and reject the others? Are any of them similar to the explanations you thought of?

Notice the following characteristics of theories:

- They are all very "large" explanatory frameworks—the basic concepts can be applied to many different situations and they are not specific to the question of consumer debt. We can use cultural theory, rational choice theory, psychoanalytic theories, or Marxist theories to provide explanations for many situations.
- Theories are not entirely incompatible with each other. They operate at different levels and we can do a little mixing and matching of the explanations. For example, we could subscribe to Theory 4 (Marxist and macrolevel) and also agree with one or the other of the first three theories that are based more on rational or irrational individual motivations and the effects of culture, interaction, or unconscious drives. Perhaps we could even agree with all four theories! Marxist theory explains what happened at the macro- or societal level, and the individual-level theories apply to different kinds of individuals—for example, some got into debt for irrational reasons, while others had to borrow money to survive. But some theorists are jealous and exclusive about theoretical explanations; they insist that a single theory is best and can encompass all of the other types of explanations—"thou shall not contemplate any other theoretical perspective!"
- **Grand theories** of this type are very difficult to disprove, or falsify (to recall a term we covered in depth previously). They are frames or discourses that indicate what we should think about as we try to explain a phenomenon (such as the U.S. debt burden). In this sense, they are not easily subject to falsifiability as are specific hypotheses, which can be challenged by research findings.
- Theories specify terms, concepts, and explanations that work within the theory. These components hang together and are connected to each other in a discourse. Theories ask us to learn a vocabulary; if we master a number of key terms and concepts, we are on our way to learning the theory. Each theory provides a set of boxes—concepts—into which we can place our observations of behaviors and actions. The boxes of psychoanalytic theory have labels such as "infantile wishes" and "irrational impulses." The boxes of Marxist theory have labels such as "unregulated markets," "class conflict over income and wealth," and "commodities." The boxes of cultural theories are labeled "frames," "media," "discourses," and "reference groups." Because each theory has its own vocabulary, theories often appear to "talk past one another."
- Some terms and explanations are not considered scientific because they have either been disproven as not very useful in understanding empirical reality or not amenable to empirical verification at all. Scientific theories do not permit us to refer to God, spirits, the Devil, or space aliens to explain social behaviors and situations. "The Devil made me do it" is not a scientific explanation of a crime or a mortgage default! Social scientists also avoid "conspiracy theories"—simplistic explanations based on the notion that a few individual masterminds are in cahoots with one another to control everything that happens in the social world. Racialist theorists that explain social behaviors in terms of the genetically inherited characteristics of a small number of distinct races have been found to be inadequate explanations.
- Theories can give priority to the macro- or microlevel, but good theories bridge these levels. For example, Marxist and Weberian theories are thought of as macrolevel, but they encompass ideas about individual actions, orientations, and interactions. Symbolic inter-action and Goffman's dramaturgical model are usually considered microtheories; the analysis begins with individuals and small interacting groups, but the observations are carried out in **institutions** and organizations such as schools, prisons, nursing homes, and

corporations, so that the researcher is constantly looking at the micro-level data within a meso-level context. Sometimes the micro-level observations can even be used to compare entire societies as in a study that compared death awareness among cancer patients and their families in the United States and Japan (Glaser and Strauss 1967).

## Connecting Theory with Research Design and Methods

Can we connect our choice of theories to our choice of research designs and methods? Theories point to research methods. We say "point to" because theories and research designs and methods are not tightly coupled, but allied by compatibility; they are more or less amenable or hospitable to one another. The research methods that we select, once we have chosen our foundational theory, have to produce data that make sense in the framework of the theory.

- For example, if we decided to use psychodynamic or RAT to explain indebtedness, we probably would use methods such as interviewing individuals, listening to focus groups, or observing the behavior of individuals and households to understand why and how they made choices that led them into growing mounds of debt.
- If we are using a theory of culture and discourses that impinged on consumer choices, we might want to carry out a content analysis of commercials and advertising, as well as interview individuals and conduct focus groups.
- If we are using Marxist theory we might carry out a historical-comparative analysis. We would explore the question which societies have high levels of debt and which don't—and why. Perhaps we might look at debt levels and lending practices in Japan, western European nations, and the United States. We would also look at the growing gap between the middle class and the highest income levels that appeared around 1990 and that widened sharply after 2000. We might look at how credit companies and mortgage lenders were regulated and why regulation declined in recent decades. At a microlevel, we could observe interactions between mortgage brokers and prospective debtors.
- Regardless of which theories we use to explain growing levels of consumer debt, we need to look at national economic data to understand the magnitude of the issue. Quantitative macro-level data are always useful background information, even when we are conducting qualitative research at a local site.

Notice that all of these theory–methods couplings are fairly loose. They are linked by choices we make; the **relationships between theories and research methods** are not specified by a set of inviolable rules. Take the case of Marxist theory as the source of explanations for growing consumer debt: Although Marxist theories usually focus on the macrolevel, we could begin our discussion with micro-level studies of individuals and households, using observation and interviews—or more generally, ethnography—to understand how individuals and families are impacted by the economy and how they respond to economic forces. Marxist theories eventually connect these micro-level observations to macro-level forces; but Marxists can use ethnographic designs, observations, and interviews as their research choices (Burawoy et al. 1991).

## When Does Theory Begin? Before the Beginning ...

Our discussion of foundational theory alerts us to the importance of thinking about theories before we start the empirical research. As indicated in Chapter 3, theories guide the formulation of research questions. In our research, we may be looking for a new application for the foundational theory. In some cases, we may be exploring which of two (or more) theories make the best sense of our empirical data. When we conclude that one theory makes better sense of the facts and observations we have collected than does another theory we cannot simply conclude that the less satisfactory theory has been "disproved" for all times, places, situations, and contexts. The challenged theory may remain "locally true" in some societies or situations but not in others, or it may require elaboration and refinement before it can be applied to the situation we are studying.

## Foundational Theories and the *Problematic* of a Research Project

Choosing foundational theories is closely related to formulating a **problematic** for the research project. A problematic is not a statement about a social problem (drug addiction, mortgage foreclosures, etc.), but a statement about the purpose of the research. It identifies the slice of social reality that we think is worth studying and presents the reasons why this situation, action, or phenomenon is of interest. It explains why this situation or topic was singled out for inquiry. In the statement of the problematic, the researcher frames the research question in the broadest terms; later the research question can be posed in a more specific way or broken down into several related questions.

Foundational theories influence the way the problematic is framed and, in turn, how research questions are worded. In our example, social psychological theories would lead us to frame the question about consumer debt largely in terms of individual and household behaviors or choices; Marxist theories would lead us to frame the question in terms of processes within capitalism, processes related to class inequalities and the social relations of production.

Here is another example of how foundational theories shape the problematic of a study and the formulation of research questions. In Chapter 3, we described a study of a tattoo shop. Notice that the problematic of the study focused on interactions, on customer–artist relationships, and on the occupation of being a tattoo artist. The theoretical foundations of these topics were linked to the work of symbolic interactionists and Chicago school sociologists who studied occupations, such as Everett Hughes (1984). We did not frame the initial problematic of the study around other possible questions with different theoretical motivations, such as "Why do people get tattoos?" or "What kinds of people get tattoos?" or "What social forces influence the choices of designs that different kinds of people choose?"

## GROUNDED THEORY IN ACTION: RESEARCH ILLUSTRATIONS

Many qualitative researchers assert that they are seeking to construct "grounded theory"—that is, they believe that theory should emerge from the empirical research rather than guide it from the start. This position was very popular during the heyday of symbolic interactionism in the 1960s. Many symbolic interactionists were explicitly challenging the frameworks in sociology in that period—structural functionalism and Marxist and Weberian conflict theories, all which made large claims about society as a whole. Symbolic interactionists believed that these macro-theoretical claims got in the way of accurate observation and attention to interaction, microprocesses, and everyday life. Not only did macrotheories interfere with accurate observation but also *reified* "society" and "social structure."

**Reification** means making terms like "society" and "structure" appear to be referring to things, when society is not a thing at all, but an ongoing set of processes, interactions, practices, and actions (Blumer 1968). For example, when we say "society does not approve of child pornography" we really mean that a lot of individuals do not approve of it, that legislatures have passed laws against it, and that law enforcement authorities arrest people who produce or consume it. It is not "society" as an abstraction that opposes child pornography; the norms are set and enforced by definite individuals and organizations. As sociologists, we cannot deal in vague abstractions such as "society," but have to focus on individuals, their discourse, and their actions. Therefore, for scholars developing grounded theory the essential first step was careful observation in specific small-scale contexts. These observations were compiled in a systematic way to develop categories and concepts.

## To See the World in a Grain of Sand

The theories that symbolic interactionists constructed in this grounded manner were theories of interaction, of gestures, of discourses, of everyday life and lived experience—in short, symbolic interactionist theories and other microtheories! It may be useful to remember here that "microtheories" are also grand theories. That sounds like a contradiction! But what it means is that microtheories specify "how the world works" just as much as Marxist or structural-functionalist theories; like these macrotheories, microtheories provide a vocabulary for identifying social actions and the conditions that matter in people's lives. Ultimately their core foundational assumption, or belief, is that "the world exists in a grain of sand"—that society is nothing without micro-level interactions; that society is made from the ordinary interchanges of daily life; and that the key to really understanding how the world works lies in the treasure chest of microsociological studies. Microtheories, like all theories, point to what is worth studying in the first place.

Symbolic interactionists began their research with observations at the microlevel but usually within organizations and institutions (the mesolevel). They emphasized that we can never observe "society as a whole," "the class structure," or "structures of racial dominance." We can only observe specific individuals, behaviors, texts, and artifacts, at specific times and places. Even research designed to produce macro-level conclusions—in Marxist and Weberian historical-comparative studies—has to begin with micro-level empirical research activities—we have to look at a specific set of documents or specific workplaces. We cannot empirically study "class structure" or "capitalism" or "bureaucracy" in general any more than we can see "dogs in general" or even "pit bulls in general." Empirically we can only observe specific instances of whatever it is we want to understand, and so all research has a micro starting point, even if it is aimed at broader conclusions.

## Key Elements of Grounded Theory

Grounded theory often led to microsociological conclusions, and it did so by offering a systematic way of organizing empirical observations, moving from observations to codes and then to categories and empirical generalizations. The key elements of grounded theory are a series of steps and operations that take the researcher from observations to theoretical conclusions (these will be discussed in more detail in Chapter 22).

- • **Comparative.** The research should always be a *comparative analysis* in which the observation and conceptualization are carried out in several groups or organizations, which may in turn be embedded in larger contexts. For example, two important developers of grounded theory, Barney Glaser and Anselm Strauss (1967), looked at the extent to which patients are aware of the fact that they have cancer. Glaser and Strauss compared practices not only at different hospitals in the United States but also at Japanese hospitals.

- **Textual database**. The research generates a *textual database*, a body of material that is subjected to a systematic analysis. This database is formed by field notes, interview notes or recordings, and documents. The researcher then examines this database (possibly using software, but it is not absolutely necessary) to identify terms and topics that appear consistently. These terms and topics provide hints about the presence of themes.
- **Open coding**. The first step in identifying these terms, topics, and eventually themes is *open coding*, in which the researcher tries to answer very basic questions: What is this interaction (or interview comment or document segment) about? What are key properties of this "whatever it is"? What is the best name or label to put on the phenomenon? As the codes are identified, the researcher begins to see them jell into categories. These categories are key themes; in quantified research, they might be the variables of the study. For example, in the study of cancer patients in hospitals, "awareness context" became a key category; in some settings, patients were in an "open awareness context" and cognizant of the seriousness of the cancer, while in other settings they were in a "closed awareness context" in which doctors and family members did not speak about the cancer and did not even use the word "cancer." Notice how these themes or categories are broader and more abstract than any single observation or remark in an interview. They were found in many parts of the textual database and they make sense in many situations, even beyond this specific set of data, although they are derived from specific observations, bounded in time and space. Open and closed awareness contexts are not limited to speaking about cancer, but could apply to other illnesses or problems.
- **Axial (relational) coding** *that identifies relationships*. The open coding that leads to the identification of key themes (or categories or properties of a situation) is followed by *axial coding*, a process of relating the elements—the categories—to each other. For example, one can consider causal relationships, variations in contexts, responses that people make (the actions they take), and the consequences or outcomes which may be both intended and unintended.
- *Comparative analysis of the relationships*. At this step, but in fact throughout the process, the analysis is comparative. How are the categories or themes different in different contexts? How do contexts vary with regard to how themes are related to each other within the context? What are the limits to generalization? The comparative analysis enables the researcher to understand how far concepts can be generalized and how the categories vary in different contexts. These considerations in turn can lead into analyzing causal relationships. For example, Glaser and Strauss observed that wards for cancer patients in Japanese hospitals were clearly labeled as cancer wards (thus instantly creating an open awareness context), whereas in the United States, at the time of their study, most hospitals practiced closed awareness. This variation within and across cultures then leads the researcher into new questions. Similarly, Coleman analyzed adolescent cultures in several high schools; although he found many similarities in these "adolescent societies," he found differences in which types of kids were in the leading crowds and what attributes made teens popular in each school. He also found differences in the way teen crowds were linked to the adult authority structure of the school and to the stratification system of the community (Coleman et al. 1981).

Notice how reminiscent the building of grounded theory is of Weber's ideal-type analysis that we discussed in Chapter 2. The concept emerges from observations, but then in turn, the comparative analysis of how concepts concretely and empirically "make themselves felt" in different contexts sharpens the concepts and increases our understanding of how far we can generalize the concepts.

## But Is Grounded Theory Really Built from the Ground Up?

We have to look critically at the claim that grounded theory construction is largely inductive; this claim is a bit debatable. The researcher appears to be using detailed observations, supported by rich down-to-earth material from the field notes, to create ideas about a type of social setting—medical schools, nursing homes, commodity exchanges, gangs, and so on. But in large measure, this appearance of groundedness, the inductive derivation of concepts and conclusions, is a sleight of hand created in the construction of a research narrative that relies heavily on observational material.

The researcher may indeed be reaching conclusions about general characteristics of this type of milieu from her observations and may be inventing new terms or concepts to encompass the actions and situations she has encountered. But the broader theoretical framework that affirms the importance of the microlevel and posits that "society" is constituted at the microlevel as a sum total of interactions, actions, discourses, symbols, and practices is not discovered in the field, but is already present in the researcher's mind before she starts fieldwork. Not only broad theoretical frameworks, but a number of more specific hunches, ideas, and loosely structured hypotheses are probably already formulated. All of these initial ideas shape the collection of data, the formulation of field-notes, and the creation of the textual database. Fieldwork (or any kind of research) provides elaboration, disproves some initial working hypotheses, and provides new concepts, but it is not by itself the source of all the theories, generalizations, ideas, and conclusions of the project. To some extent, then, one might argue that every study based on a grounded-theory approach generates foregone conclusions, findings that aren't so much "outcomes" as they are affirmations of the researcher's mental constructs as they existed prior to and received affirmation during the research period.

## The "Always Already" Contradiction of Grounded Theory

Our last word on grounded theory is a postmodern critique (Alvesson 2002). The entire process that has produced the textual database is already heavily theorized! The choice of groups or sites to compare, the process of observing and writing field notes that become part of the textual database, the choice of documents, the choice of interview subjects and topics—all of these components have already been shaped by the researchers' preexisting system of categories, which are themselves rooted in the researcher's *belief* in the superiority of micro-level frameworks and, moreover, in the belief (entirely nonfalsifiable, by the way) that the world exists in a real way only in small-scale interactions.

The researcher's material is already "oriented" and not random or all-inclusive. The researcher never goes into the field as a *tabula rasa* (as a blank slate), recording everything indiscriminately. To quote Christopher Isherwood: "I am a camera"—yes, but a camera pointed in some directions more frequently than others and with specific settings for the focal distance! Concepts and categories guide the fieldwork (or the documentary analysis) from the start and are implicit or explicit in the research questions. Whether or not we explicitly state the theoretical foundations of our work, these foundations are present; they are like a set of concept boxes which we set up and into which we start throwing the data.

The critical postmodernist would say that building grounded theory is a disingenuous depiction of the research process, because what we build is invariably the object for which we already have a blueprint in our minds very early in the research process. There is already foundational theory "at work" in producing the materials for the textual database, the choice of comparisons, and the open coding process. Critical reflection is therefore needed to identify and bring to the researcher's consciousness the choices and assumptions that underlie the entire process of building grounded theory.

# CRITICAL-REFLEXIVE THEORY IN ACTION

Let's review what we've covered. So far, we have encountered two different approaches (and two matching criticisms) to integrating theory into qualitative research.

- Foundational theory begins with a theory that helps to establish the problematic and guides the research questions. The criticism is that so much theory has already been built into the research project that it may be difficult to come up with new or alternative theoretical conclusions.
- Grounded theory appears to start with empirical observations. It seems less reified than foundational theory—less loaded down with a *priori* concepts. Although it appears to start with empirical observations at specific times and places, the criticism is that this appearance is disingenuous—not deliberately deceptive, because the researchers themselves are fooled by it. The empirical process is just as conceptually guided from the start as in foundational theory, but we are just not being as honest about it with ourselves or our readers.

These criticisms of foundational and grounded theories have led to calls for reflexive sociology. This is a mental process or practice by which researchers examine the origin and sources of the categories and concepts (and theories) which they bring to the research. These influences on research choices include the social characteristics of the researchers (class, race-ethnicity, culture, gender, nationality, religion, sexual orientation, and all the other constructed categories of social relationships), personal experiences, education, intellectual milieu, media habits, career trajectories, and the local, national, and global settings in which they work as social scientists.

## Getting Back to "Bias"—Simply but Not Simplistically

This practice should not be understood simplistically, as an encouragement to dismiss researchers' ideas on the basis of their social characteristics such as race, class, gender, and sexual orientation. Ideas must be evaluated on their own terms, not on the basis of their inventors' ascribed characteristics (such as being a dead white male, or any other combination of categories). But we should be aware of how these characteristics might mold and influence the way we think about research questions and theories. Racial phenotypes and sex categories, which seem so "natural" and important to many people, have no direct influence on ideas and research projects, but they may indirectly affect a person's ideas because they increase the likelihood of certain experiences, career contingencies, identities, and organizational affiliations. Education, religion, peer groups, and personal networks are more direct shapers of how people think and how they choose to carry out research.

Ideas, theories, categories, and concepts never simply emerge from the data and the research experience but are already there in the researchers' minds from the start in some form, however shadowy they might be. Making them conscious and explicit can lead to improvements in the research design, a more honest research narrative, and a deeper understanding of why the researchers' categories are not identical to those of their subjects.

## The Theory-Research "Dialogue"

In a good research project, theory is always both foundational and grounded in a broad sense—foundational in that it guides the research question and hence the project as a whole and grounded in that the researcher must be open to new ways of interpreting, explaining, extending, modifying, and choosing theories based on observation and comparisons.

To put it differently, research is *always* both inductive and deductive. Empirical research is never like a geometry proof (purely deductive) nor is it ever purely inductive, growing out of a naïve encounter with empirical reality. Even what we term "facts" are already highly processed stuff. For example, the fact about the rising level of personal debt in the United States did not just suddenly appear out of nowhere; it was produced in a process involving decisions by economists and government officials about what information to collect and how to measure characteristics of the economy.

## MOVING AHEAD WITH THEORY: A PRACTICAL GUIDE FOR OVERCOMING THE ABSTRACTION PARALYSIS

The material presented in this chapter has been pretty dense. So let's reorient ourselves to the practical demand of getting research done! From this point forward, we present some key issues for you to think about, write about, and generally consider as you move forward in designing your theory-informed research project. We begin with a brief review of the various levels of analysis at which you could end up operating in your study. Then, we offer a brief guide for getting your research project started and give you some tips on going from direct observation and data production to theorizing, and then back again.

### Levels of Analysis

Sociologists often talk about three levels of analysis: macro, meso, and micro.

Here, we will discuss more about these levels and the difference between types of theories and levels of analysis, though this distinction is hazy in the minds of many sociologists.

**Macro-level** analysis is about "large" entities such as whole societies like the United States and France, types of societies (such as capitalist and feudal societies), the global or world system, historical processes such as globalization or modernization, and structures such as class and racial-ethnic stratification systems.

The **mesolevel** of analysis usually includes organizations and institutions. For example, we might study Al Qaeda or the Republican Party, a mental hospital or a university. These entities can involve hundreds or thousands of people and often last beyond the lifetime of any individual. Many sociologists would also place communities at the mesolevel; they involve many people in complex interactions and persist over time.

Finally, the **microlevel** is focused on interactions and individual experiences. It is often very fleeting—actions that last only a few hours or minutes and are small scale, involving only a few people. Some theorists see the microlevel as the capillary level of larger systems and processes—just as the capillaries are the tiniest vessels of circulatory system (Foucault and feminist theorists, for example). This approach means being aware of the mesocontext—institutions and organizations—within which we are carrying out micro-level observations of interactions and individual actions. Sociologists such as Herbert Blumer (1968) insist that the "larger systems" are illusory and reified constructs to be avoided if we want to think clearly about social realities.

Like many classifications, the distinctions among these three levels of analysis appear to make sense but break down when we look at them closely. For example, we might say that "the family" is an institution and can be studied at the mesolevel; yet in practice we either observe "it" at the microlevel, in the interaction of individuals in a specific family, or analyze aggregated data from millions of specific families. It is very hard to explain how to actually study families at the mesolevel without recourse to data collected at the microlevel. (We could study family law or regulatory codes that influence the behaviors of individuals who live in families, but that is not the same thing as studying "the family.") *In this respect, research aimed at understanding meso- and macro-level phenomena is often* in practice *micro-level observation and analysis.*

**LEVEL OF ANALYSIS AND RESEARCH DESIGN AND METHODS CHOICES**    The level of analysis is closely intertwined with our choice of research designs and methods. If we are using observational methods in designs, such as ethnographies and community-based participatory research, the data are often at the microlevel. We can only observe a small number of individuals over a relatively short time span. How do we pick research designs and methods to study entities such as "Russian society" or "the global system"? An extreme position would be to argue that all empirical data originate at the microlevel and are about specific interactions or specific discourses ultimately produced by individuals, even if the researcher claims that the data are representative of a larger group or collectivity. We will confront this problem in more detail when we discuss historical-comparative research, in which the researcher claims to be studying and comparing whole societies, types of societies (social formations such as capitalism, feudalism, or socialism), large structures (such as stratification systems), and processes (such as globalization); the researcher almost always has to rely on and compile other people's research and secondary analysis in order to be able to see and discuss these very large entities.

**LEVEL OF ANALYSIS AND CHOICE OF THEORY**    The level of analysis is also linked to our theoretical choices. Macroanalysis often goes with structural functionalism or various forms of conflict theory (Marxist or Weberian)—theories that seek to classify and explain historical trajectories of types of societies such as feudalism and capitalism. Microanalysis often goes with symbolic interaction and Goffman's dramaturgical model—theories that deconstruct "society" into multiple actions and interactions.

Ethnography—which some researchers would consider the premier qualitative design—can be used for studies across a wide range of theories and at all three levels. Many methods chosen from the "methods tool-kit" will work with a wide range of designs, theories, and levels of analysis. The important thing is to be able to explain *why* we made the choices!

**WORKING AT ONE LEVEL TO UNDERSTAND ANOTHER LEVEL**    Remember that many social scientists do micro-level research in order to gain understanding at the macrolevel. Conclusions from fieldwork are not limited to the specific setting where the research was carried out. For example, Burawoy and his students (1991) conducted ethnographic research in local communities and organizations; although they were carrying out their research at a micro- and mesolevel, their foundational theory was Marxist and they wanted to understand power and resistance, processes of class conflict and collective action that had implications at the national and global level. The concept of resistance is often a way of linking micro-level observations to macro-level processes of conflict. For example, a researcher might observe at the capillary level on *one* estate, in *one* rural community, to see how sharecroppers interact with landowners and to document the "resistance of the weak"—the various strategies that sharecroppers use to defy owners and foremen. From this microresearch, the researcher may feel confident to generalize about agrarian class relations throughout the society, to sharecropping in general, and perhaps even to resistance of the weak in societies based on slavery, serfdom, and wage labor, and not just sharecropping (James Scott 1987). Maybe the researcher is even willing to stretch conclusions based on micro-observations of "resistance of the weak" to other types of hierarchies such as gender inequality.

So the macro–meso–micro levels are never separate and disconnected, although the researcher must choose to begin the study at one or another level—usually at the microlevel, because empirical research must take place at some specific time and place and focus on specific individuals, texts, or objects. In this regard, the researcher is like a novelist: even if novelists would like their work to be universally human, they can produce an exciting, readable novel only if they write about specific individuals in a specific setting. "Universal" novels about the human condition "in general" are usually unbearably abstract and boring.

## Research and Theory: A Continuous Conversation

Theory and empirical research are always in a dialog with each other (in a "dialectical relationship," if you prefer a fancier term). Empirical research helps us refine and extend theories and disproves some hypotheses derived from theories (a process that is not to be confused with the impossible dream of disproving the theories). But theory points to what we should be studying, how we should study it (at what level of analysis, and by what research designs and methods), and what concepts may be useful in selecting from and analyzing the rich "buzzing, blooming, confusion" that we encounter in the empirical world.

In this regard, the opposition of "foundational theory" and "grounded theory" is in part resolved by the scientific method. We observe loosely and open-mindedly, but we already have a broad theoretical understanding of what is important to observe. On the basis of initial observations (as well as reading the research literature), we state a problematic, identify research questions, and begin to formulate hypotheses, not necessarily formally stated as such. We test these hypotheses against further observations, now as part of a more formal research design that often has a comparative strategy so that we can see how well our concepts stretch to encompass new contexts. The exploration of the limits and causes of variation are key parts of the process. And we have to be ready to refine or even to abandon concepts and hypotheses altogether, or at least admit that there exist contexts to which they cannot be generalized. Our conclusions about the hypotheses—our *findings*—in turn lead to a strengthening and refinement of theory, to a better crafting of it.

## How Much Theory?

Social scientists differ not only in their preferences among available foundational theories but also in the extent to which they integrate theory into their research and writing. At one end of the spectrum, we find researchers who want their empirical research to be strongly, explicitly, and completely permeated by a single theory from the initial design to the final report. At the other end of the spectrum, we encounter researchers who prefer not to connect their findings (the results related to their hypotheses about what will turn up in research) to a larger body of theory or to do so only loosely and eclectically.

**THEORY-HEAVY AND THEORY-LIGHT—TWO APPROACHES**    A good example of this difference is provided by two widely read studies of school failure among young men: Paul Willis, *Learning to Labor* (1981); and Jay MacLeod's *Ain't No Makin' It* (1987). We have already discussed Paul Willis's *Learning to Labor* in Chapter 3. So we will not repeat our summary, except to remind the reader that the study is explicitly Marxist in its theoretical foundations. Paul Willis's study is permeated by Marxist ideas and in turn refines and enhances Marxist theory by moving away from conventional notions about the limited opportunities of the working class to a more sophisticated analysis of how young working-class men reject opportunities that the school system provides and what the implications of this rejection are for the political future of the class.

Jay MacLeod's *Ain't No Makin' It* (*ANMI*) formulated a similar research question to guide empirical research in an urban area of the northeastern United States. He observed two groups of young men ("Hallway Hangers" and the "Brothers") living in housing projects. One group was predominantly white, the other mostly African American men. Though the former group explicitly rejected schooling and the latter expressed more positive attitudes toward education, ultimately neither group fared well within school or in the labor market. Most of the young men ended up unemployed or sporadically and precariously employed in low-wage jobs. Some were incarcerated. Few enjoyed any degree of social mobility.

MacLeod does not insist on a single consistent foundational study for his research and leaves open the possibility of different types of theoretical perspectives, many of which he mentions in the book. For example, Pierre Bourdieu and theorists inspired by his work provide concepts of social reproduction and enable us to recognize the misrecognitions expressed by both groups of young men. The school-rejecting Hallway Hangers have misrecognized their situation, believing it to be hopeless and then acting on the basis of this self-fulfilling prophecy instead of using school as an opportunity that might lead to better jobs. But ironically, the school-accepting Brothers have also misrecognized their reality, substituting positive *talk* about the value of education for the recognition that they will need to work hard in school if they hope to benefit from educational opportunities. Bourdieu's concepts of habitus and different forms of capital are also relevant and considered by MacLeod. Alternatively, structural theories about social reproduction are applicable to these findings; and MacLeod even touches on theories of agency and rational action as he discusses why individuals in the two groups make choices about school, jobs, and their life prospects.

Theories of racial construction and dominance apply, because the Brothers are predominantly African American, while the Hallway Hangers are white and rely (somewhat but not completely mistakenly) on racial privilege to see them into good jobs. MacLeod introduces these theories but does not infuse the entire book with a single theory that consistently makes sense out of the rich mass of descriptive detail and excerpts from the many interviews conducted over the years. Without a consistent theoretical interpretation by the author, readers are "on their own" in making sense of what is happening, especially in understanding the reasons for the Brothers' apparently contradictory rhetoric and behaviors.

Notice how Paul Willis and Jay MacLeod are using almost identical research designs and methods. Both are working at macro-, meso-, and microlevels. Both are looking at interactions within groups in very specific settings, at the microlevel. Both then use these micro-level observations to gain insight into the problems of schools and education as institutions at the mesolevel and into the larger, macro-level issues of social mobility and inequalities. Paul Willis links all the levels to Marxist theory, developing a multilayered and complex Marxist theory of social reproduction and the perpetuation of the divide between mental and manual labor. The young men (and millions like them) are unintentionally perpetuating the ideology that mental labor is the prerogative of the bourgeoisie and its allied strata, while manual labor—and increasingly, unemployment—is "freely chosen" by the working class as it remains true to its "us versus them" mentality, its culture of resistance, and its lack of solidarity across gender and ethno-racial lines. Paul Willis argues that working-class rejection of mental labor ultimately prevents the class as a whole from developing a hegemonic consciousness and challenging the dominance of capitalism. Jay MacLeod's study is more descriptive and leaves open a number of avenues of theoretical analysis. Readers will differ in which they prefer: the highly theorized analysis in *Learning to Labor* that brilliantly illuminates the entire project or the descriptively rich but far less theorized research findings of *ANMI* that leave openings for interpretations from several theoretical perspectives.

## From Empirical Observation to Reflexive Theorizing: Four Steps for Getting Started

Some readers may object to the idea of beginning with theory—with the foundational theory approach. They might say that this approach assumes too much or takes too much for granted. They do not want to *start* with the ideas of Weber, Marx and Engels, feminists, Bourdieu, or microsociological perspectives, although they might be prepared to arrive at these theories later, *after* their observations. They might also believe that these theories are all too "grand"—too sweeping in their claims about "how the world works."

But how can we actually develop theory on the basis of empirical observation, especially if we are not completely committed to the microsociological and interactionist conclusions to which a grounded strategy often leads?

Here are four steps that can help researchers move from intense empirical inquiry to broader theoretical conclusions. The four steps we outline address divisions and dilemmas that have beset research in the social sciences. They provide ways of bringing a critical-reflexive orientation to our research.

As a preface to the four steps, however, we feel compelled to elucidate a few of our core assumptions, or guiding beliefs, concerning the research enterprise.

- *The **objective–subjective split**. We strongly affirm that there is a social reality "out there" and in that regard we are taking an objectivist position, consistent with our engagement with the scientific method; but we recognize the need for sensitivity to the many different experiences and ways of seeing that people bring to this reality. These subjective differences must be understood as part of our comprehension of social reality.

- *The macro–meso–micro distinctions.* We recognize that most research ultimately is based on micro-level observation and information of one kind or another—whether it is our fieldwork and participant-observation in a specific research site, the analysis of a specific document or cultural product (such as music, a building, or artwork), or the aggregation of data from individuals that produces "crime rates," "unemployment rates," "foreclosure rates," and all the other statistical data we use in studies. We want to reach comparative and macro-level conclusions with long-term validity and generalizability, but our production of data is usually specific, local, and time-bound.

- *The "them and us" division between researcher and researched.* We should not be afraid to assert that our conclusions are more accurate and in-depth—more true—than the views that our research subjects may hold. As scientists, we do *not* have to defer to the opinions of research subjects, who may be mistaken in their view of the world which they *misrecognize* (to use Bourdieu's term). Indeed, it is our responsibility to present an accurate map of the reality which we are studying, even if it challenges the perceptions and claims of our research subjects. For example, Greg Scott found that injection drug users claim to follow safe injecting practices, but his video recordings of their actual behaviors revealed that many of them did not adhere to these practices (2011). The townspeople studied by Vidich and Bensman (1969) claimed to be independent of the national economy and to be masters of their own destiny; but the research revealed that the economic and political conditions of the community were the result of processes and decisions at the state and national level. But we cannot dismiss the subjects' views lightly. To label our research subjects' views as "misrecognitions" requires critical scrutiny of our own views and assumptions, including assumptions we have absorbed from the media and the notions of our own discipline that we bring to the research.

Why can we claim to see social reality more correctly than the people whom we are studying? What is the basis for our claim?

Our "four steps to theory" are based on Diane Vaughan's strategy for studying adverse events (1996), Clifford Geertz's concept of "thick description," Michael Burawoy and his students' ethnographies of power and resistance in modern society (1991), and Loïc Wacquant's reflections on his ethnographic work (2009). Here we have taken ideas from these sources to suggest a way of planning the route from observation to theory. It is not identical to the procedure for building grounded theory that we discussed earlier in the chapter (Glaser and Strauss 1967; Strauss and Corbin 1990, 1998), but it has some points of convergence with it.

**STEP ONE: *VERSTEHEN* OR MASTERING THE VOCABULARY OF THE MILIEU YOU ARE STUDYING**   This step is crucial because it means that the researcher has made an effort to "get inside the heads" of the research subjects, to understand the perspectives of the participants, and to see everyday community life through their eyes. This is the first step of *verstehen*. *This step is usually interactive and happens in the field.* It takes place between the researcher and the research subjects. In some cases, it may mean careful reading of a text, as Weber read the words of the Protestant reformers for his study of the Protestant ethic and the spirit of capitalism (1958), or contemplation of a cultural object such as a building, song, or artwork.

There are many substeps involved. *Verstehen* may mean learning a unique vocabulary, whether it is a thieves' argot or the specialized terminology of accounting or NASA engineers. Each word in this special vocabulary encapsulates people's views of the world and their feelings about it. Sometimes these words may appear to be common words in everyday usage, but they are used with different meanings than the ordinary ones. For example, Diane Vaughan in her study of the *Challenger* launch decision and disaster (1996) found that engineers and managers at NASA and contracting firms had assigned definite meanings to the words "acceptable risk" that were not identical to the ideas that most people form when they hear the term. In most communities, the perspectives of the participants are embodied in the words they use. In addition, in a research practice called "carnal sociology" (which we will discuss later), it is not just enough to learn words, but bodily habits and gestures also have to be learned, mastered, and made "one's own" (Wacquant 2004, 2009). The perspectives of the community are deeply embedded in local lives. They reflect local knowledge and often cannot be explicitly stated either to themselves or to an outsider, so the researcher has to infer them from observations and participation. Vaughan refers to this local knowledge as *ethnocognition* (1996: 197).

This type of understanding is related to the creation of the textual database and its open coding in grounded theory. Only by immersion in the world of the subjects can we create a textual database that is more than a reflection of our own assumptions and theoretical categories. Researchers must begin by putting their own categories or concepts into a mental lockbox that is stowed away during research; they must first open themselves up to the participants' categories. We cannot pretend not to have our own categories and concepts, but we can try to put them aside temporarily. We must see the world as our subjects see it and immerse ourselves in their way of seeing, feeling, talking, and experiencing.

**STEP TWO: SORTING OUT THE DIFFERENCE BETWEEN INSIDER AND OUTSIDER MEANINGS**   The second step is the creation of distance between the *ethnocognitions* we have learned in our research and our own categories, concepts, theories, and perceptions. This step is essential for the observer who wants to do research, rather than act as a spokesperson for a community. It is not enough to learn thoroughly the perspectives of the research subjects. It is also necessary to step away from these perspectives and look at them as an outsider. There is nothing wrong with being a spokesperson for a community (especially if it is one that has few other avenues of outreach), but representing the interests of the community is not the same as research. And even the observer who would like to help a community represent its interests has to "translate" its language and its *ethnocognitions* into the language of the outside world.

The distinction between the views of the insider and the trained outsider is similar to a distinction that is referred to in anthropology as the difference between the **emic and the etic**. "Emic" is related to "phonemic," which in linguistics is the unit of sound that conveys a meaning to speakers of the language; "etic" is related to "phonetic," which refers to sounds that can be distinguished by an outside observer, regardless of their meaning to the speakers of the language. In other words, the vocabulary and meanings of participants must be understood on their own terms; but the researcher also has a distinct set of categories for making sense out of what is happening that are not necessarily shared by the participants. In fact, sometimes participants will vociferously deny these interpretations.

**This step takes place within the researcher's head.**    The researcher creates the gap between the objective and the subjective. Some researchers (especially feminists and postmodernists) believe this is a dangerous line to cross, but if we fail to cross it, we are only repeating the views of our subjects.

Wacquant (2009) does not use the metaphor of "crossing a line" or creating a gap, but of a return from the field; he says it is ok to "go native" as a step in the research, but the researcher must not stay forever in the field—in the world of the "natives"—but must come back from the field as a sociologist.

The step of grasping the difference between the subjects' views and our own is especially vital and difficult when we are conducting research on organizations and individuals who have more power and wealth than we have. The power of elites makes their categories and frames very pervasive and seductive. As Pierre Bourdieu says, elites have symbolic capital and use their economic and political power to shape discourses and framing, set the agenda of the media, introduce slogans into everyday usage, and impose their frames on public discussion. So the words and views of the rich and powerful must be subjected to even more careful scrutiny than those of other research subjects.

The tension that is felt in making the distinction between insider meanings and our own ideas helps us to bring theory into the research. Why do we see the world differently from our research subjects? This very simple question about experience and perception forces us to think reflexively and theoretically. To answer it, we have to think about our own experience and how it was shaped, and we begin to recognize the sources of the categories that we brought into the research, which could include personal experiences, the media, our own education, and the social science institutions and circles in which we work.

**STEP THREE: PRODUCING THICK DESCRIPTIONS AND THICK INTERPRETATIONS**    We begin to explain the situation or milieu that we have studied in a contextualized and complete way, which many social scientists have come to call "thick description" and "thick interpretation." At this step, the researcher has returned from the world of the participants to the world of the readers of research. In the first step, the research subjects explained their vocabulary, their meanings, and their perspectives to the researcher, and now the researcher explains the world of the research subjects to others. Researchers can only accomplish this task if they engage in "thick description and thick interpretation." The term "thick description" was coined by Clifford Geertz, an anthropologist, to mean that the description the researcher writes must be highly contextualized (1973). The researcher appears to be writing a "mere description" of what has been empirically observed, but in order for this description to make sense, every element of it must be carefully explained and its entire context must be presented. Remember how local knowledge and *ethnocognitions* are embedded in local histories and local practices? Thick description means explaining this embedding to outsiders. All the meanings, history, words, and gestures that seem taken for granted to the participants have to be explained by the researcher in order for the action and situation to make sense to the outsider. *This step takes place between the researcher and the persons who learn from the research; in effect, it often takes place on the pages of the research report or in a voice-over narration in a documentary film or audio piece.*

Thick description and interpretation are work that involves not only translation but also writing history. The event, action, or word is embedded not only in larger spatial contexts but also in many temporal layers; there is a "backstory" to the action. A murder takes place in the context of a family feud or clan rivalry; a professor loses his job after years of tension with his department; a space shuttle is launched on a freezing day after months of discussion of what constitutes "acceptable risk." Telling these backstories requires explaining culture and institutions. Often documents or cultural artifacts become a valuable supplement to the words and observed behaviors of participants; these cultural objects help to reveal the backstories and provide multiple and inconsistent versions of what happened that add depth—and controversy—to the accounts of participants. These backstories may themselves be embedded in stories of longer, historical scope that are shaped by cultures and conflicts.

As the researcher writes the thick description—the contextualized account—the explanations begin to turn toward interpretation and finally toward theory. The researcher has to make choices to write the thick description and to explain the contexts; and as the researcher thinks about these choices, they become theoretical. The theoretical categories and concepts that may have lurked in the researcher's mind in the early stage of the research now come out of their shadows and are recognized. In other words, the thick description has a reflexive side. The researcher thinks about how to contextualize and explain the actions that were recorded. This reflection is closely linked to thinking about variation in comparative analysis and to the "axial coding" in grounded theory that relates categories and concepts to contexts, causes, responses, and outcomes. The difference between this type of theorizing and grounded theory is that the researchers recognize that the categories and concepts are not just found "in the data" but already are present in part "in their own minds." Recognizing this tension, this duality between "in the data" and "already in my mind" is a key part of reflexive research.

**STEP FOUR: REFLECTING ON THE MACRO–MICRO LINKAGES**    As the researcher writes thick descriptions and struggles with the boundaries between insider and outsider understandings, the explanations begin to move from the observed microactions into a broader analysis of fields or institutions, and perhaps ultimately toward the analysis of whole societies. In modern societies, even the most remote small communities are deeply involved in national markets, governmental regulation, and institutions formed by many organizations. Local communities are influenced by larger systems of stratification, both class stratification and ethno-racial dominance. As the researcher writes about these larger social forces, theory begins to flow into the analysis. It is no longer just an account of a few people's actions, explained in their own words, but a bigger picture developed by the researcher. As the grounded theorists argue, a comparative analysis—

comparisons of two or more small groups, organizations, or situations—may greatly facilitate understanding the larger picture.

Greg Scott's "It's a Sucker's Outfit" (2004) is an example of these steps in critical and reflexive development of theory. In this article, the steps are not laid out in this schematic order, but they are clearly discernible in the argument. Scott begins by showing the tension between gang members' views of the role of the gang in integrating the formerly incarcerated into the community and the larger, objective reality of the negative impact of the gang on the goal of reintegration. He concludes with a critique of incarceration as an institution in the United States.

The same approach can be applied in the study of powerful elites; in Khurana's *Searching for a Corporate Savior* (2002), the author begins by critically summarizing the practices and discourses of corporate boards in the CEO recruitment process. He then shows that the ethnocognitions about CEO recruitment and the practices associated with the ethnocognitions led to the escalation of CEO compensation and the restriction of opportunities for people who do not fit the "old boy network." He exposes the mythology—the misrecognitions—concerning the charisma of the CEO and the belief that CEOs are extraordinary human beings with unique talents who therefore must receive enormous compensation. He traces the steps and interactions of the recruitment procedure that reinforce these misrecognitions. Khurana moves decisively from quantitative data and interviews (data collected at the microlevel) to an analysis of the corporate sphere in the United States and the implications of CEO recruitment for the U.S. economy.

## CONCLUSION

To sum up, in this chapter we have encouraged you to think about the ways that theories are integrated into and constructed through qualitative research. We urge you to reflect critically on your own research choices and to link micro-level research to larger, macro- and meso-level conclusions. We proposed four steps for getting started on these goals.

## ACKNOWLEDGEMENT

The authors thank Black Hawk Hancock for reading and commenting on an early draft of this chapter.

## Exercises

1. Use a theory text to identify two theories that you find interesting. Use one of the research topics you developed for Chapters 1 and 3 and suggest how the theories might be used to state the research questions and even to offer specific hypotheses.

2. Identify a study you have read that follows the four steps suggested in the chapter to make research more theoretical and establish macro–micro linkages. Be explicit in discussing how the research follows the four steps (not necessarily in exactly the same order in the written research report).

3. Have you ever read a study that: followed the procedures for developing grounded theory; discussed

findings in "thick description"; explicitly grappled with the challenge of distinguishing subjective and objective approaches; established macro–micro linkages (such as the relationship between stratification systems and personal interaction)? If yes to any of these, describe the study and evaluate how effectively its author accomplished the given objective.

4. As in the authors' discussion of indebtedness in the United States, pick a topic (or social issue) and identify how different theorists might view this issue or topic. Can you maintain the boundary between theory (explanation and interpretation) and ideology/opinion? Which is the best theory for

understanding this topic? Why? Are theories you considered mutually exclusive or complementary? Why? Each theory "points to" a research design and methods? Why, and how would you explain your answer?

5. Find a short "textual database" (e.g., a newspaper article, a 30-second commercial you can record, or a page of your own notes about a setting such as the campus cafeteria). Can you identify themes that appear in this text? Can you suggest "axial codings"? (This exercise is a warm-up for Chapter 22)

Do you do the coding differently for a text you created (the field notes) than for the newspaper article or the commercial. Now take the same "textual database" and apply the four steps of critical-reflexive theory building to it: identify key terms for the participants; your own understanding and interpretation; thick description of the context and background; and macro–micro linkages. Try it with a beer commercial! How would you provide a thick description of the commercial's images for a person who is unfamiliar with U.S. culture?

## Key Terms

axial (relational) coding *95*
comparative *94*
critical-reflexive theory *88*
emic and etic *104*
examples of theories: conflict theories; critical race theory; feminist theories; institutional analysis; Marxist theories; structural functionalism; symbolic interaction *88*

foundational theory *88*
grand theory *91*
grounded theory *88*
insider and outsider meanings *103*
levels of analysis: micro, meso, and macro *98*
macro–micro linkages *105*
objective–subjective split *102*
open coding *95*
problematic *93*

reification *93*
relationships between theories and research methods *92*
textual database *95*
thick descriptions and thick interpretations *104*

# II

# Choosing a Research Design

In Part II, we discuss several basic strategies or designs for qualitative research projects. Each design has a distinct organization. The simplest way to explain the differences is to say that certain research questions are best-suited to one design over the others; what matters most is how the research question is framed. Its framing will determine which combinations of methods you'll draw from the methods toolbox. These combinations of choices will tell you which research design will be most amenable to the study.

Here are the five basic strategies or designs we cover:

*Ethnography.* In this design, the research questions address a group's way of life. The research is mostly about a current situation (though we may include historical materials). There is a large descriptive component in the research—we usually have to describe the way of life before we can get into explanatory and analytical perspectives. The descriptive goal of the research almost always calls for observation, participant-observation, and some form of interviewing and interaction as our choices from the tool-kit. We are trying to construct *verstehen*—Weber's term for integrated/integrative understanding—to comprehend the existential condition of the group and the worldviews and actions of its members.

*Historical-comparative research.* In this design, the research questions deal with change in societies and social institutions and more specifically about the reasons why societies change in different ways. The research question asks why societies vary and what explains variation in their patterns of change. The fact that the change took place in the past and that many or all of the participants are dead impacts our choice of methods. Interviewing and participant-observation are impossible (or at best secondary) and we rely more heavily on the analysis of documents, discourses, and cultural artifacts. Primary or "eye-witness" documents are often important but so are scholars' secondary writings about historical events and even their interpretive and analytical essays.

*Social autopsy.* As the name implies, autopsies are dissections of things that went wrong. They examine the social causes and consequences of what are delicately called "adverse events," which include natural disasters, accidents, and crimes committed by individuals but even more so by states and movements. The logic of research begins with the event and moves forward and backward to the causes and effects of the "adverse event"—for example, hurricane and flood, nuclear power plant accident, shuttle crash, heat-wave deaths, drug overdose deaths, or genocide. The analysis contributes to knowledge about social structure, inequalities and disparities, power and dominance, the behaviors of media and government elites, conflict, and technological problems. The choice of methods is highly eclectic—even the dead tell tales—and can include almost any method in the tool-kit.

*Participatory action research or community-based participatory research.* In these designs, the researcher works *with*—and often in the service of—a community, a community-based organization, or a social movement organization to define the goals of the research. The boundaries of researcher and researched become blurry, the questions cannot be formulated in advance and unilaterally by the researcher, and choice of methods and analysis of data are negotiated between researcher and participants (who are not to be called or treated as "subjects"—nor as "objects" of the researcher's gaze). The high degree of politicization and commitment to social change of this type of research design makes it very different from the more academic designs, even the ones with a critical edge like the social autopsy.

*Discourse analysis and the analysis of cultural artifacts.* Although the analysis of discourses and cultural artifacts is a method in the toolbox, it can also be considered a design in its own right. The research question draws us into the world of the creators of the text or artwork; we ask our research questions not of living subjects/participants but of the documents and works of the imagination we see and hear. We can analyze the crumbling walls of ancient cities, contemporary TV sitcoms, the fantastical works of "outsider" artists, terrorists' audio recordings posted on Internet sites, commercials aired during the Super Bowl, and the furniture and floral arrangements of pachinko parlors—each of these cultural objects takes us into realities and irrealities of social worlds. Our measures are unobtrusive, noninterventional, and noninteractive. This design allows us to understand—again, the Weberian word *verstehen*—worlds of the past or milieus that we could never enter in person. We may end up knowing relatively little about the social conditions of production or about the impact of the discourse, but we learn about the world of the human imagination, about the images, representations, cognitive maps, and the fantasies that human beings create.

We end the overview of the designs with a short chapter on multimethod or mixed-method designs that combine qualitative and quantitative approaches.

# 7

# Ethnography:
# A Synopsis

## OVERVIEW

In this chapter, we provide an informal introduction to **ethnography**, a complex and multifaceted methodology, largely but not exclusively qualitative in nature, with a long and rich history in the social and behavioral sciences. Ethnography is a *scientific and artistic* approach to studying human societies, and it resembles the ordinary person's self-reflexive and systematic approaches to learning about the world around them, particularly when confronted with a new cultural experience. Following the informal introduction, we present some of the core elements of the "ethnographic imagination" (Willis 2000), the specific tenets that distinguish this logic of inquiry from others discussed in this book.

## AN EXAMPLE—*IN SEARCH OF RESPECT: SELLING CRACK IN EL BARRIO*

Philippe Bourgeois lived for three and a half years in East Harlem in order to document and understand the local microcosm of crack users and dealers who live in a poor and marginalized community. In his book *In Search of Respect: Selling Crack in El Barrio*, Bourgeois boils down hours of interviews and observations into a multidimensional and complex portrait of men and women coping with desperate conditions. Violence, incarceration, misogyny, heartbreak, hopes, and betrayals are elements of the story, not only in the narratives about individuals but also in the depiction of a culture as a whole.

Bourgeois didn't just drop into the neighborhood for a few days to interview passersby or take a peek into bars and crack houses, and then return quickly to a safe, orderly middle-class world. He immersed himself (and his wife and child) for a long time in the "other country" at the end of a short subway ride. His conclusions are based on months of fieldwork, reported in extensive quotes from interviews and conversations with people he came to know well, and documented by descriptions of recurrent actions and situations that he saw and recorded. The story he tells does not have a Hollywood ending nor does it offer simple conclusions and optimistic "problem-solving" interventions. He probes "the human condition" in one specific context, writing a dialogue between the voices of the people he met and his own understanding of their conditions.

Another edgy, high-risk ethnography is Greg Scott's "It's a Sucker's Outfit: How Urban Gangs Enable and Impede the Reintegration of Ex-Convicts" (2004). Scott not only describes the setting, actions, and words of the participants in a vivid and carefully documented way; he also systematically relates his data to an analysis of incarceration and the gang as an organization. Few social scientists are as prepared to take risks as Bourgeois and Scott, but ethnography is always a powerful, intense, and time-consuming design. Understanding the culture of others requires preparation, systematic ways of recording and producing data, reflexive choices in the writing, and a sociological imagination to create a coherent, insightful account.

## AN EXAMPLE—*LIQUIDATED: AN ETHNOGRAPHY OF WALL STREET*

Only a few miles away from the fieldwork site where Bourgeois lived—a short ride on the New York subway—Karen Ho found a job in investment banking and entered the world of Wall Street as an ethnographer to capture its corporate culture, a system of values and behaviors based on a sustaining belief in smartness, exploitive hours of detail-oriented work for the young analysts, absolute job insecurity, and the worldview that risk, impermanence, and the single-minded pursuit of money should become the sole principles of global society. Like Bourgeois, Ho immersed herself with no holds barred in an extreme setting (Ho 2009).

## ETHNOGRAPHY IN EVERYDAY LIFE

In some sense, everyone is an ethnographer. Even the most ordinary life ushers in a parade of ethnographic projects. As we encounter new and sometimes strange situations, we adopt an ethnographer mind-set and course of action, although we rarely think of ourselves as ethnographers. Our most ethnographic endeavors stem from major transitions or dislocations, such as changing residence, traveling, starting a new job, being hospitalized for a long period, beginning a residential drug or alcohol treatment, moving in with a lover or spouse or stranger, or getting folded into a new circle of friends. At these junctures, we adopt the ways and means of the "professional stranger"; we approach life as an ethnographer approaches a research setting. But what does this mean?

Literally, "ethnography" means "writing people" (graph = to write/depict; ethno = people). This definition is dense with meaning and implications. Ethnography is the art and craft of writing people. Performing ethnography successfully at the professional level demands a combination of science, artistic sensibility, and vocational skill and training. It is part science, part aesthetic creation, and part craft. In this chapter and in Part III "Focus on Ethnography," we offer insight into a complex methodology with a long and storied history in the social and behavioral sciences.

### Professional Strangeness

Ethnographers set out to study culture. More specifically, they seek to systematically investigate and then accurately represent (through their prose and/or pictures and/or films, etc.) the culture with an **emic**, or "inside-out" perspective. This contrasts with other forms of doing sociological research on groups or communities or organizations, where the researcher obviously assumes an "outside-in" (**etic**) vista and represents the issue or group from an outsider's perspective.

Ethnographers strive to understand a given culture on its own terms, and on the terms of the people who occupy it, dwell within it, and produce and reproduce it on a daily basis. They "write people" from a perspective as observers who participate to some extent in the lives of the people about whom they write.

The discipline of anthropology gave rise to ethnographic research but does not enjoy a monopoly of this versatile methodology. In classic anthropological studies, the ethnographer examined a primitive tribe in a foreign country, a tribe marked by sociocultural and geographic isolation (an erstwhile "fact" debated hotly in retrospect). Such "pristine" and self-contained cultures hardly exist these days, if they ever really did, and ethnographic studies in sociology are increasingly domestic. Contemporary ethnographers are just as likely to be studying "cultures within cultures" as they are to be studying indigenous cultures in some other land. Today, ethnographers come from many different disciplinary backgrounds—sociology, anthropology, economics, medicine, law, communications, international studies, American studies, and private-sphere commercial domains such as marketing/advertising and new product research and development. Although each discipline has its own standards and conventions for doing this kind of research, they share a common concern for "the cultural."

The ethnographer begins her study (which may mark a new phase of her life or serve as a rite of passage) when she assumes the status of a "professional stranger" (Agar 1986). Over the course of her time in an unfamiliar place, she gradually develops an insider's perspective. Hardly ever does the ethnographer "go native," or become a full-fledged member of whichever society she's studying. Instead, she retains "critical distance," which ebbs and flows depending upon time and circumstance. In fact, it's almost impossible for the researcher to "go native." This contrasts with the popular ethnographies we all perform as we encounter life-changing transitions. Most of us want to become a full-fledged member of the culture and society into which we have moved intentionally.

## Solving Puzzles in Reverse

Ethnography at the professional and lay levels revolves around solving the problem of culture. Think of culture as a completed jigsaw puzzle bearing an illustration of some sort. Let's assume this particular jigsaw puzzle has 10,000 pieces; it's complicated. But unlike a real puzzle, the picture we are striving to assemble is not shown on the box. As in everyday life, you must begin to assemble the puzzle, piece by piece, through trial and error, and as you slowly develop some idea of what the big picture looks like, you begin making decisions about how to put it together. However, culture is more complicated than a static illustration. Each of the 10,000 individual pieces continually changes its shape, and the total number of pieces keeps changing—increasing and decreasing without warning. And even more problematic is that the ultimate illustration also keeps changing because in the end the illustration you create is but one of many that could have been created.

In your daily life you don't think about the culture in which you live. Nor do you spend much time trying to visualize the culture *in toto*, writ large. That's because you don't have to. One of the greatest privileges in life, arguably, is the freedom from having to figure out what your culture consists of, what it "looks like," and how to operate fluently within it. Familiarity breeds "functional ignorance" in many respects. The more familiar with your culture you become, the less you will notice or see it, and the less capable of explaining it you will be. Ignorance of one's own culture is a grand luxury, for it derives from many years' worth of assimilated, embodied, rarely-if-ever challenged knowledge about oneself and one's place in the world.

When you find yourself in a new and foreign situation, you experience not only fear, trepidation, and anxiety but also a sense of excitement and thrill, and these contradictory feelings result from your being culturally disembodied. You have yet to embody the knowledge and skill necessary to function as a competent cultural actor. In short, you're an alien. Every day ushers in numerous problems that need solving. Because you have spent so many years participating and observing your own life, you know what many of these "problems" will be: feeling "at home" in your new residence; moving through the new neighborhood in which you now live; obtaining a sufficient supply of satisfactory-tasting food; getting to work or school; meeting and greeting strangers and then negotiating your way into more intense relations with them (e.g., friendship). During these moments in your life you pay very close attention to the little things—to the things people do, the words they say, the gestures they make, and how they carry themselves in public. You study the environment around you, and you try to make sense of things—you try to discern patterns in how people behave as individuals and in groups.

You do all of this in an effort to figure out what's going on, to estimate what all of these details add up to, how they are a product of and also express the "bigger picture" of life in your new community. If, say, you're living and going to school in a new city or town, you cannot get to know the entire community, the whole place. So you focus your efforts of knowing on the imme-diate circumstances, contexts, and problems. A relatively narrow frame of reference guides what you do, where you go, decisions you make, actions you take or don't take, and so forth. Your hope is that by becoming acclimated to this small sector of the larger community, you will become a competent member of the broader setting/scene/population as well. And if you competently master the local lived experience, chances are you will succeed in the eyes of the "host" society of which the local scene is one of many parts.

At some point down the road the adventure will end. You may well still be living in this place that used to seem foreign to you, but to some extent the thrill (and the need for) of concerted discovery is gone. You no longer tap into that higher level of consciousness that reflects on the rationale or strategy behind your actions or the actions of others. Rather than asking "how do I live here" while simultaneously living there, you simply live. Living in this once-foreign place has become second nature to you. As a member of the scene, even if some or many still consider you to be an outsider of sorts, you embody the practices, values, and expressions of the setting—you fit in. No longer do you think about daily life as a series of puzzles. Moreover, it's very likely that you have come to believe that how you now do things is the *only* way you could be doing them. But that isn't true.

Over time, you have participated observantly in your own life; you necessarily have been immersed in your own life (this may seem obvious, but it's not), and you have sought answers to pressing questions about your navigation through the world. Through trial and error, you have developed solutions to a good many of the problems you face. And the solutions have synched so well with the lives of others with whom you must interact that they have come to seem "natural." But they are anything but natural. You have developed them through social, economic, political, and cultural interaction with others. In short, you have constructed your life ethnographically. You have written yourself.

One of sociology's greatest thinkers, Everett Hughes, wrote extensively about the similari-ties between ethnography and everyday life. For him, the two orientations had more in common than not. In both domains one's success boils down to the capacity to assimilate information and move forward by advancing educated guesses regarding what to do next. Just as learning to live successfully and happily isn't easy, neither is learning to ethnography:

> The problem of learning to be a field observer is like the problem of learning to live in society. It is the problem of making enough good guesses from previous experience so

that one can get into a social situation in which to get more knowledge and experience to enable him to make more good guesses to get into a better situation, ad infinitum. (Everett Hughes in Junker 1960: xiii)

The point here is that ethnography is something we do every day. But our lay version is less systematic, more taken-for-granted, and less reflexive (or critically contemplated) than the professional version. Producing a good ethnography means learning the art and craft of knowing, thinking about the logic of reaching conclusions about culture, and familiarizing yourself with practices that will help you observe and write about culture.

## ETHNOGRAPHY: A LOGIC OF KNOWING

Michael Agar (2006), a long-time ethnographer whose work we highly recommend you to read (particularly *The Professional Stranger*, 1996), puts it best: "Ethnography names an *epistemology*—a way of knowing and a kind of knowledge that results—rather than a recipe or a particular focus" (2006: 57).

Ethnography is a design, an overall plan for understanding how a group exists. It generally calls for the adoption of multiple methods and then bringing the resulting data to bear on a question about a particular group's culture. Ethnography is a way of combining and using various methods, both quantitative and qualitative, and so in a strict sense, it is neither a quantitative nor a qualitative method; in any case, the guiding principle is that the ethnographic project strives to answer questions about how a group of people gets along in the world. And you, the ethnographer, assumed the responsibility of depicting how the group exists.

### The Culture Question: "How?"

"How" is arguably one of the main focal points of ethnography. It may well be *the* central question. As we've said already, we're talking about the study of culture. But what is culture? This is another taken-for-granted, oft-tossed about term whose actual meaning we rarely make explicit enough for agreement on what we're discussing. While hundreds of definitions exist, we're going to adopt a relatively simple one for the purposes of this chapter: Culture consists of a given group's members' relatively well-shared, acquired *knowledge* for the purpose of organizing behavior and also interpreting the behavior of others (on a small or very large scale). In essence, culture is a shared way of understanding the world and taking action within it. And it's always *relatively* well-shared, meaning that not everyone complies with the dominant culture's rules and forms, and most people don't conform *all* the time. But most of us comply most of the time, but to what are we complying? Figuring out the "what" is essential: "What comprises the culture I'm studying?" But to get to the "what?" question, you've gotta deal with the "how": "*How* did this culture arise and *how* do its members keep reproducing, if continually changing, it?"

At any given moment, we exist amidst a bramble of rules governing our behaviors, our actions, prescribing what we can and should do and think, and proscribing the transgressive behaviors whose carrying out we generally resist no matter how strong the urge. Some of the rules into whose province we were born are formal and official; they are laws. Most of the rules, however, are less formal and often not even spoken aloud; they are **mores**, also known as customs or conventions. Rules and knowledge are often *embodied*, experienced as ways of moving, sensing, and acting in the material world, not formed explicitly into words and ideas.

At the group- or community-level, we refer to the body of mores as "norms," patterns of expected behavior. And we generally agree on, or at least recognize and to some degree assimilate, the informal code of behavior, and it's quite obvious when someone breaks the code. Every behavior, or every action, gives shape and reinforcement to these norms, mores, and laws. They act on us, and our resulting actions act back on them ... in many ways, we are the law, and the law is us. No matter how much we like to think or tell ourselves (or others) that we are original, unique, one-of-a-kind, the fact is that we are very much alike in nearly every respect (physiologically and socially). Our behavior takes on ritualistic qualities, not necessarily in the spiritual sense, but in that our behaviors are predictable and patterned and derive in part from a commitment to conformity.

**EXAMPLE—ACCOMPLISHED INTERACTION:**    To summarize by way of illustration, let's take up the issue of noninteraction (as inspired by the work of Goffman, Blumer, Hughes, et al.). In most locations across North America, people commit informally and implicitly, without ever really discussing it, to avoid interacting with each other in certain venues: waiting room at the doctor's office, bus stop, train, car, elevator, and so on. These places all have one thing in common: They are way stations—transitional settings—places we occupy *en route* to a final destination. There's no rule against talking in these places (for the most part), and there's no law against it. And neither parents nor teachers ever tell children, "Don't talk to others when you're in the following locations ...." Curiously enough, though, nearly all of us subscribe to a deep and abiding commitment to noninteraction. We accomplish mutual avoidance in such settings. We don't think much about our accomplished noninteraction until someone breaks the rule—for example, a fellow passenger begins chatting us up, or a nervous fellow patient tries to initiate extended, meaningful conversation as we wait miserably to see the doctor.

Remember, sociology is the study of people doing things, and/or *not* doing things, together. Consistently avoiding interaction in certain specific places is something that we do, and we do it together, and our doing of it derives from a mutual commitment to uncodified rules and a reciprocal trust that we'll abide by the same unofficial code of conduct. Though perhaps trivial, this example illustrates culture—the shared ways of understanding the world and organizing our actions in it. And it offers some insight into the most important, or least most pervasive, rules and boundaries that govern behavior—the norms, mores, and customs about which we rarely speak or even think. Finally, accomplished noninteraction, as a cultural phenomenon, tells us a great deal about the ritualized quality of our public behavior.

## Culture as Process and Structure in Context

Culture is a process. It's also a structure. And, more important in terms of discussing ethnography, it is an outcome, an effect, a derivative; it is, in short, a result of human activity, both cooperation and conflict. Too often, sociologists (and journalists alike) talk about culture as though "it" causes things to happen. Culture doesn't make things happen. Rather, "it" flows from humans' attempts to adapt to their environment, to the social system in which they find themselves, to the political structures shaping their "placement" in the hierarchy of material or symbolic wealth (the economy). We develop patterns of behavior, ways of being and doing, and they have a particular substance and style. Writ large, these patterns of activity and styles of doing and ways of thinking comprise culture.

Ethnographers generally set out to understand culture as a problem to be solved, a puzzle to be understood, an enigma to be contemplated, dissected, and explained. In a word (and often-used word, in fact), we "problematize" culture. How does this particular culture come about? How can we explain its emergence? What are its various parts? How do they work together, or not work together? What sustains this culture? How did this or that given culture dissolve or expand or otherwise change?

But ethnography doesn't always involve such big questions as these. Often it's just not feasible to study or explain an entire culture. And so we pose midrange questions. Rather than trying to explain, for instance, the entire culture of homeless or precariously housed people or the culture of substance abusers throughout the United States, the ethnographer begins with a local context and a local group, defined by its participants or by outsiders. Generalizations begin to flow from the intense study of the local group in its local context.

This is exactly what James Spradley (1970) does in the classic ethnography (and a leading study in urban sociology) titled *You Owe Yourself a Drunk*. Spradley examines closely how the culture of drunks in Seattle is sustained, shaped, and generally affected by the community's "legitimate" institutions such as law enforcement, business, and political governance. One of his many findings was that the very institutions hell-bent on remedying the problems related to public drunkenness and vagrancy were the core factors responsible for sustaining these "problems." Spradley's "field" was defined and delimited by his concern for the points of contact between the culture of drunks and the institutional structures and policy enactments of the social control organizations in the community.

## Depth versus Breadth

Ethnographic logic also emphasizes depth over breadth. Earlier in this book, we argued that the primary difference between quantitative and qualitative research lies in their respective approaches to the creation of knowledge concerning some aspect of social life. Quantitative researchers generally examine only a handful of variables but a great number of cases. Their research questions lead them to administer surveys, for instance, wherein they ask a small number of questions to a large number of people. Then they analyze the responses and try to explain variance. Qualitative researchers, on the other hand, ask questions that demand deeper investigation. The answers to their research questions tend to involve a large number of factors, which means they can focus only on a relatively small number of cases. Ethnographers, much like qualitative researchers, also work with a small number of cases (sometimes only one case) and a huge number of variables (although many of them prefer not to use the term "variable," which sounds too much like traditional quantitative research). These variables include all the characteristics of the social context and all the social forces that operate within it. Ethnography is the study of a single culture or the comparative study of several cultures. In both cases, however, one examines many situations, individual experiences, and factors (or "variables") within each culture in order to develop a *holistic*, comprehensive understanding of how the culture operates.

A holistic approach requires the ethnographer to study cultural processes **in situ,** or in the natural setting of the people who occupy the culture. This approach differs markedly from typical quantitative (and many qualitative) studies, wherein the researcher first identifies a phenomenon or problem (as social science tends to be obsessed with *problems and pathologies*) and then *isolates* it, extracts the problem from the conditions that produced it, attempting to quantify or qualify the problem, and finally attempts to examine recurrences of the problem throughout a population, with a focus on explaining how the problem's distribution varies. Ethnography focuses on cultural processes *in context* and attempts to explain how cultures operate, how they produce their own problems and solutions, how they relate to other cultures (whether hostile or friendly), and so forth. Occasionally ethnographers will isolate a particular instance and build an ethnographic study around it, but this is relatively rare. In general, the ethnographer goes for depth and complexity, and ultimately attempts to understand culture itself as "the problem"—which is to say that the ethnographer asks the question, "What gave rise to this culture, and how did it become what it is?"

## Falsification

Counterintuitively, perhaps, the ethnographer achieves the ability to tell a holistic story about a culture by continually attempting to undermine the story while she tries to assemble it. Falsification is the heart of ethnographic logic. The ethnographer must continually attempt to falsify every emergent conclusion she reaches. Here, we encourage you to refer back to the "falsification principle" presented in our discussion of qualitative methodology's relationship to the traditionally accepted doctrine of the scientific method. This operation is like trying to make a puzzle piece fit into a spot and setting it aside if it is not a good fit, to continue our puzzle analogy; if it is not a good fit, we do not insist on cutting or bending it to force it into place.

Ethnography's focus on falsification is influenced by the work of Karl Popper (1963), who believed it is the basis of all scientific inquiry. But ethnography presents real problems to the process of falsification because we don't use the methods of the natural sciences and the quantitative social sciences such as probability sampling, double-blind testing, and tests of statistical significance. In ethnography, we are constantly tempted to create data that support our initial conjectures.

Regarding ethnography's near-obsession with falsification, Michael Agar (2006: 103) writes,

> Ethnographers, by and large, suffer from a disease called "chronic Popperism," if I can refer tongue in cheek to the writings of philosopher Karl Popper (1963). We keep looking for evidence that what we think is going on in fact is not. We are ambulatory falsification machines. And the falsification we seek relies heavily, though not exclusively, on questions about meaning and context. (2006: 103)

Rather than assuming you're right, even at the outset, assume that you are wrong about the reason you're seeing, what you're seeing, or hearing what you're hearing.

When I (Scott) first began working with street addicts (heroin and crack cocaine), I assumed that I could attract them to my interviews with any incentive payment (honorarium) of $10 or more. But I was wrong. Many local addicts chose not to agree to be interviewed. They were in the same economic situation as those who agreed to the interview, and their drug-addiction levels were roughly the same. So what gives? Why did some participate, while others did not?

The answers are many, but one of the most powerful explanatory factors was their relative connectedness to non-drug-using family members. No matter how badly they needed the incentive payment, they would often decline the interview out of fear that their family might read about them in my published ethnography. This obviously contravened my assumptions about their level of economic need, which was intertwined with my assumption that they couldn't care less about what others thought of them. After all, they were street junkies—how much worse could their social situations get. But many of them had too much pride and too much personal capital at stake to participate in my work.

**Chronic Popperism** is the science of ethnography, and it's an element that clearly distinguishes ethnography from journalism. Journalists don't spend a year, or often even a month, trying to figure out how they're wrong about the conclusion they've reached concerning the relationship between X and Y; instead, journalists often collect anecdotal information (which is *not* data, even in the plural), draw conclusions that they consciously or subconsciously believe will appeal to their editors (whose audience ultimately consists of those who provide the revenue stream—the advertisers), and then seek out confirmatory evidence.

Once they've submitted their "copy" (the story), someone called a "fact checker" goes through the material, follows up with sources to check the accuracy of quotes, consults authoritative texts to verify dates and other factual aspects of the piece, and so forth. But the "fact checker" checks "the facts"; they don't check the interpretation, and they *certainly* don't go looking for contravening facts! In news organizations, there's usually no one who holds the responsibility of challenging the story, providing alternative and competing explanations or narratives. Once copy is submitted, everyone's mission becomes one of confirming and ensuring the narrative's publication.

As ethnographers, we're looking out for *dis*confirming evidence, but with an eye toward developing an explanation for how certain events fit a certain pattern, and how many other events don't fit the pattern, and finally, why some events fit the pattern and many other events don't. Out of all this, we hope to develop a relatively coherent, holistic account of the culture we're studying and of the specific events, occasions, rituals, and interactions we've chosen to focus on in our study.

A word of caution: Doing ethnography can drive you crazy. With its commitment to holism and context (everything is connected with everything else) and its compulsive falsification attempts, the life of an ethnographer can be maddening. Michael Agar calls it "heartbreak of the holistic mind" (2006: 120).

## Questioning Reality

Notwithstanding the ethnographer's fascination with complexity, holism, contingency, context, situatedness, and interminable interconnectedness, the methodology's logic calls for simple, though not simplistic, explanation. Ethnography entails questioning "reality," repeatedly and critically. What everyone assumes to be real by their implicit collective agreement not to question it is exactly what the ethnographer sets to question. Through chronic Popperism, the ethnographer arrives at an answer—not inductively or deductively, but abductively.

**Abductive logic** (discussed in detail in a later chapter) means openness to both **deduction** and **induction** (the traditional logics of social inquiry) and above all, an openness to imaginative leaps. But in the end, the ethnographer strives to articulate the most economical, parsimonious explanation possible, one that identifies the culture itself as problematic ("How is this culture possible, and how does it work?") and offers the simplest possible explanatory framework. It integrates the view from the inside with the view from the outside, making sense of why insiders see the world as they claim to do.

As John Dewey (1938/1998) wrote, "Reality is what we choose not to question at the moment." That's the ethnographer's focus—everything that cultural insiders do not question. And once asked, the question cannot be answered by insiders alone, for they rarely appreciate the fact of having a culture. This is true for almost everyone. Can you tell me what your culture consists of, exactly? How is your behavior an expression/product and producer of that culture?

You see how difficult it really is. You must offer your own explanation, one that accounts for what insiders know but one that goes beyond their knowledge. But it should not be overly complex. Again, we're striving to meet the criteria of "good science."

## Parsimony and Ockham's Razor

"Good science" also means following the premise of Ockham's razor: The theory that you ultimately set forth should make as few assumptions as possible and the assumptions it does include should relate directly to the observed events. The simpler the explanatory framework, the easier it will be to test, and then to build upon—and if necessary, to discard. At the end, your theoretical base will enjoy a foundation comprised of very few core explanatory factors, but they will be intertwined with each other in infinitely complex ways. Hence, you need to develop parsimonious postulates easily tested through observation.

## The World in a Grain of Sand

Using this phrase, borrowed from William Blake's poem, as a touchstone, we conclude this chapter by emphasizing again ethnography's concern with understanding thoroughly the local, the particular, and the seemingly inconsequential. Life, death, the gods, and the devil are all in the details (to modify an old adage). But although ethnography requires deep, long-term, always taxing immersion, it's critical that the ethnographer learn how to successfully step back from the details and employ abductive logic. Many an ethnography has gotten lost in the middle of a field study, so caught up in participating in the culture that the ethnographer never finishes the study, fails to answer the research question, and so the job never gets done.

## Ethnography Holds Up a Mirror

Seeing the world in a grain of sand means performing an ethnographic study that says something important about the culture under study. But ethnography also tells the outside world something about itself. A great ethnography is a looking-glass experience for the readers. What appears at first glance to be entirely foreign, exotic maybe, turns out to be a study that says something about the "normal" world in which the published ethnography circulates. If an ethnographer can achieve this "natural generalizability," then she has accomplished a great deal. A good ethnography of a "foreign," "exotic," or "outsider" culture reveals our own lives and culture to us.

The ethnographer, whether doing a community-oriented study or a problem-centered study, always has a "problem" (not in the sense of a social problem, but an intellectual puzzle): how to explain something, how to make sense of patterns, how to accurately convey "what's really going on." Later in this book, we present several chapters on the specific techniques that comprise "doing ethnography." The endeavor may seem awfully mysterious at this point, and to some extent there is a bit of mystery in this science, as in all sciences, even physics. Science and mystery go hand in hand. As Albert Einstein (2011) remarked, "The most beautiful thing we can experience is the mysterious. It is the source of all true art and all science. He to whom this emotion is a stranger, who can no longer pause to wonder and stand rapt in awe, is as good as dead: his eyes are closed." Ethnography is the science of mystery and of mystification. Indeed, one might say that ethnography is the science of demystification done all-too-often mysteriously. In this book, we hope to unravel some of this mystery of doing ethnography.

# BOX 7.1
## Ethnography and Journalism

Many professions (and professionals) focus on writing people. Take journalism, for instance, a field we've already invoked in this discussion. For hundreds of years, professional writers have investigated the lives of humans, individuals and groups, and then rendered those lives (in varying degrees of detail and accuracy) in public forums. They identify an issue or problem with broad public appeal or relevance. Background, or archival, research furnishes knowledge they will need in order to gain entry to the community and to ask the right questions. Then they go out and try to find informants, spokespersons, people whose lives bear directly on the issue at hand. The journalist often attempts to build a trust-laden relationship with informants so that they will share with the writer sensitive information and insight into how their lives bear on the issue, and how the issue affects their lives.

Just like the ethnographer, the investigator strives to craft a *representation* of the group or culture on which she has chosen to focus. But journalists work under several constraints. They need to find "the hook" or angle that makes the story "newsworthy." To be newsworthy the angle must be salient to a very wide audience, consisting not only of highly educated, highly literate readers but also to less educated folks, especially those whose lives might be directly affected by the events. And the angle must enjoy a *du jour* quality. Journalists work under much more intense time pressures than ethnographers. News editors (print, broadcast, and Web) always ask their reporters the question "Why now?" and insist on getting the story out quickly. If the journalist cannot explain the angle in one or two sentences and/or convince the editor of its salience and timeliness, then the story doesn't get off the ground, and the journalist never even makes the first phone call.

Journalists developed standards of evidence and ethics, standards that became part of the profession by the early twentieth century, largely to shield them from World War I government propaganda and the emerging advertising and public relations industry (Schudson 1978). Professional bodies, such as the International Federation of Journalists, promulgate rules to guide journalists who report "the news." Although many codes exist, they generally share a concern for these common tenets of journalistic reporting: objectivity, truthfulness, fairness, impartiality, accuracy, and public accountability.[1]

### THE SCHOOL OF NEW JOURNALISM.

In the 1950s, journalism spawned subfields bearing a striking resemblance to ethnography, particularly a branch that came to be known as "New Journalism" (also termed as "creative nonfiction" and "literary journalism"). Norman Mailer's highly controversial 1957 portrait of the hipster as "The White Negro" sparked a journalistic movement that wove together orthodox journalism's commitment to fact and chronology, literature, creative writing's devotion to the crafting of lyrical prose, and ethnography's obsession with "thick description" of people, places, things, and events.

With the publication of Truman Capote's book-length account of the murder of a family in rural Kansas and the execution of the murderers (*In Cold Blood*, a title that refers to execution as well as murder), the "New Journalism" genre achieved prominence. Tom Wolfe's later work on hot rod culture, Hunter Thompson's dogged reporting on the 1972 campaign trail, and Joan Didion's essays on emerging lifestyles and culture (*Slouching Towards Bethlehem*, 1969) knotted this new strand of journalism firmly into the history of American prose. As the war in Vietnam escalated, the New Journalists focused on the war and became more intense in their critique of U.S. policies.

*(continued)*

---

[1] We strongly recommend that you read Jay Rosen's compelling dissection of "objectivity" in journalism, which he treats as a form of "persuasion," a system of "signs" that journalists employ to convince readers that their report is "true" in some transcendent way, a way that extends above and beyond the particulars of the moment, the daily grind of the writers' and readers' lives. Capital "T" Truth. Here's where you can find Rosen's piece: http://journalism.nyu.edu/pubzone/weblogs/pressthink/2010/07/07/obj_persuasion.html

*(continued)*

The New Journalists differed fairly dramatically from their more orthodox counterparts working in newsrooms and broadcast stations around the world. The New Journalists rejected the principle of "objectivity," arguing that in practice this fundamental tenet meant a bland, uncritical reporting of interviews conducted on all sides of an issue, a refusal to engage on any issue, and consequently a (partially unintentional) complicity in promoting the frames and agenda of powerful elites. The New Journalists insisted that "objectivity" stems from being *involved in*, not detached from, the action, the scene, the lives of the people about whom you're writing. Reporting the truth required stating their own point of view. They also eschewed the formalistic and staid aesthetic of most journalistic prose. Rather, they wrote lengthy accounts bursting at the seams with singing, lively, lyrical prose.

If you read books like Thompson's *Hell's Angels* or Joan Didion's *Slouching Towards Bethlehem*, you'll find a very different kind of writing from the increasingly standardized prose of newspaper stories. In contrast to the rather predictable sentence structure and tepid description of the standard news story, the New Journalists' report unfolds in scenes with full dialogue captured, or re-created; they don't rely on decontextualized, practically disembodied quotes from bystanders with a second- or even third-hand account of what went down. Re-created dialogue is central to the New Journalists' writing tool-kit. At the same time, though, the stories are self-consciously just that— stories. They are far less concerned with "facts" and far more concerned with conveying the "vibe," the essence of the moment as they experienced it, the expression of the writer's "interiority," for New Journalism balks at the factual, acknowledging that what is "fact" is always under contest, forever in flux, and perpetually unsteady.

The New Journalist strives to construct a *believable* (if self-referential) story, whether or not she gets the "facts" right.

The New Journalists developed the stories; they wrote people. Developing the stories meant immersing themselves, sometimes for long periods, in the situations that intrigued them. But they upheld the journalistic virtues of *experiential* accuracy (as opposed to factual accuracy), fairness, and public accountability. But impartiality, they argued, is unattainable—undesirable even. Why would anyone want to be impartial toward important, newsworthy events and people? After all, partiality—taking a perspective—is a product and producer of passion, and the best-told stories are those told passionately about passionate experiences.

Much like ethnographers, the New Journalists paid close attention to "status details," the features of the environment, the characteristics and mannerisms of the "characters" in the stories, the little things that add up to a way of life for a person. The opening sentence of *On Boxing*, by Joyce Carol Oates, illustrates the New Journalists' belief in the adage "the devil's in the details":

> The young welterweights are surely conscious of the chorus of jeers, boos, and catcalls in this great cavernous space reaching up into the cheap twenty-dollar seats in the balconies amid the constant milling of people in the aisles, the commingled smells of hotdogs, beer, cigarette and cigar smoke, hair oil.

In a pattern familiar to qualitative researchers, the New Journalists move back and forth between the concrete and the abstract, the details and the generalizations about the bigger scene of which a given moment or event is but a part. Later in the same essay, Oates pulls focus and brings the reader to a higher level of analysis, as she shares some of her inferences concerning the sport, art, and craft of boxing:

> To enter the ring near-naked and to risk one's life is to make of one's audience voyeurs of a kind: boxing is so intimate. It is to ease out of sanity's consciousness and into another, difficult to name. It is to risk, and sometimes to realize, the agony of which "agon" (Greek, "contest") is the root.

Tom Wolfe, one of this genre's founders, once remarked that the only way to figure out how people see themselves is by scrutinizing the minutiae of their surroundings. In this way, he said, we can perform a "social autopsy" of a given character in a story. The New Journalists' social autopsy looks a great deal like the social autopsy method we describe in a later chapter.

## THE JOURNALIST AND THE ETHNOGRAPHER.

The journalist and the ethnographer work in similar ways, especially if we're talking about the New Journalists and the investigative journalists who produce multivolume series. But there are some important differences between journalistic work and ethnographic inquiry.

First, there are differences in the *time frame*. Ethnographers tend to cultivate their "stories" and do their investigative work and their writing over a much longer period of time. While the journalist may consider two or three months to be a huge commitment for a single story, it's not unusual for ethnographers to spend two to three years in the field and another two to three years writing up their experiences and findings.

Second, journalists and ethnographers differ with respect to theory. By name and usually by conscious practice, ethnographers work within the social sciences. And while they argue strenuously over the politics, significance, purpose, and practice of ethnography, there is general consensus that ethnography is more than storytelling.

Third, ethnographers are more interested in *generalizing their findings*. Beyond a commitment to accuracy or "truth" in ethnographic representation-making, the ethnographer strives to say something about the so-called "human condition." The specific "case" at hand is certainly important and valuable in its own right; but the ethnographer's real interest lies in examining and relating the case in ways that help readers better understand the world in general, or at least some aspect of the more general world. Scott's (2009) **ethnographilm** *The Family at 1312*, for instance, ostensibly focuses on a "fictive kinship" system developed and perpetuated by crack smokers, prostitutes, and drug dealers. In dissecting this so-called pseudo-family, Scott's film holds up a mirror in which the viewer can see some of the fundamental dynamics that operate in the majority of the "normal" families in contemporary America.

Fourth, ethnographers and journalists impose very *different narrative structures* on their writing. Journalists like to organize their stories around conflicts, people dramatically taking opposing sides on an issue, or heroic struggles against the odds. Ethnographers do not look for or find this narrative structure in their observations of cultures in context. Nor do they organize their data to fit familiar plotlines like the quest or the Hollywood ending. Most published ethnographies don't hang on a narrative arc, nor do their writers concern themselves with presenting a coherent plotline, although they try to write in a vivid, readable way and to present their "research subjects" as real and complete human beings, not cardboard cutouts representing concepts. The plot of an ethnography, however, typically emerges not from the events and lives within the culture under scrutiny; rather, the plot consists of the *unfolding of the argument* presented by the ethnographer. And the argument generally derives from the application of the ethnographer's conceptual and analytic frame to the evidence she produces as a result of long-term interactions with the culture she has chosen to study. *The narrative structure of the ethnography is its rhetorical unfolding.*

## CONCLUSION

In this chapter, we have provided an informal introduction to the art and science called "ethnography." At this point, you should have a pretty good grasp on how ethnography compares with the kind of inquiry in which we engage when we find ourselves in new and strange situations of everyday life. We examined the building blocks of ethnography's "logic of inquiry," its focus on cultures, its attention to context, and its concern with falsifiability in a process that does not conform exactly to the scientific method practiced in the natural sciences. We also elucidated some of the similarities and differences between ethnography and journalism, its closest "ally" in the professions that involve writing about people.

# Exercises

1. Go spend a half a day in a place you've never been. It should be somewhere local, but easy to get to and safe to visit. It might be a part of town you've never visited before, a neighborhood that you know has a different way of life than your own. Before you leave, sit down and think about how you're going to become "fluent" in the ways and means of that area's culture. Write out a plan of attack. Then go forth. Keep good notes during your visit. When you return, write up your experiences. As you write, however, try to avoid falling into the trap of comparing everything you experienced to the things you already know and are comfortable with in your own culture. Evaluate the experience on its own terms, not in relation to your biography.

2. Explain how ethnography is different from how we usually come to know about a new situation or culture in daily life.

3. Explain the differences and similarities between ethnography and journalism. (Read one of the books of New Journalism mentioned in the chapter or an essay in a magazine like *Rolling Stone*.)

4. Search through published editions of a major newspaper or news magazine. Find a piece of "investigative" journalism that strikes a chord with you. Read it carefully. Now explain how the piece resembles ethnography and also how it falls short of being "truly ethnographic."

5. Identify a simple norm or custom and transgress it in a nonthreatening way in a public place. For example, wear a belt or tie wrapped around your head, or a bit more daringly, put a pair of clean underpants on your head as headgear. Observe how others react and try it out in various venues—class, a ball game, family dinner. What do you learn about rules, norms, customs, transgressions, and sanctions? (Based on a classroom performance by Noel Barker.)

6. The next time you find yourself in a relaxed, informal environment/situation with friends, family, or even your romantic partner, construct your presentation of self using a more formal structural system. For instance, when having dinner with your significant other, treat the whole interaction as an economy. When he asks you to bring him something, do it but at the same time hand him a handwritten invoice charging for your time. Basically, your goal is to turn every interaction into an economic exchange. Write up the experience. This exercise should tell you a great deal about the "culture" of your community of friends, of you and your partner's relationship, and of your family. By invoking the principles of a very different, perhaps even antagonistic, cultural system (e.g., the economy), you can really get a sense of the underlying principles of the culture you currently occupy, produce, and reproduce.

# Key Terms

abductive logic *119*
chronic Popperism *119*
culture as a process and
    structure *116*
deduction *119*
ethnography *111*

ethnographilm *123*
emic *112*
etic *112*
falsification *118*
induction *119*
in situ *117*

mores *115*
New Journalism *121*
Ockham's razor and
    parsimony *120*

# 8

# Historical-Comparative Research

## OVERVIEW

Historical-comparative (HC) qualitative research design is guided by macro-level research questions, and in that regard it is different from most qualitative research, which leans toward a microlevel of analysis and is based on observations that take months or years to unfold, but not decades or centuries. In HC research, we explain large-scale differences among societies. The unit of analysis (UAO) is usually a whole society or a type of society, such as capitalist societies or feudal societies. For example, we might be asking why societies end up with different types of political institutions, religions and values, economic arrangements, or **class structures**. We would explain these differences among societies in terms of large institutions and structures.

## HISTORY OF HISTORICAL-COMPARATIVE RESEARCH

You may remember from Chapter 2 (history of qualitative research) that HC strategies originated with Weber and other classical theorists. Certainly Marx and Engels were also engaged in HC analysis as they tried to understand the origins of capitalism and its global impact. In the late nineteenth and early twentieth centuries, a favorite explanation of societal and cultural differences was based on the notion of race; scholars as well as the general public in Europe and the Americas believed that humanity was divided into a limited number of races, each with distinct mentalities as well as physical features, and that these mentalities determined the type of society that each race formed. The great classical sociologists—the theorists of the period whose work we still read today—all rejected racial explanations and explored societal differences in terms of historical development of institutions and culture, not biologically inherited mentalities. In the view of the classical sociological theorists, small initial differences in social arrangements in ancient times (possibly related to climate and other environmental conditions) produced cumulative and expanding effects, creating major societal differences by the dawn of the modern period around 1500 C.E.

Weber and the other great classical sociological thinkers (most notably Marx and Engels, and Durkheim) introduced HC design as a two-step process. We begin by defining a situation or social arrangement as an ideal type, an abstract and extensive definition, and we then seek to understand where it occurs (in what historical periods and contexts) and why its actual manifestations (as opposed to its definition on a printed page) differ from the ideal type. To do this well, we need to immerse ourselves deeply in historical knowledge. HC research requires training in historical analysis rather than field experiences.

For example, we might define **capitalism** as an **economic and social system** characterized by **private ownership** of productive property, **markets**, and free wage labor (not slavery or serfdom); and then explore where, when, and how it emerged and what accounts for variation among capitalist societies. For example, we could try to explain why markets are more regulated in European countries than in the United States.

## Exemplary Historical-Comparative Research Studies

Let's look at several examples of historical-comparative research. The examples of HC research will clarify the logic of the design.

**PEASANT WARS**   Our first example is Eric Wolf's *Peasant Wars of the Twentieth Century*. Wolf looked at six major upheavals of the twentieth century: the Mexican Revolution that began in 1910 and continued until the 1930s; the Russian Revolution of 1917; the Chinese Revolution that began in the 1920s and consolidated a regime by 1949; the Algerian Revolution against French colonial rule in the late 1950s and early 1960s; the Vietnamese Revolution that began as a movement against French colonial rule, continued as the United States' "War in Vietnam," and finally consolidated a new unified state in 1975; and the Cuban Revolution (1999).

These upheavals were violent, multifaceted changes in political systems, class structure, culture and ideology, and economic organization. All of them took a long time to unfold and involved millions of participants. They were not just quick military coups. Journalists and social scientists would call them **"revolutions"**—indeed many of them are always labeled with that word—but for Wolf the word is only the beginning of the analysis.

Wolf's research question is focused on similarities: What led up to the armed struggles and the overthrow of the central political institutions (whether it was a state or a colonial regime)? What caused the revolutions in the first place? Was there a key precondition that all of these cases have in common, despite the fact that they are located across the globe in very different cultures?

This question could be answered in many ways. We might look at the organization of the revolutionary movements, weaknesses in the military and administrative apparatus of the central government or colonial regime, or cultural change such as the impact of Western ideals of democracy and political rights, inadvertently introduced by Western powers as they directly or indirectly controlled these regions. These explanations would have emphasized the role of elites—emerging leaders who formed revolutionary movements and established new national identities and the political, military, or cultural authorities of the collapsing regimes who lost control. Wolf does not dismiss these explanations but he subordinates them to another perspective that looks at the underlying cause that precedes these political and military shifts.

Wolf answers his research question by looking at what happened to peasant communities as capitalism penetrated the countryside. The transformation of rural social relationships into capitalist ones happened as a result of land becoming a commodity available for private ownership, growing and fluctuating markets in agricultural products, and wage labor as a replacement for traditional obligations. Wolf argues that this economic, social, and cultural transformation created the conditions on a vast scale for the uprooting of traditional peasants, their molding into a proletarianized labor force, and the consequent onset of social instability in the countryside. The destruction of traditional social relationships in the countryside was a necessary and sufficient condition for the mobilization of revolutionary movements and armies.

Notice that capitalist penetration of rural areas was the common denominator of all six cases; whatever their initial cultures and agrarian social arrangements, all six were impacted by capitalist agrarian development, whether it was introduced by a colonial regime (as in Algeria and Vietnam), by foreign companies (as in Cuba), or by national capitalists and landowners turned capitalist, orienting production toward global markets (in Mexico during the presidency of Porfirio Diaz, in Russia, and in China). This similarity explains the similarities in the outcome of all six cases.

Capitalist penetration of the countryside is the independent variable and revolution redefined as a peasant war is the dependent variable, if we reformulate Wolf's analysis in these traditional quantitative terms. And they are very big variables. Notice how these variables are not defined in measurable quantitative terms but as ideal types.

The reader may at first glance think that Wolf's hypothesis, deeply rooted in Marxist theories of capitalism as a global system, cannot be falsified. But in HC research, alternative explanations and hypotheses are just as possible as in quantitative designs or ethnographies based on participant-observation in the field.

**REVOLUTIONS**    Theda Skocpol asked a similar research question but proposed a different answer (1979). Skocpol's question was this: Why did France, Russia, and China experience massive revolutions, upheavals marked by both transformations of the political system and class conflict on a very large scale, with the annihilation of aristocracy and landowners as a class? Notice that her cases are not identical to Wolf's; she includes a case—the French Revolution—that took place before capitalism became a global economic system, and she leaves out the more recent, anticolonial cases.

Skocpol's answer is that the old regimes, protecting an increasingly oppressive agrarian class structure dominated by a landed class, not weakened in military engagements. As she words it,

> The revolutionary crises developed when the old-regime states became unable to meet the challenges of evolving international situations. Monarchical authorities were subjected to new threats or to intensified competition from more economically developed powers abroad. And they were constrained or checked in their responses by the institutionalized relationships of the autocratic state organizations to the landed upper classes and the agrarian economies. Caught in cross-pressures between domestic class structures and international exigencies, the autocracies and their centralized administrations and armies broke apart, opening the way for social-revolutionary transformations spearheaded by revolts from below. (1979: 47)

Her methods included careful examination of secondary accounts written by historians. Her conclusions offer a different view than Wolf's, encompassing Weberian as well as Marxist perspectives: The "ancien régimes" as political structures failed to protect the class structures; political actions undertaken by the regimes—specifically failed military operations—weakened the political structures that protected and defended the underlying class structure.

Goodwin and Skocpol (1989) also posed a challenge to Wolf's work in their study of Third World revolutions, a list that overlaps Wolf's although focused entirely on upheavals that culminated after World War II. This list does not include the Mexican and Russian revolutions, and for all practical purposes the Chinese Revolution, which was essentially complete by the end of World War II.

Capitalist social arrangements had appeared virtually everywhere in the world after World War II except in the Soviet bloc and China. Markets, wage labor, private ownership of productive property, and commodity production were dominant or at least major institutions of all non-Communist societies, even if not of communities in remote regions. So why did some regions and nations experience revolutions, while others, equally changed in their social structure, did not? Goodwin and Skocpol argue that although capitalist relations of production may have been a necessary condition, they were not a sufficient condition for revolution and did not in any automatic or direct way produce a revolution. They also argue that revolutions appeared only where significant parts of the population were excluded from power; it was exclusion from power, and not capitalism alone, that was the precipitating condition for revolt, armed struggle, and regime change.

Goodwin and Skocpol identify the types of societies in which exclusion was the common experience and they claim there were two of these: one was the "family-style" dictatorship in which a single extended family and its friends and cronies dominated the economy and political system, such as the Trujillos in the Dominican Republic, the Somozas in Nicaragua, and the Haile Selassie regime in Ethiopia. Segments of the population that were not connected and subservient to the dominant family were excluded from power, even if they were educated and prosperous.

The second type of regime that was toppled by successful revolutionary movements was direct colonial rule, a form of colonial administration in which little effort was made to co-opt traditional indigenous authorities such as chiefs, kings, or rajahs. These exclusionary colonial regimes did not create figurehead intermediary authorities and institutions, legitimated by the fiction that they represented the legacy of traditional rulers and authorities. The use of traditional or pseudo-traditional authorities to run a colony is called "indirect rule." The English generally favored indirect rule and were clever at promoting and inventing "native potentates" and creating symbols of traditional authority (visible not only in their overseas colonies but in the Scottish and Welsh areas they occupied in the formation of Great Britain—regiments wearing kilts, indigenous titles for English rulers of Celtic territories, etc.) (Hobsbawm and Ranger 1992). The French favored direct rule and made little effort to co-opt indigenous rulers, thereby creating a feeling of exclusion.

Two of Wolf's "peasant war" cases—Algeria and Vietnam—were French colonies; Cuba could be considered a family-style dictatorship in which Batista favored his cronies. Wolf's other cases lie somewhat or entirely outside of the period considered by Goodwin and Skocpol. Remember also that Goodwin and Skocpol are looking at successful **regime changes**; so a protracted armed struggle like the one in Guatemala does not fit into their set of cases because it was not won by the armed insurgency.

Have Goodwin and Skocpol "falsified" Wolf's hypothesis that capitalist penetration of the countryside is the precondition of Third World revolutions? Or, have they only entered an intervening variable—the presence of an exclusionary regime—into the equation, at least for the post–World War II cases? Note that they have also changed the theoretical foundations, from a predominantly Marxist perspective to one that is more closely linked to Weberian conflict theory with its emphasis on political action as a force that is co-equal in explanatory power with the economic base.

**SOCIAL MOVEMENTS**    A couple of examples of HC analysis of social movements may provide useful illustrations of this design.

Benedict Anderson (1999) asks the research question what precipitated nationalist movements and his answer is that the causal forces were western education, literacy, and awareness of common cultural interests—all inadvertently fostered by colonial rulers as they developed strata of native elites and intellectuals in the process of administering their colonies.

In his study *Imagined Communities*, Anderson's dependent variables are nationalism as an ideology and nationalist movements; these elements of collective action are the outcomes of the process he analyzes. His independent variable is communication in the colonial territory that helps to form in the minds and discourses of educated indigenous strata "an imagined community"—a cognitive map of a single nation. Nationalism is not a "natural" or "instinctual" sentiment, but a discursive and cognitive process that takes place among people with certain types of education.

Anderson's cases are located in Latin American and Southeast Asia. In Latin America in the first decades of the nineteenth century, creole (native-born of European ancestry) elites led independence movements. In southeast Asia, nationalist movements began in the twentieth century and achieved their aims in Indonesia, Vietnam, and the Philippines.

Unlike Wolf, Goodwin and Skocpol, Anderson uses not only secondary accounts but relies heavily on memoirs—life narratives—of nationalist leaders, a method we will discuss in Part III.

Martin Riesebrodt (1998) also looks at similarities in movements, in this case two recent movements, the Islamicist movement that came to power in Iran in 1979 and political religious fundamentalism in the United States. At first glance, these two movements seem quite different: one is Islamic and successfully formed a regime, while the other is Christian and a political force in the United States but not a governing power. It is not even clear that "fundamentalism" is an appropriate label for the radical Shi'a Islamic movement at all. But in Weberian fashion, Riesebrodt argues that they both represent an underlying ideal type: a stance of ambivalence toward modernity that embraces modern technology and the form of the mass media, and even the ideal of the democratic state, while rejecting modern secular forms of social relationships, gender relations, and the family. Riesebrodt argues that both movements (and by implication, similar conservative currents in Islam, Judaism, and Christianity) are propelled by the goal of reestablishing patriarchal gender and family relationships. Riesebrodt is following the lead of Weber here, in looking at religion, ideas and values, and political action as major forces in social outcomes. Weber was just as interested as the Marxists in economic and class relationships, but he was more inclined to think of religion and politics as independent variables than Marxists generally do (Zeitlin 1997: 197–207).

The recent "transition to democracy" that took place in many nations in the last decades of the twentieth century offers many opportunities for HC analysis. In this period, a number of countries "returned to democracy" after a period of military or one-party rule. This widely used expression immediately challenges us to consider whether we can establish an ideal type of "return to democracy"—Is it indeed a single phenomenon and if so, to what other social arrangements is it related?

Przeworski (1991) argues that we can indeed do this. His research question is what happened in a number of countries by the 1990s, and his cases include both Eastern European countries formerly in the Soviet bloc and under single-party state-socialist rule and Latin American countries (specifically Chile, Argentina, and Peru) that "returned" from rule by right-wing military regimes. He argues that in both sets of cases, the political transition to democracy is accompanied by an economic transition to markets (or to freer markets, in so far as the South American countries were capitalist societies throughout the period of the dictatorships). Notice the very large variables in this analysis—democracy (and its absence), the presence and structure of markets, the concept of a **return to democracy**, and the behaviors of institutional political actors such as labor and capital.

Kenneth Roberts (1998) takes a different methodological approach to a historical-comparative research project with a similar research question as Przeworski's. He explored the prospects for and barriers against a "deepening of democracy" in Peru and Chile. By **deepening of democracy**, he means extending participation in politics to a larger public and making it more meaningful and more responsive to the needs of citizens. In other words, he means citizen involvement that includes the minimal requirements of civil rights and liberties and regular competitive elections, but goes further to include ways of bringing ordinary citizens into public discussion and decision making. He examined two cases in which the minimal forms of democracy were reestablished after military rule.

Chile was ruled by a right-wing military regime from the coup carried out by August Pinochet against Salvador Allende on September 11, 1973, until the late 1980s when the Pinochet regime was forced to begin making concessions to opposition forces. Peru was dominated by an elected authoritarian government under Alberto Fujimori who had restricted democratic freedoms after consolidating his power in what many observers termed an "auto-coup," a coup against his own democratically elected presidency; his authoritarian rule was finally brought to an end in public exposure of corruption and repressive policies. The choice of these two cases creates a different logic of analysis from that of Przeworski's analysis of a return to democracy; Przeworski's cases are mostly countries that were substantially industrialized and modern with a largely literate and westernized population, both in eastern Europe and in the "southern cone" of Latin America. By comparing Chile with Peru, Roberts created a very complex set of comparisons and contrasts for analysis: Peru is a much poorer country than Chile and is characterized by a large indigenous population and a considerably lower level of industrial development. His analysis therefore must take into account cultural differences and very different class structures, despite a degree of similarity in the return of the political system to democracy.

Indeed Roberts found major differences in the way democracy deepened but only within definite limits in both countries. In Chile, movement organizations on the radical left were increasingly forced into the model of standard electoral politics—playing by the rules of electoral competition typical of developed capitalist countries; if they failed to enter this game, they recognized (or believed) that they would not be able to play an important role in Chilean politics in the period during which institutions were gradually restored to democratic functioning. On the other hand, in Peru, large parts of the left refused to play the "bourgeois game" of participating in electoral politics and instead concentrated on organizing grassroots community groups in poor neighborhoods, hoping to create social movements that could survive outside of the well-defined limits of electoral politics.

A very brief summary would be that in Chile democracy was not deepened because there were pressures on radical democratic groups to join the game of electoral politics, whereas in Peru there were also problems in deepening it because too many radical groups insisted on developing relatively limited and often competing and even antagonistic grassroots organizations leading to a disconnect between radical groups and the electoral system. Roberts examines the political choices made by the groups and parties as collective actors in the political arenas of the two countries. He interviewed political leaders and tends to interpret the outcomes in terms of their choices within the global system; these choices are constrained but not simply determined by these larger social forces, such as the collapse of the Soviet Union, which meant that the Chilean left found itself with little support for more intransigently left options. Ultimately, as in Skocpol's work, the guiding theory is probably Weberian, an emphasis on the action of individual and collective actors and the expression of their purpose in political organization; it is also compatible with Bourdieu's concept of the political field (Hancock and Garner 2009) though Roberts does not spend much time on these underlying theories.

# CHARACTERISTICS OF HISTORICAL-COMPARATIVE RESEARCH

Let's sum up what all of these studies have in common:

- They are about very large units of analysis—generally whole societies, political systems, capitalism as a global system and other types of social formations such as feudalism and tributary kingdoms, class structures, and so on. Individuals are not the unit of analysis.
- The analysis covers long time spans, processes that take decades or even centuries.
- They focus on relationships among big variables, such as the type of economic and social system, revolutions, the actions and **ideologies** of movements, and global political change. These variables are almost always defined in terms of ideal types and the values of the variables are identified categorically, at a nominal or ordinal level of measurement, not with a quantitative metric.
- The studies examine the variables in their complex contexts; variables are not "pulled out" and measured separately.
- The studies use **small samples (small N)**, generally less than 30 cases, and sometimes as few as two.
- The researchers examine large volumes of **secondary sources**, including writings by historians, **eyewitness accounts**, **life narratives** and memoirs, and **documents**; only in a few of the HC studies are interviews or observational methods used. Often "nonobtrusive measures" are needed because the actors are now all dead and not available for interactive methods.
- Weber's concept of the ideal type guides research, with the analysis focused on why and how similar institutions or transformations emerged in different situations and on reasons for variation.
- HC research faces challenges in establishing falsifiability. It is not impossible to do so, but a straightforward hypothesis-testing format is rarely employed because the situations are "large," unique in key respects, and historically situated. The large number of variables and their highly contextual character creates problems for conventional hypothesis-testing procedures, and so does the necessity of using nonrandom samples. Instead of falsifiability based on statistical tests of significance, the emphasis is more on plausibility and the absence of better explanatory frameworks; identifying preconditions rather than verified causes is the goal of the research, a situation that is prevalent in many forms of qualitative research. Short of recruiting research assistants among celestial beings who can test events in parallel universes, it is difficult to use designs such as experiments and multivariate analysis to determine causality in historical events. It is hard to say that the French king's problems in the French and Indian war against the British in North America and later his generous support of the American Revolution—generosity that doubtless also offered a chance to get back at his traditional British antagonists—"caused" the weakness of the French monarchy and precipitated the French Revolution. To truly test this proposition, we would have to run a historical experiment in which the Louis XVI wisely refrains from this foreign policy venture in one version of reality while engaging in it in the other version—or better yet, observe his choices in a statistically robust set of parallel universes to see if the choices make a significant difference in the course of French history—truly the stuff of science fiction, not sociology.
- The research questions link the big variables in big hypotheses, such as the one that argues that new, capitalist socioeconomic relations in the countryside were the precondition of the emergence of revolutionary movements in the twentieth century.

- Theories are strongly integrated into the project, and it is usually foundational theories that drive the research questions and guide the interpretation of data; and these theories are often based on Marxist or Weberian conflict theories.
- HC research leans toward a nomothetic orientation, and in that regard differs from some historical research which is more ideographic; in other words, although the canons of the scientific method have to be modified to study historical events and trends, social scientists in HC remain confident that generalization is possible and that general patterns can be discerned. This position is the nomothetic one—the one that searches for recurrent patterns and predictable relationships among phenomena, as opposed to the ideographic view that all historical events are unique and can only be recounted as interesting narratives, without the effort to find underlying patterns or regularities.

## WHEN AND HOW TO USE HISTORICAL-COMPARATIVE ANALYSIS

Now that we have looked at a number of examples of the logic of HC studies, we can say a bit more about the choice of methods and the ways in which evidence is amassed, the way the data are grown to use our farming metaphor.

- A small number of cases formed the basis of the sample—the researchers treated **societies as the units of analysis**,
- Primary and secondary documents can be important sources of information.
- Many social scientists rely on historians to do the "grunt work" of historical research, the actual labor in **archives**. They rely on their understanding of the quality of historical research and interpretation—for example, the quality and reputation of journals of historical research—and come into relatively little contact with primary data.
- Interviews and direct observation can be used only when participants are still alive, as was the case in Roberts' research; even in that situation, observation may be very limited if the movements or political groups are no longer operative or the political situation has shifted dramatically.
- Life narratives and memoirs were used by several researchers, such as Anderson.

## CONCLUSION

Doing historical-comparative research is hard work! Although operating at the **macro-level research** in terms of the dominant UOA, the research must attend painstakingly to the details within and across cases. Moreover, the researcher's job is to identify and account for their similarities and differences, and how various factors intersect, combine, converge, or otherwise "interact." In the end, the researcher must craft a persuasive and well-evidenced argument concerning how different cases came to produce similar outcomes and/or how very similar cases ended up with very different outcomes. This chapter has presented a variety of examples of HC research, and through these illustrations we have revealed the basic architecture of HC research designs (in an abbreviated manner, of course). This kind of research can be very rewarding, but at the same time frustrating because of the number of variables, the complexity of their interactions, the challenge of selecting cases, the "wiggle-room" for alternative interpretations, and the volume of potential data, whether from archives, secondary sources, or **participant narratives**. In the end, however, HC scholars produce some of the most influential and widely read texts in the field of sociology.

## Exercises

1. Identify a difference between two countries that you find thought-provoking. For example, think about the different health care systems of Canada and the United States. Read about the history of the specific institutions and of the countries and use the information to propose an explanation of the differences. What additional information would you want to collect to develop your explanation? Are there alternative explanations?

2. Think about the macro–micro level distinctions we have discussed in this book? How does this distinction "play out" in the context of HC research? Propose a research question involving a comparison of two countries that could be explored with different methods at the microlevel and the macrolevel (Example: the historical origins of the differences in French and U.S. food habits).

3. What do you find most appealing about the HC approach? What do you find least appealing? What do your answers say about you as a person (biographically speaking) and as a student of sociology? Do your answers provide any hints as to your preferences vis-à-vis daily life concerns, sociological theory, skills and capacities, and so on?

4. How would you approach an HC study of the new health care laws in the United States? What if you had to conduct the study using only domestic institutions and organizations (i.e., this would not be an international study involving other countries)?

## Key Terms

archives *132*
capitalism: commodities *126*
economic and social systems *126*
markets *126*
private ownership of the means
    of production *126*
class structure *125*
deepening of democracy *129*

ideologies *131*
institutions *125*
macro-level research *132*
political systems *126*
primary sources: documents *131*
eyewitness accounts *131*
life narratives *131*
participant narratives *132*

regime change *128*
return to democracy *129*
revolution *126*
secondary sources *131*
small samples (small *N*) *131*
social movements *128*
societies as the units of
    analysis *132*

# Social Autopsies: Adverse Events and What They Tell Us About Society

## OVERVIEW

In this chapter, we present the "social autopsy," a design that dissects social causes and consequences of **adverse events** in order to learn more about societies, institutions, and organizations. We provide several examples of autopsies in order to illustrate the goals and key components of this design. We also offer some practical guidance on designing and carrying out your own social autopsy.

## CONTEMPORARY LIFE AND THE DEMAND FOR AUTOPSIES

In the autumn of 2005, Americans watched with disbelief (and horror in many cases) as the city of New Orleans was lashed by a hurricane and a flood, thousands of its residents were herded into the Superdome and dispersed to all corners of the nation, whole neighborhoods became uninhabitable, and about 1400 people died. Hurricane Katrina and the flooding that accompanied it seemed to rip the cover off of uncomfortable truths—the poverty of so many residents of New Orleans, the poorly maintained state of the levees and canals, the confused response of both state and local government, the callous treatment of survivors, and inadequate leadership at the top level of FEMA, the federal disaster management agency. Many political leaders and pundits referred to Katrina as a natural disaster—an "act of God"—but critics pointed out—and continue to point out—the fact that human failures contributed to the differential vulnerability of New Orleanians and to the fumbling of agencies entrusted with disaster management and citizen security.

Katrina is certainly not the only instance of a disaster leading to exposures of institutional failure, organizational and governmental mismanagement, social

House in the Lower Ninth Ward in New Orleans.

disparities, and inadequate planning. In some cases, the disaster is largely natural even though the responses are shaped by social institutions; in other instances, the disaster or adverse event is a social product from start to finish. The analysis of **institutional failures** has come to be called "social autopsy" and it is the basis for a special type of case study. The disaster uncovers underlying problems, and social processes that are normally concealed or opaque become visible and **transparent**. Therefore, it is a powerful method for studying organizations, institutions, and whole societies.

The term "social autopsy" came into use especially with Eric Klinenberg's (2002) *Heat Wave*, one of the most comprehensive and widely read sociological dissections of a disaster. Klinenberg examined the distribution and causes of the deaths attributable to the 1995 heat wave in Chicago. He identifies the logic of a social autopsy in these words:

> What makes the heat wave such a meaningful event is that it represents the exemplary case of what Marcel Mauss [a French social scientist and student of theorist Emile Durkheim] called a **total social fact**, one that integrates and activates a broad set of social institutions and generates a series of social processes that expose the inner workings of the city. (2002: 32)

## TYPES OF EVENTS: NATURAL DISASTERS, ACCIDENTS, AND INTENTIONAL ACTS

The events that can be autopsied include **natural disasters**, **accidents in high-risk systems**, and **intentional acts**. Hurricane Katrina, the Chicago heat wave of 1995, the 2010 floods in Pakistan, the earthquake in Haiti, and the December 2004 tsunami in the Indian Ocean are examples of natural disasters. The social autopsy focuses on the populations that were at risk and the response of governments and relief agencies.

A second type of "adverse event" that can be autopsied are accidents, such as coal mine disasters, the sinking of the *Titanic*, the nuclear power plant accident in Chernobyl, Ukraine, the chemical leak in Bhopal, India, the BP explosion and leak in the Gulf of Mexico, and the February 2008 recall of meat from "downer cattle"—animals too sick to stand. These incidents were certainly not intentional, but neither are they "natural disasters." They are the result of decisions made in the management of an organization or errors in organizational practices and routines. The organizations are involved in a high-risk technology or are operating in a complicated natural setting, such as an iceberg-filled ocean or the depths of a mine. The organization or system in which the accident takes place operates within a larger social context—a local and national culture and a political and governmental system. For example, in some countries a high rate of coal mine accidents is considered "normal" or "acceptable," while in other countries the national culture and a strong union movement resist this naturalization of mine accidents and insist on stringent safety standards. The autopsy addresses all of these levels.

A third type of autopsy dissects an event or situation that is entirely "human made"—for instance, the torture and humiliation of prisoners that took place in the prison at Abu Ghraib in Iraq under U.S. occupation, the Watergate break-in planned by the Nixon administration, or instances of ethnic displacement and genocide. Here the analysis links the actions of lower level personnel to the larger organizational, political, cultural, and international context.

## Examples of Social Autopsies

**THE BUFFALO CREEK FLOOD**    Sociologists and social psychologists had studied disasters for decades during the period after World War II, often focusing on collective behavior and social disorder that emerged during the event or on the traumatic experiences of survivors. But one of the more comprehensive, critical, and socially contextualized studies of disaster was written by Kai Erikson (1976) about a disaster that occurred in West Virginia in 1972, the Buffalo Creek flood. His study already had many of the characteristics of the complete social autopsy.

The flood raised the question what do we mean by "natural disaster" or "act of God"? Buffalo Creek flowed through a valley in West Virginia. Pittston Coal Company, one of the large mining companies in the region, had created a series of sludge ponds high in the valley, pools that formed amid the piles of material removed from the ground during the mining process. These sludge ponds and the surrounding mud and debris became highly unstable; in a season of heavy rains the sludge ponds finally burst loose and flooded the valley with 130 million gallons of mine waste water and debris. As the water, mud, and rocks rushed through the valley it picked up additional debris—trees and houses torn from the ground. When this terrifying mass hit homes it swept them up and killed their inhabitants, drowned in the raging waters or crushed by swirling logs, housing materials, rocks, and mud. By the time the flood was over, 125 people were dead and 4000 were homeless. Many of the survivors had seen loved ones killed and had come near-death themselves. Was this a "natural disaster" or a disaster caused by human negligence?

Kai Erikson traveled to Buffalo Creek to gain an understanding of the impact of the flood on the community and the survivors. The law firm that represented survivors in a suit against Pittston Coal funded Erikson's research. His focus was not primarily on the actions of owners, managers, and employees of the coal company that had created the sludge ponds, but the experiences of the survivors; in that regard it was somewhat different from later social autopsies that focused on conditions and decisions that caused a problem in the first place. Erikson emphasized the need to understand the impact of the flood in the specific cultural and social context of

Appalachia. Although it was one of the poorest regions in the United States, its people were independent and self-reliant. They not only had strong social bonds with each other but also held to a value system of autonomy and freedom, which they linked to the rugged terrain of the Appalachian Mountains.

Erikson believed that these cultural traditions, somewhat paradoxically perhaps, made it especially difficult for the people of Buffalo Creek to cope with the disaster. Their dispersed living pattern was disrupted as they were forced into temporary housing, and they felt increasingly dependent on government aid for day-to-day survival. They were reluctant to ask for or receive government support and equally reluctant to leave their valley to start a new life where there were more jobs and economic opportunities. Their ethos of self-reliance excluded the very "help-seeking" behavior necessary for them to obtain relief. Erikson's book takes a pessimistic view of the long-term impact of the flood on **community and identity**.

**THE *CHALLENGER* LAUNCH DECISION**   Diane Vaughan's (1996) *The Challenger Launch Decision* is closer in aim and methods to Klinenberg's definition of a social autopsy. In January 1986, on a very cold day in Florida, NASA launched the space shuttle *Challenger*. Across the world, hundreds of millions of television viewers watched excitedly as the shuttle began its thunderous liftoff. Within a few seconds, the craft exploded, killing its seven occupants.

The ensuing investigation quickly focused on damage to the O-rings, large gasket-like seals between the rocket sections, as the technical cause of the explosion. It turned out that NASA had experienced a series of problems with this component. The question that Vaughan (and others) wanted to answer went beyond the technical details of exactly how and why the O-rings had failed—the question was why the decision to launch was made when there were indications that there might be problems with the O-rings, especially on such a very cold day. What sequence of behaviors, interactions, and decisions had led up to the launch decision? Vaughan was able to interview managers and engineers at NASA and at Thiokol, the contracting firm, and had access to key documents.

Vaughan proposes that the work groups charged with the development of the shuttle began to form a distinctive culture. In interaction, people create norms about how to handle ambiguous and potentially risky situations. The need to manage risk and accomplish goals leads to breaking the formal rules and developing informal rules that allow a higher level of risk-taking. These informal emergent norms are part of the **routinization of deviance**.

We can see this process in many organizations—hospitals and police departments, for example. If everyone "worked to rule" following every formal rule to the letter, it would be literally impossible to get anything done in most organizations; so formal rules are shaded and informal rules are followed that enable workers to accomplish their job. Recruits are quickly socialized to understand these informal rules, though they are not spelled out explicitly. According to Vaughan, at NASA and its contracting firms a "culture of production" was pervasive, and many people—managers perhaps more so than engineers—were prepared to take some risks in ambiguous situations in order to keep the mission on target. Furthermore, the organizational culture emphasized hierarchy, and roles were defined in a way that discouraged subordinate employees from speaking out. Thus, the culture and structure of the work groups created a situation in which managers were willing to take risks that eventually led to the needless deaths of seven people.

Vaughan's book is a detailed study, carefully based on interviews and documents. But it is not the only direction that a social autopsy of the launch decision can take. For example, Edward Tufte (1997)—in an article of only a few pages to Vaughan's 575—argues that it was poor graphing and data analysis that led to an underestimation of the risk. He provides a dramatic graph, plotting O-ring damage as a function of temperature, which would suggest to even a complete novice that a launch at a freezing temperature might be a very bad idea. Upon seeing this graph, one of the authors' (Roberta) entire social research methods class—not a single one of whom was an engineer or rocket scientist—immediately said that it was clear that there was a relationship between low temperatures and O-ring damage. Yet this simple graph plotting O-ring damage as a function of temperature for all the launches had never been developed by the space shuttle launch team. Tufte concludes that the problem was a **failure of analysis and cognition**, not work group culture and the routinization of deviance.

Charles Perrow (1999), author of a massive study of high-tech accidents, suggests yet a third explanation—closer to the ones in the popular press and public opinion at the time of the disaster. He argues that NASA allowed production pressures to override safety concerns and specifically that upper management under pressure from the Reagan administration (eager for a spectacular launch) suppressed safety concerns that were being voiced by engineers alarmed by the very low temperatures. Rather than the result of a subtle process pervading work groups throughout the organizations (NASA and its contractors), the risky launch decision was a blatant mistake at the top, caused by external **political pressure**. Perrow warns that we should never confuse culture and power—"We miss a great deal when we substitute culture for power" (1999: 380).

**THE CHICAGO HEAT WAVE**    Klinenberg's social autopsy of the Chicago heat wave focuses both on the distribution of deaths and on the social and organizational processes that allowed the deaths to happen. Unfortunately, many readers do not read far enough into the book to understand the logic of the entire design. At the start of the analysis, Klinenberg looks at who died: the victims were largely poor elderly people who lived by themselves and were isolated from their families and social support networks. They were disproportionately white and African American, and relatively less likely to be Latino or Asian American. At this point some readers stop reading, satisfied that their stereotypes are confirmed: Latinos and Asians value family and take good care of their elderly.

Of course, this is not the end of Klinenberg's study; he then analyzes death rates and the circumstances of death in two neighborhoods and provides a larger social context for the individual deaths. In a poor neighborhood with high commercial and community activity, death rates were relatively low, whereas in an even poorer neighborhood with high crime rates, vacant lots, and thinned out social activities, death rates were particularly high. The first neighborhood, South Lawndale, was predominantly Latino, but poor elderly whites living there also enjoyed the protective factor of a vibrant community life. The second neighborhood, North Lawndale, was predominantly African American, but Klinenberg emphasizes that it was not race *per se*, but the social processes of crime and urban demolition that had diminished community life, which gave it a higher death rate. People who lived there were afraid to leave their homes, there were few retail areas or safe, attractive public spaces, and social bonds had become weaker.

Klinenberg then moves to a decisive **institutional analysis**, offering yet a larger frame of analysis—municipal and national social policy. He argues that in the period of neoliberalism since the 1980s social services have not only been cut back. They have also been reorganized on a **"smart consumer" model of social services in the neoliberal era** which requires complex choices in a quasi-market situation. Public services have been restructured to create a welter of choices among many competing agencies. Finding and contacting the right agency or nonprofit provider is difficult and complex; simple entitlements to one-size-fits-all public services have ended. This reorganization has happened in many developed capitalist societies and major cities and in social service institutions from Medicare drug plans to school systems. Smart young people looking for magnet schools for their children may be able to navigate this new terrain of public-sector consumer choice with ease and assurance. Poor ill old people, living in isolation in frightening high-crime neighborhoods, were not able to get the help they needed. Someone who is very ill, isolated from family, too old to be in contact with friends and social networks, and too afraid to open the window is not likely to be making effective choices among a welter of hard-to-contact government and nonprofit agencies who might be able to provide help.

At the end of the book, Klinenberg analyzes the way the media and the public relations agencies of the city minimized the disaster and chose not to reveal the failure of social services.

## THE DESIGN OF SOCIAL AUTOPSIES

What have we learned about social autopsy as a research method from these examples? Drawing on the examples presented to this point, we now can identify some of the key elements in the design and execution of the social autopsy method.

### Appropriate Types of Research Questions

Social autopsies offer a range of approaches and perspectives. They can highlight one or more of the following:

- The structure and practices of organizations designed to manage risky technologies.
- **Organizational culture** that permits or even encourages taking "shortcuts" that circumvent safety procedures.
- **Power and hierarchy** and the role of organizational power holders in encouraging risky behavior—for example, the pressures in NASA to launch the shuttle.
- **Organizational routines and work group norms** that permit high-risk behavior.
- Problems of **resource allocation** and the impact of diminished or misallocated resources in precipitating an accident or preventing effective response to a natural disaster—for instance, the poorly maintained state of levees and canals in New Orleans.
- **Disparities** among the groups that are exposed to or affected by the accident or disaster, which in turn reveal underlying **inequalities**—for instance, the vulnerability of poor people, people of color, and populations in poor countries to both natural disasters and to the siting of high risk and hazardous technologies.
- The **response of governments and other institutions** to the event, revealing their effectiveness and concern, or lack thereof.
- The **representation of these events in the media**, and the consequent formation of **public opinion** and public concern toward the event, the survivors, and the institutions involved.

### The Logic of the Social Autopsy

Let's sum up the logic of social autopsies as a method of social research:

- Social autopsies are a special type of case study.
- Social autopsies are a way of studying organizations, power and decision making, and inequalities in the impact of disasters, accidents, and intentional acts.
- Normally secretive or "opaque" practices and organizations are exposed to view in the social autopsy.
- Social autopsies are potentially contentious; the researcher may "step on the toes" of people with power, raise questions about the functioning of institutions, or bring attention to disparities and inequalities. In some cases, the researcher may be an advocate from the outset.

## Social Autopsies Are Contentious

Social autopsies are highly **contentious interpretations**. They tend to antagonize those whose action and/or inaction contributed to the disaster's onset, unfolding, and/or adversity of aftermath. All steps in the analysis, from the discussion of disparities and vulnerable populations to the identification of organizational and institutional contexts and analysis of media coverage will cause controversy.

**SEE FOR YOURSELF**    We strongly suggest to readers a little exploration of this on the Internet, using "Chernobyl" as the search term. "Chernobyl" was a town in Ukraine (part of the Soviet Union at the time—1986), in which a major accident took place in a nuclear power plant. A number of people died directly as a result of the accident and a large cloud of radioactive material was released and floated over northern and eastern Europe. Communities near the plant had to be evacuated, and a fairly large zone remains closed off and uninhabited. Beyond this very terse description of the incident, there is little that can be said about Chernobyl that finds consensus.

Explorers online will find vastly different estimates of the toll. At one extreme, websites suggest that about 60 people died, most of them firefighters who heroically gave their lives battling the fires in the days immediately following the accident. They died within a few days or weeks of the accident. These websites—and many of them are associated with the nuclear power industry—claim that there is little evidence of longer-term effects on larger populations. At the other pole of the argument, sites that call for continued aid and support for populations in Ukraine claim that 100,000s of people—especially children—are suffering from adverse effects and illnesses such as leukemia and thyroid cancers and that everyone in the region will continue to be at risk for a long time to come. What is the quality of the evidence? Does the truth lie somewhere in between? How can we decide?

"Chernobyl" not only exemplifies disagreement over disaster and accident *impact*; there are also very large differences in the discussion of its *causes*. Some websites emphasize operator error—human error at the lowest rungs of the organization. The operators decided to run a test, but neglected to follow basic safety rules concerning the water supply. Other accounts emphasize that the design of nuclear reactors and power plants in the Soviet Union was faulty and highly risky. In this perspective, any Soviet nuclear facility was an accident waiting to happen; they were all poorly designed and failed to include safeguards for overriding inevitable human errors or at least containing their effects. Yet other observers point beyond both operators and plant design, instead placing the blame on the Soviet ideology of uncritical use of technology and disregard for consequences to human beings and the environment. In this larger perspective, the unconscionable draining of water from the Aral Sea to irrigate central Asian cotton fields is part of the same disastrous overall culture, state policy, and practice as the Chernobyl accident.

Look at these contending websites for yourself. Is it clear which site has the best evidence-based data on effects? Which interpretation of the causes of the accident seems more persuasive? In any case, exploring these questions online will give you a fascinating glimpse of why social autopsies can become one of the most contentious and highly politicized methods of social research.

## Against the "Conspiracy Theory"

Social autopsies of disasters and accidents are not conspiracy theories; the researcher is not claiming that some secret or shadowy "they" has made the disaster happen on purpose. The Daley administration in Chicago did not cause the heat wave in order to kill old people. Pittston Coal did not want the sludge ponds to flood the valley. Nobody wanted the *Challenger* to explode. Even in the case of Katrina, stating that there was gross negligence in the upkeep of the levees as well as inadequate evacuation procedures is not the same as believing that the Lower Ninth Ward was allowed to flood on purpose. (You may want to watch Spike Lee's *When the Levees Broke*, in which some of the people interviewed voice the opinion that the flooding was intentional, but it seems fairly clear that the filmmaker is keeping his distance from this position—watch it and decide for yourself.) Nevertheless, social autopsies could also be carried out for events that were intended—torture, genocide, and ethnic displacement. But even here the focus is not only on the perpetrators but also on the organizational and institutional context, and perhaps the culture and geopolitical situation as well, in which it was allowed to happen or that enabled it to continue.

Social autopsies "do not reduce complex events to a single guilty actor or causal agent," as Klinenberg notes (2002: 32). He even states that they cannot be reduced to a single social force; they are usually the result of multiple intersecting causal processes—a sort of "perfect storm" in the social structure. For example, one could argue that the *Challenger* launch decision involved both work group culture and pressure from the top and that "Chernobyl" included operator error in the context of poorly designed systems and uncritical state policies of technology development. "Katrina" was based on converging forces including poverty, racism, incompetence at the apex of FEMA reflecting the effects of cronyism and fund-raising in the federal government, deferred maintenance on public works, and failed emergency planning at the state and local level.

The highly contentious nature of social autopsies suggests that the researcher must take special precautions to limit bias once the research is underway and must be exceptionally sensitive to ensuring that falsifiability is possible in the design. If the researcher was hired by plaintiffs in a lawsuit or is working with an advocacy group, these concerns are particularly pressing.

## COMPONENTS OF A SOCIAL AUTOPSY

A social autopsy therefore is an overall research design, not a specific technique. It includes quantitative as well as qualitative analysis, interviews and observation as well as unobtrusive measures. Here are components that might be included in a full-scale, multilevel social autopsy and a few suggestions, or directives, for specific data collection methods.

### Who Was Affected?

The method involves examining risks that disproportionately affect vulnerable populations, the disparities and inequalities that contribute to heightened risk of disaster for some but not others, the spatial distribution of risk and vulnerability, and the vast range of survivors' experiences.

**VULNERABILITY AND RISK**    The focus of the study could be vulnerable groups and the disparities in the impact of a disaster or adverse event. Here official data, available from government sources, is invaluable. Klinenberg looks at the data collected by the Cook County Public Administrator's Office as well as notes kept by police and left at the Cook County Morgue. Data from government agencies such as the EPA may be useful in analyzing how siting decisions were made for dangerous processes, toxic waste sites, and other environmental hazards. These are rarely placed in communities of wealthy and powerful people. It is not surprising to find that a very poorly managed and monitored Union Carbide plant was located in a community of poor people in a city in India—Bhopal. In his analysis of the social and spatial impact of Katrina, John Logan (2006) made use of data collected by government agencies.

**DISTRIBUTION OF THE IMPACT** Who were the Individuals Affected?    At this level, several distinct sources of data and methods of analysis can be used. First of all, we might want to look at the victims of the disaster. Who were they in terms of demographic variables such as age, income level, poverty status, occupation, employment status (unemployed, underemployed, employed), race or ethnicity, gender, and length of residence in the area? In this analysis, characteristics such as income level, occupation, poverty status, and employment status are indicators of the larger, more complex variable social class.

The immediate next step is to ask whether the victims of the disaster or accident were different from other people. The analysis quickly moves to a discussion of disparities, and these in turn point to underlying structural inequalities. In order to carry out this part of the analysis, it is not enough to examine the data on victims (and survivors) but also to compare them to those who were relatively unaffected. For example, Klinenberg found that people who died in the Chicago heat wave were older, poorer, more isolated, and less likely to be Latino or Asian than other Chicagoans. If carefully collected statistics on victims are available in public data sources, a sophisticated quantitative analysis may be possible. A multiple regression model in which the relationships among variables are considered may help us to understand the relative role of age, living alone, race-ethnicity, and poverty as predictors of the outcome of death or survival, to use the example of the heat wave. Other predictor variables would be selected for other types of disasters or accidents, as appropriate to the specific situation. Since these characteristics may be interrelated, the multiple regression model allows the effects of each one to be considered separately while controlling for the others.

The quantitative analysis is complicated by the fact that in most disasters and accidents the risk of dying or other adverse effects is quite low in absolute terms. Although the death toll in New Orleans is quite horrifying and completely unacceptable, it is nevertheless the case that the vast majority of New Orleans residents survived. Therefore in the quantitative comparison, the two groups being compared—the victims and the nonvictims—are very different in size and this difference may create technical problems in the statistical analysis. Another way of saying this is that because the overwhelming majority of Chicagoans did not die in the heat wave, it is in fact difficult to compare the death rates of (for example) Latinos and non-Latinos or the wealthy and the poor—all of them had a very low **rate of absolute risk**. Although the comparison of rates is the ideal standard of analysis, in these cases, we may have to resort to comparing the demographic profile of victims to the profile of nonvictims or of the population as a whole. We also have to be careful in using expressions such as "risk factor," keeping in mind the very low absolute risk. For instance, being white or African American was associated with higher death rates in the heat wave, but we certainly do not want to jump to the conclusion that all whites and African Americans were "at risk" in this disaster in any meaningful sense of the term "risk factor."

**SPATIAL ANALYSIS OF THE DISTRIBUTION OF THE IMPACT**    At the next substep, a **spatial analysis** can be added to the model, still in the context of asking who was vulnerable. We consider not only the characteristics of vulnerable populations compared to the relatively secure or immune but also the overall spatial patterning and the effects of neighborhood or community contexts. To once again cite Klinenberg's example, poor, elderly live-alone white people in the predominantly Latino community of South Lawndale had a relatively lower death rate than people with the same individual characteristics living in other neighborhoods. Spatial context matters. Once we have determined that spatial context makes a difference in vulnerability, we need to conceptualize the way it makes a difference. The data themselves may have little to reveal

Houses in the Lower Ninth Ward in New Orleans.

about this—we need to turn to sociological theories and qualitative research to understand why neighborhood contexts are important—exactly how they "work" to make some areas more at risk than others.

We can map the impact of the disaster, identifying the spatial areas where people are most likely to experience the impact. If we do that for Katrina's effects in New Orleans we very quickly see that the most adverse consequences—death, injury, long-term homelessness—were experienced in poorer and predominantly African American areas of the city, especially the Lower Ninth Ward.

In mapping the spatial dimensions of "adverse event" impact, we need to think about the boundaries of our mapping. For example, if we study the impact of Katrina on the Gulf Coast as a whole, we would find that many white people lost their homes. The racial disparities are most evident within New Orleans and its immediate surrounding communities. How big we make our map makes a difference in how we reach our conclusions about racial disparities in Katrina's effects (Logan 2006).

This type of spatial analysis works not only for natural disasters and accidents but also for intentional acts. Hannah Arendt (1992), in a controversial book on Nazi genocide, *Eichmann in Jerusalem*, suggested that three countries in Europe—Denmark, Italy, and Bulgaria—had considerably higher rates of survival among Jews than other countries during the Holocaust. What accounted for the difference? Why were people in these three nations more likely to resist the orders of the Nazis to round up and deport Jews? Arendt suggests the reasons were quite different and deeply rooted in national cultures as well as the specific circumstances of German occupation.

Danes felt a sense of civic engagement and collective responsibility; although it had been impossible for them to defend their small, flat country against the German invasion. They were seen as "fellow Aryans" by the occupiers and not as closely and brutally monitored as "inferior peoples."

As is well known, the Danish resistance was able to get most Jews in the country—citizens and refugees from other countries alike—onto fishing boats and smuggle them to Sweden, a neutral country prepared to accept them.

In Italy, resistance to genocide was more likely to be based on individual, anti-statist values of common humanity and concern; the Fascist government cooperated with the Nazis, but many individuals risked their lives to help Jewish friends (and strangers as well) to escape. In Bulgaria, the attitude at many levels of the society was one of "Nobody can come in here and tell us what to do." When the Nazi occupiers ordered Jews to be rounded up throughout the country and brought to the capital to be deported from there to death camps, the Bulgarian head of the national security forces ordered Jews to be shipped out to remote villages in the countryside so they could not be easily found and deported. In this example, the initial mapping of the crime—the identification of countries with high or low rates of Jewish survival—is only the first step toward the analysis of cultural, institutional, organizational, and military characteristics that can be used to explain the distribution of the outcome.

**SURVIVOR EXPERIENCES VARY GREATLY, BUT PATTERNS EXIST**    Still focusing primarily on characteristics of survivors and the distribution of the event in terms of rates for demographic categories and spatial areas, many autopsies include insights into the feelings of the survivors, the impact on communities, and the human impact of specific public policies designed to manage the disaster. In this case, interviews with survivors are obviously a valuable method, and so is participant-observation in the communities that were affected by the disaster, as well as among survivors who may be scattered far away from the disaster site. Because many disasters disrupt communities and force people to seek new homes and new jobs, the researcher might have to range far from the point of impact. For example, Erikson interviewed survivors of the Buffalo Creek disaster not only to understand what had happened to them in the flood but also to understand their feelings about temporary housing and relocation. Following the tsunami, residents of fishing villages in southern India and Sri Lanka were relocated away from the coast and faced great hardship in making a living.

There are difficult issues in both sampling and interpreting survivor interviews. Sampling is difficult because in many cases there is no clear "sampling frame" that allows the researcher to enumerate all possible survivors, though this problem varies with the nature of the incident. In industrial accidents, for example, we can at least think about a list of all employees of a factory— though it might be very hard to obtain that list from the company. In natural disasters or ethnic displacement, the initial lists are hard to specify.

Homelessness and displacement are major consequences of disasters, large-scale accidents, and policies of "ethnic cleansing," so it becomes difficult to find survivors. Those who can be found—for example, those who stayed in their homes during a disaster or did not flee from ethnic violence— may be quite different from the displaced, creating problems of generalizability for the researcher.

Survivor accounts require careful interpretation. Survivors may have learned to tell a story that will obtain support or win a court case. Survivors may therefore exaggerate the impact of the incident or overestimate its long-term effects. Survivors who want to talk about their experiences may be different in many ways from those who refuse to be interviewed or take measures not to be identifiable as a survivor at all.

**Survivor interviews** may be very similar to "testimonial literature"—the collection and editing of the accounts of survivors of a large range of terrible events. This literature has been especially strongly developed in Latin America, where political activists and intellectuals have dedicated themselves to collecting and disseminating the stories of survivors of torture, massacres, and "disappearances" under military regimes (in Guatemala, El Salvador, Uruguay, Argentina, and Chile, for instance), as well as survivors of natural disasters such as the earthquake that claimed between 10,000 and 20,000 lives in Mexico City in 1985 (Poniatowska 1995).

## The Role of Organizations and Institutions

The next focus of the study is organizational culture, hierarchy within organizations, organizational routines and practices, and the resources of organizations. The analysis would probably use interviews and archival data. For example, Vaughan interviewed engineers at NASA and Thiokol and looked at documents charting O-ring damage on previous launches.

**BACKGROUND RESEARCH**    The first step for the researchers is to immerse themselves in available information. Often the social autopsy requires an understanding of complex scientific, medical, or technological knowledge. The researcher can be begin with textbooks and research articles concerning the topic or may be lucky enough to find a review essay or published review of the literature. For example, Vaughan had to learn a large amount of information about shuttle and rocket technology in order to understand what respondents said in interviews about safety procedures and risk management. Klinenberg had to understand how people die in a heat wave before he could conduct meaningful interviews with medical examiners. In order to be a credible and effective interviewer, the researcher has to acquire much of this information and knowledge before conducting the interviews.

**PUBLIC RECORDS AND ARCHIVES—COURT CASES AND HEARINGS**    Investigations by public bodies or commissions can be useful sources of this material, and court cases and public hearings are an invaluable starting point in many cases. Sworn witnesses are required to testify about a situation and the evidence provides clues to the researcher about organizational practices that may have been one of the causes of the incident. Of course, testimony must be treated with caution by the researcher; witnesses may be protecting themselves or an organization. Problems are often blamed on the lowest level of operators and higher levels of an organizational hierarchy are shielded in the evidence. Nevertheless, the public testimony and accompanying documents are a necessary starting place for the social autopsy, providing at least a baseline of information about what happened. They also help the researcher to understand the terminology of the institution—the discourses and jargon that have to be used at the next step, which is interviewing. Individuals closely involved with a technology or any type of process may not talk about it in quite the same ways as the books and articles from which the researcher has gained basic knowledge.

**INTERVIEWS WITH INDIVIDUALS IN ORGANIZATIONS AND INSTITUTIONS**    The researcher might next turn to interviews with members of the organization or institution. The warnings and strictures that apply to the role of guides in qualitative research apply to the respondents in this situation as well. People who agree to be interviewed may be angry and marginalized within the organization; they are eager to present their own behavior in a positive light (as a whistle-blower, for instance), while accusing others in the organization of having acted irresponsibly.

Alternatively, they may be "stranger handlers" in a role designed to minimize negative conclusions about the organization and assist in a cover-up or "damage control."

Sampling respondents who were or continue to be in the organizations involved in the incident presents complicated problems. Most organizations do not provide comprehensive public lists of employees, so creating anything resembling a sampling frame and a random sampling procedure is virtually impossible. If a researcher resorts to snowball sampling (asking each respondent to identify other individuals who might agree to be interviewed) the practice is likely to amplify any initial bias in the process with a repetition and confirmation of what the initial respondent in the network claims is accurate. Sampling individuals who left the organization after the incident is even more difficult and is almost certain to have to rely on snowball sampling techniques tapping into networks of probably like-minded people.

In these complicated, complex, and organizationally contextualized case studies, interview guides need to be developed that are worded nonjudgmentally. The interviewer must know enough about the situation, including underlying technology, to be ready to pose focused follow-up questions in an interactive manner; it is not enough to prepare a well-designed, initial structured interview guide.

A naïve front can be useful in the interview. Even though the interviewer must know something about the topic of the interviewers, in some cases, it may be a good tactic to ask the respondent to "begin at the beginning" and to explain the basic processes and terminology. The interviewer can compare the way the respondents talk about the process with the way it is described in textbooks or the research literature, and the comparison may be revealing, possibly containing clues about shortcuts or crucial, risky decision-points.

It is important to remember that IRB approval almost always carries with it measures to ensure confidentiality and anonymity. These safeguards may induce respondents to be frank in their discussion of organizational problems.

## Evaluate the Public Representations of the Event

Social autopsy includes the response of media and other organizations that specialize in the representation of reality—public relations firms, advocacy groups, and so on. To gauge the way the image of the disaster is formed and manipulated, the methods of content analysis and discourse analysis are useful. For example, why was the phrase "refugees" used repeatedly about people forced to leave their homes during Katrina? Were black people removing goods from stores labeled "looters," while white people doing the same thing were described as looking for items they needed to survive? Are accidents in non-Western countries given less attention by the media than those in Western or developed nations? For example, the 4000 deaths and over 200,000 serious injuries resulting from a chemical accident in the Union Carbide plant in Bhopal, India, seem to have drawn less attention than smaller accidents in North America and Europe, such as the Three Mile Island nuclear accident in Pennsylvania in which no one was killed or injured.

As terrible as Katrina was, in terms of deaths and displacement it was much smaller than an earthquake in Pakistan that took place a few weeks later, in October 2005, and caused possibly as many as 73,000 deaths and homelessness among over a million people. A student in one of Roberta's classes a few months after this earthquake said he had never heard of it and excused his ignorance by claiming he was "a victim of the media." Although the excuse is absurd, it is true that the media coverage of the quake in the United States was terse and disappeared quickly compared to Katrina coverage.

**PERFORM A CONTENT ANALYSIS**   A few basic categories for content analysis could include:

- *Typification of victims and victim behavior*. For example, are the victims portrayed as innocent or careless, irresponsible, incompetent, and even complicit?
- Typification of the rescue effort, first responders, and long-term aid
- Who is interviewed and the types of authorities and experts interviewed?
- *Point of view*. Does the coverage present different points of view on what happened? Does it assign blame or suggest that what happened was "an act of God" or not preventable?
- *Duration and positioning of coverage*. How long is the story? Does it appear on the front page or at the top of the news on TV? When does it fade from a leading spot and where does it go?

After an initial content analysis based on these simple categories, a more refined coding can be developed and applied.

## PUTTING IT ALL TOGETHER: THE NEED FOR MULTILEVEL DESIGN

The social autopsy in its most developed form—in Klinenberg's book, for example—covers all of these elements: the distribution of its impact, which in the case of larger disasters is rarely random and generally linked to social disparities; the analysis of cultural, organizational, and institutional processes that have set conditions for the adverse event or precipitated it; the impact on survivors and people indirectly affected by it; the institutional response to it; and the images and representations used to portray it. So it usually requires a multimethod approach including interviews with survivors and with decision makers, archival records and government data, quantitative and qualitative analysis, and possibly participant-observation.

### Theoretical Foundations

Throughout this book, we encourage readers to connect research design to theory. Theoretical foundations lead to a deeper analysis and help us to understand underlying processes, not just the problems of the day. Social autopsies are very easy to link to theories—here are a few examples.

Klinenberg uses ideas from both conflict theories and Emile Durkheim in his analysis of the Chicago heat wave. The two initial parts of the analysis seem strongly influenced by Durkheim's work. As Durkheim did in *Suicide*, Klinenberg looks at the distribution of deaths—who was vulnerable? The concentration of mortality among elderly people living alone also points to the significance of Durkheim's view of society. The great French theorist believed that sometimes society is dense, vibrant, and cohesive, but sometimes—and increasingly so in the modern era—it is "thinned out" and atomistic, a condition that puts elderly people at risk. This Durkheimian analysis is developed more explicitly and intensely in Klinenberg's contrast of the two communities.

The community with a dense, vital social life had better survival rates among at-risk categories of people than the community with little public sociability and a high degree of fear and isolation. Klinenberg's reference to Marcel Mauss (a student of Durkheim) and the phrase "total social fact" signal his debt to Durkheim. But in the second part of the book, Klinenberg draws on conflict theory—the Marxian subtext seems unmistakable—to point out how the withdrawal and reorganization of public social services contributed to the disaster. Heat wave deaths have to be understood in light of the major transition from "embedded liberalism" (characterized by government provision of social services and many entitlements) to "neoliberalism" with governments cutting services or reorganizing them to limit access, charging user fees, and generally making it more difficult to get help. The media failed to analyze these problems in social services in their heat wave coverage. Klinenberg's critical perspective on the media links him to conflict theories.

Durkheim and Marx are almost always good choices for sociological inspiration, but there are many other theorists whose concepts can deepen a social autopsy. For example, Michel Foucault was interested in regimes of surveillance and regulation; he used the quarantine as a key example of institutional efforts to define and contain a problem. Max Weber and Pierre Bourdieu, along with Marxists, are theorists of inequalities and stratification systems and their work can be used to understand the disparities that become evident in many disasters. Bourdieu's "symbolic violence" and "misrecognition" are concepts that draw our attention to the mis- representation of events in the media. Weber as a theorist of bureaucracy, organization, and instrumental reason contributes to understanding organizational decision making and in the analysis of failures to follow procedures, distortions produced by hierarchical relationships and the very workings of instrumental reason itself.

C. Wright Mills' (1940) concept of " vocabularies of motives"—the excuses and rationaliza- tions that are used to explain behavior—as well as the symbolic interactionists' labeling theory help us to see similarities in the way that many accidents are managed and represented—for instance, the tendency to blame them on the lowest level of the hierarchy, such as the operators at Chernobyl or the lowest-ranking soldiers at Abu Ghraib. The whole point of the social autopsy is to understand mismanaged disasters, accidents, and intentional acts as produced by larger forces than individual error or misconduct. Erving Goffman's analysis of teams in the presentation of self and impression management provides insight into organizational presentations and cover-ups often associated with accidents. Feminist theory encourages the researcher to give voice to survivors who might otherwise remain silent—or silenced—and to turn away from official histories of adverse events.

Finally, we can see a similarity between the multistage social autopsy and the progressive– regressive method of understanding human action that was suggested by existentialist philosopher Jean-Paul Sartre. Sartre began with a key event or situation in the life of the individuals about whom he wrote and then traced the *antecedents* of this event—the regressive part of the study—and its *consequences*—the progressive part. The antecedents took Sartre in the direction of preconditions and causes, ranging from childhood experiences to situations later in life and the immediate precipi- tating circumstances; the consequences showed the impact of the event on the life of the individual and the way it shaped his or her later actions and choices. Similarly in the social autopsy, we look at both the impact on survivors and communities and the causes and preconditions of the accident, disaster, or action.

So we can see—in this quick sketch—that autopsies can have deep roots in theory, as well as applications in the "real world" of policy and social change which we will briefly sketch as well.

## Related Types of Inquiries

Readers of this chapter will almost certainly be asking themselves how social autopsies differ from investigative reporting. Indeed the two kinds of writing are closely related!

Here are a few of the differences:

- The social autopsy researcher generally has more time—a time frame of years to conduct research, whereas journalists tend to be under time pressure of days or at best weeks to complete their investigation.
- The social autopsy researcher feels freer to look at larger social and cultural contexts. Although good investigative reporters are not hesitant to "go after" higher levels of officials

and the upper reaches of organizational hierarchies, they may feel pressure to avoid social science concepts such as "routinization of deviance." They may feel compelled to stick to simpler explanatory frames focused on the misconduct of individuals. This is beginning to change, however, and many journalists are comfortable using terms such as "organizational culture."

- Few reporters are eager to present readers with a complex statistical analysis.
- The social researcher must conduct the research with IRB approval, and this requirement almost certainly means the anonymity and confidentiality of sources. Names not only aren't revealed, they are also kept confidential. Journalists face the diametrically opposite problem; they are encouraged never to publish blind interviews (i.e., ones in which names are withheld) unless the interviewee is at great risk. So both professions face challenges in the management of confidentiality and with it, the public's ability to verify the evidence, but the challenges lead to opposite strategies for managing information about the respondents' identities.

Another related type of writing is the testimonial, which we have already mentioned. For an example of a powerful and moving compilation of testimonials, see Elena Poniatowska's work (1995) on the 1985 earthquake in Mexico City.

## APPLICATIONS

There are many possible applications for social autopsies beyond the impartial search for knowledge and a better understanding of what causes adverse events. Here are a few examples of applications related to **activism, advocacy research, expert witness, and the development public policy**:

Social autopsies may be part of a larger environmental justice research goal. The term **environmental justice** means that there is a growing sense that environmental hazards are not randomly or evenly distributed in most societies. Economic and racial stratification are related to heightened risk. Toxic waste sites, pollution from industrial processes, truck traffic with accompanying air pollution, hazardous mining operations, and landfills are more likely to be situated in or near poor communities or communities of racially marginalized people (people of color in Europe and the Western Hemisphere, or ethnic minorities in many parts of the world). Garbage and toxic waste are exported to poorer nations. A social autopsy can pinpoint specific harm caused to a community and trace the decision making that produced the outcome; for example, identifying the sources of air pollution that affect communities—and disproportionately often low-income and minority communities (Ash et al. 2009).

Social autopsies can be a component of **advocacy research**, specifically focused on changing a situation, pressuring policy makers, preparing testimony in lawsuits or legislative hearings.

Social autopsies can be used to improve organizational practices, both routine practices and emergency practices, as well as technology.

Social autopsies can be used to change policies regarding access to social services. Klinenberg's study made it clear that police had not been trained to identify and help elderly people at risk and that the expectation that they would perform this function had to be backed up with better preparation or assigned to other agencies.

Social autopsies can be used to call public attention to social disparities (and the underlying inequalities) and contribute to social policies to reduce disparities.

## CONCLUSION

The social autopsy can be a powerful tool for the sociological study of natural and human-made disasters (with most "disasters" being a combination of both natural elements and human frailty). It also represents a vehicle by which research can "go public" in a very controversial, social change-producing way. In this chapter, we have discussed some of the most widely read social autopsies, and from them we have drawn key lessons on how to design and implement a social autopsy of your own.

## Exercises

In this section, we impart some practical tips for doing a social autopsy by challenging you with a few exercises that range in degree of difficulty.

### 1. An Easy Exercise

Suggest an incident that would be a good topic for a social autopsy and explain your choice. (You may want to go online and find out the basic description of the incident in the media.)

Look at the following list of ideas for social autopsies. Select a specific case that sounds interesting and find out a little more about it. These suggestions were made by students in undergraduate and graduate research methods classes.

- Industrial accidents: in recent years in the United States, lives have been lost in industrial accidents in chicken processing plants, sugar refineries, coal mines, and petroleum refineries. Some of these accidents took place in high-tech systems, others in factories using simpler technologies. From 2001 to 2005, about 5000 people died each year from occupationally related accidents (National Safety Council website; Bureau of Labor statistics). Are there patterns in accident deaths? How does the U.S. record compare to other nations?
- Clubs and concerts: The E-2 nightclub incident in Chicago; the Warwick, Rhode Island, fire in a concert.
- Sports injuries and deaths, and the decision making involved: For example, find out more about the Paret–Griffith fight, which resulted in the death of Benny Paret, and the question why the ref did not stop it in time. How do coaches and refs make decisions about risk to athletes? For a contemporary example, find out more about the risk of concussion in football and how coaches make decisions about it.
- Policy brutality, wrongful death incidents, torture and abuse of foreign prisoners, and prosecutor misconduct in convictions of innocent people: For example, John Burge and Chicago Police Department District 2 torture of suspects. Why were these acts allowed to continue for so long? Who were the victims? DNA testing and the release of innocent people from prison and death row is a related issue—how many such incidents took place and under what circumstances? How did the Abu Ghraib abuse incidents happen?
- Deaths and injuries caused by medical procedures, including cosmetic surgery.
- Product recall: the February 2008 meat recall; recall of toys, including injuries resulting from magnets.
- Effects of pollution on communities: Love Canal; truck pollution near ports and international borders; siting of dangerous industrial processes; landfill siting.

### 2. A Moderately Difficult Exercise

Select an incident (from the preceding list or your own choice) and outline what you would do in a social autopsy research project. You can spell out research questions and research activities designed to answer the questions, as well as focus on specific methodological concerns such as this: Where might you find survivors to interview? How would you sample them? How would you define the area in which you would carry out a spatial analysis? What disparities in impact do you expect to find? How could you learn more about processes in organizations and institutions? What media would you analyze to reach conclusions about representations of the event? What challenges might you face in gaining IRB approval for your project? For example, how would you assure confidentiality for respondents in organizations?

Internet Exercise: Go to the Country Profile on the OFDA-CRED International Disaster Database.

What is the purpose of this database? What are the criteria for listing a disaster on it? What patterns do you see in the country profiles? (Keep in mind that countries with very large populations are likely to have more disasters and disaster-related deaths as a result of their size, so we have to be careful not to jump to conclusions about factors such as culture, union strength, or government policy.)

**3. A Difficult Exercise**
Actually carry out a research project such as the one outlined in the preceding exercise.

## Key Terms

activism *149*

adverse events: accidents; disasters *134*

intentional acts *135*

advocacy research *149*

contending interpretations of disaster data *140*

development of public policy *149*

disparities *139*

distribution of impact (differences in rates by demographic categories and spatial location) *142*

environmental justice *149*

expert witness *149*

failure of analysis and cognition *138*

inequalities *139*

institutional analysis *138*

institutional failure *135*

long-term impacts on community and identity *137*

organizational culture *139*

organizational routines and work group norms *139*

political pressures *138*

power and hierarchy *139*

public opinion *139*

public records and archives *145*

resource allocation *139*

response of governments and other institutions *139*

risk/absolute risk *142*

routinization of deviance *137*

"smart consumer" model of social services in the neoliberal era *138*

spatial analysis *142*

survivor interviews *145*

total social fact *135*

transparency *135*

# Community-Based Participatory Research or Participatory Action Research (with Krista Harper)

## OVERVIEW

As a research strategy, CBPR is distinct from ethnography and from designs in which the researcher remains "distant" from the researched, such as historical-comparative research and discourse analysis. If your topic is the French Revolution of 1789, you are obviously not "part of the action." In ethnography, the researcher is present in the action as an observer, if not a participant, but he tries not to unduly shape or influence what he is seeing and experiencing. This chapter presents an increasingly popular and ever more demanding approach to conducting qualitative research *with* the people who ordinarily would be called "research subjects." In the CBPR paradigm, the researcher puts herself in the service of the erstwhile "human subjects," who become **research participants** and take the lead in articulating the research question, carrying out the study, and presenting and making use of the results.

## WHAT IS CBPR?

CBPR breaks with the logic of the detached, objective observer in two ways: (1) The researcher is trying to help bring about change, and (2) the researcher interacts and cooperates with the researched in order to bring about changes that the researched themselves have identified as desirable. The CBPR researcher typically rejects claims of objectivity and "outsideness" and commits himself/herself instead to the interests of community members who want to cooperate with the researcher to conduct studies that will lead to favorable immediate and/or long-term changes in the community. **Activism** and **advocacy** are values that motivate many CBPR researchers.

These two simple-sounding premises lead to enormous complexity and make CBPR probably the most difficult, time-consuming, and unpredictable form of research.

## A Brief History (or Rather, "Herstory")

CBPR arose from feminist and postmodernist critiques of the claim that researchers can and should be objective outsiders, gazing at the research subjects without engaging with anyone's lives and hopes (Smith 1990a, 1992; Reinharz with Davidman 1992). It was also influenced by activism of the 1960s and 1970s and the involvement of many young social scientists of the period in community organizing. Roberta Garner remembers distinctly her unsettled and uncomfortable feeling when one of her professors, Richard Flacks, not only described participation in a movement called "Jobs or Income Now" (JOIN) in the Uptown neighborhood of Chicago but also invited one of the community activists to come to the graduate class and talk about the community and the organization. Roberta was still very much locked in an "ivory tower" view of the university and was not sure that she wanted to hear directly from a community resident and activist, instead of having the observations filtered through the theoretical and analytical lens of a sociologist! It was 1965 and the times were about to change dramatically.

Roughly 30 years later, the other of us (Greg) remembers sitting in Professor Flacks' office at the University of California–Santa Barbara talking about Greg's "area exam"[1] in social movements. At the time, Greg was involved with the "Garment Worker's Justice Center," a grassroots organization dedicated to improving the working conditions of undocumented Latino immigrant garment workers and to securing a legitimate place for them within the industry's dominant union. After listening patiently to Greg whine about how difficult it was to gain entrée to such a volatile context, Professor Flacks said, "Get off your ass and think of something to do FOR them and stop trying to think of smart ways to get something OUT OF them." This was a defining moment in Greg's career, although Professor Flacks very likely has no recollection of it. Within a week, Greg had learned that what the workers really wanted was basic instruction in ESL, with the lessons focused on the specifics of their work context. Another week later and Greg was teaching industry-specific ESL to the "vanguard" of workers, who were working hard to politicize their fellow workers and to educate the union leadership on the benefits of better responding to the needs of undocumented workers.

Working in the service of people in whose life and well-being you have a research interest is the foundation of CBPR. Now let's look more closely at the two basic principles of CBPR and see where they lead.

**THE RESEARCHER AS AN AGENT OF CHANGE**    When researchers commit themselves to social change, they typically operate on an implicit or explicit "deficit" assumption. From the outset, they assume that there is something wrong with the world as it exists and that things could be better. In other words, they are committing themselves to an "ought" rather than accepting the "is." These assumptions are shared by many social scientists with a critical perspective on society. But even the most critical observers rarely think that their role can (or should) extend beyond identifying the flaws and the problems. So the majority of "deficit-oriented" social scientists spend their career critiquing the social phenomena that intrigue them most.

---

[1] An "area exam" is a research paper, somewhat similar to a literature review, in which a doctoral student demonstrates mastery of a particular subfield of the discipline. Each area exam typically requires six to nine months' worth of solid work, resulting in a 30–50 page heavily referenced paper. At UCSB, for instance, Greg had to successfully complete two area exams ("Social Movements" and "Criminology") in addition to writing a dissertation in his primary subfield of sociology ("Ethno-Political Economy").

Many critical sociologists, on the contrary, not only feel qualified to diagnose problems and dismantle ideological myths and misrecognition but also believe that their role *should* extend beyond criticism. They feel some obligation to help the situation and/or people implicated in their studies, but the problem is that they don't feel (justifiably in many cases) prepared or confident enough to *prescribe remedies*. They may believe that the problems are too large and systemic to be resolved with the means they have available, or that intellectuals can have a role in identifying problems but are not qualified to take the lead in organizing movements for change, or they may simply just have no idea where or how to begin their quest to "make a positive difference." Whatever the case, most critical sociologists don't "take the plunge" into action.

Increasingly, however, researchers in nearly all of the academic disciplines—but especially the social sciences—not only believe that they have a legitimate role in mobilizing for change but actually find a way to get themselves into the fray. Once committed to the ideal of the scholar as an agent of change, the action-oriented researcher must figure out how and where to get involved, and then master what may be the most difficult skill of all—occupying a quasi-leadership role from a position subordinate to "the cause" about which he, as a researcher with strong political values, is passionate.

**THE COMMUNITY AS THE "EXPERT"**    CBPR rests on the assumption that the **community** (a term to which we will return) has the knowledge—at least the **local knowledge**—to contribute to remedying injustices or solving problems. CBPR researchers have a considerable amount of faith in those they are researching and believe that the community understands its situation and that community members are not in a state of misrecognition or (worse) false consciousness. The researchers accord respect to local knowledge and the information and beliefs the community brings to the project. The researchers must be prepared to learn from the researched—not only about their beliefs and worldviews (in which ethnographers are also certainly interested) but about their social realities as the community members see them. Of course, the researcher's belief in the knowledge held by the community is not naïve or unquestioning, and generally the researchers define part of their role to be expanding this knowledge.

**THE RESEARCHER FACILITATES AND DOESN'T DICTATE**    CBPR researchers have to be prepared to interact with the community and to allow or enable the community to define goals of the research and to participate in selecting specific methods and techniques. Community members are involved in interaction with the researcher to "grow the data" and have the right to redirect and redefine the research project and to engage in the choice of methods.

For example, the researcher must be prepared for **negotiation of the research question** or the goals of research with community members. Community members may have a decisive role in determining who or what gets sampled. This interaction about both goals and methods is almost certain to slow down the project and possibly to move it in directions that the researchers had not anticipated at all. There are many implications of this fact. One is that CBPR moves more slowly than researcher-driven research; it may take years instead of months to organize the project and collect even the most basic data. Another very serious implication is that CBPR can encounter problems with IRB approval. Remember that we emphasized that IRB approval must precede the research. Many IRBs are becoming more flexible in accepting innovations and improvisations that are introduced at a later date; but CBPR researchers need to consider IRB guidelines when research goals and activities are being negotiated with community members.

The research questions of CBPR are quite different from those of other designs. The basic questions are: "What can we do to address this problem or injustice? What is the root condition that needs to be changed in order for the lives of community members to be better? How do community members themselves answer these questions and how do their answers impinge on our understanding of the situation? What resources can they (and we the researchers) bring to bear on the problem? And what can we do together—researchers working with community members—to bring this problem to the attention of a larger community, the society or the public sphere as a whole, or to policy makers who can help us remedy matters?"

## What Is the Meaning of "Community"?

Let's look in closer detail at a key term in the name of the research design: "community." What is a community? Who speaks for a community? These questions point to choices that are related both to technical problems of sampling and to the politics of research. Does "the community" include power-holders who may be exploitive, discriminatory, and "part of the problem"—for example, local political bosses or gang leaders or authority figures in local organizations? Does the researcher always have the responsibility to work with the most disadvantaged people in the community? What if the community is deeply split into multiple hostile factions or divided into two opposing camps? What are we to make of demographic divisions that generally exist even within unified communities, such as the lines of age and gender? Even a community that is homogenous in social class and ethnicity may contain differences in the amount of property owned or levels of household income—distinctions that to an outsider may seem trivial and petty, but that are highly meaningful and divisive differences within the community.

These divisions frequently cut across the obvious visible racial divides in a community and the large economic divisions as well. Interventions in the community can increase divisiveness not only along demographic lines but also along more subtle lines. Racial-ethnic groups and the broad economic categories like "middle class" or "working class" may be quite divided along the lines of owners and renters, long-term residents and newcomers, people with a "decent" lifestyle and people with a "street" lifestyle (Anderson 1999). The project to improve community life may turn out to improve it more markedly for some than for others and it may fail to integrate residents in a community if they are seen as marginal by homeowners and long-term residents.

For example, Greg studied a community-based project of the Illinois Gang Crime Prevention Center (an agency of the Illinois Attorney General's office) to reduce crime in a neighborhood in a large city in Illinois; in the evaluation of the project, the researchers found that recruitment to the intervention, participation in it, satisfaction with the process and the outcomes, and even the sampling procedure to obtain feedback from residents were heavily tilted toward residents who had a stronger stake of homeownership and residential tenure in the neighborhood and who saw themselves as law-abiding "decent folk." People who did not fit under these labels were treated as unwelcome in the neighborhood, and the project actually accentuated and reinforced these previously more informal lines of division (see also Pattillo 2008).

Researchers carrying abstract theoretical concepts into the field may be shocked by how important personality clashes and dislikes are within most groups, even among people who "objectively" have shared interests and should feel solidarity with each other. Whose side are we on?—an easy question to ask among intellectuals, a harder question to answer in practice in community-based fieldwork.

## Problem-Solving? Whose Problems, Whose Solutions?

A second aspect of CBPR that requires careful thought is the question of how far is it appropriate to go with "solutions" or interventions for community conditions. Researchers need to avoid a number of pitfalls: the urge to use the community as a laboratory for testing their favorite interventions; the sense that their theoretical knowledge trumps the local knowledge of community residents; the belief that their interventions will be readily accepted and easy to implement. For these reasons, it may be wiser to think of the researcher as a **facilitator** who can contribute information and insights to community dialog and stimulate community residents to talk among themselves and evaluate options using evidence-based arguments, rather than as someone who can prescribe interventions (Stoecker 2005).

At the end of the chapter, we will return to these questioning and critical perspectives, especially when CBPR or PAR is used as a teaching tool. Before we consider the issues that emerge from PAR, let us look at an example of a PAR project and provide some practical perspectives on the design.

## PAR IN ACTION: ENVIRONMENTAL JUSTICE IN A HUNGARIAN VILLAGE

Our major example is the environmental justice project of Krista Harper who worked in a community of Roma in Hungary to bring public awareness to environmental problems.

To summarize Krista's project, we will begin by explaining the term "environmental justice" and provide a brief history of the Hungarian Roma.

### Starting with Justice

**Environmental justice** is a term that refers to efforts to reduce disparities in the impact of environmental problems. Over the years, activists and scholars have observed that various types of pollution and environmental hazards are concentrated in communities of poor people and people of color. It is rare that garbage dumps, polluting industries and hazardous waste sites are located in communities of the wealthy and powerful. Poor people and ethnic minorities are exposed to higher levels of health risk from environmental pollution and hazardous industrial processes. These disparities have been found both in the United States and in many other countries.

For example, "cancer alley"—a region with high levels of illness associated with petrochemical plants along the Mississippi River in Louisiana—is located near many African American communities. High levels of air pollution associated with truck traffic in the port of Long Beach, California, impact a predominantly Latino community near the port. These examples in the United States help us understand the goal of environmental justice—that the risks and hazards associated with industrial processes, pollution, and waste disposal should not fall disproportionately on economically and socially vulnerable communities (Ash et al. 2009).

### Getting to Know the Roma

Who are the Roma? Roma or Romani ("gypsies") are an ethnic group of Indian origin that came to Europe many centuries ago and lives scattered in many European countries. Roma have endured a long history of marginalization and exclusion, and during the period of Nazi occupation were subjected to genocide. "Roma" calls up images of colorful nomads traveling through the landscape in their horse-drawn carts, but this stereotype is completely inappropriate for Hungarian Roma who have lived in permanent settlements for close to 200 years, although they were often spatially segregated from non-Roma Hungarians. Most Hungarian Roma do not speak a distinct language and they are not markedly visually distinct from other Hungarians, despite the stereotype that they are darker complexioned. They live in segregated neighborhoods within cities and small towns and have lower incomes and less access to schooling and health care than non-Roma.

Hungarian government policy has fluctuated sharply toward the Roma, ranging from efforts to encourage assimilation to cooperation with Nazi policies of genocide during the German occupation in World War II. After the war, during the Communist regime, the official policy was that economic integration would gradually bring about social integration; and most Roma found low-wage jobs in industry (Szelenyi and Ladanyi 2006). In Sajozentpeter, the community in which Krista carried out her CBPR, Roma worked in a glass factory during the years of socialism. Once the Communist state fell, the glass factory was shut down and the Roma lost their jobs, and therefore they lost their source of income and the modest level of social and economic integration they had enjoyed previously.

Krista had been studying the environmental movement in Hungary. The movement was part of "reawakened" civil society that contributed to the collapse of the Communist regime, and Krista had made connections with environmental activists and written about the strategies and goals of environmentalist organizations in the 1980s and early 1990s. She had also published on the topic of the chemical spill in the Tisza River which affected riverine and wetland environments throughout southeastern Europe. As she became increasingly interested in the situation of Roma Hungarians, she saw that they faced many problems of health and living conditions, and that environmentally oriented collective action might be one of the ways of improving their lives.

## A Key Informant Emerges

As she explored these topics, Krista met a person who became a key guide and friend in her endeavors: Jutka Bari. Jutka was working on a university degree and was president of an activist, community-based organization, the Sajo River Association for Environment and Community Development (SAKKF). Krista comments,

> We were both interested in the connection between Roma communities and the environment, and we decided to work together on these themes. The founding members had included 'environment' in the organization's name five years earlier, with the hope of involving community members in the restoration of nearby wetlands. The group set aside these initial plans to focus on youth, community development, and public health for its first projects. Nevertheless, several members of the organization remained interested in the theme and agreed to participate in collaborative research on environmental issues.

So the project emerged from the collaboration of an **indigenous activist,** Jutka Bari, with a researcher in environmental activism, Krista Harper. Krista could bring resources and social science training to the project and enjoyed links to international organizations that would help to raise awareness of the problems, while Jutka was a resident of the community, and one with the skills and knowledge for leadership. As an educated individual, she was in an excellent position to bridge the gap between social science research and indigenous understandings and goals.

Krista provides this capsule description of the community:

> Sajoszentpeter (pop. 14,000) was a minor industrial center in northern Hungary for most of the twentieth century, producing glass and coal until the factory and mine were privatized and closed down following the collapse of state socialism in the early 1990s. The entire population of the town lost its livelihood in the space of a few months, and no new employers appeared in the subsequent decade and a half. Surrounded by fields and the Sajo River wetlands, the neighborhood in this project is over 100 years old and has 2000 residents, most of them Roma. Connected to the rest of the town by a bridge, the community is a two-minute walk to the main square where the mayor's office is located.

Although only a few minutes from the town center, the Roma neighborhood is set apart by the poor condition of the homes, the lack of clean water and modern sanitation, and illegal dumping by outsiders and residents. In many places along the Sajo River, trash heaps and dump sites marred the beautiful landscape of wetlands. Although the Roma were an excluded and segregated population, they were not isolated from or unaware of the larger society. Many of them had lived in or traveled to Budapest, the capital, and several had lived in Canada. A number of them (including Jutka) were married to non-Roma. They were not the "pristine" indigenous folk of a remote village, but a community of twenty-first-century people who are poor and considered an ethnic minority.

## Jointly Designing the Project

Krista and Jutka made key choices in their organization of the PAR project, of which three stand out: one was to enlist young people in the community as active participants; the second was to use a **photo-voice method**; and the third was to develop a photography project that would show both negative and positive aspects of the community. As is the case in many PAR or CBPR projects, resources and positive aspects of the community were included in the discourse, not just needs and negative aspects.

**PHOTO-VOICE**    Krista describes the photo-voice project:

> Six young community-based researchers (ages 18–24) participated in training sessions on photography and research ethics, leading to a discussion of critical themes: the politics of representation of Roma as a minority group, the young researchers' relationship to the rest of the community, and what it means to be on either side of the camera's lens. At the second official meeting of the research team, I distributed small digital cameras to the photographers. I presented the first theme, "environment," and asked them to define the term broadly and to include both positive and negative aspects of environmental conditions and people's beliefs and practices related to the environment. By the following week, the photographers had taken over 400 photos related to the environment. Quickly running through the photos, we noticed that almost half showed trash heaps and dumping sites in and near the neighborhood....We quickly arranged the photos as a digital slideshow and gathered around my laptop computer to discuss the images. Even though we were all aware that photos capture and condense information, we were all amazed to discover how each photo opened up stories, emotions, and new questions.

The photos showed problems and disparities such as unequal access to sewage disposal and wastewater treatment, unequal access to household water, the lack of green space and playgrounds, problems of waste management and illegal dumping, lack of access to efficient energy and fuel sources, poor housing quality, and lack of access to telecommunications. Positive aspects of the environment and the community were also revealed such as the beauty of the wetlands and fishing opportunities, use of bikes, horses, walking, carpools, and public transportation, gardening and animal husbandry, and participatory sports.

The group presented its work at a photo exhibit in Sajoszentpeter, in the street in the entrance to the neighborhood. The young photographers gave their exhibit the title "This is also Sajoszentpeter" to emphasize that the Roma and their neighborhood are also part of the town and to reject their condition of exclusion. They invited community officials, administrators, and professionals to attend. They humorously noted who was prepared to cross the bridge to attend the event on the "gypsy side of town." The exhibit was covered by a national daily, and the pictures became the framework for opening discussions about policy responses to the issues that were raised in the photographs.

The team held an exhibit in Budapest, the capital, at the Central European University. The event included a 90-minute discussion of issues raised in the photographs, facilitated by a nationally known Roma activist and an environmental lawyer. The occasion allowed SAKKF to extend its network to national human rights organizations and non-Roma organizations; grant applications were made to improve access to information technology and more public participation in environmental planning. For some of the photographers, it was the first trip to the capital city. The event thus contributed to increased public awareness on both sides—the photographers made contact with a larger sphere of human rights organizations and environmental activists, and the community broke out of an atmosphere of silence and neglect.

This project is an excellent example of a small scale and manageable CBPR project. It did not have large-scale goals but accomplished the more modest aim of reducing isolation and creating **public awareness**. The participants began to see themselves as agents, capable of reaching beyond their community, breaking the silence that had accompanied their exclusion and segregation, making contacts with other activists, and recording the situation in a way that made it visible to larger constituencies.

## AN OVERVIEW OF CBPR AS A DESIGN CHOICE

1. As we have already noted, the essentials of CBPR are that the researcher works with community leaders and the research is interactive in accord with egalitarian ideals.
2. It is effective to use methods that are readily understood by community members and that are inherently engaging and participatory. This is a major reason why photo-voice and focus groups are excellent choices for CBPR, whereas seeing an outsider writing field notes or watching him or her interview people may convey an impression of one-sidedness and power differences between the researcher and the "subjects." The contemporary technology and nonwritten character of photo-voice and digital documentary film are also appealing to people who may not be very interested in production for written media.
3. Following from point (1), we can see that the production of information in a visual or physical form—a set of photographs, a documentary film, techniques for braiding hair, an article in a magazine or newspaper, a wall mural, and so on—may be a more meaningful product than a peer-reviewed article published by the researcher in a scholarly journal. These kinds of products are more meaningful for two reasons: They are more attractive and appealing to the community members who participated in the research, and they permit much broader dissemination of the results. Many people might like to see a documentary video or look at a photo gallery, while few really want to read articles in research journals. Thus the more widely attractive product is more likely to draw the attention of a larger constituency to the issues the CBPR team wants to bring to the public. But students trying to write a thesis or professors facing tenure decisions on the basis of their publishing record may be uncomfortable with these products.
4. The researchers must be willing to assume new roles as **facilitators of interaction within the community**, as spokespersons for the community in those forums that require professional expertise, as media experts in bringing community issues to public attention, and so on. At the same time, the researchers must commit themselves to not assuming the mantle of permanent representative and spokesperson for the community; they must be prepared to

gracefully cede this position to **indigenous leadership**. There are lessons to be learned from the U.S. civil rights movement in this regard, from the instances in which predominantly white college students and activists from the north had to learn to cede their authority to local leaders.

5. Interaction between the community members and the outsider is seen explicitly not only as a way of beginning to address specific problems but, above all, as a method of breaking isolation. Disadvantaged communities easily become invisible and silent. Their poor conditions are defined to be "natural" by the larger society. The practice of CBPR creates bridges between the community and the larger society, so that members of the larger society become aware of the community not as a collection of picturesque or pathetic subjects but as a group of acting, thinking, striving, self-defining human beings like themselves. Equally important is that the community members see themselves in this way, not as victims, forgotten people, or the objects of the scientific gaze, but as agents, involved in collective action with long-term goals of improving their conditions of life.

## PRACTICAL TIPS

1. CBPR or PAR requires background knowledge of the community and contacts with community leaders. Previous research and community service experience in the specific community in which you plan to work are valuable—probably essential.

2. Try to establish multiple contacts and relationships in the community to avoid having your work become the vehicle for the interests of one individual or community-based organization. You need to form a multifaceted understanding of the goals, values, and interests of many stakeholders before entering into a definite research agreement with any one party.

3. Be patient. Developing your research design collaboratively will require frequent meetings and your research may take unexpected turns, even turns into areas which do not fit your own goals and research questions well. Do not undertake CBPR unless you have a long stretch of time available. If you are rushing to complete a senior thesis or a master's writing project, CBPR may not be the right project for you, no matter how much you share the values of CBPR.

4. Develop methods of research and dissemination of the findings that will be comprehensible and of interest to the community. Effective **methods of dissemination include photo-galleries, documentary film, and other visual methods**. This does not mean that you cannot use more traditional methods (observation with field notes, interviews, quantitative analysis, etc.) but that you will want to expand your repertoire, especially when it comes to dissemination of your findings.

## PAR AS METHOD AND OBJECT OF TEACHING: CRITICAL PERSPECTIVES

We conclude the chapter with a critical reflection on PAR and related research designs, especially when they are used as a teaching method—as pedagogy for introducing students to fieldwork. Our intention is not to dismiss PAR or CBPR but to urge careful preparation and a self-reflective approach to the limits of this design and to the ethical and political concerns associated with it, especially if you are a student researcher or training student researchers.

## A Retelling of PAR's History

In his 1981 presidential address to the American Sociological Association, William F. Whyte challenged sociologists to "rethink sociology" and to do a better job demonstrating the discipline's "practical relevance" (1982: 1). Whyte's suggested reorientation of sociology called for a sustained focus on "the discovery, description, and analysis of *social inventions for solving human problems*" (1982: 1, emphasis in the original). On the same page, he defines the social invention as (1) "a new element in organizational or interorganizational relations," or (2) "new sets of procedures for shaping human interactions and activities and the relations of humans to the natural and social environment," or (3) "a new policy in action (that is, not just on paper)," or (4) "a new role or a new set of roles." At the end of his address, Whyte argues that the study of social inventions can promote advances in sociological theory and methodology, a claim that clearly implies a common ground between "applied" and "pure" social science. Whyte adds provocatively that this in itself, this reorientation, arguably constitutes a social invention within the discipline.

According to Whyte, participatory action research is "a methodology in which the professional researcher invites one or more members of the organization studied to play more active roles than simply those of passive informants" (1989: 369). The researcher, he writes, "combines participant observation with explicitly recognized action objectives and a commitment to carry out the project with the active participation in the research process by some members of the organization studied" (1989: 369). Although Whyte's contributions have indisputably shaped the field of PAR (for he is a widely acknowledged trailblazer in the area, at least within sociology and management studies), his perspective presumes the researcher's expertise, and he neglects a consideration of research methods other than participant observation.

## Revising the Definition of PAR

A definition more consistent with our perspective comes from Deshler and Ewert (1995: 2):

> Participatory action research can be defined as a process of systematic inquiry, in which those who are experiencing a problematic situation in a community . . . participate collaboratively with trained researchers as subjects, in deciding the focus of knowledge generation, in collecting and analyzing information, and in taking action to manage, improve, or solve their problem situation.

While certainly preferable to Whyte's conception because of its emphasis on the agency and autonomy of community actors as well as its circumvention of positivistic notions (i.e., knowledge is *generated*, not discovered or found through investigation), this definition may well perpetuate the labeling and ghettoization of already marginalized communities. In essence, this conceptualization (and most others, too) of PAR require either that the community be oppressed (see, for example, Reardon 1994; Brydon-Miller 2001) or that it be experiencing "problems." The unintended consequence of this well-intentioned conceptual manipulation is that *deficiency and weakness* become the community's principal features of interest to the researchers involved. In other words, we as researchers care about the community in question mainly *because* it is oppressed, stigmatized, or otherwise harmed, and we therefore set out to improve it with the application of our skills. This approach can be almost as injurious as outright assaults on the community's integrity because no matter what we do, we still hold the community accountable for being distressed and weak.

Very few scholarly works account for, much less examine, the potential or actual unfavorable and unintended consequences of PAR. What are common adverse effects that follow from researchers' scholarly-activist pursuits with(in) communities and their organizations, formal and informal? We focus on the way these effects are multiplied when the researchers are not experienced senior scholars but students sent out into communities to have their first experiences of fieldwork. The generally valuable strategy of experiential learning faces special problems when it is linked to community intervention.

## PAR AND PEDAGOGY: THE POLITICS OF TEACHING AND LEARNING THROUGH CBPR

John Dewey (1938: 13) writes that "the belief that all genuine education comes about through experience does not mean that all experiences are genuinely or equally educative." Building on Dewey's assertion, Scarce (1997: 224) references Mills (1959): "Social experiences are not *sociological* experiences" (emphasis in original). PAR social scientists work with community members to create and apply critical frameworks to make sense of the intersection of private troubles and public issues. This can be a double-edged sword. With experiential learning, we have more time and more opportunities to do this, but in cases where we fail, everyone involved in the endeavor—researchers, students, and community members alike—face a greater likelihood of treating their experiences as proof of their preconceptions' accuracy.

### Beware the Backfire Effect: When CBPR Becomes the "Cure That Kills"

In this section, we discuss some of the **iatrogenic effects** associated with PAR projects that involve researchers ushering their students (such as yourself) into communities for the purpose of engaging in action research, which in turn serves as a form of "experiential learning" for the students and social action for the community. In other words, we discuss how attempting to bring about empirically driven, favorable social change may actually lead to the accomplishment of its opposite. ("Iatrogenic" is a term that was originally invented to refer to the adverse effects of medical interventions and practices.)

**OBJECTIFICATION**   Robert J. Hironimus-Wendt and Larry Lovell-Troy (1999: 360) report that "an uninformed service learning experience may hinder, rather than help the movement toward a just society because students may objectify community residents and blame them for their problems." Also, Grant et al. (1981: 23) describe the "zoo phenomenon," where students gaze impassively (and passively) at the people who occupy a social world, and how this activity reinforces students' stereotypes about them (see also Wright 2000: 118). Amelioration can be achieved, but is not guaranteed, when critical reflection complements the experience (Wright 2000). In the implementation of many field-based PAR experiential learning projects, which in part were designed to counter bigotry and prejudice, a countervailing outcome materializes— an even stronger tendency among some students to blame the "subjects" of their study.

**BLAMING THE VICTIM**   Hironimus-Wendt and Lovell-Troy (1999) document some of the problems they encountered in teaching courses centered on experiential learning, one of the main being the all-too-common tendency of students to "blame the victim" for his or her social and/or economic plight (see also Corwin 1996). Many students "reach unwarranted, often racist conclusions based on selective perceptions," which they develop through a "prism of prejudice and individualism" (Hondagneu-Sotelo and Raskoff 1994: 250). In short, they may decide that community actors are responsible for the conditions of their existence and that they suffer because they make poor decisions.

**PATERNALISM**    Hondagneu-Sotelo and Raskoff (1994) describe the "white knight syndrome," wherein students feel outraged by the inequalities they see in the field. A conscientization ensues, which is a generally desirable development, but their consciousness remains immature, its development arrested, as they begin to fancy themselves saviors of the less fortunate. This nonsociological, minimally reflexive position can be as dangerous as blaming the victim, at least in terms of the reification of stereotypes.

Paternalism often manifests in researchers' and students' verbal and nonverbal expressions. It may affect their tone of voice—talking in a "sing-song" manner to community members, as though they are small children. Or the researcher/student may presume to what is best for the community members and even speak and act as though they represent the community's interests. Another common misstep involves the researcher taking action on the community's behalf, presuming to be endowed with the power to speak *for* the community. This commonly stems from the researcher's arrogant assumption that she knows what is best for the community better than the community does. Paternalism can be just as damaging as objectification, and it's generally more difficult to counter.

**IDENTIFYING AND OVERIDENTIFYING WITH "THE OTHER"**    Hironimus-Wendt and Lovell-Troy (1999) illustrate how some students find it very difficult to identify with the community actors with whom they work in the context of service learning. Students and researchers may see their community counterparts as completely and fundamentally different from themselves, believing that they are nothing alike and will never be much alike. That is, the researchers refuse to acknowledge the sameness or similarities uniting them with their learning partners.

In some cases, however, the researcher overidentifies with the "the other" and ends up snuffing the autonomous agency of the "subject-partner." Typically this phenomenon stems from a combination of good intentions and a psychological process in which the researcher comes to view his own life story as one of victimization and allows this feeling to affect his relationship with the community. He internalizes the community's "pain," which then melds with his own past or current sense of hurt. At this point, the researcher identifies himself as one of the community, as someone who also has been injured or mistreated and whose misfortunes and suffering are equal in kind and degree to those of the community. Such egocentrism is fairly common in participatory action research and should be avoided. Engagement in continual "reflexivity" exercises can be preventative.

**DISILLUSIONMENT WITH CBOs**    Perhaps not an adverse—but certainly a real—consequence of working directly with nonprofits is that students learn that not all community organizations are operating effectively. Most of the CBOs (**community-based organizations**) with which PAR scholar-teachers work tend to operate as "third-tier helping organizations" (Venkatesh 1997). These organizations face demand from community residents to extend their services well beyond the parameters established by their mission. Faith-based organizations in distressed neighborhoods, for instance, routinely end up delivering to the community much more than opportunities for the expression of religious faith. In fact, their principal mission of cultivating faith may be overshadowed by the other things they do, such as operating a homeless shelter, providing a safe haven for victims of domestic violence, operating an *ad hoc* job placement service, running a food pantry for the poor, and generally providing community support for which they receive little or no funding. With pressure for service mounting in the face of scarce resources, the typical CBO often concerns itself more with staying in business than with engaging in evaluative or action research.

These forces come together to produce in many instances a series of troubling experiences for the researcher and her students. The CBO's records may be disorganized or even nonexistent; the CBO's director's and/or staff's initial enthusiasm for the research may wane swiftly as they come to realize just how much time they must spend making PAR work to their benefit; staff may resent the researcher(s) and/or perceive the researcher to be a "spy" for management; clients and staff with busy schedules that are organized around principles different from those that underpin researchers' and students' schedules may miss their appointments for interviews and other research activities; and so on. Researchers and students engaged in PAR also frequently encounter conflict within the CBO and/or between the CBO and its clients and/or community stakeholders.

All of these things taken together often spell disappointment for the researcher and students, who understandably had high hopes for the project and may have romanticized the CBO beyond reason. This is particularly likely to happen in cases where the CBO is engaged in some sort of political action that resonates deeply with the researcher and/or students. Once the CBO's "dirty laundry" is exposed, a nearly implacable gloom may settle into the researcher's/ student's perspective on—and capacity to work with—the organization.

**PRESSURE TO MISREPRESENT**   Community-based organizations tend to occupy unsteady ground in the world of activism and social service. PAR scholars gravitate to CBOs because they believe their respective missions to be "simpatico," compatible, and potentially mutually supportive and regenerative. During the course of the PAR relationship, however, a diligent researcher is bound to unearth or generate data whose analysis yields findings unfavorable to the CBO. After all, no intervention is perfect, no matter how well-meaning it is. In fact, intention has little to do with measured outcomes. Hence, the researcher finds herself in a predicament: (1) Air the "dirty laundry" (i.e., the study's unfavorable findings) and risk damaging the CBO's reputation or standing and perhaps even undermining the broader movement of which the CBO is just one part, (2) selectively present the findings in such a way as to protect the CBO and the movement, and/or (3) do nothing at all.

The first approach may be good social science, but it's probably bad politics. And this probably matters to the PAR scholar, whose own political views motivate her to get involved with this particular CBO in the first place. The second option puts the scholar at risk for ethics violations. And the third option likely will do some damage to the researcher's relationship with the CBO, who will feel "cheated" out of their promised product, and this option may also be adverse to the researcher's career—after all, the researcher's employer (probably a university) expects that significant time spent on a research project, and especially a PAR project (which is often construed as "borderline" science anyway) will yield some kind of publication on findings.

PAR's success as research and as an action project depends on the quality of the relationship between the researcher and the CBO (and its constituents). Publishing a report containing negative findings may damage this diligently cultivated relationship. This puts researchers in a position of having to choose between proper ethical conduct and heightened loyalty to the CBO and the movement of which it is a part. This dilemma arises in nearly every PAR project. And it always gets resolved, one way or the other. How it gets resolved depends on many different factors. Ultimately, though, it's the researcher's decision. As we discussed in Chapter 5, one of this book's authors (Scott) chose to publish unfavorable results of a study, and in the end it cost him his relationship with multiple organizations to which he had become very attached. We will reflect again on these issues in Part V when we discuss "telling the story" and the way this process can affect the relationship between the researcher and the people and organizations who were the subjects of the research.

## CONCLUSION

PAR can be used to achieve favorable social change along several vectors: student learning, community advancement, university integrity, and individual faculty well-being. Originally intended to be an object and method of teaching and organizational change, PAR can deliver institutional change beyond the parameters of the CBO. PAR is not, however, a turnkey enterprise vouchsafing only desirable outcomes. Rather, we have shown that like most social interventions (i.e., systematic attempts to change populations favorably), teaching and engaging in PAR is a double-edged sword. Its nuance, complexity, and subtlety work in both directions, the desirable and the undesirable, with the final result being contingent on a number of variables. For first-time PAR researchers, the simplest and most ethical approach is to begin by sharing useful skills or resources (as Greg did when he tutored ESL and Krista when she provided cameras and helped arrange a university gallery exhibit for the photos). Begin as a facilitator and good listener—and don't presume to be a community spokesperson or an expert who plans and implements a life-changing intervention—for other people.

## Exercises

1. Describe one or several communities near the campus of your university or in your city. What problems or issues do you see in these communities (examples: high unemployment rate, homelessness; lack of health care institutions; few food stores; racial isolation; high drop rate in the high schools; high crime rate). What indicators are you using to reach the conclusion that these problems exist in the community? Is there any evidence that community residents are concerned about these problems? Can you identify community organizations? What are their goals? Their strategies? Are any of them working to resolve the issues you have identified?

2. Krista Harper's research suggests that finding assets or positive aspects of a community is an important part of a CBPR project. Can you identify assets or positive features in the community?

3. Attend a meeting of a community group (Community Policing/Watch Group, Neighborhood Block Association, etc.) and write a short report of what you have observed. Who attended the meeting? Who represented the community group? What was talked about? Were any decisions reached? What procedures were followed? You can trace the results of the meeting and see if any further action was taken and what the outcome was.

4. Get involved in a community service or service learning project in the community. What have you learned about the community, its residents, and community institutions from this experience? Do you and the residents you met have the same or different views of issues, assets, and actions?

## Key Terms

activism *152*

advocacy *152*

agent of change *153*

community *154*

community-based organization *163*

environmental justice *156*

facilitating interaction in the community *159*

iatrogenic effect *162*

indigenous activist *157*

indigenous leadership *160*

local knowledge *154*

methods of disseminating findings: photo-gallery; documentary film; and other visual methods *160*

negotiation of the research questions *154*

participants, not research subjects *152*

paternalism *163*

photo-voice *158*

public awareness *159*

researcher as facilitator *156*

# The Analysis of Cultural Objects and Discourses as a Research Design (With Martha Martinez and Christopher Carroll)

## OVERVIEW

This chapter explores a wide range of designs focusing on the **cultural object**—a thing that represents a **culture.** The "object" could be the words that people say or write (a **discourse**), or a **cultural artifact** such as a painting, graffiti, a musical composition, or a style of clothing. The emphasis here is on a thing—something we can touch (or see or listen to), not the interactions, dynamics, phenomena, and practices that comprise the raw material in the designs we've presented up to this point. Arguably, compiled interview transcripts could constitute a discourse, but in this chapter we are primarily interested in objects that are produced "spontaneously," not in interaction with the researcher and not intended originally for use as research data. In fact, some sociologists would refer to this kind of activity as "unobtrusive research" because the researcher doesn't interact directly with human subjects but rather attempts to understand/explain some aspects of subjects' lives by analyzing objects they created/generated.

# WHY CONDUCT CULTURAL OBJECTS RESEARCH?

Analysis of cultural objects as a research strategy or logic of research is based on the premise that we can learn about culture and social arrangements by analyzing words and material artifacts without interacting with the people who produce them.

For either practical or theoretical reasons, or both, a researcher might find this type of design to be the most appropriate selection.

## Practical Reasons for Studying Cultural Objects

**STUDYING THE PAST**   If there are no longer any living individuals in this society or culture, we can learn about their ideas, feelings, practices, and behaviors only by studying the objects that they have left behind. For example, when Weber suggested that the ideas of the Hebrew prophets were a starting point of modern rationality or when he identified the beliefs of sixteenth-century Protestant reformers as a force in creating the spirit of capitalism, he had to look at the writings of these religious thinkers since they were no longer available for interviews.

**STUDYING INACCESSIBLE GROUPS AND ORGANIZATIONS**   It's not only the dead who are difficult to interview. Many groups, organizations, and movements may also be well-protected against outsiders. Their representatives, or "gatekeepers," decline to be interviewed or are difficult and/or dangerous to contact. Oftentimes, if they are contacted, they respond only with a repetition of "front rhetoric"—organizational formulas—that give little insight into their actual goals and practices. In these cases, it may be possible to obtain **documents** or **artifacts** that are more revealing.

## Theory-Driven Reasons for Studying Cultural Objects

There are also theoretical reasons for discourse and cultural-object analysis as research design, strategy, and logic of inquiry. We may be interested in how a type of society—of social relationships among groups and individuals—is expressed or reflected in cultural production.

**THE CULTURAL DOMINANT—ENCODED OBJECTS**   Fredric Jameson (1991), for example, argues that postmodernism is the cultural logic of late (or advanced) capitalism, the form that culture takes in the period of global capitalism. In Jameson's view, a "cultural dominant" can be recognized in every period (whether it is a whole era like feudalism or classical antiquity, or a more limited epoch within these large time spans, such as early industrial capitalism, twentieth-century "high modernity," or late advanced global capitalism). By "cultural dominant," he means a prevailing form of culture, not a culture imposed by dominant classes or nations. The "cultural dominant" is not consciously imposed by powerful social actors, but rather comes to be the unconsciously adopted template for cultural production.

Jameson argues that in contemporary culture, historical knowledge is replaced by a passion for nostalgia and "retro" styles. The anxious pursuit of inner meaning, a key theme in twentieth-century high modern literature and art, is replaced by surface intensities—excitement, thrills, and pleasure in extreme sensations. The search for a "true" or "authentic" self is abandoned. New media technologies that are characteristic of contemporary capitalism have contributed to this loss of "interiority," or the tendency toward introspective meaning-making. Others, such as Baudrillard (1998), Castells (2000), and Gerbner (2002), have similar ideas about the highly mediated, high surface intensity, and totalizing symbolic environments of our times. To study contemporary culture, we need to look at these cultural artifacts themselves, such as TV programs, contemporary works of architecture, websites, fashion design, and many other objects.

When we want to understand culture as a coherent product of a specific type of society, we do not always want or need to look at social relationships, interactions, or behaviors, either the ones involved in producing the cultural objects or the ones involved in consuming them. We can analyze the cultural objects—literature, popular culture, visual art, music, and so on without observing artists, the art market, film production companies, architects and their clients, and so on. Nor do we need to watch viewers watching television or interview people wearing the latest fashions.

**BUT HOW DO PEOPLE DECODE OBJECTS?**    Some sociologists would not agree with this perspective and would argue that we always need to look at the social relations that prevail in the institutions that produce culture as well as understand how these products are consumed. In Stuart Hall's terms, we need to understand how culture is **encoded** in cultural objects (especially media) and how consumers **decode** these messages, and this type of analysis requires observing and interacting with producers and consumers of culture (Hall 2001). But this chapter is premised on the view that we can learn from the objects themselves without knowing about practices and relationships that generate the object or that provide the context in which it is consumed.

## RESEARCH IN ACTION: EXAMPLES OF STUDYING CULTURAL OBJECTS

Let's look at a few more examples of the analysis of cultural objects:

### Entertainment

Entertainment has often subjected to a conflict-theory analysis, and one of the most important theoretical works of the heyday of **conflict theory** is Todd Gitlin's *Inside Prime Time* (1983/2000). Gitlin persuasively argued that the entertainment broadcast by the major commercial channels during prime time contained powerful ideological messages. These messages were uniformly pacifying. While they contain nods to rebellious dreams or increasingly liberal social norms, they stifle any thought of change in capitalism and class power. Gitlin identifies format and formula, **genre**, setting, character type, slant, and solution as the elements whereby **ideological hegemony** (an all-encompassing, self-referential and self-reinforcing belief system) is inserted into entertainment. For example, the formula forces a standardized time frame on the viewer. Commercial advertisements make the point that public problems (e.g., the widening divide between adult children and their aging parents) can only have personal solutions (e.g., purchasing the newest cellular phone technology).

The process of viewing is itself private, discouraging public discussion of issues, even if they are broached in the shows. The genre of the cop show and sports inculcates certain values associated with violence, law and order, and competition. Social problems that surface in the shows often are quickly solved (related also to the time frame of the format). Often the solution is a purely private one. If there is a public space or issue at stake, the solution frequently depends on violence exercised by the authorities and the state. Rebels are shown to be ineffective or duplicitous, and this portrayal undermines commitment to collective action. Gitlin views prime-time television as a "soft" method of hegemony, one that is malleable and can even stretch to contain some dissenting or resisting positions, ultimately defusing them by "partial incorporation," a strategy that provides the critical viewer with just enough satisfaction to be pacified and thereby dissuaded from inciting any truly oppositional action.

## Advertising

Many media theorists with a conflict or critical perspective are interested in advertising. It has a central role in advanced capitalism, since it lubricates the circulation of commodities. Demand is created by advertising and new consumer wants are constantly conjured into existence. Furthermore, advertising creates a magical world of its own, a fantasy realm of new desires, anxieties, and instant solutions available through product purchases (e.g., consider any one of the Apple Computer products). The fantastical, infantile, and highly visual aspects of advertising as it evolved in the age of television fascinate theorists (Williams 1999). Stuart Ewen and Elizabeth Ewen, in *Channels of Desire: Mass Images and the Shaping of American Consciousness* (1982), probed the ways in which popular aspirations, desires, and identities were shaped in American capitalism. Immigrants and poor people were drawn into the dream world of consumer goods and name brands.

The Ewens continued a Marxist perspective of ambivalence toward these powerful "sirens" of the marketplace that constantly promise abundance and liberation from narrow, impoverished conditions—especially to women who are defined by their roles as consumers—but are only selling commodities. Feelings of freedom, choice, liberation, as well as consumer goods are acquired at the price of alienated labor and loss of community and family life.

In *Advertising: The Uneasy Persuasion* (1986), Schudson developed a witty comparison between advertising, which he called "capitalist realism," and the movement in art called "socialist realism." Socialist realism had been the orthodox position on art enforced on Soviet artists during the Stalinist period. Artists were not permitted to experiment or innovate in artistic form, but had to follow rigidly classical styles of composition and representation. The subject matter and themes had to be uniformly upbeat—never "defeatist" or critical of the Communist Party—and tied to Soviet social goals, especially the collectivization of agriculture and the achievement of large industrial projects. The archetypal product of socialist realism was the painting or movie about a young man achieving his dream of bringing tractors to his collective farm, peopled by happy, glowing peasants. Schudson argues that ads are the images of capitalist realism, idealized **representations** of a world of strong beautiful people happily fulfilling their lives by the purchase of intensely wonderful objects—the commodities ("products") of consumer capitalism.

The viewer is induced by constant repetition to believe in the existence, beauty, and attainability of this magical, make-believe world of objects. Capitalist realism, like socialist realism, has the ideological function of valorizing a political and economic system and inducing individuals to perform their roles in it.

In this context it is worth noting a number of empirical studies that highlight another aspect of television imagery—the tendency to stereotype racial and ethnic minorities and to create "moral panics" about their presence in society. For example, in the United States, images of African Americans and Latinos are chosen to illustrate news stories and entertainment programs about crime and drugs disproportionately to their actual representation in crime and drug use statistics. Similar stereotyping takes place in stories about terrorism or contagious illnesses in immigrant communities in North America and Europe.

## Understanding the Religious Imaginary: *Thank You, St. Jude*!

Robert Orsi's *Thank You, St. Jude* (1999) is an example of a study focused on the analysis of documents, although Orsi supplemented his analysis of documents with interviews. The documents were letters published in the *Voice of St. Jude* between 1935 and 1958 and in *St. Jude's Journal* after 1963. These letters had been sent to the shrine of St. Jude in Chicago and expressed hope for help from the saint or thanked him for his aid. St. Jude is the saint of hopeless causes, and so the letters revealed the most severe and deeply felt problems of American Catholics in the years that spanned the Depression, World War II and the Korean War, and the assimilation of European immigrants into U.S. society. Many Catholics were first- or second-generation immigrants and lived in working-class communities. Orsi subtitles his book "Women's devotion to the patron saint of hopeless causes" because many of the writers were women and their letters give insight into the conditions in which they lived.

The hopeless causes included alcoholic and abusive husbands, health problems in their families, handicapped children, war, economic hardships, and concern about pregnancy in families and communities in which contraception was not an option. Women were expected to cope with these difficulties in a spirit of sacrifice and faith, often to the point of silence and denial. The letters to the saint provided a socially acceptable way of expressing their fears and sorrows, as well as anger about insensitive, neglectful, and abusive men. The letters also reveal how working-class Catholic Americans pictured the sacred, the **iconography** of the saint, and how women bonded together through their shared faith and the shared image of the saint. Speaking and expressing their thoughts and concerns within the community formed by their devotion to the saint enabled them to break out of isolation and despair. Orsi's systematic and sensitive reading of the letters provides powerful insights into the intimate lives of individuals, families, and communities that were almost invisible in the mainstream media and public discussion of the period.

Orsi's analysis of the letters allows the reader to enter into the minds of the letter writers in the spirit of Weber's *verstehen* and to understand **popular representations of the sacred**. Orsi emphasizes the ambiguous nature of these representations of St. Jude. On one hand, the saint served to reconcile women to their traditional and circumscribed status; but on the other hand, he also freed their imaginations and aspirations for a more satisfying life. "Jude was the site where 'reality' and 'fantasy' converged, where play, illusion, and hope intersected with the constraints of the present" (1999: 200).

## Style

Dick Hebdige's *Subculture: The Meaning of Style* is a modern classic in the examination of **style** and cultural objects. Written in 1979, it examines the meaning of punk as an emerging movement of style as well as other post–World War II British **subcultures** such as the Teddy Boys and Mods, the Rastafarians, the Rockers, the skinheads, and Glam and glitter rock. One of Hebdige's main ideas is that opposition to hegemony is not expressed in overtly political forms but "obliquely, in style. The objections are lodged, the contradictions displayed (and, as we shall see, 'magically resolved') at the profoundly superficial level of appearances: that is, at the level of signs (1981/1991: 17)."

Hebdige begins his book with a reflection in the memoirs of Jean Genet, a homosexual thief and convict (and writer), who notes how the police mocked a tube of Vaseline™ they found in his possession, identifying it with homosexual acts and thus stigmatizing it and him; but for Genet it then becomes an object of value as a **sign of a forbidden and transgressive identity**. This incident in the life of an individual considered to be in the most marginalized parts of society reveals how objects carry social meaning and can become the **site of conflict** and struggle. "These 'humble objects' can be magically appropriated; 'stolen' by subordinate groups and made to carry 'secret' meanings; meanings which express, in code, a form of resistance to the order which guarantees their continued subordination" (1981/1991: 18).

Hebdige then discusses how both fashion and music provide these elements of style. Sometimes they are mocking appropriations and transformations of the most conservative and mainstream forms, such as the absurdly elegant clothing of the "Mods." At other times, they may literally rip and mangle accepted appearances, as in the case of the tattered clothing of the punks and their use of safety pins to pierce their faces. These acts and objects represented not only their anger but also their use of their own bodies to enact the dismantling of British industry and decimation of working-class communities as Britain moved from a manufacturing economy to one focused on financial institutions and real-estate development.

Several of the subcultures appropriated black Caribbean themes and elements of style—such as dreadlocks—and these carried messages of opposition not only when adopted by blacks but also in white working–class subcultures, a process labeled by Hebdige as "White Skin, Black Masks" (a flipping of the phrase "Black Skin, White Masks" with which revolutionary psychiatrist Frantz Fanon had summed up dilemmas of black people in white societies). A number of the **oppositional subcultures** used objects made of plastic to express their contempt for the cult of authenticity; plastic accessories and neon-hued synthetic fashions signaled that the dream of an authentic—that is, more rooted and organic style—had become ridiculous and a barrier to recognition of the profoundly and irrevocably alienated character of modern capitalist society.

In adopting the cultural-objects approach in its purest form, Hebdige does not interview participants in these subcultures but goes directly to the music, clothing, **body modifications** and ornamentation, and occasionally texts written by participants.

## Architecture and Urban Design

Architecture and urban design can be analyzed as cultural artifacts. Architecture and the cityscape form a powerful, visible, and material expression of social relationships and culture (De Certeau 1999; Jameson 1991). Buildings require large amounts of private or public funds and so they reveal much about the tastes and values of people with power and money. The French theorist Michel Foucault (1999) was interested in how architecture and the use of space express power differences. Michael Sorkin (1992) in "See you in Disneyland" discovers themes in Disneyland that express ideologies and ideals in a permanent space and tangible form. Among the values that are represented by the organization of Disneyland are: movement and transportation, with the ubiquitous ride as the archetype of experience; commodification and the global marketplace; regulation, surveillance, and the orderly monitoring and management of bodies in spaces that are clean and crime-free.

## Managers' Views of Workers: Developing a Research Design and Asking a Research Question

These analyses of cultural objects are interpretive essays that make reference to specific TV shows, commercials, buildings, prayers to a saint in the form of letters to a periodical, clothing, and music as examples but they did not use quantified data to support their conclusions. So let's turn to some other projects that went further in the direction of quantifying, coding, and data analysis.

**FORMULATING A RESEARCH QUESTION**     Martha Martinez's project tackles a large and fascinating research question in the intersection of sociology, economics, and management theory: What social forces influence managers' views of labor?

Why is this a worthwhile research question and how did she go about answering it?

Many sociological theorists, starting with Marx and Engels, have asserted that managers' view of labor is always instrumentalist and focused on labor as a force of production that must be tightly controlled and reduced to the lowest possible wage rates. The Marxist position was revised

McCormick Tribune Campus Center designed by Rem Koolhaas and completed in 2003, Illinois Institute of Technology, Chicago, IL (January 2004).

and renewed in the work of Harry Braverman (1979/1998), *Labor and Monopoly Capital*, in which he argued that in the twentieth century technology was systematically used to de-skill workers and transfer control and planning to management, making workers ever more replaceable and vulnerable. Neo-Weberians as well as Marxists subscribe to this premise; for example, George Ritzer's (2000) very popular McDonaldization thesis is that management is constantly restructuring organizations to make employees' behavior more efficient, more predictable, and easier to control. Pierre Bourdieu (1977) took a similar approach, arguing that managers develop

St. Vincent's Circle, DePaul University Lincoln Park Campus, Chicago, IL (October 2010).

a *habitus*, a set of skills, knowledge, dispositions, and embodied practices, which is aimed at domination of workers, albeit sometimes in veiled or covert ways.

The management literature offers a decisively different view of managers' images of labor; management theorists are far more likely to emphasize the importance of human resources, the fact that labor is an essential asset in a firm, the value of having an experienced and loyal labor force, and the aim of creating a cooperative partnership with labor rather than an antagonistic and confrontational relationship.

So very broadly speaking, we are left with the question of which paradigm is closer to reality—the critical sociologists' belief that management always seeks to reduce the power of labor and drive down workers' share of economic rewards or the management theorists' belief that a firm prospers when labor is considered to be a valuable partner?

**HOW DO INDUSTRY CHARACTERISTICS INFLUENCE MANAGERS' IDEOLOGIES?**     The question posed in the preceding paragraph informs the project at a fundamental level, but Martinez proposes to go beyond a simple either-or and asks a more nuanced and complicated research question: Do the characteristics of an industry and its specific pattern and timing of insertion into the global economy shape management images of labor? In other words, do variation in industry characteristics and the industry's phase of globalization produce markedly different management images of labor's role in the enterprise? It is by no means obvious what the effects of industry characteristics and phases of globalization are on management images of workers. A variety of hypotheses can be formulated: For example, workers may be seen as replaceable and interchangeable in industries in which it is easy to move operations abroad. A high level of technology may lead to managers to believe that workers have valuable skills and knowledge that make them difficult to replace, or on the contrary, as in Braverman's analysis, sophisticated technology could be used to de-skill workers. These are examples of hypotheses

Dietzgen Building, 990 West Fullerton, DePaul University Lincoln Park Campus, Chicago, IL (October 2010).

*Campus architecture tells stories about the values, traditions, and self-images of universities. Rem Koolhaas's innovative campus center, built around the elevated train tracks, signals modernity and complements the legacy of architect Mies van der Rohe on the IIT campus. In contrast, DePaul architecture evokes the tradition of European cloisters in St. Vincent's Circle as well as the Chicago architectural "vernacular" of brick structures. The DePaul building that still bears the logo of drafting tool-maker and socialist Eugene Dietzgen's plant celebrates Chicago's industrial heritage as "the city that works."*

about the effects of industry characteristics and the phase of globalization on management images of labor that Martinez is testing in her study.

The answers to these questions have policy implications and great societal relevance, as economist Robert Reich (1991) clearly outlined in *The Work of Nations*. Citizens of a country would like to see its firms compete effectively in the global economy with a skilled, secure, and well-paid labor force, rather than taking the low road of de-skilling, outsourcing, and expansion of a low-wage and precarious labor tier of the national economy. The outcome depends in part on how managers view workers, because their images will shape decisions about the labor force.

**ANSWERING THE RESEARCH QUESTION**    Now let's look at how Martinez developed her research design to answer these broad theoretical research questions.

Although the research questions are complicated, the research design is straightforward. Martinez chose two markedly different industries that have both undergone a radical process of globalization in recent decades: apparel and information technology. This choice allows Martinez to accomplish two goals—examine *industry differences* and look at *changes in managers' images of labor* over time during the period of globalization.

Her general methodological approach of **frame analysis** is very much in keeping with contemporary sociological perspectives. Frame analysis was introduced by Erving Goffman in the

1960s–1970s and thereafter became the leading way to analyze culture, cognitive processes, the formation of representations and images, rhetoric, and narrative strategies. Frame analysis is widely used to study movement ideologies, media representations, and many other cultural objects. This concept and its associated methods of discourse and content analysis are very effective for studying how images change (frame transformation) and how representations of an organization are aligned with other ideologies (frame alignment). Martha's choice of frame analysis as both a guiding concept and a methodological strategy is very appropriate and in keeping with trends in the sociology and cultural studies.

Now let's move from the design (or research strategy, or logic of research) to the actual choices from the methods tool-kit and the specific techniques associated with these methods.

**CONTENT ANALYSIS**   First, she identified the most important trade journal in each field. Her units of analysis were articles in which managers expressed their views of workers. She sampled these articles by a nonrandom but systematic method of choosing which issues of the journal to examine: She decided to use the December issues because these contain a review of the events of the year in each industry and the June ones which do not. She had to decide if an article expressed management views of labor or not. For each article that did, she coded the overall perspective of the article into one of four categories: (1) labor as an asset, a positive and explicit statement, that might include favorable content about unions and high salaries; (2) labor as a factor to be controlled, with unions defined as a problem and the aim of reducing labor costs explicitly mentioned, possibly in the context of layoffs or outsourcing; (3) labor as a responsibility of business, with an emphasis on attention to the welfare of workers; and (4) labor as incidental, when the article details policies that affect labor (such as layoffs or changes in the workforce or job characteristics) but without any reference to the impact on workers.

The coded data enable her to identify the images that managers hold of workers, differences in these images between the two industries, and changes in the images as the process of globalization unfolds.

## The Invisible Metropolis (by Christopher Carroll)

Christopher Carroll (2009) found discourse analysis useful in his research on how the media and government justify the use of video surveillance by the city of Chicago to deter and respond to crime, terrorism, and emergencies. The decision to use discourse analysis came after Carroll was surprised by three trends he found in academic research and the media: (1) The research on "effectiveness" found very little support that video surveillance was effective at deterring or responding to crime and terrorism, except in limited circumstances (e.g., car break-ins inside public garages); (2) Despite little support for its effectiveness, government agencies throughout the world continued to install video surveillance technologies at a rapid rate; and (3) Despite the lack of support in the research literature for the effectiveness of the technologies, very little media discourse questioned their use.

**THE RESEARCH QUESTION**   If evidence-based effectiveness is not the driving force for the deployment of surveillance technologies, how has their use become so popular and unquestioned? Carroll used media and political discourse on video surveillance in Chicago as his object of inquiry as he set about answering this question. Using **critical discourse analysis** as the theoretical framework guiding his analysis, Carroll focused on media and political discourse as a cultural object and a social practice. By tracing how these discourses were formulated, he uncovered reasons why video surveillance has so quickly propagated throughout Chicago. Carroll concludes that the media and political discourse on surveillance is not only shaped by societal forces but is itself an active and shaping social practice.

**CREATING THE DATABASE**    Carroll limited his analysis of the media discourse to major Chicago newspapers and television reports and the political discourse to official City of Chicago press releases between June 2003 and December 2008. June 2003 was chosen as the start date because Chicago installed the first of its anticrime "blue-light" cameras or PODs (Police Observation Devices) that summer. He used Lexus-Nexus, ProQuest, Academic World News Database, Google News, and individual newspaper and television websites to ensure his sample was as comprehensive as possible. The City of Chicago website (http://egov.cityofchicago.org) was used to download the official government press releases. Each saved transcript was carefully labeled; each file name included date, source, and topic. In addition, two large documents were created, one that contained all of the press releases in chronological order and another that contained all the media reports. These two documents with the materials in chronological order facilitated systematic and manageable coding and analysis.

**CODING**    Carroll coded the media and political texts for several themes split into manifest and latent content. Five manifest themes were coded: (1) technological capabilities, (2) mission and goals, (3) effectiveness, (4) public opinion, and (5) privacy and civil liberties. Latent themes were also uncovered and coded contemporaneously with the data gathering and analysis. Whereas the manifest themes were fairly obvious and on the surface of the text, the latent themes served to frame or present the surveillance technology in Chicago, and were only discerned after a careful reading of the discourse in its entirety. Four latent themes were coded: (1) panopticism: security via visibility with the aim of altering or deterring undesired behavior; (2) security via visibility without humans: detection and predicting the future with computers, eerily reminiscent of *Minority Report* and the Philip Dick story on which the movie was based; (3) security via visibility with the aim of ensuring citizens that a benevolent government is looking after its safety; and (4) security via visibility as a technique and consequence of urban entrepreneurialism (Harvey 1989).

**FINDINGS AND CONCLUSIONS**    Carroll mapped out the media and discourse on video surveillance in Chicago finding that the City of Chicago and a majority of the media reports frame video surveillance as a panacea for the problems of crime, terrorism, and emergencies. Independent research suggesting the ineffectiveness of surveillance is left out all together from the political discourse and is either excluded or marginalized from the media discourse. In fact, Carroll found that the majority of media reports on video surveillance in Chicago merely reiterate government press releases, leaving little room for public dialogue or outside expert opinion.

Carroll's most intriguing findings and conclusions arise out of his use of critical discourse analysis as his overarching theoretical framework. In doing so, Carroll embeds the media and political discourse in the historical and social context of early twenty-first-century Chicago. For instance, he finds that the content of both the media and political discourse on surveillance is almost exclusively driven by political elites (e.g., former Mayor Richard Daley of Chicago, Chicago law enforcement officials, and Chicago aldermen). Therefore, competing discourses that challenge the video-surveillance system (e.g., concerns about privacy, civil liberties, and effectiveness) are rendered impotent or excluded all together by the hegemonic discourse.

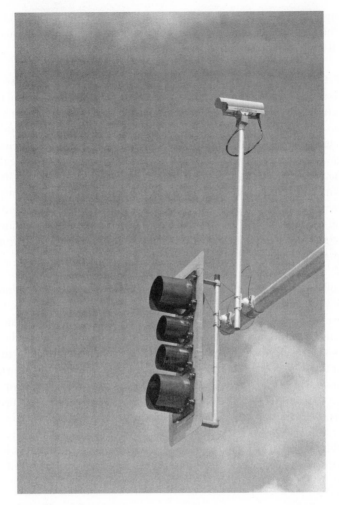

Surveillance Camera

Carroll also finds that the discourse on surveillance is framed within larger discourses of urban entrepreneurialism, a belief in the effectiveness of technological fixes for social problems, and the related belief that through creating the feeling of being watched, one will change their behavior. He calls this belief "panopticism," a term that appears in Michel Foucault's (1979) theories of social regulation in complex, modern societies. Carroll concludes that the surveillance discourse (re)inscribes and (re)legitimates the belief that video surveillance is necessary and effective, while public discussion and dissenting viewpoints are silenced or rendered invisible. Carroll's research illustrates how discourse analysis can provide insight into how new policies of social control are justified to the public, often in disregard of any evidence about their effectiveness.

## Analysis of High School Yearbooks

Paul Haubrich (1993) wanted to understand how student behaviors had changed in Milwaukee between 1930 and 1985. His analysis used different types of data, including school district records that provided insight into changes such as growing high school enrollments, larger proportions of African American and Latino students, and increasing rates of high school completion because the diploma had become a necessity and was no longer an elite privilege. But he also wanted to understand the changing role of school in the lives of adolescents. Examining yearbooks of two high schools was part of this project. The words and images in the yearbooks gave life to the quantitative data in the school system's records of enrollment and demographic data.

Haubrich realizes that yearbooks are extensively monitored and censored by the school administration, and so at a superficial level seem to be unreliable guides to student culture. But if we know how to interpret the pictures and text and especially once we begin to look at how they change over the decades, the yearbook becomes a valuable source of information about values, role expectations, self-presentations, norms, and activities. Not every student lived up to these expectations and norms, but the norms and expectations provide clues about the socialization of adolescents and the formation of their focal concerns.

Haubrich found that "[a] trend that became evident in these years was a transition from the school providing a central focus in the lives of students to a peer-oriented social system in which the adolescent was less dependent on the institution for a social life" (1993: 195). Haubrich discusses this transition as a general trend in the United States and comments,

> In Milwaukee, this meant that many of the social structures established by the early high schools diminished in importance when students began to interact in social networks only incidentally identified with school. Students turned to commercial forms of social interaction, such as movies, cars, television, radio, and home parties. Eventually part-time work financed these activities, allowing students greater control over their own development. Consequently, the school was accorded a smaller role in the transition to adulthood.
>
> (1993: 195–196)

The yearbooks provide support for this conclusion. School-based clubs and social organizations disappear from the pages, and eventually only athletics and the prom remain. Dances, plays, variety shows, and other events are no longer offered. Organizations such as Girls Club and Camaraderie, Mothers Tea, Senior Tea, the Winter Mixer, and the Faculty Tea vanish after the 1930s, and after 1950, there is a rapid decline even in academic and athletic clubs. From the 1920s to the 1950s, "adults were a significant part of the many activities that revolved around schools, and it appears that they retained a good deal of authority in the ways they interacted with students. ....The high school was central to the lives of many of Milwaukee's teenagers" (1993: 215).

Haubrich not only looks at the list of activities and organizations; he also scrutinizes clothing and captions of the images of teens and teachers. These representations of youth and adults are clues to the cultures of schools and adolescents. Formality in dress and the use of terms of respect toward teachers decreased markedly; already by the 1930s and 1940s, students are no longer formally dressed like "little adults" as they were in the 1920s, when high school was still an institution that catered to the upper-middle class. By the 1930s and 1940s, it was becoming apparent that "student styles of dress were no longer influenced by pressures from parents or other adults, and that a popular youth culture was beginning to have an impact upon style choices" (1993: 223). Teachers became less involved in extra-curricular activities. Haubrich discusses the complex interlocking reasons for this shrinking role of the school in the social lives of young people, an apparent paradox as youth were increasingly likely to attend high school and parents became more dependent on schools for socialization.

This type of analysis of discourses and objects can also be a method—a choice from the method tool-kit—within a larger, comprehensive research design. For example, Matt Char used content analysis of high school yearbooks as part of a larger project of studying an exurban community and its high school. The larger project used mixed methods, including interviews with community leaders, analysis of census data, mapping and visual recording of changes in the town, a high school survey, focus groups with high school students, and observation. Matt's portion of the study involved content analysis of the yearbooks produced at the high school from the 1950s to the 1990s in order to document change in the school and community and, above all, to understand the culture of the high school.

The community had been an agricultural community at the far edge of a metropolitan area located in the Midwest. Over the years its economy was increasingly influenced by the metropolitan economy. In the 1990s, a major electronics manufacturing company built an enormous plant in the community, but with the shift of this particular product to overseas production, the plant never even opened. Meanwhile the prevailing culture of the community was a blue-collar rural one, celebrating hunting, fishing, rugged independence, and freedom from government, big business, and the "9 to 5" routine. Yet these local values were increasingly coming under challenge from new economic forces and lifeways as urban white-collar types moved into the area and a community of Mexican immigrants grew in size and shifted from agricultural labor into more diversified activities, including opening businesses in the downtown.

Analyzing the images, activities, and symbols in the yearbooks, Matt was able to trace the declining dominance of rural white culture but the persistence of a strongly masculine tilt in the values and practices of the community and the high school—celebration of male teachers and coaches, athletics focused on wrestling, and so on. Like Martinez, Matt created coding categories for various variables describing yearbook contents. For example, he coded the demographic characteristics of people who received awards or were selected for special recognition, such as "teacher of the year" or "coach of the year." He coded the type of extracurricular activities that were featured, such as the 4-H clubs that prepared young people for modern farming in the 1950s. These findings meshed with focus group findings—the school throughout the decades was marked by greater satisfaction and a sense of participation among young men than young women. The high school yearbooks tended to document the mainstream and socially approved parts of local youth culture, while the survey and observations revealed the same culture but also elements of its "submerged" side, such as drug use and alienation from school, as well as tension between whites and Hispanics. In general, documents such as yearbooks or trade journals provide insight into the official culture of an organization or industry.

Not how well the analysis of cultural objects and discourses (the yearbooks in the work of Haubrich and Char) fits into historical-comparative research. Both researchers used their analysis of yearbooks to trace a process of change in the role of schooling that unfolded over several decades. Change in youth cultures, school policy, the meaning of a high school diploma, recreation and entertainment, and the relationships between adults and teens were all encapsulated in the yearbooks, and the design allowed the researchers to document these profound shifts in U.S. society.

## Content Analysis Exercise: Home Pages of Colleges and Universities

One of our research methods classes tried an exercise that you can do yourself. We looked at websites of colleges and universities, exploring the symbols and framing devices that the institutions used to represent themselves and make themselves attractive to the viewers. This analysis parallels Erving

Goffman's theories about the "presentation of self in everyday life" and impression management, but focuses on organizations rather than individuals. Even looking at only a small number of websites, we saw several distinct patterns emerging. There were obvious demographic differences in the types of people portrayed on the home pages. But beyond these predictable differences, we found that the more expensive and prestigious institutions tended to have more conceptual imagery, while institutions whose students were less wealthy or had more vocational aspirations reflected the down-to-earth character of their presumed viewers' needs and wants. They emphasized training for specific jobs and readily visible instructions for applying for financial aid, rather than "high concept" imagery of art objects, a postmodern iconic representation of Marilyn Monroe, or high-magnification photos of microorganisms—examples of images from selective and expensive institutions.

Colors and body language also signaled values related to the mission and demographics of the institution. The Citadel (a military institution) featured almost faceless images of men of diverse races arrayed in a neat line in uniforms and presented in steely blues and blacks, with no reference to the local environment (Charleston, SC); Rhode Island School of Design offered images of casually dressed young people, portrayed in warm, bright colors and animatedly looking at art objects in Providence, USA, and Ghana. Vassar, a historical woman's college, showed two young women jogging in the snow ("empowerment," "health," and "determination") and the large Andy Warhol iconic image of Marilyn Monroe. This image suggests that the college encourages an interest in women's issues but with a critical and deconstructionist distance from traditional representations of femininity and sex appeal. The colors of the Vassar website were surprisingly like those of the Citadel home page—cold blues, whites, and blacks—perhaps signaling seriousness of purpose.

This exercise could easily be expanded and quantified. We could draw a random sample of the colleges and universities of the United States, visit each website's home page (our unit of analysis), and code what we find for a number of variables, such as the categories of people portrayed in the images, predominant colors, type of imagery, key links, **icons,** and representations of the location. Alternatively, we might prefer to do less quantified and detailed coding, and place each website into broader more heuristic categories. Either way, the project would provide insight into institutional representations and organizational cultures; potentially we could link these data to information about the programs, demographics, finances, and student income levels of the institution and to observational and interview information about how the institution chooses to represent itself and how decision makers in enrollment management, institutional development, and web design hope to reach their potential viewers, students, donors, and others to whom they are addressing their images.

## SUMMARY: WHEN AND HOW DO WE USE THIS DESIGN?

Here are some practical tips for conceptualizing and implementing a study based on the cultural-objects approach.

### Formulate the Research Questions and Think about Relevant Theories

The great temptation to be avoided in the analysis of cultural artifacts is to rush into quantitative data analysis before the research questions have been formulated and the theoretical significance considered. Texts can be prepared for computer-aided analysis with software such as *ATLAS.ti*, but the researcher needs to first think through the purpose and theoretical orientation of the research. Identifying specific themes that appear in a text and examining their interconnections requires a broader context for the project and an interpretive framework for understanding why these interconnected themes appear. Once again we see that inductive and deductive approaches are not opposites, but mutually reinforcing.

## Carefully Specify the Units of Analysis and Organize Your Sampling

A second essential part of the research design is clarity about the units of analysis and observation. There may be several levels that have to be sampled, just as when survey researchers sample census tracts, households within census tracts, and then individuals within households. For example, Martha Martinez identified industries, trade journals published in the industries, and then articles in these journals. Matt looked at yearbooks of one high school during several decades and at the specific rubrics that appeared in the yearbooks. In both these cases, there was a multilevel analysis.

Chris used mass media databases and websites of media outlets for the analysis of media discourse on surveillance and press releases and speeches from the City of Chicago website for the analysis of political discourse. He identified June 2003 and September 2008 as the starting and ending dates of the analysis and thereby limited the number of units of analysis he included.

## Identify Key Variables to Record

We need to identify the key characteristics of the unit of analysis that we want to analyze. For example, we might decide that we want to look for key words, key themes, and/or demographic or social characteristics of individuals who are represented in the discourse, such as their gender, race/ethnicity, or social class. In Matt's yearbook study, the demographics of students in extra-curricular activities were charted, noting trends in the racial and gender composition of student organizations and other activities represented in the yearbooks. The purpose or mission of the activities was also recorded, as the activities shifted from strongly agriculturally themed (the 4-H club) to more diversified and industrial or "postindustrial." These characteristics can be recorded as variables that are associated with each unit of analysis—each activity displayed in the yearbook.

## Select Your Time Period(s)

Decisions have to be made about starting and end dates of the sampling. For example, Chris began in June 2003 because it was the date of the first "blue-light" camera deployment, a relatively practical and commonsense starting point. But in other cases, knowledge of the social context may be helpful in deciding theoretically or practically decisive moments in time; if we wanted to look at images of African American major league players in U.S. media, it would be important to know that Jackie Robinson was the first black player in the majors and that he started playing in 1947. To analyze the images in a broader context, it would be useful to know more about events and trends of this period—for example, President Truman's desegregation order for the Armed Forces, movements among African American veterans returning from World War II, a growing opposition to segregation throughout U.S. society, and the sense that the United States was entering a period of competition with the Soviet Union for favorable public opinion in newly independent nations in Asia and Africa. In some cases, we might want to organize our sample to include artifacts or discourses produced "before" and "after" a key event; in others, we might begin with a clear starting point or new trend and trace it as it unfolds. These choices need to emerge from our research questions.

## Create a Data File

In many instances of discourse analysis when we use a data file to keep track of our data, each case is an article in a newspaper or periodical or a website. These cases can then be characterized by specific variables such as the presence of a specific theme, the number of individuals in a specific demographic category that appear, or the presence of a specific key word.

Once we have placed our data in a data file we can begin to systematically answer our research questions, identifying the appearance and distribution of themes, changes over time, and differences among various media that we are comparing. It is now easy to scan text and visual materials and to create a **textual database** that lends itself to the **open and axial codings**, discussed in the section on grounded theory in Chapter 6. We will discuss these techniques in more detail in Chapter 22 for analyzing qualitative data.

## CONCLUSION

Human society is complex. And although it may seem as though sociological research should always involve interacting with humans, many exemplary studies have focused exclusively on cultural objects and have contributed enormously to our understanding of society. It's not always possible to interact with people—they may be dead, as in cases where you're studying people who lived in bygone eras, or they may be inaccessible to you, as in cases where you simply cannot achieve direct contact with the persons in whom you're interested. There also may be solid theoretical reasons for restricting your analysis to objects, as we have demonstrated in our discussion of various research projects wherein the researchers could have interacted with humans to produce their data but instead chose, for good reason, to concentrate solely on the objects pertaining to the groups of interest. At this point, you should be familiar enough with this approach to conduct your own study using the cultural-objects approach. Give it a try!

## Exercises

1. Select any one of the following and systematically describe (possibly photograph) them: buildings on your campus; graffiti near the campus; churches, mosques, synagogues, and other places of worship near the campus. What do these objects tell us about the values of their creators? What styles are used to convey meanings? Can you decipher the "iconography" of the images—what do the symbols refer to?

2. Select a popular TV program and focus on one or several variables (e.g., gender, race/ethnicity, age). How are people in the relevant categories portrayed? Create a coding system for these representations and carry out coding for a couple of episodes of the show. What can you conclude?

3. A slightly different version of Exercise 2 is to treat the show as a little microcosm and ask what are the demographic and cultural characteristics of this tiny world. For example, the world of professional football is disproportionately male and young; it is violent (though not lethally so), hierarchical, and competitive. The commercials that accompany a program can be analyzed as well and they are very revealing about the demographics for whom the show is targeted.

4. Propose your own set of cultural objects for study. Discuss theories that might help you organize your project. State your research questions. Propose categories of coding and a procedure for sampling the materials.

5. Think of a research topic and/or question that could be answered using data gathered through interactions with live human beings but that would be better answered through the study of cultural objects. In particular, in this imaginary study the reason for not talking to humans is that you have reason to believe that they won't be honest with you and that your data therefore will be invalid.

6. Carry out a systematic version of the college and university website project described in this chapter. Consider how you would sample colleges and universities and what categories you would use for coding the images and text. Develop research questions or research hypotheses to explore in your project.

7. Compare high school yearbooks with friends from diverse backgrounds. How are schools and individual students presented in these yearbooks? Do you think there is a relationship between the types of images presented in a yearbook and other characteristics of the school, such as its demographic composition, location, or type of governance (public, private-independent, religious, etc.)?

8. Look at wedding photographs of a large number of people, some of whom you know fairly well. What differences and similarities do you see? What do you learn about values, tastes, and social relationships? Can you reach better conclusions when you know the people involved, and do these situations give you any clues about how to reach conclusions from pictures of strangers?

## Key Terms

advertising *170*

artifacts *168*

body modification *172*

conflict theory *169*

critical discourse analysis *176*

cultural dominant *168*

cultural object or artifact *167*

culture *167*

decoding *169*

discourse *167*

documents *168*

encoding *169*

frame analysis *175*

genre *169*

iconography *171*

icons *181*

ideological hegemony *169*

objects as sites of
   conflict *171*

open and axial codings *183*

oppositional subculture *172*

popular representations
   of the sacred *171*

representations *170*

signs of forbidden and
   transgressive identities *171*

style *171*

subculture *171*

textual database (created from
   interviews, documents, field
   notes, etc.) *183*

# 12

# Multimethod Designs

## OVERVIEW

In this chapter we discuss studies that combine qualitative and/or ethnographic designs with quantitative methods. In recent years, the social and behavioral sciences have adopted a more welcoming and positive stance toward "mixed-method" studies. The attitudinal sea change is refreshingly free from the pointless hostility and bitterness that divided sociologists in the twentieth century. But there is still a lot to be learned on both sides of the divide and there is room for growth in terms of refining our ability to appropriately and effectively combine research methodologies in a single study.

## MIXING METHODS: THE VALUE OF TRIANGULATION

We have already discussed how in any type of design we can use a variety of tools from the methods tool-kit. Most well-designed studies use more than one method. For example, many social autopsies use interviews with survivors and documentary materials, such as police or hospital records. Community-based participatory research can bring together focus groups, observations, and photo-voice or other visual methods. In this sense, almost every large research project is multimethod. Using different methods improves the researcher's understanding of contexts and introduces **triangulation** into the study, where we use multiple techniques from multiple vantage points to gather data on a given event, relationship, organizational phenomenon, and so on. When we obtain information from different sources using different methods, we are less likely to be misled or mistaken in our conclusions.

## REASONS AND STRATEGIES FOR BRINGING METHODS TOGETHER

Researchers can bring together quantitative and qualitative methods in multimethod (or mixed method) research in many different ways. Here are some examples:

- In historical-comparative research, statistical techniques, such as **small-$n$ analysis** and fuzzy-case studies, and even regression analysis are being used to analyze variable relationships for a small number of cases, usually countries.
- Quantitative data collection and analysis is used within ethnographic studies.

- Qualitative methods such as interviewing and observation (and even full-fledged ethnographic research) are employed as a follow-up to quantitative research, providing an in-depth, grounded and more subjectively toned understanding of the variable relationships revealed in the statistical analysis.
- Qualitative analysis software such as *NVIVO* and *ATLAS.ti* is used to analyze textual databases derived from interviews, focus group transcripts, historical documents, life narratives, and field notes; and these techniques create quantitative data (see Chapter 22).

In the history of sociological research, qualitative methods were often labeled **exploratory** with the implication that they might yield valuable research questions that can then be answered more scientifically and definitively with quantitative methods based on **probability samples** and **statistical analysis** of numerical data. This view of qualitative methods as merely ways of reconnoitering the research terrain is beginning to change, and the quantitative–qualitative relationship is becoming richer and more reciprocal.

### Using Qualitative Research to Understand Forces That Produce Patterns of Variable Relationships

The order of quantitative and qualitative can be reversed from the traditional pattern in which qualitative research precedes quantitative research and functions as an early, exploratory phase of the research project. Quantitative research brings to light the patterns and helps us to identify which variables are predictors of outcomes, but it is qualitative research that allows us to understand processes and meaning-giving interactions that "create" the link between the **predictors and the outcomes**. For example, Monique Payne (2008) found that residential mobility leads to lower educational outcomes among adolescents, once variables such as family income have been controlled. Why would this be the case?

Here an observation and interview-based study of the experience of being a new kid in the classroom or of family interaction during a residential move might shed light on what forces "produce" the statistically significant relationship between mobility and lower educational outcomes. The qualitative study can illuminate the processes, experiences, interactions, and formation of "cognitive landscapes" in the minds of adolescents that impact their educational achievement.

### Including Quantitative Analysis within an Overall Qualitative or Ethnographic Design

Qualitative and quantitative research do not need to be arranged in a sequence, with one necessarily coming before or after the other. In fact, it's rarely done this way. Typically a multimethod researcher uses both methodologies simultaneously within the same study. For example, in a larger ethnographic study of injection drug use, Scott prepared visual records of 400 instances of injection practices. Each one of these records was qualitative—a short film of an individual injecting—but analyzed together they formed a large quantitative database that we can use to understand exactly what individuals do when they inject drugs. By revealing what a large number of individuals actually do when they inject drugs, the information can be used to help people discontinue dangerous and harmful practices and begin to implement safer injection practices. The way this portion of the study was integrated into a larger ethnographic design is discussed in the chapters in Part III.

Greg prepared two videos for the study: one is the injection hygiene video to help health providers and laypeople shift to safer practices, and the other is the video that gives coders instructions for how to code how to apply qualitative and quantitative codes to the videorecorded injections. These materials were used to produce a social mapping of injection drug use, to understand what injection drug users actually do when they inject, and ultimately to help them adhere to safer injection practices.

## Using Quantitative Methods to Analyze Qualitative Materials

Qualitative materials are now often converted into a quantitative database in content and discourse analysis. While each interview, historical document, life narrative, media text, or set of field notes is usually considered an item of qualitative data, together items of this type form a textual database (as we discussed in Chapter 6, in the section on grounded theory). Software can be used to identify themes and categories in the textual database and to keep track of relationships among these themes or categories.[1] When these procedures are applied to a large piece of text or many text items, the result is a large sample of material that is readily amenable to quantitative data analysis techniques.

The approach to analyzing the data can be inductive or deductive. In an inductive approach, the software scrutinizes the textual database to identify frequently repeated words, phrases, and topics and to look for contexts in which these themes connect to each other. In a deductive approach, the researchers would first identify themes and relationships among themes that they would like to examine, and the software would locate these terms and contexts.

For example, in the analysis of cultural objects and discourses (Chapter 11), we discussed how Martha Martinez is examining trade publications in two distinct industries to see how managers view workers—as valued partners of management, as antagonists to management, as a responsibility of management, or as expendable and easily replaced commodities. These are the four major categories into which articles as the units of analysis are being coded. Martinez is charting changes in the proportion of articles that take these positions and asking whether these changes are related to the integration of the industries into the global economy. Her method is basically a deductive one in which she has used her knowledge of management orientations and the global economy to identify the various positions.

Once the key codes (and categories or themes) are identified, the software can comb through large amounts of texts, not only keeping track of frequencies but also carrying out the "axial coding" of related themes and contexts.

## Using Qualitative Data to Contextualize Quantitative Data

Qualitative methods can be used to provide a **context for quantitative data**. For example, Garner et al. (2006) developed a survey instrument that was administered in several high schools in the Midwest and Northern Italy. The questions covered a wide range of topics relevant to high school students in most schools and many countries, such as parental occupations; number of siblings; post–high school plans; hours spent on homework each week; employment; grades; ratings of school characteristics on a 10-point scale; and characteristics of students that they perceived as

---

[1] See Chapter 22 on Computer Assisted Qualitative Data Analysis software programs.

increasing the chance of an individual "being in the popular crowd." The respondents also answered open-ended questions about tastes in music, school cliques, and advice they would give to a new student at their school. These data were quite rich in themselves; but they were analyzed in the context of the schools based on qualitative data about the schools.

The researchers developed the qualitative material by using methods of observation, a "parent as researcher" participant observer method (Adler and Adler 1998), focus groups, interviews with students, teachers, and administrators, and a content analysis of yearbooks. Putting together the quantitative survey data and the qualitative data about the schools and communities created an intense dialog between the universalistic variables of the survey that made sense in all the schools and the specific, local, and contextualized information about the schools that was produced by qualitative methods.

In one school, the students were predominantly African American and many of their families lived below the poverty line. Another school was in a small town at the edge of a major metropolitan area where white and Latino residents retained many habits and ideals of rural culture. Two were ethnically diverse technical schools, one of which was selective and college-oriented while at the other school students' performance on standardized tests was relatively low, drop-out rates were higher, and few graduates gained admission to selective colleges. Yet another school in the sample was an intellectually challenging and nurturing private school, many of whose students were very wealthy.

The Italian sample of schools was almost as diverse as the U.S. sample. It included predominantly male technical schools and an elite "classical" high school. In all quantitative survey research, the questions to the respondents have to "make sense" across all settings. Without contextualized interpretation, the survey information remains rather generic. The survey answers became richer and far more informative when they were interpreted in the context of the school, using qualitative information about the schools' "social climates," organizational cultures, and surrounding communities.

A similar mixed design was used in Laumann et al.'s *Sexual Organization of the City* (2004). The research team carried out a survey of sexual behaviors in four communities in Chicago: a predominantly African American community on the south side; two predominantly Latino communities, one with many Puerto Rican residents and the other mostly Mexican American; and a predominantly white community on the north side with a large gay population. The survey asked about the number and sex of partners, disputes and conflicts between intimate partners, demographic information, religious affiliation, integration into networks, and sexual histories of individuals. The survey data were statistically analyzed and the findings were reported in the book-length research report. The authors use the quantitative data to construct the "sex markets" characteristic of each neighborhood and to examine differences in sexual behavior by education, gender, sexual orientation, and culture/ethnicity.

The researchers also made use of census data and other publicly available information about the neighborhoods. These quantitative data are enhanced and contextualized by qualitative information based on semi-structured interviews with social service providers and representatives of religious organizations in the communities. The combination of quantitative data collected from a probability sample of individuals and qualitative responses from a nonrandom sample of social service providers, clergy, and representatives of community organizations enables the authors to answer questions about the social regulation of sexual behavior and the ways in which organizational interventions fail or succeed in affecting behaviors. The two types of data collected in this study balance and complement each other.

## Using Quantitative Tools in Comparative Research

In Chapter 8, we discussed historical-comparative studies that were primarily qualitative in their design, the type of data that were collected and analyzed, and the general framing of the research questions. These types of questions, suitably reframed, can also be addressed with quantitative tools. This approach requires more precise definitions of **variables**, openness to use of quantitative data, and systematic attention to the **relationships among variables**. For example, the studies we discussed Chapter 8 used concepts such as "penetration of capitalist relations of production into the countryside," "exclusionary regimes," and "deepening of democracy." Rich documentary and observational data that were intensely contextualized but accompanied by little or no quantification were used to discuss conditions under which institutions or behavior patterns emerged.

If we were to approach these research questions in a more quantitative way, we would have to make a new set of choices in how to link the concepts to specific variables and what types of data to include. For example, we could look at national statistical data to determine more precisely "penetration of capitalist relations of production into the countryside"—for instance, by looking at the ratio between acreage devoted to subsistence agriculture and acreage devoted to commercial crops in various regions of the country. In many of these studies, the quantification remains at a fairly low **level of measurement**; the variables are coded at the "**ordinal level**" (where numbers ascend or descend in a meaningful way, as in rankings) or as **dichotomous variables** (i.e., this or that, one or the other … never neither or both). For example, we might rank countries by how developed their commercial agriculture is (ordinal level of measurement) or we might simply look at the data in order to eventually place each country in one of two categories designating the predominant or most important mode of agriculture: commercial agriculture or subsistence farming.

These levels of measurement permit analysis of *necessary and sufficient conditions* for a defined outcome variable generally also coded at the ordinal or dichotomous level of measurement (such as presence or absence of a revolutionary regime change).

There are a number of techniques for quantitative approaches to comparative analysis. For example, sometimes there are enough countries in the set, precise enough measurement of variables (at the **interval-ratio level**—in other words, definite numerical measurements, not just rankings or yes/no coding), and enough data available that various types of regression analysis are feasible. Other techniques, known a bit confusingly as "qualitative comparative analysis" involve simpler coding of variables and efforts to identify necessary and sufficient presence of one variable for the presence of the another variable. When this relationship can be established, researchers consider the first variable to be a **causal factor** for the second variable. Variables may be defined dichotomously (present or not present) in "crisp-set analysis" or on a 0 to 1 scale in "fuzzy-set analysis." Finally, in small-*n* analysis, with no more than 10 cases, the comparisons are often **nominal** (a placement of countries into categories that have no inherent order) or ordinal (a ranking of the countries on the variables) and much of the analysis is fundamentally qualitative, a tracing of the processes that link the variables and that (one hopes) will be discernible in each case (Kenworthy and Hicks 2008).

As in purely qualitative historical-comparative analysis, there is no "royal road" that avoids careful study of the countries in the data set, whether by the tools of the historian or by "boots-on-the-ground" presence and fieldwork in the countries. The researcher who relies purely on publicly available statistics and statistical analysis with little attention to the cultures, histories, and contextualized situations of the cases is likely to produce results that are not very meaningful and insightful in the real world.

## Using Multimethod Research to Understand Contemporary Issues: The Example of Youth Crime and Homelessness

As we've stated repeatedly, all research methods involve numbers and text at some level. Distinctions are a matter of degree, each scholar emphasizing one more than the other depending upon skill set and study specifics, such as the nature of the research question. Over the years, however, the social sciences have become polarized between qualitative and quantitative methodology. Most researchers would place themselves in one or the other "camp," even though all researchers use numbers and all use text in every phase of a project.

Our position in this book is that the same underlying logic of inquiry drives, if not unites, both of these ostensibly discrepant methodologies. Over the past two decades, social science has witnessed a rapid increase in the number of multimethod studies, and more and more newly minted PhDs have achieved adeptness in integrating qualitative and quantitative techniques and bringing them to bear on a particular research question and/or hypothesis. We would argue that the rise in popularity and use of multiple method integration has a lot to do with the influence of criminology and public health, two very powerful (i.e., well-funded and far-reaching) fields where *applied social science* is the norm. In fact, doing applied research is prized in these two realms where social science meets up with public policy implementation.

In these fields where the "public good" tends to motivate much of the scholarly work, researchers have begun to adopt multimethod designs out of necessity if nothing else. In the face of an HIV pandemic or in the wake of mass incarceration, applied scholars join forces with each other and with their university counterparts to answer difficult questions using as many tools as they can get their hands on. Working on social problems under pressure has made the multimethod study more common in these fields than others, thought by no means has the "hybridized approach" attained the status of "normativity." The methodological distinction is more pronounced, and the multimethod study more rare, in the so-called "basic" (i.e., not applied) social sciences. Despite the relative scarcity of actual multimethod studies, it's pretty hard to find a researcher who would argue strenuously, on principle, against "triangulation," or the utilization of multiple methods to produce data whose analysis will answer a given question. Most everyone sees the value in multimethod inquiry, but very few have *mastered* it.

Mastery of multimethod inquiry is difficult to attain. For the most part, even the fields of criminology and public health, wherein multimethod studies are approaching normativity, the parochialism of professional development and training in doctoral programs, the increasing specialization of peer review panel selection, and the escalating stringency of funding agencies lead many scholars to work exclusively within one or the other domain—it's either qualitative or quantitative. However, a few award winning, widely read but seldom-imitated studies merit consideration, for they represent the "holy grail" of multiple methodology inquiry.

In 1998, a book titled *Mean Streets: Youth Crime and Homelessness* garnered resounding critical acclaim. The authors, John Hagan and Bill McCarthy, are criminologists by trade, but their multiyear, multimethod study embodies an interdisciplinary social science conceptual spirit and rests on rigorous qualitative, quantitative, and ethnographic endeavoring. Although the book advances no new theoretical propositions, its authors creatively and convincingly proceed to integrate and then test highly inventive theoretical models. The book's hallmark is its hybridization—theoretically and methodologically—in the study of how social conditions and delinquency interact dynamically over time among homeless youth.

Hagan and McCarthy point out the worsening of theoretical anemia within American criminology. Scholars of crime and delinquency in the United States have drifted from the disciplinary roots in street-level studies of deviance and have gradually adopted a singular focus on quantitative models involving the administration of surveys among high school students and other youth in controlled settings. Changes in funding priorities have led the modern criminologist astray—rapidly waning are the days of "shoe leather criminology."

These authors wear out their shoes in doing the research for this book. Much of their study takes place on the streets; even when it's not focused on street activity, the researchers maintain their connections and presence on the corners, the main strips, the back alleys, and the encampments where study subjects spend their time.

**Comparative analysis** is another distinguishing feature of *Mean Streets*. The authors focus on two cities—Vancouver, BC, and Toronto, ON, Canada. And within each city they compare two populations: street youth and school-enrolled youth. Adhering closely to the logic of qualitative research, they select these two cities out of an interest in understanding how the two cities' differences (or "variance") vis-à-vis social policy influence, and are influenced by, the "criminogenic conditions" affecting homeless youth. Interestingly, they find that Vancouver's model, which is centered on controlling crime through "target hardening" and crackdowns on street denizens, actually amplifies the very conditions that caused the homelessness and the delinquency in the first place.

Because they integrate standard survey methods—ethnographic observation, qualitative interviewing, social mapping, content analysis, and even a form of social autopsy (along with other methods discussed in this book)—Hagan and McCarthy position themselves to ascertain the convergence of multiple factors (variables), processes, and relations in the production of "foreground" and "background" contexts that explain the occurrence of homelessness and crime among youth. Ultimately, they find that the same factors explaining crime among the homeless street youth also explain crime among the housed youth still enrolled in school. How they arrive at this finding (and many other intriguing findings) is a much longer story, one we encourage you to discover by reading the book yourself.

*Mean Streets* isn't flawless. The authors' discussion of how/why homeless youth get off the streets and desist in offending is theoretically and empirically feeble compared to their analysis of the factors that explain crime. Moreover, harkening back to our "unit of analysis" discussion, a good deal of street crime (and of life in general) emerges from and reciprocally influences *social* processes at the group and/or community level. While the authors recognize this explicitly, their study focuses almost solely on *individual-level* factors and processes. This is particularly disappointing and unfortunate given their extensive utilization of ethnographic logic in conducting this research; one could say they failed to make full use of their ethnographic capacity by focusing their fieldwork at the individual level and thereby neglecting opportunities to examine communal/group-level dynamics. Although the theoretical framework for understanding youth crime and homelessness is not particularly innovative, *Mean Streets* sets a very high methodological bar.

## CONCLUSION

This chapter is intentionally brief and is designed merely to open a door to the many possibilities of combining quantitative and qualitative methods. We have provided examples of the logic of designs that combine these approaches. There are many different strategies available for combining different approaches, and the choice of strategy will vary with the research questions. The main advantage of these mixed methods is that they provide both the precision of quantitative research and the contextualized richness of qualitative studies. They offer the opportunity for *triangulation*, for learning about the social world from multiple perspectives.

## Exercises

1. Pick a single-method study you have read. Critically dissect it using knowledge you have gained thus far in reading this book. Articulate how the study could be improved by the use of multiple methods.
2. Develop your own research idea. Posit a research question that is amenable to a multimethod approach. Explain why the multimethod approach is superior to a single-method approach. Remember, adopting a multimethod model isn't inherently better than using a single-method approach.
3. Can you think of an instance when it would be inadvisable to adopt a multimethod framework? Explain.

## Key Terms

causal factor *189*
comparative analysis *191*
context for quantitative data *187*
contexualization of quantitative data *187*
dichotomous variable (present or not present) *189*

exploratory methods *186*
level of measurement: nominal, ordinal, and interval-ratio (quantified or numerical) *189*
predictors and outcomes *186*
probability sample *186*

small-*n* analysis *185*
statistical analysis *186*
triangulation *185*
variables and relationships among variables *189*

# III

# Focus on Ethnography

Because ethnographic research is such a complex undertaking and so often encompasses many other methods and designs, we have devoted an entire part to it. The four chapters in this part elaborate the themes developed in Chapter 7. The first of these four chapters discusses the broad goal of studying culture and preparing for the field, the second explores the many types of data that ethnographers produce and analyze, the third focuses on doing fieldwork and writing good field notes, and the fourth suggests strategies for producing ethnographic data.

# 13

# Ethnography: Defining, Preparing for, and Entering the Field

## OVERVIEW

In the first chapter of Part III, we discuss how to enter "fieldwork"—the defining experience of ethnography. We discuss the first steps that you need to take to prepare yourself for entering the field, such as getting acquainted with prior research and "mapping your biases." We return to the topic of how to generalize from a **sample of one** culture. We look at "mental habits" that are useful in producing an ethnography, especially reflection and the indispensable *capacity for surprise*. We end with a short discussion of how to thrive in the early days of an ethnographic field study and how to deal with people-related issues that are typically encountered as soon as you step into the terrain.

## WHAT IS ETHNOGRAPHY?

Ethnography is usually considered a qualitative method, yet an ethnographic design may encompass quantitative research and quantitative approaches to analyzing qualitative data (such as computer-assisted content analysis of interviews, documents, and field notes). Many social scientists consider ethnography to be a **third method** that does not fall neatly into either category. Earlier in the book, we discussed the primary distinction between qualitative and quantitative research in terms of variables and cases. Quantitative research entails the study of a large number of cases but a small number of variables, while qualitative research involves studying a small number of cases and a larger number of variables. Some social scientists describe the difference as being one of "depth versus breadth," with qualitative research typically digging deeper and focusing on context while quantitative research incorporates more cases and makes use of statistical techniques. In this regard, ethnographic research is probably closer to the qualitative end of the spectrum.

## The Field

Instead of trying to pigeonhole ethnography into these blurry categories, it might be better to identify what all ethnographic designs have in common: *the experience of entering a field and observing a culture.* The ethnographer goes to a special place, **the field**, and spends time there observing a culture and writing about people. The field could be a place that is very familiar to the researcher (e.g., the world of the French *haute bourgeoisie* for Le Wita, who grew up in this milieu), one that is far away and different from anything the researcher has previously experienced (the Brazilian town in which Scheper-Hughes observed child-raising, infant mortality, gender roles, and the impact of poverty, in *Death Without Weeping*), or one that is physically close but socially distant, like East Harlem in Bourgeois' study of crack dealers, a South-Side Chicago boxing gym for Wacquant, and the Brickyard community of homeless people where Scott did his fieldwork. If the researcher does not spend time in the field, the study is not ethnography.

We hasten to note here recent efforts to develop a subfield loosely termed "nonhuman ethnography," a methodological branch predicated on the notion that humans and nonhumans interact to create social worlds. Attilla Bruni (2005), for instance, conducted a four-month ethnography of a hospital's digitized clinical records software/computer system, which he views

Looking east across "The Brickyard," a functioning salvage brick company on whose grounds nearly 200 homeless heroin and crack users on Chicago's west side have created a modern-day "shantytown."

Greg's "home" on the outskirts of "The Brickyard," where he lived while carrying out his three-year ethnographic study.

as "shadowing nonhumans." In this way, he studies how nonhuman, even nonmaterial, "objects" can tell us a great deal about the humans whom these objects "shadow." Although Bruni did not embed himself in the hospital halls or patients' rooms, much less occupy the software system, he did ensconce himself in the digital "infrastructure" that in many ways defines humans as "cases" in the medical system.

In the end, however, all of these designs—whether they entail the study of a tangible or intangible "field"—have a few key features in common and entail a similar "logic path" to representation. Get your plan together, figure out what you're interested in learning, gain entry to the field, spend a considerable amount of time producing data, step back from the field and figure out what you've learned, and then write up the process and results in a scholarly or popular press article or in a book-length treatment.

## Casting a Big Light with a Small Lamp

In addition to the field and the focus on culture, there is another central common denominator of ethnographies, regardless of motivation or approach: the belief that one can study (formally or informally) a relatively small group or community to produce knowledge and insight relevant and useful beyond the confines of the culture studied. Using a limited number of instances to draw broader conclusions is actually a central feature not only of qualitative research but of science in general. For example, quantitative researchers use statistical inference to draw conclusions from sample data. The most valued and celebrated scientific accounts are those whose examinations of observed cases shed light on, or help us to better understand, *unobserved* cases. You may recall our earlier discussion of "generalizability." Every ethnographer aspires to produce a study with findings whose salience extends beyond the boundaries of the case that she spent years examining.

Ethnography is a methodology in its own right. It's neither strictly quantitative nor strictly qualitative. It has its own logic and some unique methods and techniques. Almost invariably, ethnographers focus on the study and understanding of how groups of people, often construed as "communities," engage in *the making of meaning*. In the typical case, the ethnographer aspires to examine and convey a representation of how certain people create culture, how they go about the business of developing and sustaining particular ideas, or lay theories, of how the world operates and/or should operate. The implicit, or maybe explicit, guiding assumption is that all people (even the insane) attempt to create for themselves meaningful lives. Every group, no matter how "deviant" or "bizarre" or seemingly "irrational," creates a life of purpose (not in the strict instrumental sense, necessarily). Erving Goffman, one of the most widely recognized and well-respected qualitative sociologists, articulates this presumption, which expresses the core of what Paul Willis (2000) calls the "ethnographic imagination." Goffman asserts, "Any group of persons—prisoners, primitives, pilots, or patients—develop a life of their own that becomes meaningful, reasonable, and normal once you get close to it" (Goffman 1961: ix–x).

Your challenge as a student ethnographer is to hatch a plan for studying how a given group has developed a life of its own, one that its members find normal, meaningful, and reasonable. Implementing the plan, as Goffman indicates, demands that you "get close" to the life, the world, the culture, the people you want to better understand—in short, to enter the field. Later in this chapter, we'll talk about the process of "getting close" to informants in the field, but for now let's focus on the idea behind getting close. It's necessary to get close, to get involved, to become part of the scene so that you can get a solid fix on how people understand and define the world, how they go about organizing their action in it, and how they interpret and respond to others' actions. This, you may recall, is the essence of culture. You need to become fluent in their culture before you can write people convincingly.

## GETTING READY TO GET CLOSE: PLANNING FOR ETHNOGRAPHIC WORK

"Getting close" varies in difficulty, approach, time, and intensity depending on the group you have chosen to study, who you are, and how you relate to the group. If you're planning to conduct an ethnographic study of college students, your process of getting close and the time it takes to get close will be different than if you're planning to study outlaw motorcycle clubs that engage in methamphetamine manufacture and distribution. Whatever the case, ethnographic research requires a great deal of planning, and an equally great deal of midstream adjustments to your research questions, hypotheses, goals and objectives, relationships with informants in the field, and creation of data.

### Doing Your Homework: Background Research

All research projects begin with the reading of previous research on the topic. You do background research (preparing **literature reviews** and/or annotated bibliographies), and you try to identify **gaps in knowledge** and **unsolved puzzles**. What have others learned from studying the same group or culture? What have they *not* learned? How have they approached the study of this group, or groups like this group?

You may have to read in more than one body of literature. For example, Nancy Scheper-Hughes became familiar with research about Brazil, sugar production, child raising and infant mortality, gender roles, and popular rituals like Carnival, because her study involved all of these topics.

Some folks think that ethnography entails wandering into a place, hanging around a lot, and then at some point gradually or suddenly realizing that you're interested in formalizing your hanging out into a research project. Moreover, many people who don't do ethnography hold the false impression that the ethnographer enters the field as a clean slate (*tabula rasa*), and somehow the culture into which she ventures inscribes its values, meanings, rituals, and way of life onto the researcher, who in turn conveys it to a wider audience via a scholarly article or a book-length manuscript.

The reality couldn't be more different. While ethnographers often do not spend a ton of time developing theory-derived hypotheses for testing during fieldwork, the ethnographic project almost always involves intensive investigation of the extant literature on the subject/people/community/culture of interest. Now, it's true that in many instances the ethnographer first spends time in the community before developing an active research interest in it. But even then, upon realizing that there's something worthy of critical study, she "hits the books" and starts poking around for other studies on similar subjects. In fact, the moment during which the ethnographer recognizes or becomes aware of a research angle illustrates the coming together of abstract knowledge and material lived existence.

The ethnographer, like anyone else, comes to a new situation with a wide array of ideas, preconceptions, predispositions, images, and projections about the community he will spend the next X amount of time studying. It's not possible to approach a research setting and not have these preformulated notions. There's no such thing as a blank slate or an entirely value- and idea-free frame of mind—it would require the unlikely scenario of being abducted, blindfolded, and dropped into a foreign situation.

## Reflexivity Exercises: Placing Your Vague Preconceptions in a Vivid Foreground

No matter how unfamiliar the culture is to you, even before entering it the first time you undoubtedly have ideas about it. Some of those ideas are based on reading good research but others are just stereotypes. As Becker (1998) argues and demonstrates, you very likely entertain "imagery" of the culture and the people who populate and animate it. Unchecked and unquestioned, these images and ideas and preconceived notions could become a source of data corruption down the road. In short, unless you subject your own biases to critical scrutiny, they could spell the demise of your ethnographic project.

**MAP YOUR BIASES**  So, before you enter the field (and simultaneously with reading the research literature) you can begin writing a kind of journal, or diary, or essay, or series of memoranda, or whatever format makes you comfortable. In this prose you should reflect on how you envision the culture, the people, the places, the things, the events, the interactions, and so forth. Be as specific as you can be. This is one of your first steps in exercising **reflexivity**, or the exercising of awareness of the reciprocal relationship between you and the people you're studying. In this document, or journal, you should write as openly and honestly as you can, no holds barred, no matter how negatively stereotypical or judgmental you think you sound. It's crucial at this point that you get your cognitive schemata on paper, where you can dissect them and begin to figure out how to resolve them, or at the very least, work around them when you're in the field. Otherwise, these thoughts and images will only "contaminate" the data that you manufacture.

The pre-fieldwork imagery you reduce to paper now requires critical dissection. By this point, you have probably learned that you possessed many more notions about the culture than you initially figured. You've made these implicit assumptions into explicit material that you can assess. We suggest that you continually return to the pre-field exercises during your time in the field. In fact, as we discuss later, throughout the period of your fieldwork you would be well-advised to repeatedly engage in reflexivity exercises, for they aid in monitoring how your taken-for-granted assumptions change and how they might impact the data that you produce.

**DEFINE YOUR GOALS**    In addition to plotting or **mapping your own biases**, preconceptions, stereotypes, imagery, assumptions, and so forth, you should begin to make explicit what you want to learn about the culture you've chosen to study. At this point in the process, your work makes use of the knowledge and skills to which you've been exposed in earlier chapters. You have studied the literature on the subject/culture that interests you, so you're familiar with the kinds of research questions others have asked and tried to answer. Now it's your turn. Start with the question, "What's missing?" In reading the articles, books, book chapters, reports, journalistic accounts, and so forth, what questions do you think remain unanswered? What's *not* there in the literature? This is a good question to ask whenever you're beginning a critical study of any representation. Whether it's a scholarly article or a film or even a social situation, this simple question will move you down the path of developing the necessary "critical consciousness" for conducting ethnography effectively.

## Asking Questions and Planning to Seek Answers

Qualitative research, and ethnography in particular, enjoys abundant strengths, one of which (perhaps the most important one) is its flexibility. Sensitivity to the continuous flux, the ebbing and flowing, of events occurring in the field under study is one of the most important strengths of ethnographic research—but this can also be its greatest weakness. Indeed, many quantitative social scientists decry the open-endedness of qualitative work, frequently arguing that it's "too subjective" to constitute "serious science." To counter this criticism, qualitative researchers need to communicate explicitly to their students the specific methods, techniques, assumptions, and standards that make for good (strong, valid, useful) work in this tradition. There is an artistic side to good ethnography, but novice researchers need guidance in specific methods and standards just like novice artists. Susan Silbey, a highly regarded qualitative sociologist, expresses her chagrin at the unexamined contradictions that infect so many teacher–student interactions:

> . . . some years ago I heard a colleague advise a student going out to do field work for the first time 'to be like a blank slate,' 'just tell me everything you see and hear, write it all down.' The student was completely baffled and clearly at a loss about what to do, to do first, or second, or how to begin. What would constitute telling me all you see and hear. Importantly, the student had read a lot of sociology, and knew a lot about signs and signifiers, latent as well as manifest patterns in social relations. She knew that competent social actors are not blank slates. She felt incompetent but not entirely blank. She had a project, after all.

> (Silbey, 2004: 121)

By this point in the process you are no longer a blank slate—you have developed a pretty good idea of what you want to study, why you want to study it, and what you already know, think about, and visualize of the culture or community you've chosen.

As Susan Silbey points out, scholars in both quantitative and qualitative traditions aspire to create "science" of some sort. Otherwise, they would be working in some other field, such as journalism or public sculpture. And when it comes to the science of quantitative, qualitative, and ethnographic research, they have virtually identical aspirations.

> The goal of research is to produce results that can be falsifiable and in some way affirmable by rational processes of actors other than the author. Most important is that the researcher provides an account of how the conclusions were reached, why the reader should believe the claims and how one might go about trying to produce a similar account.
>
> (Silbey, 2004: 122)

Ethnography is not about traipsing jauntily and insouciantly into someone else's life, another group's culture, or a community unknown to you and then writing about your feelings. The research experience needs to be structured, transparent, and self-reflexive (which is not the same as being all about yourself—it means being aware of what you are up to). Remember that all research orientations share the goal of creating systematic accounts that are scientific in a broad sense, even if not always positivistic.

## Prepare for Your Role on a Stage Not Your Own

Ethnography frequently seems a lot like "hanging out…with a purpose." In this way, it's very similar to how world-renowned journalist Gay Talese describes his method of reportage: "It's the art of hanging out." And to watch the ethnographer in action is to see someone who appears to be wandering aimlessly, yukking it up with folks sitting on their front porches or having a drink at the bar or milling about on the street corner. But the ethnographer is (or should be) doing these things concertedly, with a purpose in mind, and engaged in a fourfold function—**relating, reflecting, retaining, and reducing**. While in the field, every movement, every interaction, every moment demands the exercise of this "fourfold consciousness."

**RELATING**    Research requires data. This may seem like too obvious a statement to put in writing, especially at this point in the book. But where do ethnographic data come from? The ethnographer creates it. How does the ethnographer go about creating the data? Through his interaction with the people, places, and things that comprise the culture. These interactions may take the form of strict observation (watching and recording), interviewing, participating in rituals, getting involved in group discussions, or any of a number of activities.

Regardless of the venue, however, the professional stranger must be acting, talking, and relating in ways deemed appropriate by the members of that culture. This is not to say that the ethnographer is expected to behave as a "native" would behave, but she must act in accordance with the culture's expectations regarding how foreign entrants to the culture should act. This is one of the first things you will need to figure out. Before trying to determine how a native should behave, figure out how a stranger behaves, because that's what you will be for quite a while—a stranger. So you, as an ethnographer, are also a human being, a social actor trying very hard to pull off a convincing performance on an unfamiliar stage. As a nonresearcher, you've already accumulated quite a bit of experience maneuvering through analogous scenes and situations. You therefore have a sense of what's entailed here. You must relate—talk, gesture, walk, stand, sit, enter, greet, depart, laugh, and so on, even if these behaviors at first seem uncomfortable.

**REFLECTING ON RELATING**    Relating is one thing. And thinking about how you're relating is another. This second level of consciousness tends to punch in when we encounter new settings where a mystique or opaqueness obscures the rules that govern the "interaction rituals" (Goffman 1967). Hence, you must think about how you're behaving, whereas in the familiar contexts of your life you generally act without reflecting on how you're acting unless the situation is changing dramatically or something unusual is happening. When you're doing ethnography, though, you're not only reflecting on how you're relating as a social actor, but you're also reflecting *instrumentally* on how best to relate with others such that you can produce through your interactions the most valid and reliable data possible. Because you don't have access to all of your plans and your computer and books, when you're in the field you must be recalling the research questions, hypotheses, plans, and so forth that guide your inquiry. This business of relating, reflecting on relating, and reflecting on the reflections of relating is anything but easy.

It's exhausting to interact with people in this way, which is one of the reasons most ethnographers recommend (wisely, in our estimation) that you spend no more than six or eight hours in the field on any day and that you spread your field visits over time. You will need the downtime to recover, decompress, write your field notes (explored in detail below), and plan for the next outing. Even a short stint in the field, say four hours, is capable of very easily generating a tremendous amount of data, which you must be able to recall and reproduce between visits.

**RETAINING—LEARNING TO RECALL LIKE AN ACTOR DELIVERING LINES:**    Recalling field experiences—reproducing the interactions, observations, and insights you had in the field—hinges on your capacity for retaining the phenomena as they unfolded in real time in the field. Most ethnography/methods textbooks say nothing about this aspect of the field experience, or else they insist that you "show the people" to the reader of your finished product by including verbatim reproductions of natural dialogue and/or responses to interview questions. But the "how to" books and manuals and articles fail to give insight into how one goes about doing this. The reason for this neglect, or blind spot, could be fairly simple: It's different for everyone. Such relativism, though, contravenes our commitment to elucidating rigorous standards for the implementation of ethnographic research designs. In Chapter 14, we discuss strategies for producing data in the field, which will involve a more detailed account of tactics for recalling experiences and dialogue.

But in the preparatory stage, you can begin "training" yourself to recall events as well as verbatim dialogue from conversations with and between or among informants. Everyday life offers bountiful opportunities for training your senses of sound and sight, the two primary avenues by which you begin creating ethnographic data. The senses of touch, smell, and taste certainly have their place in all manner of ethnographic research (and may be very important in some studies, such as an ethnography of a restaurant). But at the outset, begin refining sight and sound using daily life as your venue. Contemporary technology can be useful in your endeavor to train yourself to "record" events retrospectively. Go on outings to ordinary places—the park, a beach, a bus stop, an ordinary street corner of your choosing. Take along with you a video recorder, or even just a cell phone that captures moving images. Sit and watch while recording what you see. Set the "begin" and "end" times and adhere to them strictly. Spend no more than three or four minutes observing and recording. Move the recording device (video camera or phone) so that it captures what you're watching. Then go home and write up what you saw, heard, and smelled but *do not* consult the video recording you made.

**REDUCING: WHAT GETS LEFT OUT OR CHANGED WHEN YOU WRITE FIELD NOTES?**   In Chapter 15, we offer some guidelines for writing your field notes, but for now just write them free-form. Once you think you've written up what you believe to be a pretty exhaustive account of your observations, watch the video recording. Keep an inventory of all the things you missed. Once you've made your list, you likely will be surprised by how many items populate the list. Now review the list and analyze the items on it. Can you place the items into categories? If so, what are the categories? Do you tend to systematically neglect certain things, or kinds of things, in the environment? The answer will be yes, for everyone wears "blinders" when they're in social settings. This exercise helps you to focus on how you are reducing what you observe and recall because you cannot retain and record everything.

## Reflecting on Reduction and Recognizing Your Blinders! A Preparatory Exercise

Over the course of our lives we have developed these blinders, or "perceptual filters" as a result of social conditioning. The "place" we occupy in the social world, the economy, the political power structure, and other macro-level conditions all influence what we see in the world and how we see/interpret these things. We constantly engage in the practice of "thin-slicing" (Gladwell 2007). Because it's impossible to notice and process *everything* we see, hear, touch, taste, and smell in any given context, we have developed perceptual mechanisms for "slicing" out what's important to us. But for a field researcher, the properties or characteristics or traits of "what's important" go by another name: bias. If you enter the field completely unaware of your biases, then your data will be corrupted quite unknowingly. You will filter out phenomena that you have come to exclude from your "viewfinder," but those may be the phenomena of greatest import to the local actors in the culture you're studying.

You can perform a similar exercise with interviewing. Pick a subject—a stranger, a family member, or a friend—and ask the person if you could interview her for 15 minutes about some topic that interests you. The actual topic doesn't really matter. When you sit down for the interview, be sure to ask your "subject" open-ended questions (i.e., questions that cannot be answered with a discrete response, such as "yes" or "no" or a single word or phrase). Your questions should require descriptive responses. Good open-ended interview questions often begin with "how," such as "How did you come to drink alcohol for the first time?" or "What do you think…", or "What do you think about the university's rules concerning plagiarism among students?"

Whatever topic you choose and however you end up asking questions, you should record the interview on audiotape and on paper. Take notes during the interview. In Chapter 18, we discuss specific interviewing techniques, so we won't go into them here. The point is that you should take notes on the conversation (and it should be approached and treated as a conversation, not an interrogation), but only to the point where you can participate effectively as a "conversation partner" with the subject. Don't let your note-taking get in the way of the "active listening" (discussed in detail in a later chapter).

After the interview, go back to your notes and try to reconstruct the subject's answers to your questions, including tangents and digressions. Then listen to and transcribe verbatim the interview. Compare the text (data) you reconstructed from your notes and from memory with the transcript of the recording. Undoubtedly you will notice quite a gap between what you re-created and what the subject "actually" said. But again, that's not the end of this learning assignment. Now you need to identify passages in the interview transcript that you either (a) totally neglected or (b) re-created (reproduced) inaccurately. Finally, you need to analyze the omissions and inaccuracies. They occurred for a reason, or for several reasons, and if you reflect on them critically you will become more sensitive to the perceptual filters that shape your way of experiencing the world.

To produce good data, you'll need to be sensitive to content and style/form, particularly when it comes to reconstructing conversations and dialogue. Later, we present a list of specific strategies for writing good field notes, but for now let us simply say that during the interview or conversation you must attend to content (what people are saying), temporality (the order or sequence in which they say things), cadence (inflection and intonation), rhythm (for everyone's speech has a distinct beat), and phraseology (the particular and distinctive catchphrases people have and generally use repeatedly and unreflectively). Training oneself to be a good observer of human behavior and speech is in some ways like learning to become an actor, but in other ways it's very different. Think of the ethnographic scene as a special kind of dress rehearsal, the one and only chance you'll get to learn your lines, learn others' lines, indeed learn the entire script. Later, in the comfort of your own setting (office, bedroom, wherever you do your work), you'll have to reproduce the entire script—including everyone's lines, the staging, the sequencing, the props, all of it—from memory. In short, when you're doing fieldwork, you are living with your "fourfold-consciousness" so that you can relive the situation later, when you're in a position to produce your data.

Becoming a good observer, a good producer of ethnographic data, develops over a long period of time and requires lots of training and practice. You will encounter many moments of frustration and long stretches of tedium. Ethnographers typically spend more time writing up their detailed notes (creating data) than they spend in the field. At least that's the case for those ethnographers whose data become known as "exemplary." You'll also learn a good deal about who you are as a person and as a member of civic life.

## THINKING ABOUT YOUR PROJECT: THE LOGIC OF ETHNOGRAPHIC DISCOVERY

You have practiced your observational and data production skills. You've thought long and hard about your project. You've surveyed the literature to find out what other researchers have learned, what knowledge they've produced on the subject and, more important, what they have neglected to learn and contribute to the knowledge fund. Now you're ready to make a list of research questions. You might even be in a position to write out some informal or formal hypotheses, or educated guesses that you plan to take into the field. It's important to keep in mind that you're seeking to understand patterns of behavior. And, more to the point, you want to ask questions and seek answers concerning **variation within a culture.**

There are two aspects to planning your project. One is to follow good practices in design and methods, and Chapters 14–16, as well as several chapters in Part III, will offer guidelines. Following these rules is the easy part of doing ethnography—engaging in hard work, but guided by straightforward and down-to-earth recommendations. The other part is beginning to think about how your project is going to yield *knowledge of a culture*—what do we even mean by that phrase? That's the hard part because we have to think about our own thought processes—to operate at a "meta-level" of reflexivity about what we are doing when we try to reach conclusions. It involves cultivating habits of mind that lead to discovery.

# MENTAL HABITS OF ETHNOGRAPHERS

In this section, we spin a few ideas about what it "feels like to be an ethnographer"—about habits of mind and ways of thinking that set the mood for producing good ethnographies.

To give a preview of this section, we are going to discuss **difference** (*and sameness*), the problems of *generalizing from a small sample*, the use of **iterative recursive abduction** (which basically means leaping to conclusions from a series of repeated observations), and the *capacity for being surprised*. These are habits of mind that may help us to produce a good ethnography; unlike our suggestions for good practices in the field, it's hard to reduce them to a linear set of instructions.

## Sameness and Difference: Not the Same Difference

In studying a culture, we want to look for uniformities, yet remain aware of differences and variation. How do we decide which to prioritize? And when does variation in behavior or outcomes amount to a real difference? (A lot of quantitative research uses the concept of "statistical significance" to answer this question, but that won't work in qualitative and ethnographic research.)

Some of the most highly regarded qualitative researchers claim that the qualitative approach in general, and ethnography in particular, concerns itself principally with sameness, or how a wide spectrum of people tend to converge on the same, relatively few, cultural forms. Howard Becker, for instance, asserts that qualitative researchers "are less interested in things that differ among the members" (thus providing the variation that is so necessary to quantitative analysis) and far more interested in characteristics or traits or beliefs common to the great majority of a culture's members (2003, p. 45).

Although the balance of interest may tilt toward sameness, we disagree with Becker's generalization. As an ethnographer, you certainly want to orient yourself to the production and sustenance of cultural forms—how do people keep this way of life going? But given that culture isn't unified bur rather disjointed, disrupted, uneven, fractured, and otherwise multifaceted, the ethnographer should possess a keen interest in the **variation within a given culture** (assuming one can even speak defensibly about "a culture" without reification).

## Generalizing from Your Sample of One: Culture X

Whatever the case, you want to understand things about the culture. You want to get a feel for difference, or variation, and for similarity, or sameness across cases. At this point, it's important to remind ourselves of the *unit of analysis* discussion from earlier chapters. An ethnography examines a single case: the culture that the ethnographer has chosen to study, although ethnographers must be sensitive to variation in behaviors and outcomes among individuals and groups who participate in this culture. Ethnographic research, "small *N*" research, and qualitative methods have a logic that is different from the techniques and vernacular of the natural sciences and the quantitative social/behavioral sciences.

Generalizability is a hallmark of the scientific method, as we discussed previously. In ethnographic research, however, you're not aspiring to **generalize** in the same way that quantitative social scientists attempt to generalize from a sample to a population when they express cautious confidence that their findings apply to **unobserved as well as observed cases** (summarized by a confidence interval or a test of significance). Instead, you pursue what we're going to call the capacity to **genericize.** Erving Goffman, a qualitative sociologist of high repute, wrote extensively about how qualitative research and ethnography should avoid falling into the trap of natural science mimicry. More recently, Small (2009) wrote that ethnography has its own logic and should be assessed according to standards and criteria different from those that govern the evaluation of quantitative work. Rather than adopting the same logic of quantitative research, we recommend that qualitative and ethnographic research unfold according to a logic of investigation that capitalizes on the "small N," the single case (i.e., culture).

The logic of ethnographic research is really quite simple and straightforward. You aspire to comprehend the parameters of a given culture. And you attempt to understand how that culture is maintained, how it changes, and how it interacts with proximal cultures and/or its "host" culture. Moreover, you develop this understanding through immersion, not through detached inquiry. You set out to "embed" yourself in the culture and, as best you can, achieve a high level of fluency as a "resident stranger" (Scheper-Hughes 2001) of the culture. As we asserted previously, becoming a "native" of the culture is an infeasible and unattainable goal, particularly when the culture isn't your own. But becoming fluent in the culture's vernacular (spoken and unspoken) is a reasonable goal. In fact, when you've reached the point in your study when nothing new is happening, when you're capable of explaining events, relations, and phenomena in the same way that "insiders" explain them, you probably can consider the data collection to be complete. When your "accounts" of cultural phenomena square up with those given by insiders, then your field-work is coming to a close.

Simply put, your ethnographic goal is to "give an account" (Agar 1980) of the culture that resonates with members of the culture and that satisfies the standards of quality for ethnographic research. This is not to say that the people in your study will agree with, or even like, your conclusions (we'll discuss this later in Chapter 24). But their assessment of your account's *accuracy* should result in high marks for you, the resident stranger who sees their culture "through a glass darkly" (Scheper-Hughes 2001). When you engage in analysis, you will not be articulating in a facile, uncritical way exactly what the insiders say and do. Instead, you'll bring to bear on their words and actions—the culture writ large—your own critical assessment, developed through a dialogue of "ideas and evidence." By this point, you will have gained a promontory point on the culture, a vantage few insiders have the capacity to achieve. In this respect, then, your representation of the culture will not be, nor could it ever be, wholly "emic." Every solid representation of a culture exhibits a blend of the emic and etic perspectives. *Remember, it's their culture, but it's your story*. This can be tricky terrain, as we'll discuss in Chapter 24.

## Iterative Recursive Abduction

"To see the world in a grain of sand…" as William Blake suggests in "Auguries of Innocence" is a special capacity. It resembles C. W. Mills' explication of the "sociological imagination": the ability to appreciate the manifestation of "public issues" within the small orbit of "personal troubles." This is the essence of ethnographic social science: appreciating the interconnections between small and the grand, the micro and the macro. Ethnographers document the details of culture for the sake of "assembling the puzzle." Large-scale, impalpable structural forces (the economy, law, politics, etc.) give rise and shape to the local, and the playing out of the local both propagates and challenges the more macro-level forces at play. Ethnography, as a logic of social science inquiry, is well-positioned to explore these intricate connections vis-à-vis culture, as a set of practices and as an institution. How do we assemble the puzzle? Here are terms that can help us in first developing an understanding of a single culture and then drawing broader conclusions from our sample of one.

**ITERATIVE AND RECURSIVE**  Ethnographic analysis is iterative and recursive. This means that we search for general rules that members of the culture seem to be applying repeatedly in the course of daily life. We find these rules through our observations of behaviors that derive from and manifest these rules. And we keep applying the general rule to common, or similar, observations until we can fairly well state what the guiding cultural rule is. In order to achieve relatively coherent view of the culture, we must observe the application of its rules in relation to the culture as a whole. And we must observe specific rules, in their actualization, across cases and contexts within the culture.

**ABDUCTIVE**  Ethnography at its best employs an "abductive" logic, as opposed to logic that is purely deductive, purely inductive, or even some blend of the two. Many methods texts describe the difference between deductive and inductive logic, but we agree with Agar that ethnographic research—probably all research—really follows an **abductive logic**.

Deductive logic means that we have theories in place that lead to predictions that we test against the empirical world and reject if they are not supported by the facts. In deductive logic, the "fact" reigns supreme, ready to "knock out" a hypothesis (and much more rarely a whole theory) that doesn't fit it. Deductive logic often relies on the research procedures you learn in quantitative methods and stats courses such as creating operational variables, stating hypotheses, drawing probability samples, and testing for significance.

Inductive logic means that we claim to be teasing out general principles by examining lots of empirical data; often we really already have these theoretical premises in mind before we "find them" in the data analysis. Inductive logic still operates in the realm of existing concepts. Within this line of thinking, one comes across "new" material, new or previously un-encountered or at least undocumented experiences and then attempts to fit them into existing concepts. One goes from the empirical, the readily accessible "facts" revealed in the course of fieldwork and then "slots" them into conceptual and/or theoretical constructs that the ethnographer invariably carries, like luggage, into the field with her. In the application of inductive logic, the concept is assumed to be "true." Moreover (and more problematically), it is assumed to be applicable to the events transpiring in the field.

Hence, the ethnographer using purely inductive logic makes an observation, thus producing a data point, and then assumes *a priori* that the empirical event instantiates some preexisting concept or theoretical proposition (which the researcher has quietly kept in the back of her mind). This is the reverse of purely deductive logic, where the ethnographer assumes the "truth" of the empirical event. In an inductive approach, empirical events somehow express, manifest, and embody some general truth that has already been identified and articulated in the form of theory although we are careful not to state it until we have "found it" in the empirical data.

*Abductive logic* differs from both of these approaches. Deductive and inductive logic both invoke a "confirmatory meta-logic," which is to say that at their core these lines of reasoning make assumptions about truth and then seek out their confirmation either through fitting new material into old ideas or manipulating (integrating, juxtaposing, appending, etc.) old ideas to square up with new empirical material. Putting it simply, both lines of reasoning are concerned with "old ideas." But where do *new* ideas, concepts, hypotheses, or theory come from? The best ethnographies deliver something "new"...Consequently, we need a logic that differs from, and goes beyond, either of these alone or even both of them combined. A lot of philosophers of science have tried to answer the question where the new ideas come from across the whole spectrum of sciences (Kuhn 1962; Feyerabend 1975), but here we want to focus on ethnography in particular.

As Agar (2006: 62) cheekily points out the demand for ethnographic work is greatest out-side of the university, particularly in social service settings and in the corporate world, two spheres in which "success" hinges on meeting clients' culturally specific needs. "The inelegant question, 'what in the hell is going on out there,' motivates organizations to seek ethnographic help. They can't *de*duce or *in*duce because old knowledge clearly doesn't work." This problem has led Agar to adopt a new logic model and develop it into a framework for doing ethnography, the model that he calls iterative reductive abduction. (Charles Peirce, 1906, a logician and semiotician, introduced the term "abductive logic" into philosophic discourse. Since then, the term has made its way into computer science, artificial intelligence, philosophy, legal studies, and anthropology.)

Remember that in ordinary speech, *abduction* means kidnapping—grabbing and carrying off someone, as when space aliens *abduct* a human. Abductor muscles move limbs *away* from the center of the body. So the main idea is that abductive logic leads us away from conventional methods of reaching conclusions. In the crudest lay terms, abductive reasoning amounts to guessing. In other words, we grab our results and carry them off, taking them a lot further than the cautious deductionists and inductionists think is safe, and we get playful with them. It's a particular kind of guesswork; it emerges from the interaction of abstract thought, empirical experience, and the mind's capacity for supposition. Coming up with "new truths" requires that we extend inquiry beyond the confines of "old idea" manipulation on which deductive and inductive logic both rest.

We engage in abductive reasoning every day, many times a day, but we don't usually recognize it as such, much less consider it to be a particularly rigorous or scientific endeavor. But, as many scholars of knowledge (epistemologists such as Paul Feyerabend [1975]) have argued, brilliant advances in science arose not from the application of formal logic or the routines of empirical data-gathering, but from the scientist's playful "hunch" that a specific empirical event/observation, or set of events, had in common a unifying principle, or law, or perhaps that they all shared a common precursor or antecedent event. Peirce et al. (1998) say it well enough themself:

> Now, that the matter of no new truth can come from induction or from deduction, we have seen. It can only come from abduction; and abduction is, after all, nothing but guessing. We are therefore bound to hope that, although the possible explana-tions of our facts may be strictly innumerable, yet our mind will be able, in some finite number of guesses, to guess the sole true explanation of them. That we are bound to assume, independently of any evidence that it is true. Animated by that hope, we are to proceed to the construction of a hypothesis.

## Speculation, Imagination, and Surprise

Albert Einstein, the Nobel Prize–winning physicist and philosopher, wrote extensively and contemplated deeply the nature of scientific advancement and the development of insight into human affairs. His position was akin to that of many scholars who specialize in the study of how scientific advances occur: Imagination is indispensable. "I think that only daring specula-tion can lead us further and not accumulation of facts," Einstein wrote in a letter to Michele Besso in 1952. He even prized imagination over knowledge, at least in the context of develop-ing new ideas. Indeed, the "study of hunches" has become a discipline, or at least a scientific focus, in its own right. Previously we discussed the value of maintaining the capacity to be surprised by your observations (i.e., your data). Imagination in light of the empirical world and knowledge of conceptual notions propel abductive reasoning...guessing is the science of everyday life.

**HOW TO GUESS**    In the context of ethnography, guessing is critical, but it also must be subjected to critical scrutiny. Peirce set forth a formal statement of abductive logic, the steps by which we arrive at guesses which in turn are based on iteration and recursion:

> *The surprising fact, F, is observed.*
> *If H were true, F would be a matter of course.*
> *Hence, there is reason to suspect that H is true. (quoted in Agar 2006: 63)*

The observation of "F" surprises us. Why? Because we haven't yet encountered any theoretical or conceptual framework that would lead us to expect or predict the occurrence of F. Nor have we necessarily observed F previously. Perhaps we observe a second instance of F, and maybe then a third. Now we have a series of Fs (and F could be anything—an argument of a certain sort, a ritual, the use of a particular phrase, a way of making money, etc.)—and that is how the recursive and iterative part comes in. Now, at some point, most likely when we least expect it, we get a hunch about F's occurrence, not just the single incident of F, but the multiple instances of F. We suspect that they have something in common. And so we now have one hypothesis concerning F's etiology, or the process by which F came to occur. But how do we formulate the idea that H somehow might be what produces F? That often happens in a flash of insight that rearranges everything we think we knew and understood.

**THE "A-HA!" EXPERIENCE**    Oftentimes, when doing ethnographic work, the product of abductive reasoning just comes to you, like a flash, the kind of sudden burst of insight commonly known as the "a-ha!" experience. Einstein, whose startling insights transformed physics, recognized the invaluable contributions of the "flight of fancy," the supposition, the brilliant flash of abductive reasoning, the guess: "I never came upon any of my discoveries through the process of rational thinking."

The sudden and quite unexpected burst of insight, the proposition that H might explain the incidence of F, is by no means the end of the road. Although few of Einstein's "discoveries" resulted from deliberate and concerted analytic work, all of his suppositions (or flights of wonder) were followed by intensive, meticulous calculation, experimentation, empirical testing, and analysis. And not all brilliant flashes in physics or ethnography will pass the rigors of *post hoc* testing.

The "a-ha!" moment is not the beginning of the road either! Because the moment does not happen in the empty tabula-rasa mind, but only after immersion in experience, observation, and reflection—it's a new way of arranging all that stuff.

Methods texts are reluctant to reveal the role of anarchy and insight in science. In the past decade, however, neurologic scientists have made terrific strides in the study of "insight," the term they use for the distinctive problem-solving process that differs in form, function, and subjective feeling from its more deliberative and mechanical analytic method for solving problems. Jung-Beeman et al. (2004), for example, find that insight solutions, as they call them, are associated strongly with a surge of high-frequency wave activity in the brain's right hemisphere anterior superior temporal gyrus. The right hemisphere of the brain governs our "creative" capacities, including but not limited to such faculties as curiosity, experimentation, metaphoric thinking, playfulness, solution finding, artistry, flexibility, synthesizing and in general, risk taking. Some neurologists claim that the right hemisphere is also opportunistic, future oriented, inclined to invite change, and functions as the center for our ability to visualize. Indeed, most "insight" brain studies reveal a tremendous amount of neural activity in the right hemisphere with simultaneous but far less significant activity in the so-called "problem solving" and "logical" left hemisphere. Psychologists emphasize the relationship between creativity and "flow" by which they mean a state of harmonious immersion and prolonged concentration in a mental activity.

You—the astute reader—may be wondering whether abductive anarchy threatens Popperian policing (the chronic fussing about falsification we discussed earlier). Yes, it does, and the tension makes for better science—and stimulating conversations with yourself.

**TALKING TO YOURSELF**    Most likely, your experiences observing F coalesced around some common theme, or perhaps some aspect of your consciousness connected the Fs to something else, or maybe even detected some theme to F (time of day, location, chronology, etc.). And some other part of your consciousness, a place where abstract knowledge and static information reside, connected the Fs, your linkage of the Fs to something else, and a blend of abstractions to which you gained some exposure previously, say in a class on sociological theory, for instance. Whatever the case, the logic and actual doing of ethnography is dynamic, dialectical. You're constantly going back and forth between the consciousness of the field and the consciousness of the intellectual in an office somewhere. When you do ethnography, you spend a lot of time talking to yourself.

Qualitative research and ethnography are open-ended modes of inquiry. As a researcher, you constantly go back and forth between what Ragin calls "dialogue" and "evidence." You go into a research setting with all sorts of explicit and latent constructs, ideas, notions, and even working theories, not to mention images and stereotypes. If you've followed our suggestion, you will have made many of these explicit and also analyzed them before going into the field.

Some professional ethnographers (see Agar 1980) even recommend strongly that you undergo psychiatric counseling prior going into the field so as to minimize the extent to which you "project" your own predispositions, cognitive maps, emotional sensibilities, and so on onto your interpretations of phenomena you experience/observe in the field. While we stop short of endorsing or recommending pre-fieldwork therapy, we do believe it's important for you to be very explicit about the "baggage" you're carrying as you sojourn into a new culture. In any event, throughout the ethnographic research process you will find yourself going back and forth between ideas/concepts/theories and the data you create based on your fieldwork experiences. While some social scientists believe this open-endedness to be a weakness of the ethnographic logic, we would argue the contrary—it might be its greatest strength.

## Maintaining the Capacity to Be Surprised

The project you have in mind the day you first step foot into the field will be very different from the project you end up completing. This is to be expected. Remaining open, maintaining the capacity to be "surprised" by your data, and actively seeking repudiation of your own working hypotheses is the ideal condition, but it's crucial that you keep a running log of how your ideas change. You can record these changes in your ideas in analytic memos (see Chapter 17). Document your working theories about the phenomena that interest you, seek to "test" these notions, and aggressively scavenge for data that will disconfirm these hypotheses. This kind of "analytic induction" will receive more complete treatment later, but for now we just want to make the assertion that the hunt for "negative cases" is one of the things that makes ethnography distinct from other logics and methodologies, and it represents one of the ways by which your research achieves a high level of integrity.

A lot of this boils down to having fun doing your research—feeling thrilled and excited about observing, reflecting and thinking. It means wanting to be involved in your research all the time, not just nine to five on weekdays, even if it is just in the form of spinning ideas or talking to yourself. The capacity for enjoyment (even of unpleasant experiences) is strongly related to intellectual curiosity and the capacity for surprise. If ethnography is not fun once you give it a try, don't do it. Like most enjoyable activities, it is improved by practice and systematic know-how—but it should never feel like a boring routine.

## ENTERING THE FIELD

Ethnography is a lonely job—sometimes terrifying, occasionally tedious, frequently thrilling, always unbounded and assailing you with self-doubt. In the preparatory stage, you might be talking with your friends, colleagues, mentors and instructors, and others who have some stake in your project, your life, and/or your well-being. But once you enter the field, you are "adrift," cut loose from the social and cultural moorings with which you had become so familiar and on which you had become so dependent. You're alone out there; you are a professional stranger (Agar 1980).

During your early days in the field, you don't know anyone. You don't know who you should get to know or how you should get to know them. At every juncture, you realize that while one "bad decision" in making connections won't be the ruination of you, a few of them in succession just might doom you to irrelevance, or worse, exile. And you have no "wing man," no backup, no friend who can buffer or broker new situations or get you out of uncomfortable interactions. Get used to this loneliness, as it's one of the defining characteristics of the trade. Later we share with you some strategies and tactics for overcoming the loneliness, which not coincidentally also improve your analytic faculties.

### New People

In Chapter 17, we will discuss sponsored and unsponsored strategies of entering the field. Here, we will focus on meeting new people, avoiding certain kinds of new people, building relationships, and learning when to keep quiet.

**GATEKEEPERS, STRANGER-HANDLERS, AND PUBLIC CHARACTERS**    Once you've entered the field, one or two locals almost undoubtedly will approach you and begin telling you what seems to be the entire story of the culture, and they might even share with you the intimate details of their biographies. You might think you've landed upon a goldmine. But in most instances, a few months in the field will bring about a disappointing revelation: Those early interactions weren't really gold; rather, they were "fool's gold."

Upon venturing into the field for the first time, you'll meet new people, and they'll likely be very talkative. They might seem to be confiding in you the "public secrets" of the group, community, or culture that you have chosen to study. Down the road, however, you likely will discover that although these early bonds were important to you, they didn't yield particularly valid data. This is because every community has informal "stranger-handlers," the people who serve as the culture's "gatekeepers." Sometimes they are self-appointed and wordlessly ratified guardians and spokespersons of the culture. Often these folks are quite knowledgeable of the culture, and they're also well-integrated with the various networks of people who comprise the culture. In some fieldwork, stranger-handling may be an official role in the organization that you hope to study, and individuals are identified by titles containing terms such as "media relations" or "community relations." Their function is to acquaint you with positive features of the organization and to keep you from prying into behaviors or topics which the organization would prefer to keep private. In other instances, however, they're relative outsiders themselves—they are the marginal among the marginalized. But they have found their niche—handling people like you.

When they are themselves marginal in the culture, you need to be cautious of forming overly tight, highly visible relationships with them even though they are easy to meet in the first days of fieldwork. Doing so may result in the community relegating you to the margins, where you'll remain for the rest of your study. While in the margins, you'll have countless interesting conversations with the stranger-handlers, but they won't amount to much. The stranger-handlers like to talk, and they're especially fond of talking about themselves. But they're not typical nor are they all that representative—the two qualities that make for a good "key informant"; and their main function may be to keep you from talking to other, more informative and candid, individuals.

An equally dubious "first contact" may be offered by the "public character." Every culture and community has the local "public character" (Jacobs 1961) who may be mentally ill or merely eccentric. They're not well-integrated into the culture. They're close enough to know what's going on, but they're not ensconced or even accepted well enough by insiders to make anything "real" actually happen. They're observers within their own cultures; like you, they're "outsiders within." This is what makes them seem like such wonderful informants. But they're not wonderful informants because they're simply not representative. The insiders, the core of the culture, generally have exiled these folks to the periphery. While they may offer valuable insight to you, you should neither rely too heavily (and certainly not unquestioningly) upon their accounts, nor should you become too closely tied to them in the eyes of the culture's "mainstream" members.

As soon as possible, seek out those who don't gravitate to you immediately. You need to develop relations of increasing intimacy with insiders who are representative (i.e., they are fluent and active in the promulgation/reproduction of the culture), but at the same time *atypical* (i.e., they are unusually analytical, reflective, capable of engaging in a higher order of thought and analysis concerning the culture they occupy). In short, the best informant is a cultural insider who enjoys uncommon access to the culture's privileged "areas" and information *and* is analytically conscious and aware of *having* a culture.

The good informant is very similar to the good ethnographer: Both have the ability to jump back and forth between what's going on (the concrete) and why it's going on (the more abstract and structural patterns of culture of which the activity is an "instantiation," or manifestation). Together, the good informant and the good ethnographer can create a good ethnographic account.

**SUBJECTS, RESPONDENTS, AND INFORMANTS**    The people you encounter in the culture you're studying go by several different names within the ethnographic tradition. Every label carries with it all sorts of intellectual rationales, political views, and pragmatic orientations. The term **subject** connotes a relatively superficial relationship, one in which the person providing data is temporarily engaged with the researcher and constitutes little more than a "case." This term is the norm in quantitative, survey-based research and in biomedical research where the researcher's detachment is expected, if not demanded and/or celebrated. A **respondent** is someone with whom the researcher has a slightly "deeper" and "more meaningful" relationship. Beyond providing data at a single point in time, the respondent might be a supplier of data for a whole day, or a couple of days. With this categorization we find more of an attachment between the researcher and the researched, but it's fleeting.

The term **informant** or "key informant" enjoys a long history in ethnographic studies. These are the people who supply you with the words and behaviors that comprise the bulk of the data you produce. For a given study, you need to develop relationships with a diverse range of informants. Selecting an informant can be a tricky enterprise, and if done poorly can lead to the demise of other relationships in the field and, ultimately, to your project's premature and very avoidable death. Informants do the job of informing you of what's happening in the field, what people are doing, what they're saying (or what they're *really* saying when they're talking). They also give you a sense of the culture's and setting's history. Over the course of your time in the field, your relations with informants will be somewhat intense. There will be lots of "give and take," though in the end (as we'll argue later), they're likely giving you more than you're giving them.

**WHEN THE KEY INFORMANT BECOMES A FRIEND**    Nancy Scheper-Hughes, in her study of "Ballybran," a dual-language "traditional" village in rural Ireland, uses the term "companion" when referring to the usually small number of culture members with whom you maintain a relationship that goes beyond that of researcher–informant. When William Foote Whyte set out to study "corner boys" and "college boys" in South Boston, early on he encountered "Doc," the unofficial but undeniable charismatic leader of the Corner Boys (a kind of street gang). Doc guided Whyte through Cornerville, introducing him to the people living there, paving his way into the private lives of families, the covert arenas of illicit activity, and even teaching Whyte how to comport himself—how to walk, talk, carry himself, interact with others, and generally just "fit in." During your time in the field, especially if you spend more than a few months doing your study, you will develop relationships akin to friendship. But it's an odd, singular kind of friendship. At heart, it's exploitative (as we noted in Chapter 4 and will discuss again in Chapter 24).

## Knowing When to Keep Quiet

Our final tip about your first days in the field is to keep quiet unless you have a strong reason to do a lot of talking; you are there to learn about a culture or organization, not to impart your wisdom to its members. Entering the field requires good sense in interacting with your new acquaintances, as the following cautionary tale illustrates. Many years ago, Roberta's graduate advisor arranged a fascinating research experience for her—a chance to observe social dynamics and clinical practice in a new community mental health center. At her first visit, she was shocked to see how the health professional (a white man) led the paraprofessionals (a dozen or so African American women) through the process of diagnosing an absent patient whose case had been briefly presented. The patient had been referred to the mental health center when neighbors called the police after he became enraged, threatened his ex-wife, and threw his mother's TV set out of the window.

The diagnostic procedure consisted of the paraprofessionals thumbing through a workbook based on the then-current *Diagnostic and Statistical Manual* and seemingly at random calling out the names of diagnostic categories that might apply to the patient. The mental health professional said "no" without any explanation for each guess he deemed to be incorrect (e.g., "bi-polar disorder"). No one said anything about the social, economic, and community context of poverty, layoffs, unemployment, racism, and lack of support for returning veterans which the patient had experienced, as could easily be deduced from the initial presentation of the "case." Roberta could not contain herself, waved her hand to be called on, stood up, and triumphantly made her point: "Of course this guy is enraged—he's got real reasons to be mad!" Everyone in the room just looked at her for a few seconds, said nothing, and then went right back to their diagnostic-label guessing game. After this incident, Roberta felt uncomfortable about going back to the site, and so a promising research opportunity for understanding professional hierarchies, labeling practices, and the social construction of mental illness was wasted. Conclusion: Keep your opinions to yourself, especially in public situations at the beginning of your fieldwork!

## CONCLUSION

In this wide-ranging chapter, we have offered an introduction to the art and science of ethnography as research that focuses on "solving the puzzle of culture." Being in the field is the *sine qua non* of ethnography. In its search for holistic, contextualized understanding and generalization from a single culture, it goes beyond the conventional deductive and inductive logics. Ethnography is one of the most powerful vehicles for understanding and explaining human culture.

## Key Terms

abductive logic versus deduction
    and induction *207*
ethnography as a third method *195*
fourfold consciousness: relating,
    reflecting, retaining, reducing *201*
gaps in the literature *198*
gatekeepers *211*
generalization *205*
genericizing; *205*

informants *213*
iterative and recursive *205*
literature review *198*
mapping biases *200*
observed and unobserved cases
    (in the context of generalizing
    and genericizing) *205*
public characters *211*
reflexivity *199*

respondents *212*
sameness and difference *205*
sample of one *195*
stranger-handlers *211*
subjects *212*
the field *196*
unsolved puzzles *198*
variation within a culture *204*

# 14

# Types of Ethnographic Data

## OVERVIEW

In this chapter, we discuss the different types of ethnographic data that you will end up collecting or creating in the field. From behaviors you observe to people's words to artifacts you collect or manufacture (as in photos or videos), anything in the field could end up becoming data in your ethnographic endeavor.

## REVIEW: DESIGNING RESEARCH, KNOWING THE DATA YOU NEED

To refresh our memory, let's review the sequence of research design "events," or principal components: developing a research question; from this question deriving one or more hypotheses you can test in the field; specifying the kind of **data** you need in order to test the hypotheses; elucidating a methodology for obtaining/producing these data; creating "instruments" for recording/producing said data (in reference to a plan for analyzing the data); collecting the data; and finally, analyzing and reporting on the results of your analysis. This all seems very straightforward and linear, as though you'll proceed in lockstep down the path of doing research. But in the real life of researchers, especially qualitative researchers and most especially ethnographers, research design and execution are anything *but* linear. It's a complicated, messy, perplexing, oftentimes byzantine, and always doubt-filled journey toward discovery. Although "research in action" never looks exactly the way it does in the textbooks (including this one), it's very important to keep these principal components in mind, as they will make your serpentine route a little more navigable and your project more feasible.

## TYPES OF DATA

Of course, relative mastery of all of these components is critical to your success as an ethnographer, but the most important domain is formed by the data you produce through your fieldwork. As you think about your project, you obviously need to be clear (at some point down the road) about your overarching research question, units of analysis, and above all, *the data that concern you most*. There are different types of data, and every type brings with it countless manifestations and instances. For now, let's divide the world of data into six categories: (1) behavior/action, (2) words, (3) nonbehavioral data such as the environment, objects, and elements of style, (4) events and rituals (which are special kinds of behaviors), (5) norms, values, and beliefs (which are complex composites of actions and words), and (6) people and their personas.

## Behavior/Action

What are people doing? How are they doing it? When are they doing it? Where? And when/where/how are they *not* doing it? These are critical questions that arise in the majority of ethnographic research projects. People engage in all sorts of behaviors, often without realizing it consciously. And they have many reasons for doing and/or not doing things. But we'll get to their reasons—and how they lie about their stated reasons—later.

Max Weber, widely considered to be one of the founders of sociology, conceived of the discipline as fundamentally concerned with "the interpretive understanding of social action in order thereby to arrive at a causal explanation of its course and consequences" (Weber 1968: 4). All sociology is interpretive, according to Weber, from whom many cultural sociologists and ethnographers take many of their cues. When studying a foreign or even somewhat familiar culture, the ethnographer works toward the development of *verstehen*, a concept originally worked up sociologically by Weber and Georg Simmel and later introduced to American sociology by Talcott Parsons in his 1937 landmark piece "The Structure of Social Action."

*Verstehen* refers to systematically developing an interpretive, processual understanding of a culture. As Weber wrote and as most sociological ethnographers still contend, the elemental unit of *verstehen*, and of interpretive sociology in general, is the individual and her actions, "the basic social unit" in Weber's terms. Noteworthy here is the emphasis on **action**, which Weber and his acolytes distinguish from behavior. This distinction guides the production of data in field work.

Social action is different from behavior, though both occur at the level of the individual person. Think of it this way: Action is behavior with an attitude. Behavior denotes simply the motor skill deployments stripped of any concern or regard for social context. Action, on the other hand, refers to human activity that exhibits (or seems to exhibit) an orientation to the behavior of other humans. In Weber's view, social action materializes when one's behavior is "meaningfully oriented" to others.

Despite ambiguities in this definition, we can say that ethnographers concern themselves with the "what, when, where, how, and why" of human activity. The important point here is that in the course of a given day we engage in thousands of movements, some of them intentional and deliberate, most of them not, for a good portion of our day is spent on "autopilot"; we're thinking and acting, but we're not necessarily acting *because* we're thinking . . . or vice versa. As an ethnographer, your job is to document the behaviors...the physical movements you observe among members of the culture you're studying but to do so within the analysis of action, of *meaningful* behavior. A good many of the activities you document (i.e., write down in your notes) will end up being virtually meaningless to the culture's insiders and probably to you too, but one of them could lead to an "a-ha!" moment.

If It's Obviously Insignificant, Then It's Obviously Very Important. Sometimes, you may document behaviors that in the future you discover to be devoid of significant meaning according

"Sapphire" Pam injects "Johnny Rocket" with heroin in "The Brickyard."

to interviews with the informants who engage in the behavior. But just because they find the behaviors meaningless from their indigenous perspective doesn't mean that they will be meaningless to you, as an outsider working within the emic–etic dialectic of observing, learning, accounting, and representing.

For example, in my studies of heroin addicts, I (Greg Scott) found myself repeatedly documenting how informants went about performing their drug injections. Invariably (100% of cases) the injection process would include several behaviors seemingly unrelated to the successful transfer of heroin from syringe to vein. Addicts would blow on the needle point, or utter a short catchphrase just before inserting the needle into the skin, or perform some other act that had nothing to do with the physical transfer of drug to body.

In several hundred cases, I videotaped addicts' injections. Much later in the research timeline, I sat down with the addicts and showed them the video recordings of their injections, and I asked them questions about every single movement, every aspect of the process, every facet of their behaviors. In response to questions about these more tangential, seemingly noninstrumental actions, they invariably said, "oh, that's nothing," "it doesn't mean anything," or "that's just something I always do." Now, had I let the sleeping dog lie, I might well have concluded that indeed these movements are simple, rote, noninstrumental, and largely irrelevant behaviors (not social actions) and are therefore unworthy of further analysis. Instead, I pushed them with "challenge questions" (Agar 1980), as in "Okay…I hear you…but if it doesn't mean anything at all, then why do you do it every time you inject?" I suspected that something was up, that they weren't "just doing it" for no reason at all. But I also didn't want to assume that they were acting rationally, deliberately. All I really knew is that each person engaged in a pattern of repetitive motion virtually identical across dozens of drug injection procedures in which they engaged.

Addicts' responses to my challenge questions were intriguing. "Well, I have always blown on the needle point right before I inject." "Always...even the very first time you shot up?" I asked. "Well, no," the response. "When did you start doing that?", a logical follow-up. "I guess I started doing it because I saw somebody else doing it." Me: "But why did you keep doing it?" Addict: "Well, because they said they did it because it brought them good luck...that it was a kind of ritual . . . then I did it, and I got really, really high. So I kept doing it. And now I just always do it for good luck . . . it sounds crazy, but I guess I think it gives me luck, too, like I'm gonna get a better high out of it, or at least not a bad high, or an overdose, or something like that." This brief snippet of my conversation with an addict typifies the responses I got from all of them. They are superstitious. They invent and quite mechanically, without much thought, perform ritualistic maneuvers that originate in superstition concerning the relationship between the drug and themselves.

Ultimately my investigation into superstitious behaviors led me into learning more about the "spiritual" (or cosmic) dimensions of heroin use. The vast majority of research, biographical, popular press, and literary accounts of heroin addiction describe and characterize the addict as disorganized, shiftless, alien to conventional values and beliefs, an immature hedonist impulsively rushing headlong into a vacation from reality, and more crucially, an escape from the bonds of civic society. By starting with questions about repetitive motions in the injection process, I ended up conducting research on the many ways that addicts view and treat heroin use as a way to accomplish and enhance, not eschew or flee, their beliefs, their connections with others. Their engagement in ritualistic, superstition-fueled behaviors indicates a concern for their mental and spiritual well-being and their social connectivity. What may appear to be meaningless, and what the actor may even say is meaningless, could turn out to be quite meaningful.

Superstition is normal, at least in the Durkheimian sense of "normalcy." It's exceptionally common in most societies. Nearly all of us have one or another kind of superstitious belief and an attendant ritualistic behavior that impedes or advances the consequences of that belief. Why would heroin addicts be any different? But the point here isn't about superstition. It's about behavior, and its relation to meaning in a broad context of doing fieldwork. People do things. You see and hear them do things. They may or may not be able to explain their reasons for doing these things. And if they can explain their reasons, they may or may not tell the truth. The reasons themselves, more to the point, may not be what's important to you. It's the pattern behind the reasons, the reason's implications or precursor beliefs.

Sociologists, especially those with quantitative leanings, tend to ignore "invariant" social phenomena, such as repetitive behaviors. We discussed this earlier. Many social scientists argue that without variation you have no real significance, and quantitative models' logic depends entirely on discovering that variation in one variable influences variation in another variable. But the ethnographer's bread and butter is sameness, or at least similarity. As Gerald Suttles points out, fieldworkers would be well-served by problematizing the **normative uniformities** they observe and report on in their work. After all, when you're studying culture, the question, "How is it that nearly everyone does/says/believes the same thing?" is just as interesting as the question, "What are the reasons that people say/do/believe different things?"

**OBSERVING WHEN NOTHING IS HAPPENING**   One final note on observing and studying behavior in the field: When you feel like nothing's happening, pay closer attention. One of the more interesting features of social life is our capacity for accomplishing *non*interaction. As Howard Becker says, sociology is the study of people doing things, and not doing things, together. Many instances of intentional noninteraction occur in daily life. Think about the contexts in which you routinely endeavor to avoid interacting with others: in the elevator, in the doctor's office waiting room, on the public bus. While it may be no coincidence that all of these places are temporary stops *en route* to a destination, the point is that we have developed all sorts of tools for curbing our own participation in interaction in these spaces, and for reducing the likelihood of others' attempts to initiate interaction. When you're in the middle of a situation and find yourself wondering "When's the action going to start?" or "When is something going to happen?", you should challenge yourself to figure out how the people in the scene managed to achieve their noninteraction with each other.

An example from a student research project on needle exchange for heroin injectors might help illustrate the point. Stereotypes of "the junky" abound. In popular imagination the junky is lazy, devious, criminal, amoral or immoral, rebellious, and so on. A few years ago a group of students in my (Scott's) ethnographic methods class decided to conduct a comparative ethnography of three different sterile syringe exchange program (SEP) sites. The SEP operates at street level, doing outreach from a modified delivery step-van, and provides injection drug users with sterile needles in exchange for used, potentially injected needles. As an aside, SEPs are the only proven intervention with respect to reducing the incidence and prevalence of HIV among drug injectors.

In the half hour leading up to the start time at each of the three sites, the students observed "nothing going on, participants just waiting in line." Their field notes would contain virtually nothing in relation to that half hour prior to the outreach van's arrival. Beyond a simple count of participants ("12 participants here") and a brief mention of their behavior ("standing in line"), the notes for this episode ("waiting for the van") said nothing. So I challenged the students to observe more carefully, to think a bit harder, and to document more thoroughly what was *really* going on. At first they were perplexed. But soon it became clear to them that a whole lot was actually going on, and that they had been ignoring some very important things.

Chicago Recovery Alliance syringe exchange van and program participants.

At this point I should inform you that during the study period the SEP hosted a research study concerning hepatitis B, a preventable viral infection of the liver that is very common among drug injectors. The study involved interviews, blood testing, and vaccinating the injectors. More important, every time a study subject showed up and successfully completed the tasks associated with a given appointment, the subject received a $15 cash stipend. Nearly all of the study's subjects were precariously housed or homeless, unemployed (or, rather, not working a legitimate job), and the going rate for a bag of heroin is $10. It should come as no surprise that during the study period the SEP interacted with more participants than usual. Participants who made it into the study would begin showing up at the SEP site 30–60 minutes before program activity commenced. But they weren't "doing nothing" or "just waiting." So what were they doing?

Once the student ethnographers (led by Erin Curtin, who now holds her PhD in Public Health) began to describe the waiting, they realized that many noteworthy things were going on. Soon their closer observations led them to conclude in more general terms that things indeed were going on: first, the "junkies" were showing up early. Second, they often were showing up with a friend whom they had brought in hopes of that friend getting into the study. Third, they were forming an orderly, quiet line, and they sustained the integrity of the order throughout the waiting period. Fourth, they were talking to each other (quietly) as they stood in line. Fifth, someone always took charge of getting the line established and keeping it orderly. Sixth, they were sanctioning one another for their "waiting behavior," rewarding those who complied with the *ad hoc* rules established by the self-appointed line leader and punishing those who became "unruly." Seventh, on occasion a small number of the subjects seemed to be "demonstrating" something to each other while they waited in line (as evidenced by one-on-one conversations, typically between pairs who arrived together, using verbal and nonverbal gestures).

What do these things mean? If nothing else, these observations demonstrate that a capacity for orderliness and organization exists among the observed addicts in the study (who, by the way, were representative in their demographics and drug use histories of Chicago heroin injectors generally). Also, when living in four- to six-hour increments (the time between heroin "doses") and continually trying to stave off ugly physical withdrawal symptoms, these addicts were quite enterprising. They nearly always brought a fellow junky with them, hoping to get that person into the study as well. Why? Out of beneficence? Occasionally. But there emerged a pattern: They tended to bring with them the running buddies who owed them money, or drugs. When the buddy was screened into the study, interviewed, and then compensated, the subject was there, waiting for payback. A high percentage of study subjects exacted a "steering fee" for turning their friends onto the paid study. Some even convinced their buddies that but for their putting in a good word for the "newbie," the friend would not have gotten into the study at all.

Their orderliness reflected their knowledge of "the game," of the staff's predilection for program rules. Being in a perpetual "underdog" position means that to survive, the junky must be a very good student of the "host society" and of the programs on which he depends for daily survival. These junkies, upon further observation and interviewing, clearly articulated their knowledge of how to play the program game; and being orderly is an important strategy for succeeding at the game. Finally, what do we make of the apparent "demonstrations"? What were they doing? Well, a good many of the study's subjects reached out to fellow drug users who were *not* drug injectors; they were crack smokers, heroin sniffers, or alcoholics. But the study focused exclusively on drug injectors. So the more enterprising addicts, while standing in line with the noninjecting friends they brought with them, were teaching their friends how to "come off" as injectors and thereby "get over" on the study staff, whose job it was to screen out the noninjectors.

The demonstrations included lessons on how to inject, how to answer the screening questions convincingly, how to pretend to be experiencing the effects of injected heroin, and so on.

Behavior and action together comprise the ethnographer's bread and butter. Words are important, yes. What people say about their world, about what they do, about what they believe are all important to the study of culture. But arguably the most important cultural dimension is that of enactment. It's critical to assess how people enact and embody their culture, and to examine how their words belie or square up with their behaviors.

## Words

When doing ethnographic research, you will find yourself awash in words. In fact, one of traditional ethnography's traits is its qualitative nature—the data you produce and the results you present will depend more heavily on words than on numbers. This is not to say that numbers are irrelevant, however. Every ethnographic study depends upon some degree of quantification and involves the recording of numeric data and the use of numbers in the crafting of cultural representation. But unless you're engaged in "quantitative ethnography," you'll be much more concerned with words than you will be with numbers. And if you come to specialize in "linguistic ethnography" (see Agar 1995, for example), you'll become obsessed with words!

Just about any sociologist would agree with the assertion that speaking is an act. In fact, the term "speech act" has become a fixture in sociological parlance. As you do your fieldwork, keep this simple notion in mind: Talk is a form of action. Talk is also one of the central means by which we "act" (i.e., take action and also "present" ourselves strategically to others). You'll want to make all sorts of differentiation in the "kind" of talk in which people, including yourself, engage.

To make a simplistic distinction for the purpose of discussion, your work with words falls into three broad categories: the words of individual insiders, the discourse of the collective (culture) you're studying, and the words you use to collect and analyze the data and to convey your findings (i.e., develop your representation of the culture you've studied).

At the individual cultural insider level, fieldwork entails countless (no pun intended) informal and formal conversations. You'll be talking casually with people, listening to them talk with each other, conducting structured and semi-structured interviews of them, reading material they've written and/or material they read, and so forth. *It's critical that you record informants' words as they occur in context (i.e., verbatim).* Reproduced words serve as your primary data source when doing ethnography. When talking with and/or interviewing people, you need to record the words they use, as they use them, and also do your best to note the ways in which they say the words—the rhythm and inflection they use. At some point, the people in your study will appear in the representations you write, and you want to maximize your fidelity to the content and style of their "speech."

At the collective level, one of the first things you'll set out to do is learn the vernacular, or argot, of the group/community you're studying. Every group—particularly if it's commonly known as a "subculture" (e.g., drag queens)—develops its own specialized terms for the people, phenomena, events, relationships, and objects that give definition/distinction to the group and/or that occupy the greatest amount of the group members' individual and collective attention, time, and energy. The term that ethnographers use for this specialized system of language is "argot," whose lay translation is **slang**.

**Insider Talk**    Slang represents an opportunity to learn about a group's behavior. Specialized terms, each in their own right, offer insight into how group members communicate with each other and how they orient themselves to meaningful action. Again, words and action are inextricably linked, even when the words and the actions are diametrically opposed. When doing fieldwork we strongly recommend that you keep track of slang terms, which may be invented and singular to the group or borrowed/appropriated from the dominant culture and applied in particularistic ways. Throughout your fieldwork, you'll want to build and continually update a "glossary of terms," each item with its definitions enumerated and notes on variations of its use. You'll also want to assess the extent to which each term is shared within the culture, because very few slang terms achieve complete consensus and total circulation.

For example, among prostitutes in Chicago there is wide variation in the term used to describe the exchange of sexual contact for money or drugs. Among activists and academics, the "politically correct" term for someone who sells sex is "sex worker." This term has a long and complicated politico-linguistic history, which we don't have the time to explore here. So let's focus on the street level. Studies of prostitution in Chicago reveal a wide range of terms, including hooker, escort, or working girl. But hardly any of the women who exchange sex for money/drugs at street level refer to themselves as sex workers. In fact, they are much more likely to use one of the terms that prostitution activists find most loathsome: hooker. Why is this the case?

On the streets the term "hooker" also has a long, complicated politico-linguistic history. And it has enjoyed a far longer and wider usage than just about any other term, especially "sex worker." By no means, however, is "hooker" a consensus term. Many women who engage in this form of revenue-generation actually abstain from the use of any single label. Their reasons for abstention are many, not the least important of which being that they believe themselves to be far more than what they happen to do for money. Nevertheless, "hooker" enjoys the most widespread adoption. At first glance, one might say that this is a result of "internalized oppression" or "poor self-esteem" or some such socio-psychopathology. Or, if one takes these women at their word (so to speak) and therefore takes seriously their rationale for use of the term, a different understanding emerges.

"Hooking" is a hustle. It's a way of making money. More specifically, it's a way of getting a guy (usually) to give up his money for something that he'd rather not pay for, or if he does enjoy the act of paying for it, then hooking entails getting him to give up *more* money than he'd like to spend. The act of hooking is complex, and it necessitates creativity, artifice, courage, cunning, and many other character traits that our culture generally deems venerable. In short, according to the women who have assumed this title, hooking is an act of agency. The term's etymology alone gives us a bit of insight into the agency involved in the act. Although there's no certainty over how the term came to be applied to prostitutes (or "ladies of negotiable affections"), etymologists concerned with the term generally agree that one of its earliest connotations related to the act of "catching hold of, and drawing in," an intended or desired object. Hookers work creatively and diligently to "get their hooks" into a "john," or client, and then employ their faculties of persuasion to reel him into the agreement to give up money he'd rather keep for himself in exchange for some kind of sexual contact. Across the term's history it also has maintained a connotative connection with fishing—the hooker being the one who uses her appearance and gestures and words as "bait" to catch the unsuspecting, relatively "dumb" fish.

On a related note, the term "john," which refers to the client of a hooker, tells us something as well about the hooking act. Since the 1800s, the name "John Doe" has held a place in the realm of jurisprudence; in legal matters it refers to "any man of unknown name." And in the early 1900s, the term "john" took hold on the streets of east coast cities as a way for men to identify themselves anonymously to prostitutes, as it was against a man's interests to allow a

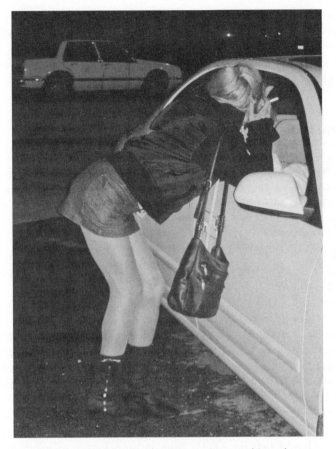

"Christine," a heroin addict for the past 25 years (since the age of 15), embraces the term "hooker" to capture the work she does on Chicago's west side.

prostitute to know his real name. The now-antiquated British slang term for penis, which developed concurrently with "John Doe," is "John Thomas." Pulling these etymological strands together, the modern-day use of "john" makes sense in light of the inspired use of the term "hooking." A john is just another man to get over on, to fleece, to exploit for money. Given all this, it makes sense that many prostitutes adopt the label "hooker" for it represents an act of agency over a man who represents little more than an anonymous, unsuspecting penis capable of being swindled (or at least enticed or seduced) into providing compensation. "Sex work," in the view of many women, denotes formality and hierarchy, and the disempowerment that characterizes so many American workplaces.

The lesson here is that language matters. And you need to keep track of it. As an aside (but one we explore in depth later), you also need to become fluent in the use of the vernacular. But we must caution you against using local slang the same way and to the same extent that insiders use it. It's of vital importance that you figure out the degree to which it is acceptable for outsiders such as yourself to use local slang so you don't sound stupid. As William Foote Whyte points out, no one really expects you to use slang, as they don't expect you to become "one of the gang." You are there to do a job. Judicious use of slang is advised. On the other hand, if everyone's using the term "hooker" and you persist in the use of "sex worker," and your usage tends to irritate many of the people from whom you're attempting to extract data, then selective use of the slang term is advised. In short, just as important as becoming fluent in the argot is becoming fluent in *the terms and conditions of its usage.*

## Nonbehavioral Data

People's actions and words will comprise the bulk of the data you produce in your ethnographic research. But every highly regarded ethnography also involves the collection and analysis of other data. In fact, much of what you experience in the field will be "beyond" words and actions. All manner of important sensory information will surround, if not bombard, you during any given fieldwork outing.

**ENVIRONMENT**    Culture emanates from humans' interconnected attempts to adapt to circumstances and conditions largely beyond their control. The natural and built environments that envelop people constitute an important dimension of human culture, and cultures differ in their capacity to control their natural and built settings. Some do it with wisdom and foresight (as in the reforestation practiced in Tokugawa Japan), while others insist on behaviors that precipitate the collapse of their way of life (as in the livestock raising practiced by Vikings in Greenland) (Diamond 2005). Hence, your fieldwork should include the documentation and analysis of the landscape(s) in which the culture operates, and how variations in the landscape correspond to variations in the cultural dynamics you're investigating. "Ethnographic mapping" has taken on terrific salience in the past 20 years of "domestic ethnography." Mapping the landscape has been staple activity of ethnographers since the inception of this research design/logic, but the integration of the mapping process and map contents into data analysis has represented a major hurdle in various fields, from anthropology to sociology to public health to commercial market research on consumer behavior.

Dead or alive, humans occupy territory, space, geography. Ignoring the geography of human behavior is deeply problematic, though discerning how the landscape shapes and is shaped by human behavior is a difficult thing to do. As an ethnographer, you'll want to map the natural landscape to the best of your ability. You also should create and update maps of the human-made environment. Without a doubt you should record how people modify their natural and fabricated environments during the course of your field study. Such behavior may well shed light on cultural phenomena of interest to you (values, norms, etc.).

Because ethnography not only requires you to attain fluency of daily life operation (as gauged in relation to how insiders operate) but also extends beyond this to include the distinct perspective that you, as a social scientist, bring to the situation, making your own maps is a necessary though not entirely sufficient attempt at mapping. Increasingly, ethnographers are making use of mapping data generated by their informants. At some point in the course of doing fieldwork, the ethnographer asks key informants (representing a diverse array of "positions" within the culture) to prepare their own maps of the natural and/or built environment (or both). Informant map-making offers insight into the landscape as the informant sees it, and in the aggregate allows you to begin to understand variation among informants as to what's important in the landscape, how different features of the landscape serve different purposes, and even what constitutes the landscape. The varying content of the maps can be analytically interesting, as can variations in the maps' aesthetics.

For example, Singer et al. conducted an ethnographic study of injection drug users (IDUs) that relied heavily upon mapping of social networks and landscapes, and how variation in landscape related to variations in social network size, composition, functioning, and so forth. In an offshoot of that study, Chicago researchers asked informants to create maps of their daily lives; that is, they mapped out the geographic "orbit" they occupy and traverse on a daily basis. They were asked to indicate the most important features of those orbits.

The two maps shown here were made by a heroin-addicted married couple—"Pony Tail" Steve and "Sapphire" Pam—who created their maps independent of one another, without communicating anything to each other about their respective map-making activities. Analyzing the content of these maps would be interesting, as would evaluating differences in the content and aesthetics related to gender, drug of choice, residential status (homeless vs. housed), and income level/type. "Indigenous maps" furnish a glance at how informants see the world spatially, which can be a very important dimension to your study. It's especially exhilarating when the informants' maps contradict the geosocial map you, as the ethnographer,

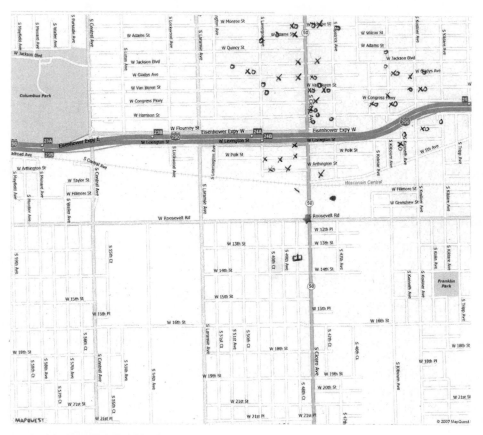

Pony Tail Steve's Map of "The Brickyard."

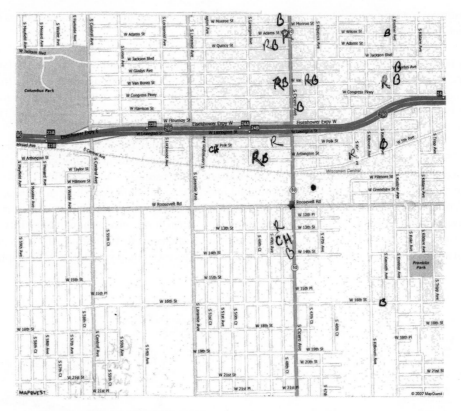

Sapphire Pam's Map of "The Brickyard."

had previously constructed and to which you previously adhered when thinking about the culture you're studying.

## Objects and Styles

Clothing, hair styles, cosmetics, automobiles, and the like are all fodder for the research and data analysis mill. In Chapter 11, we discussed Dick Hebdige's studies of style, so we won't go into detail again here. We'll simply remind you that you cannot study culture without studying style. But here we would do well to heed Weber's directive: We're not interested in individuals per se (or, rather, exclusively as individuals) but instead as "carriers of culture," for every one of us embodies, expresses, and resists dominant cultural precepts in everything we do, every day. But elements of style can be scrutinized. These and other physical objects, including all the things that make up the built environment, preserve and express the culture's internal order (hairstyles, for example), which may well be in flux (e.g., graffiti sprayed over a highbrow arts reception at a newly renovated building in a gentrifying neighborhood). The local culture's internal consistencies and contradictions often manifest in the physical objects circulating or residing within that culture. Teasing out the operating assumptions of a culture through examination of objects and artifacts can be an incredibly illuminating ethnographic activity. Every culture has an "unconscious life," and the keys to this unconscious can be found in the culture's physical objects and in the insider's stylistic practices and representational habits.

## Events and Rituals

Now we will look at types of data that are composites of actions, words, and nonbehavioral physical objects, and among the leading examples are events and rituals. Most cultures around the world, with varying frequency, sanction formal and/or informal events and rituals, whether *ad hoc* or planned well in advance. The line demarcating events and rituals is often blurred, as in the case of "coming of age" events where people gather to celebrate, to memorialize, and to affirm through ritual their belief in and commitment to the transition from the state of childhood to that of adulthood. Within this event one observes a good many socially and culturally approved rituals, or stylized though standardized behaviors infused with deeper meaning concerning the individual and her place in the world (and/or cosmos).

One of the most famous event/rituals in anthropological literature is Clifford Geertz's "Deep Play: Notes on the Balinese Cockfight" (1973c). Geertz studied the Balinese carefully, and he advocated for "thick description," the highly detailed accounting of persons, places, things, and events. But as with most ethnographers, there's more to the task than merely describing in detail a culture and its dynamics. Rather, one must describe repeatedly what one observes, and then one must step back from it and look for patterns. Geertz (and most ethnographers, especially in the anthropological tradition) sift through the detailed descriptions in an effort to identify the culture's "core ethos," its central defining trait vis-à-vis communal life. Only 10 days after arriving in the Balinese village he had set out to study, Geertz and his wife found themselves absorbed into a crowd of people (a "superorganism") encircling a seemingly raucous affair: an illegal cockfight.

Balinese society is highly stratified, and the elites of the republic, like the Dutch imperialist government before it, proscribed cockfighting out of paternalistic concern for the poor, the rural bumpkin, the primitive villager who needs to be protected against his own retrogressive leanings. The article Geertz produced, his representation of the cockfight he observed, offers a fascinating multilevel account of the special occasion. In the piece, Geertz describes his own position in relation to the fight and to Balinese society generally, and he also describes the fight as well as what the fight "means" to the Balinese (which, by the way, is his commentary on the fight as a commentary). Like so many ethnographers, Geertz finds an ineluctable dialectic of mutuality wedding the fight as an ordinary daily event to the wider structures governing Balinese society. In essence, the fight emblematizes, or tells the story of, the wider society's way of operating. Indeed, according to Geertz, the "special occasion" in any society tells the story of that society—the intended "audience" is society itself. To put it simply, the rules of the event articulate the rules of the event's host society: "As much of America surfaces in a ball park, on a golf links, at a race track, or around a poker table, much of Bali surfaces in a cock ring. For it is only apparently cocks that are fighting there. Actually, it is men" (p. 2).

The cockfight, like any special occasion in Bali or any other society, is an important event for its unfolding through ritualized "deep play," which in this case elaborates the "status rivalry" that accompanies and emanates from a highly stratified society. In the article, Geertz eschews the then-popular "structural functionalist" tradition of sociology, which would view the cock-fight as a mechanism by which Balinese participants and observers experience a reinforcement of differential status. Rather, he calls the cockfight an "interpretive" event full of ritualistic behaviors that add up to a "story" that participants tell themselves *about* themselves. It's an opportunity, of sorts, to put into ritualistic expression the complex structural machinations that assort people into value-categories. In Geertz's view, the cockfight is an auto-teaching-learning experience:

> What he learns there is what his culture's ethos and his private sensibility (or, anyway, certain aspects of them) look like when spelled out externally in a collective text; that the two are near enough alike to be articulated in the symbolics of a single such text; and—the disquieting part—that the text in which this revelation is accomplished consists of a chicken hacking another mindlessly to bits. (p. 10)

Events and rituals are microenterprises that express, illustrate, articulate, and otherwise embody (and occasionally challenge and/or alter) macro-level forces that give structure to people's lives. In this respect, then, culture may be seen as a structural feature of society, much the same in form as the economy, the polity, law, and so on. From the ethnographic view, events and rituals present an invaluable opportunity to observe social actors "playing out" society's most salient "rules," the terms by which insiders expect themselves and each other to live. And, if examined closely enough, rituals and events offer a window onto the impalpable elements of "culture as structure," including norms, values, and beliefs.

## The Intangibles: Norms, Values, Standards, and Beliefs

**Norms** are the informal rules that guide people's behavior and so tend to be fairly specific (e.g., assuming a deferential posture when dealing with authority figures). **Values** are more general, expressing the "things" that a collective identifies as "good" (e.g., "honesty"). **Beliefs** are those ideas or propositions that a group of people generally accept as "truth" (e.g., the earth is round, or at least not flat). Standards are generally clearer, as they consist of often explicit criteria that people use to assess other people within and outside of the group, and standards apply usually to very specific situations and activities (e.g., criteria for making the dean's list). In addition, people apply standards less formally but no less consequentially to evaluate the extent of a group member's commitment to the group (e.g., just how much of a "punk" are you?).

Gathering data on norms, values, beliefs, and standards can be challenging, to say the least. For the most part, these intangible but essential features of society go unspoken and unwritten, although we do attempt to codify some of them in our laws, administrative regulations, codes of conduct, and so forth. But nowhere does any culture reduce to writing all of their norms, values, and beliefs. Nor do people talk about them explicitly. For example, can you describe exactly how you learned the proper way to stand and behave while riding an elevator? Can you remember exactly how you learned the meaning of honesty and why it's "the best policy?" How about the circumstances under which you *should* deviate from the honesty policy…how did you learn to assess situations and determine whether telling a lie would actually be the "best" (most moral) route? These are complicated matters about which we rarely speak. But if you don't understand a culture's norms, values, and commonly (widely) held beliefs, then you don't understand the culture.

If people generally don't discuss these things, much less delineate them clearly and even formally, then how can you discern them, produce data on them, write definitively about them? Well, there's no easy answer. But we can provide some tips.

It's generally wise to start with standards that apply to group membership. Although social scientists tend to treat cultures and groups as "things" (i.e., we reify them) for the purposes of analysis and representation, they're usually quite nebulous and open-ended in reality. For example, in the popular imagination street gangs are tight-knit criminal operations exhibiting a high degree of organization and carried forward by unfaltering intramember loyalty. But in reality, as I demonstrate in "Sucker's Outfit," the gang is very porous and internally conflicted, and loyalty is more often a prop that more powerful criminals use to exploit younger, less powerful yet very eager, criminals-in-the-making. In Ragin's (2000) terms, most of the cultural/social/professional/ groups to which we belong are "fuzzy sets," and our involvement in them varies both qualitatively (what we do) and also quantitatively (the intensity of our membership).

This said, however, the people who occupy, inhabit, embody, and perpetuate the culture you're studying have specific ideas about who does and does not enjoy "membership" in that culture. Even though the boundaries may be somewhat arbitrary and subject to movement and/or alteration and/or redefinition, everyone affiliated with the culture most likely can describe to you the standards by which the insiders assess the potential of newcomers to become regulars. Most ethnographic studies clearly involved collection and analysis of data on membership standards.

In addition to membership standards, insiders constantly assess (often critically) each other's behavior, style, attitude, perceived motivation, speech, and so on. The culture's *core ethos* (i.e., the "guiding spirit") comes into play here. Once you have figured out the principle elements of a culture's functioning, you can begin to identify the key events and situations in which that ethos assumes greater significance. At this point, you need to observe closely how the insiders involved in the situation appraise each other's participation, and what the consequences are when someone either exhibits a high degree of consistency with the core ethos or deviates radically from the ethos.

Finally, in many cultures you'll find written standards concerning individual, group, and/or organizational activity. Even among the homeless, many ethnographers have found written rules pertaining to the appropriation of personal belongings, the use of shared space, and other features of life on the streets. Whatever the culture, seek out published and unpublished standards concerning membership and "situational ethics" (how to act in specific, defining moments) and continually engage in comparative assessment of these written rules against what you observe in action.

As for norms, values, and beliefs, the tips are meager. The first point is that you should not opt to neglect them simply because they're so difficult to assess, particularly when relying solely on observation. Interviewing people about their values and beliefs can be fruitful, but keep in mind the nearly universal gap between what people say they believe and what they actually believe (or the beliefs that their behavior betrays). In your field notes you should maintain a separate section where you can reflect on the "intangibles" in relation to the detailed observations you have made. Also, you should keep and continually update a corpus of codified standards, norms, values, and beliefs. After all, it's not likely that anyone in the culture you're studying will have these handy for you to review. So take it upon yourself. You won't be sorry.

## People and Personas

People constitute the heart of your ethnography. They should be the center of your research and the mainstay of your representations (papers, articles, presentations, etc.). Obviously humans are complicated creatures, and in your fieldwork you need to get to know them as people the best you can. But the reality is that for the most part they will be "objects of observation" in your study. It seems prudent to pause for a reminder that when doing ethnography, your job is to explain whatever culture you have chosen to study. Individual persons obviously contribute to the formation, propagation, and modification of that culture, but in the end, each person is a datum and a provider/facilitator/keeper of data. They are not your friends, though they may be your "friends" (note the quotation marks). Every person is a "representation," meaning that the person you see and come to know in the field (let alone write about) is only part of the individual as a complete human being. A sophisticated informant in one of my studies once wrote in a letter to me from his prison cell, "I am not what you see, nor am I more or less than what you see." What was he talking about?

Everyone has multiple "personas." The word "persona" is derived from the Latin term for "mask." Who we are depends upon where we are, whom we're with, what's going on, and a host of other contextual/social and psychological (as well as emotional) variables. At any given moment, one is **representing one's self**, selectively telegraphing aspects of the self to others. It's a dynamic and complex process. It's impossible to be completely oneself at any given point in time. Fragmentary representations are the best that we can do. Informants in the field represent certain aspects of themselves to others, including you. How much of their selves you see may change over time. The most you can hope for is that over time the self they represent to you will appear to be very similar to the self they represent to their peers, their fellow insiders. This process of "public identity convergence" is something you should document and track over time. In common parlance, it's a matter of "getting to know" your informants. But unlike everyday life, the process of getting to know field informants needs to be analyzed in relation to the data you produce on the basis of your interactions with them.

At a minimum, you should create and maintain a log or inventory of "persons" in the field. You may even want to make a file on them, each one containing an index card (paper or electronic) with the person's name (or pseudonym) and certain information you'll need to access quickly (age, ethnicity, relation to others in the field, characteristics of your relationship with the person, special notations on their verbal and/or nonverbal behavior and appearance, etc.). The cards themselves will be useful to you throughout the process of doing fieldwork and in your analyses of data. You'll be able to sort the cards into piles, for instance, and begin to understand patterns behind social networks—who knows and/or hangs out with whom, what they have in common, similarities and differences in social action across persons and networks, and so forth. You also can use qualitative data analysis software programs to capture, store, and manipulate this kind of information, as we discuss in Chapter 22.

The point here is that in many respects the person is an object of study—an individual is a data point. But she is also a producer of data (or co-producer, rather, as data come from your interactions with her and from your observations of her interactions with others). She is a product of her culture, in part, while also being a producer of that culture. She is valuable to you for many reasons, not the least of which being her capacity to serve your project's interests. This may seem brash and/or callous and/or reductionistic, but in many respects it's true. And it's one of the many areas of ethnography that few people discuss openly.

In our personal lives, we reduce our significant others, our acquaintances, or colleagues, and unknown others to relatively simplistic proxies of their selves. The people we know are much more complicated and multifaceted in the context of their own lives than they are in the context of ours. It's important to acknowledge this explicitly, if only privately, when doing fieldwork. In the end, your paper will reduce complex human beings to extremely simplistic representations. Reductionism is a necessity, an exigency really, of ethnographic research. If nothing else, the time and space demands of your final product (and the arbiter of your final product's quality, for example, a professor or journal editors) require you to engage in this reductionism. The only question, then, is, "How distorted will your representation be?"

Keeping accurate and detailed records on the persons you encounter in your fieldwork will improve the quality of your data, enhance your capacity for relating to informants, and in the end give you the best chance of representing your informants accurately and respectfully. It may seem paradoxical or counterintuitive, but objectifying your informants throughout the fieldwork period is the best way to represent them fairly, and as accurately and completely as possible, when it comes time to report your results.

## CONCLUSION

In this chapter, we have reviewed the major types, or categories, of data you can make in the context of ethnographic research. It's not an exhaustive list, just a start on the ones you can include as you design your own field project. The next chapter focuses on field notes, the central mechanism by which one "disciplines" field observations into analyzable data.

## Key Terms

action and behavior *216*
beliefs *228*
data *215*
events and rituals *227*
insider talk *221*

norms *228*
normative uniformities *218*
persona and the representation
  of self *229*
slang *221*

values *228*
words *221*

# **15**

# Writing Ethnographic Field Notes (with Gerald R. Suttles)

## OVERVIEW

The largest single block of work in an ethnographic field study entails keeping field notes. What are field notes? They are your notes on what happens in the field. This seems simple enough. But as is so often the case, the apparent simplicity is deceptive. Writing good (i.e., useful) field notes is much harder than one might think. In this chapter, we discuss the significance and use of field notes, how to write good notes, how to think critically by way of writing field notes, and how to make sense of them along the way.

## THE SIGNIFICANCE OF FIELD NOTES

Field notes constitute the basic evidence upon which field studies depend. Without high quality and detailed field notes, such studies would be indefensible. Field notes have two major goals: *disciplining data gathering* and *making public the basis of your interpretation*. Ideally, field notes should be written and organized such that an independent reader could take them, analyze them, and then arrive at the same interpretations, inferences, explanations, and conclusions as you did. While very few ethnographers ever achieve this ideal, it's a standard worth striving to meet. The ability to keep field notes is a "make or break" quality: If you can't keep adequate field notes, then you should reconsider doing fieldwork.

## THE BASICS OF FIELD NOTES

In this section, we offer guidance on how to develop field notes, which ultimately will constitute your study's central source of data. There are many ways to keep field notes—as many approaches as there are ethnographers, in fact. Also, there really is no "right" or

A pile of Greg's field notebooks from the Brickyard ethnography.

"wrong" way to write field notes. In fact, some highly regarded ethnographers advocate for a minimalist approach, whereby the ethnographer actually writes very few notes but rather emphasizes the participation side of participant observation—only after exiting the field, they argue, should the ethnographer begin "writing things up."

We subscribe to a different orientation. Our position is that field notes are essential to the success of the ethnographic study and therefore must be maintained rigorously, carefully, and continuously throughout the study period and even beyond the period of immersion. In our view, field notes aren't just a static collection of words on a page; rather, they represent the main venue in which the ethnographer produces and analyzes data. "Field notes" is a term that connotes active deliberation—they reflect, advance, and capture the ongoing dialogue of ideas and evidence, the interplay of which ultimately yields the ethnographic representation.

Writing good field notes is equal parts art and technical skill. Here are some tips for writing them well.

## Handling Time

This section addresses the way time is organized in field notes and has two elements—chronological order and the notion of episodes.

**CHRONOLOGICAL ORDER** Field notes should reflect the time-order in which your observations and inquiries occur. Thus, field notes should be dated, and they should unfold in a well-documented temporal progression. Changes in locale, the entry of new persons to the scene, intervening events, and other substantial changes to the scene should be identified by their nature and by the approximate time frame in which they occurred. Ordering your notes chronologically serves many purposes.

1. It assists in your recall of events, explanations, observations, and so forth. While you may not recall your observations in the precise order in which they occurred, you should attempt to do so, as this will aid in reconstructing the fieldwork experiences accurately.
2. It forces you to be as exhaustive as possible in recording what you observe and inquire about. By trying to account for what happened in each hour of the day, you will be forced to recall all or most of the day's events rather than those few which are most recent or compelling or congenial to your memory, your personality, your presuppositions and preconceptions, and/or your working theories.
3. It forces you to obtain a more representative sampling of events, observations, and responses than would result from a selective recording of just those items of information which "come to mind." This is especially important at the outset of fieldwork, when you're trying to establish a holistic account, or view, and to keep yourself from attaching yourself to, and then becoming entranced by, one or another popular or personal interpretation.
4. It provides a common framework for organizing field notes so that one does not waste inordinate personal time deciding how to write up the day's events. Moreover, it does not produce several different orderings of events so that retrieval and problems of comparability become unwieldy.
5. It preserves the "natural causal texture" of behavior in everyday life. Notice that we are using the term "causal texture" rather than causation. There's a big difference. Causal texture refers to the "face validity" of any event's or interaction's progression. First, this happened. Then, Y happened. Finally, Z occurred. This establishes a flow. Later, when you do your analysis, you can begin to tease out factors of causation and consequence as they manifest in your review of multiple similar instances. This is very different from *assuming* while you're in the field that X caused Y and that Z was the result of this causal relationship.

**EPISODES**    Field notes should consist of episodes, each one having a clear beginning and a clear ending. The episode is an ordering device that the researcher imposes on the observations to turn a flow of "stuff" into manageable chunks. Sometimes it may represent an event with a "natural" start and end, but that is not always the case. An episode consists of a paragraph or a section in your field notes, and it captures a series of events or responses (verbatim, to the extent possible) that convey a discernible and coherent "chunk of reality" as you experienced it in the field. The episode, as written in your field notes, should be responsive to, or result from, a "trigger," some occurrence that set the episode in motion (e.g., a police officer arrives on the scene of a nonviolent protest). The end marker of an episode is the point at which another occurrence (speech act, behavioral act, significant time or venue change, etc.) changes the direction of, or even brings to a close, the episode.

When you're "transcribing" a conversation or informal interview, an episode may consist of a topic, specific or general, that consumes a significant portion of time (a few minutes or more) and that could be understood in its own right (e.g., "how I decided to leave medical school" in the context of a conversation about a midwife's career path). In behavioral terms, an episode may consist of a job or a task, or at the very least, a particular act or action on the part of an informant in the field (or on your part, as the field researcher). During observation of heroin addicts, for instance, one might conceive of "copping" (i.e., going to buy their heroin from a dealer) as a single act and then convey it in an episode. In deciding on what to identify as an episode, you must think ahead to your analyses of the data you're producing.

Because all data analyses revolve around manipulating small "chunks" of data (i.e., the "coded quotation"), you would be well-served by breaking down "copping" into its constituent parts, because every "episode" is divisible, depending on the level of generalization at which you're operating. In doing fieldwork, you need to concentrate on the minutiae of others' daily lives, and you will take the same approach when analyzing your data. Manipulating these small pieces or strands of data (i.e., "data analysis") will comprise the evidentiary base on which you make generalizations about events, relationships, norms, or values in the culture. Hence, the act of "copping" should be divided into its various components, such as getting the money together, talking with other addicts about the "spot" with the best dope, traveling to the dope spot, exchanging money for dope (the transaction itself), and heading to the place where the drug will be used. Each of these episodes has its own logic, its own time frame, its own set of activities, and its own attendant normative beliefs and values. And each of them "makes sense" in terms of a how a heroin addict actually sees or understands the copping process. It's much more than just "buying heroin."

How long should an episode be? This is a tricky question. The event you observe or dialogue you hear will be of a certain length; that's a given. However long it takes to unfold in "real life" is how long it is. But remember, the term "episode" as we're using it here refers *not* exclusively to the actual event (e.g., a bullfight) but rather to your reconstruction of the event in your field notes. This is a very important distinction. There's life and then there's your written account of life. While it's true that your written episodes derive from your observation of events, they are not the same as those events. So, if you were observing a bullfight, it might consume an hour. And while writing up the entire bullfight easily could consume 25 pages of single-spaced text, you need to be cognizant of your future analytic needs. All qualitative analysis, regardless of the data, revolves around small, discrete units of text. We discuss this at greater length in Chapter 22. For now, though, let us simply state that you want to compose your episodes in such a way that you can easily "retrieve" them later. More important, each episode should (a) constitute a coherent "piece" of action, a discrete sequence of a larger event you observed, and (b) stand on its own as an intelligible representation, meaning that even though it fits into a more expansive account, one should be able to comprehend it on its own if it were extracted from the account as a whole.

For instance, if you were to break down your 25-page bullfight account into its constituent elements, you might end up with 20 distinct episodes, each of them consuming one or two substantial paragraphs. Perhaps you gained access to the "backstage" of this event, where you observed the road-weary, inured, jaded bullfighter preparing for the "big show." The preparation might be an episode. Even getting dressed could constitute an episode. Most likely, however, "putting his boots on" would not comprise an episode. Why not? How do we make such fine distinctions? That's a good question. Beyond a certain point of specification, it's difficult to operationalize or define an episode. It's a situation where "I know it when I see it." That's obviously not very helpful.

For logistical and analytic reasons, as we've said, the episode should be relatively short (1–2 paragraphs, no more than one page), and it should be coherent enough to stand on its own. But these are formalistic qualities and have nothing to do with the content of the episode. Does content matter in determining where a given episode begins and where it ends? Yes, it does. Can we specify in advance the content of an episode, in the abstract? Unfortunately no. This doesn't mean, however, that we can't specify any parameters of a currently unknown episode's content. In situations like this, we turn to a problem-solving technique known as "the axiomatic solution": a rough set of criteria for deciding what an "episode" is. Like applying criteria we use for deciding to date someone, these criteria are not explicitly and minutely spelled out in advance, but you should be prepared to review them and to account for your choices in identifying episodes.

However, we can state a few of the criteria/conditions that your written episode must satisfy content-wise. Aside from being relatively brief, easily retrievable, and somewhat self-contained (all stylistic traits), an episode matters, substantively. The events or words conveyed in the episode should have some sort of salience, or relevance, in and of themselves, either in relation to your working theoretical/conceptual notions or to the informants' frame of reference, or to both.

In a word, the episode—as you have written it in your field note—is *meaningful* to you and to the people who animate it (the informants). Now, because you are a social scientist engaged in the task of studying the culture, the meaning you attach to the episode may differ somewhat from that of the participants. But your interpretation should not be fundamentally infeasible or irrelevant or ridiculous in the eyes of the participants. You may view the bullfighter's preparation as a series of rituals executed principally to convey to onlookers that the coming event is more than just a human fighting a bull but rather expresses some greater mythic logic of humans accepting challenges with potentially fatal consequences. Now that may not be what's going through the bullfighter's head as she or he prepares to fight the bull, but the interpretation shouldn't be unreasonable in his/her view. (At a later point in your analysis, you may want to challenge the participants' understandings, but descriptive field notes are not the best place to do it. Analytic memos (described in Chapter 17) offer a better technique for recording your questioning of insider perspectives.)

## Language and Terminology: The Key to Understanding Insider Views

Language is a key to all cultures, and as we discussed in Chapter 14, words are a major element of the data you want to record.

In Howard Becker's seminal study of medical student education and professionalization, he opted to concentrate on the language, the **vernacular** or argot that emerges among people undergoing the transformation from "regular person" to "physician." One of his most thought-provoking pieces from the project examines the term "crock." For weeks on end, he heard the medical students repeatedly using "crock" when talking about patients with no discernible physiological etiology to their ailments. In a word, they were suffering idiopathic ailments. In more common parlance, they were hypochondriacs at worst, overwrought patients experiencing psychosomatic illness at best. But the reason that medical students avoided interacting, much less treating, crocks wasn't their impatience with "irrational" or "unreasonable" patients. Rather, a central feature of "becoming a respected doctor" is the extent to which one learns how to perform "cures" for identifiable, life-threatening illnesses.

Moreover, a physician's standing in the professional medical community hinges in large measure on the degree to which that physician's exercise of medical care power could not only cure a very sick patient but also, if implemented ineptly, could kill that same patient. Becker's ethnography, homing in as it did on the terminology in which medical students were steeped, led him to understand a great deal about the professionalization of doctors—this, in turn, helped him to study and then explain how doctors quite predictably and understandably, if not almost implacably, assume a posture of "defensive arrogance" when dealing with patients. Becker et al.'s (1976) published account *Boys in White: Student Culture in Medical School* embodies the highest of technical standards within ethnography, in large measure due its reliance upon Becker's vigilance in keeping detailed field notes. Also evident in Becker's work is a commitment to ongoing analysis and to keeping the "feedback loop" wide open. Throughout the study period, Becker and his co-authors collected data, reflected upon it, and then adjusted the line of inquiry according to the newly gained insights.

This brings us to an important point: Throughout the fieldwork process, many changes will occur in how you collect data, your interests, your research questions and hypotheses, and so on. How you construct and write your field notes, as derivative in part from how you behave in the field and in part from how you think about the field, therefore also should be expected to change. As you become better acquainted with the "insider's views" on the scene and what happens in it, you will do a better (more accurate) job of conveying field events in your field notes, and the way you organize episodes will gradually conform more closely with how informants view the "episodes" in their daily lives. Throughout the fieldwork period, you should engage in continual analysis of your field notes, as though they are data in themselves.

This notion of examining your own field notes harkens back to our earlier discussion of treating your pre-field exercises in which you attempt to discern the features of your taken-for-granted "perceptual filters," the generally hidden parameters (biases, assumptions, stereotypes, personal interests, etc.) that structure the way you perceive, understand, explain, and take action in the world. It's a component of *reflexivity*, a concept we've presented, defined, and illustrated in multiple ways throughout this book. Continual analysis of *how* you take field notes, with specific focus on how you structure episodes, can furnish insight into how your views of the culture change. This is one way to document the progression of your abstract understanding of the culture you've set out to study. So pay close attention to how you structure episodes, how you conceptualize them, and how the structures of your episodes change, or don't change, over time.

## Concreteness

When you write up your early sets of field notes you will find yourself repeatedly using problematic language. You'll summarize events with words that place differential value and judgment on people's actions and words. For example, you may write something like, "She got angry at him because he forgot her birthday, and his indifference to her anger made her sad." Now, what you actually saw and heard may or may not have resulted from the emotional vagaries you think you have observed. Actually, though, you have projected onto the scene your interpretation of verbal and nonverbal cues, whose particular sequence and configuration you have come to identify as "anger," "indifference," and/or "sadness."

"Projection" and judgment are two of the most insidious temptations, or conceits, to be avoided when doing fieldwork and writing up field notes. In this example, you can't adequately answer some basic questions: How do you know she was angry? What makes you think that his forgetting her birthday caused the anger? Are you certain that there weren't other variables at play in bringing about her anger (if indeed it was anger in the first place)? Your summary statements concerning the informants' words, actions, responses, motives and regarding the structure of the situation might be accurate, but at this stage they're more likely to be way off base. Regardless, you should *always* refrain from making these sorts of judgments, value assessments, and imputations of psychological motive. Instead, focus on describing in concrete terms what is going on. The key word here is **evidence**: *Describe*, don't speculate.

In the analysis phase of your project (which, as we've already discussed, isn't so much a discrete stage at the end of the project but rather an ongoing process), you will be examining the evidence you have produced from your observations in the field. Indeed you may end up drawing conclusions about anger, indifference, sadness, and their relationship to disputes between romantically connected people. But in order to draw these conclusions, you will need evidence.

Instead of projecting your own views onto the scene or making summary statements, use specific, well-chosen words to describe what is going on: "She walks more swiftly than usual into the room. Her eyes are locked on Joseph, her gaze uninterrupted. Joseph sits on the couch, slightly hunched over, a video game controller in his hand. Her progress comes to an abrupt halt about six inches from his position. Standing over him, she says at a higher volume than is customary for her, 'Why are you playing this stupid game when we're supposed to be leaving for dinner in five minutes?' Her hands are on her hips, her arms jutting outward, the spaces between her arms and torso making a triangular shape, and she's leaning slightly to her right, partially blocking his view of the television screen. Joseph continues to stare at the screen, his fingers working briskly over the controller's multicolored buttons." You get the idea: *concrete* description of concrete events.

## Present Tense

We recommend that you write your field notes in the present tense, as though you, as a future reader/evaluator of the notes, are experiencing things as they happen, in real time. Rather than writing, "She walked into the room," you instead should write "she walks into the room." There are many reasons for this seemingly trivial tip. First, writing field notes from memory is challenging. It's not easy to do. Although it gets easier over time, it's never easy. The hardest parts, not surprisingly, are recalling exactly what happened and in what order, and accurately rendering what people said. One way to increase the accuracy of your account is to write in the present tense, as though you are experiencing the events again, as you sit at your keyboard. The present tense, oddly enough, more effectively throws you back into the past, and it puts you in the role of commentator. You're watching the "replay" of events in your head, and you're narrating them with great specificity. Writing this way involves not so much "remembering" and "re-rendering." So, writing in the present tense increases the accuracy and completeness of your account.

Second, the present tense keeps your evidence "fresh." Once you have written field notes for a given outing, you will file them away and not look at them again for a while. While we recommend that you continually review past field notes, the reality is that you might go weeks without reflecting again on a set of field notes. Upon returning to notes, you'll need all the help you can get in terms of putting yourself back into the events to which you've given an accounting. An account written in the present tense is more dynamic than an account cast in the past tense, which means you'll do a better job of returning to the recollection. Finally, the dynamism of the present tense will be an asset to you when writing up the final product (or products). One marker of a good ethnography is its ability to bring the subjects alive, to bring the reader into the world described in the article or book (or film or audio segment) (Ragin 2000). Use of the past tense impedes readers' quest to enter this realm you've studied and have gotten to know so well. You want to do all you can to put them there, just as you put yourself there. In a way, the present tense constitutes a mechanism for "channeling" the field to your notes and ultimately to your reader.

## Contemporaneity

Writing in the present tense is one way to increase the accuracy of the evidence you produce when writing your field notes. Writing up your notes *promptly* is another way to maximize accuracy and completeness. While you may be able to jot notes in the field, it's not always (and under many circumstances not ever) possible to keep notes while doing the fieldwork. Jotting means writing short notes while you are in the field, noting only **key words** to jog your memory later. In Chapter 17, we discuss field contexts in which jotting is inappropriate. Whether you can't carry out any jotting at all (e.g., at a funeral) or can only do it hastily, it's very important that you reduce your observations to writing as soon as possible. Some ethnographers write their complete notes immediately upon returning from the field. Others, like me (Scott), return from the field, write a chronological outline of events accompanied by verbatim reproductions of dialogue from conversations and interviews (in sequence, of course), and then wait 12 to 24 hours before sitting down to write up a complete account of the field experience.

How Many Pages Do I Have to Write? The amount of time between a given field outing and your writing of notes will vary depending upon your personal learning style and the particularities of your information processing and memory recall faculties. This is an important thing to learn about yourself. Is your recollection more accurate immediately following a given event, or do you need time to digest and assimilate what's happened? There are no hard and fast rules governing the time lapse between observation and write-up; you should follow a pattern that works best for you. This said, however, there's a good chance that a lag of two or more days will result in greatly diminished accuracy of sequence, style, and content. With each passing day your recollections degrade. By the end of a week, you may remember only the highlights of the experience, and the potential for projection will have reached a high level.

## WRITING TO THINK, THINKING TO WRITE: WRITING *AS* THINKING

Up to this point, we have emphasized the necessity of producing detailed, chronologically ordered, accurate data based on your observations and experiences in the field. We have urged you to check your judgments at the door and to avoid the trap of projecting your own emotional biases onto the events and interactions you witness in the field. But does this mean that you should not be thinking, analyzing, hypothesizing, or reacting emotionally while writing your field notes? *No.* Not at all. In fact, it's rather impossible not to engage in these cognitive and emotional activities when writing your field notes, even if the field experiences themselves carry very little emotional charge.

Writing is a form of analysis. To illustrate with a very rudimentary example, you cannot write notes on every single thing you see, hear, smell, taste, touch during the field experience. While doing the fieldwork your perceptual filters will work very hard to keep most of the sensory experiences at bay, allowing only a relatively small stream of inputs. Upon leaving the field, the filters associated with your cognitive processing of memory will narrow even more the range of sensory experiences you just had. Finally, the process of writing notes *is* an analytic process, as you must continuously make decisions about what to write about and what not to write about. If left unexamined and unquestioned, your writing of field notes could impact negatively, perhaps even ruin, the data you produce.

As a function of time spent in the field and time reflecting on the ideas you have about how the culture works, you will experience a gradual shift in the way that you write field notes. Previously we discussed the importance of continually assessing how it is that you construct episodes—how what you consider to be the form and content of a typical episode changes over time. Well, the same kind of reflexivity applies to your writing of field notes more generally. Over time, you will begin to focus on certain aspects of the field experience. You cannot and will never be able to write up every single observation you have in the field. Even the information/input that succeeds in passing through all of your perceptual and cognitive filters will be too vast still for anything close to a complete write-up. What's important here is that you pay close and critical attention to the field experiences that you (a) recall clearly and (b) choose to write up. Writing is all about choice. On one hand, you can't write up everything, and so you must make difficult choices as to what to include and what to exclude. On the other hand, you don't want to allow unexamined systematic biases make your selection decisions for you.

Some researchers find it helpful to keep separate descriptive field notes produced throughout the fieldwork from analytic memos which become increasingly important as your work progresses. The analytic memos include reflection, conceptualization, and those "a-ha" moment ideas. See Chapter 17 for more on these types of notes.

## From the Periphery to the Core: Lessons from a Student Ethnography of a Tattoo Parlor in Chicago, IL

In Sarah and Maize's study of the tattoo parlor, they found that in the early days of the study they were writing about all sorts of things they never really figured they would either remember or write up in their field notes. They wrote highly detailed accounts of the music playing on the shop's sound system, the kind of clothing and shoes the customers were wearing, the variations in lighting over the course of the day, and so forth. After a few weeks of writing about these minute details of tattoo parlor life, they became rather frustrated, especially since I kept challenging them to tell me why these things mattered. Sure, they had made these observations. And I didn't doubt the veracity of their accounts. But what did music and customer attire have to do with their research question or hypotheses or even their interests? Gradually they came to see the point. They grew better "acquainted" with their research question, and from this they were able to develop specific *themes* to explore in the field. More specifically even, they were able to identify the "customer–artist interaction" as their fundamental *unit of analysis* (see Chapter 3). Once they achieved more focus, they had a much easier time writing their field notes. Their accounts still were detailed and evidence-driven and descriptive, but at last they were writing about the observations that mattered in relation to their bigger questions concerning interactions between tattoo artists and their customers.

## Putting the Blinders Back On: Smartly This Time!

At this point, we feel compelled to issue the same warning stated previously: Making choices in the field and in writing field notes demands that you create and put on "blinders." Your research question and hypotheses, or themes to explore, or guiding notions all serve to focus your research and make everything more manageable. At the same time, however, they create enormous "blind spots." It is therefore critical that you continually examine the way you do fieldwork and the content and style of your notes (i.e., evidence) to identify potential biases in your data. In short, the upside of increased focus is enhanced manageability, feasibility, and capacity to "go deep," which is this method's hallmark trait. The downside of increased focus, however, is that you greatly increase the risk of ignoring/excluding/omitting crucial cultural events and processes that influence the phenomena on which you have chosen to focus.

A short example may help to illustrate this double-edged sword. In her study of the rural Irish village of "Ballybran," Nancy Scheper-Hughes (2001) spent a solid year engaged in intensive immersive fieldwork. Entering the field armed with all sorts of background materials and theoretical perspectives, she intended to explore the dynamics of Irish sexuality and gender. "I had an open field before me," she writes. In the early weeks of the study, she took copious notes, examined several thousand pages of local historical records, pored over health and demographic data, talked informally with suspicious locals, and tried to make herself into a sort of human fixture in the small, relatively insular hamlet in the countryside.

At the outset of her study, as with so many ethnographers, her "lens" was exceptionally wide. Her field notes seemed nearly indiscriminate, replete as they were with detailed accounts of the village dwellers' personal histories, kinship networks, fashion, interactions, and so on. But a few months into the work, she somewhat serendipitously ended up talking with a psychiatrist who handed her a recently released report that highlighted excessive and differential rates of mental illness diagnosis and hospitalization in rural Ireland. The psychiatrist challenged Scheper-Hughes to figure out the "puzzle" of "the overproduction of young adults in severe distress whose very real problems in living were perhaps too readily diagnosed as schizophrenia" (p. 24). Hence, as is so often the case in ethnographic studies, the ethnographer's research question shifted dramatically through the interaction of contingency and curiosity. From that point forward, Scheper-Hughes refined her focus, and as a consequence her inquiries and attendant field notes became more focused and, as such, more analyzable.

## DIGITAL RECORDING TECHNOLOGY

The issue of using audio-video recording technology in fieldwork is very complicated. In thinking about whether or not to employ a digital voice recorder and/or video recorder, the fieldworker needs to contend with ethical considerations (Chapter 4), questions of data integrity, and the logistical complications that arise when trying to capture observations on digital media. We cannot cover all of these issues comprehensively, for doing so would require that we devote this entire book to "fieldwork and digital technology/electronic media." But we can address some of the most pressing issues.

### Integrity of Data

Ethics aside, the first issue is **data integrity**. Earlier we discussed the "Hawthorne Effect," and it's particularly salient when recording technology is introduced to the ethnographic scene. The behavior you're observing changes by virtue your observing it. Plain and simple. People talk and act differently when they know they're being watched. You experience this in your daily life. Ever gotten caught in the act of doing something when all along you assumed you had no "audience"? Singing in the shower, talking to yourself, making weird faces—these are things we do in private, and when we realize we're not in private, we stop doing them or change the way we're doing them. This is an extreme example to make the point: Our behavior is contingent in part upon who's watching us behave.

The literature on ethnographic methods comes alive with endless, forever unresolved debates over the merits and demerits of using AV technology in the field. Indeed, technology brings with it many important advantages. But it also has its disadvantages. Although there's no universal rule for using recording technology, you need to ask how the technology might affect the integrity of the data you're collecting. Remember, as an ethnographer your principal objective is to cultivate the trust of informants, to get them to trust you enough to be vulnerable around you such that they feel comfortable enough letting you into their private worlds. Will the presence of an audio recorder or video camera make your informant more or less comfortable revealing his soft underbelly?

It's quite obvious that the answer to this question varies by project, context, informant, subject matter or issue under discussion or consideration, and the nature of your relationship with the informant. The latter is in large measure a function of time. When your relationship with an informant is in its infancy, you generally don't want to bring a digital recorder into the mix. Being recorded makes people nervous, and when they're nervous, they reveal less of themselves and/or self-consciously reveal themselves in word and action. When deciding whether or not to record, always err on the side of caution. Only in rare instances will it be entirely unproblematic for you to whip out a recorder and press the red button.

In addition, if your data are of such complexity, depth, and/or breadth that you cannot manage to record it sufficiently in retrospect using only your field notes (or "jottings"), then perhaps you do need the assistance of a digital media recording device. But you should develop a strategy for bringing it into the field. There should be a sound basis for its use, and you should have at the ready an explanation for your informants, and this explanation should put them at ease. Also, as we discuss in Chapter 4, you'll have to employ different safeguards for protecting the confidentiality, privacy, and/or anonymity of your data and/or informants.

Whatever you end up deciding here, keep this in mind: Your recorder will fail you. It is a virtual certainty that the video camera or audio recorder will malfunction—the batteries will die, the mechanism will lock up, or you might hit the wrong button. Imagine having recorded several days' worth of conversation and events, only to accidentally press "Erase All." Then you will be left with nothing. And because you implicitly relied on the recorder to do the work of assimilating what you observed in the field, you probably didn't pay sufficient attention to be able to reconstruct what you saw, heard, felt, and smelled. The point is that even if you're using a recorder, you should proceed in your fieldwork as though you're not using one. Make your jottings in the field and write up your field notes as if you didn't record them. Then return to the recordings to flesh out your notes and to make additional, perhaps higher level, observations. Using an audio recorder to capture your verbal account of field events immediately upon exit from the field can also be immensely productive.

In many instances, a time lag will separate your exit from the field and your return to the place where you write your field notes. If you're living in the field, this may be less relevant, but not irrelevant. It's not always possible to begin reconstructing field events and writing up your notes *immediately* following departure from the field. As we've suggested, you may find that you need a bit of lag time for processing your thoughts and impressions and for forming your observations well enough to write them down coherently. Talking into an audio recorder, stream of consciousness style, can help you prepare to systematically write up your account of occurrences, conversations, and insights. If this works for you, then we suggest that immediately upon conclusion of a field outing, get some privacy for yourself and talk into a recorder. Then, a few hours or a day later, when it's time to write up your notes, return to the recording and use it to help you recall some of the highlights.

## Logistics

Aside from introducing the technology to the field and ensuring its proper functioning, other logistical concerns come to the surface when using a recorder to capture field events. First, the recordings will be lengthy. Transcribing them, even roughly, is exceptionally time-consuming. And hiring someone to transcribe them is beyond the budgets of even the most accomplished university-based ethnographers. Besides, most ethnographers agree that you should write up your own field notes, and if you've recorded interviews or events, you should transcribe them yourself. Often, this is the time when you'll think most deeply and concertedly about the data from that particular day or outing. If someone else transcribes it for you, you'll likely put the transcript into a file and then return to it weeks, months, or even years later. Reading it then will leave you perplexed, as you try to fill in the blanks from memory, attempt to recall the appropriate "subtext," and generally try to figure out why the events in print were so important and relevant to your project.

This brings up an important point about training yourself to do good ethnographic work. Recorders can be incredibly useful in this regard. In preparing to do fieldwork, we've provided you with some suggestions on how to refine your skills and creative faculties. The recorder is well-suited in this regard. As part of training yourself to recall the content of interviews, for instance, you should sit down with a friend and record a one-hour conversation with him. As you're talking, take just a few notes on what he's saying and how he's saying it, as you would do when talking with an actual informant in the field. Then, when you return to your office or home, sit down and reconstruct in your field notes the conversation as you recall it. Once you think it's complete, go back and listen to the recording while following along in your notes. You'll be stunned by how much you remembered and even more stunned by how much you neglected either to hear the first time around or recall when writing up the conversation.

Remember, an audio recording is a poor substitute for field notes. Equally poor is a video recording. Their limitations—and their tendency to inspire laziness in the fieldworker—further reduce their value to the ethnographic enterprise. However, they do have their time and place, and used wisely they can produce invaluable material for your project.

## CONCLUSION: FIELD NOTES AND PROFESSIONAL STANDARDS

Historically, the writing of field notes gets very little attention in research methods textbooks and even less attention in published ethnographies. Field notes and other forms of data often comprise the "black box" of ethnographic research: Ethnographers rarely reveal their approach to notes and even less frequently make their raw notes available to their peers, their published works' audiences, or their informants. In addition, for many years the majority of ethnographers maintained notes that were very messy, incomplete, unfinished, and usually inscrutable to an outside reader. The professional training of ethnographers tended to reinforce this norm. As a case in point, I (Scott) received virtually no formal training in how to conduct ethnography, how to formulate evidence, how to operate in the field, how to analyze data, and so on. Emblematic of my professional education was the one course on ethnographic methods I took in graduate school. Its title was "Methods Schmethods," and its instructors (two world-renowned sociologist-ethnographers) promulgated an open-ended, freeform approach to doing ethnographic research. They bristled at the talk of standards, protocols, guidelines, and they strenuously resisted any consideration of data or evidence, eschewing all of this in the name of waging war against the "imperialism of empiricism."

However, in the past 20 years, the field's professional expectations have risen, standards of evidence have emerged, and protocols for analysis have materialized. Funders and even journal editors (and peer reviewers) have erected a higher bar for assessing fieldwork and, part and parcel of this, field notes. Some of the contemporary era's leading ethnographers, Mitchell Duneier for example, have joined the call for elevated rigor, the guiding principle being replicability, a cornerstone of the scientific method. Sandelowski (1986) discusses the "audit trail," a mechanism by which the researcher constructs her field notes in such a way that an uninformed outsider not only can read and digest them but also can connect them with the trail of emergent hypothesis formulation and testing and, ultimately, with the researcher's analytic maneuvers and substantive conclusions. This is a very high standard to meet, if only because the nature of the data makes the audit trail benchmark very time consuming to attain.

The **transparency** of fieldwork, in terms of process and evidence, is arguably the most controversial and hotly debated topic in ethnographic research, and while full consensus is not likely to emerge, it seems clear at this point that nearly every discipline's criteria for assessing the validity of evidence and analysis are becoming more rigorous. This doesn't appear to be a passing phase. Ethnography is only as solid as the ethnographer's approach to the enterprise of scientific inquiry. And like any other methodology, the quality of the implementation—and thus the final product— varies widely. Bad ethnographies get published every day. But it's the excellent ethnography that transforms the way people think about certain aspects of the world. Which route will you take?

## Exercises

1. Pick an ordinary daily scene, situation, or venue to observe for 15 minutes. Prepare yourself to write field notes on what you see. Go and do your observation, then return and write up your notes. Put them away. One week later return to them. How do they look? Are they accurate? Did you omit anything? What do you think needs to be added? Most important, in reading the notes, do you feel as though you're being "transported" back in time to that place about which you've written?

2. Now, pick another place where you can observe for 15 minutes. This time, take a friend with you. Also prepare him or her to write field notes in the same way that you do. Proceed as you did before. After you've returned and written up your notes, compare the two sets of notes—yours and your friend's. What are the main differences? What do these differences say about your and your friend's perceptual filters? What are the key similarities? How would you account for these?

3. Pick a third situation or venue in which to conduct ethnographic observation for five minutes. Bring a friend. But this time, have your friend video-record (on a cell phone camera even) the five-minute segment. Instruct your friend to try very hard to keep the camera pointed in the direction in which you're looking so that the camera is roughly capturing what you're watching. Next, come home and write up your field notes. Then compare your notes to the camera recording. What are the differences? The similarities?

4. Review these three sets of field notes against the criteria we have presented in this chapter. What are your strengths? Organizing in time? Writing in episodes? What kinds of data are you best at recording? Words? Behaviors? Objects? Rituals? Why do you suppose you're better at recording some of these data types than others?

## Key Terms

chronological order *233*

concreteness *237*

contemporaneity *238*

data integrity *241*

digital recording technology *241*

episodes *234*

evidence *237*

key words *238*

language *236*

present tense *238*

transparency *243*

vernacular *236*

# 16

# Directed Strategies for Data-Making

## OVERVIEW

In this chapter, we talk about several concrete strategies for producing data in the course of doing ethnographic fieldwork. To this point we have focused on the logic of ethnographic design, as well as strategies and tactics to help you build the kind of relationships you need in order to position yourself solidly in the culture or community you're studying. We identified the main types of data that are used in ethnographies and explained how to write field notes. Now, we cover specific things you can do to make data happen.

## ETHNOGRAPHY ESSENTIALS: A BRIEF REVIEW

By this point you've done your background research, made your fieldwork preparations, entered the field, and made some unobtrusive observations. You've even begun talking casually with people as you try to figure out which end is up. And you're equipped with some general principles on how to "hang out with a purpose," and you have some basic ideas for developing relationships. But there's more to ethnography than merely hanging out, making quasi-friends, and writing stories about your experiences.

In the course of ethnographic research, you may draw upon any combination of the "tools" we've presented in this book. And there are countless other methods not presented in this book. The point is that ethnographers choose the data-making tools whose use makes the most sense in light of the cultural context, the research question(s) and/or hypotheses, and the researcher's experiences and skills. There is no single agreed-upon approach for selecting and/or deploying the many different methods/tools that comprise your study's particular methodology. Ultimately, however, the written word is your medium for making and analyzing data, as well as presenting your results.

Everything you recall having seen, heard, felt, tasted, smelled, and touched will be reduced to handwritten and then typed words on a page. Although ethnographers increasingly utilize audio-video technologies in the making of field data (A/V techniques covered in Chapter 20), the modal data form is still text, and the most common unit for organizing text is field notes. (*Note*: Even in illiterate and semiliterate cultures your data will be comprised of text, though your techniques for making data may be less text-heavy than would be the case in a literate culture.)

Some of the data-making techniques you'll use have already received some mention in this and the preceding chapters. But now we have the opportunity to explore them more fully. Below we describe in just enough detail to get you started some of the more common ways that ethnographers produce data from field experiences. It's important to recall, at this point, some of the fundamental ideas we've already discussed: First, the ethnographer is the instrument for making data. Second, data are produced as a result of the ethnographer's interactions with informants. Third, interactions with informants arise from the ethnographer's strategic composition of an interpersonal infrastructure in the culture under study. Fourth, the quality and quantity of the ethnographer's data varies in relation to the degree and type of trust and rapport in the ethnographer's relations with informants.

Fifth, the ethnographer's ultimate goal is to generate "an account" of the culture, a narrative (or "story") that is consistent *but not synonymous* with the emic ("insider") perspective on the culture. That is, the representation you craft must account for the emic view of the culture, but because insiders only rarely enjoy a critical appreciation of the culture in which they participate, the ethnographic story must be capable of explaining the culture's interior logic (i.e., its "ethos") by drawing upon social scientific theoretical and conceptual analytics. The ethnographic story is, in short, the result of a "dialogue of evidence and ideas" (Ragin 1994) and therefore amounts to much more than a detailed description of "what people do."

Sixth, in accounting for how the culture operates (or how it originated, how it is maintained, how it changes, etc.), the individual cultural insider is not the primary unit of analysis; rather, the UOA is the culture itself, as culture is the outcome of interacting individual and institutional forces. Therefore, although making data at the level of the individual informant is necessary, it is not sufficient for analysis and representation. Finally, when implementing any of the data production methods discussed here or elsewhere, it is of paramount importance that you have a clear idea of why you're using a given method, what you expect the method to yield in the way of data, and how you intend to analyze the data in relation to the study question(s) and/or hypotheses.

## THE DIRECTED STRATEGIES

### When Should I Use Directed Strategies?

Too many ethnographers rely on directed strategies and techniques *only* when they feel they need to test their hypotheses. Hypothesis-testing ordinarily occurs in a frenzy of fieldwork activities clustered at the front-end and tail-end of the ethnographic study. Prior to entering the field, you will have done a fair amount of background research, identified the specific culture and "field" on which you wish to concentrate your effort, and you will have composed some rough hypotheses. Because you've learned "just enough to be dangerous," you'll likely be tempted to begin gathering data in a very directed, perhaps even heavy-handed, manner. You may try to convince informants whom you've just met to sit down for lengthy structured interviews, for instance. Or else you'll make a huge nuisance of yourself by performing highly conspicuous measures in the field—you may, for example, develop an elaborate network-mapping protocol and then pluck it from your bag and blatantly make notes and diagrams of who's doing what with whom and where and how. Mapping is technically defined as an unobtrusive measure, but you're doing it in a way that attracts attention and disrupts the scene!

The same temptation will rear its head near the end of your field study. You'll wake up one fine day to the realization that you've tested none of the more informed hypotheses that occurred to you (but which you failed to write down) during the course of doing your study. Over breakfast you'll feverishly specify these formerly latent, foggy hypotheses and then craft a plan for "testing" them. Lickety-split you'll venture into the field and prevail upon the informants you now know very well to tolerate your three-hour life history interview. And you'll work frenetically for a few days as you try to wrap up the countless "loose ends" still dangling as the deadline approaches. This pattern, or workflow, "fits" the vast majority of published ethnographic studies. Too many of us engage prematurely in directed data production as a result of our inability to effectively manage role strain and role conflict while in the field.

Within the culture you're studying, you'll be an outsider. That will be your "status" from the cultural insider perspective. Even if you spend five years living in the culture, you'll still be considered the outsider (though if you do your job well, perhaps you'll be "the outsider who is now like one of us, but who isn't one of us . . . but at least she isn't as strange as she once was"). At least two dominant roles will be attached to this status: **participant and observer.** In the early days of fieldwork, you'll be more of an observer than participant. However, as you grow more comfortable in the field, you'll experience "role strain" (Merton 1949), a pronounced incompatibility and tension between these two roles. In a word, you'll have become more of a participant, an "observing participant."

In many cases, the ethnographer comes to identify so closely with the insiders and participates so actively in the culture that she stops producing data . . . she loses sight of the **etic** perspective. This very thing happened to William Foote Whyte in his study of "Cornerville": He became so engrossed in "doing culture" that he lost his grip on observing and examining culture. (As we stated previously, it's very difficult to perform and simultaneously analyze culture.) While he didn't "go native," for such a thing is rarely possible, he did become so immersed that he stopped doing the research and instead spent his time doing and thinking what his chums did and thought. Ultimately, Whyte had to extricate himself entirely from Cornerville—he moved far away and allowed several years to pass before he could sufficiently regain his outsider's perspective for the purpose of analyzing his experiences.

Reprioritizing roles (observer and participant in the case of ethnography) is one way to deal with the role strain of fieldwork. More commonly, however, ethnographers reprioritize roles in an incremental fashion, gradually becoming more of a participant and less of an observer until at some point they altogether discard the observer role. Then, when they realize that they must "wrap it up," they suddenly resurrect their observer role and consequently engage in highly directive data-making activities. We caution you against this pattern. Ideally, you will fulfill these roles simultaneously, but your performance should allow prioritization shifts to occur.

Depending upon timeline, nature of the project, circumstances of fieldwork, and myriad other variables, you will find yourself emphasizing (and de-emphasizing by necessity) one or the other role. This is the desirable state of affairs. However, should you end up in the less desirable state wherein you have discarded one role or the other, try to avoid sudden changes; instead, calmly, slowly, and deliberately steer yourself back into a homeostatic role-split. As in driving on icy roads, the trick is making an adjustment without turning the wheel too hard in the opposite direction and going into a spin.

**Directed techniques** should be utilized throughout the course of fieldwork, though generally speaking, it's a mistake to employ them before you've achieved sufficient rapport with informants such that your use of such heavy-handed methods will neither antagonize them nor make them suspicious of you. Once again, we reiterate the message behind much of the material we have presented thus far: Ethnography should be evidence-based, and the quality of the evidence depends heavily upon the quality of your relationships with informants. Dispensing with the preamble, let's turn to some of the techniques you should consider using in your own study.

## What Do Directed Strategies Produce?

We've discussed some tactics for inspiring in the informant the notion that he's in charge and that you can be trusted with sensitive information. In Chapter 18, we will share specific guidelines for managing the infrastructure and functions of interaction in conversations and formal interviews. Now it's time to examine some of the most commonly used questions (and sets of questions). So we're transitioning from the logistical management of interrogatory conversation to the substance of conversations with informants. What questions should you be asking?

You'll find a good deal of detailed guidance in Agar's (1980) *The Professional Stranger*, from which we take much of the following advice concerning how to ask questions. Before sharing some strategies concerning ways to ask questions, we should mention (as a reminder) that what you ask (i.e., the substance of your questions) will be determined in large measure by the research question and hypotheses guiding your project and also by the contingencies you encounter in the field. Generally, however, you'll be well-served by following some or all of the following question-forming strategies.

## Asking Questions

There's more to asking questions than meets the eye or ear. Let's talk about some of the ways you can approach the whole business—and it is a business—of asking questions of people in the field.

Ask "How . . . ?" Remember, ask a lot of "how" questions. Your job entails exhibiting ignorance, and while it's critical for you to understand the who, what, when, and where factors of the culture, people often respond best to an inquiring stranger when the questions call for descriptions of process. So you might ask, "How did you get into tattooing?" or "How did you first begin stealing as a way to make money?" or "How did you end up living here?" Soliciting process descriptions is a good way to generate a tremendously valuable data set from the get-go. It's an especially prosperous endeavor when you ask "how" questions in relation to events and/or behaviors that have become part of the culture's "public record" (see previous discussion).

**ESTIMATION**   When getting a feel for a community or culture as a whole, or when trying to establish a sense of how widespread a particular phenomenon is, ask your informants to help you out, in *their* own terms. Every ethnography involves the eliciting and analysis of qualitative and quantitative data, even if the quantitative data aren't numeric *per se*. At a fundamental level, qualitative research and ethnography are concerned with proportions: occurrences within and across the cases that comprise your sample. After all, you probably won't be too interested (analytically anyway) in an incident that has occurred only one time, in one person's life. You're on a search for patterns of sameness and difference, which means dealing in proportions of cases. So, when you're in the field, ask informants to give you with **distribution checks** and "folk estimates."

A distribution check entails nothing more than asking an informant to give you some sense of how widespread or common, or how uncommon, a particular cultural phenomenon is. And a folk estimate involves your asking an informant to provide you with a rough projection of how many or what percentage of cultural insiders experience or engage in a behavior, event, ritual, or to quantify some other issue.

The modifier "folk" underscores the importance of encouraging the informant to calculate and express the estimate using a base system that makes sense to him. You don't want to force the informant to adopt an arbitrary baseline, or some baseline that you prefer, when providing an estimate. So, if you're studying farmers, and you're interested in gathering data on how they have experienced changes in domestic agricultural subsidy policies over the past 30 years, then you need to figure out what base system makes sense to the farmers. Obviously you could force them to consider changes on your timeline, or the generally agreed-upon timeline pinned to the calendar year. However, in the local community, the farmers may have found a more meaningful way to mark the passage of time—foreclosures on family farms. Perhaps that's how local family farmers think about policy changes. If so, then you need to be sensitive to this and not force them to think your way when answering the question. Besides, the very fact that they construe time in terms of its effects on family farms rather than a mechanical unfolding of years tells you something about the community. In other words, the particularity of their base system *is* datum.

**COMPARE AND CONTRAST**    Try to get into the habit of asking "contrast questions." Quite simply, a contrast question poses a juxtaposition of two events, things, relationships, or phenomena. Contrast questions are one way of understanding variation and difference within cultures, a goal we mentioned in Chapter 13. While doing research on condom use among college students, for example, you might ask, "What are some of the differences in how you use a condom with your boyfriend versus how you use a condom when you're with someone you're not really dating?" This question allows you to elicit two different behavioral descriptions and then to discern the basis on which the informant distinguishes the two. Follow-up questions regarding what accounts for the differences and/or similarities may be very fruitful. For example, you might ask, "Can you explain some of the reasons for the difference between these two—using condoms with a boyfriend versus using them with someone who isn't really your boyfriend?"

**BAITING**    As we mention in Chapter 18, many methods textbooks discourage the practice of asking **baiting or leading** questions or any question that suggests or encourages a particular answer or category of potential answers. But in the context of ethnographic work, a leading question can be extremely useful, particularly when you want to falsify emergent conclusions you have formed. As Agar (1996) points out, the point isn't whether or not a question is leading, for every question is to some degree leading; that's what makes it a question. Rather, the point is the degree to which you, as the questioner, can control the question well enough to know where it's going and then to make use of it as an analytic device.

Sometimes it's a good idea to lead an informant. For instance, if you've interviewed and talked informally with lots of informants, and there appears to be a high level of uniformity in their responses to a question or descriptions of an event, you should consider using leading questions to falsify the emergent conclusion that you're beginning to embrace and that may arise from the favorite sayings and slogans of the community.

In Chicago's street drug addict community, for example, one of the dominant mantras is "love all, trust none." This phrase captures the necessity of making symbolic and material deposits into the greater good of the addict community out of recognition that "we're all in this together." At the same time, however, addicts realize that they shouldn't trust each other. One of the most oft-told jokes among addicts is this: "How can you tell when a junky is lying?" Answer: "His lips are moving."

"Love all, trust none." It's become a cliché, and that is why it is fair game for "baiting." When you ask how addicts' interact with each other and get this shopworn phrase in response, then you can follow up with a challenge: *Really? You love everyone? There's nobody out here that you don't love?*

"Love All, Trust None" scrawled on a piece of paving stone found near a heroin "shooting gallery" on Chicago's south side.

*And there's nobody that you actually do trust?* As an important aside, be sure that you can *safely* challenge an informant in this way, for it's not always an advisable tactic from the perspectives of personal well-being and maintaining good relations with informants. But with sufficient rapport, you can issue such a challenge. When I (Scott) did just that, I discovered a great deal of variation I didn't realize existed. More important, addicts' responses taught me a great deal about the *meaning* of love and trust. In fact, street addicts *do* love some people, and they do trust some people, but they don't always love the ones they trust or trust the ones they love. These are special terms connoting special features of special relationships. Had I met the apparent consensus with facile acceptance, I never would have learned about the complex workings of love and trust on the streets.

## Processual Interviewing

Asking your informants to vocalize thoughts, activities, and decisions as they engage in actions is a useful way for understanding the relationship between behaviors and "cognitive maps." Processual interviewing gives the ethnographer insight into a cognitive process that accompanies behaviors. The processual interview is an interview . . . and it's relatively structured, but not by you. The informant's activity, whatever it is, is the source of the interview's structure. This method yields insight into particular skills, normative activities and/or rituals, and common repetitive behaviors within a culture.

"Getting ready in the morning," for instance, can be amazingly dense with cultural references. With this technique, you reach agreement with the informant that you're going to closely observe a given behavior, and the informant is going to narrate to you exactly what he's doing, why he's doing it the way he's doing it, and so forth. Along the way you may ask specific questions to "probe" into other areas, such as particularity of circumstance or origin of the knowledge.

Again, you want to produce a detailed record of the event, and you may find value in repeating the assessment for multiple behaviors/activities in a given informant's life and/or comparing the same activity across informants. Again, it's essential that your observation be clearly linked, conceptually and empirically, to the research question you're addressing in your study. And with each record you'll want to record the informant's demographics, a description of the physical setting, the presence of others and the social roles they occupy, the special equipment or material items dedicated to the activity, a chronological record of the behavior as it unfolds, dialogue between informant and others (including you). Once you have conducted processual interviews with several informants, you can begin to analyze them, identify patterns/similarities across cases, and then begin to create "manuals" for the particular behavioral domain on which you're focused.

## Manualize

Every culture encompasses specific processes for getting things done. After all, culture *is* the sum total of all the ways that members of a particular group accomplish daily life (see Chapter 15). Culture is an accomplishment, a series of adaptations to fixed as well as flexible conditions. **Culture is knowledge**, much of it embodied in action, not in explicit verbal instructions. It is therefore critical that you identify the key behavioral domains of the culture you're studying and begin to "manualize" the core activities within each domain, making explicit the knowledge and rules that implicitly govern this activity.

A behavioral domain is a kind of collective "habitus" (Bourdieu and Wacquant 1992). It comprises an activity in which a considerable number of cultural insiders engage for the purpose of achieving a material or nonmaterial end that is sanctioned either negatively or positively by the culture writ large. Flashing gang symbols with one's hands, for example, is a behavioral domain in the culture of many street gangs across the world. This activity requires the precise execution of various interrelated mechanical operations. Also, culturally ratified rules govern the flashing of signs—when, where, for what reason, how (style), and so forth. Learning to flash signs is an integral aspect of becoming a "gang member." Once learned, the signs serve a communicative purpose within the gang and also between gang members and their opponents (rival gangs, police officers, teachers, etc.).

In doing your research, you need to identify as many of the integral behavior domains as you possibly can. You do this through observation, interviewing, and "free-listing," a data-making activity we discuss next. Once identified, you then want to proceed as though you're writing a "how-to manual" on the activity. And, as with all other forms of data recording, you need to continually update each manual as you go along. The manual should be intelligible to an outsider who knows nothing about the culture and should be written as though it's giving instruction to a newcomer who wants to master the activity. It then will become part of your data set, and you will subject the manuals to analysis.

## Free-Listing and Pile-Sorting

Upon first entering a culture, you'll be ignorant of many things. You won't really even know how to talk. Even if you technically speak the same language as the cultural insiders, they use words differently, construct their sentences with a different style and according to different rules, and the cadence and rhythm of their speech is different. Your ignorance can be traced to your lack of familiarity with the "cultural domains" inherent to the group. It behooves you to learn as many of the cultural domains early on as you possibly can. To the extent that you become fluent in the cultural domains, you will be a good asker of questions. Conversely, to the extent that you remain ignorant of cultural domains, your questions and comments will sound stupid at best, offensive at worst.

A cultural domain is an area of shared reality, or at least a shared conception of reality. Specifically a domain consists of items that belong to the same "type" of something. The "something" is typically expressed in language. Also, a cultural domain is not a personal preference; it's a perception of a public matter/issue. For example, if you're studying drug dealers, you might want to know how they think about their customers. So you might ask, "Who buys street drugs?" You want them to "free list," or provide you with an *ad hoc* tally in response to your directive about customers, a critical cultural domain in their lives. Some of your informants will give you a list of slang terms for customer. Many will give you a list of demographic attributes ("young, old, men, women, black, white, rich, poor" etc.). Others will flatly reply, "everybody." (In the latter case, you'll want to probe with something like "who is everybody?")

The point is that you want the informant to give you a sense of how they view that one small aspect of the symbolic world they share with others. Free-listing gives you insight into how cultural insiders view the world, how they organize it, and how they talk about it. Many obvious benefits accrue to you as a result of their free-listing activities, the most practical being knowing how to talk, what words to use and not use, and so forth. You can use free-listing to (1) identify the items in a cultural domain, (2) get a handle on the characteristics of each item and also the relationships among the items, which in turn will help you see how the domain is structured, and (3) assess the relative importance of items in the domain, which gives you a sense of how power circulates through the domain.

Doing a free-list with an informant is easy. You sit down with them, and you ask them a question. They talk and you write down everything they say—verbatim. For each cultural domain question, you should write each response on its own index card (or some other small piece of paper). Returning to the drug dealer example, we can ask the dealer to tell us who buys street drugs. Then, we can ask him to describe each of these customers. Third, we'll want to ask, "so if you had to group customers together, how would you do it?"

At this point, you would display in no particular order all of the cards bearing the various items the dealer gave in response to the question. Then you let him sort them into clusters, or piles (thus the term "pile-sorting"). Once the piles have been sorted and arranged, you can ask the informant to share his rationale for constructing the piles in this particular way. Perhaps he organized them by gender, by race, by drug of choice, or by economic status. You also can ask questions about each "pile," or group. One question should address what the group's members have in common aside from the primary reason the informant put them together in the pile.

Free-listing and pile-sorting are activities that typically go together, but they can be done separately. The results of free-lists can be arranged into a table indicating the frequency of each item's appearance in informants' lists taken together. Pile-sort results can be analyzed using a simple matrix listing the informants down the left side (the rows) and the item names across the top (columns). Each informant would have his own matrix, and you would cluster the groups together or use some other technique to show the various groupings. Then you would compare them across informants to look for patterns in how the informants view interpersonal groupings within the cultural domain.

## Sociometric Grid Mapping

When you're in the field it's a good idea to keep very simple tallies of who's on the scene with whom, and how the groupings change over time, across space, and in relation to external and internal forces. The "sociometric grid map" is one way to capture this information.

Quite simply, a sociometric grid is nothing more than a table, or matrix. Down the left side you list the names of all the people you may come across in the course of doing fieldwork. And you place their names in the same order, from left to right, across the top of the grid (the columns). Then, when you're out doing fieldwork and have the time and opportunity to do some unobtrusive observation, you take note of who's with whom by placing an "X" in the cell that represents the "coming together" of the people in question.

Because social constellations/groupings tend to change over time, your sociometric grid maps should be time-sensitive as well. If, for instance, you're examining the variegated use of space on a single block of a densely and diversely populated urban neighborhood, you will need to produce data in synch with changes in how the street's inhabitants change their groupings. So if a particular corner is occupied by five young men of color at 3 p.m., but by 5 p.m. they've disbanded and been replaced by seven older white ethnic women, then you'll need to capture this in your field notes, preferably directly into a blank grid sheet, such that you can capture the dynamism of the street over the course of the day. Obviously you won't know people's names if you're doing unobtrusive measuring, but you can make up names for them or simply refer to them in your notes by their physical characteristics.

However you keep track of social groupings, they can serve your study very well for they go beyond the individual level and allow you to conduct group-level analyses. For a good example of how very simple sociometric mapping, overlain on rudimentary geographic maps, can tell you a lot about group composition (e.g., hierarchy) and activity, see W. F. Whyte's *Street Corner Society* (1943).

## Daily Diary

This data production technique involves getting informants to keep semi-structured diary accounts of daily life, which the researcher collects on a regular basis (customarily on a daily or weekly basis), reviews with the informant, and ultimately analyzes as textual data. The daily diary has a long history in social science research and has been used to produce data on many different behaviors, from eating to alcohol to sex to migraine headaches to self-care among diabetics. In general, studies of this technique find enhanced reliability of self-report data, especially when the data concern "sensitive" topics, and more complete and detailed information. Informants who keep daily diaries generally feel more comfortable writing about such things as their drug use or sexual activity, as opposed to talking with a relative stranger (i.e., the researcher) about these things.

Daily diaries are generally more reliable than retrospective interviewing because the diary minimizes the probability and magnitude of recall error. Few people can accurately remember things 30 days after they happened, or even a couple of days later. In ethnographic research, you usually want real-time insight from informants on particular issues. The daily diary technique affords just that, along with more detailed data than otherwise might have been obtained. So how do you use the daily diary in your research project? Well, it's really straightforward.

First, you probably want to "sample for heterogeneity." In other words, select a wide variety of informants representing the various subgroups and subdivisions within the culture you're studying. As we've indicated already, every culture develops and rests upon some kind of stratification, or hierarchy. And each stratum, or level, of the hierarchy, is typically marked by differentiation among various groups. You need to figure out the basis of the differentiation within levels (and across levels) and then sample so that you achieve representation from as many different groups as possible. Once you have determined the structure of the culture, you can proceed with diary data collection. At this point, you might be thinking that there's always a "right time" and "right place" for this and/or any other technique we discuss, but actually there isn't. Any of these techniques can be used at any point and to any number of ends when doing your research.

The daily diary, for instance, may be used in a more exploratory way. That is, you may decide that it has value to you much earlier in the study; indeed, it might be one of the best tools for figuring out the composition and characteristics of the culture—its hierarchical arrangement, its constituent activities, its central ethos, its key domains, its organizing structures, and its most pronounced patterns. Quite simply, the daily diary can be used at any point in the ethnographic trajectory; you just need to be clear on why you're using it at this particular time, how you're going to use it, and of course, the limitations on the method given where you are in the study's life course.

Back to the mechanics of the technique: You can structure the diary in advance, or you can allow informants to make a "free form" record and then later take an inductive approach to teasing out a structure common to most/all informants or the structure unique to a person. To do this, you need to know, or at least have a rough idea, of what you want to learn from the informants' daily life experiences. After all, there's no way that anyone can write down every single thing that happens to them in the course of a given day. Even a day spent at home, on the couch, watching TV and eating cereal is far too complicated to capture *in toto* using *any* media (audio, video, written word, etc.). There's simply no way to capture all of that detail in writing. Even five minutes worth of sensory experience (all you see, feel, taste, smell, and hear) defies truly comprehensive and accurate depiction.

As discussed in an earlier chapter, we all develop and apply "perceptual filters" that allow some of the world's stimuli to "get in" to our consciousness but which keep out most of the world's stimuli. Informants in a study, just like you and everyone else, have their own perceptual filters. So if you want to begin learning what those filters constitute, then allow informants a more open-ended diary structure. If, however, you're familiar with their unique filters (culturally speaking), then provide some structure to the diary form itself.

The structure consists of content areas, or topics, that you want the informant to write about during/at the end of the day. If you're trying to understand grooming habits, then you might provide diary forms that require informants to selectively represent their daily life by focusing principally on how they get themselves ready in the morning, how they maintain physical appearance throughout the day, and how they engage in hygiene-promoting or retarding activities. These content areas, or "cues," would be typed on the form itself.

Daily diary forms may specify not just content areas (grooming processes, eating habits, sexual activity, etc.) but also the logistical dimensions of daily life. You may want to elicit data on informants' use of time—how much time they spend engaged in various activities, patterns in activities' begin and end times, or locations of select activities. In addition, the daily diary usually, but not always, consists of open-ended directives. You may decide to solicit more categorical data from informants, in which case you would include checklists, questions with response that need to be ranked in terms of importance, and/or other discrete response items that you believe to be well-suited for producing the data you need to perform the analyses necessary for answering the research question (or addressing the hypotheses) at the core of your research study.

Every data production technique raises its own confidentiality issues. The daily diary is no exception. Indeed, its use carries greater risk of confidentiality breach as compared with the retrospective interview, for instance. This issue is even more salient and consequential among informants who are engaging in illegal, illicit, and/or deviant activities. After all, you're asking them to write down the things they've done throughout the day. They therefore are creating a "paper trail" just for your benefit (setting aside whatever therapeutic value may come from their keeping of a diary). If the content of their daily diary could get them in some kind of trouble if the diary were to get into the wrong hands somehow, then you need to take extra steps to protect informants. First, informants should refrain from writing their names or other identifying information (e.g., addresses) in their diary accounts. Second, if informants are engaged in illegal, deviant, or just "secret" activities, you should work with them to develop a system of code words, sensible in their terms and according to their worldview, which in turn allows them to refer to activities, things, events, or people without divulging to unauthorized readers the exact nature of the diary's contents.

Before concluding this section, we want to discuss briefly a few limitations of the daily diary technique: legibility, accuracy, and literacy. You'll need to figure out how to ensure maximum legibility and recall accuracy of diary submissions. For the most part, informants who keep daily diaries don't write their entries contemporaneous with the events they're describing. In other words, the typical informant will experience an event and then in most cases a few hours, or as much as a day, may pass before the informant sits down to write up the day's happenings. And the write-up might be partly or wholly illegible. Moreover, if you're working with/among semiliterate or illiterate informants, then the written diary may be an infeasible technique. If you are studying people with more power or money than you have, they will probably refuse to keep a diary for you!

While these issues could be challenging, they're not irresolvable. In fact, if some portion of the population you're studying has literacy challenges, you will want to make sure you work *extra* hard to include them in your diary sample. After all, when doing ethnographic work you should be striving to sample for heterogeneity in most instances, so it's vital that you include the literate, semiliterate, and illiterate cultural insiders. Given this exigency, you'll need to be inventive when it comes to using this technique. One way to address all of these issues (i.e., legibility, accuracy, and literacy level variation) is to conjoin brief interviews with each of the informant's submission of the diary. If, for example, you're collecting the diaries every three days, then you should set up an interview schedule that allows you to meet with each of the informants for a period of time sufficient for joint review of the diary and for your asking of probing and follow-up questions. You simply want the informant to go back over the diary with you, clarify any illegible entries or entries you don't understand, flesh certain entries out with a more detailed oral description, correct recall errors if possible, and so forth. Most of the studies that have used the daily diary adopt this approach, and if you elect to do the same, make sure that you follow the same process and protocol with everyone, so as to minimize "interviewer bias."

## Ethnographic Shadowing

Reading an informant's daily diary is one way to gain valuable insight into her life. But "ethnographic shadowing" yields even more nuanced and rich data. Also known as the "day visit," this technique involves attaching yourself for a full day to a specific informant whom you have chosen purposively. Ultimately, you'll want to shadow a number of informants across the culture's many subdivisions and demarcations (again, sampling for heterogeneity). When you shadow an informant, you should do what he does, go where he goes, and to the best of your ability (and within the constraints of the law and your study's and discipline's ethical codes of conduct) emulate (without mimicking) the informant. Shadowing requires that you closely observe the informant, ask him questions about what he's doing and why he's doing it (remember, without using the word "why?"), record as much information in real time as you possibly can, and then write up a detailed account of the activities, dialogue, places visited, routes taken, people encountered, all of it organized by episode of course.

The shadowing write-up should assume the form of field notes. In addition, though, you should map out the day chronologically and spatially. Create actual maps, with narrative accounts explaining how the day unfolded, events transpired, and decisions made. You should be striving to re-create a tour of the day you've spent with the informant whom you selected through diversity sampling.

Shadowing of this sort works best when you have a specific goal or objective, even if it's merely exploratory. It also works well when you're attempting to test a working hypothesis about this or the other phenomena. Without a focal point, shadowing can become unfocused, and your resulting written account will be sprawling and directionless. Also, be sure that you and the informant establish an agreement ahead of time regarding which activities you will observe and which ones you won't. Obviously, this is especially important when studying "outlaw" or "antisocial" groups—you and the informant may have the same or different views on what you should and should not witness and, most important, what you should and should not participate in.

Shadowing can give you a tremendous amount of data on how informants view and navigate the world, what their perceptual filters are, how they acquire and use information, and how they make decisions (or don't). During the shadowing event(s), you can—and should—make use of other techniques discussed in this and other sections of the book. You might want to engage in informant mapping, pile-sorting, processual interviewing, and the like during the shadowing sojourns.

Once you've concluded a shadowing event, it's important to reduce it to a "case" for the purpose of making cross-case comparisons. You'll want to tease out similarities and differences within, between, and among cases within the same cultural subfield and across the multiple and varied fields that comprise the culture. Shadowing works best when the ethnographer and informant enjoy a high level of rapport between them. Without rapport and familiarity, the exercise can become awkward, uncomfortable, stilted, and ultimately unproductive. Having an active dislike of the informant can make the enterprise doubly challenging. So use this technique after you've been in the field a while and have gotten to know the informants you're sampling into this effort.

Finally, while shadowing an informant you want to minimize the degree to which he deviates from his usual schedule in order to "show you a good time" or "make things more exciting" for you. Informants, once they've gotten to know and like you, can be very accommodating, and their concern for your well-being and contentment can be one of your worst enemies, at least with regard to data integrity. You want them to "be real," and you can tell them as much (not in those words, necessarily) at the beginning of the shadow period. This addresses the last point we wish to make here: Before going out in the field with an informant you're shadowing, you should let the informant know when you're going to start and when you're going to stop, and then try to adhere to the schedule you've established. In this same discussion, you might want to suggest to the informant that she come up with an easy way to explain who you are—that's your "cover story." This will reduce the awkwardness of the first encounter or two, when the informant's peers ask, "Who is that odd person with you?"

## Informant Mapping: Individuals and Focus Groups

In a previous chapter in this section, we recommended unobtrusive mapping as a way for you to become familiar with the geographic area corresponding with the culture you've chosen to study. While this is valuable in terms of getting an "etic" fix on the parameters of the study area, one of the major objectives in ethnographic research is to develop an "emic" view against which you can dialectically examine the "etic" perspective that derives from your own training, background, and theoretical/conceptual framework. Informant mapping entails just what its name suggests: Informants create social and/or geographic maps corresponding with their own worldview.

Informants' maps, whether generated individually or in a group setting, will furnish you with data on how they see the social, natural, and built "ecology" of daily life, as they experience it. Decades' worth of interdisciplinary research support the basic premise that drives this technique: The natural and built environmental features we experience daily have a profound effect on the decisions we make, the things we do and/or don't do, the relationships we form or don't form, even how we think about the world and our place within it. It's almost too obvious to put into words, but the fact is *we exist in place*. We occupy physical and social space. And while we can change our positioning, we often cannot change the physical (and often social) parameters that define and delimit the range of occupancy options available to us. Hence, mapping is justified.

Singer et al. (2000) describe multiple methods for studying the "social geography" of AIDS and hepatitis risk among injection drug users. In their article (which is definitely worth reading), they discuss informant mapping. Although they do see value in having individual informants create maps of their worlds, they advise that ethnographers engage in "focus group informant mapping," which basically combines the focus group technique (Chapter 19) with individual mapping. In the rest of this section, we discuss how to engage groups of informants in the mapping process, so just keep in mind that you can use the same approach, modified only slightly, when working with individual informants.

Once you have worked with individual informants on mapping, you should begin *sampling for homogeneity* to create groups whom you assign the task of creating social and/or geographic maps. With most techniques we advise sampling for heterogeneity, but with this technique you want to facilitate the emergence of consensus regarding what constitutes the best depiction of the social/physical ecology. Once you have worked with multiple groups within each subdivision of the culture, you can make cross-group and cross-division comparisons, a necessary element of your final analysis.

Focus group informant mapping offers data on at least two levels: In the end you will have the maps themselves, and you also will want to treat the discussion itself as data. In the context of a small group, informants will be assigned the task of creating a map (e.g., a map of "dangerous and safe places for dumpster diving" when studying street-level homelessness). In the end, the group will have created a map of risky and relatively safe places within the orbits of their daily lives, but along the way they almost undoubtedly will debate the weaknesses and strengths, nature and importance of each person's contribution to the map-making enterprise. These debates should be recorded (by you) and turned into a transcript, which later you will fold into your data set. Quite simply, you (as the facilitator) are forcing the group to achieve consensus on a map. How they go about achieving that consensus—the rhetoric they use, the words they choose, the intragroup disputes that arise—is a very important data source for your study.

So how do you go about generating this important source of data? First, recruit 5–10 individuals whom you have deemed somewhat akin to each other. You need to be explicit (with yourself) about how you're determined that these are people with something in common. Make note of your decision-making and selection process. Again, the people chosen to be in each group should occupy the same subdivision of the culture you're studying. Later you can create more heterogeneous groups, but for now you're looking to figure out how like-minded and similarly situated cultural insiders view the world.

Once you have convened the group, you will serve as facilitator and therefore guide them through the mapping process. Chapter 19 offers direction in how to run a focus group. This is the same thing, basically, except that you want them to produce a commodity, a product—a map of consensus.

Where and when possible, you'll want to tape record the session (with participants' consent, of course). Give everyone mapping materials—pre-printed, bare-bones maps (the kind of maps you can get from Google Maps, for instance), pencils with erasers. Or you can use small dry-erase boards, or one big board on which you inscribe the elements that the group has decided should be on the map. Whatever the case, researchers have found it best to start these groups with a basic grid; that is, you should not simply give informants a blank sheet of paper and say, "here you go, make a map." Rather, you should give them a skeletal map comprised of street boundaries that very broadly contain the area within which they live their lives. At the outset, you should get the group to discuss whether the basic grid is too broad or too restrictive. Once you've settled on the "base map," you can proceed with the more fine-grained mapping. Then you facilitate the focus group by asking a few core, open-ended questions that get people talking about the features that should be mapped. The actual questions and substance of their discussion, and what they end up mapping, depends upon the nature of your research study.

In the Singer et al. (2000) study, informants were asked where "public injection" happens, where informants can find clean/sterile needles, what kinds of places they stay away from. In my (Scott's) study of a community mobilization program, I asked homeowners only two questions: "Where do you feel safe?" and "Where do you feel threatened?" Then they moved forward collectively to create a single map that captured all informants' answers to these questions. Subsequently, in a separate session, I asked renters the same two questions. They generated their own map. Finally, I asked the neighborhood's unhoused (i.e., homeless) occupants these questions. The maps from these groups were very illuminating, though not altogether surprising. The homeowners viewed the spaces occupied by renters and by the homeless as harboring equivalent degrees and types of danger; the renters viewed only the homeless-occupied areas as dangerous; the homeless viewed the renters' and homeowners' spaces as equally dangerous.

Ultimately this technique generates a wealth of visual and textual data that can be used for all sorts of analyses. Once you've sampled for homogeneity, you should consider (later in the study) convening groups of disparate cultural insiders—people who occupy different, perhaps even discrepant—subgroups within the culture. Proceed with caution if you do this, as it can be very difficult to facilitate a group comprised of people who don't like each other, don't get along with each other, or simply don't feel comfortable in each other's presence.

## Systematic Social Observation (SSO)

Direct participation and observation of social and physical life in urban spaces enjoys a long, rich history in the field of urban sociology. Recognizing the limitations of survey research, Chicago-based urban sociologists concerned with the connection between physical space and social interaction long ago began developing methods to assess the sights, sounds, and feel of specific neighborhoods. Lofland (1973: 22) capably articulates the central rationale for conducting SSO as a supplement to other research methods that target urban issues:

> The answer to the question of how city life was to be possible, then, is this. City life was made possible by an "ordering" of the urban populace in terms of appearance and spatial location such that those within the city could know a great deal about one another by simply looking.

Residents of any given neighborhood—regardless of economic status—frequently find it difficult to describe accurately the world they inhabit, especially in terms of the complex relationships between social and physical order. Hence, it becomes important to employ other methods that hone in on key issues in a more independent, dispassionate manner. Doing systematic social observation can be a tricky affair. This technique is best-utilized after you have gained sufficient acceptance in the community/culture such that walking around with a clipboard, writing things on a form, will not raise much ire or cause you any trouble with the informants who live there.

The point of SSO is to systematically gather qualitative *and* quantitative ethnographic data on physical and social phenomena in the neighborhood/area that encompasses the culture you're studying. With this technique, you are the one doing the observing. And even when you're taking note of the physical features and conditions of the area, you're doing so with an eye toward assessing the interplay between the physical and social dimensions of cultural life in the area. "Systematic" refers to the use of coding methods that follow explicit, largely inflexible rules that serve to enhance the method's replicability.

**SSO IN POST-KATRINA NEW ORLEANS**    A few years ago, I (Scott) conducted a "formative ethnographic assessment" of "post-Katrina" neighborhoods in New Orleans. The goal was to study the neighborhoods using qualitative, quantitative, and ethnographic methods. A good deal of the ethnographic work was quantitative, which is where SSO came into play. This method allowed my team to gather a large volume of information/data on each neighborhood in a very short period of time. In this case we were using ethnography to determine whether the methods used in a pre-Katrina study of HIV risk in New Orleans could be used again to study HIV risk.

Pre-Katrina secondary data were helpful in identifying potentially high-risk areas of the city, but without direct observation, the researchers in charge of the pre-Katrina study would have no way of knowing whether or not (a) these neighborhoods were still populated at all, (b) whether or not the repopulated neighborhoods were occupied by the same people (i.e., the same "at-risk" population) as before the storm, (c) where these neighborhoods stood with respect to recovery and repopulation potential, or (d) for parallel construction conducting *any* kind of survey, regardless of method would be feasible in these specific areas of the city.

To accomplish the twofold objective of (a) ascertaining the level and type of repopulation in the "risk areas" as defined by pre-Katrina data and (b) gauging the feasibility of conducting a post-Katrina survey among residents of these areas, I led a research team through the process of developing and then implementing an SSO effort. We painstakingly scrutinized the visible characteristics of social and physical life in every single census tract of the 25 neighborhoods where the survey had taken place before the hurricane. Major categories of interest include the state of residential and commercial structures (every structure assessed), the presence and condition of public service facilities, the quality of physical order, the nature of social interaction, and the overall quality of physical and social life in the neighborhood.

Here's how we, as a team, conducted SSO as part of the overall ethnographic research project: A minimum of three team members would travel together in an automobile. An initial drive-through of the entire tract helped all members get a "feel" for the neighborhood. Following the casual drive-through, the team would assess the tract using the SSO, going house-by-house, block-by-block, until every bit of physical space in the tract received treatment. The driver maintained responsibility for vocalizing a tally of the persons seen and automobiles present. The other team members independently rated the tract, recording their observations on the SSO form. Typically, they sat in the backseat of the vehicle, both of them recording their observations independently while the driver assisted in counting persons and vehicles present in the neighborhoods.

A "typical" neighborhood where we conducted SSO in post-Katrina New Orleans.

Several dozen residents of the St. Bernard Public Housing Development in New Orleans returned after Katrina to find that the city had closed up their homes. So they set up a village of tents and refused to heed the city's order to vacate the structures that the city insisted had been made "uninhabitable" by the storm.

In addition, the SSO protocols required that all three team members get out of the vehicle and venture forth on foot to systematically observe and code 20 percent of the census tract's total physical area. Also, whenever a team member encountered a problematic instance, such as determining how many residential units a particular structure hosted or whether or not someone was occupying a unit, the driver would stop the car and the team would discuss the issue. At the end of the discussion, the raters would record their impressions independently rather than merely reaching consensus.

Upon concluding the tract's SSO, the team would retire to a location outside of the tract, usually a restaurant, to independently clarify and refine their tallies and recorded observations. I then entered the data from the SSO forms into Microsoft Excel (which I later imported to SPSS for quantitative analysis). These became very important data in terms of analyzing the nature of social and physical life in the given tract, which ultimately factored into my supervisors' decisions regarding whether or not the neighborhoods surveyed before Katrina were sufficiently similar to the post-Katrina neighborhoods such that the original survey could be implemented again.

However you use SSO, it can produce valuable data. But as with every technique we've described in this book, you have to be very clear on why you're using it, how you're using it, and most important, how you intend to analyze the data for the purpose of addressing and/or answering your research question (or testing your hypotheses).

## CONCLUSION

In this chapter, we've presented and described several of the most common data production techniques implemented in ethnographic research. As we've already said, though, within the context of doing ethnography you can use not just these techniques but any/all of the other methods we've presented in this book (and many we haven't even covered here). Which techniques you use, and how you use them, is a matter best settled in reference to the nature of your study, the guiding research question, and the kind of data you need to make in order to answer the question(s) and hypotheses you've posed.

Ultimately your job as ethnographer is one of "translation" (derived from the original Latin term for "carry over"). You do all of this work to help an ignorant audience make sense of things that probably seem surprising to them but which are not surprising to the people among whom these things happen (i.e., your informants) and that are no longer surprising to you because you have spent time observing and developing an emic–etic understanding of them. Ethnographic analysis, the last stage in the process, involves translating cultural "occurrences" into a newly developed framework articulated in the vernacular of your peers within whatever discipline you're located.

The point (and challenge) of analysis is to figure out how the locals make meaning out of a particular phenomenon of interest to you, how they imbue it with meaning, and how the phenomenon, as an "instance," is part of a pattern that the cultural insiders may or may not discern. In the ideal case you will develop new ideas, insights that emerge from the multilateral interaction among your personal biography, the cultural context you're studying, and the theoretical frameworks elaborated within your discipline. Making sense of the data you have produced is no easy task. In the next chapter, we offer a look in more detail at observation as the single most important method for discovery, one that is used not only by ethnographers but in many types of research designs.

## Exercises

1. Pick a topic or activity that you know quite a bit about. Something simple, such as "getting ready for work (or school)" or "getting ready to go to a party." Now try your hand at asking a friend how he performs this activity. Make sure that you employ the different ways of asking questions presented in this chapter ("how," "compare and contrast," etc.). By asking this person the same basic question, in multiple ways, about the same basic activity, what did you learn?

2. Select an everyday situation, activity, venue, scene, something that you take for granted (e.g., people waiting at a bus stop). Go to the bus stop and spend an hour there. Manualize the behavior of people you see there. What kind of variation exists within this manual? Are there different manuals depending on what activity the person is engaging in (e.g., someone really waiting for a bus vs. someone just taking a break from walking vs. someone asking for spare change)?

3. At the same location chosen in Exercise 2, try your hand at network and geospatial mapping.

4. Ask a friend—someone you know very, very well—to let you shadow him/her for a whole day. This should be a pretty typical day, but one in which the friend goes places and/or does routine things for which you're ordinarily not present. Now, systematically shadow this friend and write up your notes. What did you learn about her? What did you learn about yourself? What did you learn about ethnography in general and/or the specific technique of shadowing?

## Key Terms

baiting or leading questions *249*
compare and contrast, especially as
    related to variability *249*
daily diary *253*
directed strategies and techniques
    for making data *247*

distribution check *248*
estimation *248*
etic *247*
ethnographic shadowing *255*
free-listing and pile-sorting *251*
informant mapping *256*

manualizing; culture as
    knowledge *251*
observer and participant roles *247*
processual interviewing *250*
sociometric grid mapping *252*
systematic social observation *258*

# IV

# Choices from the Methods Tool-Kit

Part IV introduces the reader to a wide range of methods and techniques that can be used to implement many different types of designs. They are not specific to the logic of any one of the designs but can be an effective part of several. For example, interviewing, observing, life narrative analysis, and focus groups could be used for ethnographies, social autopsies, and community-based participatory research. Visual methods can be used in these three strongly interactive designs, and also as "unobtrusive measures" for the analysis of cultural objects. Interviews, analysis of life narratives, and the use of software to analyze documents could also be used in historical-comparative analysis. Thus the chapters of this part provide a versatile set of tools that can be adapted and applied in markedly different designs.

# 17

# Observation, Participant-Observation, and Carnal Sociology

## OVERVIEW

In the previous section, we discussed in some detail the role of observation in ethnographic research. Earlier in the book, we mentioned observation as a tool for producing data, but to this point we have yet to elucidate the particularities of observation as a crucial data production tool in the methods tool-kit, or discuss its place in the epistemology of qualitative research. As we've said, observation is an essential component of ethnographic and community-based designs. Any design that calls for research into current conditions (rather than the past) usually includes some kind of observation. By the end of this chapter, you will have a firm enough grasp on observation to begin incorporating it into your own study.

## A SPECTRUM OF OBSERVATION: DEGREES OF SEPARATION

**Observation** and **participation** fall along a spectrum from observation without any real participation to **carnal sociology**, which entails full and embodied immersion in the milieu that is being studied.

### Unobtrusive Observation

In observation without participation, the observer is "outside of the action." The vantage point is external to the scene of interest. The activity is largely a visual and auditory one, not a kinetic and bodily experience. The observer sits quietly in a room looking and listening to what others are doing, stands near them in an outdoor setting, or hangs out with them trying to look as unobtrusive as possible. It's almost as if the observer pretends that she is invisible. The observer does not define herself as part of the group.

In the purest, least participatory form of observation, the observer sits behind a two-way mirror partition through which she can see the observed and the observed cannot see her, but only a dark reflective surface. This type of "extreme" one-wayness is rare in sociology, and almost all observation involves some degree of presence and interaction with the observed. Many textbooks characterize this mode of observation as "nonparticipant"; we disagree, however, because even when a researcher uses a two-way mirror to observe people in action, or sits quietly on a park bench watching passersby, she is still "in the picture." She is there, and she is "present" in the situation. Breathing and keeping a pulse alone make her a living creature in the scene. She may not be obtruding on the situation…but she is definitely there. Hence we prefer the term "unobtrusive" over "nonparticipant."

## "Obtrusive" Observation: A Range of Involvement

Participant-observation means that the researcher is at some level taking part in the activities of the individuals that are being observed, whether it is a sports event, a casual get-together in a bar, or an illegal activity such as packaging crack cocaine. The people being observed speak to the participant-observer and expect an answer. The participant-observer is present in the situation. Observing and participating are often associated with being "in the field." These research activities take place in a natural setting, natural in the sense that it has not been set up by the researcher.

## Carnal Participation and Observation

At the far extreme of the spectrum that runs from one-way observation to full participation, the "carnal sociologist" is fully engaged in the activities of the group and learns the **embodied knowledge** of the group, whether boxers or philosophers. The carnal sociologist not only interacts with the group but involves herself in all the behaviors in which the group engages and tries to experience what they are experiencing, using her entire body to do so. It is "carnal" in the sense of experienced in the flesh, as Loïc Wacquant has named it (2004, 2009). The researcher acquired embodied knowledge by fully participating in a practice. This research practice is closely linked to the theories of Pierre Bourdieu and to his concept of **habitus**, or embodied knowledge. All social practice and knowledge has a physical component, and we cannot claim to understand other people's cognition and views unless we have shared their embodied experiences, whether these are a homemaker's moves with a broom, a scholar's long hours at a library desk, or a boxer's moments in the gym and the ring.

**MONEY-TRADERS**    Richard Widick engaged in trading in the options exchange in San Francisco. Here is his description of this research (2003: 680):

> [The] embodied performance of trading is the object of my investigation. . . . I spent two years working on the options floor in the 1980s, during which time I worked and lived through an endless series of trades, stopping just short of becoming a trader and making floor trading my own way of life. In the 1990s, I returned to the trading pits and found them largely unchanged; their intensity, camaraderie, masculinity, and technology still told of a world apart…

He goes on to observe the fact that the traders are predominantly white men. The world of the pits is intense and physical and the most successful traders have absorbed a practical logic so that they do not have to review consciously the rules of trading. Widick does not analyze the exclusion of men of color, but he makes it clear that the pits are almost as masculine a space as the football field or the boxing ring. Globalization and technological innovation have shaped the logic of trading such that traders are at the nodes of global information networks with market conditions that change by the minute, although the actual trades were negotiated face to face in the pits.

Widick describes this physical experience (2003: 699) in a style of prose one rarely encounters in standard sociological texts but which has become the norm in works of carnal social science:

> The implosion of global information in the face to face locale helps make inhabiting the trading crowd an intense bodily practice. The pits are alive with a physical and psychological intersubjectivity. Bodies are held in rigid attention to electronically displayed economic indicators, pressing against each other in collective anticipation. An amplified excitement is palpable as the turbulent crowds sense the next tick of a stock. The smells of sweat and breath and ink and coffee texture these interludes….Waiting. Watching for a sign of recognition by the other, a bit of news, some action. Who will be the next to trade? How will the market move?…

**CLUB DANCING**    A similar entry into the habitus associated with a practice was accomplished by Black Hawk Hancock when he entered the Chicago dance scene, not only the Lindy Hop but also Steppin' an African American dance style. Entering the world of Steppin'—the clubs where it is danced on the South Side—meant entering a world in which whites were a minority (Hancock 2005, 2007). The presence of Black Hawk and his partner (both white) and their competence as Steppin' dancers produced reactions among the other guests which illuminated the construction of whiteness and blackness as they saw the unsettling of the taken-for-granted links between physical appearance and bodily knowledge, the **embodied competence** of Steppin.

The observer's choice of where to place himself or herself on this spectrum from peering through the one-way glass to participating in an embodied carnal experience has major consequences for the research and for the type of interpretation and conclusions that can emerge from the study.

## CHOOSING CARNAL SOCIOLOGY

The researcher often begins a study with a conscious choice where the research will fall along the spectrum from observation to "carnal sociology." The choice can be made on the basis of many considerations. One of them is of course the goals of the research. If the research is focused on an embodied skill or practice, participation may be necessary. Many researchers might argue that it is hard to understand the lives of boxers if a person has never been in the ring—or never participated in any contact sport whatsoever.

### The "Goodness of Fit" between Observer and Observed

The characteristics of the observer and the observed impinge on the choice to participate or to observe with little participation. A researcher who is likely to be seen as completely different from the observed is more likely to opt for observation with little participation. For example, an elderly woman studying young men in a boxing gym might learn much about their culture as a relatively detached observer, but would probably have neither a pleasant nor a productive experience if she decided to spar with them. She is more likely to look, chat, and interview than to enter the ring in boxing gear and start throwing and taking punches.

Race-ethnicity, class, age, gender, sexual orientation, level of education, occupational experience, and ways of speaking and acting can all contribute to situations in which observation appears to be a wiser or certainly easier choice than full participation; and if the observer and the observed are different in all of these respects, participation can be very difficult. The researcher will be under constant pressure to explain their incongruous presence. Gender and race (as a status defined by visible markers such as skin tone) appear to be identities that are difficult to hide and hence make full participation difficult; but speech patterns, diction, clothing and body language are often also noticeable as identity markers that are difficult to conceal. "Passing" across ethnic and class lines is difficult for many people. Yet the example of Hancock and his Steppin' experience suggest that a disruption that is brought about by carnal, embodied research can be very productive in revealing the "taken-for-granted" rules of everyday life, in this case, assumptions about "race," the ability to dance, and the nature and "naturalness" of bodily capital.

## Research Ethics and IRB Restrictions

A second influence on the choice of how much to participate in the experience being researched is the code of ethics that governs social science research. The formula of total participation can add unacceptable levels of deception to the research if the researcher blends completely into the environment she is studying and the individuals and groups under observation do not realize that they have become research subjects. We have already discussed the issue that qualitative and ethnographic research often includes this element of deception. The researcher who lives in a community and participates in its full round of life is in fact conducting research without having initially or continuously identified himself as a researcher; nor did the researcher in this case obtain the consent of all of the observed individuals.

Not all participant-observation and "carnal sociology" are deceptive in this regard, however. For example, when Loïc Wacquant conducted a study of a boxing gym on the South Side of Chicago, he did not try to disguise his identity as a Frenchman among Americans, a white man among African American men, or a university student and intellectual among working-class people. He made no effort to deceive his research subjects about who he was, although he did learn to box and took part in the Golden Gloves tournament.

## ENTRY AND GUIDES

As pointed out in the previous section on ethnography, the problem of **entry** is the leading challenge in observational methods. For all but the simplest observations in public places, the researcher has to enter a **milieu**—often an organization or a residential space such as a neighborhood or a village with its preexisting social ties. These are the concrete places and groups that correspond to those nebulous and conceptual terms "institution" and "community." When we study institutions such as higher education, the penal system, law enforcement, or the health care system, we have to enter organizations such as a specific college, prison, police station, or hospital. When we study "communities" we have to live in and interact with the residents of a specific neighborhood. "Institutions" and "communities" cannot be studied in the abstract, only in their specific instances.

Social networks and markets are also conceptual entities that are studied by observing and engaging in interaction in specific contexts. They may have less precise boundaries than an organization or a residential area, but they too must be observed at specific times, places, and by seeing a set of actions and interactions.

If we do not keep these specifics in mind, we can easily fall into a *reified* way of thinking about society and institutions, talking about them as "things" that exist apart from the actions and interactions of human beings. Sometimes abstractions such as "culture" or "institution" are useful, but we want to introduce these terms very carefully and not begin our observations at this point.

## Entry

Entry strategies vary along a spectrum from highly sponsored to entirely self-arranged. In turn, the organizations and spaces that we want to enter also fall along a continuum from very open to completely closed. Common sense tells us that we can enter a closed space or organization only with some degree of sponsorship, but apart from this obvious fact, there are a good many choices to be made about entry arrangements.

Every social milieu has its **gatekeepers**—individuals who control entry and access. In some settings, gatekeeping is entirely informal. If you want to become part of a group of neighbors who chat across the backyard fence and drop in on each others' barbecues, there are no formal gatekeepers; access is a matter of interacting sociably in such a way that you become part of the group and get invited to barbecues. At the other extreme, gatekeeping is formal and its roles are highly elaborated in many organizations such as prisons, corporations, and the faculty of university departments. It is very difficult to just "hang out" in a prison and become part of a group of prison inmates (Wacquant 2002). The spaces are physically demarcated, and the roles are clearly defined, making penetration into the organization and any specific group within it quite difficult. It is possible to enter only with the explicit consent of gatekeepers who approve contacts with other participants in the milieu. Entering these types of milieus is virtually impossible without sponsorship and support from a large number of gatekeepers.

**AN EXAMPLE OF SPONSORED ENTRY**     In highly **sponsored entry**, persons with authority both inside and outside of the site agree to place the researcher into the setting and support her presence. For example, when she was a grad student, Roberta Garner was given the opportunity to be an observer of an on-campus tutoring project for male low-income high-school students who had been identified as "underachievers." The project organizers hoped to raise the educational aspirations and attainment of the young men by exposing them to a more exciting and varied set of experiences than was available at their public high school.

Roberta was assigned to accompany the group with its college student tutors through the program's round of activities that included jazz concerts, meals in the university cafeteria, and earnest discussions of John Reed's book about the Russian Revolution, *Ten Days that Shook the World*. Her presence was formally recognized and in fact part of her role was to contribute to a qualitative evaluation of the tutoring project. Her faculty advisor had prearranged her role with the project organizers. There was no doubt about her role—she was a project observer. Although she interacted with the young men and their tutors in a friendly, informal way, she did not in any sense enter their world as a full participant, but remained an observer. This role gave her some privileges—she was able to take notes at any time—and it also created a distance between her and the participants, reinforcing the distance that already existed due to gender, age (she was older), race (she is white, the young men were predominantly African American), class (she was a middle-class grad student), and education.

The advantages of sponsorship are obvious: The observer is placed in the organization, formal entry is gained easily, and the role is clearly defined. The disadvantages are subtler: A social distance is established between the observer and the observed. The observer carries the "stamp of approval" of authority figures both within and outside of the organization, and participants will be less likely to voice critical opinions to him. The "underlife of the institution" (to use Erving Goffman's phrase) will be kept hidden.

Sponsorship can be informal, resulting in a less evident observer role and a less clearly defined reason for the observer's presence. For example, a friend may introduce the observer to individuals in the neighborhood or organization. The contact is spontaneous and open, but the researcher still has the comfortable feeling that "someone is looking out for her" and will help her to meet people and avoid missteps. An influential person in an organization may help the researcher to make contacts within the organization and even though an official observer role is not defined (as in fully sponsored entry), doors are opened on an informal basis. For example, Loïc Wacquant was introduced to the Woodlawn boxing gym by a friend—and said he wanted to learn how to box.

At the far end of the spectrum of entry, in the least formalized situation, the researcher simply enters the field site unannounced and without any personal or organizational contacts. This type of entry is virtually impossible in an organizational or institutional context and suggests that the inhabitants of the milieu have only a low degree of control over their own space. Imagine entering a corporation, university dean's office, or government agency and just "hanging out" in its space for any length of time! One of the most dramatic accounts of completely unsponsored entry is afforded by Ruth Horowitz's story (1983) of her first contact with gang members in a Latino neighborhood in Chicago. She just sat in a park until she had an opportunity to return a ball that had rolled her way and provided an opening for a conversation with one of the Lions, the local gang.

These informal self-arranged entries are virtually impossible when the unit of analysis is a wealthy or powerful organization rather than a relatively weak and porous one (such as a boxing gym in a poor neighborhood). It would be very difficult to just "show up" in the headquarters of a corporation and begin to socialize with the CEO and the board of directors. These barriers are closely related to Morris Janowitz's observation (quoted in Chapter 5) that it is easy to carry out research on the poor and powerless and difficult to do so on the rich and powerful.

## The Guide, Key Informants, and Research Bargains

Whatever the initial form of entry, many researchers quickly acquire a **guide**, a participant in the milieu who takes it upon himself or herself to "show the ropes" to the observer, help him meet other participants, and interpret the observations. The guide is both essential to the research and a major source of error! She or he is essential because only the guide can open key doors and explain unfamiliar actions; but he or she can also mislead the researcher both intentionally and unintentionally.

Motivations for acting as guide are varied, and the researcher must discern these in order to make sense of what the guide says. A few examples will illustrate the issues:

- The guide may be motivated by advantages to be gained from acting as a cultural broker. The guide plans to exchange information about and access to the milieu for the researcher's information and access to organizations and people with whom the researcher is connected.
- The guide may be genuinely interested in the research and hope to further a scientific understanding of the community.
- The guide may be motivated by specific material benefits, such as money, access to transportation, or help in obtaining resources.
- The guide is motivated by the desire to provide a correct interpretation to the observer for what is observed. He or she want to make sure that the researcher obtains the "right information" and forms the "right interpretation" of the research situation, and to preempt or prevent interpretations that might be damaging, revealing, or disrespectful to the community or organization. For instance, a gang leader may want the researcher to see the gang as a family whose members are fiercely committed to each other and to the neighborhood—and not to

see it as an enterprise in which rank-and-file members are exploited and the neighborhood rendered uninviting to legitimate businesses. This self-designated interpretive role can be extremely damaging to the research.

- In some cases, the guide may even be an individual who has the specialized role of dealing with the nosy outsider. In a formal organization, this role may be formal—the "media relations" person or "community relations" staffer are formal roles for professional guides whose responsibility it is to make sure that outsiders are steered to the right contacts and information.
- The guide may be a disgruntled group member who wants to use the researcher as a spokesperson for negative and critical views of the group or organization. This person can provide valuable information, but his views should not be taken as the only information available.
- The guide may be an "outsider within," a person who, despite enjoying technical membership in the group, is at the same time marginalized by the group and desperately in search of a friend. Although harmless in terms of interpretation of data, her attention can have a negative impact on the researcher's ability to meet more central and effective group members and can result in the researcher herself remaining marginal to the milieu.

Each of these motivations carries with it risks for the research, but of these the most serious are the ones caused by the guide who wants the researcher to observe only through "rose colored glasses." This individual will almost certainly prevent the researcher from meeting people or observing activities that would lead to critical interpretations. Unlike the disgruntled or marginalized individual, this guide has the social power and the interpretive resources to structure the experiences of the researcher and to tilt the entire observation.

What practical advice can we give to the neophyte researcher? One obvious, useful step is to cultivate more than one guide, to build relationships with several members of the group or organization. In a community, it is a good idea to explore a range of community organizations and meet representatives of each. A single guide—no matter how helpful and well-intentioned—does not provide a full range of information about a community or organization. In formal settings, or settings such as a community that includes several formal organizations, the researcher can openly and forthrightly state that she would like to meet a wider range of people, explaining to the guide that "balance" is a criterion or that it is necessary to "talk to different sides." Most people are familiar with the canons of modern journalism that emphasize balanced reporting, and they will be inclined to accept this standard as part of the research process. Make sure that the guide is not the same person who comes up with the individuals from "the other side." You must seek them out yourself.

For example, Pattillo (2008) made every effort to learn about both sides in the controversy over the placement of public housing in a gentrifying neighborhood in Chicago. She went to meetings, interviewed, and read documents that represented both the "for" and the "against" positions of residents.

If the setting is an informal one, it may be more difficult to find individuals with viewpoints different from the guides or willing to express these viewpoints. Similarly if the setting is a highly closed one—such as a corporation or a gang—it may be hard to find dissenting views or to avoid the perspective of your guide.

Floyd Mann (1970) (citing Merton) suggests "dual" or even "multiple" entry. The observer should contact both formal and informal leaders and members of an organization at lower ranks. Each of these will provide somewhat different perspectives on the organization, and an accurate picture emerges only with these multiple viewpoints.

**KEY INFORMANTS**    A different way of thinking about guides is to focus on **key informants**. The wording is a signal that this approach is seen as more under the control of the researcher and more focused on specific information rather than an all-around introduction to a social milieu. The guide is often self-appointed, manages the researcher's whole round of contacts with individuals and groups in the milieu, and offers interpretations of what is seen and heard by the researcher. The "key informant" provides information that the researcher wants to obtain. It is a more limited role than that of the guide and can inherently be held by many different individuals. "Informant" has an unfortunate resonance with the terms "police informants" and "informers" so it carries the connotation that the informant may be revealing information that the group does not want exposed to an outsider.

Whether interaction is with one or more guides or with "key informants," the observer enters into "research bargains" engaging in reciprocal or mutually advantageous relationships.

## Recording Observation and Participation: Field Notes and Analytic Memos

Observation as a method requires development of the techniques for writing **field notes**. Field notes are essential to the research. In Chapter 15, we discussed at great length the writing of field notes. Here, however, we offer a different though compatible perspective on writing notes when you're doing observation as part of a study that is not entirely (or even remotely) ethnographic.

Based on Schatzman and Strauss's (1973) classic guide to field research, we suggest two types of notes: descriptive notes and analytic memos. **Descriptive notes** convey information and summarize observations. **Analytic memos** begin the work of interpreting the observations and link them to theories and research questions.

**DESCRIPTIVE NOTES (DNS)**    The first step in creating field notes is to write descriptions of what has been seen and heard in the field situation. Observation that is not recorded in field notes is almost worthless; memory will fail or play tricks on the researcher. You can try a very simple exercise of observing in the campus cafeteria for a few minutes on three separate occasions. Sit quietly at a table and look and listen to your surroundings. On one of these occasions write up your notes several hours after your observation; in the second instance, write them immediately afterward; and for the third observation, write the notes while you are observing.

It makes a difference which order you carry out these three ways of recording your notes (writing the notes during observation will sensitize you to the amount of information you can record and may improve your retention in delayed writing), but whichever way you do it, if you wait several hours to write the notes, you will almost certainly have lost a lot of information. Your notes will become devoid of details (what was that guy wearing? How many people were at the table near the TV?). Characterizations of people will become reduced to very simple demographic categories ("Asian," "woman," etc.) without nuance, and what people said will become increasingly paraphrased and different from their actual words.

Of course, there are situations in which you cannot take notes while you are observing. If you are interacting with your research subjects it would probably be awkward. Some contexts—such as religious services, funerals, or festive meals—preclude scribbling in a notebook. You have to wait to get home to write the notes.

Notes can vary in the voice and stance of the researcher. At one extreme—fairly common in observational research—the notes are written as if the observer were external, almost as if she were watching through the one-way glass. She keeps herself and her actions largely out of the notes, unless to indicate that she asked a question or engaged in interaction of some type.

At the other and much less common extreme, the notes are primarily about the self of the observer, about his feelings, behaviors, and responses to the situation. This information is not irrelevant to the research, but it is probably best kept in a separate set of notes that might be called "self-notes" to record actions and feelings of the researcher. These self-notes may overlap **"method" notes**, in which the researcher records actions closely related to the research and keeps track of choices that were made in the field situation.

The descriptive notes should be recorded in a way that allows them to be sorted by different criteria and grouped together according to more than one classification system. In the past, the simplest way to accomplish this goal was to keep them on index cards, and this remains an excellent technique when you do not have access to a computer in the field or cannot get around to typing them for some time. Alternatively, you can put each descriptive note on a sheet of paper and keep the set in a loose-leaf binder. The advantage of computerized notes is that it facilitates textual analysis, the kinds of coding and categorization involved in grounded theory.

Each descriptive note can have several key word labels, as well as its time–date–place tag. The key word labels can be color coded—written or underlined with colored pencils or color-highlighted on the computer. For example, let's say we observed an incident in the halls of the high school which we are studying, in which we noticed a teacher encountering a couple of students and telling one of them to turn his T-shirt inside out so that the words "wish you were beer" could not be seen or read. We can label this description as related to clothing, and it can also be labeled as related to gender, cliques, informal culture, alcohol use attitudes, rebellious humor, and teacher reaction to student behavior.

Later, when we write analytic memos and later yet, sections of our research report, this single DN can be pulled together with others that share related tags. For example, we might want to write an analytic memo that discusses all the forms of *rebellion* in the high school, with emphasis on the "resistance of the weak"—relatively harmless, humorous jabs at authority. The *gender* tag on the DN would allow us to pull this incident together with other situations that show how boys and girls have different ways of expressing their feelings about school and teen life. Finally, the *authority* tag would allow us to group this relatively minor incident with more serious confrontations between students and adult authority figures.

As the DNs are entered into computerized files, these tags of course can be added to the notes, and the material is easily called up with a Search/Find command. Axial coding—coding to establish relationships among themes and topics and to identify contexts—is facilitated by entering the DN into computerized files.

## Choices about Recording: Descriptive Notes

It is not always easy to draw the line between the descriptive notes and the analytic memos. Because we are not cameras, our field notes will always have an interpretive tilt from the very start. We cannot record everything, so we are constantly making selections of what is important to record and remember. That table in the corner under the TV—does it matter what racial category you think you can assign to the individuals? Do you want to record their gender? Are their clothes worth noting? Do you need to count how many people were sitting at the table? Is the TV program playing above their heads part of what needs to be put in your descriptive notes? Do you care what food they have on their plates? Notice how your decisions to record these simple visible details are already choices associated with your research questions and the interpretive frameworks you are planning to use.

Some of these choices seem embedded in the common sense of our times or in the traditions of sociology (which overlap each other but are not identical). To record in a campus cafeteria and not note the gender or racial categories that people appear to be in would seem strange in terms of the expectations of both the discipline and our society. Sociologists think these characteristics are important because the general public thinks they matter.

Recording people's class generally seems far more difficult than identifying their gender or race. And here sociology and popular opinion part ways; sociologists place a strong emphasis on social class, while the general public gives it less attention, beyond a crude categorization of "rich," "poor," and "middle class." However, within local contexts, much finer distinctions of class and SES may be made with the use of status markers associated with consumption, such as the kind of cars individuals drive, brands of clothing and accessories, and addresses. The local status hierarchies are not well synchronized with the national class structure, however, as the following experience illustrates. Roberta asked a class if they thought it was easy to tell an individual's social class, and two women from Chicago inner-city (predominantly Latino and white) high schools said that at their schools wearing necklaces with a name spelled out in gold letters was a sign of having a lot of money; whereupon a woman from a very wealthy Northshore lakefront suburb made a little face and said, "that would hardly identify someone as upper class in *my* community."

Looking and listening to note an individual's ethnicity within the broad racial categories that Americans like to use is difficult. Beyond the first generation of immigrants, most people do not have accents that convey national origins, and visible signs of ethnicity are very confusing and complicated. A hundred years ago, many ethnic and national-origin categories were believed to be races and to be physically distinguishable; but few people would make that claim today. As you make notes in the cafeteria, can you distinguish Laotian Americans from Vietnamese Americans? Second-generation Polish Americans from descendents of Czech immigrants? Do these distinctions still matter, and if so, in which contexts?

Most ethnic categorization is far more complicated than we tend to assume. Roberta was embarrassed when a student she had assumed to be Latina turned out to have one parent who immigrated to the United States from Iran. An ethnically diverse class of students in Chicago saw a photograph of six young Roma-Hungarians and guessed that they are "Latinos, but not from Mexico—maybe Argentine." French students—not baseball fans—were quite puzzled by a photograph of White Sox manager Ozzie Guillen (whose picture they had never seen before) and were not able to identify his ethnicity and national origin.

## The Analytic Memo: A Device for Making Sense of Notes

A second major type of writing is the analytic memo. This is a note in which the researcher begins the process of interpretation. It bridges the gap between detailed concrete descriptions and more theoretical and analytical views of the field situation.

AMs have two goals. One is to take the step from description to interpretation. The description of the "the facts" is already interpretive and analytic because a selection has been made from the totality of what can be observed. Not everything is recorded in the descriptive notes. But the AMs are interpretive not only by selection and omission from the observed totality but also by explicitly adding ideas. In the AM the researcher begins to connect descriptions to research questions. Writing AMs is a way to focus observations on the goal of answering the research questions.

The second purpose of the analytic memo is to begin linking the observed descriptive details to theory. For example, in an observation-based exercise, a student of ours observed a family talking about gender roles as they sat around the dining room table during a weekend dinner (Roman 2009). The descriptive memos—rendered as "strips" or in a similar format—record what each person said about the roles and activities of men and women and also noted the gestures and facial expressions that accompanied the remarks. The DNs also included information about the individuals—their ages, relationships to each other, occupations, and level of education.

The AMs begin to interpret the interaction, linked the observed material to concepts such as negotiation, gender discourse, gender roles, framing practices, and social change. In this case the interpretation and concepts emerged from feminist theory and symbolic interactionist theory. What was new in this observation was not the theory used in the analysis, but the situation itself. The individuals interacting were young, middle-class, and well-educated, of Puerto Rican origin but two generations removed from migration from the island to the mainland. What was being negotiated was not a simple "traditional to modern" or "Hispanic to Anglo" gender-role shift, but a much more complicated and postmodern reassessment of gender and culture. "Culture" itself was very much in play, as the individuals recognized multiple cultural heritages—U.S.- American, Anglo-American, Hispanic-American, and Puerto Rican, each one of which is itself unstable and changing in terms of gender roles. The fact that the women are college educated and hold professional and managerial jobs was a key element in the situation. The observation gives us insight into the contemporary negotiation of gender roles in a setting where cultures are not seen as static traditions but as layered, overlapping, and changeable frames of reference. The AMs provide the beginnings of interpretations. They can consist of jotted phrases and ideas which are elaborated in the research report.

## HOWARD BECKER'S TIPS FOR IMPROVING OBJECTIVITY AND PLAUSIBILITY

Here, we can return to the issues we raised in Chapter 3 on the scientific method in qualitative research. Becker (1970) provides a list of activities that can help to make observation grounded in systematic ways to improve the objectivity and plausibility of observation.

### Observable Indicators

First, one should consider exactly how observable indicators are related to (and possibly tell stories about) the less observable underlying phenomena in which we are interested. Often norms are not voiced by members of the group; even identifying these norms is tabooed, an "elephant in the room." But we can infer these norms from the behaviors of group members, their refraining from mentioning certain situations, or even from their *non*engagement in certain behaviors (i.e., what they don't do can be just as telling as what they do).

### Credibility of Informants

Second, we can think about the credibility of informants and use observational clues to address this issue. We can see how others react to the informant and we can test information from a specific informant against information that we collect through observation or from interviews with others.

## Volunteered and Spontaneous Sharing of Information versus Directed Information: A Clue to the Salience of Concerns

Third, Becker suggests that whether information is volunteered or gathered through a directed statement (one directed by the researcher) is a clue to the focal concerns of the group or milieu which we are studying—to the salience of certain themes or values. For example, students in a particular major may speak frequently and spontaneously about the chance to make a lot of money that they believe they will enjoy after college graduation—or they may address their financial prospects only when they are asked about the topic. This difference is related to Becker's belief that observation "trumps" interviewing, that it provides more objective information about the values and focal concerns of a group.

By the same token, however, information that is not volunteered but only emerges in interviews or in response to questions can be very useful as a clue that points to taboos.

## Noting the Frequency and Distribution of Phenomena

Finally, Becker encourages observers to make a note of the frequency and distribution of phenomena. Although qualitative research means restraint in the quantification of information it does not completely preclude it. Becker suggests noting information such as whether every member or no member or some intermediate proportion of members volunteered a particular piece of information or came up with it in response to questions; and whether all, none, or some proportion of members engaged in behavior that supported a conclusion about the milieu.

For example, observing the council of department chairs and the dean in a college of liberal arts and sciences within a comprehensive university, one might conclude that at any given council meeting only about 10 people out of the 40 or so present make any remarks of any kind and that most of these 8–10 people make remarks at each monthly meeting, while others participate never or only rarely. The observer might note over the course of the nine monthly meetings during the academic year that consistent "talkers" are the chairs of philosophy, history, religious studies, sociology, and international studies, while chairs of science departments almost never say anything.

The observer might also note that the council never votes on any motion or measure, nor does any member call for a vote as a decision-making procedure. This type of note of frequency and distribution of remarks could be used to support the interpretation that this body is not a very active site of either contention or collective decision making. One could conclude that it is primarily a forum for announcements from the dean, including statements of policies decided by the provost and transmitted through the dean, and that it is not a council in the usual sense of a deliberative body engaged in discussion or proactive planning of policies. Notice how these observations are not based on a very precise level of quantification but "the observer takes a cue from...statistical colleagues" (Becker 1970b: 194) and gives a rough sense of proportions (about 10 out of 40 people present speak during the meeting; a third of the time is used for formal reports; the dean makes announcements and states his position for about a third of the time) and frequencies (a vote is never taken) (Becker 1970b: 194).

These relatively rough quantifications of proportions and frequencies are enough to give the reader a strong sense of how meeting time is used and how this council of chairs operates at this institution, as well as insights into norms and taboos; and these observations could then complement interviews about organizational decision making and culture at this institution.

# FIRST STEPS: MAPPING SPACE, IDENTIFYING ICONS, RECORDING TIME

An excellent way to begin observing is **spatial mapping** and creation of a **time schedule**, charting the space of your research site and recording the daily and weekly round of life. You can sketch a small map of the space, whether it is an office suite or a neighborhood. The location of activities is a good guide to their cultural meaning and importance. For example, in organizations, private offices with windows are signals that the individual enjoys a position of authority. In a neighborhood, the size and style of homes signal class and social status. In a doctor's office or a tattoo parlor, the customers/patients/clients may sit in a waiting area that is clearly demarcated from the spaces where the practitioners do their work. There may be physical barriers, such as the office area of the receptionist, that mark the distinction between the customers' space and the professionals' work area.

Similarly, government offices and public agencies create spaces for individuals who are waiting to be called up to a counter where they can interact with public employees. There may be a series of waiting rooms, each one taking the individual closer to the ultimate goal of having a document issued. Court buildings are elaborately spatially organized, with each space having its own meaning and conditions of access, from the metal detectors at the entrance to the jury assembly room to the court rooms, the judges' chambers, and the direct passageways to the jail (Bogira 2005). The spatial organization reflects the roles and the disparities in power and control over one's situation.

Although Wacquant does not provide a map of the boxing gym in which he practiced carnal sociology, he describes it in vivid detail. Wacquant not only describes the rooms and the furnishings, he also takes us immediately into the iconography of boxing, the images of Mike Tyson, Muhammad Ali, Leon Spinks, Sugar Ray Leonard, American flags, and local fighters that represent the heroes and values of the "sweet science" as practiced on the Southside of Chicago. Here, the description of the physical space overlaps the analysis of cultural artifacts, the posters and photographs that express ideals and enhance sociability among the fighters.

In the theoretical tradition of critically analyzing misrecognition, Wacquant (2004) points out that the images he saw on the walls convey a representation of continuity between the champions and the local fighters and the illusion of a "ladder of mobility" that can lead from the gym to the top of the pugilistic hierarchy:

> This visual "syntagm," this physical proximity [between the images of the champions and notices of regional fights], suggests an association, a quasi-genealogical link between the local pugs, who fight for negligible purses on regional cards, and the super-champions who divide up among themselves the fabulous fees of the prestigious events televised from Las Vegas and Atlantic City...This seemingly innocuous mural iconography...upholds the belief in an ideal by definition inaccessible to virtually all boxers and contributes to maintaining the illusion of a continuous "ladder of mobility," leading step by step from the base to the summit of the pugilistic pyramid—when everything that transpires of the social and economic organization of professional boxing indicates rather that there is discontinuity, that the networks that manage the business of bruising are less like "ladders" than strongly segmented networks, access to which is tightly controlled by those who possess the specific social capital. (2004: 35–36)

A parallel process of observation can be creation of a time schedule for the milieu that is being studied. The institution, neighborhood, community, or organization has an overall schedule or rhythm and within this larger framework, specific roles or individuals have their own schedules. For example, the boss may arrive later than others. As Widick remarked in the selection about trading earlier in the chapter, the pace of trading is frantic, and this intensity is a major characteristic of the milieu and becomes an integral, embodied aspect of the individuals in it.

The pace of a university day, week, term, and academic year create a rhythm of professors' lives that is often at odds with those of people who work 9 to 5. The professor appears to work little, because she is in class only a few hours a week and makes an appearance for office hours only occasionally. In an urban neighborhood, each day has its rhythm. In the early morning hours, the homeless have to leave shelters and begin their quest for safety, warmth, and a minimal income; later office workers head for public transportation to get to their offices by nine o'clock; in the later morning, moms appear with kids on their way to playgrounds and stores begin to open. After the workday, the streets fill with young people heading to restaurants and clubs; and a "night shift" left to police, "shady characters," and "angel-headed hipsters looking for a fix" may be evident between bar-closing time and dawn.

In some organizations, the observer can follow the time schedule of the organization—the round of activities—by **shadowing** individuals, following them through their daily activities and moving with them through different spaces and interactions. Obviously "shadowing" requires the consent and support of the individual and the organization as a whole. Police "ride alongs" are a well-documented type of shadowing.

The round of life is recorded in a special type of descriptive note, the **time chart**. Often more than one time chart has to be created to capture the schedules of people with different types of roles as well as variation among days of the week or seasons. Some enterprises have a highly seasonal character—farming and university teaching—for instance, while others are the same throughout the year.

The creation of maps and time charts is a good way to begin interaction in the setting. Creating the maps and time charts is also a good way to begin understanding the organization or neighborhood and asking relatively simple, concrete questions about it, the "how" questions that we discussed in Chapter 16. But be aware that sometimes this activity will take you directly into sensitive matters—Who got the window office? Why is Professor X never in the office? Why are there so many empty stores on Main Street? These apparently innocent questions of the newcomer can lead quickly into revelations about conflicts and dysfunctions in the setting.

## A SUMMARY OF PRACTICAL TIPS

1. Write field notes as soon as possible after the observation and during it if it is possible to do so politely and unobtrusively (see Emerson et al. 1995, for more on field notes).
2. A useful way to record information is writing **strips**, which are written like segments of a play or screenplay, showing who spoke, what they said (as close to verbatim as possible) and what gestures, actions, and facial expressions accompanied the words. Also note the characteristics of the setting (furniture, food, clothing, etc.) and basic characteristics of the individuals (age, gender, race-ethnicity, and if possible, occupation, education, and a guess about class and income). If you are in doubt what to record, let your RQs be your guide for making a selection. All DNs should be identified by date, time, and place; other tags will depend on what you think you may use the material for—and could in any case be added later as you review your notes.
3. Write AMs to link the descriptive notes to your research questions and to theories. Analytic memos do not have to be written as frequently as the DNs. They can group together material

from several DNs; indicate which DNs have been grouped together by date, time, and place. AMs should always be dated.

4. You can write AMs that create different groupings of the DN material, and you can color the DNs to link them to different AMs.

At the very least, keep a **fieldwork log** in which every day a note is made of what, when, and where observations were made, who was observed, and a phrase or two is used to record major developments of the day. But a log of this type will be inadequate for recalling major descriptive detail; for this you will need to consult the accompanying field notes.

## CONCLUSION

Observation is a very important and useful tool for doing qualitative research and a component of many types of designs. Doing it well takes a substantial investment of time and energy. As with most other activities that demand a blend of skill and style, becoming an adept social observer of human behavior takes practice. This chapter has given you a good foundation for beginning to think about how you can incorporate observation into your research designs. By now you should be able to articulate exactly how and why observation is an appropriate tool to use in your project (or, alternatively, why it's not an appropriate tool for your study).

## Exercises

1. Short observation exercise. Observe in a public place such as a park, shopping mall, or campus cafeteria for about an hour. Try to take notes as you observe. What do you see and hear? What do you think is important to include in your notes?

2. Can you organize your notes as "strips" that look like little segments of a screenplay? What are some of the problems you encounter in doing this?

3. Coordinate a "dual observation" outing with a friend, roommate, or fellow student. Both of you should go to the same place and spend the same amount of time doing the observation. You should be unobtrusive. Be sure to occupy different vantage points on the central venue of activity. After you have observed and taken notes for a short period, type them up and then compare your notes. How are they similar? How are they different? What do the similarities and differences reveal about the "scene" you both observed? What do they say about the role of the observer's perception in the making of data on the basis of observation?

## Key Terms

# Interviewing

## OVERVIEW

Interviewing is a versatile method amenable to a wide range of uses. It's one of the most commonly used tools in the methods toolbox, and it can be used in quantitative, qualitative, and ethnographic strategies and designs. The main exceptions, as we've already mentioned, are historical-comparative research—where the cases are typically societies of long ago—and designs that are entirely unobtrusive and based on the analysis of documents and cultural artifacts. You can use the interview to gain insight into the views and opinions of individuals or groups, to obtain information about practices and technical know-how, to collect life narratives and oral histories, and/or to comprehend organizational and movement ideologies. In this chapter, we provide some background information on "the interview" as a research method, or tool, describe the different kinds of interview, and give you practical guidelines and tips on how to conduct interviews in your own research study.

## BACKGROUND AND ORIENTATIONS

Our central objective when conducting an interview is to understand the meanings, ideas, opinions, and perspectives of the interviewees, the research subjects who are the actors in the situation we're studying. We also may hope to acquire insight into their actual *behaviors*, but we exercise caution (and skepticism) on this front, for we know and must always assume that when interviewees describe their behaviors, they're filtering the descriptions through **frames** and intentions that generally remain concealed from the researcher's view. In other words, people *always* give a "biased" account of the things they do and have done. In saying this, we don't mean to assert that all people are liars and cheats. However, when describing our actions—things we've done or intend to do—all of us tend to "frame" our words to suit our interests, whatever those interests may be.

Despite the ever-present veneer of self-interest that gives a certain gloss to the things people say, the interview is a valuable tool for obtaining insight into whatever research topic you've chosen. It's particularly valuable if, by use of other tools, you can discern the frames and filters that your interviewees appear to be using. Indeed, one indicator that your subjects share a common culture or societal grouping is that they all tend to use the same sorts of frames and filters (though their use of them may vary). Information collected in an interview is different from information that we gather ourselves as an informed observer, information such as the observations recorded in our field notes. It's advisable to assume that there's a gap, sometimes quite large, between what people do and what they *say* they do. So as valuable as it is, the interview shouldn't be the only basket into which you put all of your research eggs.

As with every other method, we advise that you use the interview in a critically self-conscious way, that you continually question not just the substance it yields but also the method itself. This is a matter of "good science"—the never-ending exercise of what we earlier termed "enlightened skepticism." This idea of critically reflecting on the methods we're using to collect data brings us to a discussion of the prevailing orientations that researchers adopt vis-à-vis the interview.

## Orientations toward Interviewing

In recent years, feminist and postmodernist scholars have precipitated a critical discourse around "the interview" as a research method. This discussion has yielded, among other things, a kind of "interview typology," a way of distinguishing among three prevailing **orientations toward interviewing: positivist, romantic, and postmodern** (Alvesson 2002).

- The first orientation is *neopositivism*, the traditional scientific view of research as an objective pursuit of knowledge in which the researcher has a position that is external to the world of the subjects. The researchers treat the interview as an instrument for collecting data. While maintaining a healthy skepticism toward what interviewees tell them, they do hope to glean *factual* information from it, at the very least about the opinions and perceptions of the interviewees. Those who fit within this orientation tend to uphold and defend the validity and attainability of *objective knowledge.*
- The second orientation has been termed the *romantic* one; the interview is experienced as a human encounter in which the main criterion is authenticity of the interchange between interviewer and interviewee. Considerable energy is placed into thinking about the relationship between researcher and "subject" and an effort is made to reduce this distance. Feminist thought markedly influences this position.
- The third position that has emerged in recent decades is the *postmodernist* one in which the interview constitutes a "speech act" wherein the interviewer and interviewee together *construct through dialogue* a view of social reality (Alvesson 2002: 122). The postmodern position emphasizes the local context in which the construction takes place and the discourses that both the interviewers and the interviewees put into play. The interviewers are never just eliciting information about the cultural meanings or subjective understandings held by the interviewees; the interviewers are actually creating these discourses by the questions they ask and their own actions in the local context.

## The Postmodern View

The postmodernist view of interviewing has implications for how we design interview questions and analyze interview data. We have to be aware that we are constructing social reality by the way we ask questions and that the data we have *produced* (not collected!) in the form of an interview transcript are discourses in which we participated. We therefore have to be aware that when we identify themes in the interview transcript or code it (especially using software) that our "findings" are comprised of interviewees' insights, as rendered in words, and of the words, ideas, and perspectives that *we*, the researchers, brought to the table in the form of questions.

This consideration immediately leads to a piece of practical advice. Do not confuse your research questions with the questions you prepare for your interviews! These two sets of questions are different in purpose, format, and wording, though your research questions indeed will influence the questions you choose to ask your interviewees. If you need to refresh your understanding of the RQ, then we suggest that you revisit Chapter 2.

With the postmodernist caveat in mind, we now move ahead with a discussion of the most basic way of typifying interview *structure*.

## Structured, Semi-Structured, and Unstructured Interviews

Researchers can choose from among three **types of interviews: structured, semi-structured, and unstructured**.

**STRUCTURED INTERVIEWS**  Structured interviews are used in quantitative research and produce data that are very close to being quantitative. The answers are precoded into multiple-choice categories, specific numbers (such as age or income), or points on a scale. The interviewer has little leeway in asking the questions or posing follow-up questions. The interview is highly scripted. This does not mean that rapport and a pleasant manner are unimportant or irrelevant; it just means that the establishment of rapport cannot lead the interviewer far away from the prepared set of questions.

In structured interviewing, interviewers are often employees of research organizations and highly trained in establishing rapport with the subjects, but they generally do not formulate the questions themselves and the interviewing is not part of their "own" research project. (Michael et al. 1994, *Sex in America*, present a fascinating discussion of selecting and preparing interviewers for a research project that probed intimate aspects of individuals' sexual behavior, experiences, and practices; it provides a good example of structured interviewing.)

Recording a structured interview is very easy; we simply check the precoded categories or fill in a number. The data can very easily be entered into a data file on a computer and are immediately ready for statistical analysis.

Structured interviewing is closely linked to the *neopositivist orientation* we mentioned at the beginning of the chapter. The underlying assumption is that interviews are tools for producing usable information, if not directly about behaviors or situations, at the very least about the orientations and perceptions of the interviewees. Yet paradoxically, the material collected in the structured interview is the most extensively constructed by the researchers who have imposed their framing and their categories on the questions and constrained the way the respondents can address the topic.

**SEMI-STRUCTURED INTERVIEWING**  In semi-structured interviewing, the researcher relies on an **interview guide**, a set of prepared questions that cover the basic topics and themes for the respondent to address. But there are few if any precoded answers, and respondents are encouraged to expound at length in their own words. The framing and wording of the answers are key parts of what the interviewer wants to learn, not "noise" that has to be blocked out in obtaining answers that fit the precoded categories. In structured interviewing in many surveys, the researchers are imposing their own categories on their subjects, forcing them to answer in terms of these categories; in semi- and unstructured interviewing, the researchers are interested in the categories that the respondents use to frame their answers.

The interview guide for semi-structured interviewing, however, engenders comparability among a number of interviews. It insures that respondents are answering a similar set of questions and that certain topics and themes will be addressed in all the interviews. The researchers are interested in seeing the agreements and disagreements among the respondents and the different ways in which they frame answers. For example, we might want to see if high school students have a uniform view of their principal or of the school curriculum. Semi-structured interviewing is flexible enough to allow questions to be substantially modified for individuals or different groups of respondents and to allow the researcher to improvise follow-up questions as the interview takes place.

The interview guide looks more like a series of topics than fully formulated and tightly scripted questions that must be asked exactly as they are worded. The interview guide helps the researcher to make sure that all the topics are covered and to remind her of the order in which they need to be asked.

Semi-structured interviews can be audio recorded to capture all the nuances of wording and framing that are important in the interpretation and analysis; but "in a pinch" the interviewer can record by taking notes, making sure to capture not only the respondents' meaning and intention but also the key terms the respondents use.

The structure of the interview guide assures a relatively organized flow of topics (possibly with digressions) and relatively complete coverage of themes. In semi-structured interviewing, the researcher has already identified key themes associated with the questions and does not need to select these themes from the flow of recorded material afterwards. The themes, if not the exact wording and framing, have been prepared and selected by the researcher. This preselection of themes has consequences for coding and for the construction of grounded theory; if we "put those themes" into the interview guide at the start of the project, we cannot be surprised to find them in the text of the interview that we are coding!

Semi-structured interviews are close to interviews that journalists and talk show hosts conduct; interviewers in the media usually have prepared a set of questions and guide the respondent through topics of the interviewer's choosing, rather than relying on the respondent to choose the topics.

**UNSTRUCTURED INTERVIEWING**    Unstructured interviewing is almost like a conversation among acquaintances and friends. The interviewer has a set of topics but does not feel he "needs to get through" the set. The flow of words and ideas is largely unbounded and much less predictable as compared with the structured and semi-structured interview scenarios.

Unstructured interviewing is a good technique for eliciting longer discourses and narratives. One of the most important of these is the life narrative, which we will discuss in a separate chapter. The respondent tells the story of her or his own life, probably not in a single session but over a series of encounters. Similarly an oral history—the story of a group or place—can be produced in unstructured interviewing.

In these techniques, a relatively simple stimulus sets off a lengthy and complex response: "Can you tell me something about yourself, your life, your most important experiences . . . the story of your family . . . of your community . . . how has this place changed over the years . . . ?"

If the respondent is a talkative, lively, and engaged kind of person, the answers flow easily. Only an occasional probe or follow-up from the interviewer is needed. The respondent produces material spontaneously, not according to the interviewer's script. These stories are probably not organized chronologically; they may jump around in time and be repetitive. The same person may convey the same key event in slightly different ways depending on many different variables, most notably how the interviewee wants to present herself to the interviewer. It is up to the researcher to analyze and organize the material.

The researcher must make the following types of choices in using the material from unstructured interviews:

1. *Recording the interview.* Unlike the structured and even the semi-structured interview, the unstructured interview has to be audio recorded (if not video recorded). The complex structure of the respondents' comments cannot be captured in notes; it sounds paradoxical, but it is the unstructured interview that produces the most complicated structure of responses, whereas the structured interview produces very simple answers.

2. *Editing the material.* The researcher must make editing choices at various stages, for instance, during the transcription of the recorded interview (the stage at which "ums" and "you knows" may be dropped) and again for the presentation of the interview in the research report in which repetitions may be eliminated and selections are made from the transcript to use as supporting evidence for specific interpretations. But at no point should grammar or word choice be altered by the researcher. Jay MacLeod's *Ain't No Makin' It*—a study of social reproduction in a low-income neighborhood—offers excellent examples of lively and careful transcriptions of interview material that capture the rhythms of real speech.

If the preparation of the transcript requires translation (as it well may happen in ethnographic research), very complicated dilemmas present themselves.

Transcription, editing, and interpretation of unstructured interviews are complicated research activities.

Once again we can see the contrast between quantitative and qualitative research. In quantitative research, an enormous amount of initial effort is put into preparing the survey instrument, but once the precoded categories and scales are in place, it is easy to transform the answers into data that can be statistically analyzed—all that is necessary is a bit of typing into a data file (and with online survey forms, even this step is automatic). In an unstructured interview, the first steps seem easy—just asking sociable questions to a congenial individual; but the result is a lengthy flow of communication with a complicated and even chaotic internal organization that presents formidable challenges to recording and analyzing.

We also see again how data are neither "collected" (a word that implies they are just lying on the ground waiting to be picked up) nor "constructed" solely by the researcher (a phrase that implies that we are creating them entirely by ourselves according to our imagination and our blueprints); instead the best metaphor is that data are grown in the field of interaction between ourselves and the research subjects, in this case, the interview respondents.

In quantitative research, the data are grown in neat rows into highly uniform products varying only in a limited number of predictable key features (the categories or measures of the key variable tapped by a question). In qualitative research, the data grow less neatly and predictably. Our garden or field is likely sectioned off in broad terms, but there's a lot weeds and a lot of cross-fertilization going on. The harvest is difficult, even though the initial planting seemed easy, carefree, and conversational ("Can you tell me about your life . . . .how has this place changed since you first arrived . . . .?"). It is easy to miss a particularly luscious cluster of berries amid the brambles, and obtaining something useful requires careful sorting of the variable and unpredictable results.

At this stage in unstructured interviewing and some semi-structured interviewing, researchers may turn to qualitative analysis software, such as *ATLAS.ti*, to identify themes in the transcribed text (see Chapter 22). But we need to keep in mind the postmodernists' critique of interviewing (and other types of "data collection"): the textual database formed by an interview transcript is a discourse that we have participated in creating in the first place. When we code it and find themes in it, are these not themes and categories that we put into it ourselves, not only by specific questions we posed but by the entire local context of the interview situation, who we are, what we represent, how we speak, and how we set up the encounter with the interviewee?

Now that we've got a sense of the interview's basic formats or structures, let's talk about how you actually go about conducting an interview.

## INTERVIEW PROCEDURES AND PRACTICES

Interviewers need to consider the **setting** in which the interview is conducted, especially as it makes some identities of the respondent more salient than others. Interviewing in a workplace or the offices of a social movement may produce more formal answers than interviewing in a person's home, a café, or a bar. The duration of the interview should probably not exceed a couple of hours in any one session.

The researcher must make a choice about **reciprocity**, in other words, what is "in it" for the respondent. The interview may offer an opportunity for attention, a chance to speak to a neutral party who offers a "sounding board" for complaints and concerns, or an occasion for earning money or receiving a favor of some type. Each of these incentives will attract certain categories of individuals and each one has corresponding risks—for example, that our respondents will be individuals who want attention, or want to express grievances, or need financial help, or hope to profit from connections made through networking with the researcher. But remember that many people love to be interviewed and will thoroughly enjoy the experience of having the interviewer listen attentively to their words, regardless of what material benefits you offer.

### The Sympathetic Ear: An Example of Research in Action

An interesting example of a researcher offering an attentive and sympathetic ear is provided by Larry Mayo's research experience in Guam, a Pacific Island with a quasi-colonial relationship to the United States which administers the territory and maintains a large military presence there. Statesiders (people from the United States, who formed a stratum of administrators and military personnel) recognized Larry as "one of us" and felt free to tell him about negative experiences with the Guamanians; but as an African American, Larry was seen by the Guamanians as sharing an identity as a person of color, and they felt free to reveal their negative feelings about the predominantly white Statesiders. In this case, both sides saw aspects of Larry's identity that they felt they shared and that made them comfortable talking to him about the local situation. In other instances, it may be precisely because the researcher is an outsider who appears to have very little in common with any of the respondents that makes him or her appear to be a neutral and disinterested (not uninterested) party who is willing to listen to different sides of a dispute and to be fair in making judgments.

### Believing, Disbelieving and Disbelieving Belief

Two key rules must be followed in interviewing:

- Never be judgmental.
- Never believe all you hear.

And here's a suggested corollary to the second rule: "Avoid hearing only what you believe." Schatzman and Strauss (1973: 69), two leading scholars in symbolic interactionist field research summed up the rules even more succinctly: The researcher believes "everything" and "nothing" simultaneously.

Let's look at this stance in a little more detail.

**NEVER BE JUDGMENTAL**    This dictum means truly putting on hold the feelings and opinions that you have about the situation you are studying. In Chapter 5, we discussed how many qualitative researchers undertake their research with definite political commitments. But we also reminded you of Weber's position that the researcher must be open to inconvenient truths, the facts that may lead us to modify or even abandon our initial positions.

This openness must permeate not only our research design but also our interaction with our research subjects for two reasons. One is that if we impose our initial political orientation and expectations we will not be able to find the very facts that could lead us to revisit and revise our initial positions. Our hypotheses will never be subjected to the test of falsifiability. This reason for openness emerges from the logic of inquiry itself. The second reason is a more practical and interpersonal one: If we communicate to our respondents by gestures, body language, and facial expressions as well as by words that we disapprove of what they are saying, they will pick up our negative attitude and withdraw from the interview emotionally and mentally if not actually physically. Human beings are sensitively attuned to negative feedback from people with whom they are interacting and they will not want to continue to speak honestly with us.

The dictum "Do not be judgmental" has profound implications for the wording of questions as well as comportment during the interview. It does not mean that we cannot disagree with respondents or that we always have to refrain from asking challenging types of questions, as we will see shortly, as long as we do this in a planned and aware way.

**NEVER BELIEVE ALL YOU HEAR**    This advice may appear to contradict the advice not to be judgmental, but complete openness to what respondents are saying must be accompanied by complete skepticism. Remind yourself constantly that you are not being told *the truth*, but at best *a* truth that is temporarily valid for the respondent. "Temporarily" because people themselves shift quickly in their opinions and their framing of their truths is **setting-specific**.

Interview a judge in chambers and you may hear different answers to questions about the jury system and defendants than you would over a drink in a bar. The courthouse setting calls for formality, a shared professional ideology, a sense of moral authority, while the "backstage setting" (to use Goffman's term) calls for humor, role distance, and informality. But we have to be very careful here: The "backstage" is not necessarily any truer than the formal frontstage in the courthouse (Hancock and Garner 2009). Both sets of expectations, both role performances may be true. Indeed the opportunity to "let off steam" and use the backstage setting to make fun of clients and colleagues may strengthen a serious commitment to the formal structure (as students of Carnival have long pointed out—carnival boisterousness and mockery ultimately reinforce the existing social order, Scheper-Hughes 1992).

This simple example (judge in chambers; judge in a bar) highlights a problem that was identified many years ago by Howard Becker: and that is the risk of uncovering *too much* cynicism and therefore underestimating idealism as the principle that guides the respondent. In this regard, we have to return to Goffman and remind ourselves that the backstage with its cynicism is as much a presentation of self as the frontstage with its earnest idealism. Studying medical students, Becker and Geer found both orientations in the same individual and came to believe that group settings often brought out the cynicism while the idealism was more readily elicited in one-on-one interviews. Our example of the judge suggests that settings as well as the absence or presence of peers is also an influence on the expression of cynicism or idealism. Becker cautions the researcher not to discount the idealism (1970a: 104–105).

The point is that in an interview we never receive a single simple piece of information. The information is always refracted through multiple filters: the multiple roles of respondents which may carry contradictory expectations; the multiple ideologies and worldviews they hold; the settings in which the interviews are conducted, the way researchers choose to portray themselves; and how the interviewee perceives and responds to the researcher's presentation of self.

Interviews allow us to see social reality only dimly and somewhat distortedly, through lenses and filters (some known, most unknown), or as Scheper-Hughes puts it, "through a glass darkly." This is why the best researchers often use conventionally prohibited actions such as leading questions or even direct challenges to the respondents' statements. Challenges are a deliberate gambit to induce the interviewee to elaborate and say things that might otherwise not be said. It is not the same stance as being judgmental and expressing sincerely negative feelings about interviewee's remarks.

This is one of the places where many methods textbooks—and methods instructors—go wrong: They urge you, the researcher-interviewer, to *never* contradict, challenge, unsettle, or otherwise upset your interviewee, for doing so will compromise the interview, the relationship, and quite possibly the entire study. This is a bunch of malarkey. First, in this field—as in life—it's important to "never say never." Second, the interview's purpose is not solely restricted to giving the interviewee an unfettered, unrestricted venue in which to say anything she wants. Third, the interview *is* a dynamic interaction. Fourth, what happens in the interview should be pegged to the ultimate purpose of the study—the central objective and research question. If challenging an interviewee is necessary, then that's what should be done. Finally, there is no single overarching and totalizing edict for conducting interviews. As with most things in life, how you conduct the interview, and specifically whether or not you challenge an informant, depends on a lot of things. Your job is to figure out what those things are and proceed accordingly.

In the end, what you want out of the interview—a utilitarian enterprise whose business is extraction—is the most revealing and truthful information on a given topic, event, subject, community, relationship, or phenomenon. Schatzman and Strauss suggest **four tactics for questions** that stand a pretty good chance of producing solid information (1973: 80–81), and every one of these tactics strays from the feeble advice "never contradict your interviewee."

1. **The devil's advocate question**. In this question, the interviewer asks a question from a perspective that he or she knows is counter to the position of the respondent. The response may confirm and elaborate the respondent's initial position, clarify different stands within a community or organization, or even "break open" an impasse and encourage the respondent to address alternatives and acknowledge diverging opinions.
2. **The hypothetical question**. This question asks the respondent to consider possibilities and scenarios that have not (yet) taken place, and the answer provides an elaboration of the respondent's thinking.
3. **Posing the ideal**. The respondent may be asked to discuss an ideal situation, process, or behavior; or the interviewer may suggest an ideal and see how the respondent reacts.
4. **Offering interpretations or testing propositions**. The interviewer actually "runs an interpretation" by the respondent, going beyond merely checking whether the respondent's statements are accurately understood and reproduced and testing whether the meaning and purpose of the statements or information has been grasped. Even inconsistencies may be pointed out. The respondent is being drawn into the next step of the interview method—the interpretation of the interview data. This type of question clearly requires good rapport between interviewer and respondent and an intelligent engaged respondent.

These kinds of questions run counter to other advice that is often given to interviewers, which is to get respondents to talk about actual behaviors and past actions, to avoid questions about hypothetical situations and ideals, and never to challenge respondents. Indeed Patton (2002) explicitly warns researchers not to use hypotheticals; these questions easily lead to talking about wish lists and to socially acceptable responses. And interviewing not in a research setting, but as the chair of an institutional search committee recruiting a new executive officer, Roberta was explicitly advised by the search firm never to ask hypothetical questions about what the individual would or might do if . . . , but only questions about actual decisions and behaviors in the past. This advice is of value in research as well, unless we are primarily studying myths and ideals.

**LEADING INTO CONFESSION**    A notorious example of questions that cut through the façade of the socially acceptable is provided by the Kinsey study of human sexuality, a very controversial report that relied on questionable sampling and produced startling (though probably not reliable) revelations about the extensive distribution of sexual behavior that transgressed traditional norms, especially same-sex encounters among men. The Kinsey team was encouraged to always frame a question based on the assumption that the respondent had engaged in a particular behavior: "When did you first . . . .?" Or "How often do you . . . .?" And the interviewers were instructed never to ask whether or not the respondent had engaged in the behavior, a question that would produce the **socially desirable response** "no."

As you will see in the latter part of the chapter, these gambits are not considered acceptable interview practice by many researchers and they can only be used with great care and restraint. We want to cut through the level of formulaic socially acceptable answers, but we have to remain sensitive and tactful to our respondents.

Kinsey as well as Schatzmann and Strauss were anticipating the postmodernist orientation to interviewing. They were already recognizing it as an inherently political interchange, always heavily loaded with the researchers' concepts and categories from the start, infused with theoretical assumptions, and never a simple and authentic elicitation of the interviewees' subjective meanings and experiences. By a practice of reflexivity, recognizing these assumptions and choices, we can use the interview material without illusions.

## Elite Interviews

Special mention must be made of problems that arise in interviewing elites, loosely defined as people with more power or social status than the interviewer, at least within the local context. They are individuals who can exercise control over the flow of information in a community or an organization. Their stake in managing information is larger than that of less powerful individuals; the latter are mainly concerned with their own images and resources, whereas elites have organizations, established networks, and even institutions to protect. Elites are far more likely to have a consistent well-planned discourse available that provides stock answers to interview questions. At the extreme, many elites won't give interviews at all, and will only let researchers talk to professionals in information management—press secretaries, corporate spokespersons, media relations staffers, and so on. The researcher therefore has to use two strategies to cut through elite information management and make the situation more transparent.

**STRATEGY 1**    The Element of Surprise: One strategy involves planning questions to induce more spontaneous, truthful, and revealing answers. We have already seen Schatzman and Strauss's suggestions for these types of questions. Social scientists can learn from watching TV hosts and journalists, both what to do and what to avoid. Some media interviewers are far too deferential to celebrities and authority figures and never ask hard hitting questions. This deferential posture may arise because the interviewer is genuinely respectful of the ideological aura that surrounds roles such as president of the United States or CEO of a large corporation—or merely because the interviewer relies on an ongoing, sustained, friendly relationship with the interviewees and their organizations. A pointed question that reveals that the interviewer considers the interviewee to have been dishing out an organizational line may jeopardize the relationship and make it more difficult to interview that individual in the future.

Social scientists are usually under less restraint of this kind and do not see themselves as having to sustain good relationships with an "information source" in the long run. The ethics of journalism call for revealing and naming sources, while the ethics of social science research call for the exact opposite practice—preserving anonymity and confidentiality and this commitment may encourage more open and truthful expression by respondents. But it is true that elites and organizational spokespersons may be wary of guarantees of confidentiality and anonymity offered by researchers. They also may assume that social scientists are leftists or extreme liberals who are hostile to established authority and corporations.

**STRATEGY 2** Play It As It Lays: The second strategy for coping with guarded and formulaic results of elite interviews is the orientation we have emphasized throughout this book: Researchers have the obligation to "call it as we see it" and to interpret information collected from elites as we do all information—that is, to constantly compare it to other information (such as observational data we have recorded), to analyze it theoretically, and to examine it in light of knowledge that we believe to be objective and that we have developed for ourselves. What is said in an interview—elite or otherwise—is a discourse about reality, not a simple, complete and reliable statement about reality. It often contains both deliberate prevaricating and misrecognition.

**EXAMPLE—SEX AND GOD** Laumann et al.'s (2004) study of sexual behavior in a large metropolis includes a fascinating analysis of how service providers and religious leaders see sexual issues in their communities. Much of the study is based on survey data, but a couple of chapters report findings from interviews with individuals in religious and social service organizations. The analysis by Ellingson (2004) and Ellingson et al. (2004) steps back from the words of the respondents to provide an in-depth interpretation that includes recognition of inconsistencies. Ellingson interviewed 58 providers representing 51 social and health service organizations in Chicago communities. He wanted to understand the relationship between the *causal stories* that providers told about the reasons for sexually related problems such as teen pregnancy, HIV/AIDS and STDs, and domestic violence and the *intervention strategies* that providers offered to the clients of their organizations.

Ellingson points out the gap between the rhetoric of the "causal stories," which offers structural and cultural explanations, and the intervention repertoire, which is focused on encouraging more rational and less risky behavior by individuals, almost as if these individuals were not influenced by the social and cultural environments identified in the "causal stories." Ellingson is arguing that there is a disconnect between causal discourses and available interventions; and that if the causal discourses are accurate, the interventions will probably not be very effective. The service providers seem to avoid confronting this disconnect. These interviews might have offered an opportunity for the interviewing strategies suggested by Schatzmann and Strauss, such as the "devil's advocate question" or "testing an interpretation," but Ellingson does not indicate that he employed them.

The chapter on religious leaders' views of sexual behavior reveals issues in the articulation between the official views of churches (often conservative on sexual matters) and the local sexual norms and practices; many religious leaders negotiate a relatively permissive or liberal stand with their congregations and the local community because they find it difficult to enforce official doctrine in the local, interactive context. As Ellingson et al. state, "the case studies reveal that local norms regarding sexual behavior and identity and congregations' identities and histories are usually more salient than polity, official teaching, or denominational affiliation" (2004: 347–348). In other words, Ellingson was successful in learning more from his respondents than a simple reiteration of an "official position" and he was able to analyze their nuanced, complex responses in light of the survey data and other information gathered in the study.

Journalists often use the term **expert interviews** which overlaps our term "elite interviewing" but involves significant differences. "Elite interviewing" draws more attention to power differences between the interviewer and the interviewee and it does not assume that the interviewee is an expert. The same skepticism of "believe everything, believe nothing" applies to interviewing the person who is in the role of expert as it applies to anyone else. Ellingson respected the knowledge and insights that the community health and social service providers had into the circumstances of the lives of people in the community, but he identified tensions and disconnects in their narratives. You can also look at Karen Ho's (2009) ethnography of Wall Street for a discussion of how to conduct interviews in a cultural setting—investment banks—in which individuals see themselves as supremely intelligent, risk embracing, and powerful.

In the following section, we offer guidelines for effective and ethical interaction in interviews. It elaborates the broad suggestions we made in the first part of the chapter such as "never be judgmental" and provides specifics on how to implement the principles of human subject research such as confidentiality.

## ASKING QUESTIONS INFORMALLY AND INTERACTING EFFECTIVELY

Although formal interviews, including life history interviews, will consume some of the time you spend in the field, for the most part your directed data production will occur through less formal and seemingly less structured interviews. In fact, when done properly the semi-structured ethnographic interview should look and feel a lot like a conversation wherein one party (the informant) does most of the talking and the other party (you) listens actively and attentively. When talking with informants, you can lay the foundation for a good deal of data production by adhering to seemingly obvious interactional principles and by organizing your inquiry in accordance with the "10 rules for asking questions" we present below. First, we discuss some elementary principles of interaction.

### The "10 Commandments of Informant Interviewing"

1. *Respect.* The informant is giving you time, sharing her life, and trusting you to be responsible. And she is receiving from you little or nothing in exchange. She's doing you a favor. So treat the informant like a person, not a source of data, even though in the final analysis you will be forced to objectify her and reduce her to little more than a crude token of her complete humanness. When interacting with an informant, no matter how disagreeable you find her to be, show deference. Be attentive. Be kind. And most of all, exhibit empathy.

   This principle applies not only to your interpersonal dealings with informants but equally to those many instances when you talk with your colleagues, mentors, and/or friends about the informants in your study. The stress of fieldwork manifests in all sorts of unpredictable ways, and it's common for ethnographers who've been in the field a long while to "blow off steam" among their friends in "real life" by ridiculing, mocking, or otherwise demeaning their informants in absentia. Try to resist this temptation. Obviously the informants in your study are fellow human beings, and their lives make sense to them, on their terms, and these terms may be very different from your own. But their lives should not become a source of amusement or self-congratulation in your life. Violating this principle will vitiate the data (not to mention your character) as your derogatory remarks ultimately will infiltrate the way you view, interact with, and represent the informants.

On the flip side of respecting your informant, you should behave in such a manner as to elicit respect from the informant. During the study period, you are a professional researcher. Your job is to produce analyzable data using personal interview and observational methods. While you should refrain from treating the informant like nothing more than a source of data, you also should avoid treating him too much like a friend. Somewhere between the impersonal, detached observer and the gushing buddy is where you ought to be.

2. *Understanding.* When interviewing an informant, do your best to understand his views from within his frame of reference. To use Goffman's words, every group of people finds meaning in the life it creates, and whatever life they lead is reasonable to them, on their terms. Your job is to figure out how their culture operates and how it makes perfectly good sense to them, no matter how unreasonable or "disorganized" or "erratic" or "exotic" it may seem to you (the adjectives in quotation marks all have a long and unfortunate history of use in sociological studies). Listen nonjudgmentally to what the informant says (monitor your verbal and nonverbal responses to make sure you're not sending a message of negative reinforcement). Avoid assessing his remarks against your own life (ethnocentrism). Do not attempt to measure, evaluate, or judge what the informant says to you. Do not assume you have the "right" perspective on any topic covered in the interview. Instead, assume that you know nothing about what is right or wrong in a given situation, setting, or culture. You are open to all possibilities, all forms of behavior, all manner of motives for engaging in action.

3. *Sensitivity.* Be aware of how you treat the informant, particularly when the conversation veers into a subject that he obviously deems "sensitive." If you're working from a script or an interview guide or a simple list of questions, be prepared to abandon the document if the informant begins to struggle emotionally with some aspect of the conversation. And if you encounter an informant who tells you things that necessitate responses and follow-up questions you didn't plan for, then toss your questions aside for the time being and deal with the present situation in the most compassionate way possible. When appropriate, steer the informant back to your line of questioning. Now, if you get the sense that your line of questioning is entirely inappropriate (and you'll know this when it happens), then give up your role as "interviewer" and allow the informant to take charge of the conversation. Afterwards, be sure to analyze what happened. Perhaps there is something very wrong with how you're approaching conversations with informants more generally. Or maybe the problem is specific to this particular informant. Either way, you need to know.

4. *Manners.* Minding your manners is critical to the success of the interviewing process. As an interviewer, you are the informant's "guest" for the time of the interview. As an ethnographer, you're a "guest" of the whole community you're studying. So behave as a guest, at least in the initial stages. You should try to be relaxed, confident, attentive, and always courteous when talking with informants. Keep your mind on the task at hand and your attention on the person in front of you. Try to prevent distractions from occurring. Before

the conversation begins, for instance, turn your cell phone and/or pager to "vibrate" mode (or turn it off completely). Unless unavoidable, never engage in a cell phone conversation or text messaging or web browsing (etc.) in the presence of an informant.

5. *Confidentiality/Anonymity.* Guarantee it. Abide by it. No matter how interesting an interview is, do not share it with anyone outside of this project. Do not disclose any information, from names or addresses to what a respondent said, for any reason. Also, if during the conversation the informant says, ". . . and this is off the record" or ". . . and this is just between us," or something to this effect, put down your pencil/pen, stop writing, and pay close attention to what she's saying. Use body language to show that you will keep her confidence on this. This principle is sacrosanct. It's also codified in the federal government's regulations concerning the protection of human subjects in research (see Chapter 4).

   Depending upon the situation, you may be audio- or video-recording the interview. If so, instruct the respondent to avoid mentioning his name, address, or any other identifying information. Once you have begun recording, ask the respondent, "Do I have your permission to tape record this interview?" Transcribe your tapes as soon after the interview as possible. Either destroy/erase the "tapes" (or digital media) upon their transcription or store them securely (a locked file cabinet in a lockable office/room for tapes, double-password protected folders for digital media stored on a computer hard drive).

6. *Time.* The informant is giving her time in exchange for little more than whatever gratification results from attempting to help you personally or the project more abstractly. Everyone's time is valuable, and our time theoretically (in relativistic terms) carries no greater value than does hers. Be conscious of how much time you take, and express gratitude for what you get. While being aware of the data you need to collect, avoid conspicuous attempts to hurry the informant along. No one appreciates being rushed through a very personal narrative, especially when their conversation "partner" has lured them into sharing their story. Always be sure you have allotted enough time for the interviews to occur at a pace significantly slower than usual.

7. *Propriety.* When you find yourself planning a conversation or interview or in the middle of an unplanned interaction, do your best to avoid asking questions deemed "improper." This can be very challenging in the early days of fieldwork, but it's essential to the successful development of a culture-wide data production infrastructure. If word gets around that "stranger" asks inappropriate questions, then you may well be doomed to irrelevance, a very bad place for an ethnographer. Every culture has rules pertaining to the "propriety" of question-asking. Think about the various cultures in which you participate each day. Consider your family, for instance. What sorts of unspoken, or at least unwritten, rules does your family have regarding question-asking? Are there certain questions that you're just not allowed to ask each other? Are there questions deemed inappropriate for specific contexts, such as the dinner table? Consider the culture you're studying to be a very large family, with all sorts of rules relating to all sorts of people, places, things, and words. You don't want to violate too many of these rules too early on. So stick to what you believe to be relatively "safe" questions in the early stages of research. The culture's rules will change as you grow roots in it, as you "mature" and evolve, as you progress from being a nosy outsider to a "stranger within." Whatever you do, if an informant makes it known to you that you've stepped over a line, then you better begin to backpedal. Then it's time to repair whatever rapport you had with her before you breached the boundary.

8. *Safety.* Be mindful of your personal safety, but don't obsess about it openly, as cultural insiders likely will take offense. Develop and continually modify/update your own "safety code," one

that makes sense in light of, and is sensitive to, both your own "habitus" and the particularities of the culture and/or community you're studying. Also be aware of the safety codes that your faculty sponsor/mentor and your university/college have issued. If they haven't issued any guidelines regarding your personal safety in the field, then you should ask them to do so. You need to know what their safety concerns are, and the degree to which they will be there to help you out if you get into a jam. If ever you perceive danger while doing fieldwork, exit the situation as quickly and safely as possible. Upon return to your home or office, report the incident to your faculty sponsor or mentor. Then, as with many other occurrences in the field, reflect on the adverse event and try to understand how it makes perfectly good sense that it happened. Because if it didn't "make sense," then it wouldn't have ever happened. Make sense?

Equally important, be mindful of the interviewee's safety. In some instances, as in Scott's project on street gangs in Chicago, informants don't want others to know about their participation in the research study, particularly when they could be punished for having done so. In Scott's study, some of the gang leaders worried that Scott might be handing data over to the police. They therefore prohibited their "soldiers" from being interviewed. But the "soldiers" knew better, for Scott had been hanging out with them for hours on end, day after day, and they had seen Scott himself participating in illegal activity. So they often agreed to be interviewed, even though it put them at risk of being "violated" (physically punished) by their superiors. Scott went to great lengths to ensure the safety of interviewees by conducting interviews in hidden locations, never publicizing who agreed to be interviewed, and so on. On a few occasions, Scott also had to negotiate with police officers who came to "bust" the house in which Scott was interviewing someone. In these cases, Scott had to convince the law enforcement agents that the interviewee was a participant in a *bona fide* research project and therefore should not be arrested.

9. *Preparation*. Prepare yourself well before you initiate the conversation/interview. Familiarize yourself with the questions you want to ask. Write them down and memorize them. And try to predict the asides and detours most likely to materialize. This will help you be more relaxed, comfortable, and able to anticipate and accommodate the informant's narrative. Do your best to cast your questions in the local vernacular, but don't go overboard, especially in the use of slang (discussed above). If, for example, you're going to interview college students about sexual behavior, don't use the term "prophylaxis." Instead, use "condom" or better yet, "protection" when asking about what sorts of things they do, or don't do, to keep themselves and/or their partners from contracting a sexually transmitted infection (STI). In this case, you definitely don't want to use terms such as "rubber" or any of the more esoteric, region-specific terms ("raincoat," "cock sock," "love glove," etc.).

10. *Documentation*. The quality of your study hinges on the quality of the data you collect, which in turn varies in relation to the quality of the relationships out of which you produce the data. Although many ethnographers would disagree with us on this point, the significance and value of your study is, in large part, a function of the degree of rigor characterizing your production of data. You should record data vigilantly and in painstaking detail, if not during the interview then immediately following its conclusion (if possible, and see above discussion). Take copious notes and preserve them well. If audio- or video-recording the interview, be sure to transcribe your tapes and disks as soon as you can. Keep your materials well-organized and secure.

Following these commandments will help you to run smooth and productive conversations with informants. In fact, you will be the one running the conversation, though you need to master the art (more of a craft really) of initiating and directing a conversation in such a way that the informant believes that she is actually in charge of the interaction. Indeed the informant is in the "lead role," or at least the role of "teacher," but aside from this arrangement you need to figure out how to persuade people to want to talk about things, especially sensitive subjects, in your presence. How do you pull this off? How do you get the informant to believe that she's in charge of the interview when in fact you're directing it? Below we discuss a few basic strategies related specifically to the asking of questions. Nothing communicates to the informant that she's in charge better than an elegantly and strategically constructed question.

## The Basics of Getting Informants to Engage in Revelatory Talk

First, many qualitative researchers and ethnographers (maybe even most of them) adopt the same guidelines for their inquiries as journalists use when doing interviews for a story: who, what, when, where, and how. To the ethnographer, the *how* question is the most important of them all. Why? Because ethnography is particularly well-equipped and positioned to gain insight into how humans adapt to each other, to their surroundings, and to the structural forces beyond their immediate control. Moreover, culture is the centerpiece of ethnographic inquiry, and culture is a process—a dynamic, porous, multilayered, multilateral, structural and interactional nonlinear field of adaptations and innovations. Asking the "how" question is, therefore, invaluable.

Second, you may have noticed that the "why?" question doesn't appear in the list above. Why not? Because asking "why?" often puts informants on the defensive, which means they'll either see you as an antagonist and close down or simply just close down. Either way, the interview won't be productive and, even worse, you may lose that informant forever. Instead of asking "why?" use some creative rephrasing to get the explanations you're looking for. For instance, let's say I'm talking with an informant in my study of power accumulation among medical students, and he says to me, "Then I walked right past Meredith [a fellow medical student] and didn't tell her that I had found out what the criteria are for naming the new 'chief resident' [medical student intern who supervises all of the other medical student interns]." I know that my informant isn't supposed to be privy to the criteria, and he knows it too. We both know that he obtained the information on the sly, or perhaps through serendipity.

One's natural inclination is to ask, "Well, why didn't you tell her?" In a situation like this, where there's a mild form of wrongdoing, the *why* resounds through the room and likely will cause my informant to stiffen and clam up. Instead, I might more constructively ask, "Oh, yeah? So . . . what were some of your reasons for walking on and not talking to her?" This question doesn't contain the damning word "why," nor does it resurrect the issue that we both know is at play—his covert knowledge of the criteria and his decision to keep it from her. We might even both suspect the reason: He wants to be named chief resident, and knowing the criteria gives him a competitive advantage. Sharing them with her dilutes his advantage.

Even when there's no malfeasance or questionable motive/conduct at hand, it's best to avoid asking "why?" There must be a few dozen different ways to ask any given "why" question, so be creative. Ask instead, "How did you come to that decision?" or simply "What were some of your reasons for not doing it?" Remember, the more comfortable your informant is being vulnerable in your presence, the better your data will be.

Third, engage in active listening. The ethnographic interview should resemble a conversation, as we've already noted. You need to exhibit sufficient enthusiasm to convince the informant that you're eager to hear what she has to say and enough sensitivity to convince her that she can confide in you. Characteristics of "active listening" include the following:

1. Voice modulation, or speaking in a multitonal and dynamic fashion (i.e., not in monotone);

2. Verbal and nonverbal positive reinforcement to the informant which entails making good eye contact even when taking notes, saying things like "okay," "right," "mm-hmm," "I see," and "yeah . . . ?";

3. Empathic tone with elongated enunciation, meaning don't be terse or abrupt in asking questions—instead, soften your voice, stretch out your syllables, and generally convey "warmth" in your voice;

4. Minimal prolonged silences, as "pregnant pauses" make interviewees feel uncomfortable—so don't let note-taking or some other distraction result in long pauses between the end of the informant's answer and the beginning of your next question or comment;

5. Take notes only to the extent that doing so doesn't pull you away from the conversation, and if the informant says something that you feel must be written down immediately, then ask the informant to slow down or pause for a moment "because what you're saying is really important [or fascinating or whatever], and I want to make sure I get it exactly right";

6. If you have questions written/printed out, make sure that you don't read the questions robotically—instead, familiarize yourself with the questions in advance so that you can ask them in a conversational, dynamic tone that doesn't sound like you're reading them;

7. In general, avoid prefiguring informant responses by asking loaded questions ("You would never consider using heroin . . . would you?!") or leading questions ("Would you say that you were happy that your fellow medical student dropped out of the program?"); exceptions to this rule do arise, as loading and leading questions ("baiting" the informant) can come in handy when you're trying to assess emergent hypotheses (as described above);

8. Avoid interjecting a definitive opinion concerning any topic covered in the interview; if the informant asks what *you* think about, say, the legalization of marijuana, either figure out a way to decline to answer or offer up a vague, noncommittal response, such as "Well, I think that one's kind of complicated, and I'm still sorting through what I think about it";

9. Avoid suggesting a response to an informant who's struggling to come up with an answer to your question; instead, give her time to think—while the silence may make you uncomfortable, she won't notice it if she's concentrating on articulating a response (and it's a good idea for you to come up with ways to make the silence less uncomfortable for you, such as pretending to write, or actually writing, notes in your notebook); and

10. Ask lots of "verb-centered" questions, as you want the informant to explain what she did in specific instances, step by step, action by action; and when it's necessary to discuss motivation, feelings, or "interior" states, be sure to ask the informant to distinguish between the interior states she experienced at the time and the interior states she currently applies in retrospect.

Incorporating these tactical maneuvers into your conversations with informants will make them feel validated, and the more validated they feel the more respected they will feel. And with a feeling of respect comes a certain degree of trust. And out of this trust you can elicit conversation to serve as the raw material for ethnographic data production.

## A FINAL WORD ON THE SUBJECT: OBSERVATION TRUMPS INTERVIEWING!

The example of the community health and social service providers suggests that respondents may say inconsistent or contradictory things about their views or behaviors and that it is the task of interpretation to identify these inconsistencies and make sense out of them. But beyond noting these discursive inconsistencies, the researcher can use observations to create an objective and contextualized analysis of what is said in interviews.

Participant-observation and interviewing often go together as complementary activities. Becker and Geer (1970) are among the qualitative researchers who privilege observation (and it is clear that more recently Wacquant has taken a similar position). They argue that the observer can see actions that are not mentioned and even misrepresented in the interviews. Observation provides a way to check discrepancies that arise in other researcher activities. Participant-observation is absolutely necessary to provide the "rich experiential context" for understanding what is said in interviews, life narratives, and focus groups.

The research practice of interpreting interviews in light of observations is a concrete instance of what it means to be objective in research. Far from denying the role of one's own viewpoint because it is biased, it is precisely the perspective of the trained and theoretically informed sociologist that makes sense out of what otherwise can be confusing or even deliberately misleading information. Surprisingly, the positivists and the postmodernists actually have convergent views of this! Positivists emphasize the role of the trained and objective observer. Yet also from the point of view of postmodernism and reflexivity, observations are more honest than interviews; we dispense with the illusion that the discourses we engage in with interviewees are purely elicitations of their meanings and we recognize that we have a major part in producing all data, whether it is quantitative or qualitative, interviews or observations. This recognition forces us to be more forthright about why and how we make our research choices.

## CONCLUSION

Interviewing is an art designed to support the scientific endeavor of sociological research. It's difficult to master. When interviewing, it's important to maintain a kind of "dual consciousness": The interviewer must simultaneously believe the interviewee and show this belief empathically and also disbelieve everything the interviewee is saying. It's important to engage with interviewees as real humans, as though it's an unscripted and nonscientific mode of communication. At the same time, the interviewer must engage in continuous analysis of all that's occurring in the context of the interview. In many ways, the interview is a con game—it's a venue in which your success hinges on your ability to exploit the interviewee and make them feel good about being exploited. You, the interviewer, want data from the interviewee. To get the best data, the interviewee must believe that you believe everything he says and that you care about him as a human being. In the end, however, the reality of research is that you will reduce this complex human being to an object, a category, a case, a number, a textual representation. This is a large responsibility, one that ideally you'll carry out in the most ethical way possible.

## Exercises

We propose the following exercises, which become increasingly difficult and time-consuming as you proceed through the steps.

1. Prepare an interview guide about some topic or issue of interest on your campus. First work with a partner in your class and ask each other the questions each

one of you has prepared. Make suggestions for how to improve the questions. Next, use your revised interview guide to interview friends and acquaintances. Once again, use the experience and their suggestions to improve your questions. Use the responses of your classroom partner and your friends to develop questions that use the "native language" to ask questions about the issue.

2. Now you are ready to interview a larger and more carefully selected sample: For example, you might pick one or two names at random for each of your classes (so you are not just interviewing a convenience sample of your friends) or a random sample of people who live in your residence hall.

3. After you have collected this data, write a short report about the results and your interviewing experience. You may want to summarize some of your data in quantitative form, but try to use actual quotes from the interviews, rather than just counting up answers. What have you learned about how people feel about the campus issue? What insight do you gain from the open-ended answers that you would not have learned from an entirely precoded survey? For example, what have you learned about the "native language" for framing the issue.

4. In the final step of this exercise, prepare an interview guide that you can use in an interview on this campus topic with a person of higher status or authority than yourself—for example, a professor or administrator. Do you encounter problems in the interview that you did not have in interviewing people of the same status as yourself?

5. Now think about the categories we proposed in the chapter for analyzing your answers: Were your respondents eager to volunteer their views or was it a process of directing them and even "pulling teeth"—what does that tell about the salience of the issue you picked? Were there inconsistencies in what individuals said and what do you learn from them?

6. As you write the final draft of your paper, try to include theoretical or conceptual perspectives. For example, were there systematic differences in how people framed their answers by gender, race/ethnicity, age, major, and other variables? Was there an underlying liberal–conservative dimension to this issue? What do people's view on this specific issue tell us about the institution in general or maybe about campus life throughout the nation—can your findings be generalized or "made relevant" to a larger slice of life than your research subjects?

7. Finally, use this exercise to address the questions raised in the chapter about whether "observation trumps interviewing"—Since you have the benefit of also observing campus life on an everyday basis, you can provide what Becker and Geer call "the rich experiential context" in which to interpret interview answers. To use Bourdieu and Wacquant's term, you can use your own understanding of the situation to identify misrecognition among your respondents. You can play the two methods (interviewing and observing) against each other to obtain two complementary perspectives on your topic.

## Key Terms

four tactics for questions *287*
devil's advocate *287*
hypothetical *287*
posing an ideal *287*
offering interpretations *287*
frames *280*
elite interviews *280*
expert interviews *290*

interview guide *282*
observation versus
  interviewing *296*
orientations toward interviewing:
  positivist, romantic, and
  postmodern *281*
reciprocity *285*

revelatory talk *294*
setting of interviews *285*
socially desirable
  response *288*
types of interviews: structured,
  semi-structured, and
  unstructured *282*

# Focus Groups (with Tracey Lewis-Elligan)

## OVERVIEW

One of the newest and hottest choices in the methods toolbox is the focus group. A focus group refers to a small number of people who interact with each other as they respond to a set of questions posed by the researcher. This process results in data that are usually captured on audio or video recording, and the interpretation includes the analysis of both individual responses and the way responses evolve and change in the group interaction. Focus group methods contain elements of interviews and observation. They are like interviews in that the questions are planned and systematically addressed to the participants, but the interaction calls for observation skills similar to those that are used in observation in natural settings. In this chapter, we offer practical guidance for using focus groups in your research studies.

## THE MANY USES OF AN UNNATURAL VENUE: FOCUS GROUP BASICS

We don't need to offer a long philosophic discussion of what we mean by "natural"— by most criteria of naturalness, the focus group is not in a natural setting. It is not formed spontaneously, the participants usually do not know each other and may never meet again, the setting—the room, the furnishings, the space—are not the natural habitat of the participants, and the set of questions to which they respond are often not matters that they would bring up spontaneously when they talk with friends and family. The flow of interaction is not natural because the researcher moves it along with the prepared set of questions.

The "non-naturalness" of the focus group venue *should be* an advantage to the researcher. By this we mean that focus groups should be used when the setting itself is either not the focus of the research question or desired data or when the natural setting would interfere somehow with the production of data. Most often, the focus group is used to produce interaction-level data involving a small number of people; the researcher wants to know what they say and how they say it. Given this goal, it's in the researchers' best interests to create a highly antiseptic environment, a "sterile" setting free of the "triggers" that might distract participants if they were talking together in their natural setting. The "genericizing" (making as generic as possible) of the focus group venue is also highly recommended when the participants don't share a natural setting to begin with, when they're drawn from different geographic/social/economic areas of life and you want to maximize the control you have over the environment. In short, what we're saying is that the "unnaturalness" of the focus group environment should be a strength, not a weakness. If it's a weakness, then you shouldn't be using this tool in the first place.

## One Exception: The *In Situ* Focus Group

In some instances, however, the researcher may utilize the focus group in the course of implementing another method, or design. An ethnographer, for example, might find herself in a field situation that lends itself to running a productive focus group. It may so happen that several of the informants are in the same place at the same time, and so the researcher takes advantage of the moment to get a focus group going. The purpose may be to test an emerging theory, or idea, or to get multiple views on a subject/topic/event that implicates all of the informants present. This "spontaneous" deployment of the focus group in a "natural" setting, however, is an exception to the general rule that focus groups occur in controlled, *in vitro* venues.

As with every other method/tool we've presented, you need to determine whether or not the focus group is appropriate given your research question and the data you need to answer the question. Let's talk more about this.

## Gauging Appropriateness of the Method

When is a focus group method appropriate? It is used extensively in market research, sometimes taking the place of surveys or supplementing them. It has become a widely used method in institutional research as well, for example, when a curriculum review committee at a university uses focus groups to see if students are excited and engaged by a new set of courses. It is a good method to use in CBPR because it allows the researcher to catch a glimpse of what community members hope to gain from a policy or program without conducting a large expensive survey. Focus groups can be an excellent method for social autopsies. They can help disaster survivors reflect on the experience and on the organizational culture, routines, and practices that may have contributed to the disaster. The management of disaster effects can be revealed in group interaction. In general, a focus group method is a time saver compared to both surveys (which require expensive instrument design, sampling, and interviewer time) and the long semi-structured interviews conducted by the researchers rather than paid assistants (which require long blocks of time for relatively few respondents). Although focus groups can lead to the saving of both time and money, they produce data that are not easy to analyze.

Group interaction among the participants brings out themes and perspectives that a single-person interview might not elicit. It allows the researcher to see and hear negotiation of views and opinions. It gives the researchers an idea how people talk about the topic and the way they may be influencing each other's thinking. In some respects, the focus group simulates natural interaction about these topics and gives insight into aspects of perceptions and opinions on which people are open to each other's points of view. It may reveal the limits of group influence as well as individual openness to persuasion. Watching and listening to a focus group helps the researcher understand the way group processes can jell or shape individual perceptions.

Because the topics of conversation are focused by the researcher's questions, the researcher can learn about topics and opinions that the participants would not spontaneously bring up.

We can easily see how this characteristic of focus groups is important in marketing. For example, consumers would probably not spontaneously talk about how a detergent ad makes them feel about the product; once the question is posed, however, we can hear the thinking of each individual on the topic and the way they may shift their views in response to each other.

In short, before choosing a focus group method, be sure that the focus group will help you answer your research question. Think through what observing a structured interaction will tell you that could not be learned from other methods such as surveys, interviews, and observing "natural" interactions. The interaction itself has to be part of what you want to study—otherwise you could just carry out a survey or interview individuals; these data are considerably easier to analyze than focus group interactions. One researcher suggests that it is especially valuable to use focus groups when the researcher wants to know whether the beliefs and opinions are stable or "prone to change in the situation of interaction with others, who are possibly seen as equals … and are able to challenge and modify a participant's views" (Krzyzanowski 2008: 173). In other words, focus group analysis explores the malleability of individual beliefs in interaction with others, a type of data that interviews could not reveal and that would emerge only gradually or in a happenstance way through observation of interactions.

The focus on specific topics or themes has to be an integral aspect of your research question—otherwise you could just observe "natural" interaction which would give you a better sense of what topics people like to talk about when they are left to their own devices. So both **interaction** and **focused topics** have to be relevant to your statement of the research question in order to choose a focus group method.

## GUIDELINES FOR RUNNING A FOCUS GROUP

Here is "how to do it." Compared to the logistic and emotional complexities of participant observation with its inherent formlessness and unpredictability, focus group methods seem simple and easy to outline.

1. The first step in **sampling** is to identify the population in which you are interested. As in quantitative research, try to establish a sampling frame that lists all the possible individuals whom you consider part of the population. In real life, you may have to make a number of compromises on the way to the sampling frame. If you are studying students who took a specific new curriculum at a university, the task is easy; the student records office can make the class rosters available to institutional researchers. If you want to sample community residents to see how they feel about a new cultural center in the local park, a list of addresses can be established and sampling of households and individuals within households set up, much as in opinion surveys and political polls. Or alternatively, individuals in community organizations can be sampled and invited to participate in the focus groups, though that would leave out people who are unaffiliated and perhaps apathetic, alienated, too busy with work or family, or unwilling to leave their homes. In studying communities, all organizationally based samples are problematic. If you want to study all individuals who might want to buy a new detergent when it goes on the market, the sampling is very complex and in practice has to be simplified to selection of individuals who are on the roster of a marketing firm as people who are willing to participate in focus groups.

2. Once the sampling frame is established you want to draw a sample that will yield about six to eight people per focus group. If the resources to establish several focus groups are available, that option is preferable to running only one for obvious reasons; you reduce the

problem of a quirky group that would yield inaccurate results or of a group that is belligerent, uncommunicative or hard to work with for whatever reason. You may want to arrange different focus groups for different parts of the population—for example, for young people and older community residents, for community leaders and less involved people, and so on. You may remember from your quantitative methods courses and experiences that it is best if the researcher does not prearrange the sample, setting definite proportions for different subgroups that she expects to find in the population. The practice of presetting proportions of key subgroups—tempting as it is—does not produce results that are as representative and accurate as random sampling. (Yes, we know—that is a "believe it or not" for most people who are convinced that random sampling will be too … random in the layperson's sense of the word.) A random sample of decent size will yield statistics such as means or proportions that are usually quite close to the population parameters and will randomize the distribution of variables that we failed to foresee in our prearrangement of preset numbers in our subsamples. In focus group research, however, we may want to split our population into subcategories that will go into distinct focus groups for the reason that interaction is often freer and livelier when the groups are homogenous in terms of characteristics that will seem important to them. For example, when Roberta carried out focus group research at a small-town high school, there were groups composed of freshmen boys, freshmen girls, senior boys, and senior girls. The underlying assumption was that for adolescents, gender and age are characteristics that create a feeling of difference and that individuals who differ in these characteristics may feel awkward interacting with each other.

3. It is generally considered a good practice for focus group participants not to know each other. That ideal cannot always be attained—when Roberta studied the small-town high school, it was not possible to keep all the groups composed only of strangers to each other. In institutional research in a school or an organization, it may be especially difficult to set up groups of strangers.

4. Many focus group researchers give out a pregroup questionnaire to participants to understand their views on the topics of the focus group. This information can then be matched with their remarks during the focus group process and with the final resolution or consensus (if any) that the group reaches. An interesting and effective use of a prequestionnaire was made by Fred Strodtbeck in his "method of revealed differences"; Strodtbeck (1951) worked in the field in the Southwest and asked couples in Navaho, Hispanic, and Anglo communities questions about their views of a good marriage. He asked the spouses in each couple to first state their opinions separately from each other and then to resolve their differences in interaction with their spouse. He was able to observe cultural variation in the process of resolving differences and negotiating consensus between spouses. This method is an example of how valuable information can be collected by comparing individual pregroup responses to the outcome of the group interaction. The pregroup questionnaire also yields basic information about each respondent.

5. Although some guides to focus group research may state that a group can have up to twelve participants, the reality is that a large size will make the data analysis extremely difficult. If resources are available, two groups of six would be preferable to one group of twelve. Eight may be an effective upper-limit for being able to follow the interaction, to distinguish the voices (if it is audio recorded), and to have a firm grasp on what the interaction was about, especially for a beginning focus-group researcher.

6. Prior to meeting the group, the researcher sets up a series of questions or topics in a document called a **protocol**. These questions/topics inject the focused themes into the interaction.

As in an interview guide, the questions may move from simple, congenial "warm up" questions or discussion of basic information to more complex or contentious topics. It is a good idea to pretest the questions to make sure that they make sense, that they are not offensive, and that they yield the types of information for which the researcher is looking. It is very important that these questions be questions that all the participants can answer. Participants should not feel that they are being tested or that they are being forced to reveal their ignorance of a subject. Generally, they should not be questions to which the answer might be "I don't know—I never heard of that—I don't have any experience with that." The questions need to be worded at a level that is appropriate for the participants and in a way that "speaks their language." Let's look at an example—a teen focus group on body image and eating behaviors. "How is the body mass index calculated?" is an inappropriate question for a focus group; we are not testing the participants' technical know-how! "How do you feel about your weight?" is a question that could lead to embarrassment. "Do you and your friends ever talk about weight or body image?" is a better question than the preceding two. It does not "put people on the spot" about their knowledge or personal characteristics while it encourages an interactive approach to the topic.

7. The number of questions is usually between 8 and 12. It varies depending on the number of participants, the complexity of the topic, and the degree to which the questions are specific or detailed. More than 12 will make the session seem tedious; less than eight may not be enough to collect the information.

8. The researcher needs to work closely with an assistant called the **moderator** who actually poses the questions. In some cases, the researcher has to pose her own questions because she doesn't have an assistant but this situation makes it very difficult for her to observe and think about the interaction. The moderator is ideally someone who has experience with focus group research and is comfortable with the types of individuals in the focus group. For example, in the high school focus groups, the moderator was a young man—a graduate student—who had previous experience conducting focus groups with teens on the topic of risky sexual behaviors. The moderator looks at the questions written by the researcher and should be able to make modifications; the questions must be comfortable and "natural" for the moderator to ask.

9. Focus group participants are human subjects and the regulations and norms that we discussed in Chapter 4 apply to their treatment. The room and the setting should be safe, congenial, and neutral. The researcher's home is generally not considered an appropriate venue. If the topics for discussion include the participants' views of a community organization, a business in the community, or a political official, the offices of these organizations and individuals are not appropriate places for the group to meet. Neither are the corporate offices of a company that produces a product whose marketing is the topic of the conversation. Focus group participants are often paid—always so in marketing research. The rules of common courtesy apply in the way that the participants are treated when they arrive and as they begin their conversation, within the bounds of the confidentiality and anonymity that they must be accorded. For example, their full names might not be disclosed to each other or might be kept confidential from all but the principal investigator. Since the participants see each other as well as the researcher and the moderator, complete confidentiality and anonymity are not possible. LRBs and IRBs will need to review the arrangements and may require different procedures depending on the topic of the focus group. Discussion of images of a detergent among people who wash their dishes will require less review and fewer measures of protection than a focus group composed of heroin addicts discussing the merits of methadone maintenance versus recovery programs.

10. Once everyone has been appropriately introduced to each other, the conversation begins. It is up to the moderator to accomplish two tasks. One is to make sure that everyone has a chance to address every question. This may require "going around the circle" and giving each individual an opportunity to speak. The second and somewhat contradictory task is to make sure that interaction actually takes place and flows freely. It is unfortunately easy to let a focus group turn into a sort of sequential interview, in which each participant takes a turn at answering the question under consideration, but there is essentially no interaction among the individuals. The trick is to do both at the same time—involve every individual and also keep up a flow of interaction with people addressing each other and not simply responding separately to the moderator's questions. The moderator also has a third task and that is to move smoothly from one question (or topic) to the next. When a question has "become tired"—when the answers become strained or repetitive—it is time to move on. The closer the flow of talk resembles natural interaction, the better, with the caveat that in natural conversations, individuals often are left out or decide to withdraw into silence, and this disengagement should be avoided in the focus group.

11. Generally two hours would be a maximum amount of time for a focus group and one hour probably the minimum. Focus groups with children or young teens might need to be shorter; for example, when RG studied the high school focus groups, each one only ran for 45 minutes.

12. While the moderator asks questions and the respondents answer the questions and then engage with each other on these topics, someone has to engage in **recording** what is happening! This task is essential and requires a considerable degree of technical expertise. Sophisticated marketing organizations have adequate methods of visual and audio recording. Unfortunately many student researchers (and even senior researchers in field situations) do not. Written recording alone is a challenging exercise; you may want to try it because it will force you to decide on the spot what is important in the interaction you are seeing and hearing. You cannot possibly record everything that is said, certainly not in the exact wording in which it is said and not in a paraphrase either. It is simply physically impossible. Research choices will have to be made very rapidly, and the only way this can happen is if you are fully in tune with your own research question and have already channeled your thinking toward certain issues and themes. You can then focus on those themes and issues, choosing not to try to write down everything you hear. If you have a more relaxed, inductive or "grounded theory" approach to your project and want to remain open to many new possibilities and directions, you will find recording with written notes to be hectic and frustrating. Audio recording is a good idea, but in practice it may be nearly impossible to tell who is speaking; sound quality has to be superb to make these distinctions and sort out multiple voices. It is very likely that when you listen to the tape you so diligently collected, you will not be able to tell who is who and often not even what is being said. Visual recording helps the researcher to get around these problems. Ideally, the researcher is not the recorder, any more than he or she is the moderator. The researcher should sit quietly in the room, observing everything and turning herself into a second but infinitely more intelligent and selective recording device, jotting down only an occasional note and connecting what is heard to the research question and the interpretive framework that she has in mind.

13. When you write about the results, focus on a qualitative description of the process you observed and support your conclusions with quotations from the transcript. In your **analysis** you want to produce several types of data. One is based on tracing how individuals responded to each other and how their positions changed, if at all. You can use material from

your pregroup questionnaires to describe the participants in demographic terms and to see whether the interaction impacted their initial positions. A second way of organizing the data is to look at which secondary themes emerge in response to your questions or topics; these secondary topics are ones that the participants bring up themselves. You can record and cross reference the secondary topics, noting how the attention of the participants may return to the same secondary topics in response to distinctly different prompts provided by the primary topics or themes introduced by the researcher. This procedure can alert the researcher to existence of themes that had been left out in the initial formulation of questions; it is as if the participants were saying, "Hey, you keep asking us about one thing, but we really want to talk about something else" (Krzyzanowski 2008: 174). In reporting your results, avoid meaningless quantification; generally a sample with less than 30 individuals does not lend itself to statistical analysis, and even reporting percentages is questionable. With only six to eight participants in the focus groups, quantification should just involve reporting numbers ("two out of six") or estimates ("half of the group") rather than reporting results as percentages which conveys a false sense of precision.

14. This consideration brings us to the last and most important point. As in all research, the method is only as good as the overall conceptualization and research question. A focus group can bring out the very essence of a community's multiple points of view—its areas of consensus and dissension. It can show how human beings negotiate their differences and create a collective consciousness or conscience. It provides clues about which individual beliefs are stable and which can be changed in interaction. It can reveal hidden impulses that lead to startling results in the market place. It can reproduce in a microcosm the peer pressures (as well as individual resistance to peer pressures) that impel people to make purchases, engage in or turn away from risky behaviors, and modify their bodies and their self-embodiment.

## RESEARCH IN ACTION: EXAMPLES OF FOCUS GROUP-BASED STUDIES

In this section, we present some real-life studies and use them to illustrate when and how to use focus groups effectively.

# Case Study

## Case Example: Are African American girls joining the eating disorder mainstream?

BY TRACEY LEWIS-ELLIGAN

Traditionally, focus groups have been well-suited to and frequently used in market research in order to target a niche market or to refine a brand. However, more recently, social science researchers have utilized the focus group method for several reasons—to conduct evaluation research, hone research instruments, and to investigate rarely explored or new territory in a particular area. Focus groups can be most valuable in exploratory research where little is known about the topic or a particular population.

The case example illustrated here falls under this latter domain. Little research has been conducted about African American girls and eating disorders. Historically, research has focused on middle- and upper-income white girls, so much so, that eating disorders are stereotypically described as white, affluent girl disorders. Little is known about how African American girls construct beliefs about body image and their eating behaviors or dieting practices, especially girls who come from economically stable and affluent backgrounds. Moreover, limited attention has been focused on the more normative developmental transitions among African American teen girls whose experiences are not shaped by added stressors associated with economic hardship.

For this particular topic and population, the focus group method was an ideal fit to explore the many unanswered questions about this underrepresented population. Three broad research questions guided the study: (1) What are upper-income African American girls' definitions of beauty? (2) Do upper-income African American girls ascribe to American norms of beauty which focus on thinness as an ideal body form? (3) How do African American girls negotiate or manage their body image?

Participants were purposively recruited from a nonprofit youth service organization to participate in the study. To meet the selection criteria, girls had to reside in families with a household income of $75,000 and above, were between the ages of 13–18, and self-identified as African American.

A total of 31 girls met the criteria and participated in focus groups. The participants' age ranged between 13 and 17, with a mean age of 14.30. The household income of the participants ranged from $75,000 to 1.5 million dollars with a mean income of $294,642. A majority of the girls attended predominantly white schools, and about half of the girls attended private schools.

Seven focus groups were conducted and audio-taped. The number of participants for each focus group ranged from 4 participants to a total of 12 participants per group. Girls who participated in the focus group with 12 participants were invited back to participate in a second focus group which was smaller in size—comprised of 5 and 6 participants.

Overall, the focus groups created a setting that allowed girls to share their beliefs about what a group of girls who identify as belonging to the same race and share a similar class position think about body image, eating disorders, and dieting. The strength of the focus group rested on the assumption that the participants shared common characteristics. A majority of the participants experienced living in predominantly white affluent communities and they attended predominantly white schools with competitive and rigorous academic programs. Similarly, they reported coming from similar backgrounds in terms of family structure and socioeconomic position. These common experiences contributed to the depth of discussion and created a synergistic effect that allowed girls to articulate their unique positions beyond their individual perspectives into a collective meaning or experience. Additionally, the focus groups allowed for lively discussion of a topic that was not previously discussed in a pointed or focused way. Girls expressed enthusiasm and validation that their voices were captured and that they had the opportunity to meet together to discuss issues that they felt were relevant to their unique positions.

Although the focus groups offered an appropriate method to investigate the girls' voices, a few limitations emerged. First, size matters! The largest focus group was comprised of 12 participants. This group proved to be too large primarily in terms of managing the flow and focus of the questions. The audiotape was difficult to hear and it was hard to track who was speaking. The large group was also the most diverse in terms of age, and the age diversity posed an issue in terms of older participants

*(continued)*

*(continued)*

silencing the younger participants. A social desirability factor was most at play with the younger participants searching for acceptance by the older participants.

Other issues in the research arose from the sensitivity of the topic. Participants might have been less willing to speak about specific aspects of personal struggles with eating disorders due to the public nature of the focus group. Participants were aware that their comments could not be assured to be anonymous or that their privacy would be fully protected. Measures were taken to try to minimize this risk by having participants sign assents forms as well as confidentiality agreement statements. However, participants were concerned that their parents may discover their responses and beliefs or that other participants of the group would share their comments with individuals outside of the focus group.

The focus group method allowed for several themes to emerge about how middle- and upper-income African American girls think about body image and eating disorders. First, girls struggled to define beauty or "the ideal girl." The participants could not define the ideal girl in just one way. Instead, they agreed that the definition varied based on one's point of view. They deconstructed "the ideal girl" based on three points of view: (1) the girl's, (2) the boy's, and (3) society's view. They grappled with their perception that there are both gender differences in defining the ideal girl and differences between American and African American points of view.

From a girl's view, the ideal girl was described as having intrinsic attributes rather than ones based on physical appearance. For example, Kristen described the ideal girl as "someone you want to strive to be like in your family or something." Wendy agreed, "maybe because they're smart. Or there's someone successful and you might want to be like them, but you won't be like oh she looks this way." Lilly, summed it up by emphasizing intrinsic uniqueness as an element of the girls' point of view: "it's who they are."

This perspective is different from their perception of the boy's definition of the ideal girl. In contrast to the girl's point of view, Alison stated, "When it's a guy's point of view, it's completely focused on what they look like." Rene elaborated, "Guys want what's perfect is a girl with a skinny waist, and like a medium butt and thighs that are kind of thick but not too and like a good bust size."

In terms of body size, the girls reported that the ideal size was determined in part by American culture and in part by African American culture. Nickol stated, "Black girls would be fuller in certain areas. Obviously like a black girl has a stereotype that like a big butt and like boobs and a white girl isn't necessarily described that way. And white girls are just skinnier." However, other girls were quick to add to the comment. For example, Kelly stated, "I don't think African American girls have less pressure to be thin. I think guys expect girls to be thin." Kristen agreed, "guys like smaller girls regardless of their race or where they're from." Beth offered the ideal size for a girl as being size "0–6 or maybe 0–8 but 8 is pushing it."

In terms of eating disorders, majority of the participants echoed the stereotypes depicted about eating disorders—especially in terms of extreme dieting or anorexia nervosa. Michele noted that eating disorders were a "white girl thing, and we haven't really experienced that." However, several girls observed that they had heard about some girls struggling with their weight and appearance. Jasmine noted that she was aware of one black girl who "did all sorts . . . taking laxatives, pills and starving herself to lose weight."

This research, driven by focus groups, has set the stage for a preliminary understanding of a topic and population that has gone largely unexplored. It begins to contribute to the literature and inform how to develop additional research designs that will allow for greater understanding about the diverse experiences of African American girls.

## High School Focus Groups

Here is another example that illustrates the way focus groups produce information that is similar to observational data. But they have the advantage that observations about how people discuss a specific topic might come about only by chance in many months of field-work—or perhaps never be collected—whereas the focus group is directly asked to address these topics.

Whether or not the researchers use software for text analysis and produce quantitative results, the focus groups should provide insights into social processes, cultures, and behaviors. It should answer research questions. In the following example, the focus group research was carried out two years consecutively at a high school in a small town—let's call it Grover's Corners—near the edge of a large metropolitan area in the Midwest.

The case example is based on a letter written by a member of the research team (Roberta Garner) after the second year of the study to the individual who served as moderator in the first year. Here is a little background information. During the years when the focus groups were conducted, about 20 percent of the students at the high school were Latinos and the remainder was predominantly non-Hispanic whites—"Anglos" who were not immigrants. The questions on the protocol focused on plans for the future and perceptions of the school. The questions on a brief questionnaire for all focus group participants asked about parents' occupations and education, whether they expected to graduate from high school, and how much homework they do. The research questions asked how the organizational culture of the school was related to the cultures of the community and how these cultures affected student expectations and aspirations.

Dear Matt:

I thought you might be interested in hearing about the focus groups this year. . . . Remember how last year there was not one Hispanic student in the groups, although Hispanics comprise about 20% of the students? This year we put together a list of students with Hispanic surnames and drew a random sample from it so we were able to form groups of Hispanic students. Julian (a student researcher) prepared Spanish versions of the questionnaire (a short instrument administered to all participants in the focus groups) and asked the discussion questions in Spanish for two groups composed of young men and women of Mexican origin....

When we walked into the school, we saw the usual display of athletic trophies and anti-drug posters. But the "freaks" seemed more visible this year—an Anglo boy with turquoise hair, kids with bull-ring pierces through the nasal septum, two girls with dyed spiked hair and shredded leggings lying on the floor in the entrance hall. . . .

The principal quickly dispatched us to the conference room and we waited with our Mountain Dew, donuts, and Doritos for the kids to make their appearance. Three of us—the three student researchers—rotated as moderators—and I observed and took notes throughout to supplement the audiotapes.

The first group was composed of Hispanic women, mostly sophomores and juniors. The conversation proceeded bilingually because the participants varied markedly in the length of time they had lived in Grover's Corners and in their English proficiency; two felt comfortable only in Spanish. . . . Five or ten years from now they hoped to have careers and families; they would like to be able to go to college—middle class aspirations but stated in a vague and tentative way. They saw many obstacles: financial problems, the possibility of teen pregnancy, and bad grades were mentioned. One of them said sadly but firmly that she did not think she would make it to high school graduation; her mother and brothers had dropped out of school and she felt this would happen to her. She said that the teachers favored "the preppies."

The participants expressed pride in their families. "Our parents have struggled, sacrificed and suffered for a long time to give us a better life." But parents are not mentors for technical, professional or business careers or for college. They have few mentors or role models in this regard. They feel that there is continuing prejudice, discrimination, and exclusion in the school, though fights have decreased; they do not feel that they are a vital part of the school, of its academic or social life, nor does school seem to be a vital part of their lives. When we asked them what they would like us to remember from our conversation with them: "Do not feel sorry for us." They will be OK, even if life seems very hard sometimes. A key term in the conversation was *animo*, a complex concept that encompasses spirit, will, intention, energy, mind, courage and valor.

The young Anglo men were very different in their demeanor, self representations, and aspirations. There were nine of them and they bounded into the room with a lot of noise, joking and energy. The five seniors among them were quite similar to the seniors we saw last year: Big and athletic, self-confident, boisterous in a good-natured way, polite and pleasant with adults . . . They used a discourse of individual rational choice in discussing their personal plans and aspirations, but the seniors among them presented themselves as a group and assumed the mantle of speaking for the school. They indicated that they represented the school, that they are its heart and soul, whereas we observed that the other groups (female and/or Hispanic) had to define themselves from a marginal or peripheral position, as struggling to be a part of things or as defining an oppositional identity, or some mix of the two. When the Hispanic women said "we" they mean Hispanics or Hispanic women, and similarly for the Hispanic men. The Anglo women don't use "we" much in their discourse, either about the school or about themselves as a sub-group. But when the Anglo men say "we" they mean the school—they think they are speaking for the school as a whole. They believe that sports bring everyone together. They see the school as united, while the Hispanic women saw it as unequal and divided by ethnicity and class. And the Anglo males receive the most specific and useful role-modeling and mentoring from adults.

It is the Anglo males who know the most about financial aid, sports scholarships and similar financial support for college. In short, by the time the Anglo males are seniors they are the most self-confident, well-informed and "definite" of the student categories, and the least tentative in their discourse and the least marginalized in their self images. They form the core group of the school and see themselves (and I would guess, are seen by others) as "representing" what the school is all about. This is especially true of the college-bound men, the "preppies" about whom we heard complaints from others. The Anglo senior men include more children of middle class parents in technical and business occupations such as dentist, nurse, loan officer, engineer, and vet-tech (as reported in the questionnaires collected from the focus group participants) because working-class kids are more likely to become disengaged and drop out before senior year. . . .

To sum up, the Anglo males' plans are the least "contingent," least in a state of drift, the most specific, the most definite, the best informed, the most optimistic, and the most supported by adults as mentors and role models. The Hispanic females are at the opposite end of the spectrum in "drift," lack of role models and mentors, sense of pessimism, and lack of information about definite steps to take to make dreams come true. Hispanic males and Anglo females are somewhere in-between: but at a subjective level, the Hispanic males seem more positive about their future, themselves, and the school than the Anglo females we saw, even if the former face objectively larger barriers of financial problems, English proficiency, discrimination, and lack of information about post-secondary options. Our colleague Judith Bootcheck suggests that more attention needs to be given to the role of drift and contingency in post-secondary plans.

If we add the dimension of class to gender and ethnicity, the picture is enlarged and sharpened in the expected directions. SES and parental occupations are clearly also important forces, and within the groups defined by gender and ethnicity, the class factors tend to distinguish individuals with clear plans and good information from individuals who are more adrift, less well-informed, and more negative about themselves, school, and the future. . . .

---

These excerpts from the analysis show how the researchers move from recording individual comments and responses to a more global and generalizing set of findings based on the tone and topics of the group interaction. The original research summary includes information about the comments and behavior of individuals, but here we have presented the group-level findings, abstracting from what each individual contributed. The multiple focus group design allowed the researchers to identify not only the dominant or "hegemonic" view of the school (corresponding closely to that of the Anglo males) but other currents of opinion as well. Key terms used to typify values and cliques in the school appeared in the discourse: "animo"; "preppies"; "druggies—the wrong crowd"; the use of "we"; and the absence or presence in their discourse of a "path to the future."

Thus the focus group analysis brought together many sociological concepts. These concepts include demographic categories (used to form the groups in the first place); the cognitive maps that young people form of the world in which they live; subjective responses to objective conditions; role-models and mentoring as it relates to aspirations, expectations, school engagement and disengagement; the fit between organizational culture and individual goals; and the presence or absence of "drift" and "contingency" in their understanding of their futures. These concepts guided the initial research design. For example, the demographic categories were used to produce the four focus groups and motivated the questionnaire items about parents' occupations and education. The concepts of aspirations and expectations were used to develop protocol questions. But these conceptual themes also emerged out of the analysis of the interactions. Once again we can see the ongoing dialog between initial concepts used to guide the design and the concepts that emerge from the research.

## CONCLUSION

Focus groups occupy an important place in the methods tool-kit. But they should not be over-used. The research question must *demand* the use of focus groups. It should be a question that can only be answered by **examining interaction and focusing on specific topics**. And the theory with which you're working should be compatible with the method. Too many scholars jump to the focus group immediately just because it seems inventive and interesting and easy to do. In fact, conducting an effective focus group is incredibly difficult. Now you are prepared to make a rigorous assessment of its appropriateness and to run a good focus group if your research question and theoretical framework call for it.

## Exercises

1. Select a topic of interest on your campus (it could be the same issue that you used for your interview exercises) and as a class, develop a plan for focus group research. One possibility would be assessment of a course or requirement. Write the themes and questions for the protocol. Discuss your questions to see if they "sound OK." Be sure to avoid questions that probe for factual knowledge and lead to embarrassment. ("What do you think about the current economic situation?" or "How do you see the current job prospects for college gradu-ates?" and *not* "What is the current unemployment rate?")

2. To get a very basic "feel" for focus group research, invite six to eight friends of students in the class to a focus group practice exercise. Offer them treats; try to avoid inviting people who know each other. Let several people in the class take turns as moder-ator. A good exercise is not to record the interaction at all, except for written notes, and then discuss what you observed. Here are a few questions to consider: What did you learn about "the native language"—the way people worded and framed their comments? Did people's views shift or change as a result of the interaction? Can you identify a central view that was shared by many in the focus group and then variants and alternatives put forth by smaller numbers? Remember to reject the temptation of excessive quantification ("33.3% felt that . . .").

## Key Terms

analysis *303*
focus group methods: examining interaction *and* focusing on specific topics 310

focused topics 300
interaction *300*
moderator *302*
protocol *301*

recording *303*
sampling *300*

# 20
# Life Narratives

## OVERVIEW

Life narratives are life stories told by research subjects (or participants). Analysis of life narratives is a research method that can be adapted to many kinds of qualitative designs; they can be part of ethnographic research, community-based participatory research, historical research, and social autopsies. They can be interpreted from many different theoretical perspectives. In this chapter we offer a brief history of the life narrative, featuring some of the most influential studies that relied on the life narrative method, and we provide some practical guidance for using the method in your own research. Finally, we present and describe the "life history interview," a particular technique for implementing the life narrative into a research project.

## THE LIFE NARRATIVE: A STAPLE ITEM IN THE QUALITATIVE RESEARCH METHOD INVENTORY

Life narratives are often the product of unstructured interviews. They require excellent rapport between the researcher and the life-story teller. The interpretation is easier and better when the researcher understands the social context in which the storyteller lives. In many respects, the life narrative is at the opposite extreme from pre-coded survey data; the latter is highly focused, broken down into variables, and collected from a large probability sample, while the life narrative is provided by only a small number of individuals, is marked by the complexity of having all the variables intertwined with each other, and can only be understood in context.

Life narrative collection was one of the earliest qualitative methods to be employed in the social sciences and was widely used by anthropologist-ethnographers to understand the lives and cultures of communities and ethnic groups ("tribes") outside of the literate modernized regions of the world. It continued to be a method used by anthropologists in the twentieth century, yielding valuable documents such as Leo Simmons' *Sun Chief*, the autobiography of a Hopi man (1963); Ricardo Pozas, *Juan the Chamula*, the life narrative of a Maya-speaker in Chiapas, Mexico (1962); and Mintz, *Worker in Cane* (1960), about a rural worker in Puerto Rico. These classic life narratives were collected at key times in the histories of the cultures, allowing us to trace the process by which the Western, modern world transformed ways and traditional cultures of indigenous and rural people.

These changes came about not only by violent conquest but by the influx of new ideas and religions, administrative policies and decisions of government agencies, and markets in labor and commodities such as sugar.

## The Chicago School: Exemplary Life Narrative Studies

The Chicago School produced a famous analysis of a life narrative in W. I. Thomas and Florian Znaniecki's Polish Peasant study (1918–1920). The subject of the life narrative, a Polish immigrant living in Chicago in the 1920s, recounted his life in Poland and the United States and his experiences in making the transition from rural Poland to the great industrial metropolis.

In the post–World War II period, anthropologist Oscar Lewis stirred up controversy with his publication of life narratives of individuals in Mexican, Puerto Rican, and Cuban families (Lewis 1963, 1965, 1977; Stocking 1992). He drew criticism for using the life narrative material to develop the "culture of poverty" thesis. The culture of poverty thesis posited that poor people perpetuate their condition by learned behaviors and normative patterns that prevent them from managing their lives in a rational manner that would allow them to prosper, become educated and socially mobile, and engage in politics effectively. The life narratives reveal violent relationships, impulsive sexual encounters, unexpected pregnancies, sibling rivalry, parental favoritism, and reckless consumer spending.

A "Rashomon" technique of asking several respondents to comment on the same incident in the life of the family allowed the reader to see the contradictions and disagreements in how family members perceived and portrayed each other and key events. Only in the Cuban life histories do we read about people coming to organize their lives rationally and realistically because after the Cuban Revolution they were able to respond to new opportunities and a new revolutionary culture of political awareness. The Cuban narratives broached the possibility that the culture of poverty is not as deeply ingrained and inter-generationally transmitted as the other volumes seemed to assert. Critics suggested that the Mexican and Puerto Rican life narratives presented by Lewis were highly edited to reveal negative cultural patterns and that the selection of respondents perhaps also biased conclusions about the lives of poor people. Whatever the scientific validity and theoretical persuasiveness of Lewis' work, the stories make for exciting reading.

After this controversial body of work, researchers tended to be more cautious in their use of life narratives, giving attention to the difficulties of generalizing from them, the problem of bias in the selection of respondents, and the issue of how literally any information can be taken. Among important ethnographic life histories in the later decades of the twentieth century, we can mention Sharon Gmelch, *Nan: The Life of an Irish Travelling Woman* (1991), about life in the caste-like community of Travelling People in Ireland; Ernestine Friedl's *The Women of Deh Koh* (1991), about women in an Iranian village; and Janice Boddy and Virginia Barnes' life history of a Somali woman (Aman 1995).

## The Spontaneity Factor

Before discussing how to collect and interpret life histories, we need to mention life narratives that were not produced in response to a specific request by a researcher but were more spontaneously produced by a speaker or writer. Once we include these kinds of narratives, we are of course opening the door to all autobiographies and memoirs. We mentioned these types of materials in our discussion of discourse analysis and cultural artifacts, but it is appropriate to mention them here as well.

Particularly dramatic examples include memoirs produced by individuals who are not conventionally expected to write autobiographies or perhaps to write at all, but who do so out of a powerful need to record their condition and break the silence and the barriers that have cut them off from the world of the educated, the elite, and the dominant classes and ethnic groups of the nation and the globe. One of these documents is *Child of the Dark*, by Carolina Maria de Jesus (2003), who kept a diary on scraps of paper in the slums of Sao Paolo, Brazil.

Another politically engaged autobiography is *I, Rigoberta Menchu: An Indian Woman in Guatemala* (1984). Menchu describes the experiences of her family and indigenous community during the years of dictatorship and repression by the Guatemalan military. The literal-minded complained that Menchu told the story of repression and murder as if all the events had befallen specific members of her family and they suggested that it contained inaccuracies; they missed the point that the book is a condensation and representation of the life of a people, refracted through the life of an individual, but not intended to be an exact record of events. These politically charged life narratives can have an important role in community-based participatory research and are similar to the data produced in these types of design.

Members of elites also produce spontaneous life narratives, and these can reveal conflicts and perspectives that the wealthy and powerful normally shield from public view. For example, George Marcus (1992) uses Sallie Bingham's *Passion and Prejudice*, her personal story of life and money in a "dynastic family," as an account that provides insight into the construction of family relationships and estates in the upper class. He analyzes a memoir of the H. L. Hunt family to explore how family investments changed over time and why family members tried to corner the world silver market. Like Menchu's life narrative, the sagas of the wealthy may not be literally true yet nevertheless are valuable documents for understanding life in a particular milieu.

## WHOSE LIFE, WHOSE NARRATIVE?

Not all individuals in all cultures are willing to tell a life story that is of interest in research. Cultures differ markedly in whether telling a life story is a valued or even permissible activity. In some cultures, there may be powerful cultural rules—taboos, if you will—against revealing much of one's life, especially to an outsider. In many cultures, life stories are told in highly formulaic ways. There is a "right way" to tell the story, for example, as a narrative of personal triumph and success, or on the contrary, of suffering and victimization.

Social psychologists use the terms "internal and external locus of control" for differences among individuals (and their cultures) in whether the self is seen as an agent, responsible for one's own decisions, choices, and life course, or as the passive recipient of one's fate; these social psychological and cultural dispositions may shape how the life narrative is told, regardless of how life was actually lived. As we will discuss below, very few people tell their stories as tales of random chance and mere contingency, even if random events objectively shaped their life course.

### A Suitable Topic

Cultural beliefs and practices influence which topics and events are considered suitable for inclusion and which must be left out (often sexual ones). Cultural norms impact the tone of the story. Cultures differ in the norms that guide the truth of the stories people tell about themselves, and it is often difficult for the researcher to gauge this accurately. As in interviewing, the researcher must "believe everything and nothing."

Within cultures, socially relevant demographic categories (such as the old and the young, men and women, dominant and subaltern ethnic groups) may be expected to tell different kinds of stories. For example, in U.S. culture, young people are expected to tell stories of hope and ambition, and old people, stories of satisfaction and fulfillment. In some cultures, women are expected to tell stories of suffering and sacrifice for their families, regardless of whether they have really experienced these situations or felt these emotions.

Within larger cultures and specific categories or subcultures, individuals differ in their willingness to tell stories and the kinds of stories they want to tell. People who want to tell life stories are often the same ones who want to engage the researcher and act as guides.

The researcher must consider whether the individual is a leader who is proud to communicate an exemplary and respected story to the outsider, a cultural broker intent on using the contact with the outside world to further his or her own interests and perhaps those of the community, an outcast or deviant who will shed a negative light on the community and reveal its uncomfortable secrets, an isolate who is disengaged from the community, or a person who is already bi- or multicultural and at ease in several worlds. Each of these perspectives can be valuable in research, but the researcher must be able to identify the perspective in order to interpret the life narrative. A disgruntled outcast may provide valuable insights, but they will be insights different from those offered by the proud and respected leader with moral authority who represents the ideals of the culture. This issue can only be resolved by the researcher's effort to understand the life narratives in their broader social context and by obtaining other kinds of information—from observation, from interviews with a range of respondents, and so on—that enhance understanding of who is telling the life story, how the individual relates to the community, and why he or she is telling it.

## A Suitable Life

The researcher may want to avoid **problems of self-selection** by carrying out a more systematic **sampling** of individuals for the life narrative, possibly even using standard sampling techniques to do so (for instance, by randomly sampling households in the community and then randomly sampling individuals within the households that were selected). This technique may produce a larger and less biased sample, but possibly at the cost of length and quality of the narratives. And in some communities, it may be very hard for a researcher to explain random sampling that leads to the selection of "unimportant" or "weird" individuals, while the well-respected and articulate are left out.

An example of a more systematic sampling strategy, but at the cost of less rich and detailed material, is provided by Roberta Garner's study of first-generation college students. She asked over 250 students in classes in a wide range of institutions of higher education to write life narratives, which she analyzed to understand their "vocabularies of motive" for attending college. This technique yielded a large amount of data from a non-self-selected sample (and one fairly close to a random sample). The data allowed her to focus on her research question, but there was not a lot of information in the narratives about intimate personal experiences that might have provided an in-depth psychodynamic understanding of their educational choices.

## Motivation

As in the case of interviews (apart from short structured interviews), we must reflect on reciprocity. What is "in it" for individuals who provide the life narratives? Are they delighted to share the life story? Vindicating a specific act or behavior and putting themselves in a good light? Telling a tale of woe and victimization and putting the blame on someone for all adverse aspects of their life? Demonstrating pride in their culture and way of life? Hoping to be mentioned in a book and get their name in print? Helping out a new friend (the researcher)? Making a connection with an outsider who can help them or their community? Contributing to solving or at least creating awareness of a problem in the community? Participating in the scientific project of expanding our understanding of how individual biographies intersect history? Expecting to be paid for their time and their revelations about themselves? One or more of these motivations may impel individuals to tell their stories and may shape the stories that are collected.

As in the case of interviewing, paying for life narratives has costs and benefits. The costs are the commercialization of information, confirmation that the cash nexus is the only meaningful relationship between individuals, and an infusion of market values into cultures and settings that were not yet fully capitalist, especially when the research is conducted in small traditional communities. The researcher runs the risk of not only commercializing relationships with the respondents, but setting a precedent of commercialization in all relationships with outsiders. The benefits are that the researcher and the participants are less likely to be kidding themselves about their lasting and unselfish friendship and that the researcher can be more directive and demanding about the information that is provided in the life narrative. The researcher is less dependent on the good graces of the subject and may feel less limited by the cultural constraints that could influence what is revealed. But be aware that many Institutional Review Boards frown on proposals to pay research subjects.

## THE LIFE HISTORY INTERVIEW

Most people (at least in modern cultures) love to talk about themselves especially when they can hold forth uninterruptedly, unashamedly, and without adverse consequence to them. This makes the life history interview very valuable, and relatively easy to arrange, in the early stages of fieldwork. It's a good way to rapidly gain people's interest in your project and to get them to feel more comfortable talking with you. I mean, how often does a nonthreatening "professional listener" approach you and say that she's super keen on hearing your life story? Most people—even those who express reluctance at first—find the offer to be quite flattering and the experience of doing the interview to be quite engaging, therapeutic even. Informants frequently report "feeling good" about having shared their life history with a patient, nonjudgmental, interested stranger.

### Levels of Data

Therapeutic and interpersonal benefits aside, the life history interview can elicit valuable data on at least three levels: individual, group, and network. In a life history interview the individual informant is the primary unit of analysis, for you are asking him about his life course events/development over time. But you're also asking him to report on events external to his biography, structural forces he didn't control, and the actions of other people in his life generally and in the culture specifically. In this latter respect, then, the life history respondent is also an informant on at least one small aspect of the culture you're studying. He is reporting not just on his own experience but also on his perception of others' experiences and actions. Finally, the life history interview is one "data point" of many you will collect.

The content of the interview is valuable in its own right, as evidentiary matter concerning this particular member of the culture, but it's also valuable in terms of how the informant relays the information in the interview. For instance, if you're conducting life history interviews with drug addicts, you'll almost certainly ask them about how they began using drugs in the first place. What they say, individually, will be of interest to you, but more interesting and analytically useful will be the patterns you discern across the many different "cases," or people you interview. In addition, across those cases you may discover variation in *how* addicts recollect and represent their first encounters with illicit drugs, and that the variation in form appears to be related to gender, race, socioeconomic class background, etc. As you can see, the life history interview can be an invaluable tool in your study of a culture.

## Limitations of the Life History Interview

Although the life history interview and the "ethnographic interview" (Spradley 1979) can be of tremendous importance to you, they do have their limitations (as with every other method). Here we make a few cautionary notes concerning this particular method, for life history interview data should always be treated as suspect. Not only might the data be lacking in validity, but they may also suffer from poor reliability. First, people tend to lie, embellish, and generally represent themselves favorably when talking with strangers (especially when discussing not-so-positive things they've done or experienced).

**HARD TO REMEMBER *WHY*?**    Even when they believe they're telling the truth, people suffer relatively poor recall of "interior events," such as motivation—the "why" behind their actions, the intentions they had at the time, their aspirations and hopes, the way they thought about a particular issue or event, etc. Interior events and exterior events are recorded in different parts of the brain's memory bank. Even from a strictly physiological perspective, it's easier for us to access exterior events as compared with the internal goings-on we experience. Our most accurately recalled memories are those that involved a strong implicit motivational state, which in turn interacted with an emotional arousal state, and that led to our involvement in an exterior event now memorialized in the "public record" of our social life. But for the most part, we simply cannot remember accurately why we did the things we did or even how we thought about something that at the time seemed very important. For example, can you recall the first time you thought to yourself that Santa Claus might not be real? Now try to remember the first time you told someone, probably a friend or parent, that there is no such thing as Santa Claus. The former is an interior event; the latter, exterior. You can easily appreciate the difference.

In general, we remember best those aspects of our lives—and the lives of people around us—when those events have become part of the informal "public record," when they have been "socially objectified or externalized," as Gerald Suttles puts it. To the extent that information is shared and known by others, an informant's account will be that much more accurate and therefore valid as data. But to the same extent that it's shared, it's less useful in terms of illuminating variation within the culture. This dilemma is what leads many ethnographers to focus on variation in how people represent the more hidden dimensions of their lives, rather than assuming the veracity of the content statements that people make and then treating those statements as real.

**ONE-WAY STREET TO HERE AND NOW**    "What's real?" is a nettlesome question in the consideration of data obtained through the life history interview. Yes, people lie, embellish, boast, and all the rest, and indeed we humans suffer poor recall of private events. But perhaps a bigger issue is our nearly universal penchant for viewing our personal history teleologically, as if this "here and now," the current situation is the natural outcome . . . maybe the only possible outcome . . . of a long series of antecedent events. In other words, we impose a causal pattern on our own lives when explaining who we are, how we got this way, and why we do what we do the way we do it.

How did you end up as a student in the class for which you're reading this book? How did you get to this point? In answering the question you'll very likely delineate an implicitly causal sequence of events like so many stepping stones that led you from point A to B to C to . . . X. Moreover, most of the critical events that you believe shaped your path to X were, according to you, largely a result of your own motivation, your own doing, your exercise of free will. Most people in U.S. culture tell their life stories as though they were the agent behind every development in the life course. We tend to leave little or no room for accident, coincidence, happenstance, serendipity, "being in the right place at the right time," or what the more statistically enchanted social scientists call "stochastic processes" (unexplained "error" or "noise" in the data). In other cultures, narratives may follow formulas of victimization, luck, divine providence, or destiny.

**IGNORING SERENDIPITY**   In our narratives (as we learn to tell them in the United States) we made it all happen for ourselves, and even when we didn't—even when we admit to having been in the "right place at the right time"—we take credit for having done what was necessary to get ourselves into that place, at that time. Curiously enough, when explaining or evaluating present circumstances, most of us do a pretty good job of accounting for structural forces beyond our control and for historical events that change the landscape around us and thereby change who we are or can become. Our retrospective views, however, tend to package life neatly, cleanly, and linearly. And that makes them illusory, at best.

Retrospective reasons should always be treated as suspect. When recalling why we did this or that, we often make the mistake of filtering the memory of the experience through our current way of thinking about our present lives and how past experiences fit into who we are now. In some ways this is inevitable, for in the present we "know" more than we did then; our vocabulary is different, if nothing else, and in the interim we have been exposed to more of life and more frameworks to help us make sense of life. The average person's recall and ability to engage in critical self-analysis are relatively poor. Given these limitations, what can be done?

In a life history interview, you can capitalize on moments when the informant is recalling her reasons for doing something by simply asking her whether the reasons she's giving are the reasons that she had then, or the reasons that are occurring to her now. Here's an example from my (Greg Scott's) life history interview with a high-powered trafficker of illegal firearms ("the gunrunner"):

GR:   When I was 17, I got arrested for the third time. For fighting. I had a gun in my boot, a small one. The cops found it. Then they checked my car and found several shotguns and a few pistols. They started referring to me as a gun dealer. So I figured, if that's how they're gonna see me and if this is how they're gonna treat me, then I might as well become just that.

GS:   Yeah . . . now . . . is that what you were really thinking at the time? I mean, was it that straightforward, like "the authorities call me a gunrunner, so I'm going to be one?"

GR:   No . . . no . . . I guess it was pretty complicated . . . you know, that sounds stupid, right... like I was basically just following the orders of people I hated and didn't have a fucking ounce of respect for. I guess it was just . . . I didn't really plan to run guns, and I didn't even think of myself as a dealer or runner until . . . like . . . 10 years later, I guess. I mean, other people would call me that sometimes, but shit, I didn't even sell my first gun 'til I was . . . like . . . 23 years old. And getting into it was mostly about the money. I was supporting myself and this girl that I got pregnant, and I had a baby with a different girl. And I had a lot of guns, ever since I was a kid. And a friend of mine offered to buy one of my guns, so I sold it. Then I found out he had turned around and sold the fuckin' thing to a gang-banger in Little Rock, and he got twice the fucking ticket [price] I got from him. So I'm like, fuck that. Over the next year or so I started meeting some of the guys he knew . . . and, you know, they started asking us for guns. And we knew enough straws [people who buy guns from retail shops and sell them in the underground market] . . . so there you go.

This interview ran nearly six hours, and this excerpt alone—covering how he became a gunrunner—consumes about 11 typed pages. But the point is clear: His first stated reason for becoming a runner—because that's what the authority figures called him—was inaccurate. Now, Greg could have taken this reason at face value and gone off to make much of it in terms of the labeling perspective (Tannenbaum 1938; Lemert 1951; Becker 1963). But the process was both simpler and more complex. GR's reasons for getting into gunrunning had little or nothing to do with his confrontations with the police. Rather, his reasons were rooted in a need for money, a desire to support his offspring, his envy of a friend's ability to make good money doing it, his own capacity to do it, his favorable attitude toward it, and plain old opportunity.

The *historically-specific reasons* are the ones you want to get people to articulate, when and where possible, in the life history interview. You'll notice, too, that I (that's Greg) issued a bit of a challenge to this informant: I subtly questioned his first-stated motivation for becoming a runner. Many textbooks on interviewing will strongly advise you to *always* refrain from disagreeing with the informant. But this is bunk. There are few absolutes in the realm of qualitative research, and this certainly isn't one of them. Gently disagreeing with a subject can be productive, and it's a tactic best used when trying to discern variation and/or test a hypothesis concerning a phenomenon about which informants seem to agree upon and describe with absolute statements For example, if you're interviewing addicts in a shooting gallery, and all of them tell you "there's absolutely no dope for sale around here," but you suspect otherwise, you should follow up with "Really? None at all? So how are people getting their shit?" Chances are you'll learn something new about supply and/or addicts' capacity for obtaining dope when supply is low.

### Formats Vary

A final note on the life history interview: There is no standard format for conducting it. A quick perusal of Google search results on the terms "life history interview guide" will give you a hint of the wide and diverse array of actual instruments available to you. The content of the interview depends upon the culture you're studying, your project's research question and hypotheses, and the theory or conceptual framework you're working with. Generally, but not always, the interview questions unfold in a rough chronology corresponding to the informant's life course. But even this is not a hard and fast rule.

## PRACTICAL GUIDANCE FOR BUILDING THE LIFE NARRATIVE

Here are some tips for helping to build a subject's or informant's life narrative, whether you're using the life history interview or some other technique.

### Recording

It is essential to audio record (or better yet, visually record) the life narrative which may be produced over a series of sessions and could be very long. It is virtually impossible to capture it in field notes, although field notes should accompany the recording, indicating circumstances and perhaps jotting key terms, themes, and the feeling tone of the material as it is being told and recorded. These notes are valuable aids to subsequent interpretation of the life narrative. It is equally important to record information about the setting, the date, place, and circumstances in which the narrative was produced. For instance, a life narrative told with family members present is likely to be different from one told in a more private setting.

## The Transcript

The next step is to create a transcript of the life narrative. There are specially designed recorders to facilitate this tedious and difficult process, and voice recognition software to do it automatically is becoming available though still in its early stages and often not suitable for slangy colloquial speech or dialects. As in transcribing interviews, here too the initial transcript should be complete, leaving out at most interjections such as "um" and "uh" and "you know" although the psychoanalytically inclined researcher might want to preserve even hesitations, slurred words, and slips of the tongue. Certainly grammar and vocabulary should never be altered and must be transcribed faithfully with no editing.

Even at later stages of preparing a publishable partial transcript or excerpts from the transcript, grammar and wording must not be altered, although at this stage it may be desirable to insert punctuation that can help the reader follow the text. Sometimes a life narrative becomes a book in its own right and is reproduced virtually in its entirety; sometimes most or all of it may be placed in an appendix to a book or article that interprets and analyzes it. In many cases, only excerpts or selections are actually published, so choices must be made what to keep and what to omit. These choices will be guided by the research questions and theories underpinning the study.

## Interpretation

Next comes the task of interpretation, although actually interpretation is already present in all stages of the process—deciding whose life narrative to "collect," what questions to use to stimulate the process, what probes or follow-ups to use, and even to use life narratives at all.

Here we will give a few examples of **interpretive frameworks**, most of them linked to foundational theories. An alternative approach is the grounded theory process in which the interpretation is based on an inductive search for recurrent, linked themes and categories that are brought out in open and axial coding. But even this method is influenced by theories that influence the conclusions that are drawn about the recurrent themes and their relationships.

**LIFE COURSE ANALYSIS**    Life course analysis is a currently popular approach that links microlevels to macro-trends. Life course theorists argue that we must understand experiences in light of the historical periods in which individuals live.

C. W. Mills (a leading conflict theorist of the 1950s and 1960s, inspired by Weberian and Marxist thought) anticipated this perspective when he wrote,

> What varieties of men and women now prevail in this society and in this period? . . . We have come to know that every individual lives, from one generation to the next, in some society; that he lives out a biography, and that he lives it out within some historical sequences . . . The sociological imagination enables us to grasp history and biography and the relations between the two within society. . . . No social study that does not come back to the problems of biography, of history and of their intersections within a society has completed its intellectual journey.
>
> (Mills 1959)

More recently this perspective has been developed in work such as Martina Adler's (2002) analysis of women's experiences in the former DDR (East Germany), showing how different age cohorts of women formed different expectations about work and family and faced different challenges in integrating themselves into the society and economy of a reunited Germany.

Life course analysts emphasize that life cycle phenomena (such as childhood, adolescence, adulthood, and aging) cannot be understood as purely biologically driven processes or as "stages of life" scripted by static culture. These life phases are played out within a changing historical setting. Baby boomers are not different from "Gen X" or "Millennium kids" simply because they are older. They are different because they were born at the end of World War II, lived through the civil rights era and the war in Vietnam, participated in the sexual revolution, and found themselves in the job market during the stagflation of the 1970s. It is not only their biological age, but the specific set of historical experiences that set them apart from later generations.

So in analyzing a life narrative, the life course theorist looks for (and indeed may have elicited) information about the way an individual life unfolds within historical change. Key points might be how the events of history affected the individual either directly or more indirectly by opening opportunities and limiting or closing-off other options. For example, many women of the baby boom generation were strongly affected by the way in which their mothers were pushed out of the job market after World War II and outright fired from skilled and lucrative defense-related jobs they had held during the war, or not hired for professions for which they were trained, or given subtle messages in movies and magazines to stay home and raise children.

Life course analysts look for points in the life narrative where we can see the trajectory of history touch the individual life trajectory, sometimes in a single dramatic moment (the freeing of slaves; the D-day landing on Normandy beaches in June 1944; the appearance of the first Europeans in remote communities of Papua New Guinea; 9/11), more commonly in a prolonged gradual impact through changes in government policies, cultural climates, markets, and organizational practices.

Life course analysis generally develops a chronological order of analysis. A related interpretive framework, progressive-regressive analysis, shares many of life course analysis' premises but reorganizes the time order. **Progressive-regressive analysis** is a name given by the French philosopher Jean-Paul Sartre to analysis that begins with a crucial turning point or event and then traces the circumstances that led up to it and the ones that followed from it. We have already noted the use of this method in social autopsies. It can be applied in the analysis of life narratives in any research, not only social autopsies. For example, we might interview incarcerated individuals and understand their experiences in terms of acts and events that preceded and followed a crime. Or we might interview people who left an abusive relationship and analyze the narratives in terms of the abuse and violence that preceded the "enough is enough" moment of breaking free and the way they reconstructed their lives thereafter (Linda Flagg 2002). The central event in progressive-regressive analysis could be a personal event in the life of an individual or a collective event, such as a disaster.

**PSYCHOANALYSIS**    A very different interpretive framework is offered by **psychodynamic theories** that are influenced by Freudian psychoanalysis. In this perspective, the life narrative shows the interplay of three key elements that are present in all biographies (Althusser 1971): (1) the universal "forced march" from infancy to childhood and adulthood, accompanied in every human culture by language acquisition and gendered identity; (2) cultural variation in the experiences and practices that propel this "forced march"; and (3) individual variability and uniquely individual experiences.

The "forced march" from infancy to adulthood is universal and dictated by human biology, but there is considerable room for cultural variation in the practices that shape it and the experiences that accompany it. Psychoanalytically inclined researchers are curious how strapping a baby into a cradle board, nursing it on demand, and never hitting or spanking it might produce different individuals than putting a baby into a crib, letting it move its limbs freely, giving it a bottle every four hours, and using corporal punishment. Although individuals may not remember these events in their own lives, they can provide valuable information about child-raising practices, life cycle stages, and rites of passage. In these accounts what is left out may be as important as what is said. The silences surrounding sexuality, for example, may reveal repression and deep taboos in many cultures.

**HABITUS**    A somewhat different approach from the psychodynamic one but focused on similar parts of a life narrative is offered by Pierre Bourdieu's concept of **habitus** (Bourdieu 1977; Hancock and Garner 2009). Bourdieu uses the concept of habitus as a way of reconciling free, open-ended conscious choices with predetermination by obedience to rules, roles, and norms. Bourdieu argues that social reality is both inside and outside of individuals. Habitus emphasizes the internalized set of practices, schema, knowledge, and competence that shapes our perception of the world and interactions with others. It is the result of past socialization. It is incorporated into the body, into our gestures and movements. Often habitus operates below the level of consciousness and reflexivity, so that we are not aware of its power to shape our actions. For Bourdieu, habitus is a major mechanism of social reproduction, of perpetuating class structures and other patterns of dominance. Even in a society that appears open and is supposedly endowed with equal opportunities, habitus is a force that propels individuals to behave as they "need to" or "are expected to" in order to perpetuate their social position. The concept of habitus links social psychological perspectives on the formation of individual dispositions with macro-social theories of inequality.

By using life narrative data, we can trace the steps and events through which habitus is formed in an individual, the process of socialization, and the adjustment of one's body as well as mind to the habits and actions that lead one to assume a specific social role or social destiny.

**CULTURAL AND COMMUNITY ANALYSIS**    Life narratives tell us a great deal about the collectivity, cultures, and communities. Many of the great life narratives were collected as part of an ethnographic study (such as Sun Chief) or the study of a neighborhood or ethnic community (such as the life history of the Polish immigrant and the life histories in Pattillo's study of a middle-class African American community in Chicago—1999) or a subculture (such as the Chicago School studies of the "jack roller"—a mugger—Shaw, 1930/1966—or the taxi dancer) or criminal organization (Keiser's life history of a member of the Chicago Vice Lords—1969— "Cupid's Story"). The life narrative is read to provide information about a collectivity, its shared rituals, role expectations, economic condition, beliefs, and knowledge, and in general, its shared culture. Although details may vary among individuals, we are less interested in this variation than we are in the commonalities that the account reveals.

This perspective can be linked to the psychodynamic perspective (and often was in life narratives collected in ethnographic fieldwork in the 1930s to 1960s); the individual's account of childhood experiences shows us the way in which cultural norms and practices shape the coming-of-age process.

Moving beyond the childhood portions of the life narrative, the researcher can give more attention to the formation of "cognitive maps." This term has become popular lately; it suggests that all people hold a map or image of the society and the social terrain in which they live. These maps are formed in relationships with other people as well as through the influence of the media, religious institutions, and the many other social forces that create and influence culture. Cultures and individuals vary in how elaborated, detailed, and coherent these maps are. For example, people may see the world in terms of an "us and them"—the good guys and the bad guys. They may see society as an arena of contending forces (left and right, or different contending ethnic groups). Their cognitive map may be shaped by religious texts, organized around prospects of the Rapture or the appearance of the Messiah or the Hidden Imam. Some people's cognitive maps are fragmentary and unstable; others are highly elaborated and comprehensive. Life narratives are one method for understanding these cognitive maps and offer insights into the life experiences that helped to shape the maps.

### DECONSTRUCTION: LIFE NARRATIVE AS SELF-CONSTRUCTION AND DISCURSIVE FORMULA

One of the latest trends in life narrative interpretation is to treat the narratives as texts created according to cultural and organizational rules. This approach is highly postmodern, emphasizing social construction through discourse and **framing practices**. It is linked to "believing nothing" as a research orientation; we do not take the life narrative as a literal truth about anything in the life course, but as a formula for telling a good story—a story that is socially acceptable and a way of constituting a coherent, satisfying self. Individuals construct themselves by telling stories. They tell stories in social contexts according to socially shared rules of storytelling. Their self is lodged in these stories and related performances. In this regard, life narratives "collected" by researchers are not essentially different from stories produced in any social setting.

A key moment in this type of analysis came with Norman Denzin's study of Alcoholics Anonymous (AA) (actually predating the popularity of deconstruction among intellectuals). "My name is ―― and I am an alcoholic." Denzin (1993) argued that these stories were not necessarily literal truths about the individual, though they might include experiences or states of mind that are accurate representations of events and conditions. They are above all stories told according to the cultural formula of the recovery movement, to be shared with others in the organization, and to guide the storyteller toward abstinence.

Denzin's pioneering work in treating life narratives as socially constructed accounts rested on even earlier work, well before the postmodern era of deconstruction, by C. Wright Mills (1940) on vocabularies of motives. Mills (who was strongly influenced by Weber) argued that people try to give coherent accounts of their actions and that these are phrased in standard terms or vocabularies, such as the "excuse." This influential article, as well as Goffman's (1986) work on framing and the symbolic interactionists' interest in communication, helped to set the stage for Denzin's decisive jump into the deconstruction of life narratives.

Denzin emphasized that AA life stories have two key characteristics: They follow a set formula and they are collectively constructed and shared by members of AA, who learn the formula in the organization. Denzin does not deny that the formula may help alcoholics cope with their addiction—it may have positive, life-saving functions for many people. He is simply saying that the stories alcoholics tell in AA are not the spontaneous, highly varied accounts that individuals could tell about themselves and their use of alcohol. They are stories that are produced within an organizational context according to socially learned and shared rules of narrative construction.

Denzin's work has been replicated in more recent research that uses similar deconstructionist logic to analyze how people in certain social contexts produce life narratives. For example, Snow and Anderson (1993), using the concept of frames, analyzed the stories that homeless people tell in order to maintain their dignity and self-respect. Katherine Fox carried out a similar analysis of life stories that incarcerated individuals tell.

Mason-Schrock (1996) analyzed the accounts of childhood presented by trans-sexuals and concludes that they too follow a formula shared by the community of trans-sexual and trans-gendered people, for example, insisting that a feeling of being the "wrong gender" and wanting to cross-dress appeared during childhood; the author is dubious whether these accounts are always literally true. Irvine examined the stories told by people who identified themselves as co-dependents: As in AA, the recovery movement and its constituent organizations have influenced these discourses about the self and have induced a widely disparate category of individuals to tell similar stories.

In our last example, Vaughan (1990) studied the discourses that divorced couples use to describe the dissolution of their relationships—narratives of lives that have parted ways. These are not complete life narratives but they focus on a key problematic period or moment of individuals' lives—recognition that a relationship is coming to an end and the moment of its termination. These relationships are often seen as failed relationships according to social expectations. Like the homeless, individuals telling the narratives of "uncoupling" follow a formula or a set of frames that make sense out of what might otherwise be seen as failure.

In short, deconstruction is a powerful contemporary approach to life narrative interpretation. This approach does an end run around the question whether the information in a life narrative is truthful and accurate. Instead it analyzes the narrative as a text, a story that follows a set of socially shared rules for constructing these types of stories. As French deconstructionist philosopher Jacques Derrida said, there is only the text.

If Roberta Garner were to redo her study of the 250 college students, she would be less inclined to reach conclusions about their motivations and life circumstances that led to college attendance, and more likely to see these stories as following emergent formulas or frames of self-validation that call for people to express the need to fulfill themselves through education.

## CONCLUSION

Whatever interpretive framework we use, we must remember that life narratives that we are analyzing are always reconstructions of events and experiences, not direct information about these events and experiences. The narratives provide reconstructions of events and experiences under the influence of several forces.

1. Collectively shared frames and formulas, such as the AA and other recovery narratives we discussed above. These frames or formulas for telling life stories may be cultural practices of a whole society or pertain to a specific movement, subculture, or organization, such as the recovery movement.
2. Individual choices what to tell, what not to tell, and how to tell it, related to cultural influences, but not identical to them.
3. The unconscious and conscious behavior and choices of the researcher in the process of eliciting the life narrative.

The researcher analyzing life narrative documents remains aware that the words of the text reconstruct and preserve experience, but in an "embalmed" version that is not an exact replication of the experience and the immediate feelings it aroused. Later experiences and socially conditioned definitions of the situation are injected into the remembered events. A social psychologist, writing on memory, offers observations that are helpful to researchers who use life narratives:

> The process of memory thus substitutes the conventional cliché for the actual experience. It is true that the original experience or perception usually is already, to a large extent, determined by conventional cliché, by what the person expected to see or hear,

which means by what he has been taught to expect. . . .The experience is always fuller and richer than the articulate formula by which we try to be aware of it or to recover it. As time passes, this formula comes to replace more and more the original experience, and in addition, to become itself increasingly flat and conventionalized . . .

(Schachtel 1959: 289–290)

## CODA

Life narratives, like interview information, are never "just the facts, ma'am" nor "the truth, the whole truth, and nothing but the truth." The researcher therefore has to work within this limitation in a number of ways—we suggest three:

- Comparing several life narratives from the same community to each other, and seeing if they reveal discrepancies, hesitations, and resistances; and possibly even using a larger and more systematic sampling technique to reduce bias and improve generalizability.
- Contextualizing the life narrative in other information about the individual and the community—in short, as with interviews, "triangulating" the information with direct observation, with demographic background information, and with information that has a more objective grounding and verifiability in documents, although these too are constructs and not simply factual.
- Analyzing the life narrative accepting that it is a reconstruction of events and experiences, not "the truth" but a story; emphasizing and learning from frames, wording, imagery, and narrative choices; and seeing the material as a representation of reality, not an accurate and precise copy of it. Be careful not to conclude that it is the literal truth about something that happened in the life of the individual or the community as a whole.

As we think about interpretation, we see the importance of theories in pointing to strategies for analyzing qualitative data.

For example, Marxist theories of social reproduction, Pierre Bourdieu's concept of habitus formation, standard structural functionalist perspectives on socialization, psychoanalytic theories, and deconstructionist frame analysis—all take us in different directions in our understanding of the same life narrative text. Qualitative analysis software alone cannot answer our research question; it can only confirm the presence of certain words or themes and perhaps show that some we expected to find are not present. What we can do with that information is based on theories, not computer output.

## Exercises

1. A very challenging way to begin the analysis of life narratives is to write (or record) your own, assigning yourself a reasonable number of pages (or minutes). Instead of attempting to produce a life narrative in the broadest sense, you might experiment with writing a few shorter ones that focus on a specific theme or question (family experiences, education, your most exciting moments, etc.). As you look at the material you have written, see if you can discuss and interpret it from several of the theoretical perspectives suggested in the chapter. For example, what do you learn about child-raising in the milieu in which you grew up (and can you generalize your experiences to other individuals of a similar age, social class, race, ethnicity, etc?). What does your own life narrative tell about how individuals come to make choices about their education or profession? What does it tell you about how you learned to write about yourself?

2. Read one of the life narratives mentioned in the chapter and then use a different framework to interpret the material.

3. Read a biography (or autobiography) that was not collected as part of a research project and try to discuss the material from one of the interpretive perspectives of the chapter.

4. Select one major phase or event of your life and make a conscious effort to tell it or write about it in two very different ways. Both versions should be truthful and accurate in their depiction of facts. But they should be different in wording, style, tone, emphasis, framing of themes, amount of context or additional information you provide, conclusions you draw, and so on. Keep track of the choices you are making in order to produce these two different versions.

5. Have a conversation with a friend about an incident you both experienced and keep track of similarities and differences in how you remember and tell the incident. Remembering and telling are not identical to each other; for example, you might remember the same facts but tell the story differently.

## Key Terms

habitus *321*
interpretive frameworks *319*
collectively shared discursive
    frames  *322*
culture norms and practices  *321*
deconstruction and life narrative
    as self-construction *322*

framing practices *322*
habitus and socialization *321*
life course analysis *319*
psychoanalysis and psychodynamic
    theories *320*
motivations *314*

problems of self-selection *314*
progressive-regressive analysis *320*
recording *318*
sampling *314*
transcript *319*

# Visual Methods (with Thomas Fredericks)

## OVERVIEW

In this chapter we offer a brief account of how visual methods developed as a subfield in the social sciences. We also present the basic principles of critical visual literacy, a set of perceptual and analytic competencies necessary for the enlightened, theory-sensitive consumption and production of imagery. Following this, we examine some of the core components of visual methodology. Finally, we provide practical tips and guidelines for doing your own study using visual methods, with a focus on ethnographic filmmaking, or **ethnographilm**. Of particular concern to us in this chapter is how we, as working sociologists, create visual materials to use as data. In this chapter we're less concerned with the kind of visual methods that involve the study of images or objects as cultural artifacts. We're out to learn how to create visual imagery in a purposive, directed, and research question–driven way.

## THE CENTRALITY OF "THE VISUAL"

In the minds of many, "research" boils down to the manipulation of numbers and text. From conceptualization to implementation to the presentation of findings, this view of research reveals belabored scholars drawing upon numeric and language symbol systems to do their work, most of which appears to the outsider to be mundane, if not tedious. But there's more to scholarly work than just numbers in a column and words on a page. We argue that imagery—in the broadest sense of the term—is equally important to the enterprise of social science research. Without imagery, there would be no research.

Some would argue that all sociology is "visual." Indeed, most sociologists rely heavily on their sense of sight—observing people in action, reading texts, looking at data, writing—but all sociologists invoke to one degree or another their capacity to visualize cognitively the subject matter that interests them. From the outset of a project to its publication and beyond, the sociologist works with any number of recollected visions and current visualizations in order to get the job done. Vision—and the more abstract faculty of visualization—is therefore central to the doing of sociology. Setting aside this rather general and detached way of thinking about things, over the past 50 years the discipline of sociology has spawned a distinct subfield known as "visual sociology."

## Having a Vision: The Beginning

It all starts with an idea. Every project, study, and scientific article—all of them began as a notion, a hunch, a whisper of a theoretical insight, or a glimpse of how a taken-for-granted empirical phenomenon might really be more than meets the eye. What is an idea? The word itself, "idea," derives from the Greek word for "form" or "pattern." Its root, "idein," means "to see." Any time you get an idea—any idea really—you generally concoct very rapidly a mental image expressing, animating, or otherwise pertaining to the idea as it might play out in reality. This is why we say that at a fundamental level, all research is visual—because at its point of inception, the researcher(s) had to have visualized the phenomenon, or one or more representations of the phenomenon. This act of envisioning occurs even when the project doesn't focus on individual humans. If it's a historical comparative study, perhaps the researcher visualizes nation-states in some way; or if it's a social autopsy, the researcher might visualize the most vulnerable members of the population sitting in their living rooms. On other occasions, the researcher might visualize data on a chart or in a table, or maybe catches an "internal glimpse" of a histogram or bar chart.

The researcher's mental imagery plays a critical ongoing role in the project and is even (or perhaps especially) important in the project's later stages, when the researcher is analyzing data and attempting to develop a theory that explains observations. In an earlier chapter we discussed the importance of maintaining the capacity for surprise during the course of your study. Well, when we discuss "surprise," we're really referring to experiences that contravene our preexisting imagery, however crude, of the issue, situation, scene, event, or activity we're now observing. Or in the case of data analysis, we must be capable of examining our observations, along with our visual recollections and representations of them, in a critical way, holding open the possibility that our image is inaccurate, which means allowing the data to surprise us. Surprise is the essence of the logic of inquiry; and the very notion of surprise is rooted in imagery. Hence, all inquiry following the logic we articulate in this book is steeped in the realm of "the visual."

Setting aside for the moment this elemental importance of the visual, doing research always entails receiving and processing visual stimuli, creating visual representations in the form of words, graphs, tables, charts, and of course photographs, maps, and video. Very few social scientists ever really contemplate, much less rigorously examine, the influence and effects of visual activity on their research. Even fewer self-consciously and reflexively manipulate their visual sensory input channels or employ skills/techniques for creating visual material as part of either data production, data analysis, or the presentation of findings. But with the increasing popularity and affordability of visual image production technology, the epistemological and methodological landscape in the social sciences is changing. Still, though, most researchers cling to words and numbers when doing their scientific work, even though (or maybe because) doing so requires that they suppress, ignore, and otherwise keep at bay the visualizations that inspire, shape, give rise to, and fundamentally constitute "as real" the work they do.

## THE IMAGE

Before we go any further, it's probably necessary to reflect on the idea and meaning of "the image." After all, the image is central to visual methodology. Without the image, we have nothing. In the interest of simplicity, we'll set aside most of the many roiling philosophical and theoretical debates over the very existence of "the image" as a notion, an idea, or a phenomenon. Quite simply, for our purposes, every image is a conveyer of information. An image could be static, as in a photograph; or semi-static, as in a motion picture/video; or fluid, as in facial expressions and hand gestures. Another way to think about the image is to consider whether it's material or nonmaterial—for example, a picture versus a mental view or memory. Some images are extrapolative—their existence is derived from but not necessarily synonymous with a material counterpart. For instance, how you "see" the spatial arrangements of the classroom in which you're learning about research methods isn't the same thing as a picture of the classroom, a panoramic photo of the classroom, the architectural blueprint, or the university's floor plan.

### Creator and Consumer: A Contested "Relationship"

Every image gets made. This seems obvious and straightforward enough, but actually it's not. Sometimes an image has a human maker, but this is by no means always true. A good many images flow from "nature" and even from the effects of interacting inorganic bodies of matter. For the sake of this chapter, we'll be talking about human-made images—specifically visual materials that researchers manufacture for use as data. However, in the world at large the makers of images may have many different reasons for making images. Aside from whatever motivates their image-making, they often have in mind specific purposes for the images they create—they want their images to accomplish something. Often we ask of a visual image, "What did she mean to communicate with this?"

Whoever or whatever produced them originally, images also get "consumed" by those who interact with (or "see") them. Over the past 30 years the creator–audience relationship has become the focus of much discussion in the social sciences and humanities. Until these recent debates, the commonly held assumption was that makers of images intended their images to communicate something in particular, that the images had certain author-endorsed, and therefore authoritative, meaning(s). The poststructuralist and postmodernist schools of thought, however, have questioned this basic principle and, as a result, unmoored the object from its linguistic representation (i.e., from the word it goes by, as in "chair"), and in the world of visual arts and sciences, this movement has liberated the discourse from its interpretive cage wherein the image has an intended "official" meaning, and so all other interpretations are irrelevant, worthless, or even destructive.

So while image-makers often do wish to communicate something by way of the imagery they fashion, ultimately the image will yield, inspire, encourage, and otherwise engender a multiplicity of interpretations. If you need further convincing on the point, pick any photograph or drawing out of any magazine, gather together a few of your friends, and then tell each person to write down a name for the image and explain their interpretation of it, the meaning they give it. You'll most likely find at least a few different names and as many interpretations as there are people doing the interpreting. In short, every image—whether it's a word on a page, a photograph, a scene from a movie, a map, a drawing, a sculpture, or a memory—is unstable, perhaps inherently so. As a slight aside, one irony here is that poststructuralists often assert stridently that there is nothing "inherent" about or to anything in the world, and that everything is "always already" unstable, untenable, in flux . . . etc. In other words, they're saying that every symbol, image, and representation is inherently unstable . . . with a sheepish wink and barely perceptible nod, they steer through the self-contradictory rhetoric.

## Our Basic Assumptions about Imagery

Notwithstanding the hotly contested debates unfolding in academic departments around the world, we're going to adopt a few basic assumptions, or premises, for the purpose of getting through this chapter. First, images exist. Second, someone at some point made these images.

Third, in most instances the maker did intend to communicate or accomplish something with the image, whether she had in mind an audience of millions or an audience of herself alone. Fourth, only rarely can we discern precisely the "true" or "official" or "authentic" meaning behind any given image. Fifth, on a related note, for any given image there will be at least as many interpretations/ meanings as there are humans consuming the image (we say "at least as many" because often one person will form more than one interpretation of a single image, and the interpretations may even be contradictory to one another). Sixth, the field of "visual sociology" concerns itself with image production, circulation, consumption, reappropriation, etc., and for the most part assumes every image to be "valid" in its own right—that is, the image exists and is no more or less appropriate as an object of analysis than, say, a microorganism (and/or a picture of one) might be to a biologist. Seventh, although social scientists often "reduce" (more accurately, perhaps, "transform") visual images into text for the purpose of analysis, this need not always be the case, for a textual rendering of an image is no more or less "solvent" or "worthy" than the image itself. Indeed, as we illustrate later in this chapter, the well-trained visual methodologist can create imagery for use as data, analyze the imagery without converting it to text, and even communicate the analysis and the findings using the same imagery (as is the case with ethnographic film, discussed below).

## A BRIEF HISTORY OF VISUAL METHODS IN THE SOCIAL SCIENCES

The abbreviated version of this story is that social scientists have been using visual techniques since the advent of various visual technologies. In fact, as we'll see shortly, anthropologists and sociologists were using the first generation of portable film recording equipment even before "true filmmakers" picked up the technology in Hollywood. But using visual recording technologies and developing visual methodology aren't the same thing—the former is a matter of manipulating technology while the latter entails a concerted, reflexive, and theory-pinned examination of the empirical data collection and analysis system. Only in the past 30–40 years has a visual methodology developed in its own right. Let's now turn to a brief history of sociology's dealings with the visual aspects of social life.

### In the Beginning: Photography

Most sociologists would agree that the use of visual methods/techniques and the study of society share an intertwined history. Howard Becker, for instance, claims that the science known as "sociology" and the technique known as "photography" emerged at the same point in history (circa 1840) and in the same country (France): As philosopher Auguste Comte was gaining recognition for coining the term "sociology," a fellow Frenchman, Louis Daguerre, in 1839 filed the patent for his method of transferring an image from the empirical world (e.g., a person) onto a silver-coated copper plate heavily processed by iodine and mercury (Becker 1974). Ironically, however, the early "daguerreotypes" of everyday venues, such as crowded city streets, actually showed no humans—it was as though the streets were empty!

Daguerreotype makers soon discovered that the print required such a long time for exposure and processing that anything in motion, such as people scurrying along a sidewalk, would simply not appear in the final representation. Hence, most of the early daguerreotypes were still portraits or scenes that didn't include objects or people in motion. Of course, enterprising inventors soon figured out that with faster lenses, they indeed could create static images of things and people in motion. At around this point the daguerreotype's potential uses expanded well beyond the "family portrait." In the mid- to late-1800s, as sociologists were undertaking scientific studies of society, the earliest photographers were using the daguerreotype technology with faster lenses to document the world outside of the "special event" still image. They were keen on using the image capturing technology to gather social knowledge and communicate their discoveries to others. However, critical visual social documentation didn't fully emerge until very late in the nineteenth century (Stasz 1979: 122).

**SOCIOLOGISTS, SOCIAL CRITICS, AND MUCKRAKERS**    Early photographers documented social life "at the margins," as did sociologists who employed field methods around the turn of the century. With still-image photography now well advanced beyond the daguerreotype (and much more similar to the film-based photography of the twentieth century), intrepid social critics and so-called "muckrakers" explored society and social problems ranging from the lives of underprivileged immigrants to rural poverty and race relations to urban social inequality and class stratification to social unrest. Photographers and photo-essayists, like their sociologist counterparts, concentrated their efforts on those who were most down and out in densely populated urban areas and sparsely populated, impoverished rural areas.

Some of the earliest critical photo-essays carry as much force now as they did when they were published. Lewis Hine, a trained sociologist who did his studies in Chicago (Curry and Clark 1977: 15), used photography to document the lives of immigrant and child workers in the early 1900s. In fact, a watershed moment in the history of child labor laws occurred in 1909 when he published his photographs of children working from as young as three years of age in factories, coal mines, and agricultural fields across the land. This particular book factored heavily into child labor law reform. Working in a similar vein, Jacob Riis photographed the slums of New York and presented them in *How the Other Half Lives* (1890). Dorothy Lange famously documented migrant workers during the drought in the dust bowl. Rural poverty was documented by "Stryker's FSA photographic unit." During the Great Depression, Margaret Bourke-White and Erskine Caldwell (1937) spent 18 months traversing the "Deep South" of the United States, documenting in prose and photography the hardscrabble lives of sharecroppers, resulting in the book *You Have Seen Their Faces.*

Although this pioneering work in "social justice photojournalism" set the stage for sociologists' future inquiry, as Clarice Stasz (1979) points out, visual representations and images basically disappear from sociological study at the turn of the twentieth century. Between 1896 and 1913, the *American Journal of Sociology* (Vols. 2–21), which was and still is the discipline's premiere peer-reviewed journal, contained only 31 articles that used a total of 244 illustrative and/or evidentiary photographs (Stasz 1979: 120). So just as social critics and photo-essayists were reaching their prime, the mainstream practitioners of sociology were turning away from the use of visuals. At this point, sociology fell out of synch with photography-based social criticism.

## Science Poo-Poos Pictures

What explains the divergence of paths whereby sociology began excluding visuals from its core work while photographers themselves experienced a "coming into their own"? Howard Becker (1974: 5) notes that "as sociology became more scientific and less openly political, photography became more personal, more artistic, and continued to be engaged politically. Not surprisingly then, the two modes of social exploration have ceased to have very much to do with one another" (Becker 1974: 6). In a word, sociologists were invested heavily in making their work scientific. At the time, this meant heartily embracing positivism (a la Comte), which is the epistemological framework that hinges on the belief in a world populated by data and hard "facts," a world with attributes perceived and interpreted uniformly by its sane and reasonable inhabitants. In their quest to "scientize" their discipline and thereby further legitimize their work (and themselves) in the eyes of the academy and the public, sociologists relegated photographs to the enormous realm of the "unscientific," the "anecdotal," the "political," and the "biased." And so it would be a few decades before social scientists would again take photo-imagery seriously as a form of data/evidence.[1]

## Then Came Pictures in Motion . . . The Movies

On the heels of the rise and decline of social scientists' interest in "the visual" came the invention and advancement of the "cinematograph," the earliest form of motion picture recording technology. This proved to be a revolutionary advancement in how society could be documented and then "shown back to itself." Similar to the way that sociology and photography matured together into their adolescence, moving pictures and recording "actualities" developed synchronously. Only three years after the first screening of the Lumière cinematograph, anthropologists grabbed hold of and adapted this new technology as a method for collecting data as part of their research.

The cinematograph was bulky and erratic in its functioning, and its processing of imagery was very sensitive to such factors as movement, temperature, etc. In a word, it was a delicate technology and not particularly amenable to use in the "natural settings" where photographers, sociologists, and anthropologists were working. Soon, however, a major technological shift occurred—the development of a hardy moving image–recording device—the first truly portable motion picture camera. Much like photography, the early users of this device primarily used it to document everyday life, actual life as it happened in motion. The first (or perhaps just most well-known) anthropologists to make use of motion picture recording were Gregory Bateson and Margaret Mead, whose truly multimedia studies of life in Bali would set the standard for decades to come in how visual imagery could be used as data in social scientific studies.

Still photography and motion picture cinema both contributed to the solidification of the modern social sciences, particularly sociology and anthropology. However, with few exceptions, the inclusion of visual technology in social scientific method appears to have ceased around the mid-1900s, only to reemerge two decades later (around 1970). There are many conjectures about this relative void of visual activity, but the most compelling in our view is that sociology and anthropology—the two disciplines to which visual imagery would be most relevant and potentially useful—were both striving for acknowledgment as *scientific enterprises*. Evidence of this can be seen in the disciplines' mutual embrace of structural functionalism and positivism.

---

[1] In a personal communication, Becker told me (Greg) about a conversation he once had with a neurological researcher who was obviously less than persuaded by Becker's use of photographs as actual data. Finally, Becker simply asked him (and I paraphrase here), "Well, does your field of research use images?" Clearly the answer was a resounding "Yes," as neurologists rely very heavily on brain imaging technology. The neurologist, realizing Becker's point that no one image is any better or worse, empirically speaking, than any other image, simply nodded and muttered, "I see what you mean . . ." Still, the devaluation of imagery as data in the social sciences persists even to the present, and even (sometimes especially) within the disciplines that use it most, sociology and anthropology.

Again, the practitioners in each field found themselves disparaging the photograph and motion picture alike as being "soft," "too subjective," and at best "anecdotal."

## Then Came the 1960s: Peace, Love, and Subjectivity

"The 1960s" has become an historical institution in its own right. Many of us now refer to "the 1960s" as though we know what we're talking about and on the assumption that whoever we're talking to holds the same idea of "the 1960s." The term "the 1960s" is one of the most intricate and complex terms in our vocabulary, yet it rarely goes contested. It's a signifier for so many things: civil rights, the Vietnam War, protests against the war, the peace movement, political scandal, the sexual awakening of baby boomers, a radical diversification of rock and roll music, etc. It's what some poststructuralist (or modernist structuralist) linguists might call an "overdetermined" word or concept. "The 1960s" refers to everything, and so nothing, at one and the same time.

In the world of visual methods, however, the 1960s was a truly monumental decade. The advent of handheld movie cameras with synchronized sound recording occurred in the context of radical changes in how people viewed the world and their place in it. In the academy, scholars began to criticize quite strenuously the structuralist/modernist paradigms, invoking Marxian theory and the work of the Frankfurt School to form their criticisms of society, yes, but mainly of how the venerable disciplines of science went about generating knowledge of the world. Critics were especially keen on exposing the fundamental (and in the cold, harsh light of day, untenable) assumptions that allowed scientists to do their work. Soon, university students and faculty were aswirl with talk of personal subjectivity, the "politics of me," etc. In short, this "movement" (if we dare call it that) ushered in a decentralization of theoretical frameworks and, consequently, opened the door for nontraditional research methods and techniques. The idea of "data" even underwent transformation.

By the time 1970 arrived, there were hundreds, if not thousands, of social scientists across the country who had warmed not only to the decentralized and decentered theoretical devices but also to the empirical consequences: They were making photographs and movie recordings and unashamedly referring to them as *data*! Lacking the kind of institutional support that, say, survey researchers enjoyed, these "visual" sociologists began creating their own professional associations, many of which were international in scope. Out of these associations came not only conferences but also peer-reviewed journals, scientific books, photo-essays, and even ethnographic movies intended to be educative.

## 50 Years Later . . . and . . .?

We wish we could write that visual methodology has grown into a well-established field with relatively authoritative canons, principles, practices, theoretical paradigms, and so forth. But we can't because it isn't true. In fact, this book's publication has occurred at the same time as the University of Chicago Press' publication of the first-ever textbook on "visual sociology," written by Doug Harper. While we applaud this occurrence, we're also chagrined at the failure of visual methods—visual social science in general—to develop and mature into a solid subfield. Indeed, in unprecedented numbers social scientists are using visuals in their research, and never before has the technology been so affordable, reliable, easy to use, and capable of producing broadcast quality output at consumer level prices. But still, for the most part, researchers use imagery in limited ways. They use images—photographs, maps, diagrams, and other representations of the "real world"—to illustrate their arguments, to "spice up" their texts, to give the reader of their prose-centered analysis some relief. Rarely do they use imagery as data; even less often do they use imagery as the medium through which to convey their analysis and findings.

This inertia may begin to change very soon, however. A few developments give us some hope: First, as the Internet explodes with possibilities, scholars are taking note. They can't help but take note, really, if only because they need to figure out how to compete with the Internet to keep students' attention in wireless-ready classrooms! Also, the proliferation of Internet access and the increasing sophistication of Internet venues and infrastructures have engendered a wide array of "portals" through which scholars can access all sorts of data, including images and sound, as well as text.

Researchers are figuring out new ways to utilize this ever-expanding field of online resources for the purpose of implementing visual methods in their research studies. At DePaul University, for example, we're developing a curriculum and methodological infrastructure around imagery in general and what we call **ethnographilm** in particular. Ethnographilm, which we discuss in detail below, is a specific kind of documentary film whose rhetorical structure hinges on the systematic collection, analysis, and presentation of ethnographically obtained visual data and whose blend of both substantive and aesthetic elements propels the unfolding of a story about a particular culture. More on ethnographilm later . . .

Another example: Michael Wesch, a faculty scholar at Kansas State University, has spent the better part of the past decade working with students on anthropological studies of the Internet. They call it "digital ethnography," and it has become an extraordinary phenomenon on the world's largest body of participatory video: YouTube. Wesch and his students have conducted hundreds of sociological and anthropological studies using visual methods and focusing on all manner of subjects (not just the Internet but also issues relating to student life "off-line"). To learn more about the work of the student digital ethnographers at Kansas State, visit Professor Wesch's YouTube site: http://www.youtube.com/user/mwesch.

One video in particular stands out, for its serves as testament to the movement toward using visual methods to collect, analyze, and present data and findings—it's called "An anthropological introduction to YouTube." With more than 1.5 million views, the video has caused quite a stir. Professor Wesch and several of his students created the video for his June 23, 2008, presentation at the Library of Congress, arguably the country's most distinguished and well-funded public culture information archive. Even before watching the video, you'll get a sense of what Wesch (and others, including me [Greg]) was up to: taking visual methods to the next level. Just look at this excerpt from the video's "table of contents":

0:00 Introduction, YouTube's Big Numbers

2:00 Numa Numa and the Celebration of Webcams

5:53 The Machine is Us/ing Us and the New Mediascape

12:16 Introducing our Research Team

12:56 Who is on YouTube?

13:25 What's on Youtube? Charlie Bit My Finger, Soulja Boy, etc.

17:04 5% of vids are personal vlogs addressed to the YouTube community, Why?

17:30 YouTube in context. The loss of community and "networked individualism" (Wellman)

18:41 Cultural Inversion: individualism and community

19:15 Understanding new forms of community through Participant Observation

21:18 YouTube as a medium for community

23:00 Our first vlogs

Instead of the chapter and page numbers we'd find in a standard book's table of contents, we see "time codes" (TC)! We encourage you to explore what's going on at Kansas State with regard to digital ethnography and to watch/read/listen to this "anthropological report" in particular. But don't just watch it passively; instead, be critical as you make your way through the video. Exercise your *critical visual literacy* skills. What? You're not sure what critical visual literacy skills entail? Well, let's talk about that right now.

## (CRITICAL) VISUAL LITERACY

In one way or another, it seems everyone's talking about **visual literacy** these days. More specifically, people appear to be concerned about the degree to which today's youth are learning and using *critical* visual literacy skills. You've probably heard, and by now are tired of hearing, your elders lamenting the rise of the "video game generation," the "Nintendo Kids," and so forth. By this point in your college education, you've probably heard your instructors complaining about the Internet, new social media, video games, and the like. Why are they complaining? Because it's a relatively new medium, yes. Because only a fraction of university professors likely comprehend the vastness of the Internet's content and practical uses, yes. But much of the worry stems from this particular medium's capacity for growth, change, malleability, and infiltration of daily life. In the span of a few hours, entire swaths of new social media can undergo fundamental transformation that sends reverberations throughout "real life" situations (e.g., think about the implications of Facebook's decision to replace "Become a Fan" with the "Like" symbol, and the impact of certain recent "viral videos").

Things are changing fast, and many say that the world is becoming more visual . . . more image-dominant. And there are many who fear this. Why? One possible reason is that in the minds of the fearful, "literacy" is a zero-sum game, a finite domain. Therefore, the ascendancy of "the image" necessarily means the descent in the importance of the word. We disagree with this knee-jerk reaction; it's an extreme view, and it's not based on empirical data. (On the contrary, studies show that in some societies—most notably Japan—large segments of the population are literate and active consumers of both word and image media.) Our view is that the world is and always will be replete with multiple stimuli. What's important is not which stimuli tend to be dominant but rather that we do our best to become critical consumers and astute makers of these stimuli. And so we wish to talk for a moment about visual literacy and how to be a *critical consumer* in a world of images.

## Visual Intelligence and Literacy

Before we can help you figure out how to employ visual methods in your own research—which entails becoming a *critical creator* of sociological imagery—we feel compelled to spend some time on the issue of image consumption. Generally speaking, in Western societies most of us learn to read, or at least learn the building blocks of reading, before we learn to write. There's a lot of debate over the relative merits of learning one before the other, or learning them in tandem, but for now we're going to set aside those debates and simply adopt the "learn to read and then learn to write" paradigm in our discussion of visual literacy.

Definitions of "visual literacy" vary widely, but we find Baca's (1990) treatment of the concept, with her list of 186 accepted constructs of visual literacy, to be the most comprehensive. We therefore adopt her definition of visual literacy: "the use of visuals for the purposes of communication, thinking, learning, constructing meaning, creative expression, [and] aesthetic enjoyment" (Clark-Baca 1990: 65).

An increasingly common refrain in many academic circles, from film theory to communication to sociology, is that "images have a vernacular/language of their own." Images "speak" to us; they convey information, alter our cognitive landscape, manipulate our emotions for the better or worse, inspire in us new capacities, and so on. If we can agree that imagery—whether still or motion, material or nonmaterial, palpable or mental—has its own language, then we may be able to agree that to effectively "read" that language one must possess basic literacy of its key terms (vocabulary), syntax, and grammar. Establishing the common ground that visuals and images do, in fact, communicate is the first step in consuming and then producing images.

**VISUAL SYNTAX**    The term **visual syntax** denotes the form an image takes, its building blocks, and how the blocks are arranged. Scholars often analogize visual language with text-based written language. Noam Chomsky (1957) and Paul Wendt (1962), for instance, focus on the syntactic structures of images and the language of pictures. In examining the syntax of images, one should pay attention to the graphical composition as a whole—the shapes, colors, lines, placement of objects within the frame, etc. But as Bamford (2003) explains, syntactical study also includes asking and answering questions—and then critically interpreting those answers—about where the camera was placed when it made the image, how the image was edited and/or juxtaposed with other images, and what the point of view (POV) might say about the image's overall meaning (e.g., Bamford uses the example of a picture made from a low, or down-up, angle, a syntactic maneuver designed to make the image's subject appear more "imposing" or authoritative).

Every "syntactical device" contributes to the composition—and therefore the meaning—of a given image. When Greg was shooting footage for an acclaimed and widely viewed national cable television program on the history of American street gangs, the producers sent him a "spec sheet" for cinematographers. In this case, BET had elucidated differential syntax depending on whether the footage focused on "a victim" or "a gangster." For victims, Greg had to adjust his camera settings and manipulate the camera in certain ways so as to achieve a "sympathetic and soft" feel. BET wanted viewers to feel connected with the victims of gang violence, thus the close-up (CU) and extreme close-up (ECU) shots detailed on the spec sheet. When filming the gangsters, the spec sheet called for camera settings and placement that would yield footage with a very different look: "harsh," "cooler" (in color temperature), and "imposing." With adjustments to the camera's aperture, shutter speed, frame rate, and placement (eye level, "dead on"), the final image made the gangster look anything but "soft" like his victims.

When critically examining the syntax of any given image—and for a critical study you *must* look at its syntax—we suggest that you pay special attention to the following characteristics:

Scale (proportionality among people/objects/figures in image)

Dimension and contrast

Motion (direction, type, flow, implications)

Arrangement of objects/people

Framing

Depth of field (how far back "into" the photo you can see things in focus)

Light and shadow

Perspective and point of view

Contrast and color saturation

Use of foreground and background for differentiation

Metaphor and symbolism

**VISUAL SEMANTICS**    The term **visual semantics** originates in the study of written languages and refers to how meaning is made, rendered, and formed. To ascertain the meaning of images, it's fairly commonly accepted that one must scrutinize how images relate to the historically specific world conditions out of which the images arose and through which they circulate. Bamford (2003) tells us, "visual semantics refers to the ways images fit into the cultural process of communication" (2003: 3). As we stated earlier in this chapter, every image gets made, and usually it gets made for a reason (or at least out of a set of motivations, however well or not well known they may be to the maker of the image). Every image gets consumed. In this consumption lies the act of meaning-making. The area of visual semantics concerns this very issue—how do we make sense of a given image, in a critical fashion? We agree with some of the suggested questions that Bamford lays out:

What is the form and structure of the image? What does its form say about its possible interpretations?

Who created the image? When was it created? In what context? Was it a commissioned image? Who commissioned it and why? What were the terms of the commission?

What was the image's original purpose? Who was its intended audience?

What, if anything, does the image "say" about its historical context, the society that its creator inhabited?

What does this image say about class, race, gender, sexuality, religious affiliation and other dimensions along which society is organized?

Finally, and this is our favorite: What is NOT in the image but conceivably or reasonably could be in the image? What is omitted, excluded, or "glossed over"?

At the end of the chapter we present some exercises to get you practicing these syntactic and semantic devices when critically studying an image. But there's no stopping you from doing it right now. So why not take a break from reading and pick up a magazine or newspaper? Even a clothing or furniture catalogue will do. Exercise your newly acquired knowledge of the visual literacy basics . . . and in the process become more critically literate![2]

## VISUAL LITERACY AND SOCIOLOGY

"How to see" has become a central thought in visual literacy generally and in visual sociology more specifically. At various points in this book we've invoked the "sociological imagination" as a device for thinking critically about social issues. Visual literacy and the corresponding syntactical and semantic devices we just discussed dovetail nicely with the sociological imagination. We must learn how to see or at least possess an intelligent way of looking so that we may see *as sociologists*. Consistent with this book's guiding notions—stated clearly in the introductory chapter—we believe that images do indeed communicate and that we can subject them to empirical study and theorizing. As a sociologist, you'll need to practice your visual literacy skills consistently and thereby develop a specialty, a discipline within the discipline of sociology, a discipline concerned principally with the critical study of all things visual. John Dillenberger—historian, philosopher, and theologian—applies a "discipline of seeing" to the whole of life saying, "A discipline of seeing does not come by being told how to see, though that might be helpful, even necessary; it comes primarily by seeing and seeing and seeing over and over again" (Dillenberger 1980: 241). Indeed, coming into acuity with respect to visual analysis does take practice, but the payoff is worth the effort!

### How Sociologists Approach Visual Material and Methods

A small though significant portion of sociologists have taken a visual approach to the empirical study of social life. At our disposal are several practical methods for incorporating the visual into our studies. First, and most common, we analyze images that were created by another person— most often a member of the group, organization, or population we're studying. This approach usually revolves around some kind of *content analysis*, which we've discussed already. Or we might treat these visual materials as cultural artifacts and consequently analyze them as such. Again, we've covered *cultural artifacts* already in this book. Second, increasingly sociologists are using a technique called *photo elicitation*, or *PhotoVoice*, wherein the researcher asks the subjects to respond open-endedly to photographs pertaining to the subjects' culture/society. The researcher may have taken these photographs, or she may have tasked the subjects with taking and then explaining them. You may recall our discussion of PhotoVoice from the chapter on community-based participatory research.

The third approach to visual methods entails the researcher making, analyzing, and/or reporting results via culturally and socially specific imagery. Most often, the researcher creates these images using a still camera and treats the pictures much the same way an ethnographer treats observations in her field notes. In this case the photographs combined serve in place of lengthy, detailed notes, though many researchers who work this way do write detailed notes about the pictures they've taken. Less commonly, researchers use video recording (i.e., motion picture) cameras to produce footage concerning the phenomena that interest them. Here, too, the

---

[2] You might also be interested in reading Bamford's (2003) which provides a useful table for organizing image critique: http://www.adobe.com/uk/education/pdf/adobe_visual_literacy_paper.pdf

researcher may use the footage in place of field notes but more likely than not ends up writing notes on the clips, which she will have organized thematically in most instances.

## The Data *Are* and *Must Be* Images

We believe it's important to pause here and remind you that in our view, every image is a potential datum, observation, or maybe even constellation of data points. Images as data of social relations represent a person, place, or event at a specific place in time and space, and each image can be interpreted just like a survey, interview, or participant (field) observations. Every image possesses an extraordinarily large amount of information. As the saying goes, "A picture is worth a thousand words," as a social researcher you need to pick out the words you want to focus on and communicate. A social researcher, being critically visually literate, needs to notice all of the elements in a picture—pedestrian traffic, clothing, cars' makes, etc. The elements of the image might become useful variables. The photograph/image is a record just like field notes and interview transcripts.

In terms of methodology, however, we wish to make four important points: First, you must determine whether or not your particular study *demands* the collection and analysis of visual data. How do you know this? You go back to your research question. Would the research question be answered best through the making and manipulating of visual data? If not, then you may end up using visual methods for purely illustrative purposes. This methodological query we've posed might be one reason accounting for the relative scarcity of "truly visual" studies: The canons of sociology have yet to fully embrace visual methodology; hence, practitioners of the discipline rarely train their students to think in *visual methodological* terms, and if you're incapable of thinking this way, you're not likely to be asking many research questions best answered by visual data. It's a paradox.

Second, if you've decided that your research question would be answered best by visual data, then you must determine what kind of visual data should be made and then select the appropriate methods for making these data. Should the data be photographs? If so, who should take them? Should the data be images created by people who inhabit the culture you're studying? Should the data be comprised of video recordings?

Third, in evaluating the data you collect, you're going to experience "analytic paralysis" because indeed every picture (image) speaks a thousand words. When you're assessing and coding, say, an interview transcript, you have words shaped into sentences on a page. Certainly any of these words could carry multiple meanings, but the "multiplicity factor" is much higher when you're working with visual data. So, in analyzing your visual data, you're going to have to make lots of decisions and thousands of choices along the way. In terms of content, which parts of the images do you examine? In terms of the syntax, where do you place your focus? These are very tough questions with no easy answers. Again, though, we encourage you to return to the beacon in the night, your research question. As with any volume of data regardless of type, the research question will help you figure out where to focus your energy. Remember the tattoo parlor study that Maize and Sarah did, and remember how at first they were writing field notes on the music playing over the store's stereo system, the clothing that customers were wearing, and all sorts of other things that ultimately had nothing to do with their research question? Well, the potential for getting lost when working with visual data is much, much higher than when working with text or numeric data.

Finally, let's talk briefly about transparency. In Chapter 2 we discussed the core principles of the scientific method. One of them, reproducibility, has considerable bearing on visual methodology in particular (and qualitative data generally). When a quantitative researcher uses a "secondary data set" (survey data anonymized and published for public use) for her study, the final product (article or book) will make clear which data she used and how she analyzed the data. This is a form of transparency that allows other researchers to reproduce her study and (dis)confirm her study. The qualitative researcher, however, often must keep the sources of his data "secret" by giving pseudonyms to the locations and people with whom he interacted to produce the data. Requiring qualitative researchers to keep subjects and places secret is part of standard operating procedure among Institutional Review Boards. This secrecy, when combined with the fact that qualitative researchers rarely share their entire data set and instead allow the reader (and therefore colleagues in the field) to see only those bits of data they have selected for inclusion in the published article, makes the qualitative study very difficult to replicate.

A study that employs visual methodology is even more difficult to replicate. Moreover, the data shown in the final product will be subject to innumerable interpretations. In an interview-based study, for instance, you might include interview transcript excerpts that you believe illuminate the theme at hand. Readers may or may not agree with your interpretation of the words on the page. In a visual study, you'll be presenting visual data . . . and even a single photograph will open the door to many more interpretations than will a sentence or paragraph from an interview (as a general rule). Doing visual research means really "putting yourself out there." Showing your data and arguing that *your interpretation is the best one* out of thousands can be a pretty scary prospect.

Now it's time to start making images of our own . . . or at least learn how to make them in a critical, sociological way.

## IMPLEMENTING VISUAL METHODS: KEY IDEAS

In the remainder of this chapter we focus exclusively on making visual imagery for the purpose of sociological inquiry (i.e., research). Our central concern will be the moving image, the motion picture (video/film). The objective here is to get you out into the world collecting visual data for a qualitative or ethnographic study of some issue that demands visual treatment. You don't have a fancy video/film camera? No worries. Your cell phone will do the job well enough. The cost or quality of the equipment has no necessary bearing on the quality of the final product. For proof of this, ask yourself how many terrible Hollywood movies you've seen. A lot? Well, every one of them was made with cameras that cost more than your entire college education. So grab a cheap handheld video recorder or just use your (or a friend's) cell phone camera, and let's make images!

### Straddling the Great Divide: The Image as an Objective-Subjective Matter

Before we get our hands dirty with practical guidance, we need to discuss one relatively abstract, though critical, point concerning "the image" as data. Every image is generated, or produced, in a particular set of circumstances; it is both "objective" and "subjective." You can think of an image as a document of some thing, or things, at a specific point in time and space. The image represents that which you see but also that which you don't see. From our visual literacy discussion earlier, we know that the image "says something" about the objects in the image, but it also says a great deal about the person who made the image. It's of vital importance to keep in mind—and to record in your notes—as much as you can about the circumstances in which you make a given image and about how you, as a person doing research, might be affecting the image and/or what the image is capturing. This is the kind of critically self-reflexive activity we've discussed repeatedly throughout this book. Reflexivity is essential to the scientific method, and it's particularly important when it comes to making images for use as data.

As you think about critical reflexivity, keep in mind that making images is all about making decisions, or choices, such as the following: Should I pick up the camera or not? Which direction do I point the lens? What do I include in the frame? What do I exclude? Do I make a wide shot or zoom in for a close-up? Should I shoot in black and white or color? How exposed should the picture be? Manufacturing high-quality visual data is predicated on how effectively you can answer these and many other similar questions. Once again, if you're stuck and can't seem to come up with an answer, revisit your old friend the research question to get some guidance.

Actively acknowledging the subjectivity of image-making is the key to strengthening the image *as data*. To the extent that you can identify how the image-making process is shaped by, and in turn shapes, you, the subjects of the picture, your relationship to the subjects, and the context in which the picture is made, you will have positioned yourself well to deal with the many forms and degrees of "bias" that inhere to *all* data and their production. There's a risk here, though, of becoming so enmeshed in critical reflexivity, in the teasing out of subjective "bias," that you lose sight of the image's meaning in relation to your project. So as you move forward in the visual data production process, we advise that you consciously strike a healthy and useful balance between reflexivity (identifying subjectivity bias) and dealing with the images *as data in their own right*.

Now we want to offer some practical applications for implementing visual methods in general and using images as data in specific. It is our hope that these practical applications will both help to establish some boundaries for images and help to navigate through the process of visual data collection.

## The *Practice* of Image-Making

Visual sociologist John Grady offers a very important insight with respect to analyzing images, and we feel strongly that it applies to sociologists and laypersons alike. Regardless of what other research projects or activities you have going on in your life, you should always take time to make images for yourself, on as regular a basis as possible (Grady 2001: 101). We're not talking about just snapping pictures higgledy-piggledy; rather, you should set aside time to make images that evidence a high degree of critical visual literacy. The production of your own images will provide the experience for understanding the limitations of the media and for appreciating what others have accomplished. We agree wholeheartedly with Grady: "The more you shoot in an intentional way, the more you will come to understand the choices that go into the production of images" and "producing images will help train and refine your eye" (Grady 2001: 101–102). So the first rule is practice, practice, practice.

## Video (as) Documentation

At the end of your study you will have produced a document—a moving document, or "movie," but a document nonetheless. That **document** will be comprised of potentially thousands of "sub-documents" called "frames." The camera you're using probably records at a rate of 30 (actually 29.97) frames per second (FPS). This means that in a single minute of the movie, there are 1,800 individual frames passing by. A 10-minute research film consists of 180,000 individual frames! Every frame is important. Every frame should somehow convey, advance, embody, or otherwise relate to the central argument you're making. After all, the research movie you're making, just like a research paper, strives to make an argument about something. It has a rhetorical structure. One of the differences, of course, is that the characteristics of the research paper, as a document, are very different from the movie's characteristics as a document.

So what are a document, documentary data, and a documentary? A document is something that is written, photographed, or recorded via audio/video means that provides reliable evidence and information. **Documentary data** consist of theory-linked images and sequences of images that advance the rhetorical "spine" (i.e., the principal argument) of the movie. A documentary movie is a completed body of work based on or consisting of the documents and documentary data. Therefore, in order to document something one must create a factual record of it. After the factual recording of evidence (documentary data) has been completed, one can use a combination of the documents by which to create a documentary movie.

Imagery has long been used for illustrative purposes, as we've said. Only occasionally have social science researchers treated imagery seriously as data. And when they have used imagery as data, in nearly every case the imagery has been static (e.g., photographs, drawings, objects). Very rarely have visual sociologists or anthropologists not only analyzed images as images (i.e., without converting them to text), but also presented the findings via imagery. The most rare work of visual social science of all is the research movie, or what we refer to as "ethnographilm" throughout the remainder of this chapter.

## ETHNOGRAPHILM: A PARTICULAR KIND OF DOCUMENTARY MOVIE

Ethnographilm, as we mentioned briefly early in this chapter, is a specific kind of documentary film whose rhetorical structure emerges from and rests upon the systematic collection, analysis, and presentation of *ethnographically* obtained visual data and whose blend of both substantive and aesthetic elements propels the unfolding of a story about a particular culture. Note here that we're speaking of a filmic *ethnography*; we're *not* talking about a movie based on interviews with 10 people, or a fancy motion PowerPoint presentation. The ethnographilm is a movie that addresses a particular research question through the gathering and subsequent logical sequencing of video clips. It might help to think of the ethnographilm as the movie version of a book-length or article-length ethnographic study. Above all else, the ethnographilm tells a story; the story may or may not inhere in the lives of specific people. Indeed, the "narrative arc" consists of the argument's unfolding as the movie plays on.

### The Heart of Ethnographilm Is Ethnography

Ethnographilm's primary concern is the substantive issue that you have set out to explore as the ethnographer wielding a video camera. The realm of aesthetics is of secondary importance, which doesn't mean that it should be ignored entirely. A good ethnographilmmaker will put nearly as much effort and intelligence into her filmmaking style as she invested in the actual doing of the ethnography. At the end of the day, however, the ethnographilm concerns itself more with substance than style (though we must realize that style can be substantive, and the substance can come across as stylistic).

There's a lot of debate over what constitutes an ethnographic film. By no means can we say that sociologists or anthropologists or any other field has reached consensus on its definition, its defining features, what it is or isn't. But why should we let that stop us from moving forward?

Some say ethnographic film is and *must be* about *other* (not one's own, and preferably non-Western, indigenous) cultures, subcultures, customs, or social practices. Others say it should at

Greg video-recording "Copper Kevin" as part of Greg's ethnographilm about "The Brickyard" (photo by Erin Scott)

least fall under the rubric of documentary filmmaking. Social scientists argue that it should be more scientific and be subject to a systematic study and academic rubric. Jay Ruby goes as far as making the claim that an ethnographic film can only be made, directed, or produced by a trained ethnographer. One should "use ethnographic field methods that can be peer reviewed in order to maintain academic integrity" (1975: 105).

## Ethnographilm and Documentary Film: A Shared History

Ethnographic filmmaking is not a new idea (though the term "ethnographilm" is). As discussed earlier in this chapter, it was a large part of anthropological research up until the 1930s and reemerged in both anthropology and sociology about 1970. Arguably, the doorman for this kind of filmmaking was technological advancement in film recording: Soon after the handheld movie camera with synchronized sound recording hit the market, anthropologists were in the field making movies about the cultures they were studying. In fact, social scientists picked up the technology at least 10 years before Hollywood filmmakers would even consider touching it.

Notwithstanding its long history, academia has been slow to recognize ethnographic filmmaking as a legitimate method of gathering, much less presenting, social scientific data, at least not without an explanatory accompanying manuscript. It seems that the virtual nonexistence between 1930 and 1970, of which we spoke earlier, may be due to the academy's belief that ethnographic filmmaking lacked the necessary scientific rigor. This is no surprise. Throughout history the academy has privileged text over imagery in almost all "serious" disciplines. However, since its reemergence in the 1970s much has been established in the world of visual social science, including the peer-reviewed journal *Visual Studies* established by the International Visual Sociology Association (IVSA) and *Contexts* (a quarterly magazine dedicated to making sociology interesting and relevant, available through the American

Sociological Association). The IVSA also hosts an annual conference dedicated to the study and presentation of visuals in sociological study. There have also been several sociology departments (colleges and universities) that have developed visual methods and visual sociology classes and/or curriculums. Even with all of this academic development in the scholarly world there is still a need for further growth in the use of visual methods and, perhaps, none more than the use of film/video, what we call ethnographilm. Image creation and presentation should have a greater role in the researcher's tool-kit.

## So What Exactly Is an Ethnographilm?

The current challenge to the discipline and making of ethnographilm is to understand what makes something an ethnographilm. There is a need to establish a set or rules or criteria by which to base the methods of understanding and using images beyond the notion of photo elicitation and content analysis. Before we attempt to establish a set of guidelines for creating ethno-graphilm, let us briefly consider what it means to document through video.

An ethnographilm is a reflective process and approach to filmmaking and gathering data. One must reflect on both the science involved and the art of film and communication. More so than traditional documentary or fiction filmmaking, an ethnographilmmaker must consider the framing, the edit, the angle, etc., and what each will convey to an audience. The camera can be used as a catalyst to reveal social tension or as a means to provoke thought and further academic discourse. In some ways you are capturing social life in a moment in time and then reserving the right to frame and edit that reality any way you want. This brings in accountability and detailed explanation of methodology and theoretical framework that the researcher is applying to the study. Another challenge of ethnographilm is acknowledging the presence of the social scientist as filmmaker and to reflect on this reflexively.

Ethnographilm is basically the equivalent of the traditional pad of paper and pencil, the camera being the pencil and the recording medium the pad of paper, and is now getting closer and closer to being considered as important as the notebook is in a research project. Pad and pencil, the traditional tools used in social documentation, are no longer the only tools by which a social scientist can record field observations. As the notebook moves over a bit to make space for the camera as a tool, a social scientist must understand the potential of the camera and must have a clear understanding of why he or she is using it to gather data. A social scientist should not be taking pictures simply to take pictures. The value in the camera is maintained in its ability to record what the human eye cannot. A film controls time; film can slow down or stop time, or can compress hours into seconds.

## Approaches You Can Take

Ethnographic filmmaking falls into the documentary filmmaking spectrum. One could argue that the "ethnographic film" is one of several genres of documentary film. But for our purposes it makes more sense to borrow from the traditional taxonomy of documentary film to provide some direction on how you might structure your film. In other words, we see the different types of traditional documentary film as being transferable into ethnographic filmmaking. Let's look at some ways you could put structure to your film.

**HISTORICAL**   Doing historical ethnography can be difficult, particularly if the persons who made up the culture/society are dead. But many scholars have conducted historical ethnographic studies of more contemporary groups and cultures. In this approach you might document with video historical trends and/or make a comparative association of eras on a specific subject (or on specific groups/cultures), attempting to show all aspects in an objective approach.

**ADVOCACY** This approach would entail doing politically motivated ethnographic work, where your goal is to understand the inner workings of a group in order to advocate for it or to battle against it. Rigor is always important when it comes to assessing research products. With an advocacy ethnographic film, it's especially important to make explicit your "biases" and political alignments. Ultimately you want the film to be educative, to serve as a kind of intervention that changes the way people think about, for instance, a marginalized group or a dominant discourse. Whatever the case, you render your argument with rich, textured ethnographic visuals. This approach often works well in community-based participatory action research studies.

**VISUAL ESSAY** A visual essay can be used to deliver your data using the images alone. You could also add a commentary or narration voice-over (NVO) to a visual essay to help describe the events and findings; however, the most compelling visual essays are those whose images "speak for themselves" (actually, they speak for you) and therefore have no need for the overbearing, stentorian voice-over that explains everything.

**PROFILE OR CASE STUDY** This genre of ethnographilm relies heavily on the case study method used fairly widely in the social sciences (see Ragin 1994). Profile ethnographilms can be compared with the life history studies we discussed earlier in this book. Some of the most famous life history/narrative studies (e.g., Clifford Shaw's *The Jack-Roller*, 1930) could have been an amazing ethnographilm, showing the life and attitudes of one person, a juvenile delinquent, and how his life reflects, refracts, and impacts the group(s) in which he circulates and the social structures into which he was born and through which he must navigate.

**SOCIAL COMMENTARY** This is the most general branch of ethnographilm, for it's concerned with just about anything related to people, society, and the world in general. In doing the work, you might blend forms, such as doing a comparative case study of two different organizations, or perhaps doing a visual essay on a particular aspect of a specific culture or community.

## Some Basic Rules of Ethnographilmmaking

You've learned how to do ethnography. Now you want to make an ethnographilm. It's not quite as easy as just picking up a camera and filming everything you see (an approach known in the film world as "hosing," as in pointing a garden hose in every direction to cover as much ground as possible). As with ethnography wherein field notes comprise the central data mode, one must be discerning when making an ethnographilm. In previous chapters we've talked about some of the many complications associated with introducing any recording technology to the scene—it can ruin what little trust/rapport you might have built up with informants; it can compromise your and their safety and privacy, etc. Other than these very important concerns, which we must heed at all times, there are other basic rules you should follow when making an ethnographilm. Let's cover some of the most important of them.

1. Make sure that your research question demands an ethnographic approach. Then make sure that your ethnographic endeavor necessitates the use of videographic data or at least that videographic data will be no less robust than any other kind of data.

2. Determine which "type" of ethnographilm is best suited to your project and to your personality.

3. Figure out early on how you're going to use video to deliver ethnographic insight into the issue/group/culture you're studying. At this point you should determine whether or not it's feasible to deliver ethnographic insight using ethnographilm.

4. Throughout the filmmaking process you need to keep your research question at the fore of your mind while also reflecting on the nature of the sociological content, theory, and basic information the viewer needs (remember, good voice-over is possible, but bad voice-over is more likely).

5. As you collect your visual data (i.e., video clips), you need to begin organizing them in the same basic way that you would organize field notes. Open, focused, and axial coding processes can be applied to the organization of video clips. You should develop an organizational scheme (i.e., a folder system) at the very outset and then change it as necessary along the way. Early and ongoing coding/organization of video clips might prevent you from losing your mind at the end of the process, when you need to complete the film.

6. Know your film's "narrative spine," also called the "narrative train," which is the sequencing of concepts/ideas that carries the story along from beginning to end. Most often, the ethnographilm's narrative arc is the structure of the argument, not the course of action, or "plot," experienced by the characters in the film. There are good ethnographilms, however, where the rhetorical narrative and the character narrative are intertwined.

7. As you organize your film clips, be ruthless in assessing them. Don't prioritize a clip just because "it's so beautiful!" Its beauty is of no importance whatsoever if its content bears no relation to the story you're trying to tell, and it's especially useless if it doesn't somehow advance your argument. This is because *every ethnographilm is an argument about something.*

8. While video-recording, keep in mind your research question. Don't be a hoser.

9. Lay out your film clips into a beginning, a middle, and a conclusion. Think about how you're going to set up the issue/problem/question (introduction) and what you want the viewer to take away from the viewing experience (conclusion). Then start working on the body, which is the argument of the film.

10. Arranging clips into scenes and scenes into sequences is especially difficult in the middle portion of the film, the argument. You need to make your argument without the benefit of words. What you have available to you are images. So the first step is to be very clear on the argument you want to make. Then think about the material you have and how it could be arranged. One helpful tip is to think about your footage as an experience you've had (which is true). Now think about encountering an old friend, someone you haven't seen in years, and realizing that she's now very different from you in her beliefs. You suspect, in fact, that she holds the exact opposite beliefs as you on this particular subject. It's your job to tell her the story of what you've experienced in such a way as to persuade her that you're right. When telling stories of experiences we've had, we typically draw very heavily on visual references, our recollections of visual cues, etc. This very same technique can help you figure out the arrangement of your film's main body.

We offer you a number of resources, including a short "how-to" guide for video recording. In this guide we discuss the more technical aspects of making a film, such as focal length, depth of field, film speed, aperture settings, white balancing, and so forth. All of these things can be

Greg editing the "money shot" in a scene from his ethnographilm "Matrimony" (photo by Erin Scott)

manipulated to produce footage whose aesthetic dimensions add to (or detract from) the value of the content. We also offer tips on how to record good sound. High-quality audio is essential to the making of a good film. Finally, on the website you'll find a series of ethnographilms made by students of faculty members at DePaul University, as well as a video-taped interview with Greg on the topic of ethnographic filmmaking.

## Why Make an Ethnographilm?

During the famous Navajo Film Project by Sol Worth (1970), an effort to teach American Indians filmmaking techniques, Worth conveys an over-quoted but highly applicable story. An elder from the tribe, Sam Yazzie, asked, "Will making movies do sheep any harm?" T345  he response, "No," reassured him that making movies would not do the sheep any harm. He then asked, "Will making movies do the sheep any good?" The response was, "Not necessarily." To this Yazzie inquired, "Then why make movies?"

This is a great question, "Why make movies?" and although each ethnographilmmaker will need to decide this for him or herself, the answer found within the conversation is a great starting point, "Will making movies do the sheep any harm or good?" It is an ethical dilemma. We can turn back to Lewis Hine, who said, "Show something that needs to change." Or Tim Asch, who expressed the necessity to explore how to represent one's own understanding and experience of a culture. Only you can decide if ethnographilmmaking is right for you, if it's appropriate for your project, if it's consistent with your ethical and/or political views, if you've got the wherewithal and moxie to do it, and if indeed doing so will do any good. There's no medium more powerful than film . . . do you dare to try your hand at it?

## CONCLUSION . . . ACTUALLY, WE'VE ONLY JUST BEGUN

We believe firmly that in today's world everyone should possess a high level of critical visual literacy. As Jay Ruby writes, "Pictorial media will undoubtedly become more commonly recognized as an important part of almost every human being's cultural identity, and therefore something that anthropologists can and should study." Now more than ever before, laypersons and social scientists alike are finding themselves in need of developing their visual literacy skills, even if they're not doing visual research, strictly speaking. In this chapter we've laid one of many possible foundations on which you can become more visually literate. We've also tried to help you think through some of the issues related to working in visual media. In particular, we have focused on the "ethnographilm," the visual rendering of ethnographically obtained insight into how cultures, organizations, groups, and societies operate. We hope that you'll invest some time in doing the exercises below, visiting the companion website to learn more about this exciting methodology, and ultimately that you'll grab a camera and hit the streets, hell-bent on making your very own ethnographilm. If you do make one, be sure to send us a copy . . . we might want to post it on our website!

## Exercises

1. Find a public place where you and a few of your fellow students can observe and take photographs of this specific place at significant and constant time intervals. Each of you also should write field notes. Analyze both visuals and field notes.
2. Pick a social problem. Define it in visual terms. If possible use current day issues. What does this problem look like? What are the images in your mind? What evidence exists to support these images? Are you familiar with the evidence? Is it compelling? Scientific? This verbal visualization process will help you begin to develop your abilities to analyze, criticize, and synthesize research and the social world visually.
3. Make a short observational film, about two minutes in length, focused on purely descriptive images/sequences visually expressing common/daily routines and acts. Be prepared to explain how your short film is sociologically compelling and relevant.
4. Visit the companion website and participate in some of the interactive exercises associated with this chapter. We encourage you to seek out, in particular, those exercises dealing with how to edit your footage into scenes and sequences.

## Key Terms

document *340*
documentary *341*
documentary data *341*

ethnographilm *326*
visual intelligence *335*
visual literacy *334*

visual semantics *336*
visual syntax *335*

# 22

# Computer Software for Qualitative Data Analysis (with Sarah Korhonen and Rachel Lovell)

## OVERVIEW

Modern computer technology has crept into nearly every aspect of our daily lives, making many ordinary tasks simpler and less time-consuming. Our belief in the power of computer technology to transform our personal and work activities is wide-ranging and ever deepening. The world of social science research is no exception. In this chapter we explore the increasingly widespread use of computer software programs for the analysis of qualitative research data. We try to keep it simple, avoid getting overly technical, and instead focus on providing you with a conceptual understanding of how the two popular[1] software programs are organized, how they function, and how and when you can use them to support your data organization, analysis, interpretation, and reporting. By the end of the chapter you'll know enough about the two leading qualitative data analysis software programs to decide which one, if either, is appropriate for your project and to perform basic analytic functions in your program of choice.

## CADA

Computer-assisted data analysis (CADA) has flourished in the behavioral and social sciences since the advent of "main-frame" (i.e., larger than a dorm room) computer technology in the 1950s. CADA is particularly mature in the realm of quantitative

---

[1] We have chosen to focus this chapter on two of the many available software programs for qualitative data analysis: ATLAS.ti and NVivo. We chose these two programs because they're widely used by faculty researcher-instructors and students, but also because you can download and use trial versions (somewhat limited in their features but still robust) of both programs for your own research project(s).

data analysis. In the years before computer technology, most quantitative social researchers wrote their statistical equations by hand, performed power calculations using hard copy tables, or "ran" regressions with paper, pencil, and lots of erasers. Nowadays, performing the most complex quantitative analyses is a "point and click" matter, provided you know where to point, what to click, and how to make sense of the output you receive.

## New Tricks for Old and Young Dogs

For their part, qualitative researchers working in the "pre-microcomputer era" gathered their data with pen and paper. Although many of them also recorded their interviews and observations on audiotape or even film, in the end all of the data were reduced to words written on paper. Qualitative researchers would accumulate long typed transcripts of interviews and combine these with hand-drawn geographic and network maps showing the use of space and distribution of people in their study areas. Then they might have hand-completed observation sheets—complex tallies of people coming and going, organized by behavior or type of person. Somewhere along the line the "olden day" researcher would sit down with all of these data piled in front of him, faced with the question, "What the hell am I going to do with all of this stuff?" Then, in many cases, he would fall into a catatonic state, only later to be found by colleagues and rushed off to the nearest "insane asylum."

Clearly we're jesting here. The spirit of the point remains, however. It's really difficult to "make sense" of all the data you collect in doing a qualitative research study. There are no "industry standard" formulae, equations, procedures, or interpretive benchmarks. *But make sense of it you must.* Although many qualitative researchers, young and older, still manipulate their data "by hand," most of us have moved—to a greater or lesser degree—into the world of software-based analysis.

"Migrating" from manual data analysis to computer-assisted analysis is difficult for many reasons. First, there's no available software program that mimics—or even emulates to an acceptable degree—the manual tasks that we "old timers" usually perform when it comes time to analyze the data.[2] It's commonplace for a qualitative researcher to hear the siren song of a new software program. Immediately the researcher grows excited and experiences a near-Pavlovian response to the promise of a "point and click" program that will accomplish in seconds (or even microseconds) jobs that used to consume hours, days, or weeks of the researcher's time. The researcher goes online, downloads a "trial version," and double clicks to open it up for the first time ever. What the researcher then sees on her computer screen might as well be hieroglyphics (provided, of course, that she isn't fluent in ancient Egyptian symbology). This is what we might call the "anticlimax" of the "manual-to-automatic" transition in the realm of qualitative data analysis.

In most cases the researcher tinkers around, points here and clicks there, and without benefit of comprehension, closes the program (X Program Menu → Quit). Then she goes back to her pile of typed transcripts, 3×5 index cards neatly assorted into categories, and continues plodding the path of manual data analysis.

---

[2] One notable exception is Qualrus, a qualitative data analysis program that has a "note card" function, which allows you to "write" information on virtual "index cards," which in turn you can sort into piles and otherwise manipulate.

The transition from written materials analysis to computer-assisted analysis is difficult for at least a couple of reasons: First, as we've indicated, software programs—even those we focus on in this chapter—don't imitate manual processes or hard copy materials. This alone can be and often is disconcerting to researchers, students, and faculty alike. Second, every software program requires the user to learn how to use it. Some programs have a steeper "learning curve" than others. Veteran researchers invested years, maybe decades, in developing their manual, hard copy–based data analysis systems; the prospect of spending several months learning a computer program that *appears* to bear no resemblance to their "real life" processes is stomach-turning. Finally, perhaps the main reason that new and senior researchers either avoid or quickly discard computer-based analysis approaches is that they had unreasonable expectations to begin with.

## The Importance of Setting Reasonable Expectations

Garbage in, garbage out (GIGO) is a long-standing principle of computing. It's a shorthand way of saying that no computer or software program is going to do anything beyond what you tell it to do. It's not going to make something on your behalf. It won't do the work for you. While the use of a qualitative data analysis software program will expedite many of the formerly manual procedures that many of us employ, and while it most certainly will broaden the range of analytic options beyond that available to those who stick to manual manipulation of data, it's not going to perform miracles.

Although the development of computer software programs for qualitative research has lagged far behind the proliferation of sophisticated programs for organizing and manipulating numeric data, programs such as those we present in this chapter offer the researcher highly sophisticated tools for organizing, managing, analyzing, interpreting, and reporting the results of qualitative empirical studies. Breakneck developments in the field of qualitative data analysis software programming have yielded a whole new range of analytic options for researchers, and they can help save a lot of time over the long haul. Yet there still exists a considerable gap between how researchers are accustomed to working and how these programs operate. Consequently, if one wishes to use a software program to analyze data, one must invest the necessary time and energy into learning what it will do, what it will *not* do, and most important, how to bridge the gap between the researcher's "old habits" and the "new habits" required by the software programs.

So as you set out to read the remainder of this chapter, bear in mind that both of these programs—and any other program worth its salt—take a little while to master. While they have a pretty low threshold when it comes to basic analytics, it's going to require a significant investment of time on your part if you want to learn how and when to use their more sophisticated tools and functions. Most of all, as you move ahead in this chapter, remember that there's no program known to humankind that will do your data collection, data analysis, interpretation of results, theory building, hypothesis testing, or reporting of results *on your behalf*. In the end, the product of your research will be only as good as the data, and no better than your ability to make sense of—and articulate the significance of—those data.

Now we turn to the principal aim of this chapter: a comparative review of the two most widely used software programs for qualitative data analysis—*NVivo* (Ver. 8) and *ATLAS.ti* (Ver. 6). Beyond merely describing each of them, we offer our view of their relative merits and delineate the kinds of projects best-suited for each one.

## INTRODUCTION TO CAQDAS

Computer Assisted Qualitative Data Analysis software (**CAQDAS**) refers to binary code–based (0 and 1) graphical interface programs[3] housed within microcomputer hardware that allow for the manipulation of **nonnumeric structured data** and **unstructured data** for the purpose of discerning patterns in the data. The data are almost always textual—either at point of origin (e.g., an interview with its resulting transcript) or after "translation" (e.g., written descriptive commentary on video gathered in a field study). By "structured data" we're referring to materials gathered consistently and systematically across "cases" (e.g., transcripts from structured interviews of unemployed postal carriers, all of whom you asked the same questions in roughly the same order).

"Unstructured data" refer to everything else—all of the other materials that you have decided should be included in the analysis. (By the way, you should be able to make a convincing argument as to why any given piece of data should or should not be included in your analysis.) Most often, unstructured data come in the form of field notes written in a prose-like manner (i.e., without categories guiding observation), transcriptions of video recorded events, pictures of people/places/things, audio recordings of ambient sound, etc.

Whether structured or unstructured, the software programs in this chapter treat the material all the same. You have at your disposal the same organizational, analytical, and theory-building and theory-testing tools regardless of the data's degree of "structure." Besides, one person's "structured data" is another person's stinking hot mess undeserving even of the label "unstructured." The distinction is highly subjective, contested, and ultimately arbitrary. All you really need to know is that programs such as these deal with qualitative data no matter what form it takes or shape it's in.

### A Brief History of CAQDAS

The emergence of CAQDAS coincided with the advent and proliferation of microcomputers (i.e., computers small enough for personal use in the home or office). The first CAQDAS programs were created in the 1970s and were mostly data management and storage programs. These CAQDAS programs primarily functioned to store, retrieve, and organize data by assigning codes and categories; essentially they were designed and used for manipulating, searching, and reporting data. As computers became more powerful and sophisticated, so did CAQDAS programs.

The 1980s gave rise not only to horrible fashion and "New Wave" music but also to software programs that could execute analytic procedures on *textual* data. Although this may seem less than titillating to you, back then we qualitative researchers were in a real fervor, having spent years watching our quantitative-oriented colleagues using microcomputers to process their data punch cards and then spit out results of statistical calculations that they had programmed into the computer's operating systems and/or software programs. Within the domain of qualitative data software, the "breakthrough" was the newly achieved ability to generate and test theories about social life through the use of automated **Boolean logic operators** (strategic manipulations

---

[3] As an aside, *all* computer programs—from the social networking websites such as Facebook to Microsoft Word to iMovie—operate on a binary code foundation rooted in the collaborative mutual exclusion of zero and one (0,1). So everything you experience on the computer screen—from words ("eagle") to numbers ("451") to photographs to video clips to songs—is the result of thousands upon thousands of binary code permutations. Every element is nothing more or less than a particular series of zeroes and ones. Mind-blowing, isn't it?

of data that rely upon central "operators" such as "AND", "OR", "NOT", etc.). Before you heap scorn on the geeks like us who appreciated this innovation, let's take a look at two examples of research projects where the simple computerization of Boolean logic commands can/did make life much easier and more interesting.

**BOOLEAN LOGIC, SEX, AND DRUGS** First, let's say we're interested in teenagers' experimentation with drugs. In particular, we want to know more about the contexts and other events going on in their lives around the time they first experiment with an illicit substance. We've interviewed 100 teens and have asked them to reflect back a few years on their first drug experiences. Once we've collected the data, we're now poring over 100 interview transcripts, and we begin to notice what appears to be a pattern: Teens who experiment with drugs before the end of puberty also tend to experiment with sex. In the old days, we would have had to do a lot of work to test this working hypothesis—cutting, pasting, sorting, hand tabulating, etc. With the advent of automated Boolean commands, however, the researcher simply writes a command instructing the computer to retrieve only those interviews—or only those passages within interviews—where respondents said that their first drug experiences *and* their first sexual encounters occurred contemporaneously. What do we find? A distinct pattern. We observe in the data a tendency among pubescent youth to get involved in both—drugs and sex go together like biscuits and gravy—*but* not when the drug use was known and condoned, or even facilitated, by the young person's parent. This ability to discern patterns with simple Boolean command structures substantially changed, we dare say improved, the qualitative researcher's analytic tool-kit. A command containing two key words—*but* and *and*—allowed us to see a social phenomenon at work.

**BOOLEAN LOGIC AND INFIDELITY** Another example is divorcing spouses. With regard to the romantic coupling and uncoupling of adults, our "pretend" researchers who had conducted hundreds of interviews with both parties were left with a veritable mountain of printed transcripts. Using Boolean logic as their foundation, they wrote commands that yielded interview segments constituting a provocative pattern—when one person in a relationship is unhappy, his or her decision to leave the relationship occurs when the experience of dissatisfaction *and* the experience of meeting someone else to whom he or she is attracted occur close together in time, *but* the "decoupling" isn't going to happen if that "someone else" has lower "social standing" and represents lower net worth than the partner with whom the respondent is unhappy. Another social phenomenon revealed! Yes, in both instances the researchers might have arrived at these very same conclusions. But it would have taken them a lot more time to get there. More important, ascertaining these patterns would have required the analyst to perform several complex tasks by hand, such as coding/tagging, sorting, indexing, cross-indexing, tabulating, and so forth. Such maneuvers leave a lot of room for errors. This is where the power of CAQDAS is best illustrated—it expedites organizational and analytical functions, and it makes no mistakes of its own.

Note in the above examples that the computer didn't "do" the research or the theorizing on the researchers' behalf. The computer didn't spit out the "answer." Rather, the researchers had the working knowledge, the know-how, and sufficient familiarity with the data to *know* what to do with the data and which commands to issue the computer. The same goes for all software programs. Take Facebook, for example. When you find a profile of someone you know and want to befriend him, you simply drag the mouse or move the cursor to the button "Add Friend." Then you click and voila! A "friendship" request message endeavors to the other person's mailbox.

Facebook didn't make any of this happen. The program didn't know that you knew this person (though its algorithms allow it to predict with better than average odds whether or not you know someone, but that's a different story). Nor did the program calculate the costs and benefits or run through the various possible problems or issues involved in asking this person to be a friend ("well, he doesn't really know me that well, and I just broke up with his roommate . . . what if he thinks I'm trying to" . . . etc.). *You* brought the necessary knowledge/information to the table, and you were responsible for the deliberation and the ultimate decision to click "Add Friend." Facebook's software interface did add tremendous value, however. After all, making contact with that person—and by extension all of that person's contacts—would have been pretty hard to do yourself, in "real life"; you would have spent months driving, walking, talking, and writing. And you likely would have made some mistakes along the way, ultimately failing to connect yourself with all of your friend's other friends.

The moral of the story here is *manageability*. CAQDAS programs make large amounts of nonnumeric data more manageable, more manipulable, and more amenable to analysis. In the end, the program facilitates *storytelling* by disciplining a large, often somewhat amorphous mass of text data and thereby allowing you, the storyteller, to identify the key elements of the story.

## Reduction: The Key to CAQDAS

Hurling invective and ridicule at "reductionism" and "reductionistic explanations" is *de rigueur* in the social sciences and the humanities.[4] In an earlier chapter we referred to "reductionism" vis-à-vis theory and interpretation; we defined it as the tendency to distill complex social phenomena to an individual level dynamic (e.g., crime is a result of genetics or psychological pathology). Explaining the concept of reductionism in its many forms is well beyond the scope of this book. Suffice it to say, however, that you don't want to get caught up in an academic argument wherein you are characterized as a reductionist! While we're sidetracked, here's another piece of advice: Avoid saying or doing things that lead your fellow classmates to call you a "functionalist"! If ever you do wander haplessly into a situation where others are calling you these names, we suggest the following retort: "Well, I may or may not be a reductionist (or functionalist), but you are most certainly an *essentialist*!"

Now, asides aside, in this chapter we use the term "reduction" in a different way, a more mechanical and utilitarian way, and specifically in relation to data management/analysis. Here we focus on how qualitative data analysis software programs operate and, more specifically, how they can help you improve your research studies. How do they operate at a fundamental level? By **reduction**. Today's CAQDAS programs, more aesthetically pleasing and easily manipulated than their ancestors, still follow the same basic principle they always have: The *generating logic* of transforming open-ended data into malleable and manipulable "chunks" of "instances." That is, they provide you the tools necessary to reduce voluminous materials to manageable pieces of data.

---

[4] "Reductionism" takes many different forms and occupies conversations in various academic and non-academic circles, but it's particularly fashionable to talk of reductionism—and to be anti-reductionistic—in the social sciences and humanities. In the "hard" sciences, scholarly opinion is more varied, lively, and critically reflexive than it is in the social sciences. Some scientists strive for reductionism in theory and method as they attempt to delineate the most economical, parsimonious theory possible . . . or reduce their explanatory frameworks to the fewest possible elements. Ironically, "critical" theorists in the social sciences almost instinctively blanche at and reject wholesale the term "reductionism," often without even really knowing what it means (and it can mean a lot of different things, by the way).

## Back to the Future: The Primacy of the Binary

What the data consist of is up to you. Ideally, the data reflect and/or relate to and/or derive from the theory-driven research question(s) and/or hypotheses that have guided your research study to this point. As we've said, contemporary programs permit the manipulation of "nontext" files, such as audio, video, and still images. However, beneath whatever on-screen representations one sees (printed word, moving image, photograph) or hears (sound file) lies a numeric system comprised of 0's and 1's. That is, everything that you see on the screen is the result of countless iterations of **binary code**. It's this basic organizational scheme that enables the transformation of rather nebulous, open-ended information into manageably, moveable, and analyzable data.

## Garbage In, Garbage Out—Revisited with an Addendum Regarding False Hope

CAQDAS programs can complement a researcher's skills, but they cannot substitute for *or even improve* upon them. Nor will using a CAQDAS program make you a better person, help you quit smoking or lose weight, or reduce your student loan debt by 50 percent. We also want to let you know that CAQDAS programs do not perform analyses in the same way that their quantitative counterparts do. In quantitative software programs such as SPSS (now PASW Statistics), with which you might be very familiar at this point (or soon will be), the programs actually conduct analyses (e.g., chi-square, regression). By comparison, CAQDAS programs manipulate and organize data, but they cannot interpret them. So you cannot import data into the program, click on the "analyze" button, and then gleefully lap up the results. This is a very important point: A CAQDAS program can support and streamline your analyses, but it cannot do them for you. It can do only what you tell it to do. Moreover, once it has done what you've told it to do, *you* have to interpret the outcome of its actions. Basically, a CAQDAS program's analyses are only as good as you are. Yes, we've said this already . . . but repetition of important points is one key to success in the methodology textbook market; so please, bear with us.

Also, CAQDAS programs do not transcribe audio or video recordings or make coding decisions for you. Instead, CAQDAS functions like a low-level word processing program. It can no more do your work for you than, say, Microsoft Word can write a class paper on your behalf. The CAQDAS program is like a garage stocked with pretty decent tools. But neither the garage nor its inventory of tools is of any use without a skilled mechanic on the premises. In this example, by the way, *you* are the mechanic and the broken-down car is your project's data set. (Note: We mean you no disrespect with the clunker comparison.)

This said, however, CAQDAS programs, like the two we review in this chapter, can add tremendous value to your data analysis effort: They allow you to analyze data in a faster, more streamlined manner, and they provide a more advanced and powerful method for coding, sorting, and "**running queries** on" (interrogating) the data. CAQDAS programs also facilitate detailed recordkeeping, which adds transparency to the research process and validity to the results by meeting the **audit trail** standard discussed earlier in this book. Finally, CAQDAS programs facilitate more efficient and effective visualizations of inductively, deductively, and abductively achieved theories.

## The Magic Moment: Al Green or Alanis Morissette?

CAQDAS programs are not appropriate for all situations in which a researcher has qualitative data. For small-scale and/or less complicated qualitative projects, the researcher must decide if the software is necessary. As we've mentioned, every program has a learning curve, and it might be a better use of the researcher's time to conduct the analyses by hand, without the assistance of a CAQDAS program. Or, in some cases, you might want to do your analyses mostly by hand but also with the help of a spreadsheet program (e.g., MS Excel) or one of the many freeware GTD ("Getting Things Done") programs, such as Evernote, Journler, etc., all of which allow you to organize, tag/code, and otherwise make some sense of the data you've collected.

In addition, when a researcher has data that cannot be transformed into an editable text format, CAQDAS might not be appropriate. For example, a historian working exclusively with archival data that are in image form may find his or her analysis options limited because the detail in the digitized data cannot be easily coded with text tags. Yes, most CAQDAS programs do enable the text coding of still images, video clips, and audio recordings, but in some cases, like the historian analyzing thousands of miniature ceramic butterflies handcrafted in the eighteenth century, using CAQDAS might not be worth all the time and effort required to transform those butterflies into manipulable text representations.

Okay, one last cautionary note about using CAQDAS programs: Researchers often try to analyze qualitative data in a quantitative manner simply because CAQDAS programs do have functions designed to accomplish numeric tasks, or even to analyze numeric data; most have functions for "counts" and for calculating "reliability" scores. The pressure to "quantify" qualitative data can be overwhelming at times, and there's a long history of tension between qualitative and quantitative methodologists (see Part I). Rather than rehashing this long debate and once again establishing the legitimacy of qualitative research methodology, we want to issue a simple warning: Don't get all quantitative with your qualitative data just because you think it will make your study seem more "valid" or "reliable" or "good" or "rigorous." Good science lies not in a given study's label (i.e., "quantitative" vs. "qualitative") but rather in the degree to which the study meets the standards of quality we presented and explained in Part I.

## Remembering Meaning

Remember, qualitative data analysis is usually more concerned with the meanings people ascribe to their experiences, to phenomena in the world, and to the relationships and events of their lives. It's less concerned (though not entirely unconcerned) about counting how many people ("cases") experience this, that, or the other thing. How do people make meaning? What are some of the more consequential implications of all this meaning-making? What meaning am I to make of their meaning-making? These are the kinds of questions we ask in qualitative research, and the CAQDAS programs we present in this chapter are particularly effective tools in helping arrive at some answers.

## Path Forward

With all of these advantages and limitations in mind, let's proceed with our discussion of the two dominant CAQDAS programs in the behavioral and social sciences: NVivo and ATLAS.ti. Just remember, neither of these programs—and no other program—will do any of your analytic work for you. Your analysis is only as good as . . . well . . . your analysis. The computer has little to do with it.

## THE CONTENDERS: NVivo VERSUS ATLAS.ti

In this section we present NVivo 8 and ATLAS.ti 6, two of the most common CAQDAS programs. We will not be providing you with a "user manual" for either program. Instead, we're going to describe to you the logic behind these programs' central functions. By "logic," we mean the underlying mechanism by which the programs read, organize, and display the data. These two programs vary considerably in their foundational logic; the variations, in turn, impact how you can use the programs, what functions the software can perform, etc.

At some point you must decide whether or not to use one of these programs, or any program, to facilitate your data analysis. Understanding each program's core logic will help you figure out whether or not to use a software program at all. If you do decide to go with CAQDAS, knowing each program's fundamental operational scheme will help you determine which program's logic is better suited to the logic by which *you* have framed, organized, and conducted *your research* and the logic by which you have compiled your data. Only then will you be able to decide which program is the appropriate choice.

Below we explain how each program works with data, how the logic impacts the functions performed by the software, and the implications the logic has on using the program. By expanding on the logic of these programs, we strive to aid the reader in using the software with greater ease. It is our opinion that CAQDAS programs are easier to use when the program's foundational logic is understood.

We also discuss which type of qualitative data is best suited for which program by focusing on the major differences in the programs. In the end, we hope that you will be able to determine, based upon your research question, which software program is more appropriate. Cutting to the chase a bit, we'll tell you now that in general, when your project consists principally of structured qualitative data (structured interviews, systematic observations, etc.), we recommend NVivo. If, however, your project has generated a large volume of unstructured data (open-ended field notes, semi-structured interviews and/or life histories, etc.), then we recommend that you use the ATLAS.ti program. Take note, however, that these are our own recommendations and that other researchers—and even the software developers themselves— may disagree with us.[5]

## A Note on Grounded Theory: Inductive and Deductive Approaches to Making Sense

Although researchers often use CAQDAS as a way to inductively work their way toward a **grounded theory** (Glaser and Strauss 1967) of their chosen social topic, *both* programs we discuss in this chapter can be valuable tools in a more deductive, theory/hypothesis-testing approach. Don't let anyone tell you otherwise—these programs can help you build theory out of empirical data, and/or they can help you test existing theory. Which approach you take depends on your methodology, the project's substance, the quality and quantity of data you have, and the manner in which you have framed your research question. Again, it all comes back to you . . .

The choice between inductive and deductive approaches directly affects your data discovery process: If you adopt a grounded theory approach, you'll use **inductive coding** to work toward discerning patterns in your observations, and on the basis of these patterns you'll form one or more working hypotheses that you can test using the data you have or additional data you'll have to collect. The inductive approach typically means that you don't have a pre-identified

---

[5] (Disclosure: Scott prefers ATLAS.ti, though he's an infidel when it comes to data analysis software programs. He stays true to no particular program and instead opts to practice CAQDAS polyamory. On any given project, Scott may use a combination of ATLAS.ti, Evernote, Journler, MS Excel, Grapher for Mac, Movie NoteTaker, etc.). Again, the point is that you, as the researcher in charge of your study, need to figure out which software tools, if any, will best perform in the service of your study and its research question, hypotheses, and data parameters.

scheme to follow when sifting through your data—that is, you didn't produce the data using highly structured instruments, nor did you organize the data, once produced, in a highly ordered fashion.

By contrast, **deductive coding** begins with hypotheses that delineate the patterns you should expect to see in the data, followed by various forms of "testing" to see if those patterns actually exist. With this approach, the researcher has a predefined **coding scheme** (also known as a **coding tree**) customarily derived from the instrument used to produce the data (which was itself derived from the research question[s] and hypotheses), and then inspects the data, assigning codes to those "chunks" of text that seem to constitute evidence of factors or instances defined by the hypotheses (Bazeley 2007; Lewins and Silver 2007).

## Coded Chunks of Text: The Foundation of Qualitative Data Analysis

All qualitative data analysis—regardless of data type or approach to theory development—revolves around the coded "chunk" of data (a.k.a. **coded quotation**). The **chunk** might be a word, a phrase, a sentence, a paragraph, or an image, a video clip, or a sound bite; the **code** is a word, a phrase, or a number that categorizes, interprets, and conceptualizes the data. **Coding data** allow you to see patterns in the vast pool of information collected on your desk—the hundreds of field notes pages, thousands of interview transcript pages, or hours of video footage you have collected—and begin to build or test hypotheses.

The code is essential to qualitative data analysis. Around the code revolves everything else. It makes the world (or at least your study) go 'round. A code is like an abbreviation of something much longer. Whether it's a word or a number, it *stands for* an idea, theme, event, dynamic, observation, or statement whose expression on paper is too long to be easily manipulated. When you create a code, you're basically making an unmanageable portion of data into a manageable and manipulable "proxy."

Here is a very simple example of how a code works:

Say you're interested in the relationship between expectant mothers' child birthing preferences and their satisfaction with their birth experience. In this case you might develop a system for coding interviews in which mothers describe the labor and delivery of their child(ren). When mothers talk about their birth experience, you might have codes for what they say and how they say it. Here's an extract from an imaginary interview with an imaginary mother, "Kula," who gave birth in a hospital:[6]

> Kula: Well . . . from the time I got wheeled in the front door of the hospital until the moment I got wheeled out—less than 24 hours later, by the way—I felt like I had no real say in what was going on, what was happening to me, or even what the possible responses might be . . . like what could be done to deal with what was happening to me. Everyone but me was making decisions about me and about my baby. It felt to me like they just saw me as incapable of contributing anything . . . as though I were a comatose victim of a car crash . . . I had no authority, basically. No legitimacy. That's it . . . I had no legitimacy *as a mother* . . . I was only "legitimate" as a patient, a sick person . . . no, not even a sick *person* . . . I was just a "case", or an "illness", a "condition" to be treated. The

---

[6] Although the study is "imaginary" and "Kula" is a pseudonym, there really is a woman who had this experience and conveyed it to Scott in conversation. This is an accurate reproduction of her account. We use it here with her permission. Thanks, "Kula"!

fact that I'm a person was hardly relevant. The more I tried to assert myself, the more detached and clinical they got. The only time they even came close to treating me as a human being was when I let them do whatever they wanted to me and my baby ... The more I acted like a baby, the more humanely they treated me. So when I was at my most passive was when they treated me like a human. Ironic, huh?

At this point, if we were in a classroom, I'd ask you and your classmates to tell me what to do. How do we code this passage? Where do we begin? Most likely my question would meet up with a deafening silence, punctuated only by the sound of students squirming in their seats, the sound of people trying to go unnoticed. Why? Because it's a hard question with no "right" or "wrong" answer. Where we begin, what we do, how we code are questions whose answers—however provisional they may be—lie in the relationship between this **observation** and our guiding research question(s) and hypotheses. However we end up coding this, the point is that Kula's description is too long and therefore unwieldy in terms of data analysis. Therefore, we must *reduce* it to a code, or more likely, multiple codes.

One way to start is to look at the principal nouns in this passage: hospital, baby, decisions, car crash, victim, authority, legitimacy, mother, patient, person, case, illness, condition, human. Now look at the modifiers, the adjectives: incapable, comatose, detached, clinical, passive. Next, identify the central verbs, and take note of whether they're in active or passive voice: wheeled in (passive), was happening, deal with, contributing, tried to assert, treating, act. Finally, examine the adverbs, the words that modify the verbs and adjectives. What do we find here? Arguably, this passage contains only one significant adverb: "humanely."

Okay, we've got our start. By this point you should be able to see a bit more clearly what's "happening" in this passage and also how we might go about *reducing* it to a coded quotation (i.e., a code), thus making it more manageable analytically. Kula's account overflows with code possibilities. We could apply **inductive codes**, which stay very close to the words/text generated by the "subject" or informant. If in this case, for example, we're interested in how women talk about their perceptions of birth-giving, we might apply codes such as "excluded from making decisions," "legitimacy/authority," "illness," "detachment," "humane," "made passive."

Or we might take a different approach, more theory-driven, and create more abstract and **abductive codes**, which are codes that serve to bridge theory with empirical data. If our theory concerns the ways birthing mothers elicit humane treatment from medical professionals—the doctors and nurses in the maternity ward—we might apply a code such as "self-infantilize" to capture Kula's insight that "acting like a baby" (i.e., adopting a passive, sick patient countenance) is one strategy for inspiring humane, if demoralizing, treatment from the doctor. Figure 22.1 shows some of the ways we might apply codes to this passage.

## Inductive and Abductive Coding: Not Mutually Exclusive

Coding qualitative data early in a project may be purely descriptive, or inductive, but become more analytic, or abductive or even deductive, as you move through the research process (Bazeley 2007). Descriptive codes contextualize data through topics and themes and are used as devices to signify elegantly the **manifest meaning** of data (e.g., how women describe their child birthing preferences). **Analytic coding** involves manipulating codes and examining their relationships to one another, to get at the **latent meaning** which in turn points to the explanatory factors behind the phenomenon of interest (e.g., women's preferences for laboring and delivering their children as a reflection of their attitudes toward the childbirth experience and beliefs about the role medicine ought to play).

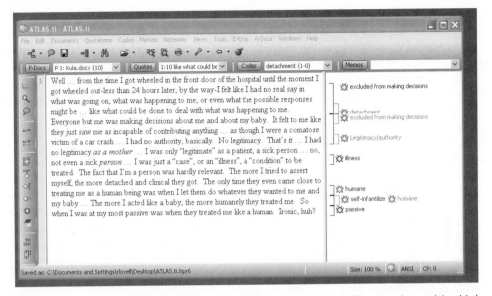

**FIGURE 22.1**    Applying abductive codes in ATLAS.ti to Kula's account of her experience giving birth

While the stage of a research project may determine which type of coding is more appropriate, most qualitative research studies incorporate both. In fact, discovering qualitative data often requires multiple iterations of coding often referred to as first-run coding (e.g., open, mostly descriptive coding) and second- (or third- or fourth-) run coding (focused, more analytic coding) (Emerson et al. 1995). If in one of the interviews an expectant mother talks about how she planned a natural, nonmedicated birth, you might create a code "natural" into which you would collect/deposit all references to preferences for natural childbirth across interviews. This allows you to go back through the many interviews and determine how often mothers discussed their preference for natural childbirth. It also allows you to discover additional themes as you turn from open to focused coding. For instance, as you inspect the data coded "natural," you may discover different kinds of natural childbirth: Mothers who used doctors, mothers who used midwives, mothers who used doulas, and mothers who used any combination of the above.

Knowledge of the coding process and its logic is essential to understanding the CAQDAS programs we feature below. In fact, it's vital no matter which program you use. Using a program successfully demands that you know how coding works because there's no available program that will create a coding scheme particular to your theory and data, code all of your data, and then make sense of it. Once again, we find ourselves reminding you that your use of CAQDAS will be no better or worse than your analytic abilities.

Now let's turn to the CAQDAS programs we've decided to present and explain to you: NVivo and ATLAS.ti. We encourage you to visit their respective websites and download free (therefore somewhat limited) trial versions of one or both programs.

## LOGIC OF NVivo AND ATLAS.ti

Every CAQDAS program, including NVivo and ATLAS.ti, acts as a "container" for your data. Once your data and the software come together as a project, the programs function much like file cabinets, or mail sorters in a post office—they are comprised of user-defined labeled categories (analogous to files or mail slots) into which you place chunks of text to which you have applied codes (e.g., Kula's description of feeling excluded from decision making plus the descriptions of, say, 25 other women whom you've interviewed, with all of these descriptions gathered together under the code "exclusion from decision making").

These software programs can "hold" the data either internally or externally. Programs that hold the data internally simply copy the files, originally created in a word processing program such as Microsoft Word, directly into the program; thus, data are actually imported into the software and can be directly manipulated (coded, annotated, appended, shortened, edited, etc.) in the program. Other programs, however, do not contain your actual documents/data but rather refer, or link, to the data, which can be stored anywhere and in any binary-code friendly program (Word, Excel, Adobe, etc.). In this case, what you see once you've opened the software program is a facsimile, a representation, of your data file. If it's an interview transcript, then you're seeing a two-dimensional replica of the original MS Word file. It's important to note here that "internal data" programs allow you to change the original document that you're treating as data, whereas the "external data" programs do not allow you to change the file's contents. (Actually, with an external data program you *can* change the original file within the program's interface, but it creates all sorts of potential problems, so we recommend against the practice.)

NVivo is an **internal data program**; ATLAS.ti is an **external data program**. This is a major distinction in the logic of both programs and has significant implications for how to use the software programs. This difference also factors heavily into the decision concerning which program to use for any given kind of qualitative data and/or method. We'll return to this in more detail later in the chapter. For now, just keep in mind that NVivo allows you to import your data files and then change them within the program, whereas ATLAS.ti creates "snapshots" of your data files whose originals (created, for instance, in MS Word) cannot be altered within ATLAS.ti.[7]

## Logic of NVivo

NVivo operates as an internal database and stores the data by directly importing text, audio, video, and picture files into the program. NVivo uses the term "Internals" to refer to these imported documents (everything you import is technically a "document" even if it's a movie, image, or audio file). This internal structure allows for direct manipulation of the data in the program. For example, in the case of textual data, when you assign a code to a passage of text, that code is attached directly to the text chunk, analogous to putting a sticker on a file folder. In other words, all manipulations to the text (coding, annotations, etc.) are always connected to the original data documents no matter from which file/slot you view your data chunks.

The original data documents are accessible from any of the various files/slots in which you chunk or gather data allowing for flexibility in viewing your data and referring back to the original context. "Externals," on the other hand, are not internal (obviously) documents, and their codes are linked, not attached directly. Examples of "externals" include nondigitized and/or nondigitizable objects, reference materials, and websites. In many instances, though, it's easy to transform "externals" into "internals" by simply taking a digital photograph of the object or even the text, a screenshot of the website (saved as a document), or a video clip or audio recording of the "event" you wish to analyze.

---

[7] Note: Even though ATLAS.ti allows you to work only with copies of your original data files and does not allow you to change your original data files from within its interface (except for .RTF files), you *can* apply codes and otherwise manipulate the data file copies.

NVivo Project Interface

**THE INTERFACE**    NVivo's software interface looks similar to Microsoft Office and is fairly easy to navigate and understand (see the screenshot of NVivo's project interface). This familiarity makes it relatively easy for the novice researcher to use. For example, many of NVivo's most commonly used functions are done by right-clicking—no need to waste time trying to find the functions in the drop-down menus or icons. NVivo comes with a number of "bells and whistles" (e.g., easy-to-use, predesigned functions), such as the matrix coding query, coding stripes, and inter-rater reliability statistics, which makes its features easier to learn and use. These bells and whistles are most effective with structured or semi-structured data because, as compared with ATLAS.ti, NVivo's functions are more difficult to customize. Thus, as with most easy-to-navigate software programs, what the researcher gains in ease-of-use, she loses in specificity and in capacity to create customized analyses.

The bottom line is that if your data are relatively structured, and if you went into the study with a clear research question and now have some testable hypotheses, then we would recommend that you work with NVivo, particularly if you're drawn to software programs with graphical, easy-to-use interfaces.

## Logic of ATLAS.ti

ATLAS.ti operates on the basis of an external database structure. This program functions as a "window" that displays your data "documents," which remain in their place of origin on your computer. In other words, as we've mentioned, ATLAS.ti does not import or work with your original data files; instead, it creates and allows you to manipulate facsimiles of your data files. ATLAS.ti merely displays the data. Unlike NVivo, this program does not distinguish between internal and external documents, as *all* of the documents you "import" are considered external. Thus, all data will physically remain outside of the program. Instead of importing files into ATLAS.ti, you simply tell the program which documents should be linked to the project (in ATLAS.ti language, "assigned").

**UNIT OF ANALYSIS THE CODED QUOTATION, CAPABLE OF STANDING ALONE**    In ATLAS.ti the unit of analysis (UOA) is the "coded quotation" (CQ). The CQ is simply the passage of text, or segment of video or audio, onto which you have placed a code. Take note here: Because the program operates as an external structure for data, once you assign a phrase or sentence or paragraph or any segment of data a code, it becomes a CQ and then stands on its own, independent of the data. What we're saying is that ATLAS.ti functions analytically at the "text-level" as compared to document level, and it's the only program that treats coded quotations as independent objects. Thus, quotations are separate entities that can be coded, annotated, linked, and visualized separately from the text (Lewins and Silver 2007).

This can be really helpful, especially when you want to analyze *how you coded your data* (an analysis of your analysis, or a kind of meta-analysis).

Remember our earlier discussion of perceptual filters and biases and how they structure the way we see the world? Well, ATLAS.ti's capacity for treating CQs as independent means that you can treat your own codes—and the data they capture/reflect/reduce—as data points in their own right. So, if you're interested in getting a bird's eye view of patterns in your review/analysis of the data, you can analyze CQs as data. This, by the way, is very cool, ultra-hip stuff! If this excites you as much as it does us, then you're truly a research geek (or "research bum" as we used to say). One warning: Describing in detail your passion for conducting meta-analyses of CQs in ATLAS.ti isn't the sort of thing that "civilians" find interesting. It's definitely not good first date (or even second or third date) material.

The external database structure also allows you to fold nontextual data into your project (i.e., graphic, audio, and video). Within the ATLAS.ti venue you can mark, code, notate, and retrieve nontext data using the same process you would follow when working with text files because, when it comes down to it, all representations in the ATLAS.ti venue can be considered "text" (though based in the binary 0/1 system of computer language). Thus, ATLAS.ti allows for the greatest flexibility in analyzing a far greater range of types of data due to its external database structure (Lewins and Silver 2007).

A basic understanding of how ATLAS.ti "reads" the data is a prerequisite for knowing the processes for linking, saving, backing up, altering, and moving your data (Lewins and Silver 2007). We will expand on this in the "Importing Data with ATLAS.ti" section below.

**UGLY BUT SMART**    The ATLAS.ti interface is less visually stimulating as compared with NVivo, and this alone often scares off students and professional researchers alike (see the screenshot of ATLAS.ti's project interface—it's like a bad mug shot of a software program, right?). On the screen ATLAS.ti looks more like a database, but when used properly it can be a very powerful mechanism for making sense, and therefore making meaning, out of your data.

Yet, as we said previously, it's often the case (and it's certainly true here) that what you gain in user-friendliness you lose in analytic robustness. ATLAS.ti and NVivo possess roughly the same core functions but differ in how the functions are performed. Comparatively speaking, ATLAS.ti has fewer easy-to-use, preprogrammed functions. However, it allows the researcher to perform most tasks in a greater number of ways. In fact, there are almost always at least four ways to do one function in ATLAS.ti (and only one way for each function in NVivo) but it's up to you, the researcher, to determine which way best suits your needs.

This difference—ease-of-use versus customizability—is analogous to "point-and-click" versus "writing syntax/code" in the world of quantitative data analysis software, where point-and-clicks make it easier to conduct analyses but you get more customizability and reliability with syntax. Thus, we recommend using ATLAS.ti if your data are less structured (e.g., non-category-driven field notes) and/or you went into the study with less clear research questions and hypotheses. Since it functions at the quotation level and not the document level like

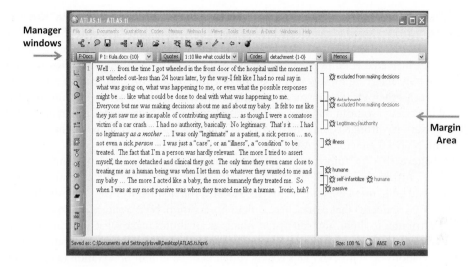

Manager windows →

← Margin Area

ATLAS.ti Project Interface

NVivo, how the data are structured matters very little to ATLAS.ti. Additionally, ATLAS.ti is preferable if you need/prefer to customize your analysis and are comfortable learning new software—especially software that lacks an easy(ier)-to-use interface.

## THE TRINITY OF UNITS: ANALYSIS, OBSERVATION, AND MANIPULATION

With any CAQDAS, it is important to keep in mind the units of observation, analysis, and manipulation throughout the process of coding and analysis. The unit of observation (e.g., individual interview) could very well be the unit of analysis (i.e., the individual person behind the interview), but this is not always the case. For example, in interviews with mothers about their childbirth experiences, the units of observation and analysis are the same: the mothers. Here the mother, as a person, and the interview of the mother are homologous—we treat them as identical. The transcript of the interview serves to "represent" the mother; hence, in discussing your findings, you'll be talking about mothers and their experiences. However, as part of your investigation of mother's experiences with childbirth you may choose to interview prenatal care providers to learn more about their individual practices and childbirth philosophies.

Mothers who attend group practices for prenatal care may interact with several practitioners and/or doctors, so you may wish to individually interview staff members and doctors at the practice. For this, the unit of observation is the individual interviews with staff and doctors, but the unit of analysis is *the practice itself*.

Finally, it's important to note that while the units of observation and analysis can be at the same or different levels, the **unit of manipulation** is always different from the units of observation and analysis; units of manipulation are the coded text or quotations that are used as building blocks for your analysis. (Note: The "unit of manipulation" is really just another way of saying "the software program's unit of analysis," as though the software were a person. It's really just a matter of identifying the centerpiece around which logical analysis revolves.)

**ORGANIZING DATA USING "ATTRIBUTES" TO TRANSFORM UNIT OF OBSERVATION INTO UNIT OF ANALYSIS**    Keeping the distinction between **unit of analysis** and **unit of observation** in mind is important because it can determine how you organize your data. Generally, in both programs it's considered good practice to organize your data around the *unit of observation*. By "organize" we are referring to how you label the documents and files, where you put them in relation to each other, etc. Once you've organized around the unit of observation (e.g., the individual interview), you can build up to the unit of analysis (if it is, in fact, different from the unit of observation) through coding the data in the interview transcripts; however, this is more so the case with NVivo than with ATLAS.ti.

We believe that to fully utilize NVivo's preprogrammed menu functions, such as "Autocoding," "Attributes," and "Relationships," it's best to organize the data around the unit of observation and build up to the unit of analysis. How do you do this? By assigning "Attributes" to every case (i.e., document) that represents a unit of observation. NVivo allows you to create cases and assign attributes to them. You can assign whatever attributes make sense for your project— age, race/ethnicity, religious affiliation, geographic location of residence, occupation, sexual preference, relationship status, etc. This is how you flesh out a unit of observation (a document) and make it stand for something much more meaningful (a person you interviewed).

For instance, in the above example of maternal childbirth practices where the individual interviews with staff and doctors are the unit of observation, you might want to assign **attributes** to the interviewees, such as age, race/ethnicity, number of years working in the obstetrics and gynecology field, etc. You might also want to assign **relationships** such as the connection between the type of practice (midwifery, obstetrics) and the birth setting (hospital, alternative birthing center, home birth), so "type of practice → *impacts* → birth setting." In NVivo, these functions work to their fullest extent if the data are organized around the unit of observation.

As for ATLAS.ti, most of its functions can be customized, so it doesn't really matter to the program how you organize your data. ATLAS.ti's coding functions allow for the same sort of coding (e.g., *attributes, relationships*). You can ascribe an attribute by simply coding the *entire text* of, say, the interview with the interviewee's age, race/ethnicity, geographic location, etc. You can also designate relationships through the **Codelinks** or **Network** functions without having to structure the data in a certain way before conducting analyses.

Now that we have explored the basic logic—the underlying schematic—of each program, let's take a closer look at how each program operates specifically.

---

## BOX 22.1
### Specifics of the Program Software

In this section we provide background information to help you determine which type of documents the programs support and how to navigate the programs' functions. For more detailed information on actual use, you should consult the programs' user's manuals, easily located online.

**THE NVivo WORKSPACE**

As noted earlier in this chapter, NVivo's software interface looks similar to Microsoft Office and is fairly easy to navigate. The elegant and inviting, or at least nonthreatening, interface makes the user feel at home, comfortable in the belief that "this is a program I can work with." Within this interface you can choose from among a variety of different "views," each of which has its uses. The "Navigation View" displays the main project components and offers the following navigational tools: *Sources, Nodes, Sets, Queries, Models, Links,* and *Classifications.* You simply decide which project component and tool you want to use and then make your selection. The "List View" displays items contained in project component folders and subfolders. The "Detail View" presents the contents of whichever list view item happens to be open at the time. See the screenshot of NVivo's project interface.

As we've noted, every CAQDAS program has its own vernacular. Though there are similarities across programs, with some programs even using identical terms, there's sufficient variation to demand some study on the part of a new user. So here are some key terms that you need to know when working with NVivo.

- **Internals**—primary source materials imported into a project (i.e., raw data) such as field notes, audio interviews, video footage.
- **Externals**—proxy sources representing materials that cannot be imported but are integral to the project (e.g., websites, reference materials, hand written documents).
- **Nodes**—the unit of analysis; "containers" for descriptive or analytic themes and topics within the data (i.e., codes). Codes are physically attached to the data and are linked to any additional manipulations of the data (e.g., overlapping codes, document links). There are five types of Nodes.

  - **Free Nodes**—stand-alone nodes containing codes that do not contain subthemes.
  - **Tree Nodes**—hierarchical nodes with a main descriptive or analytic theme (parent node) and a subtheme (child node). For example, during first-run, descriptive coding of interviews in which mothers' talk about their birth-giving experiences, you may chunk data into a parent node "reflections on childbirth" with children nodes "positive" and "negative."
  - **Case Nodes**—nodes that store all information for a unit of analysis including all data associated with a unit of analysis and any attributes that have been assigned to it.
  - **Relationship Nodes**—nodes representing a connection between two project items; can be associative or directional.
  - **Matrix Nodes**—cross-tabulated nodes created through a matrix coding query;

allows you to ask questions of your data (e.g., do birth settings differ by mothers' age?).

- **Annotations**—comments, reminders, and questions appended to data; indicated as blue highlighted text in source documents; cannot be coded.
- **Memos**—documentation recording the thoughts and insights that occur to you while working with the data. Memos can be linked to either a document or to a node and can themselves be coded. Throughout your analysis it's good practice to write memos to yourself about the patterns you're discovering, coding decisions you've made at different stages of analysis, tentative hypotheses that occur to you, insights regarding additional data to collect, etc. NVivo sets a limit of one memo per document or node. So, for the most part, you'll want to use the Memo function as a way to keep track of observations and insights about the data. Any given memo can be linked to its corresponding document as a whole, but not to specific content within it (see See Also Links below for content-specific links).
- **See Also Links**—a link, or bookmark, from a specific point in a source document to another project item; can be linked between whole source documents or specific content including specific content of a memo or another source document; no limit to the number of See Also links one may have in any source document. See Also links are useful as a reminder to the analyst to consider other content in relation to current content (e.g., like observations, contradictions, memo content).
- **Memo Links**—link connecting memos to source documents; each source document is limited to one memo; specific content cannot be linked; indicated as an icon next to a source document in List View.
- **Attributes**—project component that allows you to create attributes for and assign values to case nodes (units of analysis).
- **Relationships**—project component that allows you to define associative or directional

(continued)

*(continued)*

ties between data, cases, or nodes; created/-defined in *Classifications* and are stored as nodes.

- **Models**—allows you to conduct various kinds of visualization—theoretical, empirical, meta-analytic, etc.

## THE ATLAS.ti WORKSPACE

As previously mentioned the ATLAS.ti screen interface looks like a database and is less visually appealing when compared to NVivo. (But isn't beauty in the eye of the beholder, after all?) Unlike NVivo, ATLAS.ti's interface does not contain multiple views for navigating through your project; instead, it presents one central workspace called the Hermeneutic Unit (HU) Editor (HUE).[8] The "HU Editor" displays the contents of the main documents (called primary documents or PDs) you "imported." It's also the editing tool and provides access to all the other tools. Additionally, although there aren't a number of views, ATLAS.ti has four drop-down selection boxes (P-Docs, Quotes, Codes, and Memos). If you click on any of these the buttons, a "Manger" will open.

These four main Manger windows (P-Docs Manager, Quotes Manager, Codes Manager, Memos Manager) function similar to Navigation View in NVivo—they allow you to interact with your data and perform your analyses. These four Managers display lists of various "objects" in ATLAS.ti windows that can be opened, moved, cascaded, and filtered as desired in order to see the HU Editor and Mangers at the same time. To view the data, select one of the P-docs, which opens a large scrollable window with the document on the left and wide blank area on your right. This area on your right is the "Margin Area," which is particularly useful because it allows you to see the Codes, Hyperlinks, Comments, and Memos that are linked to the coded quotations. See the screenshot of ATLAS.ti's project interface.

ATLAS.ti uses a language different from that of NVivo. Here are some of the key terms you'll need to know.

- **Hermeneutic Unit (HU)**—the overall ATLAS.ti project file; each project has one HU, and it contains all of the "primary documents" (PDs), codes, memos, and other files associated with the project. The HU Editor Window provides a macro-view of your project and its various elements.

- **Primary Document (PD)**—your data; documents (can be text, graphics, audio, PDFs, Google Earth data, etc.) to whose contents you need to assign codes. Because the HU is the ATLAS.ti project you're working on, there will be multiple PD files between and among which you can switch back and forth using the P-docs Manager. Regardless of how many PDs you have, for any given project there will be only one HU.

- **Quotation**—the level at which ATLAS.ti operates, the fundamental unit of data (any continuous stretch of data, any rectangular portion of a picture, or any length segment of audio or video). Remember, segments of data are layered on top of the PD (really, a facsimile of the PD), but the original PD is unaltered and unalterable from within ATLAS.ti.

- **Codes**—descriptive or analytical terms assigned to text, image, etc.; each code has two numbers after it; the first number is termed *grounded*, which tells you how many quotations are linked to the code, and the second number is called *density*, which tells you how many other codes are linked to any given code. In practical terms, these two numbers can be really helpful. If you have 50 interviews with birthing mothers, for example, and you've got a code for "excluded from decision making," you will be able to tell how many times this particular issue arose in your interviews (*grounded* score) and how many other codes are connected to this code (*density* score). Regarding the latter, once you've done the initial open coding, you'll want to start trying to discern patterns in the data. Certainly, the number of times a given issue comes up is one kind of pattern. Even more sophisticated, however, is the practice of determining how codes are related to one another. This is where theory building and/or

---

[8]Note: You must create a new, or open an existing, HU in the File menu to achieve this view.

theory testing comes into play. You may, for instance, want to find out where/when/why/how "exclusion from decision making" occurs. More advanced coding allows you to place this phenomenon in relation to other phenomena. So you might find that exclusion occurs in the interviews only when birthing mothers are describing hospital births but never when they're talking about midwife-assisted births. Finally, the *density* score tells you how *central* the phenomenon is in relation to other phenomena. A low number means that whatever phenomena the code captures/summarizes are somewhat ancillary, whereas a large number refers to phenomena that are quite likely integral to the topic at hand.

- **Relations**—the "power" links connecting pairs of codes or quotations; similar to Relationships in NVivo.
- **Memos**—stand-alone documents written by you, the research analyst. Commonly used as a reference or for commenting on your coding

decision methodology, emerging theories and explanations, tentative hypotheses to test later, etc.

- **Comments**—similar to memos except that are not independent; they are attached to other objects (codes, PDs, Memos, etc.) and can be printed along with those objects.
- **Families**—groups of code in families; used primarily for "filtering" data (e.g., you may want to examine only the experiences of birthing mothers who utilized midwifes and exclude, for the moment, those observations of mothers who gave birth in hospital).
- **Networks**—graphical representations of objects (codes, coded quotations, interviewees, etc.) and the relationships among them.
- **Supercode**—groups of codes; used primarily for "queries," which are commands that you tell the software to execute on the data (e.g., "retrieve all instances where 'exclusion from decision making' code is applicable"; P.S. Yes, in case you're wondering, the Supercode icon is a cape.)

## BOX 22.2
### Data Preparation

We now understand the basic logic, purposes, and limitations of CAQDAS programs. And we know the vernacular of NVivo and ATLAS.ti. We're now ready to get started. Where do we begin the analysis? At the beginning, of course. Let's import our data so that we can get down to business.

### IMPORTING DATA WITH NVivo

NVivo supports text, picture, video, and audio files, which are directly imported into a project as Internals. Although pictures, video clips, and audio files cannot be edited in NVivo, text documents (.doc, .docx, .txt, .rtf, text-based PDF) are fully editable (including formatting). This utility can be an asset or a liability. It's helpful in that you can format document headings while in NVivo for use in "Autocoding" (discussed later). But it's also a potential liability (and a huge one at that) because it's easy to accidentally alter data without knowing

you've done so until much later, maybe as late as the very end, when you realize that a simple typographical or clerical error has rendered your findings invalid and useless. Then you have no choice but to return to square one. And square one is an unhappy place to be—not even a nice place to visit, much less live.

Therefore we advise you to perform all editing and formatting of your documents (interview transcripts, field notes, etc.) *before* you import them into NVivo. Then, upon importation, you should designate them as "read only" to avoid lethal data alteration accidents. This practice is particularly important when working in a team project environment. You should note that while "read only" text files are code-able, you cannot work with picture, audio, and video files that are marked as "read only." If you're working with nontext files and discover that you

*(continued)*

*(continued)*

can't code, annotate, or transcribe them, check the "read only" preference to make sure it is not accidentally set.

Organizing your data in NVivo is relatively easy, assuming you've organized your documents in a way that makes sense for your project (e.g., separate individual interviews with expectant mothers and prenatal care practitioners). Within the Internals project component, you can create subfolders similar to a file directory in any Windows operating system. This allows you to group interviews from different stages of data collection, by interview type (mothers, practitioners), or however it makes sense for you to group your data.

## IMPORTING DATA WITH ATLAS.ti

ATLAS.ti (Ver. 6) can use all forms of text (.doc, .docx, .txt, .rtf, etc.), graphic (jpeg, bif, pdf, etc.), audio and video format (WAV, MP3, WMA, SND, AVI, MPG, WMV, MOV, etc.), and Google Earth data files. Google Earth can be used in ATLAS.ti in several ways. ATLAS.ti actually embeds Google Earth into the software as a PD. Locations are defined as quotations. You can also create snapshots from Google Earth as PDs, which you then can code as you would any other graphical PD. However, Google Earth requires a great deal of computer processing memory when it is integrated into ATLAS.ti.[9]

As we've already mentioned, your data are not actually imported into ATLAS.ti. It's more accurate to say that facsimile replicas of your digitized materials are made available to the HU. You make your materials available to the HU by "assigning documents." Assigning documents tells ATLAS.ti (really the HU that corresponds to your project) where to look for the data by specifying a path to that data. Thus, you must be careful when changing, renaming, and moving PDs. We strongly advise you to create a library of documents in a clearly marked folder on your hard drive (e.g., a folder on the desktop, or in the "Documents" place if you're working on an Apple computer). RTF files are the only types of files that can be altered within

the program, but we strongly caution that you *never* alter your data (i.e., PDs) after you have assigned them to the HU.

If you do alter a primary document without reassigning the documents, the HU will no longer know where to find the data. If you move your documents to different computers or different folders on the same computer without reassigning, ATLAS.ti will also not be able to find them. In fact, one of the most common errors for ATLAS.ti beginners pertains to not be able to find data because you have now moved or altered your documents or changed computers. Again, we strongly recommend that you create a project folder where you save the HU and move all your data documents into this folder. If you need to move your HU, you should create a "Copy Bundle" and then move the bundle. A Copy Bundle is a compressed file, similar to a .zip folder which contains your HU as well as you PDs. But rather than going to all this trouble, just follow our advice and *never* alter the contents of your PDs once you've assigned them to the HU, and *never* move your PDs from whatever folder you initially placed them in.

Now, it's easy to say "never" do these things when you're writing a textbook. The reality is that once you've assigned PDs to your HU, you'll discover an error in one or more of them. This happens to us all the time. We've set up the HU, created the PD folder, dropped all of the PDs into the home folder, assigned all of the PDs to the HU, and then we realize that one or more of the interview transcripts, for instance, contains errors. Yes, it's tempting to try and change them within ATLAS.ti, but try your best to resist the forbidden fruit-like shortcut and instead go back to the original document(s), make the corrections, delete the copy of it you placed in the home folder that ATLAS.ti knows how to find, and then drop the corrected document into the home folder. This approach, while a little more time-consuming at the front end, will save you from hours of frustration, embarrassment, and anger down the road.

---

[9]It's important to note that ATLAS.ti cannot work with Excel spreadsheets, and certain steps must be taken when using tabular data of any kind (even tables in Word). Consult the ATLAS.ti User Manual for further direction.

# WORKING WITH DATA

Now that you've imported your data (the originals or facsimile copies, depending on whether you're using NVivo or ATLAS.ti, respectively), the question is, "What do I do with all of this stuff?" That's not a crazy or uncommon question. Far from it. In fact, it's not only a sane question, but one of the best questions to ask at this point. Here you are, facing what seems a veritable mountain of documents that amount to tens of thousands of words, and your job is to make sense of it all, to find patterns, and ultimately to tell a good, convincing, data-grounded sociological "story." Ideally, you'll tell a story good enough to earn you an "A" on the project. That about right? Well, without further dallying, here's the answer to the reasonable question you've asked: Code the data. Only by coding it will you be able to reduce it. And only by reducing it will you be able to manipulate it. Only by manipulating it will you be able to find patterns and in the end tell a good story about how those patterns arose, how they play out, and/or what they mean in the lives of the people you've chosen to study.

## Coding

Coding is the core function of *all* CAQDAS programs. Generally speaking, there are two approaches to coding: "broad-brush" coding (first-run, or open coding) and detailed coding (second-, or third-, or fourth-run, or focused coding) (Bazeley 2007). With flexibility in working with codes, both NVivo and ATLAS.ti are amenable to both approaches. In both programs, once text is coded, the codes can be dragged and dropped or merged into different nodes/quotations. In this respect, broad-brush coding allows you to "grab" chunks of observations, and code them for later detailed analysis. Broad-brush coding is useful in capturing contextual components and determining general themes in the data, and for preliminary data analyses (Bazeley 2007).

Once first-run, open coding (Emerson et al. 1995) is complete, you can move toward more focused, detailed coding using several of the programs' coding features, such as *queries and models/networks* (discussed later). In NVivo the node is the code, and in ATLAS.ti the quoted quotation is the code. Below we discuss the main coding procedures in each program.

As mentioned in our discussion about the logic of the programs, NVivo's internal database structure means that the documents you import into a project are housed in NVivo—rather than as replicas as in ATLAS.ti. This means that any coded data will have that code attached to it, no matter how else you manipulate or view your data. This is worth mention because, if there was a reason that you needed to edit your data—fix typos, remove superfluous material—the code affixed to the data would not be affected, unless, of course, you fully delete all the material for a particular code. That said, the rule of thumb still stands—it is good practice to set your text data as "read only" so that you do not accidentally alter your data.

Coding to free nodes, tree nodes is a simple process in NVivo. While you can always access full coding options from the main toolbar, most coding tasks can be accomplished through accessing the short menu by right-clicking. Once you have selected a segment of text, NVivo offers coding: (1) in vivo, or in the respondents' own words, when local terms or an unusual use of language is important; (2) at existing nodes when a node structure for the code already exists; or (3) at a new node when creating a new node structure. In addition to using the short menu, you can also drag and drop selected material into existing nodes by having the nodes visible in List View as you work through a document in Detail View.

We've mentioned that NVivo offers flexibility when working with coding schemes. Often as you move through different stages of analysis (e.g., from broad-brush coding to more detailed descriptive coding and on to analytic coding), you may discover that you have redundancy in how you created your node structure and want to collapse two nodes into one, or you may discover that certain nodes are not as viable as you anticipated via the "References" column in the Nodes "List View." "References" gives you information on how many times a particular theme arose in the source materials—much like the grounded score in ATLAS.ti—and can help you discern which nodes are more viable than others and how you may want to modify your coding scheme. If your coding scheme needs modification, you may easily merge nodes that contain coded material by selecting and copying the redundant node, highlighting the destination node and choosing to "Merge Into Selected Node." Likewise, you can code any material within a node to another node the same way you would code content from a source document.

When working with nodes, you can also expand the coded material to view the context that surrounds it. There are five options for viewing the context of a code: (1) None—only showing the content that was selected for coding; (2) Narrow—showing the coded content as well as the five words that precede and succeed it; (3) Broad—showing the coded content in the paragraph where it is located; (4) Custom—where you can specify the number of words you wish to see that surround the code; and (5) Entire Source—showing the whole source document where the code is located. When examining the context of a code, if you decide you want to incorporate the surrounding context into the code, you can choose to "spread coding" in any of the ways discussed above.

All of this is possible because the code is actually embedded in the source document; no matter how you view your data, you are actually seeing the slices of data directly from the source document. This is one of the advantages of NVivo—every data manipulation that you perform is linked to the source material throughout the project, from wherever you view your data.

**CODING IN ATLAS.ti**    Remember, ATLAS.ti isn't showing you the original document that you created in, for instance, MS Word. It's displaying an unchangeable facsimile of that document, as though you're looking at it through a window (in fact, this *is* what you're doing). ATLAS.ti's external database structure—its insistence on referring to but not giving residence to the original documents—means that your codes, as independent objects, are tied or pinned to documents (e.g., interview transcripts), but they're not housed within them. More specifically, codes are "stuck to" specific points in the document (e.g., the "exclusion from decision making" code is stuck to a specific series of alphanumeric characters [e.g., a sentence or phrase] in line number 57 in the transcript of the interview with Kula).

So, in ATLAS.ti a code is like a word or phrase that you've written on a post-it note, which you've then *attached to the window frame*. Consequently, if you go back to the original document and change the text or anything about it, then the document's appearance in the window might change. In the example we're using, the words/phrase you've coded in line 57 might now appear in line 47 because you went back to the document and deleted 10 lines of text or even blank space from an earlier point in the document. Now, because the document is shorter but the ATLAS.ti window is unchanged (and unchangeable), your code is out of place. Again, you must be careful not to change the document once you have imported and coded it in ATLAS.ti.

Because codes are independent of the actual document that contains the data, you can work with them as objects, much the same way you would work with data. You can comment on them, diagram them in a network (asking which codes are related to or co-occur with which other codes, for example), and link codes together. This is an especially useful feature for data analysts who want to conduct micro-level interactions, where every utterance truly matters (Lewins and Silver 2007).

As mentioned previously, there are numerous ways to code in ATLAS.ti, but probably the most common is to select the segment of text you want to code and then select one of the four types of coding option provided by the program: (1) open coding—when you want to create a new code; (2) code-by-list—when you want to assign a code from a list of existing codes; (3) in-vivo coding—when you want the selected text to be the name of the code; and (4) quick coding—when you want to assign the previously used code to the currently selected text, providing a quick way to assign the same code to consecutive text segments.

For greater detail on different types of coding procedures, see Box 22.3.

---

## BOX 22.3
### Additional Coding Procedures

**COLOR CODES**

Both NVivo and ATLAS.ti offer color coding functions, although NVivo's color coding is more advanced. In NVivo, the color coding feature is called *Coding Stripes*. Activating coding stripes in NVivo lets you see "at a glance" how content has been coded. They show the nodes to which the content of a document has been coded: When text is coded to a node, colored stripes appear in the far right window as you scroll through the document. NVivo's coding stripes are particularly useful if you are working with a merged team project. You can see which team member coded to a node by hovering the cursor over a coding stripe. In addition to providing a visual representation of how content is coded, you can see how coding density fluctuates throughout the document. The gray coding density bar shows the overall coding density—as the number of nodes at a particular point in the document increases, the coding density bar becomes darker. This is similar to the density score in ATLAS.ti, though an actual score is not given in NVivo. The color coding stripes show coding density by team members—as the number of team members coding to a particular node, the color coding stripe becomes darker.

ATLAS.ti's color coding features allow the user to change the color of codes and, like those of NVivo, help you see "at a glance" how data have been coded. You can select different colors based upon whatever makes the most sense to you (or whatever tickles you), such as different colors for hierarchical codes, for codes that need to be refined, for codes that represent different or competing theories, etc. This color coding feature is particularly useful when printing or saving coded data.

**AUTOCODING**

In ATLAS.ti **Autocoding** is a "quick and dirty" method for getting a quick glance at patterns in a primary document/data file. Autocoding is useful when you want to quickly and automatically find passages that contain certain words and have them automatically coded. For example, in the above example of experiences in childbirth, you might want to code every instance where a woman says "indifferent" or "uncaring." With autocoding, each instance would have its own node/quotation.

In NVivo, autocoding is performs a different function. It provides another way to organize your data to help streamline analysis. If you have a series of structured interviews, you can use autocoding to compile all answers to a question into a node or you can compile all responses from a particular respondent in a focus group into a node. NVivo *accomplishes this* by recognizing user-defined heading styles (i.e., each question in an interview has to have the same heading style within and across interview transcripts; each respondent in a focus group must be identified the same way and with the same heading style). NVivo does autocoding through recognizing user-defined heading styles. This means that for NVivo to be able to autocode, you must first organize your data into recognized heading styles before you begin coding. ATLAS.ti does this through the Auto Coding Dialog window, where the user is given a number of options regarding how they want to set up the autocode. In ATLAS.ti you don't need to organize your data in any predetermined manner before you begin autocoding.

# BOX 22.4
## Queries

Queries allow you to "ask questions" of the data. Queries search the data for the criteria that *you* define and then gather all relevant material (i.e., "query result"). Queries are particularly useful after you have performed the initial broad-brush coding of the data. They provide you with a more complex view of your codes. Queries themselves, as well as their results, can be saved for further analysis.

### "TEXT SEARCH" AND "CODING" QUERIES: BASIC TO MORE ADVANCED

The coding queries range from simple to complex. Both NVivo and ATLAS.ti have a simple *text* search query (in NVivo, *Text Search Query* and in ATLAS.ti, *Object Crawler*), which allows you to search the text using terms you define. This is especially helpful in early stages of coding where you might find a topic or theme of interest and want to see if it is prevalent in the remainder of the data, or in later stages of coding where you want to quickly assess if a new theme or hypothesis is viable enough for further exploration (Bazeley 2007).

NVivo's and ATLAS.ti's *coding* queries (which differ from text queries in that now you are making queries of codes and not text) range from simple to complex. The most basic code query allows you to retrieve all of the coded material at a particular node/quotation. More complex queries are useful when you want to go beyond searching text and actually begin asking questions of data. These code queries allow you to create a sophisticated set of criteria or a "formula" with which to search the codes. They are the "antidote to sliced or fractured data" (Bazeley 2007: 113); that is, it allows the you to see patterns among codes, particularly for intersected coding (Bazeley 2007) where the same text has been coded several times. An example a simple formula would be "retrieve all nodes/quotations that are coded to Code A and also Code B" (using the AND operator—Boolean Logic again!) while a more complex example would be "retrieve all nodes/quotations that are Code A and Code B but not Code C and overlap with Code D." In NVivo, this is done through *Coding Queries* and by *Matrix Coding*. In ATLAS.ti this can be accomplished with the *Query Tool.*

Another notable feature of the *Matrix Coding Query* in NVivo is that it makes within-group comparisons using nodes and attributes and returns results in a matrix, much like crosstabs in quantitative statistics. The result is a table where each cell represents the number of sources that reference the combination of node and attribute (e.g., Do child birthing preferences [node] differ by age group [attribute]?). This query tool also allows you to specify the search criteria: whether the relation between rows and columns represents the *intersection* of the row and column using Boolean expressions (AND, OR, NOT) or the *proximity* of the row and column terms to each other using proximity expressions (NEAR, PRECEDING, SURROUNDING).

NVivo also offers *Compound Queries*, which combine features of text search and coding queries, allowing you to create either two text search queries, two coding queries (similar to matrix coding), or a combination of a text search and coding query. Finally, NVivo allows for *Coding Comparison* queries for use in team project environments, which provide a way for a project manager to easily examine coding similarities and differences among team members coding the same text. Coding Comparisons return results in a table and show the percentage of agreement/disagreement among coders and provides a statistical measure of inter-rater reliability with Cohen's Kappa.

It should also be noted, however, that you can perform several of these same tasks in ATLAS.ti. For example, ATLAS.ti can create a PASW Statistics (formerly known as SPSS) file that displays quotations as cases and codes as variables, where a "1" indicates the presence of a code and a "0" the absence of a code. The program doesn't provide the same sort of preset functions for these types of queries although, overall, it has a stronger, customizable query tool.

In both programs, the query tool is versatile because it allows for searches of all or selected documents through the use of Boolean operators (OR, NOT, AND) to find phrase combinations and/or proximity operators (in NVivo—NEAR, PRECEEDING, SURROUNDING; in ATLAS.ti—

WITHIN, ENCLOSES, OVERLAPPES, BY, FOLLOWS) to retrieve words or quotations that have a defined proximity to or are embedded within each other (e.g., in NVivo using the *NEAR* search character, "~" [i.e., "doctor midwife~15" would return any instances where doctor and midwife existed in the text within 15 words of each other]). In ATLAS.ti one way this search can be performed is with the use of COOCCUR operator and Semantic operators (DOWN, UP, ACROSS), which accumulates codes up, down, and across hierarchies that you have already intentionally created by linking codes.

Overall, our view is that ATLAS.ti has a stronger query tool in that it allows you a great deal of flexibility in customizing your queries when compared to NVivo's. In fact, ATLAS.ti's query tool is one feature that makes this program superior to NVivo. However, like most ATLAS.ti's functions, although the query tool is stronger, it is more difficult to use because you actually write your own query "formulas." However, like other functions in these two programs while ATLAS.ti allows for more customizability, NVivo has more predetermined functions that can be very helpful but are not be easily customized.

### HYPERLINKS

In addition to the query tools already discussed, NVivo has several other query functions that are worth mentioning. You can link codes together through *Hyperlinks*. Hyperlinks allow you to create links between any source document (Internals or Externals) to nonproject items on a computer or the Internet. There is no limit to the number of hyperlinks one may use in a source document; however, they cannot be coded or searched.

## RELATIONS/RELATIONSHIPS

In addition to identifying concepts and patterns in the data by coding, understanding relationships that exist among the data is indispensable to theory building (Bazeley 2007). NVivo allows you to define relationships between cases, nodes, and even whole source documents using *Relationship Nodes*. Relationship Nodes convey connections between two project items. Relationships between project items are created and stored within the *Nodes* component of an NVivo project, but types of relationships are created within *Classifications*. Through *Classifications*, you can define the connection (associative, directional) between project items that are then used when creating a relationship node. For example, say through coding you discover that mothers who have and stick to a detailed birth plan report positive birth experiences more often than women without one. You may create a one-way directional relationship type called "impacts" in *Classifications* and then construct a relationship in *relationship nodes* that shows "birth plan ‹ impacts ‹ positive birth experience."

In ATLAS.ti you can establish a relationship between codes or quotations using the *Relation* tool. ATLAS.ti uses the term *Relation* for links between pairs of codes or pairs of quotations. For linking pairs of codes, you can make a *Codelink*. Codelinks are separate "objects" and have their own Manager, where you can see a list of all pairs of linked codes and the relation names you have used to pair them, such as *causes, associated with, contradicts, is, context of, property of*, etc. You can use the relation names provided by the program or you can create your own via the Relation Manger. You can also link codes though the *Network* tool, discussed below. The term *Relation* in ATLAS.ti also refers to links between pairs of quotations, which are also called Hyperlinks. Hyperlinks in ATLAS.ti are quotations that are connected. Often those quotations are codes that are linked but do not necessary have to be codes to be hyperlinked. Quotations can also be linked within primary documents (PDs), between PDs, or between different types of media.

## EYEBALLING AND BEYOND: A GRAPHICAL VIEW OF YOUR RESEARCH

Graphical models can be very helpful in visually representing the theoretical concepts of research. Modeling helps you explore hypotheses and develop ways of testing them. Creating models at each stage of a project (initial perceptions, early hypotheses, stages of coding) not only helps you refine your hypothesis and analysis, but also provides an "audit trail" of the research process, which in turn enhances your study's reproducibility factor. Models can be used for reflecting on the research at hand and for reporting purposes. NVivo has two types of models: (1) *Static Models* simply allow you to visually demonstrate various aspects of the research including hypotheses, conceptualizations, and relationships among data. (2) *Dynamic Models* allow you to visually present connections among the data that are clickable and lead back to the data.

In ATLAS.ti, you create a model through the *Network* tool. In Networks, the objects (which are usually codes but can also be quotations, memos, PDs, and families) are called Nodes. You can create a model of your data by linking your codes together and designating how they are linked (*property of, contradicts, intervening condition,* etc.). Networks can be saved and exported as regular image files. All Networks are dynamic in that they allow you to click on the objects and then direct you back to the data.

## CONCLUSION

CAQDAS, like any other complex mechanism, takes a good bit of time to learn and a great deal of time to master. For short-run and relatively small projects, it makes little sense to use either of the programs we've discussed in this chapter. But if you're doing a project that involves more data than you can manage using old-fashioned manual methods (index cards, post-it notes, printed coding trees, highlighter markers, etc.), then you should consider learning one or the other of these programs. Depending on the nature of your study and the kind of data you're collecting, you now should know enough to make an informed decision and move ahead with some basic analyses (in consultation with the program's user manual, of course).

## Key Terms

abductive coding *358*

analytic coding *358*

attributes *364*

audit trail *354*

autocoding *371*

binary code *354*

Boolean Logic Operators *351*

CAQDAS *351*

chunk *357*

code *357*

coded quotation *357*

codelinks *364*

coding data *357*

coding scheme *357*

coding tree *357*

deductive coding *357*

external data program *360*

grounded theory *356*

inductive codes *358*

inductive coding *356*

internal data program *360*

latent meaning *358*

manifest meaning *358*

network *364*

nonnumeric structured data *351*

observation *358*

reduction *353*

relationships *364*

running queries *354*

unit of analysis *364*

unit of observation *364*

unit of manipulation *363*

unstructured data *351*

# V

# Telling the Story

Part V helps you produce a report on your research and obtain closure on the experience. The first chapter outlines the basic elements of a research report. We focus on how to write a standard or "canonical" research report, such as the ones that are published in professional research journals, and also discusses other ways of sharing your research. Visual methods of course produce different forms of data, as discussed in Chapter 21.

The last chapter is also part of "telling the story" because it is about how the experiences of qualitative research will become part of your own story. It briefly covers possible "aftereffects" of the experience such as legal complications; but it is primarily about feelings that may be unsettling after the conclusion of your research. It reassures you that these feelings are not uniquely yours and that they are a normal part of the intensity of research, especially fieldwork.

# 23

# The Research Report

## OVERVIEW

At this point you are ready to write up a research report. You have gone from the early stages of playing around with ideas to developing a research question to collecting and analyzing data . . . and you've even begun to interpret the results. It's time to put it all down on paper. This can be a daunting prospect. Terribly daunting. Paralyzing for many. "Where do I begin?" is the question we hear from nearly every student who's gone through the research process and finds herself now facing the challenge of reducing a complicated, messy, and perhaps meandering experience to a coherent and persuasive representation—a compelling sociological story. In this chapter we help you get it all organized and written up, just like the professionals.

## THE CANONS OF FORM AND THE CANONICAL RESEARCH REPORT

When researchers follow the canons—the rules—of the scientific method, the results of their studies are generally reported in a conventional format, a narrative called a research report.

The body of the research report follows a **standard outline**:

1. **The research problem (aka "the problematic")**. A statement of the research question and the hypotheses (in those cases where specific hypotheses were formulated). This introduction discusses the research question and provides motivation for it, often in or immediately preceding a **literature review** that covers previous empirical research and theoretical perspectives.
2. A **methods** section (sometimes referred to as "Methodology" though that is not quite the right term—we prefer "Methods"). The researcher discusses the choice of design and specific methods, including sampling, and by implication addresses the issue of generalizability or relevance.
3. **Findings**. The major results are presented and related to the research question. If hypotheses were stated, the researcher indicates whether or not he found support for the hypotheses in his analysis of the data. Qualitative material, such as interview quotes or "strips" from field notes, appears as support for the statement of findings.

**4. Discussion or conclusion**. The researcher provides a broader and more theoretical conclusion than was offered in the findings section. An overview of the research is provided, and the researcher reflects on the implications of the findings for questions in the research and theoretical literature. The researcher may also consider the significance of the findings in terms of social policy and/or program development, or future research directions.

## Voice

The research report is usually written in the third person ("the author . . ." "The researchers . . .") and the narrative sustains the fiction that the results "were found" as opposed to having been *created* by the researcher's various actions and choices. The methods section makes clear that the researcher made choices and emphasizes the transparency of the project. The reader must be able to trace the researcher's choices through the data analysis and into the findings section. It must be possible for the reader to at least ask (if not fully answer) the question whether different choices would have led to different findings. The methods section of the report addresses the concerns we raised in Chapter 3: ("Asking Research Questions"), such as, How generalizable is this project? To what situations or populations is it relevant? Was the research subject to the criterion of falsifiability? Was the research hypothesis ever at risk of being unsupported? Could the results have been otherwise? How did specific decisions about sampling, observation, guides, entry processes, content analysis of documents, interview choices, or any other aspect of the study lead to these results?

The research report should tread the fine line between convincing the reader of the veracity, plausibility, relevance, and objectivity of the results and leaving open the possibility that different research choices might have produced somewhat different (or in some cases radically different) results. To say that a study was "objective" implies that different research choices might have led to somewhat different specific results, but that the larger meaning and findings of the result are an excellent representation of social life, an excellent guide to the "world out there."

## Play It Straight

The canonical research report touches only lightly on personal feelings, experiences, and opinions of the researcher. It is not about the writer! These feelings and experiences are kept entirely in abeyance throughout the writing and are not a main theme of the narrative. At most they might be recognized in a brief footnote that acknowledges a personal reason for pursuing the research. Including excerpts from field notes is another way of introducing the researcher's feelings—you can see, for example, how Greg Scott (2004) handles the description of his experience being left alone by his guide and forced by other gang members to participate in packaging drugs.

## Or Play It Not So Straight

It is essential for researchers to know how to write a canonical research report. But we should be aware of other options and alternatives. Our repertoire must include the canonical version but many researchers are now experimenting with new forms and new media. Chapter 21 addressed one of the most important of these, and Chapter 10 emphasized the role of these methods when research findings need to be disseminated beyond the readership of scholars in the discipline. In the remaining pages of this chapter we discuss mixed methods—not only of doing research but of reporting it as well. One of these methods, visual methods, emphasizes the importance of imagery at all stages of the research process, from the concept to the final product.

## BOX 23.1
### Writing Lit Reviews

Writing a "lit review" is a well-developed craft in all scientific fields. The lit review demonstrates that the researcher is familiar with prior research on the topic and building on this foundation and is not merely "reinventing the wheel." In the lit review, first the topic is delimited and the boundaries of the area under investigation are defined. Then the methods of research and findings of each relevant study are summarized. In writing the lit review the researcher's goal is to demonstrate how the proposed study is *necessary* in some way: It fills a "void" in the extant knowledge of the subject; it presents a new way of looking at old issues; it applies existing methods to new phenomena; it replicates previous studies in an attempt to reinforce the strength of existing theory and/or findings/knowledge of an issue.

Lit reviews differ in the degree to which the quality of the prior research is assessed or evaluated. In some lit reviews, this evaluation is left to the reader who is assumed to be able to judge the quality of a research project by reading about its methods. For example, a national probability sample probably renders more generalizable results than a small local convenience sample. But in other cases, the writer of the lit review may be more directive and judgmental, labeling some of the predecessors' work as more important, generalizable, reliable, or stimulating than other studies. Disagreements about the results of prior studies certainly must be identified. In fact it is often these disagreements that provide the motivation for new research questions. The research question is formulated in an effort to settle the disputes and resolve the inconsistencies among prior studies. The research question is an effort to solve the puzzle created by disagreements among the findings of prior research.

In quantitative research and those qualitative studies that include a quantifiable component, the lit review may be amplified into a meta-analysis, an effort to create a statistically analyzable pool of the findings of two or more studies. This statistical synthesis requires specialized training in statistical techniques.

## BOX 23.2
### Other Elements of the Research Report: Practical Tips

The canonical report also includes a **title**, an **abstract**, and a **works-cited** or reference section.

The *title* is guided by the research question and should give the reader an idea of the purpose, scope, and generalizability of the study. It is not a sensational headline from the *National Enquirer*, but a sober, limited, and exact caption.

The *abstract* is written after the report and helps people who are searching computerized databases of articles and reports to locate studies that may be of interest. It is usually of 150–250 words and compresses the entire research report into a paragraph that states the research question, provides some motivation from the empirical or theoretical literature, identifies the methods, and summarizes the findings and discussion.

Finally the **reference or works-cited** section is an alphabetical listing of all the work that was cited in the review of the literature or any other part of the research report. It must include any work that was directly quoted or from which facts, ideas, opinions, or conclusions were drawn. It includes works of theory that inspired the research question or influenced the discussion. When in doubt, include anything you read in the works-cited section.

Each discipline has its own precise style of handling citations, so you will hear people say things like **ASA style citations** (referring to the American Sociological Association) or "APA style" (referring to the American Psychological Association). In sociology, the in-text cite in the body of the research

*(continued)*

*(continued)*

report must include last name of author(s), year of publication, and if needed, page number, all within parentheses. [If we were to cite our own book, the in-text cite for material we placed on p. 312 would look like this: (Scott and Garner 2012: 312).] It has to come in or at the end of the sentence in which a work is mentioned or material from the work is discussed.

Each in-text cite must be matched by an entry in the works-cited section that in the case of a book includes the full name of author, the title of the book, and the publisher, with the date and place of publication. In the case of an article, the citation must include the full name of the author, the title of the article, the title of the journal, and the date, issue, and page numbers of the article. Any specific information from a source and any direct quote must include in the in-text cite the page number on which that information or quote was found.

## BOX 23.3
### What Is Paraphrasing and Why Is It Often a Problem?

Writing the Literature Review section of a research report provides ample opportunities for the demons of **plagiarism** to tempt the writer. The writer has to summarize the main findings of many studies. It seems tempting to just copy text—for example, an abstract or a key paragraph of conclusions—in order to summarize each study. The authors of the works under review seem to have said everything so well—how could the author's summary ever be improved and why should it be restated when the original seems so perfect? Why don't I just highlight that paragraph and pop it into my text. . . . This whispered temptation from the plagiarism devil must be rejected in no uncertain terms. Not only copy-and-paste must be avoided scrupulously but also the practice of copying with only minor modifications. Writers should either quote from a source, setting off the material in quotation marks or indenting and single-spacing it, or they should write about the material in their own words and sentences. **Paraphrasing** means using material from a source but not copying it verbatim as an attributed quotation. Unfortunately it is often a sloppy and deceptive practice.

Paraphrasing all too often means that the sentences of the original source material have been changed only in small details, so that the structure and rhythm of the sentences are still recognizable. The new text is not identical to the original but it is very similar. No one will believe you if you say it was "an honest mistake." You run the risk of failing a course or even being dismissed from a university. You may be put in a public pillory—in print or online—by reviewers and colleagues. Paraphrasing without a major change in wording and sentence structure is always a bad practice, and a number of well-known scholars and professional writers have found themselves in very embarrassing situations, essentially facing charges of plagiarism. If your sentence has the same structure and rhythm as a sentence in the source material, even if a few words are different, it is not acceptable! Under no circumstances should a reader be able to think "gosh, this sounds a lot like a sentence I have seen somewhere before . . ."

One way to avoid even the hint of plagiarism in paraphrasing is to make notes on the source material that consist of only key words and brief phrases of facts. Do not record or copy whole sentences. Then close the book or article, walk away from your desk, and stay away from it long enough to forget the exact wording of any sentence you read. After the forgetting is complete, return to your notes and create new sentences that are in your own words and sentence structure. Use only key technical terms or precise numerical facts from the source, but embed them in new sentences that you write by yourself. Your sentences should bear no resemblance to the original sentences. You will still need to provide a citation for the facts and ideas that you used from the source.

A number of postmodern and currently popular styles of research narrative allow more attention to the writer's experiences and feelings. For example, in carnal sociology there is far more use of the first person as the researcher describes what he or she learned from the embodied performances in which he or she participated. We can see that in Widick's accounts of trading and Wacquant's writing about boxing, the experiences of the researcher are an important part of the data. The researcher is *not* recounting these stories to communicate how he felt about his research or to make it more lively and colorful for the reader, but to explain exactly what *the embodied performance or knowledge tells us about the setting and the conditions in which participants live.* The researcher recounts and analyzes her personal experiences as they though constitute objective knowledge of a particular slice of social life, an accurate representation of a social milieu.

A more extreme personalization takes place in the "postmodern narratives" in which the entire research narrative is organized around the feelings and experiences of the writer. In these narratives, the topic is no longer the objective representation of social life (which may require descriptions of the researcher's experiences in order to clarify how knowledge is embodied), but the probing of the feelings and self of the writer. The research setting and the behavior of other participants are only props to further our insights into the feelings of the writer (Adler and Adler 2008). In these accounts, the writer is not temporarily "going native" and then returning to the world of social research with new insights, but has thoroughly gone over to the elaboration of his or her own subjectivity—some would argue that the postmodern report reveals indifference to the question of what is objectively true about the social world. Others might say that the postmodern or self-centered form of writing challenges the very notion of objectivity.

Notice that in carnal sociology as practiced and described by Wacquant, the goal of objectivity is not rejected at all; on the contrary, Wacquant believes that the researcher's embodied experience and knowledge contribute to a better objective understanding of the world. Adler and Adler note that in the postmodern genre, the canonical outline disappears and the boundaries among research questions, theory, personal experiences, feelings, observational data, the author's actions, and discussion of methods are thoroughly disrupted; all of these elements are swirled together in a narrative that may be closer in tone and structure to fiction and personal memoirs.

Adler and Adler (2008) provide a more elaborate classification of ethnographic writing (much of which could apply to other types of qualitative research writing as well). They distinguish **four types of ethnographic writing: the classical, mainstream, postmodern, and public**. Both classical and mainstream ethnographies follow the canons of research writing that we have described in the preceding pages, but with slight differences. Classical ethnographic writing is addressed to a broad readership in the social sciences. Both it and mainstream ethnography generally follow the outline and somewhat impersonal style that we have described here as the canonical form, but mainstream ethnography is in the Adlers' words "tighter, stiffer, and [in] a more formal voice (11)." It makes a strong effort to adhere to the canons of scientific writing and is very close to the rhythms of quantitative research writing, eliminating some of the simple, direct style of the classical ethnography. The Adlers emphasize that for some scholars classical ethnography "revolves around the use of extensive, persuasive, high-quality, descriptive data (9)." It tries to be readable and at the same time grounded in reality, a feeling that is evoked by vivid use of material from interviews, field notes, and other data production methods. This material is organized and presented in a way that is both accurate and gripping to read.

Classical ethnographies provide inspirational, exciting models for student readers—many of them make the newcomer to social science research eager to run into the streets, kitchens, homes, bars, hospitals, and restaurants of the metropolis and start observing everyday life. By contrast, mainstream ethnographies may seem cautious, impersonal, and exhaustive in their lit review and documentation of methods, and a bit too detached and dry. In the mainstream ethnography, there may be more of a fiction of total objectivity created in the writing style and a retracing of the research process that makes it appear highly planned and deductive, rather than inductive and evolving.

The public ethnography, in the four-fold classification proposed by Adler and Adler, addresses the largest audience, hopefully all readers interested in public issues. It is animated by political concerns and C. W. Mills' goal that the sociological imagination will enable us to see personal troubles as public issues. It is less concerned with introducing theory than classical and mainstream writing and does not include an extensive review of research and theoretical literature. At its borders, it blurs with critical traditions in journalism (see Chapter 7). An example of a book at this borderline is Barbara Ehrenreich's *Nickel and Dimed* (2001), an account of the author's experiences in low-wage work in the United States. Although the popular book had elements of postmodern ethnography as well (it included a lot of description of the author's feelings and experiences), its main purpose was a "muckraking" exposure of the desperate circumstances of the nation's large number of insecure, underpaid, overworked workers in jobs such as retail sales in big-box stores, restaurant serving, nursing-home assistants, and hotel housekeeping.

CBPR research accounts pose special problems, as we have already noted in the CBPR chapter. Because of the interactive nature of the research, the involvement of individual community residents and community organizations as coinvestigators, the value of including participants' voices in the research, and the expected social change outcomes, the report is difficult to squeeze into the canonical form. At some level, one can even question who should write this report. If the social science researcher writes it, what keeps it from slipping into the traditional patterns of subjecting relatively powerless people to the scientific or intellectual "gaze" and then claiming to "speak for them" as if they could not speak for themselves? For this reason, CBPR results are often presented as visual products, documentary films, or photo-gallery projects, so that they can have an impact on a larger audience and detach themselves from the gatekeeping and writing canons of the academic establishment, especially the "peer-reviewed journal."

## TRUTH: THE BIG ONION

In the first pages of this chapter we discussed the outline of the research report. In this section we will return to a topic we broached in Chapter 3 ("Asking Research Questions"), the topic of establishing the truth—or at least, the plausibility—of our conclusions. This topic was closely linked to a discussion of the rules of sociological storytelling, and it is therefore appropriate to return to it in the chapter about writing the research report, that is, telling the story of what we did and found in our research.

We can think of the truth as a big onion, composed of many different layers.

The first layer we will call **presence**. Presence means—were you there? It reiterates our view that the trained, theoretically informed observer is the single most important "research instrument" there is. An incident or action that you witnessed is true in your report in a different way than any other information you choose to include. Establishing your presence is not at all the same as writing about yourself; it just means that you are reporting things you saw, heard, and experienced directly. In reporting your findings, let your account be guided by your capacity for **surprise, seeing, and "the visual"** (whether it means literally using visual methods or describing your observations vividly).

The second layer of truth is based on **informant credibility**. We mentioned this problem in the context of inference and proof in the chapter on observation (Becker 1970b). When we include material that is not directly based on our own observations in the field but on accounts of others, we need to inform the reader who the informants are, whether they agreed with each other, what details each one provided, whether their accounts are independent of each other, and which ones are the most reliable and why you have come to that conclusion. Informants may be included as respondents to interviews or may appear in field notes as people who have commented on an incident or action. If we cannot determine informant credibility, we must at the very least identify the information informants provide as information that we did not establish directly by our own observations. Informant credibility applies to documents and other cultural artifacts as well as to verbal accounts.

The third layer of truth depends on *accurate description.* The more detailed the description, the closer we are to the "objective truth" of the action or incident. As the information becomes vaguer and blurrier because of the passage of time and skimpy notes, we lose our connection to the truth of the events. The need for **accurate description** is closely related to the problem of eyewitness testimony that plagues law enforcement and the judicial system. We know that eyewitness accounts are very unreliable. Even a few seconds after an event has occurred, many people have forgotten key facts that could establish the identity of persons involved in it—what they wore, their age, their race, their comportment, the words they uttered, the objects they were carrying. Eyewitnesses subconsciously allow their biases and prejudices to shape their memories. A very famous old study that asked subjects to describe a picture of an altercation in a subway car found that many subjects in remembering the picture switched the threatening razor from the hand of the white man to the hand of the black man! Studies of cases in law enforcement have also revealed that eyewitness accounts are easily manipulated by influence from police or attorneys and by leading types of questions. These studies alert us to the need for care in keeping and using field notes.

The rough quantification that was acceptable in qualitative research in the past also requires careful scrutiny. On the one hand, approximate or loosely worded statements about frequency and distribution are acceptable, and in fact, too much precision in reporting numbers is inappropriate or even suspect in qualitative research. To say that 66.66% of the participants in a focus group of six people reported a behavior or opinion is an inappropriate and incorrect use of a percentage and gives a false air of precision. Yet at the same time, we need to be careful in very loose and approximate reporting of frequencies and we should always report the reason why we feel we can include the numerical information. As we discussed in Chapters 12 and 22, careful quantification is entirely appropriate in qualitative research and is even becoming an expected part of the research, replacing the tolerance of the past for vague and careless handling of quantitative information.

These considerations form the obvious outer layers of the big "truth onion." The denser and more complex layers have to do with the truth of **interpretation**, the selection of the appropriate **context** for interpreting the data, and the **theoretical links** that are established. Truth in interpretation means that the observer understands the viewpoints of the subjects but does not always agree with them; the observer can distinguish between the meanings assigned by actors (which are always important to understand) and the possibility that some of these meanings are misrecognitions. The researcher learns the language of the subjects, but does not confine herself to this language; she is always bi-lingual and can talk about the meanings in the language of sociology. Furthermore, the researcher has to make choices about the **context** of interpretation, as we saw in our discussion of Wacquant's (2002) "Scrutinizing the Street"; objectivity and truth mean a conscious decision about which context is best for understanding what is happening in the social world under study. In the example of Wacquant's article we had to ask ourselves, "Do we scrutinize the street in the context of the street itself or within the larger framework of analyzing class inequalities and labor markets?" Finally, the theoretical links can contribute to establishing these larger frameworks of truth. These complex inner layers of the "truth onion," taken together with the more obvious outer layers, together establish the truth and objectivity of the results.

Let's take a very simple example. You are writing about security issues at a large urban university. Here is an incident you want to discuss in your paper:

> *A homeless woman got into the building and fell asleep on the little wooden bench in the washroom. Someone called Security and they went into the washroom, woke her up, and escorted her out of the building. Incidents like this happen several times a term.*

**PRESENCE**    How much of this incident did you see for yourself?

**ACCURACY OF DESCRIPTION**    How accurately and completely can you reproduce the details, either from your own observations or from the accounts of others? How old was the woman? How was she dressed? How would you describe her race or ethnicity? How many security guards were involved? What did she say to them? How did she speak to them? What did they say to her? How did they speak to her? How long did the incident take? At what time of day did it happen? Were there bystanders present and what did they say or do? Why do you state "incidents like this happen several times a term"—what evidence do you have for that statement?

**CREDIBILITY OF ACCOUNTS**    For any part of the incident that you did not see for yourself, who provided an account? Was the account collected in a formal interview or heard from bystanders? Did you hear different versions of what happened? Who are the people that told you about it and do you have any reason to believe any version of the narrative?

**UNCLEAR DETAILS**    There are a number of statements in our provisional account that are unclear—can they be clarified? What do we mean by "got into the building?" Entry requires a card-swipe. Did someone hold the door open for the woman? (a common courtesy extended to students and faculty but possibly also to any individual who happens to be standing near the door) Was the ID swipe out of order? (a common occurrence that leaves the door open for anyone who tries to open it) Did faculty or students prop the door (commonly done by smokers so they can easily get back into the building), thereby leaving it open for the woman to enter? Who contacted security? How do we know the woman was homeless (as opposed to just being tired or down-and-out or disoriented)? How do we know that incidents such as this one occur several times a term?

**INTERPRETATION**    Why have you introduced this incident into your paper? Remember your research question. How does discussing this incident help to answer this question? Does it support a specific hypothesis associated with your research question? Is this incident a piece of plausible evidence to support a thesis or an answer to the research question? What is this incident about—to what conclusions is it relevant? Is this incident about university–community relationships? About campus security policies, practices, and behaviors?

**CONTEXT AND THEORY**    What theories could offer a "big picture" way of understanding the incident? Are we linking this incident to Durkheimian or Foucaultian theories of social control and normative regulation? To a Marxist view of how urban universities deal with poverty and social disparities in their surrounding communities? To feminist theories that highlight the additional challenges faced by homeless women whose needs for safety and personal hygiene are even more acute than those of homeless men? To a critical view of how institutions committed to values of social justice nevertheless have to deal with immediate security problems, and how these tensions are negotiated on a day-to-day basis within the institution? Any one (or several) of these perspectives can provide context and meaning to the incident you chose to report. But these perspectives cannot be allowed to distort your description of what happened or induce you to "cherry pick" only those observations and accounts that conveniently support your position.

Hopefully you feel a strong tension between the imperatives to develop interpretation, context, and theory, on the one hand, and to report as accurately as possible, on the other. Two voices in your head are in dialog—one says, "this is the interpretation that makes the most sense, that is the most powerful explanation of what I saw and heard." And the other voice says, "Where are the facts—the observations—the data to support this interpretation? What is the context that allows you to offer this explanation and not some other?" This dialog is the driving force of truth and objectivity. **Truth and objectivity** emerge out of the ongoing conversation between interpretation/theory and observation/experience.

## TRUTH AND OBJECTIVITY

"Truth" and "objectivity" are lodged in the choices you make to interpret, contextualize, and describe this incident; they are a sum total of what you do in your writing.

Here is also the point to remind ourselves of the four steps toward building theory that we discussed in Chapter 6 on integrating theories.

### Understanding the Participants' Point of View

Have I presented the participants' ideas, vocabulary, local knowledge, "ethno-cognitions," and experiences as clearly and accurately as possible? Have I understood these meanings and experiences, if necessary by "walking—or dancing—in their shoes?" Does my representation draw on the perspectives and experiences of several participants rather than only one guide or a single document?

### Distinguishing the Insider and the Outsider's Perspectives

Have I contrasted and compared the participants' perspectives with my own as a trained observer? Where are the points of agreement and disagreement, the convergences and divergences in interpretations? What does my training as a sociologist add to our understanding of the situation as a whole?

### Developing Thick Description

Have I understood the historical and social context of what I observed? Can I place my observations in a larger framework of knowledge? Can I explain my observations to my readers?

### Considering Macro–Micro Linkages

Do I understand the "big picture" in which the observations were made? Can I link my observations to institutions, social inequalities, historical processes, and "fields" of organizations?

Each of these steps should be reflected in the final research report; they apply to the analysis of documents and other cultural artifacts as well as to fieldwork. As they are developed both during the research and later, in writing the report, they reinforce the effort to achieve plausibility, to answer research questions, to build theory, and to present the truth as a complex, multilayered representation of a culture, milieu, community, event, or situation.

## THEORY–METHODS LINKAGES IN THE RESEARCH REPORT

Throughout this book we have emphasized the linkage of theory and methods. Theories shape our research questions and choices, and we strive to use our research project to contribute to theoretical understanding—to a large, long-term, conceptual, and contextual understanding of "how the world works."

To achieve this goal we need to be clear on how we construct and use theories. We have used two terms—"critical" and "reflexive"—and here is an opportunity to clarify these terms further and distinguish them from other ways of doing research.

We will distinguish a critical and reflexive approach to research from two other approaches: the positivist-empiricist and the postmodern. The positivist-empiricist approach has been popular for a long time in sociology; "positivist" was a term put into circulation in the early nineteenth century by August Comte, the "father of sociology." He used it to mean adherence to the methods of the natural sciences and their application to the study of society. "Postmodern" on the other hand is a term that became popular in the late twentieth century to refer to a deconstructionist approach to knowledge in which all knowledge and information are seen as contending narratives or cultural constructs that do not refer to any bedrock of knowledge that can be known objectively.

The following chart outlines basic ways of thinking about research espoused by each of these three positions. Of course, this is a bit schematic—in fact a good researcher often participates in each of these three positions and there is a quite a bit of overlap. Rather than a triangle with three very sharply separated points, we should think of these positions as overlapping circles. We need to be careful not to caricature the positivist-empiricist and postmodern positions. Few social scientists adhere to either one in a rigid or uncritical way, so our summaries must be taken with a grain of salt.

The **positivist-empiricist** position has a long history because it is closely associated with the growth of the natural sciences. Its basic premise is that the scientific method as developed in the natural sciences makes sense in the social sciences as well. The researcher can be an external observer who collects knowledge about a world that has an objective existence, separate from his

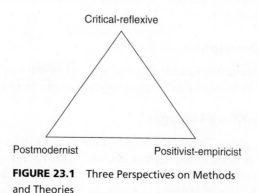

**FIGURE 23.1**    Three Perspectives on Methods and Theories

or her research activities. Research should be designed to provide as accurate a picture of this knowable world as possible. According to positivists, social and natural scientists are agreed that some version of the scientific method is useful in this endeavor and that procedures such as defining variables, measurement, hypothesis testing, statistical analysis of sample data, and consideration of generalizability and falsifiability are useful in both the social sciences and the natural sciences.

The **postmodernist** position is of recent vintage, having developed with deconstruction in philosophy. The postmodernists emphasize discourses and the social construction of reality. They are highly suspicious of claims about objective knowledge and any kind of "bedrock" of social phenomena, such as the material base of a society (a favorite "bedrock category" of the Marxists). Categories that once seemed taken for granted, even biologically based, such as gender/sex and race are also seen as constructed in discourses. Postmodernists tend to write with a lot of quotation marks around words to show that these are only terms of discourses and do not refer to categories that have an existence apart from the discourses in which they show up. Postmodernists believe that the operations and procedures that positivists like to follow to ensure the scientific validity of their findings are only agreed-upon, socially constructed routines whose claims to producing objectively valid knowledge are highly problematic.

Positivists tend to be relatively uninterested in history, although one can apply positivist methods to historical analysis by careful sampling of documents and artifacts and precise operational coding for these materials. Positivists are believed to lean toward quantitative methods and statistical analysis, although not all of them do so; and these strategies are certainly used by critical-reflexive theorists as well. Although positivists recognize the existence of conflicts and may in fact study them, positivists do not assume that conflict underlies all human actions and interactions.

Postmodernists are cautious about historical analysis because the multiple, conflicting narratives that people construct are particularly difficult to tease out when we try to study the past. For example, the influence of postmodernists can be seen in the reorganization of Civil War museums in the United States, some of which now present three different perspectives: the Confederate perspective, the African American perspective, and the Union perspective. For post-modernists it is not enough to say that different categories of people had different experiences and interests in the conflict and that we (the outside observer in the twenty-first century) can understand these points of view from an external, objective, and contextualized perspective. The postmodernist is suspicious of this claim to external, objective knowledge and prefers to encounter the three distinct narratives, each one of which is in turn composed by the discourses of many individuals. Unlike the positivists, the postmodernists assume that conflict and contention over "facts" (note the quotation marks) are always present.

The **critical-reflexive** position that we have developed in this book borrows from both positivism and postmodernism but reintegrates the borrowings into a distinct perspective. Critical-reflexive social scientists embrace the idea of objective knowledge and the possibility of the trained external observer developing an independent and comprehensive understanding of a situation. But this understanding requires constant vigilance and reflection on one's own social location, experiences, and **preexisting mental imagery**, as well as scrutiny of our research choices. Objectivity is not guaranteed by any "recipe" of technical procedures of measurement, sampling, and quantitative data analysis. To adapt Wacquant's remark, "go native, but come back a sociologist"—"go positivist, but come back a critical-reflexive sociologist." In other words, valuable methods of rigorous scientific inquiry can be learned from the positivist-empiricists, but these methods need to be examined and questioned. The scientific method can be applied to human societies and actions, but requires modification from natural science practices. One of these modifications is consistent attention to history, because the **historical context** is a particularly important force shaping current situations and circumstances. Another important element is recognition of conflicts and the role of discourses; this discursive contention must not be lost in a rush to operationalize variables and test hypotheses.

Critical-reflexive sociologists are influenced by postmodernism (and its critique of positivism), but ultimately reject the position that there are only contending discourses with no prospect of establishing objective knowledge that enables us to sort out the discourses. Critical-reflexive sociologists strive to understand the viewpoints and discourses of their research subjects, but they do not just report and repeat these without considering the context in which the discourses have emerged. **Macro–micro linkage** is especially important in this regard. The researcher has an understanding of larger and longer-term social circumstances and forces than the research subjects; the researcher must contextualize what the subjects say and do within this "big picture." **Thick description** is one way of accomplishing this. Thick description and micro–macro linkage are practices that help link qualitative research (which is often micro-level analysis) to a wider range of theories.

In this book we have provided numerous examples of research that has a critical-reflexive orientation.

For example, Greg Scott maintained a critical distance from the opinions and points of view that the gang members expressed about the gang, that it was "like a family" and that it helped the formerly incarcerated reintegrate into the community. He tried to understand why individuals formed these ideas, but he did not repeat them uncritically. His own contextualized analysis contrasted to the subjects' views. He also provided macro–micro linkages, linking his community-level (or micro- and meso-level) observations to a critical view of the effects of the U.S. corrections systems and mass incarceration on communities and individuals.

Another example: Martha Martinez provided a critical, external view of the managers' orientations toward workers. She analyzed these orientations in terms of the type of industry represented by the trade journals (and the managers) and the trajectory by which these industries became integrated into the global economy. These larger economic processes were part of the "bedrock" for understanding why managers adopt particular discourses about the labor force in their industry.

A third example: The two studies of yearbooks (the Milwaukee study and Matt Char's smaller study in Grover's Corners) related a micro-analysis of words and images in the yearbooks of a small number of high schools to nation-wide changes in the functions of high schools and in youth culture. In Milwaukee, high schools shifted from being elite institutions that provided a full round of social life to having more limited functions for a broader base of students whose social life was increasingly formed by mass media and peer groups. In Grover's Corners, Matt was able to trace the decline of rural pursuits at the center of a homogenous community and the emergence of a more diverse, fragmented, and economically diversified local society.

We also traced the critical-reflexive orientation in the works of Wacquant and Burawoy and his students. Wacquant used carnal sociology to immerse himself fully in the life of the boxing gym and thereby understand how the young men formed their perceptions of the world around them. But he did not hesitate to provide the context of economic and racial inequalities in the United States to analyze how these perceptions were formed. He entered the microcosm of the boxing gym, but he also returned from it to his role as an objective observer of social inequalities.

Similarly Burawoy and his students related their micro-level findings to the larger context of conflicts and inequalities in the United States. Their efforts to report these findings to their research subjects helped them to confront the reality that the researcher does not see the world in the same terms as the subjects and to understand this gap in experiences, perceptions, and discourses.

## BOX 23.4
### Critical-reflexive sociology (Bourdieu, Wacquant, Burawoy)

- Distinguish objective and subjective understanding
- Consciously and critically think about objectivity
- Recognize the value of the scientific method; consider generalizability and falsifiability
- Recognize the validity of an external viewpoint
- Consider contexts of research findings, micro–macro linkages, historical contexts, conflict as a social process, and material and structural forces as influences on action

| Positivist-empiricist | Postmodern |
|---|---|
| External viewpoint | Construction of social categories |
| Measurement, metrics, operational variables | "It's all point of view" |
| Objectivist stance but not critically viewed | Emphasis on discourses |
| Little attention to conflict | Multiple conflicts, not prioritized |
| Data | Narrative |
| Rigid use of scientific method | Scientific method is deconstructed |
| Little critical reflection; nothing problematized | Everything is problematized |
| Little attention to historical context | "History" is multiple narratives |
| Little attention to the material base of action | "Economy" and "class" are deconstructed |

Just to summarize once again the four steps we recommend for developing a critical-reflexive analysis of the material you are producing—the data, to use a positivist term, whether they be data based on observation and interviews or data based on documents and artifacts:

1. Understand the views, perceptions, discourses, and experiences of the research subject as thoroughly and nonjudgmentally as you can, if necessary through a carnal immersion in the experiences of the subjects (*verstehen*).
2. Distinguish the views of the research subjects from those of yourself as the trained researcher; consider the tension between subjective meanings (the world of the research subjects) and objective analysis (your world as a trained social scientist).
3. Produce thick description, providing the historical and social context for the actions and views of the subjects and explaining what you have observed.
4. Develop micro–macro linkages, placing local, micro-level experiences and interactions into a larger context which is in turn linked to the objective analysis.

## CONCLUSION

Writing a research report is very hard work. Doing it successfully means making sense out of an enormous swamp of data, memos, thoughts, theories, images, numbers, maps, and so forth. You must impose upon the giant blob known as "my research project" a kind of "false linearity."

Writing text is a very linear process, or at the very least it's a process out of which one must tease a very linear, straight-looking, orderly product. The vast majority of research methods textbooks fail to inform the reader of just how messy this whole enterprise really is. On top of it all, to be successful you must bring incredible discipline to the materials that make up your project, which means disciplining yourself. Where do you start? Anywhere. One recommendation Greg often makes when students ask, "Where do I begin?" is this: "Sit down and write me a letter explaining what you did your research project on, why you did it, and what you learned." (In Chapter 19—"Focus Groups"—you can see Roberta's letter to Matt Char as an example.) But wherever you get started, what matters most is where you finish. Best of luck to you in the endeavor of representing reality!

## Exercises

1. Write up your own research report! To break this down a bit, first try to describe one "episode" within what would be a larger study of your campus (or your family, community, workplace, etc.). Try writing it in different styles, for example "canonical" or "postmodernist."

2. Pick a topic that interests you and find three articles in the scholarly research literature about this topic (not in popular magazines, but in peer-reviewed journals of your field of study). Try to summarize each article in about a page without copying or closely paraphrasing. Then use the main ideas of the articles to formulate a new research question on the topic.

## Key Terms

abstract *379*
accurate description *383*
ASA style citations *379*
canonical form of the research report and its standard outline (statement of the problem, lit review, methods, findings, and discussion/conclusions; other elements of a research report: title, abstract, and references or works-cited section) *377*
critical-reflexive *387*

historical context *388*
informant credibility *382*
interpretation *383*
macro–micro linkages *388*
plagiarism and paraphrasing *380*
positivist-empiricist *386*
postmodernist *387*
preexisting mental imagery (of the researcher) *387*
presence *382*
problematic *377*
references or works cited *379*

surprise, seeing, and "the visual" *382*
standard outline *377*
theoretical links *383*
theory–methods linkages *386*
thick description *388*
truth and objectivity *385*
four types of ethnographic writing: classical, mainstream, public, and postmodern (Adler and Adler 2008) *381*

# 24

# Wrapping It Up

## OVERVIEW

This chapter is about ending your research. It encourages you to think about what you might encounter as your project—possibly encompassing many valuable relationships—comes to a close.

## CHALLENGES ABOUND

Researchers occasionally face external hassles—for example, field notes about their observations of illegal activities may be subpoenaed. But the real difficulties are more likely to be relational and emotional. The relationship with "subjects" winds down and the researcher is forced to wonder whether it was really a friendship. Subjects read what the researcher has written and feel disappointed, disrespected, or even mocked. The excitement of field work ebbs away and the researcher is left drained and aimless.

In this chapter we want to reassure you that these feelings are normal and that while you need to be prepared for them, you should not be left depressed or frightened by them.

We discuss four examples of issues that researchers face after their study is completed.

### Legal Complications

Let's begin with the external hassles first. Of these, the most serious are probably the legal complications that can arise from observing illegal activities or even engaging in them. Legal complications can arise when the researcher has interviewed individuals who may be involved in illegal activities or identified as suspects in a criminal investigation. Researchers should be aware that their field notes and collected materials can be treated as evidence and that they can be compelled to disclose them. Several cases suggest that this question is not fully settled one way or the other, but that there are no assurances whatsoever against compelled disclosure (Polsky 1969; Brajuha and Hallowell 1986; Scarce 1994, 2005; O'Neil 1996).

The IRB process and protection of human subjects can be very helpful in protecting both the researcher and the subjects from legal ramifications. Fully **de-identified records** and **waivers of documentation of informed consent** (so that there are no signed forms with real names available anywhere) can in some cases allow the researcher to state truthfully that no individuals can be identified in the collected data or field notes. In other instances, these claims cannot be easily made.

The best known case is that of Rik Scarce, a sociologist and doctoral student at Washington State University at the time of the incident. Scarce was studying radical environmental movements and specifically the Animal Liberation Front, when a break-in occurred at an animal lab on campus. One of the individuals whom Scarce had interviewed in the course of his study was considered a suspect. A federal grand jury subpoenaed Scarce and called for disclosure of notes he had made about conversations with the suspect. Scarce refused, citing First Amendment rights and **confidentiality privileges**. The judge ruled that these privileges did not apply to scholars and journalists (unlike attorneys). Scarce refused to disclose the notes and spent 159 days in jail in 1993 for contempt of court although he had never been arrested, tried, or convicted of any crime. You can read more about this case in Scarce, Contempt of Court (Scarce 1994, 2005) (and read his study of the movement, *Eco-Warriors*, 2005). The case also figures prominently in several works about researcher privilege and higher education law such as: Robert O'Neil (1996—also available online at www.law.duke, retrieved May 9, 2009). The gist of the story is that researchers must be aware that their materials are subject to compelled disclosure.

A similar case took place in 1984 when a SUNY doctoral student, Mario Brajuha, worked as a waiter as part of a research project on restaurants. The restaurant mysteriously burned down and Brajuha was asked to turn over his field notes to a grand jury so the jurors could decide whether notes on a conversation with a fellow waiter could provide evidence that a particular individual was responsible for the fire. Brajuha protested but agreed to provide edited notes; eventually the subpoena was dropped without the notes having been disclosed (Brajuha and Hallowell 1986).

Sheldon Zink (Wilson 2003) was observing in a hospital and took notes on the case of a patient who had received an artificial heart. When he died several months later, his wife sued the hospital, the makers of the artificial heart, and his original patient advocate. The defendants subpoenaed Zink's notes but she refused to turn them over. Eventually the request was dropped but like the other cases we described, this case left substantial doubt as to whether researchers' field notes are protected from disclosure.

In some cases, careful **de-identification** of individuals in all of the research materials would have enabled the researcher to maintain confidentiality, although this practice would not have protected Zink from pressure arising from her observation of the artificial heart implants. The other cases underline that confidentiality is a part of the informed consent relationship, and not simply a matter of putting names and notes into a safety deposit box or of obtaining a waiver of documentation of consent. Confidentiality has to be built into the field notes, so that names and locations are unidentifiable throughout the process. Even these precautions cannot, however, fully protect researchers (and therefore their subjects) from **compelled disclosure** in courtroom testimony where they may be asked to state names and reveal research sites. Journalists have typically enjoyed a higher degree of protection from compelled disclosure than social scientists, but it is not guaranteed for them either.

Daniel Wolf wrote about his fieldwork with an outlaw motorcycle gang (1991). A police officer who read the published report claimed that the reading qualified him as an expert witness in testimony against a gang member. Wolf was dismayed that anyone could claim to be an expert witness on the basis of reading his book and he also had to face the anger of his research subject (the gang member) about this **unintended consequence of the research project**.

### Holding Up the Mirror: Research Subjects See Themselves in Your Report—the Issue of Representation

Beyond the possible legal complications, researchers have to face showing their conclusions and research reports to their subjects. Almost any representation of one individual by another can lead to disappointment. If you were ever interviewed by a reporter, you probably have experienced that feeling of disappointment—the reporter used too little of what you had to say, you were not quoted absolutely accurately, your words were placed in a context that you did not control or choose, and so on. For example, you may have been interviewed by the university newspaper about the men's basketball team, and a critical remark of yours was used in the article while a more positive and balanced comment was left out. When even a brief interview with a reporter can lead to disappointment, it is easy to see that a book-length ethnography is almost certain to arouse negative feelings among the subjects when they see it.

There are several causes inherent in this disappointment. One is the sense that observed behaviors or interview excerpts are too short and are used out of context. The subjects may feel that carefully contextualized longer excerpts and observations would represent them better.

A second concern among subjects is that the researcher has actually misunderstood them and misrepresented them out of ignorance and perhaps even willfulness. This type of subject dismay is especially likely to occur when the researcher has revealed misconduct or misrecognition among his subjects. The subjects may feel that the researcher has never "walked in their shoes." For example, police may believe that the researcher has not grasped what it is like daily to confront liars, crooks, and a heavily armed public. Attendants in mental hospitals and facilities for the severely mentally or physically disabled may feel that some degree of coercion and force are needed to get through daily routines. Most occupations that involve "people work" have to deal with recalcitrant people and have "routinized deviance" to cope with these situations (Hughes 1984). From the subjects' point of view, the researcher who records and writes about this routinized misconduct looks "holier than thou." Carnal sociology is one way of managing this reaction from subjects; it bolsters the researcher's claims to understanding the experience of the subjects—of having "walked in their shoes."

The researcher's **revelation of misrecognition among subjects** is a similar issue. When the researcher reveals misconduct (for instance, a corrections officer beating an inmate), the account suggests brutality or indifference; when the researcher reveals misrecognition, it suggests ignorance, stupidity, hypocrisy, or lack of self-awareness among the subjects. For example, Vidich and Bensman (1968) took a critical view of small town residents' values of independence and community. They exposed these self-images as instances of denial and misrecognition of dependence on larger forces and the existence of inequalities in the town. The townspeople came across as self-deluded and willfully unaware of their real conditions. It was not a portrait that won Vidich and Bensman many friends in the small town they studied.

But even a generous and positive research report may radiate a quality of ironic distance. The subjects are "being written about" and they are exposed to the gaze of readers, a bit like insects pinned into a specimen display box. And this **gaze** may take on a sarcastic quality, moving from "distance" into "parody" especially when the subjects are very close in culture and lifeways to the researcher. Nowadays it is highly unlikely that a researcher would be so insensitive as to write in a mocking way about the lives of people in a remote region or a poor community; but amusing status distinctions may be featured freely when the subjects are privileged and demographically similar to the researcher.

This issue was already clearly brought up in David Riesman's introduction to Seeley et al.'s *Crestwood Heights*, an ethnography of an affluent suburban community in Canada whose residents were similar to the researchers in education, SES, and ethnic backgrounds. Riesman asks whether it is he who brings to the text a **sardonic reaction** or whether the sardonic feeling has been put into the text, for instance in the authors' description of the "efficiency" of a household or in the sentence "the giving of presents in this family is a highly regarded token of love and esteem." He compares the writing to the work of a novelist (Mary McCarthy) who is able to make a fictional character appear ridiculous by what seems to be a very simple description: "the professor came into the room, carrying his briefcase" (Riesman 1956: ix).

When Greg had finally finished his short documentary film called "The Brickyard," which chronicles the life of an outdoor encampment of homeless and precariously housed drug addicts and prostitutes, he took the film into a crack house and showed it to one of the lead "characters" in the film, a self-professed "professional crackhead" by the name of Jeff. The film begins with Jeff giving an account of how he was brutally beaten in his sleep by three young neighborhood boys who had been hired by a local drug dealer from whom Jeff had stolen money. Near the end of Jeff's monologue he begins to cry. His sobbing becomes so obtrusive that he can no longer talk. He waves the camera away and tells Greg, "I can't do this right now."

As Greg sat there next to Jeff watching the opening scene, Greg grew very nervous, wondering how Jeff—who in his typical representation of self comes off as "hyper-masculine," the proverbial "street thug"—might react to this representation, which clearly contradicted Jeff's vigilantly maintained self-image. As the scene progressed, Jeff (as viewer) became visibly agitated, issuing comments such as "What the fuck is wrong with me?" and "What the fuck is going on?" At this point Greg became certain that Jeff would turn violent and notwithstanding their close relationship beat Greg senseless. Once the scene ended, Jeff stood up and pushed the "pause" button on the DVD player. Jeff turned around and noticed that a crowd of nearly a dozen fellow drug addicts had gathered in the room. Jeff stared at Greg, and just as Greg prepared himself to be attacked physically, Jeff's face brightened as he shouted, "Yeah, baby, now that is keeping it real . . . NOBODY keeps it real like this mothafucka . . . hell yeah, man, that is what it's like out here. Shit . . . none of you motherfuckers can even touch that shit!"

Greg hunched over in relief and emotional exhaustion. Jeff resumed play of the DVD. At the end of the film everyone in the room applauded. Although some of them flat out said that they "hated" seeing themselves portrayed "that way" in the film, they also said that Greg had done a great job of "keeping it real" and representing Brickyard life "the way it really is." By the way, in the film Greg's central purpose was to reveal Brickyard residents' "misrecognitions" of their communal bonds, their "family" ethos, their professed "love" for fellow outlaws, and so forth. In essence, the film shows them to be cultivators and perpetuators of necessary delusions concerning their Selves and their "community."

Another example: Roberta wrote a very positive account of a classroom in an Italian elementary school, emphasizing the encouragement that children received from teachers and the complex skills that children learned when they created projects that combined artwork, writing, and critical thinking about their social environment; but she did not feel comfortable enough with the research report to show it to teachers and parents because the act of **writing about** seemed to subject the teachers, children, and parents to the research "gaze," regardless of the positive tone of the report.

In short, "friends don't write books about friends," and the act of writing about people always creates distance, even when the account is favorable. Film and visual methods are less distancing because the media themselves seem more familiar to people and closer to the normal

Jeff and Greg in a crack house after watching "The Brickyard" movie.

representational activities of everyday life (taking snapshots, making home movies). These media also involve less use of **scholarly jargon** (which contributes to a sense of distance and objectification as research specimens). The visual representations seem closer to the actual self of the people about whom they are made, and less processed by the words and concepts of the social scientist.

Michael Burawoy et al. (1991) conducted a graduate seminar in participant-observation in which each student carried out a research project that explored a facet of "power and resistance in the modern metropolis." In keeping with the political tilt of the seminar, the students were encouraged to present their findings to their research subjects, and we discuss two examples.

Ann Arnett Ferguson (Ferguson in Burawoy et al. 1991) provides a lengthy description of this experience, starting with the confession that she did not look forward to sharing her findings with her subjects, workers in a bakery collective. "I knew I would have to go back to the collective and present my paper sooner or later. But I tried to put it off for as long as I possibly could" (1991: 130). . . . She decided to first show her paper to one member of the collective, who eventually had copies made for all the workers and encouraged her to present it at a meeting. Her presentation, which included critical analytic remarks about members, was met by silence. "I get up and make a quick exit so the rest of the long agenda can be covered" (1991: 130). But later one member of the collective sent her a six-page single-spaced response, and in conversations with him she discovered that he was challenging some of her basic formulations. Others also ended up telling her that they felt she had not presented the full picture with all possible perspectives on the organization. Yet after this feedback, she actually became more confident about her conclusions which had now been exposed to critical reflection.

Another student, Charles Kurzman, observed the seminar itself and thereby reflected on the creation of sociological knowledge. He identifies four reasons for sharing field notes and the final paper with subjects: to allow them to correct errors; to create a sense of cooperation; to empower subjects as agents in the analysis of their own social reality; and to keep the writing "clean"—that

Pony Tail Steve and Sapphire Pam's "House Rules" for governing the large volume of invited and uninvited fellow addicts who visit their shanty home in "The Brickyard."

is, the researcher is forced to think about how the subjects would react to what he is saying about them. Yet Kurzman claims forcefully, "Unfortunately, these are also the very reasons *not* to share written analyses with subjects" (Burawoy et al. 1991: 265). He explains that subjects are likely to be upset when they see mistakes and to become hostile to the researcher. Subjects are likely to be uninterested in the theoretical aspects of the project and therefore their involvement in the writing will lead to less theoretical integration. Subjects do not necessarily feel empowered by the offer to participate in the analysis. And finally, subjects are likely to be particularly offended by simple descriptive details, such as their age, appearance, clothing, or food habits.

The researcher should avoid intentional insults and jokes, but beyond this basic sensitivity and tact, he or she cannot constantly fret about what is appropriate to put in field notes. As Kurzman puts it, "Knowing that the subjects are going to read one's field notes can make a sensitive researcher second-guess every detail" (Burawoy et al.1991: 268). The sociology graduate students observed by Kurzman in fact reacted in exactly these ways to his project. He concludes that "every social scientific analysis objectifies its subjects to a certain extent." When generalizations are formulated by the researcher, the analysis tends to diminish the strong sense the subjects have of themselves as unique individuals. Kurzman ends the essay with practical advice:

> In sum, then, the idea of sharing one's writings with one's subjects is fraught with problems. I am not suggesting that researchers refuse to show their writings to their subjects, merely trying to make the issue complex. My view is that field notes should not be shared; they are too raw and too liable to offend. However, I feel that the subjects have a right to see and comment on least one draft of the researcher's final paper.

> (Kurzman in Burawoy et al. 1991: 268)

## Promises to Keep (and Some to Break): Sharing Findings

Yet another problem of seeing the research report (or visual document) arises when the researcher has promised sponsors, gatekeepers, and guides that the findings will be shared with them. For instance, after Roberta (and her colleagues Judy Bootcheck and John Koval) had completed much of their multimethod study of Grover's Corners High School, they prepared a summary report of their findings for the principal who had generously enabled them to conduct the research. He had helped them obtain parental permissions for student participation and enabled them to set up focus groups with students, interview teachers, collect survey data, examine yearbooks, and observe classroom interaction. This report was fairly easy to write for several reasons. No individuals were identified by name. Data were reported in a statistical summary form in terms of percentages. Interview and focus group quotes and descriptions of individual behavior were not included. The principal was doing an effective job as an administrator and had been able to reduce tensions between Hispanic and Anglo students; he had taken steps to improving the performance of students on tests and in college admissions. Therefore the report was largely positive, and no major problems or misconduct were described in it. In general it conveyed a favorable impression of the school, teachers, and administration, and the researchers felt comfortable in showing it to the principal. But researchers cannot always count on being able to present relatively problem-free feedback to gatekeepers and sponsors.

A student of ours who was observing a project for teens found herself with the dilemma that she had promised a report on the findings to the program administrator and then discovered negative feelings about the program among the young women. With only a small number of women in the program, it was difficult to completely de-identify the comments. The solution was to write only a short summary (shorter than the one for the high school principal described in the preceding paragraph), which avoided using any lengthy interview comments that might have breached the confidentiality of the interview data and the privacy of the participants. Perhaps in some instances, it would be tactful for the researcher writing the executive summary to frame the subjects' concerns in the form of positive suggestions for improving the program rather than in verbatim quotations of negative comments, complaints, and criticisms. There is a thin line between tact and cover-up that researchers must face.

A rather dramatic instance of negative reactions came in the wake of Whyte's (1943/1993) *Street Corner Society*. You may remember that we discussed this classic of field research in the context of the role of guides in field research; Doc made possible many of Whyte's insights into the life of the Italian American neighborhood. Long after the research was completed and Doc had passed away, one of Doc's sons made a formal complaint to the American Sociological Association, claiming that not only had Whyte exploited Doc but Doc did not even know that

Whyte had written a book about the community and that he did not agree with many of the conclusions that Whyte was formulating about the community.

In this dispute, we can see many of the issues we have discussed: the charge that subjects or informants are exploited in research and that guides (or important informants) may feel betrayed and used; the discomfort that subjects may feel at the representations of themselves and their milieu; and the question of whether there can be multiple truths about a community—that of the residents and that of the researcher, so that the researcher does not have to simply repeat exactly what the residents tell him. Whyte had already stated the view that Doc had disowned information he gave Whyte because he (Doc) knew that the other community members would not be happy with the representations and the information that was revealed about their world. The case did not result in litigation, but the bad feelings persisted.

At the end of his essay on the outlaw motorcycle ethnography, Wolf reflects on the way his study began and therefore had to end when he wrote his ethnography:

> I saw the outlaw biker subculture as a human experience, a system of meaning in which I, as an anthropologist, had to involve myself—experience—in order to develop an adequate explanation of what was being observed. My involvement demanded the intensity of a highly emotional reaction. Each encounter was an escalation toward an outlaw biker identity. I conducted these entry and participation phases well: too well. As an outlaw biker the final phase of research, the prospect of writing an ethnography for the eyes of outsiders, was nothing short of betrayal.

> (Wolf 1991b: 223)

## The Fading of Friendship

Moving to a closely related issue in leaving fieldwork, we need to say a bit about what happens to friendships formed in fieldwork. Researchers often convince themselves that they have become friends with their subjects, especially with their guides and main informants. The subjects themselves often agree and encourage this feeling. After all, when people engage in exchanges they do become friendly and they like to feel that these relationships are affectionate and not merely arrangements of mutual convenience, let alone relationships of unequal power and resources imposed by a researcher on a vulnerable community.

This issue has become increasingly sensitive as currents of feminism and postmodernism flow into research relationships. Once upon a time, a white, male, well educated, middle-class researcher studied people with fewer resources and in less advantaged social categories than himself (sic). He (sic) was trained in fieldwork traditions of objectifying research subjects, and there were fewer illusions about the equality of the relationship or the possibility that it would turn into a lasting friendship.

In the last few decades, this orientation has become less acceptable (Smith 1990, 1992; Reinharz and Davidman 1992), and many researchers make an effort to connect to their subjects and to avoid objectifying them. But even participation and empathy do not prevent an unsatisfactory end to the relationships. Frida Kerner Furman, who conducted a study of elderly Jewish American women, contrasts the objectifying researcher to the more relationally involved one, but she comments, ". . . the ethnographer who becomes a full participant may enjoy closeness with study participants while the study lasts but then may walk away from people, as well as from the setting. She enters a 'culture of indebtedness' but may not readily know how to reciprocate" (1997: 13).

Let's look at a few examples of the fading friendship. In the last paragraph of Wolf's essay on his high-risk study of a motorcycle gang, he says very directly, "I simply faded away. . . . the special world that sustained our intense comradeship was gone."

The growing distance may be created by movement away on either side or both. Gallmeier (in Shaffir and Stebbins 1991) felt ambivalent about his experience observing a hockey team; he was put off by the players' sexism (their endless "pussy talk" and classification of women into "pigs," "star-fuckers," "team girls," "blow jobs," and "bimbos"), their locker-room pranks such as drawing a happy-face on the head of the penis and "strutting around the locker room performing a ventriloquist act" (1991: 227), and their good-natured physicality which involved hitting him, filling his shoes with shaving cream, putting him into a head lock, and knuckling his hair, as well as brawls among themselves. He makes clear that in many ways it was a relief to end the research; and it is not surprising that the player with whom he kept in touch longest was college-educated and most similar to him in outlook and habits. When he returned to the stadium and the locker room the following season, he did not recognize all the players because of the high turnover, and he reports feeling "embarrassed and detached" (1991: 229). Yet he is touched to hear that players saved his seat on the bus as a special place and would not let newcomers sit in it until they became recognized as veterans.

Taylor (in Shaffir and Stebbins 1991) had to contend with even more questionable behavior in his observations of a ward in a facility for severely developmentally disabled people; he saw attendants engage not only in mild abuse of a verbal sort but also severe instances such as making inmates swallow burning cigarettes, scrub feces and urine with their bare hands, and perform fellatio on each other. He comments, "A common way of leaving the field is 'easing out' (Junker 1960, cited in Taylor 1991) or 'drifting off'" (Glaser and Strauss 1967/1968, cited in Taylor 1991: 244). These expressions mean gradually reducing contacts without a definite break while avoiding leaving bad feelings behind. Taylor says,

> During my year on the ward, I had conflicting feelings about the attendants, On the one hand, I had come to like some of them personally and was grateful how they had opened up to me. On the other hand, I was offended morally by the conditions on the ward and the attendants' treatment of the residents under their charge. I knew that when I wrote up my study it would be critical of the institution and the attendants' activities.
>
> (1991: 244)

This is a relatively extreme example and one can understand why the researcher is not all that keen on maintaining these contacts as friendships and has at best ambivalent feelings about the relationships.

The researcher may learn that the community and the individuals have not fared well, and this information may tinge the research experience with sadness and the sense that social scientists are powerless to help the people who helped them. For example, Newbold Chinas (1993) learned that the community in southern Mexico that she studied in the late 1960s was undergoing hard times with the opening of a petroleum refinery nearby, a diminishing water supply, environmental degradation, and increasing violence. By the 1990s conditions improved with more jobs, better municipal services, access to health services, and acquisition of consumer goods that made life easier. Nevertheless, the author conveys a feeling that the life of the community is shaped by factors well beyond the control of either residents or friendly outsiders like herself, and that there is actually little that she was able to do—no matter how energetic and well-intentioned—to make life better for her research participants. The recognition that the researcher can do little to transform the life of the community participants is especially unsettling in CBPR.

A similar sense of sadness and powerlessness appears on the last page of *Dancing Skeletons*, Katherine Dettwyler's account of the cultural and social context of health conditions, nutrition, and infant mortality in Mali: "Moussa [her translator and field assistant] writes that he is fine, and that people are guardedly optimistic about the new government . . . Moussa also writes that my lovely little friend Ami succumbed to malaria in the fall of 1990. He sends no news of Daouda..." (1994: 164). Dettwyler has given a portion of her royalties to Freedom from Hunger to support the fight against malnutrition in Mali, and provides contact information so that her readers can make contributions to an organization that supports women's access to credit.

## Post-Project Blues

Fieldwork (which is a part of most of the designs we have discussed) creates a feeling of excitement and intensity that other types of research do not spark as dramatically. Of course many researchers are thrilled by statistical analysis of secondary data; waiting for the results of regression analyses and tests of significance to appear on the computer screen can provoke the same breath-holding, adrenaline-rush sensation as seeing the final card turn up in blackjack or the ball settle into the groove of the roulette wheel. Any situation in which the outcome is unpredictable is exciting, whether it is fieldwork or statistical analysis. But because in fieldwork powerful feelings of curiosity are amplified by personal relationships and entry into new spaces and contexts, the sensation can be more intense and prolonged than the ones produced in quantitative data analysis in the lab or analysis of documents in the library. Novelty may be accompanied by a sense of physical risk in some contexts; and as the novelty and risk wear off they may be replaced by affection and sympathy. This mix of feelings, extended over months or years of fieldwork, cannot easily be turned off when the fieldwork is over and the report written.

All of these emotions—the fading of friendship, the parting of ways between the researcher and the researched, the unease about the act of writing, and the ebbing of the intensity of the experience—are captured beautifully in the last paragraph of Loïc Wacquant's *Body and Soul: Notebooks of an Apprentice Boxer*. Wacquant has just lost a fight in the Golden Gloves, but he lasted through it despite his cuts, bruises, and battered ribs. When he returns to the gym the next day, he is warmly greeted by the men, including Ashante, his friend and sparring partner. But the final word in the book is given to Dee Dee, the head coach. Wacquant dedicates the book to the memory of Dee Dee and clearly they cared about each other, yet in this scene Dee Dee expresses an unsentimental view of the relationship between the researcher and the researched.

> But all this hurting vanishes upon my triumphant return to the gym. . . . I surprised everyone at the gym—starting with myself. From now on, I am fully one of them: "*Yep, Louie's a soul brother.*" Ashante is eagerly inquiring about my next fight when Dee Dee shuts the party down: "There ain't gonna be no next time. You had yo' fight. You got enough to write your damn book now. You don't need to get into d'ring."
>
> (2004: 255)

# CONCLUSION

At some point and for one or another reason, you must "wrap it up." Many researchers fall in love with the doing of research and a fair number never really do wrap it up. They just continue doing research, collecting data, and although they may even conduct analyses and make some sense of it all, they simply fail to call it a wrap and proceed to write it up and publish it to the world. By now you probably have a few ideas concerning how this happens. Ideally, you know enough about the challenges of wrapping it up to ward them off and/or overcome them when they manifest in your own research study. Finishing a study is really much harder than starting one, nearly every time, regardless of the nature of the project. So beware of the siren song of the field . . . it can keep you in its enchantment forever and a day. As hard as it may be, you must divorce yourself from the people, places, and things you have come to know, and very likely love, so that you can finish things up. Good luck to you.

## Exercises

1. Pick a topic for a research project that you find intriguing but that you think could lead to "legal complications." Why might they ensue? Are there any steps you could or must take to reduce this risk? What would you write in your IRB protocol as steps to protect your subjects? Would a different way of framing the research question or planning the research design reduce the risks of legal complications?

2. Describe a situation in which a close friendship (or intense relationship) gradually "faded" or in which you came to see the actions of your friend in a new light. How did this happen?

3. What do you think the researcher "owes" the researched? Then select an ethnography you have read and discuss your view of "indebtedness" in this instance.

4. Write a page of notes about an episode in your own research methods class (e.g., a discussion or some other episode in which a number of individuals interact). Be as detailed, honest, and objective as possible. Read it out loud to the class.

5. Much of this chapter appears addressed to leaving the field. Do you think any of the challenges apply to historical-comparative research, analysis of cultural objects, and other largely nonobtrusive or nonparticipatory designs?

## Key Terms

compelled disclosure *392*
confidentiality privileges *392*
de-contextualized quotes *391*
de-identification *392*
de-identified records *391*
friendship issues and the fading of friendship *398*
"the gaze" of the readers and the researcher *393*

legal complications *391*
post-project blues *400*
revelation of the misrecognitions or misconduct of research subjects *393*
sardonic reaction *394*
scholarly jargon *395*
sharing findings with sponsors, gatekeepers, guides, and research participants *397*

unintended consequences of research *392*
waivers of documentation of informed consent *391*
writing about *394*

# BIBLIOGRAPHY

Adler, Marina. 2002. "German Unification as a Turning Point in East German Women's Life Course: Biographical Changes in Work and Family Roles." *Sex Roles* 47: 83–98.

Adler, Patricia A. 1985. *Wheeling and Dealing: An Ethnography of an Upper-level Drug Dealing and Smuggling Community.* New York: Columbia University Press.

Adler, Patricia A. and Peter Adler. 1987. *Membership Roles in Field Research.* Newbury Park, CA: Sage Publications.

Adler, Patricia A. and Peter Adler. 1998. *Peer Power: Preadolescent Culture and Identity.* New Brunswick, NJ: Rutgers University Press.

Adler, Patricia A. and Peter Adler. 2008. "Of Rhetoric and Representation: The Four Faces of Ethnography." *The Sociological Quarterly* 49: 1–30.

Adorno, Theodor W., Else Frenkel-Brunswik, and Daniel J. Levinson. 1993. *The Authoritarian Personality.* New York: W. W. Norton.

Adorno, Theodor and Max Horkheimer. 1999. "The Culture Industry," in Simon During (ed.), *The Cultural Studies Reader.* London and New York: Routledge, pp. 31–41.

Agar, Michael H. 1980. *The Professional Stranger: An Informal Introduction to Ethnography.* New York: Academic Press.

Agar, Michael H. 1995. *Language Shock: Understanding the Culture of Conversation.* New York: William Morrow.

Agar, Michael H. 1996. *The Professional Stranger: An Informal Introduction to Ethnography,* 2nd ed. San Diego, CA: Academic Press.

Agar, Michael H. 2006. "An Ethnography by Any Other Name . . . . ," *Forum Qualitative Sozialforschung/Forum: Qualitative Social Research,* 7(4). Retrieved from http://www.qualitative-research.net/index.php/fqs/article/view/177/395.

Albert, Alexa. 2001. *Brothel: Mustang Ranch and Its Women.* New York: Random House Publishing Group.

Althusser, Louis. 1971a. "Freud and Lacan," in *Lenin and Philosophy.* New York: Monthly Review Press, pp. 189–220.

Althusser, Louis. 1971b. "Ideology and the State," in *Lenin and Philosophy.* New York: Monthly Review Press, pp. 127–186.

Alvesson, Mats. 2002. *Post Modernism and Social Research.* Buckingham, UK and Philadelphia, PA: Open University Press.

Aman, Virginia Lee Barnes, and Janice Boddy. 1995. *Aman: The Story of a Somali Girl.* Toronto: Knopf.

American Sociological Association. *Code of Ethics.*

Anderson, Benedict. 1983/1999. *Imagined Communities.* London: Verso.

Anderson, Benedict. 1999. *Imagined Communities: Reflections on the Origin and Spread of Nationalism.* London: Verso.

Anderson, Elijah. 1999. *Code of the Street.* New York: W. W. Norton.

Anyon, Jean. 1980. "Social Class and the Hidden Curriculum of Work." *Journal of Education* 162(1): 67–92.

Arendt, Hannah. 1992. *Eichmann in Jerusalem: A Report on the Banality of Evil.* New York: Penguin Books.

Ash, Michael, James K. Boyce, Grace Chang, Manuel Pastor, Justin Scoggins, and Jennifer Tran. 2009. "Justice in the Air." Creative Commons, http://creativecommons.org

Atkinson, P. 1992. *Understanding Ethnographic Texts.* Thousand Oaks: CA: Sage Publications.

Baltzell, E. Digby. 1989. *Philadelphia Gentlemen: The Making of a National Upper Class.* New Brunswick, NJ: Transaction Publishers.

Baltzell, E. Digby. 2008. *The Philadelphia Gentlemen.* New Brunswick, NJ: Transaction Publishers.

Bamford, Anne. 2003. *The Visual Literacy White Paper.* Sydney, Australia: Adobe Systems Pty. Ltd, http://www.adobe.com/uk/education/pdf/adobe_visual_literacy_paper.pdf

Banks, Marcus. 1990. "The Seductive Veracity of Ethnographic Film." *Visual Anthropology Review* 6(1): 16–21.

Barry, Ann Marie Seward. 1997. *Visual Intelligence: Perception, Image, and Manipulation in Visual Communication.* New York: State University of New York Press.

Bateson, Gregory and Margaret Mead. 1942. *Balinese Character: A Photographic Analysis.* New York: New York Academy of Sciences.

Baudrillard, Jean. 1970. *The Consumer Society.* Translated by Chris Turner. London: Sage Publications.

Baudrillard, Jean. 1998. *The Consumer Society: Myths and Structures.* London: Sage Publications.

Bazeley, Pat. 2007. *Qualitative Data Analysis with NVivo.* London: Sage Publications.

Becker, Howard S. 1963. *Outsiders: Studies in the Sociology of Deviance.* New York: Free Press.

Becker, Howard S. 1967. "Whose Side Are We On?" *Social Problems* 14: 239–247.

Becker, Howard S. 1970a. "Interviewing Medical Students," in William J. Filstead (ed.), *Qualitative Methodology: Firsthand Involvement with the Social World.* Chicago: Markham Publishing Company, pp. 103–106.

Becker, Howard S. 1970b. "Problems of Inference and Proof in Participant Observation," in William J. Filstead (ed.), *Qualitative Methodology: Firsthand Involvement with the Social World.* Chicago: Markham Publishing Company, pp. 189–201.

Becker, Howard S. 1970c. "Whose Side Are We On?" in William J. Filstead (ed.), *Qualitative Methodology: Firsthand Involvement with the Social World.* Chicago: Markham Publishing Company, pp. 15–26.

Becker, Howard S. 1974. "Photography and Sociology." *Studies in the Anthropology of Visual Communication* 1: 3–26.

Becker, Howard S. 1995. "Visual Sociology, Documentary Photography, and Photojournalism: It's (Almost) all a Matter of Context." *Visual Studies* 10(1/2): 5–14.

Becker, Howard S. 1998. *Tricks of the Trade: How to Think about Your Research While You're Doing It.* Chicago: University of Chicago Press.

Becker, Howard S. 2002. "Studying New Media." *Qualitative Sociology* 25: 3.

Becker, Howard S. 2007. *Telling about Society.* Chicago: University of Chicago Press.

Becker, Howard S. 2008. *Art Worlds.* 25th Anniversary Edition, Updated and Expanded. Berkeley and Los Angeles, CA: University of California Press.

Becker, Howard S. and Blanche Geer. 1970. "Participant Observation and Interviewing: A Comparison," in William J. Filstead (ed.), *Qualitative Methodology: Firsthand Involvement with the Social World.* Chicago, IL: Markham Publishing Company, pp. 133–142.

Becker, Howard, Blanche Geer, Everett Hughes, and Anselm Strauss. 1976. *Boys in White: Student Culture in Medical School.* New Brunswick, NJ: Transaction Publishers.

Benjamin, Walter. 2002. *The Arcades Project.* Edited by Rolf Tiedemann. Translated by Howard Eiland and Kevin McLaughlin. Cambridge, MA and London: Belknap Press of Harvard University Press.

Berg, B. L. 2001. *Qualitative Research Methods for the Social Sciences.* Boston, MA: Allyn & Bacon.

Berger, John. 1972. *Ways of Seeing.* London: British Broadcasting Corporation (BBC) and Penguin Books.

Blumer, Herbert. 1968. *Symbolic Interactionism.* Englewood Cliffs, NJ: Prentice-Hall.

Bogira, Steve. 2005. *Courtroom 302: A Year Behind the Scenes in an American Criminal Courthouse.* New York: Knopf.

Bootcheck, Judith. 2006. *Personal Communication about the Role of Drift in Post-secondary Occupational and Educational Choices.* Chicago, IL: DePaul University.

Bourdieu, Pierre. 1977. *Outline of a Theory of Practice.* Translated by Richard Nice. Cambridge, UK: Cambridge University Press.

Bourdieu, Pierre and Loïc J. D. Wacquant. 1992. *An Invitation to Reflexive Sociology.* Chicago, IL: University of Chicago Press.

Bourgeois, Philippe I. 2002. *In Search of Respect: Selling Crack in El Barrio.* New York: Cambridge University Press.

Bourgois, Philippe I. 2002. *In Search of Respect: Selling Crack in El Barrio.* Cambridge: Cambridge University Press.

Bourke-White, Margaret and Erskine Caldwell. 1937. *You Have Seen Their Faces.* New York: Viking Press.

Brajuha, Mario and Lyle Hallowell. 1986. "Legal Intrusion and the Politics of Fieldwork." *Journal of Contemporary Ethnography* 14(4): 454–478.

Braverman, Harry. 1998. *Labor and Monopoly Capital.* New York: Monthly Review Press.

Brewer, John and Albert Hunter. 2006. *Foundations of Multimethod Research: Synthesizing Styles.* Thousand Oaks, CA and London: Sage Publications.

Bruni, Attilla. 2005. "Shadowing Software and Clinical Records: On the Ethnography of Non-Humans and Heterogeneous Contexts." *Organization* 12: 357–378.

Brydon-Miller, Mary. 2001. "Education, Research, and Action: Theory and Methods of Participatory Action Research," in D. L. Tolman and M. Brydon-Miller (eds.), *From Subjects to Subjectivities: A Handbook of Interpretive and Participatory Methods.* New York: New York University Press, pp. 76–89.

Buck-Morss, Susan. 1989. *The Dialectics of Seeing: Walter Benjamin and the Arcades Project.* Cambridge, MA: MIT Press.

Bulmer, Martin. 1984. *The Chicago School of Sociology: Institutionalisation, Diversity and the Rise of Sociological Research.* Chicago, IL: University of Chicago Press.

Burawoy, Michael et al. 1991. *Ethnography Unbound: Power and Resistance in the Modern Metropolis.* Berkeley, CA: University of California Press.

Carroll, Christopher. 2009. *The (In)visible Metropolis.* Chicago, IL: DePaul University, MA Thesis, unpublished.

Castells, Manuel. 1996. *The Rise of the Network Society.* Malden, MA: Blackwell.

Castells, Manuel. 2000. *The Rise of the Network Society: Rise of the Network Society.* Oxford: Blackwell.

Char, Matt. 1997. *Yearbooks.* Chicago, IL: DePaul University, MA Thesis.

Chomsky, Noam. 1957. *Syntactic Structures.* Berlin: Walter de Gruyter.

Chomsky, Noam. 1989. *Necessary Illusions: Thought Control in Democratic Societies.* New York: South End Press.

Clark-Baca, Judy and Roberts Braden. 1990. "The Delphi Study: A Proposed Method for Resolving Visual Literacy Uncertainties," in R.A. Braden, D.G. Beauchamp, and J. Clark-Baca (eds.), *Perceptions of Visual Literacy.* Rochester, NY: International Visual Literacy Association.

Coleman, James, John Johnstone, and Kurt Jonassohn. 1981. *The Adolescent Society: The Social Life of the Teenager and Its Impact on Education.* Westport, CT: Greenwood Press.

Collier, John. 1967. *Visual Anthropology: Photography as a Research Method.* New York: Holt, Rinehart and Winston.

Cookson, Peter W. and Caroline Hodges Persell. 1985. *Preparing for Power: America's Elite Boarding Schools.* New York: Basic Books.

Corwin, Patricia. 1996. "Using the Community as a Classroom for Large Introductory Sociology Classes." *Teaching Sociology* 24(3): 310–315. Published by: American Sociological Association.

Curry, Timothy J. and Alfred C. Clarke. 1977. *Introducing Visual Sociology.* Dubuque, IA: Kendall/Hunt Publishing Co.

De Certeau, Michel. 1999. "Walking in the City," in Simon During (ed.), *The Cultural Studies Reader.* London and New York: Routledge, pp. 126–133.

De Jesus, Carolina Maria. 2003. *Child of the Dark: The Diary of Carolina Maria de Jesus.* New York: Signet.

Denzin, Norman K. 1970. *The Research Act: A Theoretical Introduction to Sociological Methods.* Chicago, IL: Aldine.

Denzin, Norman K. 1993. *The Alcoholic Society: Addiction and Recovery of the Self.* Edison, NJ: Transaction Publishers.

Denzin, Norman K. 1996. *Handbook of Qualitative Research.* Thousand Oaks, CA: Sage Publications.

Denzin, Norman K. and John M. Johnson. 1995. *The Alcoholic Society: Addiction and Recovery of the Self.* New Brunswick, NJ: Transaction Publishers.

Denzin, Norman K. and Yvonna S. Lincoln (eds.). 2000. *Handbook of Qualitative Research.* Thousand Oaks, CA: Sage Publications.

Deshler, David and Merrill Ewert. 1995. "Participatory Action Research: Traditions and Major Assumptions." *The Cornell PAR Network News* 3(1): 1–4.

Dettwyler, Katherine. 1994. *Dancing Skeletons: Life and Death in West Africa.* Prospect Heights, IL: Waveland Press.

Dewey, John. 1938. *Experience and Education.* New York: The Macmillan Company.

Dewey, John. 1938/1998. *Experience and Education.* 60th Anniversary Edition. Indianapolis, IN: Kappa Delta Pi.

Diamond, Jared. 2005. *Collapse: How Societies Choose to Fail or Succeed.* New York: Viking Books.

Dillenberger, John. 1980. "The Diversity of Disciplines as a Theological Question: The Visual Arts as Paradigm." *Journal of the American Academy of Religion* 48(2): 233–243.

Domhoff, G. William. 1975. *The Bohemian Grove and Other Retreats: A Study in Ruling-Class Cohesiveness.* New York: Harper Torchbooks.

Douglas, Jack D., Patricia Adler, Peter Adler, Andrea Fontana, C. Robert Freeman, and Joseph Kotarba. 1980. *Introduction to the Sociologies of Everyday Life.* Boston, MA: Allyn and Bacon.

Drake, St. Clair and Horace R. Cayton. 1945/1993. *Black Metropolis.* Chicago, IL: University of Chicago Press.

Drake, St. Clair and Horace R. Cayton. 1993. *Black Metropolis: A Study of Negro Life in a Northern City.* Chicago, IL: University of Chicago Press.

Duneier, Mitchell. 1994. *Slim's Table: Race, Respectability and Masculinity.* Chicago, IL: University of Chicago Press.

Duneier, Mitchell. 1999. *Sidewalk.* New York: Farrar, Strauss, and Giroux.

Duneier, Mitchell. 2001. *Sidewalk.* New York: Farrar, Straus, and Giroux.

Dunn, J. 1988. *The Beginnings of Social Understanding.* Cambridge, MA: Harvard University Press.

During, Simon. 1993. *The Cultural Studies Reader.* London and New York: Routledge.

During, Simon. 1999. *The Cultural Studies Reader.* London and New York: Routledge.

Durkheim, Émile. 1897/1951. *Suicide.* New York: Free Press.

Durkheim, Émile. 1951. *Suicide: A Study in Sociology.* Glencoe, IL: Free Press.

Ehrenreich, Barbara. 2001. *Nickel and Dimed: On (Not) Getting by in America.* New York: Metropolitan Books.

Einstein, Albert. 2009. *The Collected Papers of Albert Einstein, Volume 11: Cumulative Index, Bibliography, List of Correspondence, Chronology, and Errata to Volumes 1–10.* Princeton, NJ: Princeton University Press.

Einstein, Albert. 2011. (Authorized English translation of the volume "Mein Weltbild," original copyright 1956). New York, NY: Open Road Integrated Media.

Ellingson, Stephen. 2004. "Constructing Causal Stories and Moral Boundaries: Institutional Approaches to Sexual Problems," in Edward O. Laumann, Stephen Ellingson, Jenna Mahay, Anthony Paik, and Yoosik Youm (eds.), *The Sexual Organization of the City.* Chicago, IL: University of Chicago Press, pp. 283–308.

Ellingson, Stephen, Martha Van Haitsma, Edward O. Laumann, and Nelson Tebbe. 2004. "Religion and the Politics of Sexuality," in Edward O. Laumann, Stephen Ellingson, Jenna Mahay, Anthony Paik, and Yoosik Youm (eds.), *The Sexual Organization of the City.* Chicago, IL: University of Chicago Press, pp. 309–348.

Emerson, Robert M., Rachel I. Fretz, and Linda L. Shaw. 1995. *Writing Ethnographic Fieldnotes.* Chicago, IL: University of Chicago Press.

Erikson, Kai. 1976. *Everything in Its Path: Destruction of Community in the Buffalo Creek Flood.* New York: Simon and Schuster.

Esterberg, Kristin. 2001. *Qualitative Methods in Social Research.* New York and London: McGraw-Hill.

Evans-Prichard, E.E. 1950. *Social Anthropology.* Glencoe, IL: Free Press.

Ewen, Stuart and Elizabeth Ewen. 1982. *Channels of Desire: Mass Images and the Shaping of American Consciousness.* New York: McGraw-Hill.

Feyerabend, Paul. 1975. *Against Method: Outline of an Anarchist Theory of Knowledge.* London: New Left Books.

Fine, Gary A. 1996. *Kitchens: The Culture of Restaurant Work.* Berkeley, CA: University of California Press.

Flagg, Linda. 2002. "Enough Is Enough: Life Narratives of Women Who Left Abusers." Chicago, IL: DePaul University, Unpublished.

Foucault, Michel. 1965a. *Madness and Civilization: A History of Insanity in the Age of Reason.* New York: Pantheon Books.

Foucault, Michel. 1965b. *Madness and Civilization: A History of Insanity in the Age of Reason.* New York: Vintage.

Foucault, Michel. 1979. *Discipline and Punish: The Birth of the Prison.* (Panopticon). New York: Vintage Books.

Foucault, Michel. 1995. *Discipline and Punish: The Birth of the Prison.* New York: Vintage Books.

Foucault, Michel. 1999. "Space, Power, and Knowledge," in Simon During (ed.), *The Cultural Studies Reader.* London and New York: Routledge, pp. 134–145.

Friedl, Ernestine. 1991. *The Women of Deh Koh: Lives in an Iranian Village.* London: Penguin Group.

Furman, Frida Kerner. 1997. *Facing the Mirror: Older Women and Beauty Shop Culture.* New York and London: Routledge.

Gallmeier, Charles. 1991. "Leaving, Revisiting, and Staying in Touch: Neglected Issues in Field Research," in William Shaffir and Robert Stebbins (eds.), *Experiencing Fieldwork: An Inside View of Qualitative Research.* Newbury Park, London, New Delhi: Sage Publications, pp. 224–231.

Gans, Herbert J. 1962a. *The Urban Villagers: Group and Class in the Life of Italian-Americans.* Glencoe: Free Press.

Gans, Herbert J. 1962b. *The Urban Villagers.* New York: Free Press.

Garfinkel, Harold. 1967. *Studies in Ethnomethodology.* Englewood Cliffs, NJ: Prentice-Hall.

Garner, Roberta. 1966. *Beyond Vocationalism: The Meaning of Post-Secondary Education: A Life-History Analysis.* Chicago, IL: Universitiy of Chicago, PhD dissertation. Unpublished.

Garner, Roberta. 2007. *Social Theory: Continuity and Confrontation,* 2nd ed. Toronto: Broadview/University of Toronto Press.

Garner, Roberta, Judith Bootcheck, Michael Lorr, and Kathryn Rauch. 2006. "The Adolescent Society Revisited: Cultures, Crowds, Climates, and Status Structures in Seven Secondary Schools." *Journal of Youth and Adolescence* 35(6): 1023–1035.

Geertz, Clifford. 1973a. *The Interpretation of Cultures: Selected Essays.* New York: Basic Books.

Geertz, Clifford. 1973b. *The Interpretation of Cultures.* New York: Basic Books.

Geertz, Clifford. 1973c. "Deep Play: Notes on the Balinese Cockfight," in *The Interpretation of Cultures,* pp. 412–453. New York: Basic Books.

Gerbner, George. 2002. *Against the Mainstream: The Selected Works of George Gerbner.* New York: Peter Lang Publishers.

Gerth, H. H. and C. Wright Mills. (eds.) 1946/1965. *From Max Weber.* New York: Oxford University Press.

Gitlin, Todd. 2000. *Inside Prime Time.* Berkeley, CA: University of California Press.

Gladwell, M. 2007. *Blink: The Power of Thinking Without Thinking.* New York: Back Bay Books.

Glaser, Barney and Anselm Strauss. 1967. *The Discovery of Grounded Theory.* Chicago: Aldine.

Glesne, Corrine. 1999. *Becoming Qualitative Researchers: An Introduction.* New York and Don Mills, ON: Longman.

Glesne, Corrine. 2006. *Becoming Qualitative Researchers.* New York: Pearson Allyn and Bacon.

Gmelch, Sharon. 1991. *Nan: The Life of an Irish Traveling Woman.* Prospect Heights, IL: Waveland Press.

Goffman, Erving. 1959. *The Presentation of Self in Everyday Life.* Garden City, NY: Doubleday.

Goffman, Erving. 1961. *Asylums: Essays on the Social Situation of Patients and Other Inmates.* Garden City, NY: Doubleday.

Goffman, Erving. 1963. *Stigma: Notes on the Management of Spoiled Identity.* New York: Simon and Schuster.

Goffman, Erving. 1967. *Interaction Rituals.* New York: Pantheon.

Goffman, Erving. 1986a. *Frame Analysis.* Boston: Northeastern University Press.

Goffman, Erving. 1986b. *Frame Analysis: An Essay on the Organization of Experience.* Boston: Northeast University Press.

Goodwin, Jeff and Theda Skocpol. 1989. "Explaining Revolutions in the Third World." *Politics and Society* 174: 489–509.

Grady, John. 2001. "Becoming a Visual Sociologist." *Sociological Imagination* 38(1/2): 83–119.

Grant, Linda, Max Heirich, Stephen S. Martin, and Ellen Van Eck. 1981. "The Detroit Tour: Experiential Learning within the Framework of a Large Lecture Course." *Teaching Sociology* 9: 15–29.

Hagan, John and Bill McCarthy. 1998. *Mean Streets: Youth Crime and Homelessness.* Cambridge: Cambridge University Press.

Hall, Stuart. 1996. "Cultural Studies and Its Theoretical Legacies," in Simon During (ed.), *The Cultural Studies Reader.* London and New York: Routledge, pp. 262–275.

Hall, Stuart. 1999a. "Encoding, Decoding," in Simon During (ed.), *The Cultural Studies Reader.* London and New York: Routledge, pp. 507–517.

Hall, Stuart. 1999b. "Cultural Studies and Its Theoretical Legacies," in Simon During (ed.), *The Cultural Studies Reader.* London and New York: Routledge, pp. 97–109.

Hall, Stuart. 2001. "Encoding/Decoding," in Simon During (ed.), *The Cultural Studies Reader.* London and New York: Routledge, pp. 166–176.

Hammersley, M. and P. Atkinson. 1995. *Ethnography: Principles in Practice.* London: Routledge.

Hancock, Black Hawk. 2005. "Steppin' Out of Whiteness." *Ethnography* 6(4): 481–515.

Hancock, Black Hawk. 2007. "Learning How to Make Life Swing." *Qualitative Sociology* 30: 113–133.

Hancock, Black Hawk and Roberta Garner. 2009. *Changing Theories: New Directions in Sociology.* Toronto: University of Toronto Press.

Haney, C., W.C. Banks, and Philip G. Zimbardo. 1973. "Interpersonal Dynamics in a Simulated Prison." *International Journal of Criminology and Penology* 7: 69–97.

Harper, Douglas. 1992. *Working Knowledge: Skill and Community in a Small Shop.* Berkeley, CA: University of California Press.

Harper, Douglas. 2000. "Reimaging Visual Methods: Galileo to Neuroromancer," in N. K. Denzin and Y. S. Lincoln (eds.), *Handbook of Qualitative Research,* 2nd ed. Thousand Oaks, CA: Sage Publications, pp. 717–732.

Harper, Krista. 2010. "Across the Bridge: Using PhotoVoice to Investigate Environment and Health in a Hungarian Romani (Gypsy) Community." *European Association of Social Anthropologists (EASA).* Available at http://works.bepress.com/krista_harper/15.

Harvey, David. 1989. "From Managerialism to Entrepreneurialism: The Transformation Urban Governance in Late Capitalism." *Geografiska Annaler B* 71: 3–17.

Harwood, Don. 1975. *Video as a Second Language: How to Make a Video Documentary.* Bayside, NY: VTR Pub. Co.

Haubrich, Paul. 1993. "Student Life in Milwaukee High Schools, 1920–1985," in John Rury (ed.), *Seeds of Crisis: Public Schooling in Milwaukee Since 1920.* Madison: University of Wisconsin Press.

Hebdige, Dick. 1981/1991. *Subculture: The Meaning of Style.* London: Routledge.

Hironimus-Wendt, Robert J. and Larry Lovell-Troy. 1999. "Grounded Service Learning in Social Theory." *Teaching Sociology* 27 (October): 360–372.

Ho, Karen. 2009. *Liquidated: An Ethnography of Wall Street.* Durham and London: Duke University Press.

Hobbs, Dick and Richard Wright (eds.) 2006. *The SAGE Handbook of Fieldwork.* London: Sage Publications.

Hobsbawm, Eric and Terry Ranger (eds.). 1992. *The Invention of Tradition.* Cambridge, UK and New York: Cambridge University Press.

Hollingshead, August de Belmont. 1975. *Elmtown's Youth and Elmtown Revisited.* New York: John Wiley.

Hondagneu-Sotelo, Pierrette and Sally Raskoff. 1994. "Community Service-Learning: Promises and Problems." *Teaching Sociology* 22: 248–254.

Horowitz, Ruth. 1983. *Honor and the American Dream: Culture and Identity in a Chicano Community.* New Brunswick, NJ: Rutgers University Press.

Horowitz, Ruth. 1985. *Honor and the American Dream.* New Brunswick, NJ: Rutgers University Press.

Horowitz, Ruth. 1986. "Remaining an Outsider: Membership as a Threat to Research Rapport." *Urban Life* 14: 409–430.

Hughes, Everett Cherrington. 1984a. *The Sociological Eye: Selected Papers.* New Brunswick, NJ: Transaction Publishers.

Hughes, Everett Cherrington. 1984b. *The Sociological Eye.* New Brunswick, NJ: Transaction Publishers.

Humphreys, Laud. 1970. *Tearoom Trade: Impersonal Sex in Public Places.* Chicago: Aldine.

Jacobs, Jane. 1961/1993. *The Death and Life of Great American Cities.* New York: Random House.

Jameson, Fredric. 1991. *Postmodernism or the Cultural Logic of Late Capitalism.* Durham, NC: Duke University Press.

Jay, Martin. 1996. *The Dialectical Imagination: A History of the Frankfurt School and the Institute of Social Research 1923–1950.* Berkeley, CA: University of California Press.

Jesus, Carolina Maria de and David St. Clair. 2003. *Child of the Dark: The Diary of Carolina Maria de Jesus.* New York: New American Library.

Johnson, Dale D. and Bonnie Johnson. 2006. *High Stakes: Poverty, Testing, and Failure in American Schools.* Lanham, MD: Rowman & Littlefield Publishers.

Jones, James. H. 1993. *Bad Blood: The Tuskegee Syphilis Experiment.* New York: The Free Press.

Jung-Beeman, Mark, Edward M. Bowden, Jason Haberman, Jennifer L. Frymiare, Stella Arambel-Liu, Richard Greenblatt, Paul J. Reber, and John Kounios. 2004. "Neural Activity When People Solve Verbal Problems with Insight." *PLoS Biology* 2(4): 0500–0510.

Junker, Buford H. 1960. *Field Work: An Introduction to the Social Sciences.* Introduction by Everett C. Hughes. Chicago and London: University of Chicago Press.

Katz, Jack. 1988. *Seductions of Crime: Moral and Sensual Attractions in Doing Evil.* New York: Basic Books.

Katz, Jack. 1990. *The Seductions of Crime.* New York: Basic Books.

Keiser, R. Lincoln. 1969. *Vice Lords: Warriors of the Streets.* New York: Holt, Rinehart, and Winston.

Kenworthy, Lane and Alexander Hicks. 2008. *Method and Substance in Macrocomparative Analysis.* Houndsmill, UK and New York: Palgrave Macmillan.

Khurana, Rakesh. 2002. *Searching for a Corporate Savior: The Irrational Quest for Charismatic CEOs.* Princeton, NJ: Princeton University Press.

Kinsey, Alfred. 1948/1998. *Sexual Behavior in the Human Male.* 1st ed. Bloomington, IN: Indiana University Press.

Klinenberg, Eric. 2002. *Heat Wave: A Social Autopsy of Disaster in Chicago.* Chicago and London: University of Chicago Press.

Kozol, Jonathan. 1992. *Savage Inequalities: Children in America's Schools.* New York: HarperPerennial.

Krzyzanowski, Michal. 2008. "Analyzing Focus Group Discussions," in Ruth Wodak and Michal Krzyanowski (eds.), *Qualitative Discourse Analysis in the Social Sciences.* Houndsmill, UK and New York: Palgrave Macmillan, pp. 162–181.

Kuhn, Thomas. 1962. *Structure of Scientific Revolutions.* Chicago, IL: University of Chicago Press.

Ladányi, J. and I. Szelényi. 2006. *Patterns of Exclusion: Constructing Gypsy Ethnicity and the Making of an Underclass in Transitional Societies of Europe.* East European Monographs. New York: Columbia University Press.

Laing, R.D. 1966. *The Divided Self: An Existential Study in Sanity and Madness.* Baltimore, MD: Penguin Books.

Laing, R.D. 1970. *The Divided Self.* New York: Pantheon Books.

Laumann, Edward O. 2004. *The Sexual Organization of the City.* Chicago, IL: University of Chicago Press.

Lauren Rivera. 2010. "Status Distinctions in Interaction: Social Selection and Exclusion at an Elite Nightclub." *Qualitative Sociology* 33(3): 229–255.

Lemert, Edwin. 1951. *Social Pathology.* New York: McGraw Hill.

Le Wita, Beatrix. 1994. *French Bourgeois Culture.* Translated by J.A. Underwood. Cambridge, UK: Cambridge University Press.

Lewins, Ann and Christina Silver. 2007. *Using Software in Qualitative Research: A Step-by-Step Guide.* London: Sage Publications.

Lewis, Oscar. 1961. *The Children of Sanchez Autobiography of a Mexican Family.* New York: Vintage Books.

Lewis, Oscar. 1963. *Children of Sanchez.* New York: Vintage.

La Vida. (1965/66). Cuban Revs; Children of Sanchez. New York: Random House.

Lewis, Oscar, Ruth Lewis, and Susan Rigdon. 1977. *Four Women: Living the Revolution.* Urbana: University of Illinois Press.

Lieberson, Stanley. 1991. "Small N's and Big Conclusions: An Examination of the Reasoning in Comparative Studies Based on a Small Number of Cases." *Social Forces* 70(2): 307–320.

Liebow, Elliott. 1967. *Tally's Corner: A Study of Negro Streetcorner Men.* Boston: Little, Brown.

Lindesmith, Alfred and Anselm L. Strauss. 1956. *Social Psychology*, 2nd ed. New York: Henry Holt.

Lindesmith, Alfred Ray and Anselm L. Strauss. 1958. *Social Psychology*. New York: Holt Rinehart & Winston.

Lindemann, Danielle. 2012. *Dominatrix: Gender, Eroticism, and Control in the Dungeon*. Chicago, IL: University of Chicago Press.

Lofland, John, Lyn Lofland, Leon Anderson, and David Snow. 2005. *Analyzing Social Settings: A Guide to Qualitative Observation and Analysis*. Belmont, CA: Wadsworth.

Lofland, Lyn. 1973. *A World of Strangers: Order and Action in Urban Public Space*. New York: Waveland Press, Inc.

Logan, John R. (2006). "The Impact of Katrina: Race and Class in Storm-damaged Neighborhoods." Providence, RI: Brown University, www.s4.brown.edu/Katrina/report-pdf. Retrieved August 23, 2010.

Lynd, Robert Staughton and Helen Merrell Lynd. 1930/1959. *Middletown: A Study in Modern American Culture*. New York: Harcourt Brace Jovanovich.

Lynd, Robert Staughton and Helen Merrell Lynd. 1956. *Middletown: A Study in American Culture*. New York: Harvest Books.

Lynd, Robert Staughton and Helen Merrell Lynd. 1965. *Middletown in Transition: A Study in Cultural Conflicts*. New York: Harcourt, Brace, World.

MacLeod, Jay. 1987. *Ain't No Makin' It: Leveled Aspirations in a Low-Income Neighborhood*. Boulder, CO: Westview Press.

Mailer, Norman. 1968. *The Armies of the Night: History as a Novel, the Novel as History*. New York: Signet/New American Library.

Mailer, Norman. 1995. *The Armies of the Night*. New York: Plume.

Malinowski, Bronislaw. 1922a. *Argonauts of the Western Pacific*. London: George Routledge and Kegan Paul.

Malinowski, Bronislaw. 1922b. *Argonauts of the Western Pacific: An Account of Native Enterprise and Adventure in the Archipelagoes of Melanesian New Guinea*. London and New York: G. Routledge & Sons; E.P. Dutton & Co.

Malinowski, Bronislaw. 1935/1965. *Coral Gardens and Their Magic*. Bloomington, IN: University of Indiana Press.

Malinowski, Bronislaw. 1967. *A Diary in the Strict Sense of the Term*. New York: Harcourt, Brace & World.

Mann, Floyd. 1970. "Human Relations Skills in Social Research," in William J. Filstead (ed.), *Qualitative Methodology: Firsthand Involvement with the Social World*. Chicago: Markham Publishing Company, pp. 119–132.

Marcus, George, with Peter Dobkin Hall. 1992. *Lives in Trust: The Fortunes of Dynastic Families in Late Twentieth-Century America*. Boulder, CO: Westview Press.

Mariampolski, H. 1999. "The Power of Ethnography." *Market Research Society* 41: 75–86.

Mason-Schrock, Douglas. 1996. "Transsexuals' Narrative Construction of the 'True Self.'" *Social Psychological Quarterly* 59(3): 176–192.

Mattley, Christine. 2002. "Voicing Gender: The Performance of Gender in the Context of Phone Sex Lines," in Patricia Gagne and Richard Tewskbury (eds.), *Gendered Sexualities: Advances in Gender Research*, Vol. 6. London: JAI/Elsevier Science Ltd., pp. 79–102.

Mayo, Larry. 1991. "Chamorros: An Ethnic Minority?" in Mario Zamoras and Bjorn Erring (eds.), *Fieldwork in Cultural Anthropology*. New Delhi: Reliance Publishing House, pp. 111–121.

Maysles, Albert. 2007. *A Maysles Scrapbook: Photographs/Cinemagraphs/Documents*. New York and Gottingen, Germany: Steven Kasher Gallery and Steidl Publishers.

McRobbie, Angela. 1999. "The Place of Walter Benjamin in Cultural Studies," in Simon During (ed.), *The Cultural Studies Reader*. London and New York: Routledge, pp. 77–96.

Mead, Margaret. 1935/2001. *Sex and Temperament in Three Primitive Societies*. New York: Harper Perennial.

Menchú, Rigoberta. 1984a. *I, Rigoberta Menchu: An Indian Woman in Guatemala*. London: Verso.

Menchú, Rigoberta. 1984b. *I, Rigoberta Menchú: An Indian Woman in Guatemala*. Edited and Introduced by Elisabeth Burgos-Debray. London: Verso.

Merton, Robert K. 1949/1968. *Social Theory and Social Structure*, Enlarged ed. New York: The Free Press.

Michael, Robert, John H. Gagnon, Edward Laumann, and Gina Kolata. 1994. *Sex in America*. Boston, MA: Little, Brown, and Company.

Milgram, Stanley. 1963. "Behavioral Study of Obedience." *Journal of Abnormal and Social Psychology* 67: 371–378.

Miller, Jody. 2009. "The Status of Qualitative Research in Criminology." http://www.wjh.harvard.edu/nsfqual/Miller%20Paper.pdf. Retrieved September 25, 2009.

Mills, C. Wright. 1940. "Situated Actions and Vocabularies of Motives." *American Sociological Review* 5(6): 904–913.

Mills, C. Wright. 1959. *The Sociological Imagination*. Oxford, NY: Oxford University Press.

Mintz, Sidney Wilfred. 1960. *Worker in the Cane: A Puerto Rican Life History*. New Haven: Yale University Press.

Moerman, Michael. 1969. "A Little Knowledge," in S. A. Tyler (ed.), *Cognitive Anthropology*. New York: Holt, Rinehart & Winston, pp. 449–469.

Morgan, David L. 1997. *Focus Groups as Qualitative Research*, 2nd ed. Thousand Oaks, CA: Sage Publications.

Morris, Meaghan. 1999. "Things to Do with Shopping Centres," in S. During (ed.), *The Cultural Studies Reader*. Oxford: Oxford University Press, pp. 391–409.

Mulhall, A. 1993. *Farewell House, Farewell Home. An Ethnography of a Residential Home for the Elderly*. London: Brunel University, MSc Thesis, unpublished.

Muntaner, C. and M.B. Gomez. 2003. "Qualitative and Quantitative Research in Social Epidemiology: Is Complementarity the Only Issue?" *Gac Sanit* 17: 53–57.

Newbold Chinas, Beverly. 1993. *La Zandunga: Of Fieldwork and Friendship in Southern Mexico*. Prospect Heights, IL: Waveland Press.

Newman, Katherine S. 1999. *No Shame in My Game: The Working Poor in the Inner City*. New York: Knopf and the Russell Sage Foundation.

Newman, Katherine S. 2000. *No Shame in My Game: The Working Poor in the Inner City*, 3rd ed. New York: Vintage.

Norman K. Denzin. 1989. *The Research Act: A Theoretical Introduction to Sociological Methods*. Englewood Cliffs, NJ: Prentice Hall.

O'Neil, Robert M. 1996. "A Researcher's Privilege: Does Any Hope Remain?" in Joe Cecil and Gerald T. Wetherington (eds.), *Court-Ordered Disclosures of Academic Research: A Clash of Values of Science and Law*. Vol. 59 of *Law and Contemporary Problems*, Summer 1996, pp. 35–51.

Orsi, Robert A. 1998. *Thank You, St. Jude: Women's Devotion to the Patron Saint of Hopeless Causes*. New Haven, CT: Yale University Press.

Orsi, Robert A. 1999. *Thank You, St. Jude: Women's Devotion to the Patron Saint of Hopeless Causes*. New Haven and London: Yale University Press.

Padilla, Felix M. 1992. *The Gang as an American Enterprise*. New Brunswick, NJ: Rutgers University Press.

Pan, M. Ling. 2008. *Preparing Literature Reviews: Qualitative and Quantitative Approaches*. Glendale, CA: Pyrczak Publishing.

Park, Robert, Ernest W. Burgess and Roderick D. McKenzie. 1925. *The City*. Chicago, IL: University of Chicago Press.

Pattillo, Mary E. 1999. *Black Picket Fences: Privilege and Peril among the Black Middle Class*. Chicago, IL: University of Chicago Press.

Pattillo, Mary E. 2007. *Black on the Block: The Politics of Race and Class in the City*. Chicago, IL: University of Chicago Press.

Pattillo, Mary E. 2008. *Black on the Block*. Chicago, IL: University of Chicago Press.

Patton, Michael Quinn. 2002. *Qualitative research and evaluation methods*. Thousand Oaks, CA, London, New Delhi: Sage Publications.

Pauwels, Luc. 2002. "The Video- and Multimedia-article as a Mode of Scholarly Communication: Toward Scientifically Informed Expression and Aesthetics." *Visual Studies* 17: 2.

Payne, Monique. 2008. "Does Moving on Mean Moving Up? Exploring the Relationship between Residential Mobility and Academic Attainment." *Annual Meetings of the American Sociological Association*, Boston, MA, July 31, http://www.allacademic.com/meta/p241219_index.html.

Peirce, Charles Sanders, Nathan Houser, and Christian J.W. Kloesel. 1998. *The Essential Peirce: Selected Philosophical Writings, 1893–1913*. Bloomington, IN: Indiana University Press.

Perrow, Charles. 1999. *Normal Accidents: Living with High-risk Technologies*. Princeton, NJ: Princeton University Press.

Polakow, Valerie. 1993. *Lives on the Edge: Single Mothers and Their Children in the Other America*. Chicago, IL: University of Chicago Press.

Polsky, Ned. 1969. "Research Method, Morality, and Criminology," in *Hustlers, Beats, and Others*. New York: Doubleday and Company, Anchor Books edition, pp. 109–143.

Poniatowska, Elena. 1995. *Nothing, Nobody: The Voices of the Mexico City Earthquake*. Philadelphia, PA: Temple University Press.

Popper, Karl. 1963a. *Conjectures and Refutations*. London: Routledge and Keagan Paul, pp. 33–39; from Theodore Schick (ed.), *Readings in the Philosophy of Science*. Mountain View, CA: Mayfield Publishing Company, 2000, pp. 9–13.

Popper, Karl. 1963b. *Conjectures and Refutations*. London: Routledge and Kegan Paul.

Powdermaker, Hortense. 1966. *Stranger and Friend: The Way of an Anthropologist*. New York: W. W. Norton.

Pozas, Ricardo. 1962. *Juan the Chamula: An Ethnological Re-creation of the Life of a Mexican Indian*. Berkeley, CA: University of California Press.

Pretzlik, U. 1994. "Observational Methods and Strategies." *Nurse Researcher* 2: 13–21.

Przeworski, Adam. 1991. *Democracy and the Market: Political and Economic Reforms in Eastern Europe and Latin America*. Cambridge and New York: Cambridge University Press.

Radway, Janice. 1999. "The Institutional Matrix of Romance," in Simon During (ed.), *The Cultural Studies Reader.* London and New York: Routledge, pp. 564–576.

Ragin, Charles C. 1987. *The Comparative Method: Moving beyond Qualitative and Quantitative Strategies.* Berkeley, CA: University of California Press.

Ragin, Charles C. 1994. *Constructing Social Research: The Unity and Diversity of Method.* Thousand Oaks, CA: Pine Forge Press.

Ragin, Charles C. 2000. *Fuzzy-Set Social Science.* Chicago: University of Chicago Press.

Reardon, Kenneth M. 1994. "Undergraduate Research in Distressed Urban Communities: An Undervalued Form of Service-Learning." *Michigan Journal of Community Service Learning* 1(1): 44–54.

Reich, Robert B. 1991. *The Work of Nations: Preparing Ourselves for 21st-century Capitalism.* New York: Alfred A. Knopf.

Reinharz, Shulamith. 1992. *Feminist Methods in Social Research.* New York: Oxford University Press.

Riesebrodt, Martin. 1998. *Pious Passion: The Emergence of Modern Fundamentalism in the United States and Iran.* Berkeley, CA: University of California Press.

Riesman, David. 1956. "Introduction," in John Seeley, R. Alexander Sims, and Elizabeth Loosley (eds.), *Crestwood Heights.* New York: Basic Books.

Riis, Jacob. 1890. *How the Other Half Lives. Studies Among the Tenements of New York.* New York: Charles Scribner's Sons.

Ritzer, George. 1996. *The McDonaldization of Society.* Thousand Oaks, CA: Pine Forge Press.

Ritzer, George. 2000. *The McDonaldization of Society.* Thousand Oaks, CA and London: Pine Forge.

Roberts, Kenneth M. 1998. *Deepening Democracy: The Modern Left and Social Movements in Chile and Peru.* Stanford, CA: Stanford University Press.

Roberts, Kenneth M. 1999. *Deepening Democracy: The Modern Left and Social Movements in Chile and Peru.* Stanford, CA: Stanford University Press.

Robinson, William S. 1950. "Ecological Correlations and the Behavior of Individuals". *American Sociological Review* 15(3): 351–357.

Roman, Nicole. 2009. "Observation of Family Gender-role Negotiation." Senior Research Project, DePaul University.

Rosaldo, Renato. 2004. "Grief and a headhunter's rage". In McGee, Jon R. and Richard L. Warms (editors), *Anthropological Theory: An introductory history.* 3rd ed. New York: McGraw-Hill, pp. 579–593.

Rouch, Jean and Steven Feld. 2003. *Cine-Ethnography: Visible Evidence, First edition.* Minneapolis, MN: University of Minnesota Press.

Rubin, Lillian B. 1976. *Worlds of Pain: Life in the Working-class Family.* New York: Basic Books.

Ruby, Jay. 1975. "Is an Ethnographic Film a Filmic Ethnography?" *Studies in the Anthropology of Visual Communications* 2(2): 104–111.

Ruby, Jay. 2006. *Oak Park Stories.* CD-ROM and DVD Series. Watertown, MA: Documentary Educational Resources.

Sánchez-Jankowski, Martín. 1990. *Islands in the Street: Gangs in American Urban Society.* Berkeley, CA: University of California Press.

Sánchez-Jankowski, Martín. 1991. *Islands in the Street: Gangs and American Urban Society.* Berkeley, CA: University of California Press.

Sandelowski, M. 1986. "The Problem of Rigor in Qualitative Research." *Advances in Nursing Science* 8: 27–37.

Sartre, Jean-Paul. 1993. *The Family Idiot: Gustave Flaubert 1821–1857.* Translated by Carol Cosman. Chicago, IL: University of Chicago Press.

Scarce, Rik. 1994. "(No) Trial (But) Tribulation: When Courts and Ethnography Conflict." *Journal of Contemporary Ethnography* 23: 123–149.

Scarce, Rik. 1997. "Field Trips as Short-term Experiential Education." *Teaching Sociology* 25: 219–226.

Scarce, Rik. 2005. *Contempt of Court: A Scholar's Battle for Free Speech from Behind Bars.* Lanham, MD and Walnut Creek, CA: AltaMira Press.

Schachtel, Ernest G. 1959. *Metamorphosis: On the Development of Affect, Perception, Attention, and Memory.* New York: Basic Books.

Schatzman, Leonard and Anselm L. Strauss. 1973. *Field Research: Strategies for a Natural Sociology.* Englewood Cliffs, NJ: Prentice-Hall.

Scheper-Hughes, Nancy. 1992. *Death Without Weeping: The Violence of Everyday Life in Brazil.* Berkeley, CA: University of California Press.

Scheper-Hughes, Nancy. 2001. *Saints, Scholars, and Schizophrenics: Mental Illness in Rural Ireland.* Berkeley, CA: University of California Press.

Schor, Juliet. 1998. *The Overspent American: Upscaling, Downshifting, and the New Consumer.* New York: Basic Books.

Schudson, Michael. 1978. *Discovering the News: A Social History of American Newspapers.* New York: Basic Books.

Schudson, Michael. 1981. *Discovering the News: A Social History of American Newspapers.* New York: Basic Books.

Schudson, Michael. 1986. *Advertising, the Uneasy Persuasion: Its Dubious Impact on American Society.* New York: Basic Books.

Schwalbe, Michael. 2004. *The Sociologically Examined Life: Pieces of the Conversation*, 3rd ed. New York: McGraw-Hill.

Scott, Greg. 2004. "It's a Sucker's Outfit: How Urban Gangs Enable and Impede the Reintegration of Ex-Convicts." *Ethnography* 5(1): 107–140.

Scott, Greg. 2008. "They Got Their Program, and I Got Mine": A Cautionary Tale Concerning the Ethical Implications of Using Respondent-Driven Sampling to Study Injection Drug Users." *The International Journal on Drug Policy* 19(1): 42–51.

Scott, Greg. 2011. "Getting Off Right . . . and Left . . . and Sideways: Drug Injections in the Real World, the Persistence of Hepatitis C, and the Failure of 'Total Hygiene' Interventions." *Harm Reduction Communication* 16: 3–10.

Scott, Gregory S. 1998. *Sewing with Dignity: Class Struggle and Ethnic Conflict in the Los Angeles Garment Industry.* University of California, Santa Barbara. *ProQuest Dissertations and Theses*, http:// search. proquest.com/docview/304417055?accountid=10477.

Scott, James C. 1987. *Weapons of the Weak: Everyday Forms of Peasant Resistance.* New Haven, CT: Yale University Press.

Seidman, Irving. 1998. *Interviewing as Qualitative Research: A Guide for Researchers in Education and the Social Sciences*, 2nd ed. New York: Teachers College Press.

Shadish, W.R. 1995. "The Logic of Generalization: Five Principles Common to Experiments and Ethnographies." *American Journal of Community Psychology* 23: 419–428.

Shaffir, William and Robert A. Stebbins. 1991. *Experiencing Fieldwork: An Inside View of Qualitative Research.* Newbury Park, London, New Delhi: Sage Publications.

Shaw, Clifford. 1930/1966. *The Jack Roller: A Delinquent Boy's Own Story.* Chicago, IL: University of Chicago Press.

Shrum, Wesley, Ricardo Duque, and Timothy Brown. 2005. "Digital Video as Research Practice: Methodology for the Millennium." *Journal of Research Practice* 1(1), Article M4.

Silbey, Susan S. 2004. "Designing Qualitative Research Projects." *Workshop on Scientific Foundations of Qualitative Research*, July 11–12, 2003. Arlington, VA: National Science Foundation.

Simmons, Leo. 1963. *Sun Chief: The Autobiography of a Hopi Indian.* New Haven, CT: Yale University Press.

Singer, Merrill, Tom Stopka, Cara Siano, Kristen Springer, George Barton, Kaveh Khoshnood, April Gorry de Puga, and Robert Heimer. 2000. "The Social Geography of AIDS and Hepatitis Risk: Qualitative Approaches for Assessing Local Differences in Sterile-Syringe Access Among Injection Drug Users." *American Journal of Public Health* 90: 8.

Skocpol, Theda. 1979. *States and Social Revolutions: A Comparative Analysis of France, Russia, and China.* Cambridge and New York: Cambridge University Press.

Small, Mario Luis. 2009. " 'How Many Cases Do I Need?': On Science and the Logic of Case Selection in Field-based Research." *Ethnography* 10(5): 5–38.

Smith, Dorothy E. 1990. *The Conceptual Practices of Power: A Feminist Sociology of Knowledge.* Lebanon, NH: University Press of New England.

Smith, Dorothy E. 1992. "Sociology from Women's Perspective: A Reaffirmation." *Sociological Theory* 10: 88–97.

Snow, David A. and Leon Anderson. 1993. *Down on Their Luck: A Study of Homeless Street People.* Berkeley, CA: University of California Press.

Sorkin, M. 1992. *See You in Disneyland.* Cambridge, MA: MIT Press.

Spradley, James P. 1979. *The Ethnographic Interview.* New York: Holt, Rinehart and Winston.

Spradley, James P. 1980. *Participant Observation.* New York: Holt, Rinehart and Winston.

Stack, Carol B. 1974. *All Our Kin: Strategies for Survival in a Black Community.* New York: Harper & Row.

Stake, R.E. and D.J. Trumbull. 1982. "Naturalistic Generalizations." *Review Journal of Philosophy and Social Science* 7: 1–12.

Stallybrass, Peter and Allon White. 1999. "Bourgeois Hysteria and the Carnivalesque," in Simon During (ed.), *The Cultural Studies Reader.* London and New York: Routledge, pp. 382–388.

Stasz, Clarice. 1979. "The Early History of Visual Sociology," in Jon Wagner (ed.), *Images of Information: Still Photography in the Social Sciences.* Beverly Hills, CA: Sage Publications, pp. 119–136.

Stocking, G.W. 1992. *The Ethnographer's Magic and Other Essays in the History of Anthropology.* Madison, WI: University of Wisconsin Press.

Stoecker, Randy. 2005. *Research Methods for Community Change.* Thousand Oaks, CA, London, New Delhi: Sage Publications.

Strauss, Anselm L. 1987. *Qualitative Analysis for Social Scientists.* Cambridge: Cambridge University Press.

Strauss, Anselm L. and J.M. Corbin. 1990. *Basics of Qualitative Research: Techniques and Procedures for Developing Grounded Theory*, 2nd ed. Thousand Oaks, CA: Sage Publications.

Strauss, Anselm L. and J.M. Corbin. 1998. *Basics of Qualitative Research: Techniques and Procedures for Developing Grounded Theory.* Thousand Oaks, CA: Sage Publications.

Strodtbeck, Fred L. 1951. "Husband-Wife Interaction Over Revealed Differences." *American Sociological Review* 16(4): 468–473.

Sullivan, Mercer L. 1998. "Integrating Qualitative and Quantitative Methods in the Study of Developmental Psychopathology in Context." *Development and Psychopathology* 10: 17.

Szelenyi, Ivan and Janos Ladanyi. 2006. *Patterns of Exclusion: Constructing Gypsy Ethnicity and the Making of an Underclass in Transitional Societies of Europe.* Boulder, CO: East European Monographs.

Talayesva, Don C. and Leo W. Simmons. 1963. *Sun Chief. The Autobiography of a Hopi Indian.* New Haven, CT and London.

Tannenbaum, F. (1938). *Crime and the Community.* Boston: Ginn and Co.

Taylor, Steven J. 1991. "Leaving the Field: Research, Relationships, and Responsibilities," in Shaffir, William and Robert Stebbins (eds.), *Experiencing Fieldwork: An Inside View of Qualitative Research.* Newbury Park, London, New Delhi: Sage Publications, pp. 238–247.

Tilly, Charles, Louise Tilly, and Richard Tilly. 1975. *The Rebellious Century: 1830–1930.* Cambridge, MA: Harvard University Press.

Tufte, Edward. 1997. *Visual and Statistical Thinking: Displays of Evidence for Making Decisions.* Cheshire, CT: Graphics Press.

Van Maanen, J. 1988. *Tales of the Field: On Writing Ethnography.* Chicago, IL: University of Chicago Press.

Vaughan, Diane. 1990. *Uncoupling: Turning Points in Intimate Relationships.* New York: Vintage.

Vaughan, Diane. 1996. *The Challenger Launch Decision: Risky Technology, Culture, and Deviance at NASA.* Chicago, IL: University of Chicago Press.

Venkatesh, Sudhir Alladi. 1997. "The Three-Tier Model: How Helping Occurs in Urban, Poor Communities." *Social Service Review* 71(4): 574–606.

Venkatesh, Sudhir. 2002. *American Project: The Rise and Fall of a Modern Ghetto.* Cambridge, MA: Harvard University Press.

Venkatesh, Sudhir. 2004. "A Note on Science and Qualitative Research." *Workshop on Scientific Foundations of Qualitative Research*, July 11–12, 2003. Arlington, VA: National Science Foundation.

Venkatesh, Sudhir. 2006. *Off the Books: The Underground Economy of the Urban Poor.* Cambridge, MA: Harvard University Press.

Vidich, Arthur J. and J. Bensman. 1968. *Small Town in Mass Society.* Rev. ed. Princeton, NJ: Princeton University Press.

Vidich, Arthur J. and J. Bensman. 1969. *Small Town in Mass Society.* Princeton, NJ: Princeton University Press.

Wacquant, L.J.D. 2004. *Body & Soul: Notebooks of an Apprentice Boxer.* Oxford: Oxford University Press.

Wacquant, Loïc. 2002a. "Scrutinizing the Street: Poverty, Morality, and the Pitfalls of Urban Ethnography." *American Journal of Sociology* 107: 1468–1532.

Wacquant, Loïc. 2002b. "The Curious Eclipse of Prison Ethnography in the Age of Mass Incarceration." *Ethnography* 3(4): 371–397.

Wacquant, Loïc. 2009. "The Body, the Ghetto, and the Penal State." *Qualitative Sociology*, 32(1): 101–129.

Waddington, D. 1994. "Participant Observation," in C. Cassell and G. Symon (eds.), *Qualitative Methods in Organizational Research: A Practical Guide.* London: Sage Publications, pp. 107–122.

Warner, Lloyd, J.O. Low, Paul Lunt, and Leo Srole. 1963. *The Yankee City Series.* New Haven, CT: Yale University Press.

Warner, W. Lloyd. 1963. *Yankee City.* New Haven, CT: Yale University Press.

Warren, Carol and Tracy Xavia Karner. 2005. *Discovering Qualitative Methods: Field Research, Interviews, and Analysis.* Los Angeles, CA: Roxbury Press.

Warren, Carol and Tracy Xavia Karner. 2010. *Discovering Qualitative Methods.* New York: Oxford University Press.

Waterman, H. 1998. "Embracing Ambiguities and Valuing Ourselves: Issues of Validity in Action Research." *Advances in Nursing Science* 28: 101–105.

Weber, Max. 1958. "Science as a Vocation." In H.H. Gerth and C. Wright Mills, *From Max Weber: Essays in Sociology.* New York: Oxford University Press, pp. 129–156.

Weber, Max. 1968. *Economy and Society: An Outline of Interpretive Sociology.* New York: Bedminster Press.

Weiss, Robert S. 1994. *Learning from Strangers: The Art and Method of Qualitative Interview Studies.* New York: Free Press.

Wendt, Paul R. 1962. "The Language of Pictures," in S.I. Hayakawa (ed.), *The Use and Misuse of Language.* Greenwich, CN: Fawcett, pp. 175–193.

Whyte, William Foote. 1943/1993. *Street Corner Society: The Social Structure of an Italian Slum.* Chicago: University of Chicago Press.

Whyte, William Foote. 1982. "Social Inventions for Solving Human Problems." *American Sociological Review* 47(1): 1–13.

Whyte, William Foote. 1989. "Advancing Scientific Knowledge Through Participatory Action Research." *Sociological Forum* 4(3): 367–385.

Widick, Richard. 2003. "Flesh and the Free Market: (On taking Bourdieu to the options exchange)." *Theory and Society* 32: 679–723.

Williams, Raymond. 1999. "Advertising: The Magic System," in Simon During (ed.), *The Cultural Studies Reader.* London and New York: Routledge, pp. 410–423.

Willis, Paul E. 1979. *Learning to Labor: How Working Class Kids Get Working Class Jobs.* New York: Columbia University Press.

Willis, Paul E. 1981. *Learning to Labor: How Working Class Kids Get Working Class Jobs.* New York: Columbia University Press.

Willis, Paul E. 2000. *The Ethnographic Imagination.* Malden, MA: Polity Press.

Wilson, Robin. 2003. "Penn Anthropologist Fights Subpoenas for Field Notes in Medical Case." *Chronical of Higher Education*, March 21.

Wodak, Ruth and Michal Krzyzanowski. 2008. *Qualitative Discourse Analysis in the Social Sciences.* Houndsmill, UK and New York: Palgrave Macmillan.

Wolf, Daniel. 1991a. *The Rebels: A Brotherhood of Outlaw Bikers.* Toronto, ON: University of Toronto Press.

Wolf, Daniel. 1991b. "High Risk Methodology: Reflections on Leaving an Outlaw Society," in Shaffir, William, and Robert Stebbins (eds.), *Experiencing Fieldwork: An Inside View of Qualitative Research.* Newbury Park, London, New Delhi: Sage Publications, pp. 211–223.

Wolf, Eric. 1999. *Peasant Wars of the Twentieth Century.* Norman, OK: University of Oklahoma Press.

Worth, Sol and John Adair. 1970. "Navajo Filmmakers." *American Anthropologist* 72(1): 9–34.

Wright, Mary. 2000. "Getting More out of Less: The Benefits of Short-Term Experiential Learning in Undergraduate Sociology Courses." *Teaching Sociology* 28: 116–126.

Zeitlin, Irving. 1997. *Ideology and the Development of Sociological Theory*, 6th ed. Upper Saddle River, NJ: Prentice Hall.

Zorbaugh, Harvey. 1929/1976. *The Gold Coast and the Slum.* Chicago, IL: University of Chicago Press.

# INDEX

NOTE—Locators followed by n. refer notes.

## A

Abductive logic, 119, 207
Abstract, 379, 380
Abu Ghraib prison in Iraq, 136, 148
Academic World News Database, 177
Acceptable risk, 103, 105
Accidents
  Bhopal, chemical leak, 136
  BP explosion and leak in the Gulf of Mexico, 136
  Chernobyl, nuclear power plant accident, 136
  recall of downer cattle, Feb. 2008, 136
  *Titanic*, sinking of, 136
Accidents in high-risk systems, 135
Accomplished noninteraction, 32–33
Action, 216
Action and interaction, 26
Active listening, 294–295
Activism, 149, 152
Activism: from spokesperson to CBPR
  limited access to power, 81
  overview, 81
  struggling communities, assist, 82
  vocalizing for others, 81–82
Actuality differential, 62, 63
Adler, Martina, 319
Adversarial system, 33
Adverse events, 134, 135–136
Advertising, 170
*Advertising: The Uneasy Persuasion* (Schudson), 170
Advocacy, 152, 344
Advocacy groups, 82
Advocacy research, 149
AFDC ("welfare"), 78
Affective, 53
Africa, 18, 72, 181
African American
  Lower Ninth Ward, 143
  sympathetic ear, the, 285
  using qualitative data to contextualize quantitative data, 188
African American communities, 73, 156, 188, 321
African American girls (case study), 304–306
African American men, 54, 76, 101, 268
  *Ain't No Makin' It* (ANMI) (MacLeod), 101
African American South Side, 72
African American veterans, 182
Agar, Michael, 115, 118, 247–248
  *The Professional Stranger*, 115, 248
Age, variable of, 41
Agent of change, 153–154
A-ha! experience, 209–210, 216
AIDS, 257
*Ain't No Makin' It* (ANMI) (MacLeod), 100, 101, 284
Alcohol Anonymous (AA), 322
Algerian Revolution, 126, 127, 128
Ali, Muhammad, 277
Allende, Salvador, 130
*All Our Kin* (Stack), 76
Alteration of documentation of informed consent, 61
AM. *See* Analytic memos (AM)
Amazon region, 17, 18
American Catholics, 171
*American Gangster*, 335–336
*American Journal of Sociology*, 74
American Journal of Sociology (Vols. 2–21), 330
American Psychological Association (APA), 379

American Sociological Association (ASA), 59n., 161, 343, 379
Analysis
  CADA, 348–350
  CAQDAS. *See* Computer Assisted Qualitative Data Analysis software (CAQDAS)
  content analysis. *See* Content analysis
  cultural and community, 321–322
  cultural objects and discourses, 167–184
  of documents, 17
  focus groups, 303–304
  HC research, 132
  high school yearbooks, 178–180
  levels of, 98–99
  life course analysis, 319–320
  of research methods, 82–85
  spatial, 16, 142–144
Analytic memos (AM), 236, 240, 272, 274–275
Analytic paralysis, 338
Ancien régimes, 127
Anderson, Benedict, 128–129
  *Imagined Communities*, 129
Anderson, Elijah, 74
Anglo communities, 301
Animal Liberation Front, 392
Antecedents—the regressive part, 148
Anthropology
  ethnographic research in anthropologists (early 1900s), 18
  overview, 17–18
  sociology and, 18–19
Anyon, Jean, 78
Appalachia, 137
Aral Sea, 140
Archives, 132
Area exam, 153n.
Arendt, Hannah, 143–144
  *Eichmann in Jerusalem*, 143–144
Argot, 221, 254
Artifacts, cultural objects research, 168
The art of hanging out, 201
Asch, Tim, 346
*Asylums* (Goffman), 15
ATLAS.ti (Ver.6). *See also* CAQDAS
  autocoding, 371
  Codelink, 373
  codelinks, 364
  coding, 370–371
    quoted quotation is the code, 369
  coding queries, 372–373
  color coding, 371
  cultural objects approach, 181
  hyperlinks, 373
  importing data with, 368n.
  inductive codes, applying, 359
  internal data program, 360
  interviewing, 284
  logic of
    "assigned", 361
    coded quotation (CQ), 361–362
    interface, the, 362–363
    unit of analysis (UOA), 361
  models, creating, 374
  multimethod designs, 186
  network functions, 364
  networks, 374
  Network tool, 374
  nodes, 374
  primary documents (PD), 373
  project interface, 362
  quotations, 373
  Relation (use of term), 373
  text, 362

  text search, 372–373
  versus NVivo
    coded chunks of text, 357–358
    grounded theory, 356–357
    inductive and abductive coding, 358–359
    logic of NVivo and ATLAS.ti, 359–360n.
    overview, 355–356n.
    workspace, 366–367n.
Audio-video (A/V) technologies, 241, 245, 318. *See also* Visual methods
Audit trail, 243, 354
Auguries of Innocence (Blake), 206
Autonomy, 56
Axial (relational) coding, 95, 183, 187

## B

Baby boomers, 320
Backfire effect, 77, 162
Background contexts, 191
Backstage setting, 286
Backstory, 105
Baiting, 249–250
Bali, 18
Balinese cockfight, 227–228
Ballybran, 213, 240
Baltzell, Digby, 80
Barnes, Virginia, 312
Basic social sciences, 190
Bateson, Gregory, 18, 331
Batista, 128
Becker, Howard, 69, 218, 236, 286, 329, 330–331n.
Begin at the beginning, 146
Behavioral outcomes, 39
Beliefs, 228–229
Believability, 34–35
Belmont Report, The, 56
Beneficence, 56
Benjamin, Walter, 19
  Paris Arcades, 19, 20, 21, 22
Besso, Michele, 208
Bhopal, India, 136, 141, 146
Bias
  critical-reflexive theory, 97
  image-making, 340
  interviewer, 255
  mapping your, 199–200
  personal bias, limiting, 68–69
  recognizing your, 203
  selection of respondents, 312
  social autopsies, 140, 146
Biased account, 280
Binary code, 354
Binary code foundation, 351n.
Bingham, Sallie, 313
  *Passion and Prejudice*, 313
Black box, 243
Black Entertainment Television's (BET), 335
*Black Metropolis* (Drake and Cayton), 17
Blake, William, 120, 206
  Auguries of Innocence, 206
Blame the victim, 162–163
Blinders, 203–204, 240–241
Blumer, Herbert, 98
Boddy, Janice, 312
*Body and Soul: Notebooks of an Apprentice Boxer* (Wacquant), 400
Body modifications, 172
Bohemian Grove, 80
Boolean logic operators
  Facebook, 352–353
  and infidelity, 352
  logic commands, 352
  sex and drugs, 352